Market Volatility

Market Volatility

Robert J. Shiller

The MIT Press
Cambridge, Massachusetts
London, England

Seventh printing, 2001

First MIT Press paperback edition, 1992

© 1989 Massachusetts Institute of Technology

This book was set in Palatino by Asco Trade Typesetting Ltd., Hong Kong, and printed and bound in the United States of America.

Library of Congress Cataloging-in-Publication Data

Shiller, Robert J.
  Market volatility/Robert J. Shiller.

    p.   cm.
  Includes index.
  ISBN 0-262-19290-X (HB), 0-262-69151-5 (PB)
  1. Stocks—Prices. 2. Stock-exchange. 3. Bonds—Prices. 4. Real property—Prices.
I. Title.
HG4636.S49   1989
332.6'42—dc20   89-32028
                                                                      CIP

To Ginny

Contents

Preface

The origins of price movements are poorly known in all speculative markets: markets for corporate stocks, bonds, homes, land, commercial structures, commodities, collectibles, and foreign exchange. Why do stock prices often change up or down 20% or more in a year's time? Why do long-term bond prices sometimes change up or down as much? Why do we sometimes find "hot" markets for homes, with prices sometimes jumping 20% or more in a year, after years of stable prices?

This book presents basic research on the ultimate causes of price volatility in speculative markets—on the causes that make good economic sense and on the causes that are psychological or sociological in origin. The research, conducted over the last dozen years, includes both my own work and joint research with John Y. Campbell, Karl E. Case, Sanford J. Grossman, and Jeremy J. Siegel.

The research in this book explicitly concerns the stock market, the bond market, and the market for houses, but the aim of these studies is to uncover patterns of human behavior responsible for movements in speculative prices. As such, the book concerns matters of unusually broad interest, of interest to just about everyone who deals in, makes policy for, or does research on speculative markets.

To make the book more readable, I organized it so that parts of it can be read profitably by persons with little background in mathematics or economic theory. Each of the more technical parts of the book begins with an overview chapter that serves to guide the reader through the remaining chapters in the part, and contains no mathematics. Some of the chapters, on the other hand, are quite technical. These chapters are included to give a full presentation of the statistical methods and models that are used to back up some of the controversial theories in this book.

A reading program for someone who wants to get an impression of the basic results here without delving into the technical details would be to start with the introduction, the material in chapter 1 preceding section 1.2, and all of chapter 2. These give a basic perspective on the theories of this book, their contrast with other theories, and the controversy over these conflicting theories. Then the reader might proceed through chapter 3, which sets forth, in an entirely intuitive manner, the basic notions of ex-post value and of variance bounds, concepts that are referred to subsequently in the book. Following that, the reader might go through chapter 12 on the bond market, chapter 17 on the real estate market, chapters 19 and 20 on business fluctuations, chapter 22 on opinion changes and their market impacts, chapter 23 on the stock market crash of 1987, chapter 24 on the causes of recent booms in real estate, and chapter 25, which offers some concluding observations.

About two-thirds of this book consists of selected articles that I (often with coauthors) have published previously in various professional journals. I have kept the previously published articles intact, without cutting or substantial alteration. This was done partly in deference to the coauthors of some of the articles. Moreover, because some of the articles have incited considerable controversy I thought it would be useful to have the significant papers of this body of work reprinted here substantially unchanged. The only changes were correcting of typographical and working errors, adding of cross references within the book, and editing to make the layout of the papers conform to that of this book; the articles have not been updated. Because the articles are intact, there is some unavoidable repetition of themes, but this has been kept to a minimum.

The remaining third of this book is previously unpublished material put down here as an elaboration of and expansion on basic conclusions, a review of the literature, a discussion of critics and of alternative approaches, and a closing off of loose ends. The purpose of this new material is to establish the generality of principles and to complete ideas that have been under debate.

Acknowledgments

Much of the research reported in this book was done with colleagues: the coauthors of papers in this volume, John Y. Campbell, Karl E. Case, Sanford J. Grossman, and Jeremy J. Siegel; and coauthors of related work, Franco Modigliani, Pierre Perron, and John Pound. This book is intended to serve as an interpretation, summary, and source book for this research. However, the coauthors may not agree with all of my conclusions here.

I want to thank a series of research assistants who, over the dozen years of research covered here, put in much of the effort that made this book possible. Christine Amsler, Paula Andres, Leslie Appleton, Dale Ballou, Jie Cao, Catherine Christensen, Maura Doyle, Victoria Evans, Janet Hanousek, Roger Huang, Edward Hendricks, Michel W. Ewing, Angelo Melino, Charles Plosser, and Ellen Wolfson deserve special thanks. I want also to thank Lois Jason and Glena Ames for their help in manuscript preparation.

John Campbell gave a careful reading of the manuscript, which improved it greatly. Thanks, too, go to Andrea Beltratti, Giancarlo Corsetti, Michael Hobbs, Jeeman Jung, Wooheon Rhee, Gregory Sutton, and Martin Werner for their help in ironing out flaws in the final product. Others who have given helpful comments or suggestions for some of the papers reprinted here include Donald Andrews, Peter Bernstein, Olivier Blanchard, William Brainard, Fischer Black, Philip Cagan, Gregory Chow, Michael Darby, Robert Engle, Benjamin Friedman, Irwin Friend, Gary Gillum, Stephen LeRoy, Milton Friedman, Arnold Kling, Richard Meese, Burton Malkiel, Alicia Munnell, George Perry, Peter Phillips, Richard Roll, Stephen Ross, Kenneth Rosen, Richard Thaler, and Kenneth West. Others who have helped with data collection include Bryan Allworthy, George Bulkley, Peter Garber, Fumiko Konya, Rudolph Richter, Anna Schwartz, and Ian Tonks.

I am indebted, too, to the various critics of and commenters on my statistical work on the testing of the efficient markets hypothesis, who have pointed out the weaknesses, as well as strengths, of the methods used. Some of these are cited in the succeeding pages. Others who have spoken to me directly at professional meetings and at graduate student classes and seminars are not. The number of people who have offered me insights is too numerous to list by name, and so a blanket thanks will have to suffice.

The research here was done with the support of a series of research grants awarded me over the past twelve years by the National Science Foundation. I am also indebted to the Cowles Foundation at Yale University, The Federal Reserve Bank of Boston, the Federal Reserve Bank of Philadelphia, and the National Bureau of Economic Research for further support.

I thank the following copyright holders for permission to reprint:

for chapter 1, the Brookings Institution (© 1984);

for chapter 2, Oxford University Press (© 1988);

for portions of chapter 3, the American Agricultural Economics Association (© 1988);

for chapters 5, 18, 20, and 21, the American Economics Association (© 1981, 1989, 1987, and 1981, respectively);

for chapters 7, 14, 15, and 16, The University of Chicago (© 1988, 1977, 1979, and 1987, respectively);

for chapters 6, 8, and 10, the American Finance Association (© 1981, 1988, and 1989, respectively);

for chapter 9 and portions of chapter 19, Elsevier Science Publications (© 1989);

for chapter 24, The Federal Reserve Bank of Boston (© 1988);

and for series 1, 2, and 3 of chapter 26, Standard and Poor's/McGraw-Hill.

Market Volatility

Introduction

This is a book about the sources of volatility in prices of speculative assets, prices of corporate stocks, bonds, homes, and other things held at least in part for their uncertain investment potential. The basic question to be addressed is, what, ultimately, is behind day-to-day movements in prices? Can we trace the source of movements back in a logical manner to fundamental shocks affecting the economy, the shocks to technology, to consumer preferences, to demographics, to natural resources, to monetary policy or other instruments of government control? Or are price movements due to changes in opinion or psychology, that is, changes in confidence, speculative enthusiasm, or other aspects of the worldview of investors, shocks that are best thought of as coming ultimately from people's minds? Most analysts do not devote research effort directly to such a basic question, and attend to the details as if the question had a well-established answer. The answer is not well established; in the broad public there is no consensus at all on its answer.

This book presents evidence, from my own work and work with coauthors, on the importance to speculative price movements of both changes in economic fundamentals and changes in opinion or psychology, with the objective of presenting a balanced view, and some sense of the relative importance of each. What is most unusual about this book, when compared to other scholarly books on speculative prices, is its devotion of serious research to the role of changes in opinion or psychology in causing price changes. Much of the testing here of theories of the impact of fundamentals on prices was done with social psychological alternative theories in mind. I present here evidence that while some of the implications of the efficient markets hypothesis (that speculative prices always represent the best information about true economic value) are substantiated by data, investor attitudes are of great importance in determining the course of prices of speculative assets. Prices change in substantial measure because the investing public en masse capriciously changes its mind.

That prices change for no good reason is of great importance for many purposes. Prices of speculative assets guide very many economic activities in our society. When an asset is underpriced, incentives are created to neglect or abuse it. When it is overpriced, incentives are created to invest too much resources in it. The possibility that these prices may show repeated tendencies to move for no sensible reason matters greatly not only to those managing financial portfolios, but also to regulators, legislators, lawyers, corporate managers, builders, homeowners, collectors, conservators, and others. A better understanding of the importance of such price changes may ultimately set the stage for people to take actions that will reduce their impact.

That price changes occur because of changes in opinion is hardly a new idea. The research in this book *is* new in presenting statistical evidence challenging the efficient markets hypothesis, which asserts that *all* price changes derive logically from these fundamental shocks. The presumption in academic finance has long been that statistical evidence overwhelmingly supports the efficient markets hypothesis. The results here provide new perspectives on just what aspects of the efficient markets hypothesis are supported by the evidence. The research reported in this book also sets out the beginnings of a systematic study of the opinion changes that contribute to market volatility. There has been virtually no scholarly effort aimed at setting down general principles concerning the changing world views that guide investors.

Part I of the book sets out basic issues relevant to all markets in which prices make movements for speculative reasons. In part II the stock market is analyzed, in part III the bond market, and in part IV the real estate market. Part V pursues relations of these speculative prices to macroeconomic activity, and generalizes some of the analysis beyond the study of speculative markets themselves, to that of the macroeconomy.

The parts on the stock and bond markets include papers I have written that caused considerable controversy. The most controversial claim made in these is that there is evidence of excess price volatility, relative to the predictions of efficient markets theories, particularly in the stock market. Stephen LeRoy and Richard Porter independently made the same claim, although their interpretation of the excess volatility appears to be rather different. By excess volatility I mean that the very variability of price movements is too large to be justified in terms of efficient markets models, given the relatively low variability of fundamentals and given the correlation of price with fundamentals. Excess volatility means that if price movements were rescaled down in some sense to be defined, so as to be less variable, then price would do a better job of forecasting fundamentals.

At the same time, while excess volatility is evidence of a failure of the efficient markets model, there may still be implications of the efficient markets model that are borne out by the data. We shall see, for example, that while stock price indexes appear to be driven largely by noise that is unexplained in terms of the efficient markets model, long-term interest rates show distinct tendencies to anticipate the future, in a certain sense, in accordance with efficient markets models. The conclusion here is not that we should make no further reference to efficient markets theory, but rather that we should consider it an extreme example that we may use selectively to help us understand actual markets.

The next task of this book, to help us develop alternatives to efficient markets theory, is to study what I shall refer to as popular models. Popular models are the models of the economy held by the general public. These are not systems of equations, as are economists' models. As with popular music or popular periodicals, popular models are usually simple, un-sophisticated, and spontaneous. Popular models consist of qualitative descriptions of causes, anecdotes as suggestions of what may happen, and presumed correlations, cycles, or other simple patterns of variation of economic variables. Associated with the transmission and implementation of popular models are patterns of investor behavior: communications patterns, reaction lags, habits, and social norms, which will also be studied. Part VI of this book reports on research directly aimed at collecting information about these popular models and behavior patterns. The research consisted of asking investors about their thoughts and actions during each of two dramatic episodes: the stock market crash of 1987 and the booms in real estate prices in certain cities in the 1980s.

For an example of a popular model, consider the sequence of price movements surrounding the stock market crash of October 28, 1929, as a model for what might happen again. People who use this popular model think that these price movements might repeat themselves, in a similar sequence, at a later date. This model is extremely easy for the general public to understand and use; it is easy because it allows them to ignore any economic variables that are different, or changing differently through time, around the later date when compared with the period around 1929. This popular model was receiving a lot of attention just before the stock market crash of 1987; there was even an article advancing it (with a plot of stock prices in the 1920s and 1980s) in the *Wall Street Journal* on October 19, 1987, the very morning of the day of the stock market crash. Now it is true that the period from 1924 to the 1929 crash and the period from 1982 to the 1987 crash were both periods of fairly steady increases in stock prices, but the shorter-run oscillations actually did not match up well between the two periods, so the similarity was not so striking as to compel writers to take note of it. Singling out 1929 for so much attention is actually rather arbitrary, even though that year did see record one-day movements in stock prices. History provides many more episodes that might be used for comparison than are actually in the public mind. Other dramatic stock market episodes (e.g., the record 83% month-to-month *increase* in the Dow Jones Industrial Average between July and August of 1932) are largely forgotten, and parallels with these other episodes are generally overlooked.

In this book popular models are studied to help us interpret the apparent excess volatility in speculative markets. Popular models cause people to react incorrectly to economic data, and changing popular models themselves cause price movements that bear no relation to fundamentals. For example, if people believe that the sequence of price movements surrounding the stock market crash of 1929 is likely to repeat, then they may make it do so, in response to some events, such as initial price movements that call to mind the 1929 episode. At some times the popular models may create a feedback loop or vicious circle, whereby people's reaction to price changes causes further price changes, yet more reaction, and so on. This does not imply that there is excess volatility at all times or in all markets: popular models may as well cause people to underreact to information about fundamentals.

Popular models must be examined directly because in understanding economic behavior, where people take actions with purpose, it is critical to describe their views on what will happen if I do this, or if someone else does that. Understanding economic behavior requires more than observing patterns and correlations of behavior. People are purposeful animals; their actions are undertaken with some intentions. When we say we want to know why they behave as they do, we are asking what intentions inform their actions and what is the logic underlying their behavior.

The study of such popular models is, in a sense, a step beyond the rational expectations revolution in economics, which has been based on the approximation that economists' models and popular models are the same. That approximation allowed theorists to model human behavior without collecting information on the public models of the world, and allowed economists to produce complete and elegant theoretical models. That approximation has distinct limitations, nowhere more apparent than in the study of speculative markets.

I

Basic Issues and Alternative Models

1 Stock Prices and Social Dynamics

Fashion is the great governor of this world: it presides not only in matters of dress and amusement, but in law, physic, politics, religion, and all other things of the gravest kind: indeed, the wisest of men would be puzzled to give any better reason why particular forms in all these have been at certain times universally received, and at others universally rejected, than that they were in or out of fashion.

Henry Fielding[1]

Investing in speculative assets is a social activity. Investors spend a substantial part of their leisure time discussing investments, reading about investments, or gossiping about others' successes or failures in investing. It is thus plausible that investors' behavior (and hence prices of speculative assets) would be influenced by social movements. Attitudes or fashions seem to fluctuate in many other popular topics of conversation, such as food, clothing, health, or politics. These fluctuations in attitude often occur widely in the population and often appear without any apparent logical reason. It is plausible that attitudes or fashions regarding investments would also change spontaneously or in arbitrary social reaction to some widely noted events.

Most of those who buy and sell in speculative markets seem to take it for granted that social movements significantly influence the behavior of prices. Popular interpretations of the recurrent recessions that we observe often include ideas that the shifts in, say, consumer confidence or optimism are also at work in other aspects of the business cycle, such as interest rates, inventories, and so on. Academic research on market psychology, however, appears to have more or less died out in the 1950s, at about the time the expected-utility revolution in economics was born. Those academics who

Reprinted with minor editing from *Brookings Papers on Economic Activity* 2 (1984):457–498; © 1984 the Brookings Institution.

write about financial markets today are usually very careful to dissociate
themselves from any suggestion that market psychology might be important, as if notions of market psychology have been discredited as unscien-
tific.[2] There is instead an enormous recent literature in finance that takes
one of the various forms of the efficient markets hypothesis for motivation
and a related literature in macroeconomics that is based on the assumption
of rational expectations. In academic circles there has certainly been an
interest in speculative bubbles, but pursued within the framework of rational expectations models with unchanging tastes.[3]

It is hard to find in the large literature on the efficient markets hypothesis any discussion of an alternative hypothesis involving social psychology in financial markets.[4] Yet the impression persists in the literature and
in casual discussions that there are very powerful arguments against such
social-psychological theories. Arguments confined to an oral tradition,
tacitly accepted by all parties, and not discussed in the scholarly literature
are particularly vulnerable to error. It is thus important to consider explicitly these arguments against a major role for mass psychology in financial
markets.

Returns on speculative assets are nearly unforecastable; this fact is the
basis of the most important argument in the oral tradition against a role for
mass psychology in speculative markets. One form of this argument claims
that because real returns are nearly unforecastable, the real price of stocks
is close to the intrinsic value, that is, the present value with constant
discount rate of optimally forecasted future real dividends. This argument
for the efficient markets hypothesis represents one of the most remarkable
errors in the history of economic thought. It is remarkable in the immediacy
of its logical error and in the sweep and implications of its conclusion. I will
discuss this and other arguments for the efficient markets hypothesis and
claim that mass psychology may well be the dominant cause of movements
in the price of the aggregate stock market.

I have divided my discussion into four major sections: arguments from a
social-psychological standpoint for the importance of fashions in financial
markets, a critique of the argument for the efficient markets hypothesis, a
proposed alternative model based on social psychology, and some exploratory data analysis suggested by the alternative model.

The first section discusses what we know about changing fashions or
attitudes in light of everyday experience, research in social psychology and
sociology, and evidence from postwar stock market history. This will not
be direct evidence that people violate the principle of expected-utility
maximization, nor is the evidence of great value in judging how far we

should carry the assumption of rationality in other areas of economics (although I think social psychology is of value in understanding the business cycle). Rather, I will be motivated here by the relatively narrow question of why speculative asset prices fluctuate as much as they do.

The second section sets forth and evaluates the efficient markets model and the presumed evidence against a role for social psychology in determining prices. The fundamental issue is the power of statistical tests in distinguishing the efficient markets model from the important alternatives. If statistical tests have little power, then we ought to use the sort of qualitative evidence discussed in the first section to evaluate the efficient markets model.

The third section offers a simple though rather incomplete alternative model of stock prices that admits the importance of social-psychological factors. This model involves "smart-money investors" and "ordinary investors" and is intended to demonstrate how models of financial markets might better accommodate the econometric evidence on the near unforecastability of returns, evidence that is widely interpreted as favoring the efficient markets model.

The fourth section uses U.S. stock market data to explore some relations suggested by the alternative model. Using Standard and Poor's composite stock price index, I examine various forecasting equations for real returns. I consider whether stock price movements seem to follow simple patterns, as in an overreaction to dividends or earnings news, and whether this overreaction induces a sort of forecastability for returns. In doing this I present a time series model of the aggregate real dividend series associated with Standard and Poor's composite stock price index. I also propose a hypothetical scenario using the alternative model that shows for recent U.S. history what the smart-money investors may have been doing, the fraction of total trading volume that might have been accounted for by smart-money trades in and out of the market, and the extent to which ordinary investors may have influenced stock prices.

1.1 Evidence on Fashions and Financial Markets

Fashions in Everyday Life

Isn't it plausible that those who are so enlightened as to be readers of this might find themselves caught up in capricious fashion changes? Those of us involved in the current fashion of running for exercise may say that we do it because it is good for our health, but the health benefits of such exercise were known decades ago.[5] Talking with runners suggests that far more is at work in this movement than the logical reaction to a few papers in medical journals. Why wasn't the joy of running appreciated twenty years ago? Why are we thinking about running these days and not about once-popular leisure activities now in decline, such as leading Boy Scout troops or watching western movies?[6]

Fashions in one country may often move in one direction while those in another country are moving in a different direction. In politics, for instance, we have seen in the last decade a drift toward conservatism in some Western countries and a drift toward socialism in others. The objective evidence for or against socialism cannot have moved both ways. Something about the social environment, collective memories, or leadership is different and changing through time differently in these countries. Is there any reason to think that social movements affect investments any less strongly than they do these other activities? We know that attitudes toward investments are very different across cultures. In West Germany today investors are notably cautious; it is hard to raise venture capital, and the stock market itself is very small. Isn't it plausible that attitudes that change across countries should also change within a country through time?

Some may argue that investing is less likely than other activities to be influenced by fashions because people make investment choices privately, based on their perception of the prospects for return, and usually not with any concern for what people will think. It is, however, plausible that these perceptions of return themselves represent changing fashions. The changing fashions in "physic" that Fielding noted are analogous. Sick people in Fielding's day asked physicians to bleed them because they thought they would get well as a result and not because they thought that they would impress other people by having it done. Therapeutic bleeding is an excellent example of a fashion because there has never been any scientific basis for it; the belief in its efficacy arose entirely from the social milieu.

Who Controls Equity Investments?

It is important first to clarify the identity of investors in corporate stock. It is widely and mistakenly believed that (1) institutional investors hold most stock, (2) most wealthy individuals have delegated authority to manage their investments, and (3) smart money dominates the market. By suggesting that the market is more professionalized than it is, these misconceptions lend spurious plausibility to the notion that markets are very efficient.

It is true that the importance of institutional investors has been growing in the postwar period. Institutional holdings of New York Stock Exchange stocks as a percent of the total value of the stocks rose from 15.0% in 1955 to 35.4% in 1980.[7] Still, nearly 65% of all New York Stock Exchange stocks were held by individuals in 1980.

Most individually held corporate stock belongs to the wealthy. In 1971, the 1% of U.S. families (including single individuals) with the largest personal income accounted for 51% of the market value of stock owned by all families, while the 10% of families with the largest income accounted for 74% of market value.[8] Wealthy individuals are of course part of the same society as the rest of us. They read the same newspapers and watch the same television programs. They are different, however, in one important way. For them, information costs are quite low relative to the income from their investments. One might be inclined to think that they would in practice delegate to experts the authority over their investments.

A 1964 Brookings study (Barlow, Brazer, and Morgan [1966]) interviewed 1,051 individuals with 1961 incomes of more than $10,000 (or about $34,000 in 1984 prices) concerning their investment habits, among other things. The 1961 median income for the sample was about $40,000 (or about $135,000 in 1984 prices). "Only one-tenth reported delegating some or all authority over their investments, and this proportion reached one-fourth only for those with incomes over $300,000. Only 2 percent of the entire high-income group said they delegated 'all' authority."[9] Instead of delegating authority, most made their own investment decisions with some advice: "About three-fourths of the high-income respondents who managed their own assets said that they got advice from others in making their investment decisions. One in three of those seeking advice said they 'always' sought advice when investing, while two out of three said they did 'occasionally.'"[10] Two-thirds of the investors said they tried to keep informed, and more than half said they made use of business magazines, but "only one-tenth of those trying to keep informed said that they read the financial statements and other reports issued by the corporations in which they were considering an investment."[11]

What is really important for one's view of financial markets is not directly the extent to which institutional investors or wealthy individuals dominate the market, but the extent to which smart money dominates the market. One commonly expressed view is that intelligent individuals can be assumed to take control of the market by accumulating wealth through profitable trading. This argument overlooks the fact that individuals consume their wealth and eventually also die. When they die they bequeath it

to others who have perhaps only a small probability of being smart investors as well. In assessing this probability, one must bear in mind that the
class of smart-money investors does not correspond closely to the intelligent segment of the population. What is at work behind smart money is
not just intelligence but also interest in investments and timeliness. Presumably the probability is fairly low that heirs are smart investors.[12]

There are several factors that serve to mitigate the effects of higher
returns on the average wealth of smart-money investors. One is that most
people do not acquire most of their maximum wealth until fairly late in the
life cycle and thus do not have as much time to accumulate. Another factor
is that in a growing population, younger persons, whose portfolios have
had less time to accumulate, will figure more prominently in the aggregate
of wealth. Yet another factor is that saving early in the life cycle tends for
institutional reasons to take the form of investing in a house rather than in
speculative assets.

Roughly speaking, one can expect to live thirty years after receiving a
bequest on the death of one's parents. A representative smart-money heir
who earns and accumulates at a rate n greater than a representative ordinary investor in the middle of the thirty years will thus have on average,
if original bequests were equal, roughly $(1 + n)^{15}$ times as much wealth. If
n is 2% per years, this is 1.3; if 5% per year, this is 2.1. As long as the
percentage of smart investors is small, returns that are higher by this order
of magnitude will not cause the smart money to take over the market.

Of course, it is unlikely that smart-money investors are pure accumula-
tors; because we lack data on their savings patterns versus the savings
patterns of ordinary investors, it is impossible to say anything concrete
about how much money smart investors accumulate. If the smart investors
behave like good trustees of the family estate and consume at exactly the
rate that would preserve the real value of the family wealth, then smart
money will not accumulate at all, regardless of the return it earns.

The Ambiguity of Stock Value

Stock prices are likely to be among the prices that are relatively vulnerable
to purely social movements because there is no accepted theory by which
to understand the worth of stocks and no clearly predictable consequences
to changing one's investments.

Ordinary investors have no model or at best a very incomplete model of
the behavior of prices, dividends, or earnings of speculative assets. Do
projections of large future deficits in the federal budget imply that the price

of long-term bonds will go up or down? Does the election of a conservative U.S. president imply that earnings of General Motors will go up or
down? Does a rise in the price of oil cause the price of IBM stock to go up
or down? Ordinary investors have no objective way of knowing.

Ordinary investors are faced with what Frank Knight in 1921 called
"uncertainty" rather than "risk":

> The practical difference between the two categories, risk and uncertainty, is that in
> the former the distribution of the outcome in a group of instances is known (either
> from calculation *a priori* or from statistics of past experience), while in the case of
> uncertainty this is not true, the reason being in general that it is impossible to form
> a group of instances, because the situation dealt with is in a high degree unique.
> ... It is this *true uncertainty* which by preventing the theoretically perfect outwork-
> ing of the tendencies of competition gives the characteristic form of "enterprise"
> to economic organization as a whole and accounts for the peculiar income of the
> entrepreneur.[13]

Ordinary investors also cannot judge the competence of investment
counselors in the way they can that of other professionals. It is very easy
to learn whether a map company is producing correct maps: we can
therefore take it for granted that others have done this and that any map
that is sold will serve to guide us. It is much harder to evaluate investment
advisers who counsel individual investors on the composition of their
portfolios and who claim to help them make investments with high returns.
Most investors lack data on past outcomes of a counselor's advice and on
whether the current advice is based on the same approach that produced
these outcomes. Moreover, most investors do not understand data analysis
or risk correction, necessary knowledge for evaluating the data.

It is also much easier to change one's mind on one's investments than on
one's consumption of commodities. The former has no apparent immediate
effect on one's well being, whereas to change one's consumption of
commodities, one must give up some habit or consume something one
formerly did not enjoy.

Suggestibility and Group Pressure

Since investors lack any clear sense of objective evidence regarding prices
of speculative assets, the process by which their opinions are derived may
be especially social. There is an extensive literature in social psychology on
individual suggestibility and group pressure. Much of this literature seeks
to quantify, by well-chosen experiments, how individual opinions are influenced by the opinions of others. A good example of such experiments is

Muzafer Sherif's classic work [1937] using the "autokinetic effect." In this experiment, subjects were seated in a totally darkened room and asked to view at a distance of five meters a point of light seen through a small hole in a metal box. They were told that the point of light would begin to move and were asked to report to the experimenter the magnitude, in inches, of its movements. In fact, the point was not moving, and the viewer had no frame of reference, in the total darkness, to decide how it was moving. When placed in groups so that they could hear answers of others in the group, the individuals arrived, without any discussion, at consensuses (differing across groups) on the amount of movement. Subjects, interviewed afterward, showed little awareness of the influence of the group on their individual decision.

In another well-known experiment, Solomon Asch [1952] had individuals alone and in groups compare the lengths of line segments. The lengths were sufficiently different that, when responding alone, subjects gave very few wrong answers. Yet when placed in a group in which all other members were coached to give the same wrong answers, individual subjects also frequently gave wrong answers. Through follow-up questions, Asch found that even though the subject was often aware of the correct answer, and the answer was completely inoffensive, the subject was afraid to contradict the group.

The research shows evidence of flagrant decision errors under social pressure but not of abandonment of rational individual judgment. It does help provide some understanding of possible origins of swings in public opinion. The Asch experiment suggests that group pressures do serve at the very least to cause individuals to remain silent when their own views appear to deviate from the group's, and their silence will prevent the dissemination of relevant information that might establish the dissenters' views more firmly.

The Diffusion of Opinions

The dynamic process by which social movements take place is the subject of an extensive literature by social psychologists and sociologists, and the basic mechanisms are well known. The ideas that represent a movement may be latent in people's minds long before the movement begins. An idea may not become a matter of conviction or active thought until the individual hears the idea from several friends or from public authorities. This process takes time. The process may be helped along if some vivid news event causes people to talk about related matters or slowed if a news event distracts their attention.

Social movements can take place in a matter of hours after so vivid an event as the onset of a war. Or changes in attitudes can take decades to diffuse through the population, as evidenced by the fact that many fashion changes in dress seem to happen very slowly. The communications media may, if attention is given to some event, speed the rate of diffusion. However, the general finding of research on persuasion is that "any impact that the mass media have on opinion change is less than that produced by informal face-to-face communication of the person with his primary groups, his family, friends, coworkers, and neighbors."[14] This fact is recognized by television advertisers who, in promoting their products, often try to create with actors the illusion of such communication. Katona has used the term *social learning* to refer to the slow process of "mutual reinforcement through exchange of information among peer groups by word of mouth, a major condition for the emergence of a uniform response to new stimuli by very many people."[15] Thus, it is not surprising that in surveys in the 1950s and 1960s "the answers to the two questions 'Do you own any stocks' and 'Do you have any friends or colleagues who own any stocks' were practically identical."[16]

Such diffusion processes for news or rumor have been modeled more formally by mathematical sociologists drawing on the mathematical theory of epidemics.[17] For example, in what has been referred to as the "general epidemic model" (Bailey [1957]). It is assumed, first, that new carriers of news (as of a disease) are created at a rate equal to an "infection rate" β times the number of carriers times the number of susceptibles and, second, that carriers cease being carriers at a "removal rate" τ. The first assumption is that of the familiar model that gives rise to the logistic curve, and the second assumption causes any epidemic or social movement eventually to come to an end. In this model a new infectious agent or an event interpreted as important news can have either of two basic consequences. If the infection rate is less than a threshold equal to the removal rate divided by the number of susceptibles, the number of carriers will decline monotonically. If the infection rate is above the threshold, the number of carriers will have a hump-shaped pattern, rising at first and then declining.

The removal rate and the infection rate may differ dramatically from one social movement to another depending on the characteristics of the sources, media, and receivers. One survey of the literature on removal rates after persuasive communications concluded that "the 'typical' persuasive communication has a half-life of six months" but that different experiments produced widely different half-lives.[18] Changes in the infection rate or removal rate may be what accounts for the sudden appearance of some social movements. A rise in the infection rate, for example, may cause an attitude long latent in people's minds to snowball into a movement.

We might expect then to see a variety of patterns in social movements: long-lasting "humps" that build slowly (low removal and infection rate) or that rise and fall quickly (high removal and infection rate); news events with a subsequent monotonic decline of infectives (zero infection rate) or followed by a monotonically increasing number of infectives (zero removal rate). Of course, such patterns may not be seen directly in prices of speculative assets, as the "alternative model" I present later in this chapter will show.

Social Movements and The Postwar Stock Market

The real price of corporate stocks, as measured by a deflated Standard and Poor's composite stock price index (figure 1.1), shows what appears to be a pronounced uptrend between the late 1940s and the late 1960s and since then a downtrend (or, more accurately, a single major drop between 1973 and 1975). The postwar uptrend period, the last great bull market, has often been characterized as one of contagious and increasingly excessive optimism. Is there any evidence of such a social movement then? Is there evidence that such a social movement came to an end after the late 1960s?

Such evidence will not take the form of proof that people should have known better than to price stocks as they did. The postwar period was one of rapidly growing real earnings and real dividends, and that the growth should be expected to continue was an idea backed by plausible reasons, such as:

the constant speed-up in business research in order to cut costs and bring out ever newer and more competitive products: the extension of business expansion planning farther and farther into the future, which means that such plans are carried forward regardless of any jiggles in the trend of business: the improvement in business techniques that offset the effects of seasonal fluctuations: the advance in methods of monetary management by the Federal Reserve Board: and the similar advance in general understanding of the effects of the Government's tax and other economic policies.[19]

How was anyone to know whether these reasons were right or not?

The evidence for a social movement driving the bull market will come instead from other sources. The evidence will be the growing numbers of individuals who participated in, were interested in, or knew about the

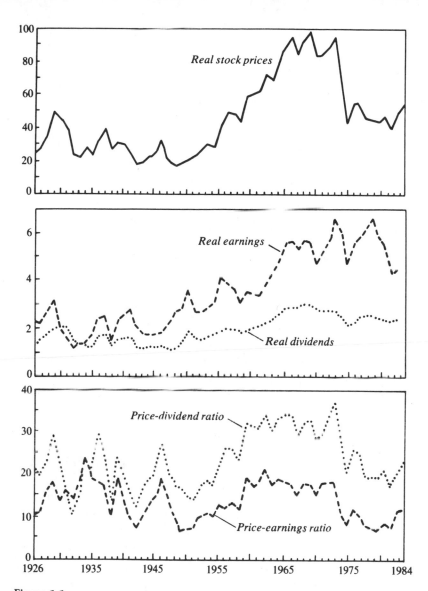

Figure 1.1
Standard and Poor's stock data, 1926–1984: annual data, 59 observations from 1926 to
1984. (Top panel) Composite stock price index for January (1941–1943 = 100) divided
by the January producer price index, all items, times 100. (Middle panel, *Real earnings*)
Four-quarter total for the fourth quarter of Standard and Poor's earnings per share adjusted
to the stock price index, divided by the January producer price index, times 100. (Middle
panel, *Real dividends*) Four-quarter total for the fourth quarter of Standard and Poor's
dividends per share adjusted to the stock price index, divided by the January producer
price index, times 100. (Bottom panel, *Price-dividend ratio*) Computed by dividing the stock
price series by the dividends series for the preceding year (in nominal terms). (Bottom
panel, *Price-earnings ratio*) Computed as for the price-dividend ratio, with earnings in place
of dividends. Source: Calculated from data from Standard and Poor's Statistical Service and
the U.S. Bureau of Labor Statistics.

market: the changes in relations between investor and agent; and the changes in attitudes that might plausibly affect the valuation of stocks. The evidence is not intended to provide a tight theory of the movements of stock prices but to show that large social movements appear to have occurred that might plausibly have had a great impact on stock prices. In fact, there is a superabundance of plausible reasons for the movements of the market.

Evidence for the growing numbers of individuals who participated in the market can of course be found most directly in the rising quantity of stocks held by institutional investors. The most important component of this increase was pension funds. The rise of employer pension funds in the postwar period might even be considered a social movement that probably caused an increased demand for shares. Individuals may, by saving less themselves, offset the saving done on their behalf by firms; but because most people do not hold any stocks, it is not possible for them (without short sales) to offset the institutional demand for stocks by holding fewer shares. Such changes in demand by institutions are likely to be important in determining asset prices but are not my main concern here. Others (e.g., Friedman [1982]) have studied such changes using flow-of-funds methodology.

The period of rising stock prices also corresponds roughly with a period of a dramatic increase in the number of people who participated directly (not through institutions) in the stock market. The New York Stock Exchange shareownership surveys showed that the total number of individual shareowners as a percent of the U.S. population rose from 4% in 1952 to 7% in 1959 to a peak of 15% in 1970.[20] The corresponding numbers for 1975, 1980, and 1981 varied from 11% to 12%.[21]

The increase in individual stockownership appears to correspond to an increase in knowledge about and interest in the market. The 1954 New York Stock Exchange investor attitude survey, consisting of interviews of several thousand individuals, was motivated by the question, Why is it that "4 out of 5 doctors, lawyers, major and minor executives, engineers and salesmen *do not own* stock in publicly owned corporations?" (New York Stock Exchange [1955, p. 54]). What came out of the survey was a sense of lack of information or interest in the stock market and vague senses of prejudice against the stock market. Only 23% of the adult population knew enough to define corporate stock as "a share in profit," "bought and sold by public, anyone can buy," or "not preferred or a bond."

By 1959 there appeared a "much better understanding of the functions of the Stock Exchange as the nation's marketplace." The number of Americans who could "explain the functions of the Exchange" rose nearly 20%. The number who knew "that companies must meet certain standards before the Exchange will permit their stocks to be listed for trading" increased 36% in the same five-year period (New York Stock Exchange [1960, p. 67]).

The growth of numbers of people who knew about or were involved at all in the stock market is important evidence that something other than a reevaluation of optimal forecasts of the long-run path of future dividends was at work in producing the bull market. Any model that attributes the increase in stock prices to a Bayesian learning process will not stand up to the observation that most of the investors at the peak of the bull market were not involved or interested in the market at all at the beginning of the increase.

Evidence about changing relations between individual investors and their agents takes two forms: evidence regarding the rise of stockbrokers and of publicity campaigns from them and evidence regarding the investment club movement.

Between 1954 and 1959 stockbrokers were growing in reputation. In the 1954 New York Stock Exchange survey 30% of the adult population said they would turn first to a broker for investment advice; by 1959 this figure had risen to 38%. During this five-year period, stockbrokers replaced bankers as the first source of investment advice. An estimated 9 million adults said they were contacted by brokers in 1959, compared with fewer than 5 million in 1954 (New York Stock Exchange [1960, p. 14]).

The New York Stock Exchange initiated an investors' education program as part of a broader shareownership program. Begun in 1954, the program by 1959 had a list of 2,500 lecturers in 85 cities. Lectures were held in local high schools as part of adult education programs by lecturers "bent on carrying the investing gospel ... wherever there were ears to hear."[22]

By 1959 the program had conducted 4,500 lecture courses reaching 525,000 persons or about 4% of the total number of shareholders in 1959. The investor education program used all the media, including advertisements in newspapers and magazines and on radio. As early as 1954, when the program was only six months old, 5% of the adult population in the United States could identify the New York Stock Exchange as the source of the slogan "Own Your Share of American Business" (New York Stock Exchange [1955, p. 10]).

In contrast the 1970s was a period of low profits for the New York Stock Exchange and advertising in newspapers and magazines was suspended. In 1975 competitive commissions were established and amendments to the

Securities Act threatened the viability of the New York Stock Exchange. Prices of seats on the exchange dropped. In response to the problems, the exchange in 1977 severely cut back the investors' education program and dropped the adult education program. Lack of public enthusiasm for the program was also offered as a reason for the cutback. The same factors that caused the New York Stock Exchange to suspend its investors' education program may have also had the effect of decreasing the efforts of individual brokers to promote corporate stocks. Such factors as competitive commissions, which reduce the profits in conventional brokerages, have "tended to shrink the numbers of people who are out there trying to encourage individual investors into this market place."[23]

Investment clubs are social clubs in which small groups of people pursue together a hobby of investing. Interest in such clubs might well give some indication of how much stocks were talked about and how much people enjoyed investing. The number of clubs in the National Association of Investment Clubs rose from 923 in 1954 to a peak of 14,102 in 1970 and then fell to 3,642 in 1980.[24] The total number of individuals directly involved in investment clubs and their aggregate wealth is of course small. However, the investment club movement is plausible evidence of a national movement that is not reflected in the membership rolls.

There is in the postwar period evidence of substantial changes in behavior big enough to have a major impact on the market. For example, the percentage of people who said that religion is "very important" in their lives fell from 75% in 1952 to 52% in 1978.[25] The birth rate hovered around 2.5% throughout the 1950s and then began a gradual decline to around 1.5% in the 1970s. These changes may reflect changing attitudes toward the importance of family, of heirs, or of individual responsibility for others.

Of all such changes, the one with perhaps the most striking importance for demand for shares in the postwar period is the pervasive decline in confidence in society's institutions after the bull market period. According to poll analyst Daniel Yankelovich,

We have seen a steady rise of mistrust in our national institutions.... Trust in government declined dramatically from almost 80% in the late 1950s to about 33% in 1976. Confidence in business fell from approximately a 70% level in the late 60s to about 15% today. Confidence in other institutions—the press, the military, the professions—doctors and lawyers—sharply declined from the mid-60s to the mid-70s.[26]

To Yankelovich's list we may add stockbrokers. One of the finding of the New York Stock Exchange 1977–1978 survey was that "a negative image of brokers and firms permeates all subgroups and even top quality clients have an unfavorable impression of the industry" (New York Stock Exchange [1979, p. 5]). By their very pervasiveness, the negative attitudes toward institutions suggest a prejudice rather than an informed judgment.

1.2   The Efficient Markets Model

The observation that stock returns are not very forecastable is widely thought to mean that investor psychology could not be an important factor in financial markets. Why is it thought so? If investor fads influenced stock prices, the argument goes, then it would seem that these fads would cause stock price movements to be somewhat predictable. Moreover, because dividends themselves are somewhat forecastable (firms in fact announce changes in their dividends from time to time), and in spite of this we are unable to forecast well any change in returns, it must be true that stock prices in some sense are determined in anticipation of dividends paid. Thus, stock prices should be determined by optimal forecasts of dividends.

The above argument can be formalized by representing the unforecastability of returns by $E_t R_t = \delta$, where E_t denotes mathematical expectation conditional on all publicly available information at time t, R_t is the real (corrected for inflation) rate of return (including both dividends and capital gain) on a stock between time t and time $t + 1$, and δ is a constant. Here, R_t equals $(P_{t+1} - P_t + D_t)/P_t$, where P_t is the real price of the share at time t and D_t any real dividend that might be paid in the time period. This is a first-order rational expectations model of the kind familiar in the literature that can be solved, subject to a stability terminal condition, by recursive substitution.[27] Out of the negative result that we cannot seem to forecast returns we thus get the powerful efficient markets model:[28]

$$P_t = \sum_{k=0}^{\infty} \frac{E_t D_{t+k}}{(1 + \delta)^{k+1}}. \tag{1}$$

Equation (1) asserts that real price is the present discounted value of expected future dividends, and in this sense price anticipates optimally (that is, takes into account all publicly available information) the stream of dividends that the stock will pay in the future.

There is a fundamental error in this argument for the efficient markets model: it overlooks the fact that the statistical tests have not shown that returns are not forecastable; they have shown only that returns are not *very* forecastable. The word *very* is crucial here, since alternative models that have price determined primarily by fads (such as will be discussed below) also imply that returns are not very forecastable.

We can get some idea at this point of the power of the regression tests of the efficient markets model against importantly different alternatives. Consider an alternative model in which the true (theoretical) R^2 in a regression of aggregate returns of corporate stocks on some set of information variables is 0.1. Given that the standard deviation of the real annual returns on the aggregate stock market is about 18%, such an R^2 implies that the standard deviation of the predictable component of returns is about 5.7% per year. Thus, under this alternative model we might well predict real returns of 14% in one year and 2% in another (these are one-standard-deviation departures from mean return). In an unusual year we might predict a real return of 19% or -3% (these are two-standard-deviation departures from the mean return). Yet if the alternative model is true with thirty observations (thirty years of data) and one forecasting variable, the probability of rejecting market efficiency in a conventional F-test at the 0.05 level is only 0.42. With two forecasting variables, the probability of rejecting is 0.32, and the probability becomes negligible as the number of explanatory variables is increased further.[29] As I have argued in a paper with Pierre Perron [1984], increasing the number of observations by sampling more frequently while leaving the span in years of data unchanged may not increase the power of tests very much and may even reduce it.

Someone may well wonder if there is not also some direct evidence that stock prices really do anticipate future dividends in the manner represented in equation 1. There is anecdotal evidence that the prices of some firms whose dividends can be forecasted to fall to zero (bankruptcy) or soar to new levels (breakthrough) do anticipate these movements. But these anecdotes do not show that there is not another component of the volatility of prices, a component that might dominate price movements in the stocks whose dividends are not so forecastable. For the aggregate stock market, there is no evidence at all that stock price movements have been followed by corresponding dividend movements (Shiller [1981, chapter 5]).

Some may argue that the constancy of discount rates in equation (1) may not be an appropriate feature for a general model of market efficiency. There are, of course, many variations on this model, such as the recent "consumption beta" models.[30] It is not possible to address all these alternatives here. Equation (1) is chosen as the most commonplace version of the efficient markets theory and a version that seems to have figured most prominently in the arguments against market psychology. Moreover, arguments about the power of tests of equation (1) may well extend to some of the other variants of the efficient markets hypothesis.

1.3   An Alternative Model

Let us postulate the existence of smart-money investors who, subject to their wealth limitations, respond quickly and appropriately to publicly available information. Consider a story that tells how they might alter the response of the market to the behavior of ordinary investors. This story is no doubt oversimplified and restrictive, but then so is the simple efficient markets model, with which it is to be compared.

Smart-money investors in this model respond to rationally expected returns but to an extent limited by their wealth. Suppose that their demand for stock is linear in the expected return on the market (or if the model is applied to an individual firm, the expected return on a share of that firm) over the next time period:

$$Q_t = \frac{(F_t R_t - \rho)}{\varphi}. \tag{2}$$

Here, Q_t is the demand for shares by smart money at time t expressed as a portion of the total shares outstanding, and $E_t R_t$ is the expected return starting at time t, defined as it is above. The symbols ρ and φ represent constants. Thus, ρ is the expected real return such that there is no demand for shares by the smart money. The real return at which $Q_t = 1$ is $\rho + \varphi$; that is, φ is the risk premium that would induce smart money to hold all the shares. The terms ρ and φ reflect the risk aversion of the smart money as well as the total real wealth of those smart-money investors who have evaluated the stock, the riskiness of the stock, and characteristics of alternative investments.

Ordinary investors include everyone who does not respond to expected returns optimally forecasted. Let us suppose that they overreact to news or are vulnerable to fads. We will not make assumptions about their behavior at all, but merely define Y_t as the total value of stock demanded per share by these investors.[31] Equilibrium in this market requires that $Q_t + Y_t/P_t = 1$. Solving the resulting rational expectations model just as we did to derive equation (1) gives us the model

$$P_t = \sum_{k=0}^{\infty} \frac{E_t D_{t+k} + \varphi E_t Y_{t+k}}{(1 + \rho + \varphi)^{k+1}}, \tag{3}$$

so that real price is the present value, discounted at rate $\rho + \varphi$, of both the expected future dividend payments and φ times the expected future demand by ordinary investors. The limit of this expression as φ goes to zero (that is, as smart money becomes more and more influential) is the ordinary efficient markets model that makes price the present value of expected dividends. The limit of this expression as φ goes to infinity (as smart money becomes less and less influential) is the model $P_t = Y_t$, so that ordinary investors determine the price.

Equation (3) and the efficient markets model [equation (1)] could be equally consistent with the usual finding in the event-studies literature that announcements have their effect on returns as soon as the information becomes public and have little predictable effect thereafter. Equation (3) has, however, a very different interpretation for the jump in price that coincides with the announcement. The jump does not represent only what the smart money thinks the announcement means for future dividends. It also represents what the smart money thinks the announcement means for the demand for stock by ordinary investors. Equation (3) implies that the price effect of changes in the outlook for future dividends will be governed by equation (1) if Y_t is not also affected by these changes. However, if Y_t is always positive, the discount rate $\rho + \varphi$ in equation (3) is necessarily greater than or equal to the expected return on the market, which is the discount factor in equation 1. If $\rho + \varphi$ is high, then factors affecting expectations of distant dividends will have relatively little effect on price today.

The more persistent is the behavior of the variable Y_t through time (that is, the less we can expect changes in Y_t to be offset by subsequent changes in the opposite direction), the less the moving average in expression (3) will reduce its variance and the more, in general, will be its influence on P_t.

I argued above that models of the diffusion of opinions suggest a number of possible patterns of response, among them a hump-shaped pattern in which Y_t would rise for a while, level off, and then return to its normal level. The implication for real price P_t of such a hump-shaped response of Y_t to a piece of news depends on the time frame of the response relative to the discount rate $\rho + \varphi$. Suppose the hump can be predicted to build up very quickly and dissipate, say, in a matter of weeks. Then equation (3) implies that there will be very little impact on price. The relatively long moving average in equation (3) will smooth over the hump in Y_t so that it is observed, if at all, only in a very attenuated form. The demand for shares by ordinary investors will show the hump-shaped pattern as smart money sells shares to them at virtually unchanged prices only to buy the shares back after the ordinary investors have lost interest.

If the hump-shaped pattern takes longer to evolve, the effect on price will be bigger. Then as soon as the news that gives rise to the hump-shaped pattern becomes known to the smart money, the price of the stock will jump discontinuously. This jump will be instantaneous, taking effect as soon as the smart money realizes that the price will be higher in the future. After the initial jump, the effect of the news will be to cause the price of the stock to rise gradually as Y_t approaches its peak (not so fast as to cause higher than normal returns after the lower dividend-price ratio is taken into account); the price will peak somewhat before Y_t does and then decline. Returns, however, will tend to be low during the period of price rise.

A more explicit yet simple example along these lines will illustrate why tests of market efficiency may have low power even if the market is driven entirely by fashions or fads. Suppose that the dividend D_t is constant through time, so that by the efficient markets model [equation (1)] price would always be constant. Suppose also that $Y_t = U_{t-1} + U_{t-2} + \cdots + U_{t-n}$, where U_t is white noise; that is, U_t is uncorrelated with U_{t-k} for all k not equal to zero. Suppose current and lagged values for U are in the information set of the smart money. Here, Y responds to an observed shock in U with a rising, then falling (or square hump) pattern. Under these assumptions, $Y_{t+1} - Y_t$ is perfectly forecastable based on information at time t. However, $P_{t+1} - P_t$ will be hardly forecastable from information at time t. It follows from equation (3) that P_t will equal a constant plus a moving average of U with substantial weight on U_t. The theoretical R^2 in a regression of $P_{t+1} - P_t$ on P_t is only 0.015 for the case $n = 20$ years, $\rho = 0$, and $\varphi = 0.2$. If one included all information (the current and twenty lagged U values) in the regression, the theoretical R^2 would rise, but only to 0.151. If the U_t are for each t uniformly distributed from 0 to 1, and if the constant dividend is 0.5 (so that the mean dividend price ratio is 4%), then the theoretical R^2 (as estimated in a Monte Carlo experiment) in a regression of the return R_t on D_t/P_t is only 0.079.

Let us now consider three alternative extreme views of the behavior of Y_t: that it responds to exogenous fads whose origin is unrelated to relevant economic data, that it responds to lagged returns, and that it responds to dividends.

The first extreme view is that Y_t is independent of current and lagged dividends: it is exogenous noise caused by capricious fashions or fads. In this view, Y_t may respond systematically to vivid news events (say, the president suffering a heart attack) but not to any time-series data that we observe. It is reasonable also to suppose that Y_t is a stationary stochastic process in that it tends to return to a mean. Thus, if demand by ordinary investors is high relative to the mean of Y_t it can be expected eventually to decline. If dividends vary relatively little through time, an argument can then be made that would suggest that return is positively correlated with the dividend-price ratio D_t/P_t. In the next section this correlation will be examined with data.

The second extreme view is that Y_t responds to past returns, that is, Y_t is a function of R_{t-1}, R_{t-2}, and so on. Together with equation (2) this gives a simple rational expectations model whose only exogenous variable is the dividend D_t. If we were to specify the function relating Y_t to past returns and specify the stochastic properties of D_t, we would be left with a model that makes P_t driven exclusively by D_t. Depending on the nature of the function and the stochastic properties of D_t, price may overreact to dividends relative to equation (1).

The third extreme view is that Y_t responds directly to current and lagged dividends, that is, Y_t is directly a function of D_t, D_{t-1}, D_{t-2}, and so on. For example, dividend growth may engender expectations of future real dividend growth that are unwarranted given the actual stochastic properties of D_t. Such expectations might also cause price to overreact to dividends relative to equation (1). Such an overreaction (to dividends as well as to earnings) will be studied econometrically below.

My suggestions about the possible behavior of Y_t are perhaps too extreme and special to provide the basis for serious econometric modeling now. However, these possibilities and equation (3) provide the motivation for some exploratory data analysis.

1.4 An Exploratory Data Analysis

Stock Prices Appear to Overreact to Dividends

Aggregate real stock prices are fairly highly correlated over time with aggregate real dividends. The simple correlation coefficient between the annual (January) real Standard and Poor's composite stock price index P and the corresponding annual real dividend series D between 1926 and 1983 is 0.91 (figure 1.1).[32] This correlation is partly due to the common trend between the two series, but the trend is by no means the whole story. The correlation coefficient between the real stock price index P and a linear time trend over the same sample is only 0.60.[33] Thus, the price of the aggregate stock market is importantly linked to its dividends, and much of the movements of the stock market that we often regard as inexplicable can be traced to movements in dividends. One reason that most of us are not accustomed to thinking of the stock market in this way is that most of the data series cover a smaller time interval (years rather than the decades shown in the figure) and sample the data more frequently (monthly, say, rather than the annual rate shown in the figure). The correlation coefficient between real price and real dividends might be much lower with data from the smaller, more frequently sampled time interval or might appear to be more dominated by trend.

The correlation between real price P and the real earnings series E for 1926 to 1983 is 0.75. This number is closer to the correlation of P with a linear time trend. Although the correlation coefficient between P and D is fairly high, the real price is substantially more volatile than the real dividend. If P is regressed on D with a constant term in the 1926–1983 sample period, the coefficient of D is 38.0 and the constant term is -0.28. The average price-dividend ratio P/D in this sample is 22.4. The real price moves proportionally more than the real dividend, and as a result P/D tends to move with real prices. The correlation in this sample of P/D with P (0.83) and with D (0.67) is strong enough that it can be seen in the figure. The volatility of stock prices relative to dividends is another reason why we tend not to view the stock market as driven so closely by dividends.

One would think that if the efficient markets model [equation (1)] is true, the price-dividend ratio should be low when real dividends are high (relative to trend or relative to the dividends' average value in recent history) and high when real dividends are low. One would also think that the real price, which represents according to equation (1) the long-run outlook for real dividends, would be sluggish relative to the real dividend. Therefore, short-run movements in the real dividend would correspond to short-run movements in the opposite direction in the price-dividend ratio.

The observed perverse behavior of the price-dividend ratio might be described as an overreaction of stock prices to dividends, if it is correct to suppose that dividends tend to return to trend or return to the average of recent history. This behavior of stock prices may be consistent with some psychological models. Psychologists have shown in experiments that individuals may continually overreact to superficially plausible evidence even when there is no statistical basis for their reaction (Tversky and Kahneman [1974]). Such an overreaction hypothesis does not necessarily imply that the ultimate source of stock price movements should be thought of as dividends or the earnings of firms. Dividends are under the discretion of managers.[34] John Lintner [1955], after a survey of dividend setting behavior of individual firms, concluded that firms have a target payout ratio from earnings but also feel that they should try to keep dividends fairly constant through time. In doing this, managers, like the public, are forecasting earnings and may become overly optimistic or pessimistic. In reality, the dividends and stock prices may both be driven by the same social optimism or pessimism, and the "overreaction" may simply reflect a greater response to the fads in price than in dividends. The apparent response of price to earnings could also be attributed to the same sort of effect to the extent that reported earnings themselves are subject to the discretion of accountants. Fischer Black [1980] has claimed that the change in accounting practices through time might be described as striving to make earnings an indicator of the value of the firm rather than the cash flow. An individual firm is substantially constrained in its accounting practices, but the accounting profession's concepts of conventional accounting methods may be influenced by notions of what is the proper level of aggregate earnings, and these notions may be influenced by social optimism or pessimism. (The observed tendency for price to move more than dividends is largely caused by the post–World War II hump in prices, which was larger than the corresponding hump in dividends. John Campbell and I discuss this on page 309.)

The relation between real price and real dividend can be described perhaps more satisfactorily from a distributed lag regression of P on D, that is, a regression that predicts P as a weighted moving average of current and lagged D. One sees from rows 1 and 2 of table 1.1 that when the real price is regressed with a thirty-year distributed lag on current and lagged real dividends, the current real dividend has a coefficient greater than the average price-dividend ratio (22.6 for this sample), and the sum of the coefficients of the lagged real dividends is negative. The sum of all coefficients of real dividends, current and lagged, is about the average price-dividend ratio. Thus, this equation implies that the price tends to be unusually high when real dividends are high relative to a weighted average of real dividends over the past thirty years and low when dividends are low relative to this weighted average.

Rows 5 and 6 of table 1.1 show the same regression but with real earnings as the independent variable. The coefficient of current earnings is less than the average price-earnings ratio (13.0 for this sample). Compared with dividends, earnings show more short-run variability; therefore these results do not contradict a notion that prices overreact to earnings as well as to dividends. The lower $\bar{R}^2$ in this regression might be regarded as a reflection of the fact that dividends are not really well described by the Lintner model [1955], which made dividends a simple distributed lag on earnings. The $\bar{R}^2$ is high enough that some major movements in stock prices are explained by this regression. For example, the decline in earnings between 1929 and 1933 explains more or less the decline in P over that

Table 1.1
Distributed lag regressions for real stock prices or returns on real dividends or earnings, selected periods, 1900–1983[a]

Sample period	Dependent variable[b]	Constant	Coefficient of current independent variable	Sum of coefficients of lagged independent variable[c]	Coefficient of lagged error	Sample statistic				
						F	Significance level of F	$\bar{R}^2$	Durbin-Watson	Standard error
Independent variable is real dividends[d]										
1900–1983	P	−0.08 (−2.95)	34.64 (14.16)	−11.79 (−4.34)	—	257.3	0.00	0.90	0.82	0.07
1900–1983[e]	P	−0.07 (−1.20)	28.25 (9.13)	−5.37 (−1.14)	0.66 (7.89)	44.49	0.00	0.68	1.86	0.06
1900–1982	R(t + 1)	0.09 (1.21)	−6.57 (−1.03)	9.62 (1.40)	—	2.72	0.05	0.06	2.06	0.19
1926–1982	R(t + 1)	0.17 (1.33)	−7.62 (−0.94)	5.17 (0.57)	—	1.52	0.22	0.03	2.05	0.20
Independent variable is real earnings[f]										
1900–1983	P	0.10 (2.61)	11.73 (5.61)	−5.83 (−2.29)	—	57.59	0.00	0.67	0.27	0.13
1900–1983[e]	P	0.17 (1.07)	7.98 (6.52)	−2.58 (−0.48)	0.90 (18.35)	10.74	0.00	0.32	1.61	0.06
1900–1983	R(t + 1)	0.09 (1.51)	−5.77 (−1.90)	7.45 (1.91)	—	2.19	0.09	0.04	1.97	0.19

a. Numbers in parentheses are t-statistics. Distributed lags based on second-degree thirty-year polynomial with far endpoint tied to zero were used throughout. The regression method is ordinary least squares except where noted otherwise. The stock price index throughout is the Standard and Poor's composite stock price index.
b. Dependent variable P is the stock price index for January divided by the January producer price index. Dependent variable R(t + 1) is the real return from January of the following year to January of two years hence (deflated by the producer price index) based on the stock price index and Standard and Poor's composite dividend series.
c. The sums are for the twenty-nine lagged values and do not include the coefficient of the current independent variable, which is shown separately.
d. Standard and Poor's dividends per share adjusted to the stock price index, total for four quarters, divided by the January producer price index.
e. Method is Cochrane-Orcutt serial correlation correction and sample statistics are for transformed regression.
f. Standard and Poor's earnings per share adjusted to the stock price index, total for four quarters, divided by the January producer price index.

period (the regression had positive residuals in all these years). While the reasons for the market decline on particular days in 1929 may forever be a mystery, the overall market decline in the depression is explained fairly well as a reaction (or an overreaction) to earnings.

It is important to investigate whether the pattern of coefficients in rows 1 or 2 (or 5 or 6) of table 1.1 might be optimal given equation (1). The easiest test of equation (1) suggested by the pattern of reaction of real prices to real dividends documented here is to regress future returns on current and lagged dividends. The efficient markets model of equation (1) implies that returns are unforecastable and the overreaction alternative suggests that D can be used to forecast returns. Such a distributed lag appears in row 3 of table 1.1. The coefficient of the current dividend is negative and the sum of the coefficients of the remaining lagged dividends is positive. Indeed, as our overreaction story would suggest, when dividends are high relative to a weighted average of lagged dividends (so that stocks are by this interpretation overpriced) there is a tendency for low subsequent returns. An F-test on all coefficients but the constant shows significance at the 5% level.[35] A similar pattern of coefficients found when E replaced D in the regression (row 7) suggests a similar overreaction for earnings, but the result is significant only at the 9% level.

By looking at the time-series properties of real dividends, one can better see why the pattern of reaction of prices to dividends causes returns to be forecastable. The class of models by Box and Jenkins [1977] that employ autoregressive integrated moving averages (ARIMA) has been very popular, and it would be instructive to see how the real dividend series could be represented by a model in this class. Unfortunately, time-series modeling methods are partly judgmental and do not lead all researchers to the same model. In applying such methods one must decide whether to detrend the data prior to data analysis. In previous work I estimated a first order autoregressive model for the log of dividends around a deterministic linear trend. In this model, with the same annual real dividend series used here, the coefficient of lagged log dividends for 1872–1978 was 0.807, which implies that dividends always would be predicted to return half the way to the trend in about three years (Shiller [1981b, chapter 6]). This result does not appear sensitive to the choice of price deflator used to deflate dividends. Taking account of the downward bias of the least squares estimate of the autoregressive coefficient, one can reject by a Dickey-Fuller test at the 5% level the null hypothesis of a random walk for log dividends in favor of the first-order autoregressive model around a trend. Some, however, find models with a deterministic trend unappealing and prefer models that make dividends nonstationary. With a model of nonstationary dividends one can handle the apparent trend by first-differencing the data. The following model was estimated with the real annual 1926–1983 Standard and Poor's dividend data:

$$\Delta D_t = 3.285 \times 10^{-3} + 0.850\ \Delta D_{t-1} + u_t,$$
$$(1.498)(11.753)$$
$$u_t = a_t - 0.981 a_{t-1},$$
$$(-69.434)$$

(1)

where a_t is a serially uncorrelated zero mean random variable. This is what Box and Jenkins called an ARIMA (1,1,1) model. It merely asserts that the change in real dividend is a linear function of its lagged value plus an error term, u_t, that is a moving average of a_t. The t-statistics, in parentheses, are misleading in that the likelihood function for this model has other modes with almost the same likelihood but very different parameter estimates. However, this model will suffice to tell how it might be plausible, given the past behavior of dividends, to forecast future dividends. The model cannot be rejected at usual significance levels with the usual Ljung-Box Q-test. It is noteworthy that when the same model was estimated with the sample period 1871–1925, almost the same parameter values emerged; the coefficient of ΔD_{t-1} was 0.840 and the coefficient of a_{t-1} was -0.973.

This estimated model is one that exhibits near parameter redundancy: the coefficient of a_{t-1} is so close to -1 that the moving average on a_t almost cancels against the first-difference operator. In other words, this model looks almost like a simple first order autoregressive model for dividends with coefficient on the lagged dividend of 0.850. It is more accurate to describe this model as a first-order autoregressive model around a moving mean that is itself a moving average of past dividends. One can write the one-step-ahead optimal forecast of D_t implied by equation (4) in the following form:

$$E_t D_{t+1} = 0.869 D_t + 0.131 M_t + 0.173,$$

(5)

$$M_t \equiv (1 - 0.981) \sum_{k=0}^{\infty} (0.981)^k D_{t-k-1},$$

where M_t is a moving average of dividends with exponentially declining weights that sum to one. Since 0.981 is so close to 1.00, the moving average that defines M_t is extremely long (0.981 even to the twenty-fifth power is 0.619), and thus the term M_t does not vary much over this sample. Thus, for one-step-ahead forecasts this model is very similar to a first-order autoregressive model on detrended dividends.

If real dividends are forecasted in accordance with equation (5), then equation (1) (with discount rate $\delta = 0.080$) would imply (using the chain principle of forecasting) that stock prices should be a moving average of dividends given by

$$P_t = 5.380D_t + 7.120M_t + 11.628. \tag{6}$$

Note that the distant past has relatively more weight in determining the price today (a weighted average of expected dividends into the infinite future) than it does in determining the dividend next period. This model thus accords with the intuitive notion that to forecast into the near future one need look only at the recent past, but to forecast into the distant future one need look into the distant past. Equation (6) implies that P_t, just as D_t, is an ARIMA $(1,1,1)$ process.[36] If I had modeled the real dividend series as a first-order autoregressive model around a trend, then P_t would be a weighted average of D_t [with about the same weight as in equation (6)] and a trend.

Equation (6) is very different from the estimated relation between P and D. The coefficient of D_t in equation (6) is 5.380, which is far below the estimated value in rows 1 or 2 of table 1. The coefficients of the lagged dividends sum to a positive number, not a negative number.

In summary, it appears that stock prices do not act, as they should, like a smoothed transformation of dividends over the past few decades. Instead dividends look like an amplification of the departure of dividends from such a transformation. It is as if the optimism of investors is too volatile, influenced by departures from trends rather than by the trends themselves.

Forecasting Regressions That Employ Dividend-Price and Earnings-Price Ratios

The most natural test of equation (1) is to regress return R_t on information available to the public at time t. Analogous tests of related models might regress excess returns on information at time t, or regress risk-corrected returns on information at time t. If the F-statistic for the regression (that is, for the null hypothesis that all coefficients save the constant term are zero) is significant, then we will have rejected the model. The simplest such tests use only price itself (scaled, say, by dividing it into earnings or dividends) as an explanatory variable and use the conventional t-statistic to test the

Table 1.2
Forecasting real returns based on the dividend-price ratio, selected periods, 1872–1983[a]

Sample period	Constant	Coefficient of dividend-price ratio	Sample statistic $\bar{R}^2$	Durbin-Watson	Standard error
1872–1983[b]	−0.10	3.59	0.06	1.85	0.17
	(−1.52)	(2.85)			
1872–1900[h]	−0.02	2.26	0.00	2.05	0.14
	(−0.20)	(0.96)			
1909–1945[b]	−0.14	3.89	0.03	1.46	0.21
	(−0.88)	(1.42)			
1946–1983[b]	−0.16	5.23	0.14	1.80	0.17
	(−1.70)	(2.62)			
1889–1982[c]	−0.13	4.26	0.09	1.85	0.17
	(−1.94)	(3.15)			
1926–1982[d]	−0.17	5.26	0.10	2.01	0.21
	(−1.73)	(2.71)			

a. Numbers in parentheses are t-statistics. The stock price index throughout is the Standard and Poor's composite stock price index. The dependent variable is the real return on the stock price index from January of the year to January of the following year (average for the months) except where otherwise noted. The return is the sum of the change in the stock price index plus Standard and Poor's four-quarter total of the composite dividends per share as adjusted to the stock price index, all divided by the stock price index. The independent variable is total dividends in the preceding year (which is Standard and Poor's four-quarter total of the composite dividends as adjusted to the stock price index) divided by the stock price index for July of the preceding year.
b. Price deflator is the producer price index.
c. Price deflator is the consumption deflator for nondurables and services.
d. Nominal returns were cumulated for the end of January until the end of January of the following year from monthly data in "Common Stocks Total Returns." Roger Ibbotson and Associates. The price deflator is the January producer price index.

model. If fads cause stocks to be at times overpriced, at times underpriced, and if these fads come to an end, then we would expect a high dividend-price or earnings-price ratio to predict high returns and a low dividend-price or earnings-price ratio to predict low returns. This would mean that the most naive investment strategy, buy when price is low relative to dividends or earnings and sell when it is high, pays off.

However, it is not easy to carry out such simple tests. One confronts a number of econometric problems: the independent variable is not "non-stochastic," so that ordinary t-statistics are not strictly valid; the error term appears nonnormal or at least conditionally heteroskedastic; and risk correction, if it is employed, is not a simple matter. There is no agreed-upon way to deal with such problems, and I will not attempt here to deal rigorously with them. It is, however, worthwhile to note that high dividend-price or earnings-price ratios do seem to be correlated with high returns.

Whether stocks with a high earnings-price ratio will have a relatively high return has been the subject of much discussion in the literature. It was confirmed that there is a simple correlation across firms between such ratios and returns (Nicholson [1968]). The question then arose, can such a phenomenon be explained within the framework of the capital asset pricing model if there happens to be a positive correlation between the ratio and the beta of the stocks, or does firm size, which correlates with the ratio, affect expected returns? Recently, Sanjoy Basu [1983] concluded that risk-adjusted returns are positively correlated with the earnings-price ratio even after controlling for firm size. As Basu notes, however, his tests depend on the risk measurement assumed.

It is apparently accepted today in the finance profession that expected returns fluctuate through time as well as across stocks. These results are interpreted as describing the time variation in the "risk premium."

The dividend/price ratio or earnings/price ratio has not figured prominently in this literature. Instead the variables chosen for forecasting were such things as the inflation rate (Fama and Schwert [1977]), the spread between low-grade and high-grade bonds (Keim and Stambaugh [1984]), or the spread between long-term and short-term bonds (Campbell [1984]).

Table 1.2 shows that a high dividend-price ratio (total Standard and Poor's dividends for the preceding year divided by the Standard and Poor's composite index for July of the preceding year) is indeed an indicator of high subsequent returns.[37] Thus, for example, the equation in row 1 asserts that when the dividend-price ratio (or "current yield") is one percentage

Table 1.3
Forecasting real returns based on the earnings-price ratio, selected periods, 1872–1983[a]

Sample period	Constant	Coefficient of earnings-price ratio	$\bar{R}^2$	Durbin-Watson	Standard error
1872–1983[b]	0.01	0.85	0.01	1.90	0.18
	(0.24)	(1.41)			
1872–1908[b]	0.00	1.28	−0.02	2.16	0.15
	(0.02)	(0.63)			
1909–1945[b]	0.08	0.03	−0.03	1.59	0.21
	(0.72)	(0.02)			
1946–1983[b]	−0.09	1.86	0.09	1.71	0.17
	(−1.09)	(2.13)			
1889–1982[c]	0.01	0.78	0.01	1.96	0.18
	(0.19)	(1.24)			
1901–1983[b]	−0.04	1.57[d]	0.05	1.81	0.19
	(−0.68)	(2.38)			

a. Numbers in parentheses are t-statistics. Dependent and independent variables and price deflators are as in table 1.2, with earnings in place of dividends.
b. Price deflator is the producer price index.
c. Price deflator is consumption deflator for nondurables and services.
d. Earnings-price ratio is computed by forming the average real earnings for the previous thirty years (not counting the current year) and then dividing by the real stock price index for January of the current year.

point above its mean, the expected return on the stock is 3.588 percentage points above its mean. Thus, the high current yield is augmented by an expected capital gain that is two and a half times as dramatic as the high current yield. In contrast, equation (1) would predict that a high current yield should correspond to an expected capital loss to offset the current yield. The efficient markets hypothesis thus appears dramatically wrong from this regression: stock prices move in a direction opposite to that forecasted by the dividend-price ratio. This is true in every subperiod examined.[38]

In table 1.3, rows 1–5 show analogous regressions with the earnings-price ratio (total Standard and Poor's earnings for the preceding year divided by the Standard and Poor's composite index for July of the preceding year) in place of the dividend-price ratio. These forecasting regressions work in the same direction (price low relative to earnings implies high returns) but are less significant.[39]

Excess Volatility of Stock Prices

Regression tests of the efficient markets model may not fully characterize the way in which the model fails. A simpler and perhaps more appealing way to see the failure of the model represented by equation (1) follows by observing that stock prices seem to show far too much volatility to be in accordance with the simple model.[40] The most important criticism of the excess volatility claim centers on the claim's assumption that stock prices are stationary around a trend of the dividend series[41] Here I discuss the volatility tests in light of this criticism and present tests in a slightly different form that deals better with the issue of nonstationarity.

I showed that if the dividend D_t is a stationary stochastic process, then the efficient markets model [equation (1)] implies the variance inequality

$$\sigma(P - P_{-1}) \leqslant \frac{\sigma(D)}{(2\delta)^{0.5}}, \tag{7}$$

that is, that the standard deviation of the change in price $P - P_{-1}$ is less than or equal to the standard deviation of the dividend D divided by the square root of twice the discount factor (Shiller [1981a, chapter 5]). If we know the standard deviation of D, then there is a limit to how much $P - P_{-1}$ can vary if equation (1) is to hold at all times. If the market is efficient, then price movements representing changes in forecasts of dividends cannot be very large unless dividends actually do move a lot. The discount factor δ is equal to the expected return $E(R_t)$, which can be estimated by taking the average return. Before we can use this inequality to test the efficient markets model, we must somehow deal with the fact that dividends appear to have a trend: in an earlier paper, I handled the problem by multiplying prices and dividends by an exponential decay factor as a way to detrend them. This method of detrending has become a source of controversy. Indeed, as I noted in the original paper, the trend in dividends may be spurious, and dividends may have another sort of non-stationarity that is not removed by such detrending (Shiller [1979, chapter 15]). Thus, violating inequality (7) in these tests should not be regarded by itself as definitive evidence against equation 1. Most of the criticism of the variance-bounds inequality has centered on this point.[42] On the other hand, the violation of the variance inequality does show that dividend volatility must be potentially much greater than actually observed historically (around a trend or around the historical mean) if the efficient markets model is to hold; and this fact can be included among other factors in judging the plausibility of the efficient markets model.

Table 1.4
Sample statistics for detrended price and dividend series, selected periods, 1871–1984[a]

Sample period	Left-hand side of inequality	Right-hand side of inequality
1877–1984	$\sigma(P5 - P5_{-1}) = 2.83$	$\sigma(D5)/(2\delta)^{0.5} = 3.52$
1887–1984	$\sigma(P15 - P15_{-1}) = 2.93$	$\sigma(D15)/(2\delta)^{0.5} = 1.64$
1902–1984	$\sigma(P30 - P30_{-1}) = 3.39$	$\sigma(D30)/(2\delta)^{0.5} = 1.38$

Source: Equations (7)–(10).
a. The variables P5, P15, and P30 are the real stock price index detrended by dividing by the 5-year, 15-year, and 30-year geometric average of lagged real earnings respectively: σ denotes sample standard deviation. The variables D5, D15, and D30 are the corresponding dividend series as defined in the text. The constant δ equals 0.08, the average real return on the Standard and Poor's composite stock price index over the entire period 1871–1983.

Table 1.4 displays the elements of the above inequality but with the data detrended in a different and perhaps more satisfactory manner that depends only on past information. Let us define detrended price series P5, P15, and P30 and corresponding dividend series D5, D15, and D30 by

$$Pk_t = \frac{P_t}{Nk_t}, \qquad k = 5, 15, 30, \tag{8}$$

and

$$Dk_t = \frac{D_t}{Nk_t} + P_{t-1}\left(\frac{1}{Nk_t} - \frac{1}{Nk_{t+1}}\right), \qquad k = 5, 15, 30, \tag{9}$$

where

$$NK_t = \prod_{j=1}^{k} E_{t-j}^{1/k}, \qquad k = 5, 15, 30. \tag{10}$$

The detrended price and dividend series have the following property: returns calculated with Pk and Dk in place of P and D in the formula for return R_t are the same as if P and D had been used. Thus, if equation (1) holds for P_t and D_t, then equation (1) holds where Pk_t and Dk_t replace P_t and D_t, and the same variance inequality (7) should hold for Pk and Dk. One can think of Pk and Dk as the price and dividend, respectively, of a share in a mutual fund that holds the same fixed portfolio (whose price is P_t and whose dividend is D_t) but buys back or sells its own shares so that it always has Nk_t shares outstanding. The variable Nk_t is a geometric moving average of lagged real earnings. This may cause the dividend of the mutual fund to be stationary even if the dividend D_t is not. A plot of D30, for example, shows no apparent trend and does not look unstationary. If, for example, the natural log of E is a Gaussian random walk and is thus nonstationary, and if $D_t = E_t$, then Pk_t will be a stationary lognormal process, and Dk_t will be the sum of stationary lognormal processes.[43] We see from table 1.4 that inequality (7) is not violated for $k = 5$ but is violated for $k = 15$ and $k = 30$. The detrending factor Nk_t gets smoother as k increases.

Implications of the Forecasting Equations in Connection with the Model

If we choose hypothetical values for ρ and φ in equation (2), we can use one of the equations forecasting R_t and produced in tables 1.1–1.3 to estimate the paths through time of Q_t and Y_t. Such an estimate will be admittedly quite arbitrary, and of course these forecasting regressions are not prima facie evidence that it would be "smart" to behave as will be supposed here. Considering such an estimate may nonetheless give some insights into the plausibility of the alternative model. We learn immediately in doing this that φ must be very large if swings in Q_t, the proportion of shares held by smart-money investors, are not to be extraordinarily large. This problem arises because stock prices are actually quite forecastable: the standard derivation of the expected return implied in many of the forecasting equations is so large that unless φ in equation (2) is large, Q_t will often move far out of the zero-to-one range.

Figure 1.2 shows a hypothetical example with estimated values of Y_t and Q_t implied by equation (2) and the forecasting equation based on the dividend-price ratio in row 1 of table 1.2 for $\rho = 0$ and $\varphi = 0.5$. Also shown is the real price P_t. For these values of ρ and φ, Q_t is always positive and thus Y_t is always less than P_t. The demand for shares by ordinary investors, Y_t, looks on the whole fairly similar to the price P_t itself. This arises because the forecasting equation is related to the dividend-price ratio and because dividends are fairly sluggish, so that Q_t itself resembles the reciprocal of P_t. However, Y_t is somewhat more volatile than P_t, showing a tendency to be lower proportionally at lows and higher proportionally at highs. The overreaction to dividends is more pronounced in Y_t than in P_t. The presence of smart money thus serves to mitigate the overreaction of ordinary investors. The year 1933 stands out for a very large proportion of smart-money investors and a low proportion of ordinary investors. This was the year when the dividend-price ratio reached an extreme high and when the highest returns were forecasted. The late 1950s and early 1960s were times of low demand by smart-money investors: the dividend-price

Figure 1.2
Hypothetical demand for shares by ordinary investors and smart-money investors. (Top panel, *Real stock prices*) Real stock price index (P_t) as described in figure 1.1. (Top panel, *Ordinary investors' demand for shares*) The hypothetical demand for shares by ordinary investors, equal to $P_t(1 - Q_t)$, where Q_t is the hypothetical demand for shares by smart-money investors. (Bottom panel, *Smart-money investors' demand for shares*) The variable Q_t from equation (2) with $\rho = 0$ and $\varphi = 0.5$ and based on the forecasting equation for returns in row 1 of table 1.2.

ratio was low then and so they were "smart" ex ante to get out market, though of course ex post they would have liked to have stayed in the market. The demand by smart money is currently neither high nor low because the dividend-price ratio is not far from its historical average. The weighted average return ($\Sigma Q_t R_t / \Sigma Q_t$) for 1926 to 1983 was 12.9%, in contrast to the average return (mean of R_t) for this period of 8.2%.

The volume of trade implied by the movements in and out of shares by smart money between t and $t + 1$ is $|Q_{t+1} - Q_t|$; the average value of this measure for the sample shown in figure 1.2 is 0.055. In this sample, the New York Stock Exchange turnover rate (reported annual share volume divided by average of shares listed) was between 9% (1942) and 42% (1982), except for the early depression years, when turnover was extremely high (New York Stock Exchange [1983, p. 68]). Thus, the story told in figure 1.2 is not one of an implausibly high volume of trade. Because corporate stock constitutes less than one-third of all wealth, we are also not talking about implausibly large wealth movements on the part of smart money.[44] Of course, not all household wealth is very liquid. The ratio of the market value of corporate equities to deposits and credit market instruments held by households ranged from 47.7% in 1948 to 136.2% in 1968.[45]

The results shown in figure 1.2 are not insensitive to the choice of forecasting equation, though as long as the forecasting equation is a simple regression on the dividend/price ratio (as in table 1.2), changing the equation has no more effect than changing ρ and φ. If an equation that forecasts with the earnings/price ratio (row six of table 1.3) is used to compute $E_t R_t$, the pattern through time of Q is somewhat different: Q is still high (though not as high in figure 1.2) in 1933 and low in the late 1950s and early 1960s. The weighted average return for smart money over this period would be 11.4%.

A discount rate $\rho + \varphi$ of 50% in equation (3) may or may not imply very forecastable returns, depending on the stochastic properties of Y_t. In the hypothetical example, the behavior of Y_t is sufficiently dominated by long (low-frequency) components that returns are not more forecastable than would be implied by the forecasting regression in table 1.2. A discount rate of 50% per year amounts to about 0.1% per day (compared to the standard deviation of daily return of about 1 percentage point), so that for event studies involving daily stock price data the discount rate is still very small. If equation (3) were to be applied to individual stocks, we might choose a smaller value of φ and hence a smaller discount rate.

1.5   Summary and Conclusion

Much of this chapter relies on the reader's good judgment. A great deal of evidence is presented here that suggests that social movements, fashions, or fads are likely to be important or even the dominant cause of speculative asset price movements; but no single piece of evidence is unimpeachable.

The most important reason for expecting that stock prices are heavily influenced by social dynamics comes from observations of participants in the market and of human nature as presented in the literature on social psychology, sociology, and marketing. A study of the history of the U.S. stock market in the postwar period suggests that various social movements were under way during this period that might plausibly have major effects on the aggregate demand for shares. Must we rely on such evidence to make the case against market efficiency? Yes; there is no alternative to human judgment in understanding human behavior.

The reason that the random-walk behavior of stock prices holds up as well as it does may be twofold. First, the aggregate demand of ordinary investors may itself not be entirely unlike a random walk. Fashions are perhaps inherently rather unpredictable, and ordinary investors may over-react to news of earnings or dividends, which behavior may also make their demand relatively unpredictable.

Second, and on the other hand, as shown by the model in equation (3) the ordinary investors' predictable patterns of behavior are prevented from causing big short-run profit opportunities by the limited amount of smart money in the economy, so that returns may be nearly unpredictable, and tests of market efficiency may have little power. However, in preventing large profit opportunities the smart money may not be preventing the ordinary investors from causing major swings in the market and even being the source of volatility in the market.

Data on stock prices show evidence of overreaction to dividends, and the forecasting equations for returns are consistent with such overreaction. However, an alternative interpretation for the correlation of prices to dividends might be that firms that set dividends are influenced by the same social dynamics that influence the rest of society. There are also other possible interpretations of this correlation; that is why I presented the data analysis as merely confirming that notions of overreaction suggested by qualitative evidence are consistent with the data.

It should also be emphasized that the model in equation (3) involves a present value of expected dividends and that it shares some properties of the efficient markets model. Despite all the inadequacies of the notion of market efficiency, modern theoretical finance does offer many insights into actual market behavior. The robustness of the models to variations like those here is a matter deserving more attention.

Notes

1. Henry Fielding, *The True Patriot*, no. 1, 1745, in James P. Browne, ed., *The Works of Henry Fielding, Esq.*, vol. 8 (London: Bickers and Son, 1903), p. 69.

2. The recent literature on behavioral economics associated with survey research has apparently not touched substantially on speculative markets. Some of their findings are relevant and will be cited below.

3. For example, David Cass and Karl Shell [1983] refer to market psychology in motivating their discussion of extraneous uncertainty, but they then assume economic agents are expected-utility maximizers with unchanging tastes. There is, however, a sense in which they and others are wrestling with some of the same issues that are of concern in this paper.

4. There are some casual arguments in the literature against such a role for mass psychology. The most-cited reference may be Eugene F. Fama [1965]. The argument consists of no more than a few paragraphs pointing out that "sophisticated traders" might eliminate profit opportunities, thereby tending to make "actual prices closer to intrinsic values" (p. 38).

5. A few minutes spent with an index to periodical literature will confirm that the idea that regular exercise helps prevent heart disease was part of the conventional wisdom by the mid-1950s.

6. There seems to be the same superabundance of theories to explain the decline of boy scouting since 1973 as for the decline in the stock market over the same period. See "Whatever Happened to . . . Boy Scouts: Trying to Make a Comeback," *U.S. News and World Report* (May 7, 1979), pp. 86–87. Those who think that people simply got tired of westerns will have to explain why it took a generation for them to do so.

7. See New York Stock Exchange [1983, p. 52]. This source says that institutional investors accounted for 65% of all public volume on the New York Stock Exchange in the fourth quarter of 1980 (p. 54). Thus, institutional investors trade much more frequently than do individual investors. Data that are probably more accurate on institutional holdings are in Irwin Friend and Marshall Blume [1978]; they estimated that 24.9% of all stock was held by institutions and foreigners in 1971, up from 17.9% in 1960 (p. 32).

8. See Marshall E. Blume, Jean Crockett, and Irwin Friend [1974]. In 1981, 7.2% of households had income above $50,000 (*Statistical Abstract of the United States, 1982–83*, p. 430).

9. Robin Barlow, Harvey E. Brazer, and James N. Morgan [1966, p. 26].

10. Ibid., p. 68.

11. Ibid., p. 71. These findings were also confirmed in other surveys. See George Katona [1975, p. 269].

12. The median correlation (from 12 studies) between IQs of natural parents and of their children is 0.50. See H. J. Eysenck and Leon Kamin [1980, p. 50].

13. Frank H. Knight [1964, pp. 232–233].

14. William J. McGuire, "The Nature of Attitudes and Attitude Change," in Gardner Lindzey and Elliot Aronson, eds., Handbook of Social Psychology (Addison Wesley, 1969), p. 231.

15. See Katona [1975, p. 203].

16. Ibid., p. 267.

17. See for example, David J. Bartholomew [1967].

18. McGuire [1969, pp. 253–254]. A description of recent research in marketing journals on the removal rate is in Bagozzi and Silk [1983]. See Bartholomew [1967] for a discussion of empirical work on the infection rate.

19. George Shea, Wall Street Journal. October 12, 1955, reprinted in Shea [1968, pp. 42–43].

20. New York Stock Exchange, Share-ownership 1952–1970 (NYSE, 1953–1971). The rise before 1970 of shareownership involved a trend toward somewhat more egalitarian distribution of stock. In 1958, 83.2% of stock value was owned by individuals with the top 10% of income. By 1970, this had fallen to 75.4%. See Blume, Friend, and Crockett [1974, p. 27].

21. New York Stock Exchange, Share-ownership 1975, 1980, and 1981 (NYSE, 1976, 1981, and 1982).

22. See New York Times, September 20, 1959.

23. Robert M. Gardiner, chairman of Reynolds Securities, Inc., as quoted in New York Exchange, Share-ownership 1975 (NYSE, 1976). p. 21.

24. Data from the National Association of Investment Clubs.

25. See "Religion in America," The Gallup Report, no. 222 (March 1984).

26. From a speech, April 1977, quoted in Seymour Martin Lipset and William Schneider, The Confidence Gap: Business, Labor and Government in the Public Mind (Free Press, 1983), p. 15. The Gallup Poll also documents a fairly steady decline in confidence in all major institutions over the years 1973–1983. See Gallup Report, no. 217.

27. One rearranges the equation to read $P_t = bE_t D_t + bE_t P_{t+1}$, where $b = 1/(1 + \delta)$, and then uses the fact that $E_t E_{t+k} = E_t$ if $k > 0$. One substitutes in the above

rational expectations model for P_{t+1}, yielding $P_t = bE_tD_t + b^2E_tD_{t+1} + b^2E_tP_{t+2}$. One repeats this process, successively substituting for the price terms on the right hand side. The terminal condition assumption in the text is that the price term, $b^nE_tP_{t+n}$, goes to zero as n goes to infinity.

28. Paul Samuelson [1977] explains the relationship of this model to the random walk model. It should be emphasized of course that there is no agreement on the precise definition of the term "efficient markets model" or whether it corresponds to equation (1). For example, in his well-known survey [1970], Eugene Fama says only that "a market in which prices always 'fully reflect' available information is called 'efficient.'" The empirical work he discusses, however, tests the hypothesis that price changes or returns are unforecastable.

29. These power computations are based on the usual assumption of normal residuals: as a result the conventional F-statistic is, under the alternative hypothesis, distributed as noncentral F, with $k - 1$ and $n - 1$ degrees of freedom and noncentrality parameter $(n/2)R^2/(1 - R^2)$, where R^2 is the theoretical coefficient of determination under the alternative hypothesis.

30. My own discussion of these and their plausibility in light of data may be found in Shiller [1982].

31. That is, Y_t is the total shares demanded at current price times current price divided by number of shares outstanding. If we assume that demand elasticity by ordinary investors is unitary, we might regard Y_t as exogenous to this model.

32. The correlation of P with D for the years 1871–1925 was 0.84. In this chapter, dividend and earnings series before 1926 are from Cowles [1938] who extended back to 1871 the Standard and Poor's composite stock price index: series Da-1 and Ea-1. All series are deflated by the producer price index (January starting 1900, annual series before 1900), where $1967 = 100$.

33. The correlation of P with time for 1871–1925 was 0.43.

34. Marsh and Merton [1983] claimed that dividends are determined by management's optimal forecast of long-run earnings.

35. Tests for heteroskedasticity as proposed by Glejser [1969] were run using D, time, and a cubic polynomial in time as explanatory variables. Heteroskedasticity appeared remarkably absent in this regression.

36. For this result in a more general form, see John Y. Campbell, "Asset Duration and Time-Varying Risk Premia" [1984].

37. There is evidence that the strategy of holding stocks with high dividend-price ratios has actually paid off for those investors who followed it. See Lewellen, Lease, and Schlarbaum [1979].

38. The same regressions were run using a different price deflator (row 5 of table 1.2) and a different measure of return (row 6 of table 1.2) with little change in results.

39. The lower significance appears to be due to the relatively noisy behavior of the annual earnings series. If the earnings-price ratio is computed as the average annual Standard and Poor's earnings for the preceding thirty years divided by the Standard and Poor's composite index for January of the current year (row 6 of table 1.3), then the relation between returns and the earnings-price ratio looks more impressive.

40. The arguments for excess volatility in financial markets were put forth independently by LeRoy and Porter [1981] and by me (Shiller [1979]—chapter 15, [1981a]—chapter 5).

41. In the case of LeRoy and Porter [1981], the earnings series, instead of the dividend series, was assumed to be stationary.

42. For example, see Flavin [1983], Kleidon [1983], and Marsh and Merton [1984].

43. If $\log D_t - \log D_{t-1} = u_t$, where u is serially uncorrelated and normal with zero mean and variance s^2, then $E_t D_{t+k} - D_t h^k$, where $h = \exp(s^2/2)$. Calling $g = 1/(1 + \delta)$, then if $hg < 1$, it follows from equation (1) that $P_t = gD_t/(1 - hg)$. Substituting this into equation (8) and using equation (10) will provide the stationarity result for Pk and Dk noted in the text.

44. Between 1945 and 1980 corporate shares held by households and private financial institutions as a proportion of household net worth including tangibles and government debt ranged from 12.6% in 1948 to 31.8% in 1968. See Board of Governors of the Federal Reserve System [1981]. 45. Ibid.

References

Asch, Solomon E. 1952. *Social Psychology*. Prentice Hall.

Bailey, Norman T. 1957. *The Mathematical Theory of Epidemics*. London: C. Griffin.

Bagozzi, Richard P., and Alvin J. Silk. 1983. "Recall, Recognition, and the Measurement of Memory for Print Advertisements," *Marketing Science* 2:95–134.

Barlow, Robin, Harvey E. Brazer, and James N. Morgan. 1966. *Economic Behavior of the Affluent*. Washington: Brookings.

Bartholomew, David J. 1967. *Stochastic Models for Social Processes* New York: Wiley.

Basu, Sanjoy. 1983. "The Relationship between Earnings' Yield, Market Value, and Return for NYSE Common Stock: Further Evidence," *Journal of Financial Economics* 12:129–156.

Black, Fischer. 1980. "The Magic in Earnings: Economic Earnings vs. Accounting Earnings," *Financial Analysts Journal* November/December: 19–24.

Blume, Marshall E., Jean Crockett, and Irwin Friend. 1974. "Stockownership in the United States: Characteristics and Trends," *Survey of Current Business* 54:16–40.

Board of Governors of the Federal Reserve System. 1981. *Balance Sheets for the U.S. Economy*. Washington: Federal Reserve Board.

Box, George E. P., and Gwylim M. Jenkins. 1977. *Time Series Analysis, Forecasting and Control*. Oakland California: Holden Day.

Campbell, John Y. 1984. *Asset Duration and Time-Varying Risk Premia*, unpublished Ph.D. dissertation.

Campbell, John Y. 1984. "Stock Returns and the Term Structure," unpublished paper, Princeton University.

Cass, David, and Karl Shell. 1983. "Do Sunspots Matter?" *Journal of Political Economy* 91:193–227.

Cowles, Alfred, and Associates. 1938. *Common Stock Indexes, 1871–1937* Bloomington Indiana: Principia Press.

Eysenck, H. J., and Leon Kamin. 1980. *The Intelligence Controversy*. New York: Wiley.

Fama, Eugene F. 1965. "The Behavior of Stock Market Prices," *Journal of Business* 38:34–105.

Fama, Eugene F. 1970. "Efficient Capital Markets: A Review of Empirical Work," *Journal of Finance* 25:383–417.

Fama, Eugene F., and G. William Schwert. 1977. "Asset Returns and Inflation," *Journal of Financial Economics* 5:115–146.

Flavin, Marjorie A. 1983. "Excess Volatility in the Financial Markets: A Reassessment of the Empirical Evidence," *Journal of Political Economy* 91:929–956.

Friend, Irwin, and Marshall Blume. 1978. *The Changing Role of the Individual Investor*. New York: Wiley.

Friedman, Benjamin M. 1982. "Effects of Shifting Saving Patterns on Interest Rates and Economic Activity," *Journal of Finance* 37:37–62.

Glejser, H. 1969. "A New Test for Heteroskedasticity," *Journal of the American Statistical Association* 64:316–323.

Katona, George. 1975. *Psychological Economics*. Elsevier.

Keim, Donald B., and Robert F. Stambaugh. 1984. "Predicting Returns in the Stock and Bond Markets," unpublished paper, University of Pennsylvania.

Kleidon, Allan W. "Variance Bounds Tests and Stock Price Valuation Models," unpublished paper, Stanford University.

Knight, Frank. 1964. *Risk, Uncertainty and Profit*. Augustus M. Kelley.

LeRoy, Stephen F., and Richard D. Porter. 1981. "The Present Value Relation: Tests Based on Implied Variance Bounds," *Econometrica* 49:555–574.

Lewellen, Wilbur G., Ronald C. Lease, and Gary C. Schlarbaum. 1979. "Investment Performance and Investor Behavior," *Journal of Financial and Quantitative Analysis* 14:29–57.

Lintner, John. 1955. "Distribution of Incomes of Corporations among Dividends, Retained Earnings and Taxes," *American Economic Review* 46:97–113.

Lipset, Seymour Martin, and William Schneider. 1983. *The Confidence Gap: Business, Labor, and Government in the Public Mind.* Free Press.

McGuire, William J. 1969. "The Nature of Attitudes and Attitude Change," in Gardner Lindzey and Elliot Aronson, eds., *Handbook of Social Psychology* Addison Wesley.

Marsh, Terry A., and Robert C. Merton. 1983. "Aggregate Dividend Behavior and Its Implications for Tests of Stock Market Rationality," Working Paper 1475–83, Cambridge: Sloan School of Management, M.I.T.

Marsh, Terry A., and Robert C. Merton. 1984. "Dividend Variability and Variance Bounds Tests for the Rationality of Stock Market Prices," Working Paper No. 1584–84, Cambridge, Sloan School of Management, M.I.T.

New York Stock Exchange. 1960. *The Investors of Tomorrow.* New York: NYSE.

New York Stock Exchange. 1983. *New York Stock Exchange Fact Book.* New York: NYSE.

New York Stock Exchange. 1955. *The Public Speaks to the Exchange Community* New York: NYSE.

New York Stock Exchange. 1979. *Public Attitudes Toward Investing: Marketing Implications.* New York: NYSE.

Nicholson, Francis. 1968. "Price Ratios in Relation to Investment Results," *Financial Analysts Journal* 24:105–109.

Samuelson, Paul A. 1977. "Proof that Properly Discounted Present Values of Assets Vibrate Randomly," in Hiroaki Nagatani and Kate Crowley, eds., *The Collected Scientific Papers of Paul A. Samuelson,* Cambridge: MIT Press.

Shea, George. 1968. *Forty Years on Wall Street.* Princeton: Dow Jones.

Sherif, Muzafer. 1937. "An Experimental Approach to the Study of Attitudes," *Sociometry* 1:90–98.

Shiller, Robert J. 1982. "Consumption, Asset Markets, and Macroeconomic Fluctuations," in Karl Brunner and Allan H. Meltzer, eds., *Economic Policy in a World of Change,* Carnegie Rochester Conference Series in Public Policy, Amsterdam: North Holland.

Shiller, Robert J. 1981a. "Do Stock Prices Move Too Much to be Justified by Subsequent Changes in Dividends?" *American Economic Review,* 71:421–436.

Shiller, Robert J. 1981b. "The Use of Volatility Measures in Assessing Market Efficiency," *Journal of Finance* 36:291–304.

Shiller, Robert J. 1979. "The Volatility of Long-Term Interest Rates and Expectations Models of the Term Structure," *Journal of Political Economy* 87:1190–1219.

Shiller, Robert J., and Pierre Perron. 1984. "Testing the Random Walk Hypothesis: Power vs. Frequency of Observation," unpublished paper, Yale University.

Tversky, Amos, and Daniel Kahneman. 1974. "Judgment Under Uncertainty: Heuristics and Biases," *Science* 185:1124–1131.

2

Fashions, Fads, and
Bubbles in Financial
Markets

For hundreds of years it has been commonly accepted that prices in speculative markets are influenced by capricious changes in investor sentiments,
changing fashions, fads, or bubbles. In the past few decades this commonly
accepted view has been strongly challenged by academic researchers in
finance. They have posed, as an alternative to this view, the hypothesis of
market efficiency and have claimed extensive statistical support for the
hypothesis.

The usual definition of market efficiency given in introductory finance
textbooks, while it is not as precise as we'd like, may capture the most
commonly understood meaning. Sharpe [1985] wrote, "A (perfectly) efficient market is one in which every security's price equals its investment
value at all times."[1] Brealey and Myers [1984] wrote, "We recommend that
financial managers assume that capital markets are efficient unless they
have a strong, specific reason to believe otherwise. That means trusting
market prices, and trusting investors to recognize true economic value."[2]

I wish to argue here that this fundamental notion of market efficiency is
not quite right and that, in fact, there is evidence that fashions, fads, or
bubbles *do* importantly influence prices of speculative assets. The view of
speculative markets that I wish to urge, however, is not just a return to the
common views of thirty or more years ago; rather my position is, in fact,
heavily influenced by the efficient-markets literature.

Investors, of course, vary in their investment savvy. Ordinary investors
are influenced by extraneous information or fads in their investment decisions and overemphasize some investments and overlook others. Other
investors, whom we may call "smart money," systematically search over
investments for abnormal returns. The latter group, limited in wealth,

Reprinted with minor editing from *Knights, Raiders and Targets*, edited by J. Coffee,
S. Ackerman, and L. Lowenstein, 1988, Oxford: Oxford University Press, pp. 56–68; ©
1988 Oxford University Press.

prevents the demands of ordinary investors from feeding directly into prices but does not prevent them from influencing prices. The "smart money" probably does not correspond closely to investment professionals: Among them are both ordinary investors and smart money. In one study (Pound and Shiller, [1987]) survey evidence was found that suggests that among institutional investors one can find both "diffusion investors," whose interest in individual stocks is spurred by interpersonal communications, and other "systematic investors."

One possible formal model of the influence of fashions, fads, or bubbles on financial markets was discussed in an earlier paper (Shiller [1984]— chapter 1). In this model prices are the present value of expected (by smart money) future dividends *plus* a term proportional to the present value of the expected (by smart money) future demands by ordinary investors.

With a model like this one, we would expect that in takeovers the price increase of target firms might well be understood, in some cases at least, in terms of the management inefficiency, synergy, or information effects theories discussed in the literature. However, the model would also suggest that firms may be takeover targets because they are overlooked by ordinary investors, or that their price increase at the time of takeover may not be understood without reference to the behavior of ordinary investors.

2.1 Traditional Evidence on Fads in Financial Markets

The old view of fads in financial markets was supported by anecdotal evidence. Some of the anecdotes are so well known as to be part of our popular culture: the stories of the tulipomania in the seventeenth century, the South Sea Islands bubble and John Law's Mississippi scheme bubble of the eighteenth century, the U.S. stock market boom of the late 1920s, the Florida land price bubble of the 1920s, the great bull market of the 1950s and early 1960s, the Canadian stock boom of the early 1950s, the growth stock craze of 1959–1961, and the high-tech boom of the early 1980s.

What is common to all of these anecdotes is the claim that people are sometimes excessively enthusiastic for certain speculative assets and that their judgment is then not sound. For example, speaking of the tulipomania of the seventeenth century, Mackay [1841] wrote, "In 1634 the rage among the Dutch to possess them [tulips] was so great that the ordinary industry of the country was neglected and the population, even to its lowest dregs, embarked in the tulip trade. As the mania increased, prices augmented until, in 1635, many persons were known to invest a fortune of 100,000 Florins in the purchase of 40 roots.... Houses and land were offered for sale at ruinously low prices, or assigned in payment of bargains made at the tulip mart."[3]

Speaking of the stock market boom of the late 1920s, Galbraith [1972] wrote, "By the summer of 1929 the market not only dominated the news. It also dominated the culture. That recherché minority which at other times has acknowledged its interest in Saint Thomas Aquinas, Proust, psychoanalysis and psychosomatic medicine then spoke of United Corporation, United Founders and steel.... Main street had always had one citizen who could speak knowingly about buying or selling stocks. Now he became an oracle."[4]

Speaking of the "growth stocks craze" of 1959–1961, Malkiel [1981] wrote, "Growth took on an almost mystical significance, and questioning the propriety of such valuations became, as in the generation past, amost heretical. These prices could not be justified on firm foundation principles."[5]

These anecdotes necessarily concern extreme and unusual events, selected as they are for dramatic effect. The tellers of these stories wished to convince us that human judgment is sometimes faulty, and they had to pick extreme examples if the faulty judgment is to be readily apparent. It is natural, however, to suspect that if such extreme examples are indeed correctly reported, then it must also be the case that in the usual course of trading, less dramatic fads or fashions are an important cause of price variability; various speculative assets are at times overvalued because they are fashionable and have attracted undue attention, while other speculative assets are subject to adverse prejudice or are just ignored and hence underpriced.

Advocates of market efficiency correctly point out that such anecdotal evidence does not constitute solid proof that human judgment was ever faulty. The problem with the anecdotes is that they hinge on the judgment of the teller of the story (or of others the teller cites) that people did *not* have good reasons to behave as they did. Even if we believe the teller's assertion that people were unusually excited or optimistic that does not prove that they were not also right to feel so. The fact that the expected future price increases did not materialize does not prove that their methods of forecasting prices were not sound. A good method of forecasting will sometimes fail, and selecting these failures for special attention may not be a good way of evaluating the method.

2.2   The Evidence for Market Efficiency

Despite the weakness of the anecdotal evidence, the evidence does *suggest* that there is an important influence of faddish behavior in financial markets.

Why is it, then, that so many in academic finance strongly assert the opposite position, that fads have no influence on financial prices? There is nothing in *theoretical* finance that implies that market prices ought not to be influenced heavily by changing fashions or fads among a portion of investors. Some people seem to think that there is such a theoretical argument. If such fashions or fads influenced price, then there would be "profit opportunities" for smart money. The smart money would then, through profitable trading, take over the market and thereby eliminate the profit opportunities. There is something to this possibility, and it does give a reason to doubt that there are spectacular profit opportunities. But the argument is not strong enough to rule out the possibility that actual price changes are not heavily influenced by changing fashions or fads. Such fashions or fads may not create spectacular profit opportunities if the future paths of the fashions or fads are not very predictable. If there exist only modest (and uncertain) profit opportunities for smart money, then the tendency for smart money to accumulate wealth through profitable trading may be a slow one and may not keep up with other tendencies that would tend to spread wealth through the population. Consider those people who, in the late 1950s and early 1960s in the United States, thought that the bull market had gone on too long and that stocks were overpriced. Even if they *knew* that the market would eventually fall, there was no way for them to get rich quickly from this knowledge. They had to wait years to be vindicated; they could not predict when the bull market would end. In fact, those people who thought the market would fall hardly took over the market.

If there is any evidence for the efficient-markets model, then it must be empirical. There is in fact a really vast statistical literature that bears on the issue of market efficiency. There are, however, fundamental problems with this literature that make it of questionable relevance to the issue at hand. The first problem is that there is no agreed-upon way to define the terms *investment value* or *true economic value* in the definitions of market efficiency, nor to define the *abnormal returns* due to departure of prices from these values. The null hypothesis of market efficiency is ill defined. The second problem is that there has been virtually no explicit consideration in this literature of how fashions or fads might be expected to influence markets. The alternative hypothesis also remains ill defined. No amount of statistical evidence can resolve such ill-defined hypotheses.

The null hypothesis of market efficiency cannot be defined just as the absence of an "abnormal profit opportunity" without defining carefully what such a profit opportunity is. It cannot be considered proof of a profit opportunity just to show that some investment strategies yield more on average than do others. The strategy of investing in stocks yields more on average than the strategy of investing in bonds. The higher return may be considered just a compensation for the higher risk of investing in stocks versus bonds. To show that markets are not efficient, one must find an investment strategy that achieves higher average return without achieving higher risk. To show this, one must rely on a model of the risk-return relationship.

The capital asset-pricing model that is the basis of many studies has been criticized on a number of theoretical grounds (Roll [1977]), and so rejection of it does not constitute evidence that markets are not efficient. Finance theorists have gone on to test rather different and new models, like the consumption-based, asset-pricing model of Breeden [1979] that measures risk by correlation of returns with consumption; but no consensus has emerged on these models. It is plain that the finance profession does not agree on how to measure risk or even on whether it can be measured with existing data.

In addition to the problems of risk, there is the problem of taxes. Investors are concerned with after-tax returns (which are influenced differentially across stocks by the dividend-price ratio), but investors differ in their tax brackets and holding periods for capital gains. Thus, the "after-tax return," which ought to be the basis of efficient-market studies, is unmeasurable.

In the absence of such a well-defined null hypothesis, critics of the basic notion of market efficiency are in a difficult position. In effect, they must try to show spectacular evidence of market inefficiency that is so dramatic that it would appear to contradict any of the different versions of the hypothesis. But perhaps it is just such spectacular evidence that we would not expect to find, if spectacular evidence means spectacular profit opportunities.

The second problem with the existing literature testing market efficiency is its lack of consideration of a well-defined alternative representing fashions or fads in financial markets. The efficient-markets literature is often described as finding only "small" departures from market efficiency. But how large are the "anomalies" that we would expect to find if fashions or fads did in fact dominate financial markets? I have argued elsewhere (Shiller [1984]—chapter 1), as has Summers [1986], that big valuation errors may generate only "small" abnormal profit opportunities. It is not hard to see that this is a possibility. If, let us say, a stock with a dividend yield of 4.5% is bid up by enthusiastic investors so that its price is doubled, and if the enthusiasm is unpredictable and there is no reason to think it will subside in the near future, then the anticipated yield falls only to 2.25%. This yield does not produce any dramatic, riskless profit opportunity through short sales or option markets. Similarly, if the stock is overlooked and its price falls by a third, then the anticipated yield rises by 2.25 percentage points to 6.75%. Buying this stock would not make one rich quickly. It is hardly obvious, given the uncertainties, that "smart money" will do anything effective in response to the 2.25% yield differential to prevent the mispricing of the stock.

However, the efficient-markets literature has indeed found a number of "small" anomalies of the sort that one might expect to find if fashions or fads dominated financial markets. I will cite here only those anomalies that are related to price relative to some simple measure of firm value. Returns have been found to show a small correlation with the earnings-price ratio, even after beta has been taken into account. Basu (1983) found that firms in the highest quintile in terms of the earnings-price ratio had an abnormal return (i.e., risk-corrected excess return) over the market of 4.4% per year.[6] High-earnings-price-ratio stocks tend to do slightly better, as if stocks whose price has fallen due to investor disinterest become underpriced and hence a good investment. Low-earnings-price-ratio stocks tend to do slightly worse, as if their low ratio is often the result of a fad pushing the price up, so that the stock is overpriced and a poor investment. Other studies (e.g., Black and Scholes [1974]; Blume [1980]; Litzenberger and Ramaswamy [1982]; Morgan [1982]) have shown that the dividend-price ratio predicts abnormal returns, just as does the price-earnings ratio, though this evidence is ambiguous since the dividend-price ratio also has tax consequences whose value depends on the tax bracket of the investor. More recently, Rosenberg [1985] has shown that stocks with high (by his criterion) book-value-price ratios tend to do slightly better, with an abnormal return of 4.4% per year. DeBondt and Thaler [1985] showed that stocks whose price has dropped dramatically (by their criterion) in the last three years show an abnormal return of 6.1% per year over the succeeding three years.

Another group of studies has investigated whether professional analysts have any ability to beat the market. If markets are inefficient, then it would seem to follow that some professional investors ought to be able to profit systematically from this information. It is tricky, however, to evaluate by any casual reading of this literature whether fashions or fads exist. Most of the studies in the literature report, on average, weekly or monthly returns of some special group of investors over a relatively short calendar interval.

In many of these studies investors who are doing the right thing for the long run may well do poorly owing to chance. Moreover, even if there are fashions or fads in financial markets, it does not follow, of course, that *all* professional investors will profit from them. One might think, though, that they as a group would be less vulnerable to fads and would therefore do better.

Dimson and Marsh [1984] surveyed 27 studies of the performance of brokers' advisory service recommendations. These studies reported returns over various horizons after each recommendation was made. The weighted-average return over prerecommendation price in all these studies was 0.6% on the publication day, 1.5% after one day, and 1.1% after one week.[7] To someone trained in finance, the natural next question to ask is whether transactions costs might substantially diminish the profit opportunity, or whether one could take advantage of these profit opportunities with substantial amounts of money without destroying them. But for the purpose of confirming that fashions or fads influence financial markets, these considerations are irrelevant.

While most of the efficient-markets literature turning up "anomalies" does not give us a clear idea as to the source of valuation errors, another avenue of research actually shows that the data are consistent with the notion that movements in the aggregate stock market over the past century may be attributed almost entirely to fashions and fads. This work (Shiller [1981b]—chapter 5, [1981c]—chapter 6; similar to work by Shiller [1979]—chapter 5; LeRoy and Porter [1981]; West [1984]; Mankiw et al. [1985]; and others) shows that aggregate, real-stock price indexes have moved much more than the present value of the corresponding real-dividend series, the present value behaving much like a trend through time. Some of the interpretations of this result made by these authors have been criticized (Flavin [1983]; Kleidon [1986]; Marsh and Merton [1987]; and others). These criticisms do not deny, however, that movements in aggregate, real stock prices over the past century were without any validating movements in fundamentals. If the data had shown, instead, that real, aggregate stock prices moved as if they were *successfully* forecasting fundamentals, we would indeed have evidence for the efficient-markets hypothesis. Since they have not, it is hard to see how any further statistical tests could be construed as proving the efficient-markets hypothesis for the aggregate stock market.

That speculative asset price movements appear to be influenced by things other than fundamentals is further suggested by some work of Roll [1984] and French and Roll [1986]. Roll showed that news about the weather seems to dominate news cited with reference to orange juice futures, and yet most price movements in orange juice futures appear to be unrelated to the weather. Moreover, the variance of orange juice futures price changes is not as high over the weekend, when there is just as much news about the weather, as it should be. French and Roll found that the variance of stock price changes from Tuesdays to the immediately following Thursdays was lower in periods when the stock market was closed on Wednesdays, even though it would seem that as much information was forthcoming then.

2.3 Diffusion Models and Fashions, Fads, and Bubbles

The availability to investors of instances or associations regarding speculative assets is a random process influenced by a number of factors. News stories or commonly noted events that remind people of the stock may make it more likely that individuals will talk about the stock. Thus, for example, news of severe weather in one part of the country may suggest conversation about companies headquartered there. The rate of spread of interest in one stock is likely to be inhibited by the spread of interest in another stock, since people can talk seriously about a limited number of stocks at a given time. Thus, for example, a big earnings announcement in a different firm may cause conversations that displace conversations about the stock. The lumpiness of media attention is also a factor inducing randomness in the behavior of diffusion traders. Opportunities to talk seriously about a given stock with others may be influenced by patterns of social interaction that may vary irregularly over time. Receptiveness to new interest may vary depending on economic or other circumstances.

A fad is a bubble if the contagion of the fad occurs through price; people are attracted by observed price increases. Observing past price increases means observing other people becoming wealthy who invested heavily in the asset, and this observation might interest or excite other potential investors. In the simplest bubble model, price increases themselves thus cause greater subsequent price increases until price reaches some barrier; then the bubble bursts and price drops precipitously, since there are then no further price increases to sustain the high demand. This model contrasts with the simple models of the transmission of attitudes offered by mathematical sociologists, as in Bartholomew [1982], in which increases in the intensity of the fad are related to the number of (not the increase in) involved people and the number of potentially involved people. These fad models tend to produce hump-shaped patterns, with the intensity of the fad gradually increasing, then gradually decreasing.

It is quite plausible that the effect of past price increases on demand for stocks is variable: Sometimes, people are encouraged by past price increases; at other times, discouraged. Past price increases may discourage investors by suggesting that the asset is becoming overpriced, and whether it does suggest this may depend on popular theories which may change from time to time. *Fashions* or *fads* are more general terms than *bubble*, and it will be easier to establish the existence of the former.

2.4   Evidence From Psychology

The notions of speculative excesses associated with the anecdotes discussed previously are inherently psychological. More specifically, they are social-psychological, relating as they do to the behavior of crowds rather than to isolated individuals. It is logical, therefore, to look in the psychological literature for evidence on the rationality of judgments of groups of people. Presumably, the fads or fashions in financial markets would be just one manifestation of a human tendency that can be documented in a wide variety of circumstances.

There is, in fact, a truly vast psychological literature on the process of human judgment and on the behavior of individuals in groups. There are several reasons why the literature has not had much impact on finance. One reason is that psychologists are often unconcerned with the possibility that their subjects are making rational decisions, and do not construct experiments in which it is possible to prove that they are not fully rational. Experimental psychologists often give problems to their subjects that strike economists as ill posed, so that it is impossible to tell whether they are responding rationally. Instead of trying to rule out the possibility that subjects are acting rationally, psychologists often try to tabulate behavior patterns that are not directly of interest to economists. The literature on contagion of attitude (e.g., see Wheeler [1966]) has emphasized such things as whether the authority or sex of the transmitter of attitudes has an impact on the rate of transmission, or whether such things as hunger, lack of social commitment, or recent chastisement affected the susceptibility of individuals to attitude change. Psychologists interested in group behavior have also concentrated on phenomena in which group ties are strong and consume much of the attention or emotional energy of the participants. They are often interested in the behavior of angry mobs, of fringe religious groups that try to cut members off from the rest of society, or of charismatic political movements. The informal communications among most investors usually do not take place in a large mob on a street corner nor even in the intense group sessions of many experiments.

There is still, apparently, a lot to be learned from the psychological literature if the reader is willing to generalize from human behavior in rather different situations.

2.5 Gambling Behavior

When the expected utility revolution in theoretical economics was born, there was some discussion of the importance of gambling behavior for economics. Now that the assumption of expected utility maximization is firmly entrenched in conventional economic theory, discussion of gambling behavior seems to have subsided in economics journals and has not kept pace with research in psychology. Studies of the behavior of gamblers reveal some aspects of human behavior that are likely to be especially important for understanding financial markets.

Gambling behavior reveals a universal aspect of human behavior and not an aspect of an individual culture: "In various forms it occurs universally in all cultures, all ages and is participated in widely by those of all societies, and social strata. Anthropological studies indicate its frequent occurrence in the most primitive of societies, and our modern games of chance are frequently more sophisticated versions of games once played by our forebears."[8]

Kallick et al. [1975], under the auspices of the Survey Research Center at the University of Michigan, undertook a study of gambling in 1975 in which more than two thousand randomly selected people in the United States were each interviewed for more than an hour about their attitudes and behavior regarding gambling. They found that 61% of the adult population placed some kind of bet in 1974; 48% placed bets on one or more of the popular commercial forms of gambling, with (among those betting) an average total wager on these in 1974 of $387 (or about $850 in 1985 prices).

The importance of the gambling urge can be underscored by the observation that in many people the urge becomes a compulsion. Compulsive gambling is a sufficiently important phenomenon that such groups as Gamblers Anonymous have arisen to deal with it.

Compulsive gambling was characterized by Custer [1975] as "preoccupation and urge to gamble with frequent gambling activity.... The gambling preoccupation, urge, and activity characteristically are progressive and with significant increases during periods of stress. Problems which arise as a result of gambling lead to an intensification of gambling behavior."[9]

Kallick et al. [1975] concluded that according to this characterization of compulsive gambling, 1.1% of American men and 0.5% of American women are "probably compulsive gamblers" and an additional 2.7% of the men and 1% of the women are "potential compulsive gamblers."[10]

Psychologist Igor Kusyszyn [1977] described gambling as a form of adult play yielding a sort of "high": "The gambler, very quickly, usually as soon as he or she begins to contemplate making the first wager, transports his or her self into a play world, a fantasy world in which he or she stays suspended until jarred back into reality by the finish of the last race or the disappearance of his or her money.... The uncertainty of the event and the risk that is an integral part of it provide for the cognitive-emotional-muscular arousal of the individual."[11]

Investing in speculative assets clearly shares with gambling the element of play. Lease et al. [1974], in a survey of 2,500 individual investors who had accounts at a large, national retail brokerage house, asked them to rate a number of attitude statements about investing on a scale of 1 to 5 (1 meaning strongly disagree, 5 meaning strongly agree). They gave a score of 4.09 to the statement "I enjoy investing and look forward to more such activity in the future." None of the other ten attitudes [including "I am substantially better informed than the average investor" (3.31) and a variety of other statements] was given as high a score.

The satisfaction afforded by gambling is related to the individual's ego involvement in the activity; and thus individual investors must themselves play to achieve satisfaction, and most do not rely on others for decisions. Lease et al. [1974] found that the average rating given to the statement "Relying exclusively upon mutual fund investments reduces the personal satisfaction I obtain from making my own investments" was 3.94. Of their respondents, only 20% said that they "rely primarily on brokerage firm or account executive for recommendations," and only 7% said they "rely primarily on paid investment newsletters or investment counselors' advice." Similar results about reliance on others for decisions came from surveys by Barlow et al. [1966] and Katona [1975].

While there is apparently no survey of institutional investors comparable to those of individual investors, it is even more likely that the aspect of play motivates them. The institutional investors are those who have chosen investing as an occupation, and it is reasonable to assume that they enjoy it as least as much and are as ego-involved as is the average investor.

If investing is, in part, play and is done for such motivations, then we will expect some judgment errors from investors like the judgment errors of gamblers. People who take chances may not require that there be really sound reasons to expect to win. Of course, the compulsive gambler at the racetrack is not deterred by losses and must know rationally and from past experience that he or she can generally expect to lose.[12] It is thus also plausible that investors whose interest is piqued by some speculative asset may go ahead and invest in that asset even after their further analysis indicates that their initial reasons to invest in it are not really good. Not playing would result in a sort of psychological letdown.

Speculative bubbles may provide a clear example of such behavior. If the price of an asset has gone up and made some of one's friends considerably richer, one's attention is drawn to that asset. The gamble posed then by investing in the asset will certainly seem interesting. On reflection, one may well realize that one has no way of knowing whether the price of the asset will continue to go up or even reverse itself and drop. The "chain letter" nature of the speculative bubble may even be readily apparent to market participants. But by the time that one has realized this, the game may have so captured one's imagination and involved one's ego that one is sorely tempted to play.

Roll's "hubris" theory of takeovers [1986] would also appear to be related to such an effect. In his theory, managers who are fully capable of understanding the "winner's curse" persist in their beliefs because of "overweaning pride," i.e., because of their ego involvement.

If one yields to the temptation to play, then one is likely to feel the need to justify the decision on grounds other than a gambling urge. One is likely to tell one's friends that the investment has good prospects. A front will be erected to conceal the gambling aspect of the decision.

As a form of play, the satisfaction afforded by gambling is affected by how well the game captures one's imagination. The observation of one's friends involved, the stories and gossip that surround a particular investment, all might contribute to the pleasure and thus to the judgmental "errors" that result. The Survey Research Center study on gambling concluded that "we have found repeatedly that the incidence of gambling on different types of games is associated with exposure to others who gamble."[13] Thus, although gambling itself is not always a social activity, the biases on judgment that it creates may tend to be social.

2.6   Salience and Judgment

The diffusion models of fashions or fads discussed earlier relied on the notion that people do not behave systematically and allow their judgment to be influenced by what happens to catch their attention.

Tversky and Kahneman [1974] asserted in what they called the "availability heuristic" that judgments are influenced by "the ease with which instances or associations come to mind." Many experiments have sought to confirm that more vividly presented arguments (involving pictures. anecdotes, etc., that would seem to make the arguments more easily remembered) have more of an effect on human judgment. The "vividness" literature, however, has not demonstrated many sharp failures of human judgment. In a survey of this literature, Taylor and Thompson [1982] concluded that "the vividness effect, at least as it has been studied to this point, is weak if existent at all.[14]

The "vividness" literature, however, has worked within some narrow bounds that may have excluded the relevant behavior. Taylor and Thompson [1982] noted that in the experiments that they cited, experimental design ensured that subjects were equally exposed to arguments whether or not they were vividly presented. Experiments confirming the effects of "salience" on judgments differ from the vividness experiments in that the former allow vivid and nonvivid presentations to compete for the subjects' attention. Taylor and Thompson find that the evidence that salience affects judgments is much stronger. Thus, a well-documented human judgment error is that people fail to collect evidence systematically and allow themselves to be distracted by attention-grabbing events.

2.7 Group Polarization of Attitudes

A number of choice dilemma experiments and observations of people gambling indicate that people in groups tend to take greater risks than do individuals separated from a group. This phenomenon, as surveyed by Clark [1971], has been called the "risky shift." Further experimental research, however, did not always confirm the risky shift, and indeed in some experiments groups behaved more cautiously than individuals.[15] It was found, though, that groups whose individual members were cautious relative to the population average tended to become even more cautious in groups, and that individuals who were less cautious relative to the population average tended to become on average even less cautious in groups. Thus, the risky-shift hypothesis was abandoned and replaced with the "group polarization" hypothesis: "The average postgroup response will tend to be more extreme and in the same direction as the average of the pregroup response."[16] A large number of studies have confirmed such a group-induced polarization of attitudes in a wide variety of decision problems, not just those involving decisions regarding risk. One survey concluded of the group polarization effect that "seldom in the history of social psychology has a nonobvious phenomenon been so firmly grounded in data from across a variety of cultures and dependent measures."[17]

The phenomenon of group-induced polarization of attitudes would suggest that social movements might be begun by any events that cause a subgroup of the population to form to talk about the matter in question. For example, an advertising campaign that reminds people of a product may, if it engenders conversation by an already favorable subgroup, heighten the favorable attitude. (It might equally well cause a less favorably disposed subgroup to develop a very negative attitude.) Social movements may end when the events cease to enforce the group interaction.

Much of the literature on the polarization effect will seem unsatisfactory to economists, who are inclined to ask whether any observed human behavior might be reconciled with an optimizing paradigm. In fact, the "group polarization of attitudes" observed in many experiments may well be consistent with rational decision making if groups pool the information of individual members. If the experiments can be described as asking groups to estimate a parameter on which each member has some information, and if the group members are optimal Bayesian decision makers, then the group estimate may behave like an amplified transformation of the average estimate that members of the group would give without pooling information. Such an information-pooling argument was used by Burnstein et al. [1971] and by Bordley [1983] to dismiss the whole literature on group polarization as only discovering rational behavior.

This criticism of the group polarization literature is not effective against all of the studies demonstrating group polarization because in many of these studies there was no conceivable information to be pooled. Many experiments asked people not to respond to questions of fact but to make decision making. For example, there is some analysis of the process by could not have any information.

There are other reasons canvassed in this literature to think that the group polarization phenomenon may not be consistent with Bayesian decision making. For example, there is some analysis of the process by which the observed group polarization occurs. It has been found that there is a tendency for groups to concentrate in their discussions on facts and arguments supporting the dominant attitude of the group (see Lamm and Myers [1978]). Janis [1972], after a series of case studies of real-world groups that made disastrously bad judgments, found that there was a tendency for self-appointed censors to appear who would try to discourage discussion of arguments contrary to the emerging group judgment.

2.8 Conclusion and Summary

The notion of market efficiency has proven a useful one in many ways in the finance literature over the past couple of decades. In many ways it is a big improvement over notions that preceded it. But the academic finance profession has carried it too far, so that alternative notions based in part on the sort of psychological research discussed in this chapter are almost totally ignored in finance journals. Since psychological alternatives are virtually never discussed in academic finance journals, the profession at large is generally uninformed about these alternatives. The profession does not generally connect the various pieces of "anomalous evidence" regarding market efficiency with such alternatives and is in the habit of describing the anomalies as "small," even though they may be the consequence of sizable valuation errors.

Modern psychology does not reduce human behavior to a simple model like the expected utility model that underlies theoretical finance. The literature on gambling behavior shows the plausibility of the claims made in the usual anecdotes that there is sometimes excessive enthusiasm for certain financial assets and thus that other financial assets are sometimes ignored. The literature on salience and human judgment makes plausible the claims in the anecdotes that popular attention to certain speculative assets was capricious. The literature on group polarization of attitudes adds some further plausibility to the claim in the anecdotes that groups of individuals may tend to act together, reaching the same decisions around the same times.

How much of the variance in price changes may be attributed to changing fashions and how much to fundamentals as measured by information about future dividends? The answer will differ from one speculative asset to another, depending on how much variation there has been in dividends. For the aggregate stock market over the past century, the aggregate dividend stream has been sufficiently trendlike that we might attribute most of the price variation to fashions or fads. For some individual stocks, on the other hand, there have been very dramatic movements in dividends or other measures of fundamental value, movements sometimes spanning orders of magnitude. Clearly, price movements for these stocks primarily reflect fundamentals.

How much credence should we attach to theories in the literature on takeovers that "undervaluation" of target firms and subsequent price changes around the date of a takeover are to be understood in terms of information about fundamentals? Again, the answer will differ across firms. When, for example, there is clear evidence that the target firm is mismanaged and that the takeover will clearly imply that a new management will be installed, then it is entirely plausible to interpret the premium paid for the target firm at the time of takeover in terms described in the literature on mismanagement theories. But we should not feel compelled to interpret prices in terms of such fundamentals, and we can be just as confident that instances occur where entirely different interpretations are appropriate where, for example, the undervaluation may be due to investors' overlooking the stock, or the takeover premium may reflect an overvaluation by those who acquire the firm.

Notes

1. Sharpe [1985, p. 67].

2. Brealey and Myers [1984, p. 784].

3. Mackay [1841, pp. 141 and 147]. Mackay notes that 100 florins would then buy ten fat sheep, a suit of clothes, or a complete bed (p. 143).

4. Galbraith [1972, pp. 79–80].

5. Malkiel [1981, p. 53].

6. Reinganum [1981] instead concluded that the "size effect" (small firms tend to show abnormal returns) largely subsumes the E/P effect. Basu, however, found that while slightly weaker for larger firms, the abnormal return predicted by the earnings-price ratio is present in all quintiles of firm size, and he criticized Reinganum for his failure to correct for risk. Peavey and Goodman [1983] found that the P/E effect is even more dramatic among a group of firms whose market value in 1980 exceeded 100 million and after controlling for an "industry effect."

7. Dimson and Marsh [1984, p. 1260].

8. Bolen and Boyd [1968, p. 617].

9. Custer [1975] cited in Kallick et al. [1975].

10. Kallick et al. [1975, p. 75].

11. Kusyszyn [1977, pp. 25–26].

12. Note that both pari-mutuel racetrack betting (horse racing is the most popular commercial sport in the United States) and the picking of stocks involve direct competition in a marketplace against other players and the subsequent thrill of watching the horse (price) move.

13. Kallick et al. [1975].

14. Taylor and Thompson [1982, p. 172].

15. Kusyszyn [1977] argued that these group experiments do not accurately represent real-world gambling in that they fail to generate the ego involvement and enthusiasm of actual gamblers.

16. Myers and Lamm [1976, p. 603].

17. Lamm and Myers [1978, p. 146].

References

Barlow, R., H. E. Brazer, and J. N. Morgan 1966. *Economic Behavior of the Affluent.* Washington. D.C.: Brookings Institution.

Bartholomew, David J. 1982. *Stochastic Models for Social Processes.* 3rd ed. New York: Wiley.

Basu, Sanjoy 1983. "The Relationship between Earnings, Yield, Market Value and Return: Further Evidence," *Journal of Financial Economics* 12: 129–156.

Bishop, G. D., and D. G. Myers 1974. "Informational Influence in Group Discussion," *Organizational Behavior and Human Performance* 12: 92–104.

Bjerring, J. H., J. Lakonishok, and T. Vermaelen 1983. Stock Prices and Financial Analysts' Recommendations," *Journal of Finance* 38 (1): 187–204.

Black, Fisher and Myron Scholes 1974. "The Effects of Dividend Yield and Dividend Policy on Common Stock Prices and Returns," *Journal of Financial Economics* 1: 1–22.

Blume, E. 1980. "Stock Returns and Dividend Yields: Some More Evidence," *Review of Economics and Statistics* 62: 567–577.

Blume, E., J. Crockett, and I. Friend 1974. "Stockownership in the United States: Characteristics and Trends," *Survey of Current Business* 54: 16–74.

Bolen, D. W., and W. H. Boyd 1968. "Gambling and the Gambler: A Review and Preliminary Findings," *Archives of General Psychiatry* 18 (5): 617–629.

Bordley, R. F. 1983. "A Bayesian Model of Group Polarization," *Organizational Behavior and Human Performance* 32: 262–274.

Brealey, R., and S. Myers 1984. *Principles of Corporation Finance.* New York: McGraw-Hill.

Breeden, Douglas 1979. "An Intertemporal Asset Pricing Model with Stochastic Consumption and Investment Opportunities," *Journal of Financial Economics* 7: 265–296.

Burnstein, E., H. Miller, A. Vinokur, S. Katz, and J. Crowley 1971. "Risky Shift Is Eminently Rational," *Journal of Personality and Social Psychology* 20: 462–471.

Clark, R. D., III 1971. Group-Induced Shift Toward Risk: A Critical Appraisal," *Psychological Bulletin* 76:251–270.

Custer, R. L. 1975. *Description of Compulsive Gambling.* Manuscript prepared for the American Psychiatric Association Task Force on Nomenclature.

DeBondt, Werner, and Richard Thaler 1985. "Does the Stock Market Overreact?" *Journal of Finance* 40:793–805.

Dimson, E., and P. Marsh 1984. "An Analysis of Brokers' and Analysts' Unpublished Forecasts of UK Stock Returns," *Journal of Finance* 39 (5):1257–1292.

Figlewski, S. 1981. "The Informational Effects of Restrictions on Short Sales: Some Empirical Evidence," *Journal of Financial and Quantitative Analysis* 16:463–476.

Flavin, Majorie 1983. "Excess Volatility in the Financial Markets: A Reassessment of the Empirical Evidence," *Journal of Political Economy* 91:929–956.

French, Kenneth R., and Richard Roll 1986. "Stock Return Variances: The Arrival of Information and the Reaction of Traders," *Journal of Financial Economics* 17:5–26.

Friend, Irwin, and Marshall Blume 1978. *The Changing Role of the Institutional Investor.* New York: Wiley.

Galbraith, J. K. 1972. *The Great Crash, 1929.* 3rd ed. Boston: Houghton Mifflin.

Hall, Robert E. 1985. Intertemporal Substitution in Consumption. Reproduced, Stanford University.

Janis, I. L. 1972, *Victims of Groupthink.* Boston: Houston.

Jarrow, R. 1980. "Heterogeneous Expectations. Restriction on Short Sales, and Equilibrium Asset Prices," *Journal of Finance* 35:1105–1113.

Kallick, M., D. Suits, T. Dielman, and J. Hybels 1975. *A Survey of American Gambling Attitudes and Behavior.* Ann Arbor: Survey Research Center. Institute for Social Research, University of Michigan.

Katona, George 1975. *Psychological Economics.* New York: Elsevier.

Kleidon, Allan W. 1986. Variance Bounds Tests and Stock Valuation Models. *Journal of Political Economy* 94:953–1001.

Kusyszyn, I. 1977. "How Gambling Saved Me from a Misspent Sabbatical," *Journal of Humanistic Psychology* 17:19–34.

Kydland, Finn E., and Edward F. Prescott 1982. "Time to Build and Aggregate Fluctuations," *Econometrica* 50:1345–1370.

Lamm, H., and D. G. Myers 1978. "Group-Induced Polarization of Attitudes and Behavior." In *Advances in Experimental Social Psychology*, Vol. 11, ed. L. Berkowitz, 145–195. New York: Academic Press.

Lease, R. C., W. G. Lewellen, and G. G. Schlarbaum 1974. "The Individual Investor: Attributes and Attitudes," *Journal of Finance* 29:413–433.

LeRoy, Stephen, and Richard Porter 1981. "The Present Value Relation: Tests Based on Variance Bounds," *Econometrica* 49:555–574.

Litzenberger, R. L., and K. Ramaswamy 1982. "The Effects of Dividends on Common Stock Prices: Tax Effects or Information Effects," *Journal of Finance* 37: 429–443.

Lucas, Robert E. 1978. "Asset Prices in an Exchange Economy," *Econometrica* 46:1429–1445.

McGuire, W. J. 1969. "The Nature of Attitudes and Attitude Change." In *The Handbook of Social Psychology*, 2nd ed., Vol. III, ed. G. Linzey and E. Aronson. Reading, Mass.: Addison-Wesley.

Mackay, C. 1841. *Memoirs of Extraordinary Popular Delusions*. London: Bentley.

Malkiel, Burton G. 1981. *A Random Walk Down Wall Street*. 2nd ed. New York: Norton.

Mankiw, N. G., D. Romer, and M. Shapiro 1985. "An Unbiased Reexamination of Stock Price Volatility," *Journal of Finance* 40:677–687.

Marsh, T. A., and R. C. Merton 1984. "Earnings Variability and Variance Bounds Tests of the Rationality of Stock Market Prices," *American Economic Review* 76: 483–498.

Morgan, I. G. 1982. "Dividends and Capital Asset Prices." *Journal of Finance* 37, 1071–1086.

Myers, D. G., and H. Lamm 1976. "The Group Polarization Phenomenon," *Psychological Bulletin* 83:602–627.

New York Stock Exchange 1960. *Investors of Tomorrow*.

New York Stock Exchange 1979. *Public Attitudes Toward Investing: Marketing Implications*.

New York Stock Exchange 1955. *The Public Speaks to the Exchange Community*.

Paget, E. H. 1929. "Sudden Changes in Group Opinion," *Social Forces* 7:440–444.

Peavey, J. W., III, and D. A. Goodman 1983. "The Significance of P/E's for Portfolio Returns," *Journal of Portfolio Management* 9:43–47.

Pound, John, and Robert J. Shiller 1987. "Are Institutional Investors Speculators?" *Journal of Portfolio Management*. Spring, 46–52.

Reinganum, M. R. 1981. "Misspecification of Capital Asset Pricing: Empirical Anomalies Based on Earnings Yields and Market Values," *Journal of Financial Economics* 9:19–46.

Roll, Richard 1977. "A Critique of the Asset Pricing Theory's Tests. I. On Past and Potential Testability of the Theory," *Journal of Financial Economics* 4:129–176.

Roll, Richard 1984. "Orange Juice and Weather," *American Economic Review* 74: 861–880.

Roll, Richard 1986. "The Hubris Hypothesis of Corporate Takeovers," *Journal of Business,* 59:197–216.

Rosenberg, Barr 1985. "Persuasive Evidence on Market Inefficiency," *Journal of Portfolio Management* 11:9–16.

Sharpe, W. F. 1985. *Investments.* 3rd ed. Englewood Cliffs, N.J.: Prentice-Hall.

Shiller, Robert J. 1979. "The Volatility of Long-Term Interest Rates and Expectations Models of the Term Structure," *Journal of Political Economy* 87:1190–1219.

Shiller, Robert J. 1981a. "Alternative Tests of Rational Expectations Models: The Case of the Term Structure," *Journal of Econometrics* 16:71–87.

Shiller, Robert J. 1981b. "Do Stock Prices Move Too Much to Be Justified by Subsequent Changes in Dividends?" *American Economic Review* 71:421–436.

Shiller, Robert J. 1984. "Stock Prices and Social Dynamics." In *Brookings Papers on Economic Activity,* 457–497. Washington, D.C.: Brookings Institution.

Shiller, Robert J. 1981c."The Use of Volatility Measures in Assessing Market Efficiency," *Journal of Finance* 36:291–304.

Shiller, Robert J., and P. Perron 1985. "Testing the Random Walk Hypothesis: Power Versus Frequency of Observation," *Economics Letters* 18:381–386.

Summers, Lawrence H. 1986. "Does the Stock Market Rationally Reflect Fundamental Values?" *Journal of Finance* 41:591–602.

Taylor, S. E., and S. C. Thompson 1982. "Stalking the Elusive 'Vividness' Effect," *Psychological Review* 89:155–181.

Teger, A. I., and D. G. Pruitt 1967. "Components of Group Risk Taking," *Journal of Experimental and Social Psychology* 3:189–205.

Tversky, Amos, and Daniel Kahneman 1974. "Judgment Under Uncertainty: Heuristics and Biases," *Science* 185:1124–1131.

West, Kenneth D. 1984. "Speculative Bubbles and Stock Price Volatility." Memo No. 54, Financial Research Center. Princeton University, Princeton, N.J.

Wheeler, L. 1966. "Toward a Theory of Behavioral Contagion," *Psychological Review* 73:179–192.

II The Stock Market

3   Overview[1]

Price movements in the stock market appear to show excess volatility; that is, they appear to be mostly unjustified in terms of simple statistical representations of the efficient markets hypothesis. The chapters in this part of the book present evidence for this claim from analysis of historical data on prices, dividends, earnings, and short-term interest rates.

The basic notion that opinion changes are a source of price fluctuations, and that popular models tend to cause people to react inappropriately to some kinds of information, does not itself imply that there should be excess volatility. Popular models might, at certain times or in certain markets, result in prices being less variable than they should be. But the evidence on excess volatility does help dispense with the notion that efficient markets models always work extremely well, and does help to tell us something about the nature of popular models that have been prevalent in the stock market.

The chapters in this part of the book, by testing whether we can justify price in terms of efficient markets models, represent a substantial departure from the sort of analysis that has been usual in most of the finance literature, which tends to emphasize the analysis of data on returns, rather than price or value. Now, of course, data on returns can be cumulated to yield a measure of value, but this cumulation has not been the focus of most statistical analyses in the finance literature. In this part of the book, we shall compare price with a measure of value that will be called ex-post value. The concept of actual value, while very simple, is not a familiar one.

3.1   Ex-Post Value or Perfect-Foresight Price

The ex-post value of an asset is defined here as the value of an investment in the asset, taking into account the actual future payoffs that the invest-

Portions of this chapter © 1988 the American Agricultural Economics Association.

ment will yield, the actual future dividends that the investor will receive.[2] If the investment will do very well in coming years, that is, will yield high dividends, then we say that the ex-post value is high today. Clearly we do not generally know the ex-post value today of an investment today— although we have imperfect indicators of it—because we do not know the future dividends. Ex-post value should not be confused with the more common terms "economic value" or "investment value," which refer to the value we place on an asset given only the information available about it today.

Throughout this book P_t will denote the price of an asset at time t, and P_t^* will denote the ex-post value. In this book, ex-post value will always be some sort of present value of the current and future dividends, D_t, D_{t+1}, D_{t+2}, ... If investors knew these future dividends, then there would be no forecasting problem, and price P_t should, by the efficient markets theory, equal ex-post value P_t^*. For this reason, we may also call the ex-post value the "perfect-foresight price" or "ex-post-rational price."[3]

Having defined ex-post value, then, we can state the efficient markets theory as asserting that price equals the best possible forecast of ex-post value. Formally, $P_t = E_t P_t^*$, which is read as "P_t is the (mathematical) expectation conditional on information available at time t of P_t^*." The mathematical expectation means the optimal forecast, taking account of probabilities seen from the vantage point of time t.

While ex-post value P_t^* is not known today (time t), it can be computed later (at a time greater than t) after dividends become known. Note that in computing true ex-post value afterward we ideally make no use of price of the asset (although terminal price may sometimes be used in approximations to ex-post value). If an investment will do well in the sense that its price will rise a lot, this does not mean that the ex-post value is high. True ex-post value includes only the payoffs that the investment itself produces, not the capital gains or losses one obtains by selling the share to another investor who will pay more or less for the asset. If the efficient markets theory is right, these capital gains or losses are just reflections of changes in, or of changing information about, ex-post value. If the efficient markets theory is wrong, these capital gains or losses may have nothing to do with ex-post value.

It should be clear that under the efficient markets theory, the price of a share can change for either of two reasons. First, it may change because P_t^* changes through time. A firm may go through a temporary period of paying out high dividends, after which the firm does poorly and pays out very little in dividends. The ex-post value P_t^* is high just before the high dividend payments, since the investor in the stock then will receive those payments. It is low after the high dividend payments because an investor who buys the stock then will not receive them. Second, price may change because new information arises about P_t^*. Investors may learn something that causes them to revise their forecast of future dividends, and this will change P_t even if P_t^* itself does not change.

In some of the succeeding chapters P_t^* is plotted in various transformations against time along with actual price P_t as a way of learning about the efficient markets model. Look, for example, at figure 5.1 on page 106. Here, ex-post value (detrended) is taken as the simple present value of future dividends using a constant discount rate, with an assumption about dividends after the end of the sample.

At the very least, one learns from figure 5.1 that actual aggregate stock price movements around the trend of smoothed earnings cannot be justified in terms of the first reason above, that is, in terms of short-run movements in ex-post value. People (such as some news journalists) are making a big mistake who often interpret drops in the stock market as rational responses to news about a recession around the corner that will temporarily affect corporate profits and hence dividends. Big movements in P_t could be accompanied by big movements in P_t^*, but they are not. For example, when the stock market dropped from its peak in 1929 to its bottom in 1932, there was no validating drop in P_t^*: earnings and dividends dropped for only a few years, and those few years had relatively little impact on the present value of dividends; a few years' dividends matter relatively little to ex-post value, which depends on all future dividends. The depression that followed 1929 was just too small and temporary an event to have much impact on P_t^*. There has never been a big enough short-term event that would justify such a price drop.

No one seems to question the conclusion that short-run movements in price P_t in theory could correspond to but in fact do not correspond to short-run movements in ex-post value P_t^*. We know that P_t^* is itself a long moving average of dividends; P_t^* will not make sharp movements unless dividend movements are much sharper, and they are not much sharper. The more contentious issue here is whether there is also something more to learn from these data, namely whether the variability of P_t is too great to be justified in terms of *either* changes in ex-post value or changing information about ex-post value. For this, we need some more conceptual apparatus.

3.2   The Variability of Forecasts

The basic concept here is that a good forecast should be less variable than, or at most as variable as, the quantity forecasted. How much less variable depends on how good the forecast is. A forecast that is very poor, i.e., that bears little relation to the outcome, should be a lot less variable than is the variable forecasted. At the other extreme, if the forecast contains no error, then it should be as variable as the variable forecasted, but no more.

That this is so follows from the requirement that it should be impossible to predict the forecast error of an optimal forecast. Suppose that the forecast x_t at time t (say, x_t is P_t above or a transformation of it) of a random variable x_t^* (say, x_t^* is P_t^* above or the corresponding transformation of it) is as variable as x_t^* but not very highly correlated with it. Then when an unusually large value of x_t is drawn, the variable x_t^* is probably not also unusually large, because of the weak correlation between x_t and x_t^*. Thus a large value of the forecast x would tend to predict a negative forecast error. Large values of x_t need not, of course, always correspond to negative forecast errors, but there would be a tendency for that, and such a tendency is inconsistent with optimal forecasting. We could use our knowledge of the tendency to improve the forecasts. Conversely, when an unusually small value of x_t occurs, the variable x_t^* is probably not also unusually small, and so a positive forecast error would tend to occur.

It should be understood that an optimal forecast $E_t x_t^*$ need not be highly correlated with the variable forecasted x_t^*. By an optimal forecast, we mean a forecast that makes best possible use of available information. If the information available about x_t^* is only weakly correlated with x_t^*, then the information should still be used in the optimal forecasting scheme, and hence the forecast should be only weakly correlated with x_t^*, but the forecast x_t should be much less variable than is x_t^*. Then despite the poor correlation between x_t and x_t^*, high values of x_t will not tend to be correlated with negative forecast errors. This is because the weak correlation between the optimal forecast x_t and the variable forecasted x_t^* is enough to cause x_t^* to tend to be, when x_t is high, just as high as x_t, given the greater variability of x_t^*, and conversely when x_t is low. Such a forecast x_t is truly optimal, though not highly successful. It is optimal in the sense that no one could forecast the forecast errors, not highly successful in the sense that the (absolute) forecast error is large.

The chapters in this part of the book look at various transformations of ex-post value as x_t^* and corresponding transformations x_t of price, as ways of evaluating market efficiency, to see whether x_t behaves like an optimal forecast of x_t^*.

The analysis consists, however, of fundamentally more than just looking at plots like these to evaluate efficient markets models. Such an approach, in neglecting any consideration of statistical models, would be hazardous. There may in fact be a spurious tendency for plots of P_t^* to look less variable than P_t even under the efficient markets model, if the behavior of dividends is such that there are no bounds to its potential variability or if the sample period is sufficiently short. Looking at plots is only *part* of the analysis of market volatility.

3.3   Organization of This Part of the Book

The chapters in this part were written over a period of years, addressing this issue in various ways. The next chapter in this part, chapter 4, introduces these chapters in more technical way, and compares them with criticism they have received.

The earliest chapters in this part, chapters 5 and 6, originally published in 1981, compare simple variance measures of price with variance measures of fundamentals. These chapters run parallel to the independent work of Stephen LeRoy and Richard Porter. Later work with John Campbell, represented here by chapter 8, looks at much more than the simple variances, estimating vector autoregressive models for price, dividends, and other information variables.[4]

The claim that stock prices show excess volatility met with strong opposition; many papers were written criticizing it. Often, the criticism brought us back to fundamental issues about what we mean by variability, whether we expect time series to be mean-reverting, or whether statistical tests are robust to certain departures from usual assumptions. I include in this part of the book, chapter 7, my response to one of my critics. The work that John Campbell and I have done, of which chapter 8 is an example, is also partly a response to the critics. Moreover, chapter 9, written with John Campbell, explicitly addresses some issues associated with the criticism that might still be applied to chapter 8.

Some of the generality of these results is indicated by the remaining two chapters in this part. Chapter 10 generalizes the variance bounds analysis to vectors of prices, so that covariances as well as variances can be considered. This chapter shows that the excess volatility that we observed in the stock market can also be described as excess comovement of individual stock prices, and shows as well that there is a tendency for aggregate stock prices across countries (the United Kingdom and the United States) to move together too much. Chapter 11 looks at principal components of subindexes of the Standard and Poor Composite, and finds that evidence is weaker that there is excess volatility for other principal components.

Notes

1. Portions of this chapter were taken from my paper "The Volatility Debate," published in *American Journal of Agricultural Economics*, 70 (1988): 1057–1063.

2. The idea of using actual value to study efficient markets models derives from some unpublished work of Jeremy Siegel in 1969. We used essentially this concept (without this name) in Shiller and Siegel [1977] (chapter 14). Stephen LeRoy and Richard Porter independently used such a concept.

3. Recently, the terms P and P^* have acquired a great deal of publicity from their different definitions at the Board of Governors of the Federal Reserve System. Jeffery J. Hallman, Richard D. Porter, and David H. Small have defined P as the GNP implicit deflator and P^* as the money stock (M2) times the long-run value of the GNP velocity of money divided by potential real GNP. If there is an analogy to the concepts in this book, it is a weak one.

4. Chapter 16, in the part on the bond market below, includes an analysis of the stock market that is superseded by chapter 8. Chapter 16 was included here primarily because it lays out some fundamental concepts and includes an analysis of the term structure of interest rates.

Stock Price Volatility: An Introductory Survey

This chapter is a survey of my own and related work on statistical analysis of stock prices and of the criticisms of this work. It will serve as an introduction to the remaining chapters in this part of the book. The chapter begins by looking at some of the fundamental issues raised by the literature over excess volatility, expanding on basic simple concepts that seem not so obvious in view of this literature, and describing these concepts in more general terms than is done in the other chapters in this part. An interpretation is given of the debate over the excess volatility claims.

4.1 The Efficient Markets Model and a First Look at the Data

There is no universally accepted definition of the term "efficient markets model." However, references to the model usually imply some form of expected present value relation. As formulated in the chapters in this part, the simple efficient markets model asserts that the price P_t of a long-term asset (let us say a stock, though it could also be bonds, land, structures, or other things) is the expected present discounted value of future dividends (or coupons, rents, or other income accruing to the owner of a unit of the asset) D_{t+k}, $k \geq 0$, discounted by future one-period interest rates r_{t+k}, $k \geq 0$. As in chapter 5 and elsewhere, we can write the simple efficient markets model in the following two equations:

$$P_t = E_t P_t^*, \tag{1}$$

$$P_t^* = \sum_{k=0}^{\infty} D_{t+k} \prod_{j=0}^{k} \gamma_{t+j}. \tag{2}$$

Here, P_t^* is the ex-post value, i.e., ex-post-rational or perfect-foresight price, and γ_{t+j} is a real discount factor equal to $1/(1 + r_{t+j})$, where r_{t+j} is the short (one-period) rate of discount at time $t + j$.

Now there is a serious problem in evaluating this simple model, namely, that P_t^* is not fully observable, even long after time t, since the summation in (2) extends to infinity and we always have only a finite record of dividends and discount rates. However, we can get an approximation to P_t^*, some time later, at time T after time t, under the assumption that the discounting in (2) makes the present value of future dividends after T small enough to be of little account in determining P_t^*. We can use (2) to produce an estimate of P_t^* if we only are willing to impose some assumption about the present value of dividends at the end of our period over which we have data on dividends.

Figure 5.1 on page 106 from my 1981 paper shows both real price P_t and ex-post value P_t^* made for the years 1871–1979 with such an assumption about dividends after 1979. This plot represents the constant discount rate case ($r_t = r$) and uses data from Standard and Poor Composite Index. Both P_t and P_t^* were detrended in that plot by dividing by an exponential trend line. Detrended P_t appeared to be much more volatile than did detrended P_t^*. This plot attracted a great deal of attention, as it appeared to show in very impressive terms that the stock market was much too volatile to be accounted for in terms of fundamentals.

Figure 4.1 is essentially the same plot, as updated through 1988, using the Standard and Poor Composite Index deflated by the producer price

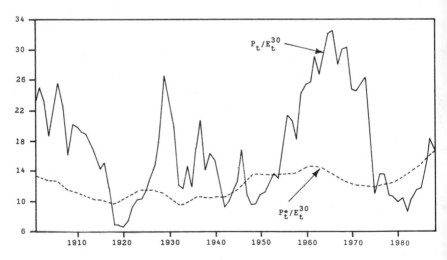

Figure 4.1
Price-earnings ratio $\bar{P}_t \equiv P_t/E_t^{30}$ and ex-post value-earnings ratio $\bar{P}_t^* \equiv P_t^*/E_t^{30}$ 1901–1988, constant discount rate case. Earnings E_t^{30} are 30-year moving average of actual real earnings; the discount rate used in equation 2 to compute P_t^* is 8.32%.

index 1982 = 100. This plot is slightly different from my original plot (it corresponds more closely to the data described in table 1.4 on page 37): what are shown are not exponentially detrended real price P_t and detrended real P_t^* but $\tilde{P}_t \equiv P_t/E_t^{30}$ and $\tilde{P}_t^* \equiv P_t^*/E_t^{30}$, where E_t^{30} is a 30-year moving average of real earnings. E_t^{30} is a moving average for years $t-1$ to $t-30$ of real earnings on the Standard and Poor Index; it is similar to the measure used in chapter 8, and is also analogous to a measure used by LeRoy and Porter [1981].[1] For figure 4.1, P_t^* was produced assuming that the present value of future real dividends in 1988 was equal to the 1988 price. That is why $\tilde{P}_t$ and $\tilde{P}_t^*$ coincide at the end, in 1988. The real discount rate r was taken as 8.32%, the sample mean real return on stocks. Dividing P_t and P_t^* by E_t^{30} is essentially just a slightly different way of detrending them. Since a 30-year moving average of real earnings is very smooth, almost a trend line, this plot does not look much different from the one in my 1981 paper (although the averaging lost us the first 30 years of the plot). The use of a 30-year interval to average is not essential to the appearance of the figure; dividing by any long average of real earnings will yield a similar-looking plot, as will any long average of real dividends or real price. I used the long moving average to detrend to eliminate any objections that information not known at time t was used in producing detrended price at time t.[2]

It appears that the variable $\tilde{P}_t$ plotted in figure 4.1 does not look like such an optimal forecast of $\tilde{P}_t^*$, and this is the basic motivation for the analysis here. This intuitive notion can be stated more formally in terms of variance bounds.

4.2   Variability of Prices and Variance Bounds

If $x_t = E_t(x_t^*)$, where E_t denotes mathematical expectation conditional on all publicly available information at time t, then

$$\sigma(x_t) = \rho(x_t, x_t^*)\sigma(x_t^*), \tag{3}$$

where σ denotes standard deviation and $\rho(x, x^*)$ denotes the correlation coefficient between x_t and x_t^*. This relation, which is a formalization of an intuitive notion described in the preceding chapter, says that unless the correlation between x_t and x_t^* is quite high, the variability of the forecast x_t must be substantially less than that of x_t^*.

In interpreting equation (3), it should be borne in mind just what the standard deviation of x_t or x_t^* means. In practice, we will be studying time series data, and there are many alternative measures of the volatility of these data. The measure used in equation (3)—the simple unconditional standard deviation of the time series—should not be confused with a measure of how jagged or choppy the time series looks when plotted. In fact, $\sigma(x_t)$ is large if x_t tends to wander substantially from its mean value. If x_t is plotted on the vertical axis against time on the horizontal axis and a horizontal line is drawn through its mean, then the standard deviation is a measure of how much the time series deviates from that horizontal line. Technically, the standard deviation is the square root of the mean square deviation. The standard deviation may be the same whether or not the deviations from the horizontal line occur in long slow swings or in sharp frequent oscillations. (See also the appendix in chapter 15.)

When one considers the relatively low frequency or long-run movements of some of the variables to which (3) is applied, one sees why the literature on excess volatility in financial markets has tended to use long historical time series data. Obviously, if the time series x_t makes long, slow, movements through time, then we will need a long time series (spanning many years) before we can measure the true tendency of the variable x_t to deviate from its mean. Getting many observations by sampling frequently (say, through weekly or even daily observations) will not give us much power to measure the standard deviations $\sigma(x_t)$ or $\sigma(x_t^*)$ if the total time span in which our data are contained is only a few years long. That is why it is difficult to do analogous volatility tests with some assets other than stocks, assets such as land or real estate, where good data on prices and the rents that correspond to dividends usually cover a shorter time span.

4.3   Formal Derivation of Variance Relations

To derive equation (3), note that $x_t = E_t(x_t^*)$ implies that $x_t^* = x_t + u_t$, where u_t is a zero-mean forecast error uncorrelated with all information available to the market at time t, and hence is uncorrelated with x_t. Thus, $\mathrm{cov}(x_t^*, x_t) = \mathrm{cov}(x_t + u_t, x_t) = \mathrm{cov}(x_t, x_t) + \mathrm{cov}(u_t, x_t) = \sigma^2(x_t)$. Using the definition of the correlation coefficient, $\rho(x_t, x_t^*) = \mathrm{cov}(x_t, x_t^*)/(\sigma(x_t)\sigma(x_t^*))$, the result follows directly. Another way to see the validity of equation (3) is to start from the proposition that if x_t is an optimal forecast of x_t^*, then when x^* is regressed on x and a constant term, the coefficient of x should be 1.000. The coefficient of x in a regression is $\mathrm{cov}(x, x^*)/\mathrm{var}(x)$. Setting this to 1.000, equation (1) follows directly.

The correlation coefficient, which must be positive given the requirement that $x_t = E_t x_t^*$, cannot exceed 1.000. Thus, there is an upper bound to the variability of price x given that of x_t^*:

$$\sigma(x_t) \leqslant \sigma(x_t^*). \tag{4}$$

We may examine whether (3) or (4) holds as a way of evaluating whether x_t is indeed an optimal forecast of x_t^*. Examining via (3) whether $\sigma(x_t)$ is too large to be justified in terms of $\rho(x_t, x_t^*)$ is equivalent to regressing x_t^* on x_t and a constant and examining whether the coefficient of x_t is less than 1.00. If the regression coefficient is less than 1.000, this means that the variability of x_t should be reduced; x_t should be scaled toward its mean, to improve the forecast. However, if we find that the coefficient of x_t is less than one, we still do not know that the variability of x_t is itself too high, given the possibility that other information might be available to forecast that is not used properly in x_t. If (4) is violated by the data, then we know that there never could be any available information that could justify the variability of x_t. Violations of (4) thus point to a narrower class of alternatives to the model $x_t = E_t x_t^*$ than do violations of (3).

One common criticism of the use of the inequality (4) is that for certain alternative hypotheses and under certain circumstances a test of the efficient markets null is no more powerful than an ordinary regression test, of regressing $x_t^* - x_t$ on x_t and testing for the significance of the coefficient of x_t using an ordinary t test. If we have observations on both x_t^* and x_t that are aligned properly, and are interested just in general alternatives, then we may indeed wish just to run such regressions. This was the point made by Frankel and Stock [1987], who considered the application to testing the efficiency of the foreign exchange market by regressing spot rates on futures rates.[3] Similar points were made by Geweke [1980] and Melino [1980].[4] Their arguments do not directly apply to the stock market and other applications, where x_t^* is a present value of an infinite dividend stream, and there are circumstances where a test of a variance inequality may have more power than a regression test, see chapter 6, section 6.5. The regression tests do not make use of certain information: that price at the end of the sample period must be justified by the present value of dividends beyond the sample, and that the latter are generated by the same process as dividends within the sample.[5]

Inequality (4) is dramatically violated by the data plotted in figure 4.1, if sample standard deviations are taken as population standard deviations. The sample standard deviation of $\tilde{P}_t$ for the years 1901–1987 is 6.706, while that of $\tilde{P}_t^*$ is only 1.611. Thus, $\tilde{P}_t$ is too volatile in terms of (4) by a factor of 4.163. The violation of the equation (3) is even more dramatic, since the correlation between $\tilde{P}_t$ and $\tilde{P}_t^*$ is only 0.296.

When we allow time-varying discount rates, the violation of the inequality (4) is less dramatic. Figure 4.2 shows the same plot where the discount rate equals the ex-post real commercial paper rate plus a constant risk

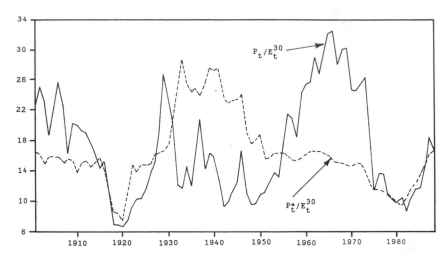

Figure 4.2
Price-earnings ratio $\tilde{P}_t \equiv P_t/E_t^{30}$ and ex-post value-earnings ratio $\tilde{P}_t^* \equiv P_t^*/E_t^{30}$ 1901–1988, time-varying discount rate case. Earnings E_t^{30} are 30-year moving average of actual real earnings. The commercial paper rate plus a constant risk premium is used to discount in equation 2 to compute P_t^*.

premium (chosen to make the sample mean of the discount rate equal the sample mean of the real return on stocks). Note that the time-varying discount rate induces a lot more volatility into $\tilde{P}_t^*$; its standard deviation in figure 4.2 is 4.657, so that the inequality (4) is violated by a factor of only 1.440.[6] However, the correlation between the two series plotted in figure 4.2 is only 0.048, again suggesting strong violation of equation (3).

4.4   A Variance Bound for Returns or Price Changes

There are also other ways of testing for, or of characterizing, the excess volatility of stock prices. My first papers on the volatility of stock market prices actually did not stress the inequality (4) described here. Of the inequalities discussed, the inequality (4) is the simplest one to interpret intuitively, and therefore has received the most response. The inequalities stressed more in the 1981 paper (chapter 5), which were analogous to an inequality studied in the 1979 paper on the term structure (chapter 15), were, in the constant discount rate case where $\gamma_t = \gamma = 1/(1 + r)$ is constant through time:

$$\sigma(\delta_t P_t) \leqslant \sigma(D_t)/\sqrt{r_2}, \tag{5}$$

$$\sigma(\Delta P_t) \leqslant \sigma(D_t)/\sqrt{(2r)}, \tag{6}$$

where $\delta_t P_t$ is the innovation in price defined as $P_t - E_{t-1} P_t = P_t + D_{t-1} -$ $(1 + r) P_{t-1}$, r_2 is the two-period interest rate $(1 + r)^2 - 1$, and $\Delta P_t = P_t - P_{t-1}$.[7] When the data were detrended as in chapter 5, these inequalities were violated quite strongly for the Standard and Poor data. These inequalities are cleaner than (4) in the sense that they do not involve approximations for P_T^*, the present value of dividends at the end of the sample. I thought then that these inequalities might also have better sampling properties than would the tests using (4) because they rely on measuring the standard deviation of dividends rather than the standard deviation of P_t^*, which is a smoothed dividend. The actual sampling properties of tests based on these inequalities depend of course on the method used to detrend dividends, if any, and the assumed stochastic properties for dividends.[8]

4.5   The West Inequality

Kenneth West [1988b] showed a different approach to testing for excess volatility. One can easily show from (1) that in the constant discount rate case ($\gamma_t = 1/(1 + r)$ is constant through time) $P_t^* - P_t$ is the present value of the innovations (or forecast errors) in price:[9]

$$P_t^* - P_t = \sum_{k=1}^{\infty} \gamma^k \delta_{t+k} P_{t+k}. \tag{7}$$

Since the innovation $\delta_{t+k} P_{t+k}$ cannot be forecasted, it must be uncorrelated with $\delta_{t+j} P_{t+j}$ $j < k$, and so the variance of the sum in equation 7 equals the sum of the variances of the terms in the summation, and $\text{var}(P_t^* - P_t)$ equals the innovation variance $\text{var}(\delta_t P_t)$ times $\gamma^2/(1 - \gamma^2)$. Now, $P_t^* - P_{St} = (P_t^* - P_t) + (P_t - P_{St})$, where P_{St} is the optimal forecast of P_t^* based on a subset S_t of the information set used by the public, $P_{St} = E(P_t^* | S_t)$. Since $P_{St} - P_t$ is known at time t it must be uncorrelated with the forecast error $P_t^* - P_t$ and hence $\text{var}(P_t^* - P_{St}) = \text{var}(P_t^* - P_t) + \text{var}(P_t - P_{St})$ and hence $\text{var}(P_t^* - P_{St}) \geqslant \text{var}(P_t^* - P_t)$. For West, P_{St} was the optimal forecast of P_t^* based on the history of dividends, $D_t, D_{t-1}, \ldots$, and on a time series model for dividends, an autoregressive model or integrated autoregressive model. Call $\delta_t P_{St}$ the innovation in P_{St}, $\delta_t P_{St} = P_{St} - E(P_{St} | S_{t-1})$. By (7) applied to P_{St} we have that $\text{var}(P_t^* - P_{St}) = \text{var}(\delta_t P_{St})$ times $\gamma^2/(1 - \gamma^2)$. This gives us the West [1988b] inequality:[10]

$$\text{var}(\delta_t P_t) \leqslant \text{var}(\delta_t P_{St}). \tag{8}$$

One applies (8) to examine the data by estimating a forecasting model for dividends and computing from the model the implied $\text{var}(\delta_t P_{St})$. This is a stronger version of inequality (5) above: in setting an upper bound on $\text{var}(\delta_t P_t)$ inequality (5) looks only at the variance of dividends, and relies on the worst case [i.e., maximizing $\text{var}(\delta_t P_{St})$ for given variance of D_t] in terms of the information structure about future dividends, whereas (8) allows us to make use of our knowledge not just of the variance of dividends but its covariance of dividends with lagged dividends, and even with other information variables. West found that this variance inequality was strongly violated with the Standard and Poor (S&P) composite stock price data using simple autoregressive models for dividends. Simply put, the autoregressive models forecast P_t^* so well that the variance in stock returns cannot be justified as due to forecast errors.[11]

4.6 The Debate over Alleged Excess Volatility

It is unfortunately difficult to summarize this rather extensive literature. As with most professional debates, the real issues are subtle, and not easily expressed. Competing concepts tend to be presented by disputants as diametric opposites when in fact they are merely rephrasings that give emphasis to some of these subtleties. Often the substance of a critique may be found already addressed in the work criticized.[12]

The debate over the alleged excess volatility is argued on statistical issues. The question is whether observed standard deviations are good measures of the population standard deviations in the expressions (3), (4), or their analogues. A problem encountered in attempting to describe the volatility debate is that there are actually a number of different varieties of tests that have been used to test for excess volatility relative to the efficient markets model, and critics often focus on specific details of the various tests.

In my original 1981 paper (chapter 5), the variables P_t and P_t^* were divided by a simple growth trend $\lambda^t = e^{bt}$ to detrend them. Since the parameter b was estimated over the entire sample (by regressing log price on time and a constant), the detrended price for time t depended on information not available at time t. Many people thought that perhaps the apparent excess volatility had to do with a spurious estimated trend, or a spurious estimated constant term in the regression, or both.

Such arguments were advanced by various critics. To illustrate his point, Allan Kleidon found a special case (similar to one used by Flavin [1983] to study variance bounds in the term structure) for the dividend process for which the volatility tests may often give false signals. This is the case where log dividends are a random walk (with constant positive expected change). As it well known, since sample paths of random walks are smooth, a trend line can be fitted to a random walk, even if the random walk has no drift to it at all. The estimated trend is spurious, and should not be extrapolated. Kleidon concluded by stochastic simulation methods that in this random walk example the methods I used (chapter 5) will generally find apparent excess volatility even when the efficient markets model (1) is true. Marsh and Merton [1986] derived an analogous result analytically. The aspect of their model that produces their results is a unit root in the dividend process (see Shiller [1986]). For the unit-root dividend process they assumed (based on a dividend smoothing model for firm managers) the variance inequality with sample variance computed as I did it in chapter 5 must always be violated in any finite sample, even when the model (1) is true.[13] Dybvig and Ingersoll [1984] showed that the variance bounds tend to be violated in a model where the growth rate of dividends is a first-order autoregressive stochastic process. Wandzura [1987] extended Kleidon's argument to a case where both log dividends and discount rates are stochastic.[14] LeRoy and Parke [1988] showed that in the case where dividends follow a geometric random walk, a modified variance bound can be computed for the variance of the price-dividend ratio, and that this variance bound is not violated with the data.

The Kleidon, Marsh-Merton, Dybvig-Ingersoll, Wandzura, and LeRoy-Parke results make the useful point that simple violations of the variance inequality (4) should not be considered plain and obvious evidence against the efficient markets model. Indeed, although I had earlier expressed doubts about the small sample properties of tests using this inequality, I learned from their exercises: the small sample properties of that inequality can be worse, given their assumptions about generating process for dividends, than I might have guessed. However, one should note that none of these papers provided examples where the violation of the original variance bounds would be expected to be as dramatic as it in fact was reported in my original papers (chapters 5 and 6). In my comment on Kleidon's paper (chapter 7), I showed that, after correcting a couple of errors in his analysis, Kleidon's own Monte Carlo methods imply that the probability of a gross violation of the variance inequality is less than 1% even under the random walk model.[15] It was indeed the gross nature of the violation that had been singled out for attention in the original papers (LeRoy and Porter [1981], and chapters 5 and 6 here); these papers recognized the possibility of biases like those documented later by others.

The reason that the critics' (Flavin, Kleidon, Marsh and Merton, Dybvig and Ingersoll, and Wandzura) analyses explain some portion of the excess volatility is that they assume a dividend process such that any change in dividends from year to year tends to cause a major change in all expected future dividends. This is a strong assumption, and is not implied just by the notion that dividends do not tend to revert to any fixed trend or by the assumption that the dividend stochastic process has a unit root. In the log random walk case for dividend, if the dividend increases by 10% from one year to the next, then all subsequent optimally predicted dividends out to infinity are also increased by 10%. Therefore, these models build in a lot of price volatility. The critics show that in these models the sample standard deviation of detrended price tends to be greater than the sample standard deviation of detrended ex-post value; this is consistent with the efficient markets model. While detrended price may appear to be too volatile to be justified in terms of the variability of detrended ex-post value, more apparent volatility of the latter will be found when more dividend data arrive, allowing a longer sample period. This does not appear to be what happens with actual dividend data; i.e., the sample standard deviation of price or ex-post value does not appear to grow with the sample period as the random walk model would imply. Dividends seem to show short-run oscillations contrary to the random walk assumption. What this amounts to is that the log random walk model for real dividends does not appear to be a good one. Real dividends appear to show a tendency to revert to trend or to a long moving average of their own lagged values. This is not to say that the dividend process lacks a unit root. See chapters 1, 6, Kleidon [1986], and Perron [1987] for a discussion of these points.[16]

Marsh and Merton claimed that there was reason to *expect* a dividend process like their process. They claimed that the work of John Lintner [1956], who interviewed managers on their dividend-setting behavior, implied that managers set dividends in proportion to "permanent earnings," which is proportional to the firm's "intrinsic value." Since, under efficient markets, price equals intrinsic value, managers in effect set dividends in response to price. Since intrinsic value is the present value of expected dividends, there is an implied permanence to shocks to dividends. Any shock to dividends is expected to be permanent since it affects estimates of intrinsic value, and hence price and therefore, by the managers' dividend setting rule and the random walk character of price, all future dividends. The Marsh-Merton model seems oddly circular, in that it relies *only* on the managers' dividend setting behavior and the efficient markets assumption, and makes no reference to the earnings potential of the firms, which had seemed central to the evaluation of the variance bounds violations (see Shiller [1986]). The Modigliani-Miller notion that dividend policy is irrelevant is taken to make such a circularity possible, if only managers decide to behave that way. I think that their claim that the Lintner results provide evidence that managers do behave this way was a little hasty; Lintner found that managers cited many considerations in deciding on their dividend policy, such as investment opportunities, and never explicitly mentioned the permanent earnings theory.

Another factor in dividend setting behavior is likely to be a desire to smooth *nominal* dividends, simply not to change these dividends too fast. Nominal dividends rather than real dividends are likely to be a concern of managers; they may boast, for example, of never cutting a *nominal* dividend. Their concern with nominal dividends is consistent with many popular models that do not take proper account of inflation. Smoothing nominal dividends will tend to impose transient noise on the real dividend process: shocks to the inflation rate would tend to produce deviations in real dividends until the nominal dividend is fully adjusted to the inflation shock.[17]

The basic import of all this criticism of the variance bounds tests is that small sample properties may be unreliable, and that if there is nonstationarity then even large sample properties of the processes may be unreliable. Another approach to dealing with these criticisms is to change the method of detrending, so that the detrended variables ought to be nonstationary and so that future data are not used to infer the detrending factor at time t.

One can reestimate the trend every period using only past data. Bulkley and Tonks [1988] found that, with U.K. data, and a somewhat unusual way of estimating the trend, the simple variance inequality (4) is not violated when this is done. They still concluded, using different methods, that there is an element of excess volatility in U.K. stock prices. In response to their work, I did a similar exercise with U.S. data 1871–1987. What I did is essentially duplicate the methods of my 1981 paper (chapter 5) but reestimate the time trend each year using only past data. I computed P_t^* using the data here (chapter 26, series 1, 2, and 5) using the mean real return over the sample to discount and the terminal real price as the terminal condition. I estimated the time trend for each year from 1900 to 1987 by regressing log real price p_t on time using data from 1871 to that year. Both P_t and P_t^* were divided by $\exp(\hat{p}_t)$, where $\hat{p}_t$ is the fitted value at time t of the regression whose sample ended in time t. The standard deviation 1900–1987 of the detrended P_t was 2.124 times the standard deviation of detrended P_t^*. Perhaps the violation appears in my U.S. result,

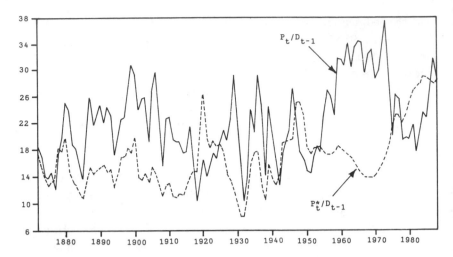

Figure 4.3
Price-dividend ratio P_t/D_{t-1} and ex-post value dividend ratio P_t^*/D_{t-1} 1872–1988, constant discount rate case. The discount rate used in equation 2 to compute P_t^* is 8.32%.

but not in Bulkley and Tonk's U.K. data because of a longer sample period with the U.S. data. Alternatively, one can detrend by just subtracting or dividing by a variable known at time t. For the case where r_t is constant through time a comparison (Mankiw, Romer, and Shapiro [1986, 1989]) of the variance of $x_t^* = P_t^* - D_t/r$ with that of $x_t = P_t - D_t/r$ shows that the variance of $P_t - D_t/r$ was larger, although when a weighted variance was computed (weighted by price to account for heteroskedasticity) the violation of the variance inequality was only marginal, depending sensitively on the value of r chosen.[18]

Plotted in figure 4.3 are ex-post value dividend ratios, P_t^*/D_{t-1}, computed with a constant discount rate r (equal to 8.32%, the average real return on stocks over the sample), and P_t/D_{t-1}, both for January.[19] The standard deviation of the P_t/D_{t-1} series plotted in figure 4.3 is 6.030, only slightly greater than the standard deviation of P_t^*/D_{t-1} equal to 4.703, but the correlation between the two is only 0.133.[20] The relation (3) is thus strongly violated. Figure 4.4 shows the same plot but where P_t^* is computed with time-varying discount rate, as in figure 4.2. Now, the standard deviation of P_t^*/D_{t-1} is 7.779, slightly greater than the standard deviation of P_t/D_{t-1}, but the correlation between the two ratios is only .060.

These results suggest that the efficient markets model does not fit the data well at all. The price-dividend ratio actually observed is at least as variable as, but bears almost no correlation with, the variable it is supposed

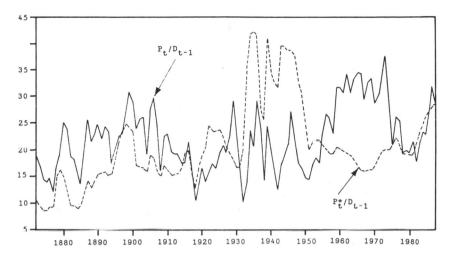

Figure 4.4
Price dividend ratio P_t/D_{t-1} and ex-post value dividend ratio P_t^*/D_{t-1} 1872–1988, time-varying discount rate case. The commercial paper rate (plus a constant risk premium) is used in equation 2 to discount to compute P_t^*.

to forecast. There is excess volatility of the price-dividend ratio in the sense that forecasting would be improved if the dividend-price ratio were scaled toward its mean, reducing its variability. It has been shown (Scott [1985]) that if $x_t^* = P_t^*/D_t$ is regressed on $x_t = P_t/D_t$ and a constant, the coefficient of P_t/D_t is nearly zero. Scott used a method of Hansen and Hodrick to correct the standard errors of the ordinary least squares regression. Strong rejections of the hypothesis that the slope coefficient is 1.00 were reported. His Monte Carlo experiments, done in the context of a simple model of dividend setting, provided some evidence that the rejections were not spurious.

The violation of market efficiency revealed by comparisons like Mankiw, Romer, and Shapiro's or Scott's is rather different from what I (chapter 5) claimed to find.

I claimed that detrended price appears to be too variable for efficient markets. That is not at all the same thing as Scott's conclusion that the forecasting ability of the dividend-price variable could be improved by scaling it toward its mean. Even if the dividend-price ratio were reduced to its historical mean, then the variability of the implied real price would still be large, just because the variability of real dividends is large. Moreover, when Mankiw, Romer, and Shapiro deal with heteroskedasticity by dividing by price, they are at the same time introducing price volatility into their measure of ex-post value.

The comparisons of ratios of price or ex-post value to smoothed earnings are more to the point for the purpose of testing for the kind of excess volatility I described (chapter 5). The simple expedient used above of detrending by dividing by a long moving average of earnings makes the specific arguments of Kleidon, and Marsh and Merton, inapplicable, as no future data were used in the detrending.

It is still the case, however, that there is an element of truth to the critiques that still might invalidate the tests of excess volatility where E_t^{30} is used to detrend. Equation (2) makes P_t^* a long moving average of dividends. Such a moving average has little short-run variability. Since E_t^{30} is *also* a smoothed series, one might say that it is not surprising that P_t^*/E_t^{30} has little variability in short samples. The finite sample estimate of $\sigma(P_t^*/E_t^{30})$ will tend to be downward biased measure of the true standard deviation. If P_t^*/E_t^{30} makes long smooth swings through time then over a short sample period, we may not observe its potential variability; we may observe only a fraction of a long swing. Since P_t is not smoothed for figure 4.1, P_t/E_t^{30} may be less smooth than P_t^*/E_t^{30} and hence tend to sho   ⸱ ⸱ᴸ:ₗ:ₗᵥᵧ
in short samples even though in a long enough sample
to have less variability.

To evaluate the potential bias, I ran Monte Carlo experiments that relied on the same log random walk model for dividends that Kleidon found was a particularly bad case for the volatility tests. For conformity to the data plotted in the figures here, in each iteration I generated 118 observations of real dividends. Earnings were assumed proportional to dividends, and a constant discount rate of 8.32% was used to compute P_t^*. In 1,000 iterations, there were 758 cases where $\sigma(P_t/E_t^{30})$ exceeded $\sigma(P_t^*/E_t^{30})$; there is indeed a tendency for spurious violation. But the spurious violation is less dramatic than is the case where prices are divided by an exponential growth variable λ_t. The mean across iterations of the ratio $\sigma(P_t/E_t^{30})/\sigma(P_t^*/E_t^{30})$ was 1.443, greater than 1.000 but substantially less than with the 4.163 observed in the actual data. In only one of the 1,000 iterations was $\sigma(P_t/E_t^{30})$ more than 4.16 times $\sigma(P_t^*/E_t^{30})$.

Model (1) implies that if P_t^*/E_t^{30} is regressed on P_t/E_t^{30} and a constant, the slope coefficient should be 1.000 and the constant zero. However, ordinary t-tests of the hypothesis that the slope coefficient is one or the constant zero are not valid, because of serially correlated residuals, and so a correction for this serial correlation should be made.

I ran regressions (Shiller [1988]) analogous to Scott's where a 30-year earnings average was used to detrend, rather than the dividend. My results confirmed the strong rejections of the model. The Monte Carlo experiments showed that there may be a downward bias to the slope coefficient, but the downward bias does not appear sufficient to account for the rejections.

Fama and French ran what are essentially Scott-type regressions, and also strongly rejected the efficient markets model.[21] They too did Monte Carlo experiments that confirmed that the rejection was not spurious. They were apparently unaware of Scott's work and described their method in very different terms, that of regressing long-horizon returns on dividend-price ratios. John Campbell and I have shown (chapter 8) that the Fama-French long-horizon return is analogous to $(P_t^* - P_t)/P_t$, where actual price at the end of the sample is used to compute P_t^*. The principle difference between their results and ours is that their holding period is of fixed length while ours is to the end of the sample. Some papers that did what they described as a modification of the variance bounds procedures to keep the terminal condition used to calculate P_t^* at a fixed distance from t (rather than the end of the sample) come even closer to the Fama and French methods (Joerding [1988], Mankiw, Romer and Shapiro [1989], Rhee [1989], and Shea [1986]).

Durlauf and Hall [1988a,b, 1989] have used Scott-type regressions to provide estimates of the noise components in stock prices. They produce time series plots of the estimated noise component for the constant discount rate case with U.S. data; the estimated noise closely resembles price itself.

Poterba and Summers [1987] found positive serial correlation in returns for short time intervals and negative correlation over long time intervals, Cutler, Poterba, and Summers [1988] found that a regression of four-year aggregate returns on the log dividend-price ratio has a statistically significant positive slope coefficient in postwar data for 14 of 15 countries. DeBondt and Thaler [1985] found that long horizon returns of stocks that had done poorly over previous years tended to be unusually high, and long-horizon returns of stocks that had done very well over previous years tended to be unusually low. Clark [1987] did an econometric decomposition of U.S. stock prices into a stationary and nonstationary trend component and found that the stock index showed wide stationary swings around a relatively smooth nonstationary fundamental component. However, the relative amplitudes of the stationary and nonstationary components were not well measured.

4.7 A Log-Linear Vector Autoregressive Analysis of Volatility Relations

Since most of the criticism of the excess volatility literature appeared, John Campbell and I have extended the framework of analysis that enables a deeper examination of volatility issues and dispenses with assumptions of stationarity assailed by critics. A technical advance in the econometric literature made this possible: the development of an econometric theory for cointegrated vector autoregressive models. For a discussion, see my paper with Campbell reproduced here as chapter 16 in part III. We derived vector autoregressive models that are not subject to the same stationarity concern that was the basis of much of the criticism, and we included (a transformation of) price in the vector, so that the full information set of the market finds its way into the analysis. By including price in the vector autoregression, we have an analysis that may be described as a vector generalization of the West procedure, in which the inequality becomes an equality since the full information of the market is incorporated in the vector.

While chapter 16 sets out the basic concepts the econometric results reported in chapter 8, which came later chronologically, supersede those in chapter 16. That is because in chapter 8 we use a model (described in greater length in Campbell and Shiller [1988]) that is log-linear in prices, dividends, and discount factors. Log linearity in (real) dividends allows us to do time series models for the change in dividends that are homoskedastic despite the increasing scale of the market over the last century, and impose nonnegativity constraints. Log linearity in discount factors eliminates the nonlinearity in r_t in (2), which is helpful for time series purposes.

The log-linear approximation to the model (1) is derived (following Campbell and Shiller [1988]) by first linearizing the log return $\log((P_{t+1} + D_t)/P_t)$ to yield the approximate log return ξ_t:

$$\xi_t = \rho(p_{t+1} - p_t) + (1 - \rho)(d_t - p_t) + k, \tag{9}$$

where p_t is log price per share, d_t is log dividend per share, ρ is the discount factor (analogous to $\bar{\gamma}$ in chapter 5) around which the return was linearized and k is a constant. This discount factor ρ equals $1/(1 + \bar{r})$, where $\bar{r}$ is the average dividend-price ratio. The approximate return is just a weighted average of the growth rate of price $(p_{t+1} - p_t)$ and of the log dividend-price ratio $d_t - p_t$ where most of the weight is put on the growth rate of price, plus a constant. Approximation error is analyzed in various ways in the appendix to Campbell and Shiller [1988].

Once we have the log-linear approximation (1') to (1), we can develop an efficient markets model that makes expected approximate return equal expected discount factors:

$$E_t \xi_t = E_t r_t \tag{10}$$

where r_t is a discount rate. As above, it follows that

$$p_t = E_t p_t^*, \tag{1'}$$

$$p_t^* = (1 - \rho) \sum_{k=0}^{\infty} \rho^k d_{t+k} - \sum_{k=0}^{\infty} \rho^k r_{t+k} + k/(1 - \rho). \tag{2'}$$

According to (2'), the ex-post value p_t^* is equal to a weighted average of future log dividends minus a term proportional to a weighted average of expected future one period interest rates. The latter term, represented by the second summation in (2'), is related to the log of the perfect foresight long-term (perpetuity) interest rate whose expectation is, under the linearized expectations hypothesis of the term structure, the market long-term interest rate. Note the similarity between (1')–(2') and the consol yield formula, which states that the log price of a consol equals the log coupon minus the log consol yield.[22] The same model can also be restated so that the log dividend-price ratio depends on a long-term interest rate minus a long-term growth rate for dividends, a sort of dynamic Gordon model.

The fundamental conclusion from our empirical work with this model, (chapter 8) is that the variance of the approximate log return ξ_t should be less than it is, given the vector of information that includes price. Table 8.2 compares the standard deviation of ξ_t with that of ξ_t', the theoretical log return at time t predicted by the model. The latter is only a quarter as large. With time-varying discount rates the standard deviation of $\xi_t' - r_t$ is still only half that of $\xi_t - r_t$. Moreover, price turns out to be a better forecaster of fundamental value if it is scaled down towards a long moving average of earnings. Figure 8.2 plots price and the optimal forecast from this model of the present value of dividends; note how much more stable the latter is.

This conclusion is not likely to be assailed on grounds of nonstationarity of variables in the vector autoregression, as these variables are ratios rather than levels of the variables in the earlier analyses. However, there are still potential problems in applying the asymptotic distribution theory in small samples. A Monte Carlo experiment (chapter 9) offers some reassurance.[23]

Beltratti [1989] has done a more extensive Monte Carlo evaluation of the techniques used in chapter 8, involving bootstrapped as well as independent normal residuals, including other information variables in the generating process, and extending the number of lags. He found that increasing the number of lags was particularly damaging to the linear Wald test; with three lags a test at the 5% level rejected in 29% of the replications, even with the estimated generating process (compared with table 9.2B). When he restricted himself to one lag, as Campbell and I do in chapter 8, his results are roughly comparable to those we report in chapter 9.

One tantalizing observation that John Campbell and I made in chapter 8 deserves discussion: while the efficient markets model is rejected, and ξ'_t is much less variable than ξ_t, the two are quite highly correlated. In the constant discount rate case, the correlation between ξ'_t and ξ_t is 0.915. This would seem to suggest that while returns are too volatile to accord with market efficiency, the source of stock return volatility *is* nonetheless information about future dividends. This suggests, for example, that the stock market crash of 1987 would likely be due to genuine information about future dividends, and that while investor overreaction would be at work, it would likely be overreaction to fundamentals rather than to each other. Elsewhere in this book I argue that investor interaction was a likely source of stock price volatility; this result would seem to suggest that such interaction plays a minor role at best in generating stock price volatility.

I think that this is too strong a conclusion to draw from the results of chapter 8, and the reason points up a weakness in our methods. The weakness is the inability to handle the possibility that the market has superior information, when compared with our data set, when the efficient markets model is not valid. The correlation between ξ'_t and ξ_t is consistently estimated in the superior information case only under the null hypothesis that says that the correlation ought to be 1.000. Under an alternative to the efficient markets hypothesis [say, equation (3) of chapter 1] the estimate of the correlation may be biased.

The chapter 8 results show that price helps forecast future dividends, and while price gets a weight of only about 1/4 in the forecasting equation for the present value of future dividends, since the price variable is much noisier than the smooth earnings variable, its changes dominate the changes in the optimal forecast p'_t. But, nonetheless, while price carries information, its short-run noise may be due primarily to fashions and fads, say. If another information variable were included in the autoregression, a variable that captures the information but not the noise, it might reduce the weight of price in the equation, and cause the correlation of ξ_t and ξ'_t to fall dramatically.[24] By the same token, the estimate of $\sigma(p'_t)$ might not be robust to superior information, in contrast to the simple variance bounds inequalities described above.

4.8   Interpretation

The simple present value model represented by equations (1) and (2) does not seem to be supported by the data. But there are many ways to interpret this result, and others would interpret this as evidence for something other than the popular models or opinion change that is emphasized in this book.[25] I emphasize investor psychology and popular models in the stock market for reasons beyond the statistical results here—the arguments were given in chapters 1 and 2. The statistical results serve primarily to overturn the impression that statistical tests in the efficient markets literature prove that investor psychology can play no role in speculative markets.

Let us, however, consider some alternative interpretations of the statistical results here.

One alternative, discussed in chapters 5 and 6, is that stock prices might be heavily influenced by information about a major disaster (such as a nationalization or defeat of one's country by a foreign power). If the disaster is big enough, the changing probability of it might be enough to cause major fluctuations in stock prices, even though the disaster did not occur in the last century. The price movements caused by the changing probability might have no correlation with observed P_t^*. There is some reason to doubt that the disaster model saves the efficient markets notion. Since dividends cannot be negative, the worst possible disaster is one that drives price to zero. Changing probabilities of such a drop may not be big enough to cause observed stock price volatility unless the probabilities of disaster are frequently fairly high. High probabilities of disaster may be inconsistent with the fact that the disaster has never occurred (see Shiller [1985] and Mankiw, Romer, and Shapiro [1989]). Schwert [1987] has pointed out that war times in the United States have not been periods of relatively high volatility of stock prices, even though these times correspond to high volatility for a number of other macroeconomic variables. Periods of high stock price volatility do not seem to be associated with any information about a widely discussed potential disaster. Still, such stories of unobserved potential variability of dividends should be borne in mind in interpreting the apparent excess volatility. Even if they sound implausible as complete explanations of the apparent excess volatility, such stories might conceivably explain some part of it.

Another important explanation for excess volatility is that prices are disturbed by "rational bubbles." It is well known that the constancy of expected returns does not imply that prices cannot show a tendency for above average returns to be followed by above average returns and below average returns to be followed by more below average returns. The model requires only that the conditionally *expected* returns be independent of past information. It could be that after a period of high returns, subsequent returns are likely to be above average but not much above average, and are unlikely to be below average, but if below average, very much below average. For a discussion of such possibilities, see Mandelbrot [1966]. That such a possibility can occur because of "animal spirits" was suggested by Blanchard [1979]."[26] Rational bubble models have been studied by Blanchard and Watson [1983], Diba and Grossman [1988], Quah [1985], and West [1987, 1988b]. Flood, Hodrick, and Kaplan [1986] have pointed out that some of the evidence of excess volatility of financial markets is not really evidence in favor of such rational bubble alternatives. Rational bubble models have the property that expected excess returns are unforecastable, a property shared by the efficient markets model. If there is a rational bubble like that proposed by Blanchard, then in regressions of P_t^*/D_t onto P_t/D_t or of P_t^*/E_t^{30} onto P_t/E_t^{30} the slope coefficient will still tend to be 1.000, because the terminal price condition used to estimate P_t^* causes P_t^* to be afflicted with the same bubble as affects P_t. Putting it differently, Campbell and I pointed out (chapter 8) that regressions of P_t^* (and transformations thereof) onto (transformed) P_t and testing for a unit slope coefficient are analogous to regression tests of the hypothesis that long-period holding returns are unforecastable, and the latter are unforecastable in a rational bubble. Still, other methods of testing for excess volatility discussed above [such as tests based on variance bounds (5), (6), or (8) or on variance comparisons with the vector autoregressive methods used in chapter 8] do have power against rational bubble alternatives.

My own attitude toward the rational bubble models is that they are too narrow a class of models to focus much attention on, given the much broader class of "near-rational" (a term of Akerlof and Yellen [1985] from another context) alternatives.[27] These are alternatives in which stock prices are not consistent with (3) above, but in which excess returns are still not very forecastable. Some of these were described in chapter 1; see also Summers [1986]. With such alternatives, there may indeed be a major role for popular models and investor psychology in determining price movements.

Yet another rational interpretation of the excess volatility results is that the volatility is due to the impact of the business cycle on rates of discount. For example, in times of prosperity the demand for stocks is high, and so their price is bid up to high levels. In times of depression, there is little demand for stocks, and so the price of stocks must fall. This interpretation suggests that another representation of the discount rate r_t in (2) might relate it somehow to aggregate macroeconomic variables. Such a theory was the subject of the paper Sanford Grossman and I wrote in 1981 (chapter 21), and is discussed also in chapter 19.

Notes

1. LeRoy and Porter [1981] applied the present value model not to dividends but to detrended earnings E_t/k_t and detrended price P_t/k_t, where k_t is an estimate of the quantity of physical capital to which corporate equity is title. The latter was defined recursively by $k_t = k_{t-1} + (E_t - D_t)/P_0$ from an initial condition $k_1 = 1$. Gilles and LeRoy [1988] proposed a different recursion for k_t based on the assumption that the value of the firm is represented by the number of "machines" it owns, and that retained earnings are used to purchase more machines at a price given by the share price. Then $k_t = k_{t-1}P_t/(P_t + D_t - E_t)$.

2. This detrending does not handle all objections to my interpretation of the plot, and may introduce different small sample considerations, to be discussed below.

3. The monetary approach to the modeling of exchange rates makes the exchange rate a function of a present value of future money growth rates. Variance bounds tests can be profitably applied to these models (see Huang [1981], Meese and Singleton [1983], Vander Kraats and Booth [1983], Diba [1987], and Froot [1987]).

4. Durlauf and Phillips [1988] and Froot [1987] pointed out that tests of the inequality (4) also have a regression interpretation. The inequality (4) can be written as $b \geqslant -0.5$, where b is the slope coefficient in a regression of x_t on $x_t^* - x_t$. By including a time variable also in the regression, the asymptotic theory developed by Phillips [1986, 1987] for the spurious regression problem can be applied to assess the role of detrending in the variance bounds tests. The probability that the sample standard deviation of detrended x_t is less than c times the standard deviation of detrended x_t^* under a unit root null can be inferred from Phillips theory applied to the regression of $cx_t^* - x_t$ on x_t. It should not be inferred that (3) and (4) are equivalent; the Durlauf-Phillips condition has no relation to the correlation coefficient ρ in (3).

5. The power arguments advanced in chapter 6 apply to variance bounds tests not involving P_T, price at time T, the end of the sample, proxying for P_T^*. Durlauf and Hall [1989] show regression tests that also make no use of P_T in determining P_T^*.

6. In chapter 5 it is noted that changing real rates of discount could justify the observed variability of stock prices only if the real rates were much more volatile than they have been in recent memory. But real interest rates were much more volatile before World War II than after.

7. Note that $P_t = E_t P_t^*$ does not imply that $\Delta P_t = E_t \Delta P_t^*$ and so $\sigma(\Delta P_t)$ need not be less than or equal to $\sigma(\Delta P_t^*)$. For an example where it is not, consider D_t as unforecastable white noise so that $P_t = \gamma D_t$.

8. We shall see below (note 15) that in one sense the sampling properties may be worse for (5) and (6) than for (4).

9. The germ of this idea was also in LeRoy and Porter [1981].

10. West's original paper, before publication, had a longer proof. This shorter proof is due to John Campbell.

11. Durlauf and Hall [1989] have pointed out that the inequality var$(P_t^* - P_{St}) \geq$ var$(P_t^* - P_t)$ is equivalent to the coefficient less than 0.5 in a regression of $P_t^* - P_t$ onto $P_{St} - P_t$; the present value model implies further that the coefficient should be zero.

12. All three points in the abstract to Kleidon's [1986] critique of my work were made in my earlier papers. The first point, that P_t need not be smoother than P_t^*, was carefully made in my 1979 paper (chapter 15, page 278). In that paper, the context was the term structure of interest rates, but the mathematical model was the same. The second point, that nonstationarity may invalidate the variance bounds tests, I made in 1981 (chapter 6, page 140). The third point, that other variance bounds inequalities valid under nonstationarity exist and are not violated, I made in 1981 (chapter 6, page 139).

13. The Kleidon and Marsh-Merton criticisms do not apply directly to the LeRoy-Porter [1981] variance bounds tests, since they used a different way of detrending. See Christian Gilles and Stephen LeRoy [1988].

14. Wandzura's analysis was couched in continuous time so that the theoretical price can be written in terms of an expression (involving modified Bessel functions) with current dividend and current interest rate as arguments. The Kleidon, Marsh-Merton, and Wandzura results rely on the fact that in my paper the sample periods over which price and ex-post rational price and measured are the same. With random walks, the estimated standard deviations tend to increase with sample period.

15. With the other inequality, (5) or (6), the probability in Kleidon's example of a gross violation under the null hypothesis may be much higher. If the program that produced the table in chapter 7 is changed to replace the inequality (4) with the inequality (5) or (6), then for $r = .05$ the proportion of replications with a gross violation (the sample estimate of the left-hand-side exceeds that of the right-hand side by a factor of five or more) rises to 10.9% for inequality (5) and 9.0% for inequality (6).

16. Some other observations are relevant. The Kleidon model predicts a constant dividend price ratio, which we do not observe. Kleidon's example thus leaves an infinite amount of excess volatility of the dividend-price ratio.

17. John Campbell [1988b, and chapter 16] and I have argued that the econometric work that Marsh and Merton [1987] claimed supported the model may be spurious. Their parameter estimates have an interpretation just in terms of the time aggregation of their data and simple characterizations of the persistence of dividends.

18. Mankiw, Romer, and Shapiro also studied the small sample properties of their variance bounds tests with Monte Carlo methods [1989].

19. Dividend-price ratios are computed with lagged dividends so that the denominator will be in the information set at time t. In this chapter, real dividends and real earnings in year t, which are received continuously throughout the year, are deflated by the producer price index for January of year $t + 1$. This way the producer price index drops out of the ratios.

20. See also the discussion of Scott [1985] below.

21. K. C. Chan [1988] has pointed out that their statistical significance disappears if the depression years are omitted from the sample.

22. Note that the weights on d_{t+k} in (2') sum to one, but that the weights on r_{t+k} sum to $1/(1 - \rho)$. The reason the latter sums to more than one is that the second sum (plus the constant) is a sort of log interest rate, not log of one plus the interest rate. Note also that the weighting given to future interest rates in the second summation in (2') is not necessarily the same as we would give future one period interest rates in an expectations model of the consol yield. These weights reflect the discount factor and growth rate of dividends for the stock.

23. Shea [1988] has in fact criticized my paper with John Campbell (chapter 16) for small sample bias as applied to the stock market. Our work in chapter 9 applies methods similar to Shea's for our log-linear model, described below, which we feel is superior to the model of stock prices given in chapter 16. See also Mattey and Meese [1986] and the reply to that by Campbell [1986].

24. Beltratti [1989] has explored the use of some other information variables in this model.

25. Stephen LeRoy, indeed, has put a very different interpretation on the violation of the variance bounds. He wrote [1984, p. 184], "In contrast with the dominant interpretation, my article with Richard Porter [1981] regarded the violation of the variance bounds inequalities as an anomaly, nothing more. Our conclusion was not that evidence had been provided in favor of some alternative to market efficiency.... If the various criticisms of the variance bounds tests are accorded a more sympathetic interpretation here than in Shiller's work, that is because the criticisms support rather than conflict with LeRoy-Porter's conclusion, which was that something *must* be wrong with the tests, or the variance inequalities would not have been violated!"

26. Flood and Garber [1980] spoke of an analogous concept, but in the context of a hyperinflation where bubbles may continue indefinitely.

27. West [1987, 1988a] presents tests for rational bubbles but concludes that the tests "are probably not able to discriminate between a bubble and 'noise' that is almost but not quite a bubble" [1988, p. 650].

References

Akerlof, George A., and Janet L. Yellen. 1985. "A Near-Rational Model of the Business Cycle, with Wage and Price Inertia," *Quarterly Journal of Economics* 100: 823–838.

Baillie, Richard T. 1987. "Econometric Tests of Rationality and Market Efficiency," unpublished paper, Michigan State University.

Beltratti, Andrea. 1989. *Essays in Stock Market Efficiency and Time-Varying Risk Premia*, unpublished Ph.D. dissertation, Yale University.

Black, Fischer. 1986. "Noise," *Journal of Finance* 41:529–43.

Black, Fischer, and Myron Scholes. 1973. "The Pricing of Options and Other Corporate Liabilities," *Journal of Political Economy* 81:637–659.

Blanchard, Olivier J. 1979. "Speculative Bubbles, Crashes, and Rational Expectations," *Economics Letters* 3:387–389.

Blanchard, Olivier J., and Mark W. Watson. 1982. "Bubbles, Rational Expectations, and Financial Markets," in Paul Wachtel, ed., *Crises in the Economic and Financial Structure*, Lexington Books: Lexington, Massachusetts, pp. 295–315.

Bulkley, George, and Ian Tonks. 1988. "Are UK Stock Prices Excessively Volatile?" University of Exeter.

Campbell, John Y. 1986. "Comment," *Econometric Reviews* 5:241–245

Campbell, John Y., and Robert J. Shiller. 1987. "Cointegration and Tests of Present Value Models," *Journal of Political Economy* 95:1062–1088.

Campbell, John Y., and Robert J. Shiller. 1988a. "The Dividend-Price Ratio and Expectations of Future Dividends and Discount Factors," *Review of Financial Studies* 1:195–228.

Campbell, John Y., and Robert J. Shiller. 1988b. "Interpreting Cointegrated Models," *Journal of Economic Dynamics and Control* 12:505–522.

Campbell, John Y., and Robert J. Shiller. 1988c. "Stock Prices, Earnings, and Expected Dividends," *Journal of Finance* 43:661–676.

Chan, K. C. 1988. "Production Uncertainty, Production Shocks, and Mean Reversion in Long Horizon Stock Returns," reproduced, Ohio State University.

Clark, Peter K. 1987. "Stationary Variation and Trend Reversion in U.S. Equity Prices," reproduced, Stanford University.

Cowles, A., 3rd, and Associates. 1939. *Common-Stock Indexes*, Second Edition, Bloomington Indiana: Principia Press.

Cutler, David M., James M. Poterba, and Lawrence H. Summers. 1988. "International Evidence on the Predictability of Stock Returns," reproduced, Massachusetts Institute of Technology.

DeBondt, Werner F. M., and Richard H. Thaler. 1985. "Does the Stock Market Overreact?" *Journal of Finance* 40:793–805.

DeBondt, Werner, F. M., and Richard H. Thaler. 1989. "A Mean Reverting Walk Down Wall Street," *Journal of Economic Perspectives* 3:189–202.

Diba, B. T. 1987. "A Critique of Variance Bounds Tests for Monetary Exchange Rate Models," *Journal of Money, Credit and Banking* 19:104–111.

Diba, B. T., and Hershel I. Grossman. 1988. "Explosive Rational Bubbles in Stock Prices?" *American Economic Review* 78:520–530.

Durlauf, Stephen N., and Robert E. Hall. 1988a. "Bounds on the Variances of Specification Errors in Models with Expectations," reproduced, Stanford University.

Durlauf, Stephen N., and Robert E. Hall. 1988b. "Determinants of Noise in the Dividends Based Stock Price Model, reproduced, Stanford University.

Durlauf, Stephen N., and Robert E. Hall. 1989. "Measuring Noise in Stock Prices," reproduced, Stanford University.

Durlauf, Stephen N., and P. C. B. Phillips. 1988. "Trends Versus Random Walks in Time Series Analysis," *Econometrica*: 56:1333–1354.

Dybvig, Philip, and Jonathan Ingersoll, Jr. 1984. "Stock Prices Are Not Too Variable: A Theoretical and Empirical Analysis," Notes for the Finance Seminar, University of Chicago.

Fama, Eugene F., and Kenneth R. French. 1988a. "Dividend Yields and Expected Stock Returns," *Journal of Financial Economics* 22:3–25.

Fama, Eugene F., and Kenneth R. French. 1988b. "Permanent and Temporary Components of Stock Prices," *Journal of Political Economy* 96:246–273.

Flavin, Majorie. 1983. "Excess Volatility in the Financial Markets: A Reassessment of the Empirical Evidence," *Journal of Political Economy* 91:929–956.

Flood, Robert P., and Peter M. Garber. 1980. "Market Fundamentals versus Price-Level Bubbles: The First Tests," *Journal of Political Economy* 88:745–770.

Flood, Robert P., Robert J. Hodrick, and Paul Kaplan. 1986. "An Evaluation of Recent Evidence on Stock Market Bubbles," NBER Working Paper No. 1971.

Frankel, Jeffrey A., and James H. Stock. 1987. "Regression vs. Volatility Tests of the Efficiency of Foreign Exchange Markets," *Journal of International Money and Finance* 6:49–56.

Froot, Kenneth A. 1987. "Tests of Excess Forecast Volatility in the Foreign Exchange and Stock Markets," NBER Working Paper No. 2362.

Geweke, John. 1980. "A Note on the Testable Implications of Expectations Models," Social Science Research Institute, University of Wisconsin, Madison, #8024.

Gilles, Christian, and Stephen F. LeRoy. 1987. "The Variance-Bounds Tests: A Critical Survey," unpublished paper, University of California Santa Barbara.

Gilles, Christian, and Stephen F. LeRoy. 1988. "Econometric Aspects of the Variance Bounds Tests," reproduced, University of California at Santa Barbara.

Hamilton, James D. 1986. "On Testing for Self-Fulfilling Speculative Price Bubbles," *International Economic Review*: 27:545–552.

Hamilton, James D., and Charles H. Whiteman. 1985. "The Observable Implications of Self-Fulfilling Expectations," *Journal of Monetary Economics* 16:353–373.

Hansen, Lars Peter, and Robert J. Hodrick. 1980. "Forward Exchange Rates as Optimal Predictors of Future Spot Rates: An Econometric Analysis," *Journal of Political Economy* 88:829–853.

Huang, Roger D. 1981. "The Monetary Approach to Exchange Rates in an Efficient Foreign Exchange Market: Tests Based on Volatility," *Journal of Finance* 36:31–41.

Joerding, Wayne. 1988. "Are Stock Prices Excessively Sensitive to Current Information?" *Journal of Economic Behavior and Organization* 9:71–85.

Kleidon, Allan W. 1986. "Variance Bounds Tests and Stock Price Valuation Models," *Journal of Political Economy* 94:953–1001.

LeRoy, Stephen F. 1984. "Efficiency and the Variability of Asset Prices," *American Economic Review* 74:183–187.

LeRoy, Stephen F., and William C. Parke. 1987. "Stock Price Volatility: A Test Based on the Geometric Random Walk," reproduced, University of California, Santa Barbara.

LeRoy, Stephen F., and Richard D. Porter 1981. "Stock Price Volatility: Tests Based on Implied Variance Bounds," *Econometrica* 49:97–113.

Lintner, John V., Jr. 1956. "Distribution of Incomes of Corporations among Dividends, Retained Earnings, and Taxes," *American Economic Review* 46:97–113.

Mandelbrot, Benoit. 1966. "Forecasts of Future Prices, Unbiassed Markets, and Martingale Models," *Journal of Business* 39:242–255.

Mankiw, N. Gregory, David Romer, and Matthew D. Shapiro. 1985. "An Unbiased Reexamination of Stock Market Volatility," *Journal of Finance* 40:677–687.

Mankiw, N. Gregory, David Romer, and Matthew D. Shapiro. 1989. "Stock Market Efficiency and Volatility: A Statistical Appraisal," reproduced, Harvard University.

Marsh, Terry A., and Robert C. Merton. 1986. "Dividend Variability and Variance Bounds Tests for the Rationality of Stock Market Prices," *American Economic Review* 76:483–498.

Marsh, Terry A., and Robert C. Merton. 1987. "Dividend Behavior for the Aggregate Stock Market," *Journal of Business* 60:1–40.

Mattey, J., and Richard A. Meese. 1987. "Empirical Assessment of Present Value Relations," *Econometric Reviews* 5:171–234.

Meese, Richard A., and Kenneth J. Singleton. 1983. "Rational Expectations and the Volatility of Floating Exchange Rates," *International Economic Review* 24:721–733.

Melino, Angelo. 1980. "Volatility Tests of the RE Model of the Term Structure: Some Comments," reproduced, Harvard University.

Pesaran, M. Hashem. 1988. "On the Volatility and Efficiency of Stock Prices," reproduced, Trinity College, Cambridge.

Phillips, P. C. B. 1986. "Understanding Spurious Regressions in Econometrics," *Journal of Econometrics* 33:311–340.

Phillips, P. C. B. 1987. "Time Series Regression with a Unit Root," *Econometrica* 55:277–301.

Poterba, James M, and Lawrence H. Summers. 1988. "Mean Reversion in Stock Prices: Evidence and Implications," *Journal of Financial Economics* 22:26–59.

Quah, Danny. 1985. "Estimation of a Nonfundamentals Model for Stock Price and Dividend Dynamics," unpublished manuscript, M.I.T.

Rhee, Wooheon. 1989. "The Power of Tests of the Present Value Model Based on Ex-Post Rational Stock Prices," reproduced, Yale University.

Roll, Richard, and Stephen A. Ross. 1980. "An Empirical Investigation of the Arbitrage Pricing Theory," *Journal of Finance* 35:1073–1103.

Schwert, G. William. 1987. "The Causes of Changing Stock Market Volatility," reproduced, University of Rochester.

Scott, Louis O. 1985. "The Present Value Model of Stock Prices: Regression Tests and Monte Carlo Results," *Review of Economics and Statistics* 67:599–605.

Shea, Gary. 1986. "Excess Volatility in the Stock Market: An Examination of Unbiased Test Methodology," reproduced, Pennsylvania State University.

Shea, Gary. 1988. "Ex Post Rational Price Approximations and Empirical Reliability of the Present Value Relation," presented at the NATO Advanced Research Workshop, A Reappraisal of the Efficiency of Financial Markets," Sesimbra, Portugal.

Shiller, Robert J. 1978. "Rational Expectations and the Dynamic Structure of Rational Expectations Models: A Critical Review," *Journal of Monetary Economics* 4:1–44.

Shiller, Robert J. 1985. "Financial Markets and Macroeconomic Fluctuations," in James L. Butkiewicz et al., eds., *Keynes Economic Legacy*, New York: Praeger.

Shiller, Robert J. 1986. "The Marsh-Merton Model of Managers' Smoothing of Dividends," *American Economic Review* 76:499–503.

Shiller, Robert J., 1988. "A Scott-Type Regression Test of the Dividend-Ratio Models," forthcoming, *Review of Economics and Statistics*.

Shiller, Robert J., and P. Perron. 1985. "Testing the Random Walk Hypothesis: Power Versus Frequency of Observation," *Economics Letters* 18:381–386.

Shiller, Robert J., and John Pound. 1989. "Survey Evidence on Diffusion of Interest and Information Among Investors," forthcoming, *Journal of Economic Behavior and Organization*.

Singleton, Kenneth J. 1980. "Expectations Models of the Term Structure and Implied Variance Bounds," *Journal of Political Economy* 88:1159–1176.

Summers, Lawrence H. 1986. "Does the Stock Market Rationally Reflect Fundamental Values?" *Journal of Finance* 41:591–601.

Tirole, Jean. 1985. "Asset Bubbles and Overlapping Generations," *Econometrica* 53:1499–1528.

Vander Kraats, R. H., and L. D. Booth. 1983. "Empirical Tests of the Monetary Approach to Exchange Rate Determination," *Journal of International Money and Finance* 2:255–278.

Wandzura, S. M. 1987. "Stock Price Volatility: Evidence of Excess?" reproduced, Hughes Research Laboratories, Malibu, California.

West, Kenneth D. 1987. "A Specification Test for Speculative Bubbles," *Quarterly Journal of Economics* 102:553–580.

West, Kenneth D. 1988a. "Bubbles, Fads and Stock Price Volatility Tests: A Partial Evaluation," *Journal of Finance* 43:639–655.

West, Kenneth D. 1988b. "Dividend Innovations and Stock Price Volatility," *Econometrica* 56:37–61.

5   Do Stock Prices Move Too Much to Be Justified by Subsequent Changes in Dividends?

A simple model that is commonly used to interpret movements in corporate common stock price indexes asserts that real stock prices equal the present value of rationally expected or optimally forecasted future real dividends discounted by a constant real discount rate. This valuation model (or variations on it in which the real discount rate is not constant but fairly stable) is often used by economists and market analysts alike as a plausible model to describe the behavior of aggregate market indexes and is viewed as providing a reasonable story to tell when people ask what accounts for a sudden movement in stock price indexes. Such movements are then attributed to "new information" about future dividends. I will refer to this model as the "efficient markets model" although it should be recognized that this name has also been applied to other models.

It has often been claimed in popular discussions that stock price indexes seem too "volatile," that is, that the movements in stock price indexes could not realistically by attributed to any objective new information, since movements in the price indexes seem to be "too big" relative to actual subsequent events. Recently, the notion that financial asset prices are too volatile to accord with efficient markets has received some econometric support in papers by Stephen LeRoy and Richard Porter [1981] on the stock market, and by myself [1979, and chapter 15] on the bond market.

To illustrate graphically why it seems that stock prices are too volatile, I have plotted in figure 5.1 a stock price index p_t with its ex-post rational counterpart p_t^* (data set 1).[1] The stock price index p_t is the real Standard and Poor's Composite Stock Price Index (detrended by dividing by a factor proportional to the long-run exponential growth path) and p_t^* is the present discounted value of the actual subsequent real dividends (also as a propor-

Reprinted with minor editing from *American Economic Review* 71 (1981): 421–435; © 1981 the American Economics Association.

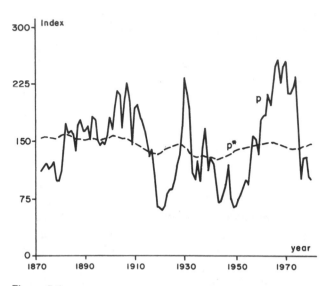

Figure 5.1
Real Standard and Poor's Composite Stock Price Index (solid line *p*) and ex-post rational price (dotted line *p**), 1871–1979, both detrended by dividing by a long-run exponential growth factor. The variable *p** is the present value of actual subsequent real detrended dividends, subject to an assumption about the present value in 1979 of dividends thereafter. Data are from data set 1 in the appendix.

tion of the same long-run growth factor).[2] The analogous series for a modified Dow Jones Industrial Average appear in figure 5.2 (data set 2). One is struck by the smoothness and stability of the ex-post rational price series p_t^* when compared with the actual price series. This behavior of p^* is due to the fact that the present value relation relates p^* to a long-weighted moving average of dividends (with weights corresponding to discount factors) and moving averages tend to smooth the series averaged. Moreover, while real dividends did vary over this sample period, they did not vary long enough or far enough to cause major movements in p^*. For example, while one normally thinks of the Great Depression as a time when business was bad, real dividends were substantially below their long-run exponential growth path (i.e., 10–25% below the growth path for the Standard and Poor's series, 16–38% below the growth path for the Dow Series) only for a few depression years: 1933, 1934, 1935, and 1938. The moving average that determines p^* will smooth out such short-run fluctuations. Clearly the stock market decline beginning in 1929 and ending in 1932 could not be rationalized in terms of subsequent dividends! Nor could it be rationalized in terms of subsequent earnings, since earnings are rele-

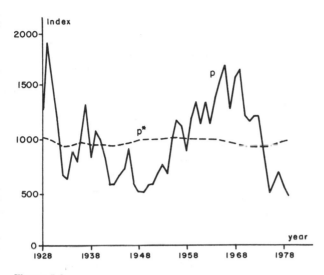

Figure 5.2
Real modified Dow Jones Industrial Average (solid line p) and ex-post rational price (dotted line p^*), 1928–1979, both detrended by dividing by a long-run exponential growth factor. The variable p^* is the present value of actual subsequent real detrended dividends, subject to an assumption about the present value in 1979 of dividends thereafter. Data are from data set 2 in the appendix.

vant in this model only as indicators of later dividends. Of course, the efficient markets model does not say $p = p^*$. Might one still suppose that this kind of stock market crash was a rational mistake, a forecast error that rational people might make? This chapter will explore the notion that the very volatility of p (i.e., the tendency of big movements in p to occur again and again) implies that the answer is no.

To give an idea of the kind of volatility comparisons that will be made here, let us consider at this point the simplest inequality that puts limits on one measure of volatility: the standard deviation of p. The efficient markets model can be described as asserting that $p_t = E_t(p_t^*)$, i.e., p_t is the mathematical expectation conditional on all information available at time t of p_t^*. In other words, p_t is the optimal forecast of p_t^*. One can define the forecast error as $u_t = p_t^* - p_t$. A fundamental principle of optimal forecasts is that the forecast error u_t must be uncorrelated with the forecast; that is, the covariance between p_t and u_t must be zero. If a forecast error showed a consistent correlation with the forecast itself, then that would in itself imply that the forecast could be improved. Mathematically, it can be shown from the theory of conditional expectations that u_t must be uncorrelated with p_t.

If one uses the principle from elementary statistics that the variance of the sum of two uncorrelated variables is the sum of their variances, one then has var(p^*) = var(u) + var(p). Since variances cannot be negative, this means var(p) $\leqslant$ var(p^*) or, converting to more easily interpreted standard deviations,

$$\sigma(p) \leqslant \sigma(p^*). \tag{1}$$

This inequality (employed before in the papers by LeRoy and Porter and myself) is violated dramatically by the data in figures 5.1 and 5.2 as is immediately obvious in looking at the figures.[3]

This chapter will develop the efficient markets model in section 5.1 to clarify some theoretical questions that may arise in connection with the inequality (1), and some similar inequalities will be derived that put limits on the standard deviation of the innovation in price and the standard deviation of the change in price. The model is restated in innovation form, which allows better understanding of the limits on stock price volatility imposed by the model. In particular, this will enable us to see (section 5.2) that the standard deviation of Δp is highest when information about dividends is revealed smoothly and that if information is revealed in big lumps occasionally the price series may have higher kurtosis (fatter tails) but will have *lower* variance. The notion expressed by some that earnings rather than dividend data should be used is discussed in section 5.3, and a way of assessing the importance of time variation in real discount rates is shown in section 5.4. The inequalities are compared with the data in section 5.5.

This chapter takes as its starting point the approach I used earlier [1979, and chapter 15], which showed evidence suggesting that long-term bond yields are too volatile to accord with simple expectations models of the term structure of interest rates.[4] In that paper, it was shown how restrictions implied by efficient markets on the cross-covariance function of short-term and long-term interest rates imply inequality restrictions on the spectra of the long-term interest rate series that characterize the smoothness that the long rate should display. In this chapter, analogous implications are derived for the volatility of stock prices, although here a simpler and more intuitively appealing discussion of the model in terms of its innovation representation is used. This chapter also has benefited from the earlier discussion by LeRoy and Porter [1981], which independently derived some restrictions on security price volatility implied by the efficient markets model and concluded that common stock prices are too volatile to accord with the model. They applied a methodology in some ways similar to that used here to study a stock price index and individual stocks in a sample period starting after World War II.

It is somewhat inaccurate to say that this chapter attempts to contradict the extensive literature of efficient markets (as, for example, Paul Cootner's [1964] volume on the random character of stock prices, or Eugene Fama's survey [1970]).[5] Most of this literature really examines different properties of security prices. Very little of the efficient markets literature bears directly on the characteristic feature of the model considered here. that expected *real* returns for the aggregate stock market are constant through time (or approximately so). Much of the literature on efficient markets concerns the investigation of nominal "profit opportunities" (variously defined) and whether transactions costs prohibit their exploitation. Of course, if real stock prices are "too volatile" as it is defined here, then there may well be a sort of real profit opportunity. Time variation in expected real interest rates does not itself imply that any trading rule dominates a buy and hold strategy, but really large variations in expected returns might seem to suggest that such a trading rule exists. This chapter does not investigate this, or whether transactions costs prohibit its exploitation. It is concerned instead with a more interesting (from an economic standpoint) question: what accounts for movements in real stock prices and can they be explained by new information about subsequent real dividends? If the model fails due to excessive volatility, then we will have seen a new characterization of how the simple model fails. The characterization is not equivalent to other characterizations of its failure, such as that one-period holding returns are forecastable, or that stocks have not been good inflation hedges recently.

The volatility comparisons that will be made here have the advantage that they are insensitive to misalignment of price and dividend series, as may happen with earlier data when collection procedures were not ideal. The tests are also not affected by the practice, in the construction of stock price and dividend indexes, of dropping certain stocks from the sample occasionally and replacing them with other stocks, so long as the volatility of the series is not misstated. These comparisons are thus well suited to existing long-term data in stock price averages. The robustness that the volatility comparisons have, coupled with their simplicity, may account for their popularity in casual discourse.

5.1 The Simple Efficient Markets Model

According to the simple efficient markets model, the real price P_t of a share at the beginning of the time period t is given by

Table 5.1
Definitions of principal symbols

γ = real discount factor for series before detrending; $\gamma = 1/(1 + r)$

$\overline{\gamma}$ = real discount factor for detrended series; $\overline{\gamma} \equiv \lambda\gamma$

D_t = real dividend accruing to stock index (before detrending)

d_t = real detrended dividend; $d_t \equiv D_t/\lambda^{t+1-T}$

Δ = first difference operator $\Delta x_t \equiv x_t - x_{t-1}$

δ_t = innovation operator; $\delta_t x_{t+k} \equiv E_t x_{t+k} - E_{t-1} x_{t+k}$; $\delta x \equiv \delta_t x_t$

E = unconditional mathematical expectations operator; $E(x)$ is the true (population) mean of x

E_t = mathematical expectations operator conditional on information at time t; $E_t x_t \equiv E(x_t | I_t)$, where I_t is the vector of information variables known at time t

λ = trend factor for price and dividend series; $\lambda \equiv 1 + g$ where g is the long-run growth rate of price and dividends

P_t = real stock price index (before detrending)

p_t = real detrended stock price index; $p_t = P_t/\lambda^{t-T}$

p_t^* = ex-post rational stock price index [expression (4)]

r = one-period real discount rate for series before detrending

$\overline{r}$ = real discount rate for detrended series; $\overline{r} = (1 - \overline{\gamma})/\overline{\gamma}$

$\overline{r}_2$ = two-period real discount rate for detrended series; $\overline{r}_2 = (1 + \overline{r})^2 - 1$

t = time (year)

T = base year for detrending and for wholesale price index; $p_T = P_T$ = nominal stock price index at time T

$$P_t = \sum_{k=0}^{\infty} \gamma^{k+1} E_t D_{t+k}, \qquad 0 < \gamma < 1, \tag{2}$$

where D_t is the real dividend paid at (let us say, the end of) time t, E_t denotes mathematical expectation conditional on information available at time t, and γ is the constant real discount factor (also see table 5.1). I define the constant real interest rate r so that $\gamma = 1/(1 + r)$. Information at time t includes P_t and D_t and their lagged values, and will generally include other variables as well.

The one-period holding return $H_t \equiv (\Delta P_{t+1} + D_t)/P_t$ is the return from buying the stock at time t and selling it at time $t + 1$. The first term in the numerator is the capital gain; the second term is the dividend received at the end of time t. They are divided by P_t to provide a rate of return. The model (2) has the property that $E_t(H_t) = r$.

The model (2) can be restated in terms of series as a proportion of the long-run growth factor: $p_t = P_t/\lambda^{t-T}$, $d_t = D_t/\lambda^{t+1-T}$, where the growth factor is $\lambda^{t-T} = (1 + g)^{t-T}$, g is the rate of growth, and T is the base year.

Dividing (2) by λ^{t-T} and substituting one finds[6]

$$p_t = \sum_{k=0}^{\infty} (\lambda\gamma)^{k+1} E_t d_{t+k} = \sum_{k=0}^{\infty} \bar{\gamma}^{k+1} E_t d_{t+k}. \tag{3}$$

The growth rate g must be less than the discount rate r if (2) is to give a finite price, and hence $\bar{\gamma} \equiv \lambda\gamma < 1$, and defining $\bar{r}$ by $\bar{\gamma} \equiv 1/(1 + \bar{r})$, the discount rate appropriate for the p_t and d_t series is $\bar{r} > 0$. This discount rate $\bar{r}$ is, it turns out, just the mean dividend divided by the mean price, i.e., $\bar{r} - E(d)/E(p)$.[7]

We may also write the model as noted above in terms of the ex-post rational price series p_t^* (analogous to the ex-post rational interest rate series that Jeremy Siegel and I used to study the Fisher effect, or that I used to study the expectations theory of the term structure). That is, p_t^* is the present value of actual subsequent dividends:

$$p_t = E_t(p_t^*), \tag{4}$$

where

$$p_t^* = \sum_{k=0}^{\infty} \bar{\gamma}^{k+1} d_{t+k}.$$

Since the summation extends to infinity, we never observe p_t^* without some error. However, with a long enough dividend series we may observe an approximate p_t^*. If we choose an arbitrary value for the terminal value of p_t^* (in figures 5.1 and 5.2, p^* for 1979 was set at the average detrended real price over the sample), then we may determine p_t^* recursively by $p_t^* = \bar{\gamma}(p_{t+1}^* + d_t)$ working backward from the terminal date. As we move back from the terminal date, the importance of the terminal value chosen declines. In data set 1 as shown in figure 5.1, $\bar{\gamma}$ is .954 and $\bar{\gamma}^{108} = .0063$ so that at the beginning of the sample the terminal value chosen has a negligible weight in the determination of p_t^*. If we had chosen a different terminal condition, the result would be to add or subtract an exponential trend from the p^* shown in figure 5.1. This is shown graphically in figure 5.3, in which p^* is shown computed from alternative terminal values. Since the only thing we need know to compute p^* about dividends after 1978 is p^* for 1979, it does not matter whether dividends are "smooth" or not after 1978. Thus, figure 5.3 represents our uncertainty about p^*.

There is yet another way to write the model, which will be useful in the analysis which follows. For this purpose, it is convenient to adopt notation for the innovation in a variable. Let us define the innovation operator $\delta_t \equiv E_t - E_{t-1}$ where E_t is the conditional expectations operator. Then for

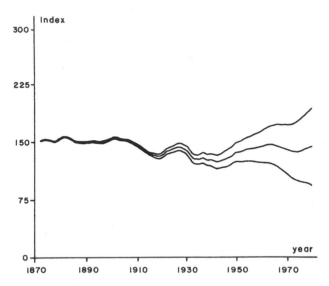

Figure 5.3
Alternative measures of the ex-post rational price p^*, obtained by alternative assumptions about the present value in 1979 of dividends thereafter. The middle curve is the p^* series plotted in figure 5.1. The series are computed recursively from terminal conditions using dividend series d of data set 1.

any variable X_t the term $\delta_t X_{t+k}$ equals $E_t X_{t+k} - E_{t-1} X_{t+k}$ which is the change in the conditional expectation of X_{t+k} that is made in response to new information arriving between $t - 1$ and t. The time subscript t may be dropped so that δX_k denotes $\delta_t X_{t+k}$ and δX denotes δX_0 or $\delta_t X_t$. Since conditional expectations operators satisfy $E_j E_k = E_{\min(j,k)}$ it follows that $E_{t-m} \delta_t X_{t+k} = E_{t-m}(E_t X_{t+k} - E_{t-1} X_{t+k}) = E_{t-m} X_{t+k} - E_{t-m} X_{t+k} = 0$, $m \geqslant 0$. This means that $\delta_t X_{t+k}$ must be uncorrelated for all k with all information known at time $t - 1$ and must, since lagged innovations are information at time t, be uncorrelated with $\delta_{t'} X_{t+j}$, $t' < t$, all j; i.e., innovations in variables are serially uncorrelated.

The model implies that the innovation in price $\delta_t p_t$ is observable. Since (3) can be written $p_t = \bar{\gamma}(d_t + E_t p_{t+1})$, we know, solving, that $E_t p_{t+1} = p_t/\bar{\gamma} - d_t$. Hence $\delta_t p_t \equiv E_t p_t - E_{t-1} p_t = p_t + d_{t-1} - p_{t-1}/\bar{\gamma} = \Delta p_t + d_{t-1} - \bar{r} p_{t-1}$. The variable that we call $\delta_t p_t$ (or just δp) is the variable that Clive Granger and Paul Samuelson emphasized should, in contrast to $\Delta p_t \equiv p_t - p_{t-1}$, by efficient markets, be unforecastable. In practice, with our data, $\delta_t p_t$ so measured will approximately equal Δp_t.

The model also implies that the innovation in price is related to the innovations in dividends by

$$\delta_t p_t = \sum_{k=0}^{\infty} \bar{\gamma}^{k+1} \delta_t d_{t+k}. \tag{5}$$

This expression is identical to (3) except that δ_t replaces E_t. Unfortunately, while $\delta_t p_t$ is observable in this model, the $\delta_t d_{t+k}$ terms are not directly observable; that is, we do not know when the public gets information about a particular dividend. Thus, in deriving inequalities below, one is obliged to assume the "worst possible" pattern of information accrual.

Expressions (2)–(5) constitute four different representations of the same efficient markets model. Expressions (4) and (5) are particularly useful for deriving our inequalities on measures of volatility. We have already used (4) to derive the limit (1) on the standard deviation of p given the standard deviation of p^*, and we will use (5) to derive a limit on the standard deviation of δp given the standard deviation of d.

One issue that relates to the derivation of (1) can now be clarified. The inequality (1) was derived using the assumption that the forecast error $u_t = p_t^* - p_t$ is uncorrelated with p_t. However, the forecast error u_t is not serially uncorrelated. It is uncorrelated with all information known at time t, but the lagged forecast error u_{t-1} is not known at time t since p_{t-1}^* is not discovered at time t. In fact, $u_t = \sum_{k=1}^{\infty} \bar{\gamma}^k \delta_{t+k} p_{t+k}$, as can be seen by substituting the expressions for p_t and p_t^* from (3) and (4) into $u_t = p_t^* - p_t$, and rearranging. Since the series $\delta_t p_t$ is serially uncorrelated, u_t has first-order autoregressive serial correlation.[8] For this reason, it is inappropriate to test the model by regressing $p_t^* - p_t$ on variables known at time t and using the ordinary t-statistics of the coefficients of these variables. However, a generalized least squares transformation of the variables would yield an appropriate regression test. We might thus regress the trans formed variable $u_t - \bar{\gamma} u_{t+1}$ on variables known at time t. Since $u_t - \bar{\gamma} u_{t+1} = \bar{\gamma} \delta_{t+1} p_{t+1}$, this amounts to testing whether the innovation in price can be forecasted. I will perform and discuss such regression tests in section 5.5.

To find a limit on the standard deviation of δp for a given standard deviation of d_t, first note that d_t equals its unconditional expectation plus the sum of its innovations:

$$d_t = E(d) + \sum_{k=0}^{\infty} \delta_{t-k} d_t. \tag{6}$$

If we regard $E(d)$ as $E_{-\infty}(d_t)$, then this expression is just a tautology. It tells us, though, that d_t $t = 0, 1, 2, \ldots$ are just different linear combinations of the same innovations in dividends that enter into the linear combination in

(5) that determine $\delta_t p_t$ $t = 0, 1, 2, \ldots$ We can thus ask how large var(δp) might be for given var(d). Since innovations are serially uncorrelated, we know from (6) that the variance of the sum is the sum of the variances:

$$\text{var}(d) = \sum_{k=0}^{\infty} \text{var}(\delta d_k) = \sum_{k=0}^{\infty} \sigma_k^2. \tag{7}$$

Our assumption of stationarity for d_t implies the $\text{var}(\delta_{t-k} d_t) \equiv \text{var}(\delta d_k) \equiv \sigma_k^2$ is independent of t.

In expression (5) we have no information that the variance of the sum is the sum of the variances since all innovations are time t innovations, which may be correlated. In fact, for given $\sigma_0^2, \sigma_1^2, \ldots$, the maximum variance of the sum in (5) occurs when the elements in the sum are perfectly positively correlated. This means then that so long as $\text{var}(\delta d) \neq 0$, $\delta_t d_{t+k} = a_k \delta_t d_t$, where $a_k = \sigma_k / \sigma_0$. Substituting this into (6) implies

$$\hat{d}_t = \sum_{k=0}^{\infty} a_k \varepsilon_{t-k}, \tag{8}$$

where a hat denotes a variable minus its mean: $\hat{d}_t \equiv d_t - E(d)$ and $\varepsilon_t \equiv \delta_t d_t$. Thus, if var($\delta p$) is to be maximized for given $\sigma_0^2, \sigma_1^2, \ldots$, the dividend process must be a moving average process in terms of its own innovations.[9] I have thus shown, rather than assumed, that if the variance of δp is to be maximized, the forecast of d_{t+k} will have the usual ARIMA form as in the forecast popularized by Box and Jenkins.

We can now find the maximum possible variance for δp for given variance of d. Since the innovations in (5) are perfectly positively correlated, $\text{var}(\delta p) = (\sum_{k=0}^{\infty} \overline{\gamma}^{k+1} \sigma_k)^2$. To maximize this subject to the constraint $\text{var}(d) = \sum_{k=0}^{\infty} \sigma_k^2$ with respect to $\sigma_0, \sigma_1, \ldots$, one may set up the Lagrangean:

$$L = \left(\sum_{k=0}^{\infty} \overline{\gamma}^{k+1} \sigma_k \right)^2 + v \left(\text{var}(d) - \sum_{k=0}^{\infty} \sigma_k^2 \right), \tag{9}$$

where v is the Lagrangean multiplier. The first-order conditions for σ_j, $j = 0, \ldots \infty$, are

$$\frac{\partial L}{\partial \sigma_j} = 2 \left(\sum_{k=0}^{\infty} \overline{\gamma}^{k+1} \sigma_k \right) \overline{\gamma}^{j+1} - 2 v \sigma_j = 0, \tag{10}$$

which in turn means that σ_j is proportional to $\overline{\gamma}^j$. The second-order conditions for a maximum are satisfied, and the maximum can be viewed as a tangency of an isoquant for var(δp), which is a hyperplane in $\delta_0, \sigma_1, \sigma_2,$

... space, with the hypersphere represented by the constraint. At the maximum $\sigma_k^2 = (1 - \bar{\gamma}^2)\,\text{var}(d)\bar{\gamma}^{2k}$ and $\text{var}(\delta p) = \bar{\gamma}^2\,\text{var}(d)/(1 - \bar{\gamma}^2)$ and so, converting to standard deviations for ease of interpretation, we have

$$\sigma(\delta p) \leqslant \sigma(d)/\sqrt{\bar{r}_2}, \tag{11}$$

where

$$\bar{r}_2 = (1 + \bar{r})^2 - 1.$$

Here, $\bar{r}_2$ is the two-period interest rate, which is roughly twice the one-period rate. The maximum occurs, then, when d_t is a first-order auto-regressive process, $\hat{d}_t = \bar{\gamma}\hat{d}_{t-1} + \varepsilon_t$, and $E_t\hat{d}_{t+k} = \bar{\gamma}^k\hat{d}_t$, where $\hat{d} \equiv d - E(d)$ as before.

The variance of the innovation in price is thus maximized when information about dividends is revealed in a smooth fashion so that the standard deviation of the new information at time t about a future dividend d_{t+k} is proportional to its weight in the present value formula in the model (5). In contrast, suppose all dividends somehow became known years before they were paid. Then the innovations in dividends would be so heavily discounted in (5) that they would contribute little to the standard deviation of the innovation in price. Alternatively, suppose nothing were known about dividends until the year they are paid. Here, although the innovation would not be heavily discounted in (5), the impact of the innovation would be confined to only one term in (5), and the standard deviation in the innovation in price would be limited to the standard deviation in the single dividend.

Other inequalities analogous to (11) can also be derived in the same way. For example, we can put an upper bound to the standard deviation of the change in price (rather than the innovation in price) for given standard deviation in dividend. The only difference induced in the above procedure is that Δp_t is a different linear combination of innovations in dividends. Using the fact the $\Delta p_t = \delta_t p_t + \bar{r}p_{t-1} - d_{t-1}$ we find

$$\Delta p_t = \sum_{k=0}^{\infty} \bar{\gamma}^{k+1}\delta_t d_{t+k} + \bar{r}\sum_{j=1}^{\infty} \delta_{t-j}\sum_{k=0}^{\infty} \bar{\gamma}^{k+1}d_{t+k-1} - \sum_{j=1}^{\infty} \delta_{t-j}d_{t-1}. \tag{12}$$

As above, the maximization of the variance of δp for given variance of d requires that the time t innovations in d be perfectly correlated (innovations at different times are necessarily uncorrelated) so that again the dividend process must be forecasted as an ARIMA process. However, the parameters of the ARIMA process for d that maximize the variance of Δp will be different. One finds, after maximizing the Lagrangean expression [analogous to (9)], an inequality slightly different from (11),

$$\sigma(\Delta p) \leqslant \sigma(d)/\sqrt{2\bar{r}}. \tag{13}$$

The upper bound is attained if the optimal dividend forecast is first-order autoregressive, but with an autoregressive coefficient slightly different from that which induced the upper bound to (11). The upper bound to (13) is attained if $\hat{d}_t = (1 - \bar{r})\hat{d}_{t-1} + \varepsilon_t$ and $E_t d_{t+k} = (1 - \bar{r})^k \hat{d}_t$, where, as before, $\hat{d}_t \equiv d_t - E(d)$.

5.2 High Kurtosis and Infrequent Important Breaks in Information

It has been repeatedly noted that stock price change distributions show high kurtosis or "fat tails." This means that, if one looks at a time-series of observations on δp or Δp, one sees long stretches of time when their (absolute) values are all rather small and then an occasional extremely large (absolute) value. This phenomenon is commonly attributed to a tendency for new information to come in big lumps infrequently. There seems to be a common presumption that this information lumping might cause stock price changes to have high or infinite variance, which would seem to contradict the conclusion in the preceding section that the variance of price is limited and is maximized if forecasts have a simple autoregressive structure.

High sample kurtosis does not indicate infinite variance if we do not assume, as did Fama [1965] and others, that price changes are drawn from the stable Paretian class of distributions.[10] The model does not suggest that price changes have a distribution in this class. The model instead suggests that the existence of moments for the price series is implied by the existence of moments for the dividends series.

As long as d is jointly stationary with information and has a finite variance, then p, p^*, δp, and Δp will be stationary and have a finite variance.[11] If d is normally distributed, however, it does not follow that the price variables will be normally distributed. In fact, they may yet show high kurtosis.

To see this possibility, suppose the dividends are serially independent and identically normally distributed. The kurtosis of the price series is defined by $K = E(\hat{p})^4/(E(\hat{p})^2)^2$, where $p \equiv \hat{p} - E(p)$. Suppose, as an example, that with a probability of $1/n$ the public is told d_t at the beginning of time t, but with probability $(n - 1)/n$ has no information about current or future dividends.[12] In time periods when they are told d_t, $\hat{p}_t$ equals $\bar{\gamma}\hat{d}_t$, otherwise $\hat{p}_t = 0$. Then $E(\hat{p}_t^4) = E((\bar{\gamma}\hat{d}_t)^4)/n$ and $E(\hat{p}_t^2) = E((\bar{\gamma}\hat{d}_t)^2)/n$ so that kurtosis equals $nE(\bar{\gamma}d_4)^4)/E((\bar{\gamma}d_t)^2)$, which equals n times the kurtosis of the normal distribution. Hence, by choosing n high enough one can achieve an arbitrarily high kurtosis, and yet the variance of price will always exist. Moreover, the distribution of $\hat{p}_t$ conditional on the information that the dividend has been revealed is also normal, in spite of high kurtosis of the unconditional distribution.

If information is revealed in big lumps occasionally (so as to induce high kurtosis as suggested in the above example) var(δp) or var(Δp) is not especially large. The variance loses more from the long interval of time when information is not revealed than it gains from the infrequent events when it is. The highest possible variance for given variance of d indeed comes when information is revealed smoothly as noted in the previous section. In the above example, where information about dividends is revealed one time in n, $\sigma(\delta p) = \bar{\gamma}n^{1/2}\sigma(d)$ and $\sigma(\Delta p) = \bar{\gamma}(2/n)^{1/2}\sigma(d)$. The values of $\sigma(\delta p)$ and $\sigma(\Delta p)$ implied by this example are for all n strictly below the upper bounds of the inequalities (11) and (13).[13]

5.3   Dividends or Earnings?

It has been argued that the model (2) does not capture what is generally meant by efficient markets, and that the model should be replaced by a model that makes price the present value of expected earnings rather than dividends. In the model (2) earnings may be relevant to the pricing of shares but only insofar as earnings are indicators of future dividends. Earnings are thus no different from any other economic variable that may indicate future dividends. The model (2) is consistent with the usual notion in finance that individuals are concerned with returns, that is, capital gains plus dividends. The model implies that expected total returns are constant and that the capital gains component of returns is just a reflection of information about future dividends. Earnings, in contrast, are statistics conceived by accountants that are supposed to provide an indicator of how well a company is doing, and there is a great deal of latitude for the definition of earnings, as the recent literature on inflation accounting will attest.

There is no reason why price per share ought to be the present value of expected earnings per share if some earnings are retained. In fact, as Merton Miller and Franco Modigliani [1961] argued, such a present value formula would entail a fundamental sort of double counting. It is incorrect to include in the present value formula both earnings at time t and the later earnings that accrue when time t earnings are reinvested.[14] Miller and Modigliani showed a formula by which price might be regarded as the present value of earnings corrected for investments, but that formula can be shown, using an accounting identity to be identical to (2).

Some people seem to feel that one cannot claim price as present value of expected dividends since firms routinely pay out only a fraction of earnings and also attempt somewhat to stabilize dividends. They are right in the case where firms paid out *no* dividends, for then the price p_t would have to grow at the discount rate $\bar{r}$, and the model (2) would not be the solution to the difference equation implied by the condition $E_t(H_t) = r$. On the other hand, if firms pay out a fraction of dividends or smooth short-run fluctuations in dividends, then the price of the firm will grow at a rate less than the discount rate and (2) is the solution to the difference equation.[15] With our Standard and Poor data, the growth rate of real price is only about 1.5%, while the discount rate is about 4.8% + 1.5% = 6.3%. At these rates, the value of the firm a few decades hence is so heavily discounted relative to its size that it contributes very little to the value of the stock today; by far the most of the value comes from the intervening dividends. Hence (2) and the implied p^* ought to be useful characterizations of the value of the firm.

The crucial thing to recognize in this context is that once we know the terminal price and intervening dividends, we have specified all that investors care about. It would not make sense to define an ex-post rational price from a terminal condition on price, using the same formula with earnings in place of dividends.

5.4   Time-Varying Real Discount Rates

If we modify the model (2) to allow real discount rates to vary without restriction through time, then the model becomes untestable. We do not observe real discount rates directly. Regardless of the behavior of P_t and D_t, there will always be a discount rate series that makes (2) hold identically. We might ask, though, whether the movements in the real discount rate that would be required are not larger than we might have expected. Or is it possible that small movements in the current one-period discount rate coupled with new information about such movements in future discount rates could account for high stock price volatility?[16]

The natural extension of (2) to the case of time varying real discount rates is

$$P_t = E_t\left(\sum_{k=0}^{\infty} D_{t+k} \prod_{j=0}^{k} \frac{1}{1 + r_{t+j}}\right),$$ (14)

which has the property that $E_t((1 + H_t)/(1 + r_t)) = 1$. If we set $1 + r_t = (\partial U/\partial C_t)/(\partial U/\partial C_{t+1})$, i.e., to the marginal rate of substitution between present and future consumption where U is the additively separable utility of consumption, then this property is the first-order condition for a maximum of expected utility subject to a stock market budget constraint, and equation (14) is consistent with such expected utility maximization at all times. Note that while r_t is a sort of ex-post real interest rate not necessarily known until time $t + 1$, only the conditional distribution at time t or earlier influences price in the formula (14).

As before, we can rewrite the model in terms of detrended series:

$$p_t = E_t(p_t^*),\tag{15}$$

where

$$p_t^* \equiv \sum_{k=0}^{\infty} d_{t+k} \prod_{j=0}^{k} \frac{1}{1 + \overline{r}_{t+j}},$$

$$1 + \overline{r}_{t+j} \equiv (1 + r_t)/\lambda.$$

This model then implies that $\sigma(p_t) \leq \sigma(p_t^*)$ as before. Since the model is nonlinear, however, it does not allow us to derive inequalities like (11) or (13). On the other hand, if movements in real interest rates are not too large, then we can use the linearization of p_t^* (i.e., Taylor expansion truncated after the linear term) around $d = E(d)$ and $\overline{r} = E(\overline{r})$; i.e.,

$$\hat{p}_t^* \cong \sum_{k=0}^{\infty} \overline{\gamma}^{k+1} \hat{d}_{t+k} - \frac{E(d)}{E(\overline{r})} \sum_{k=0}^{\infty} \overline{\gamma}^{k+1} \hat{\overline{r}}_{t+k},\tag{16}$$

where $\overline{\gamma} = 1/(1 + E(\overline{r}))$, and a hat over a variable denotes the variable minus its mean. The first term in the above expression is just the expression for p_t^* in (4) (demeaned). The second term represents the effect on p_t^* of movements in real discount rates. This second term is identical to the expression for p^* in (4) except that d_{t+k} is replaced by $\hat{\overline{r}}_{t+k}$ and the expression is premultiplied by $-E(d)/E(\overline{r})$.

It is possible to offer a simple intuitive interpretation for this linearization. First note that the derivative of $1/(1 + \overline{r}_{t+k})$, with respect to $\overline{r}$ evaluated at $E(\overline{r})$ is $-\overline{\gamma}^2$. Thus, a one percentage point increase in $\overline{r}_{t+k}$ causes $1/(1 + \overline{r}_{t+k})$ to drop by $\overline{\gamma}^2$ times 1%, or slightly less than 1%. Note that all terms in (15) dated $t + k$ or higher are premultiplied by $1/(1 + \overline{r}_{t+k})$. Thus, if $\overline{r}_{t+k}$ is increased by one percentage point, all else constant, then all of these terms will be reduced by about $\overline{\gamma}^2$ times 1%. We can approximate the sum of these terms as $\overline{\gamma}^{k-1} E(d)/E(\overline{r})$, where

$E(d)/E(\bar{r})$ is the value at the beginning of time $t + k$ of a constant dividend stream $E(d)$ discounted by $E(\bar{r})$, and $\bar{\gamma}^{k-1}$ discounts it to the present. So, we see that a one percentage point increase in $\bar{r}_{t+k}$, all else constant, decreases p_t^* by about $\bar{\gamma}^{k+1}E(d)/E(\bar{r})$, which corresponds to the kth term in expression (16). There are two sources of inaccuracy with this linearization. First, the present value of all future dividends starting with time $t + k$ is not exactly $\bar{\gamma}^{k-1}E(d)/E(\bar{r})$. Second, increasing $\bar{r}_{t+k}$ by one percentage point does not cause $1/(1 + \bar{r}_{t+k})$ to fall by exactly $\bar{\gamma}^2$ times 1%. To some extent, however, these errors in the effects on p_t^* of $\bar{r}_t$, $\bar{r}_{t+1}$, $\bar{r}_{t+2}$, ... should average out, and one can use (16) to get an idea of the effects of changes in discount rates.

To give an impression as to the accuracy of the linearization (16), I computed p_t^* for data set 2 in two ways: first using (15) and then using (16), with the same terminal condition p_{1979}^*. In place of the unobserved $\bar{r}_t$ series, I used the actual four–six-month prime commercial paper rate plus a constant to give it the mean $\bar{r}$ of table 5.2. The commercial paper rate is a *nominal* interest rate, and thus one would expect its fluctuations represent changes in inflationary expectations as well as interest rate movements. I chose it nonetheless, rather arbitrarily, as a series that shows much more fluctuation than one would normally expect to see in an expected *real* rate. The commercial paper rate ranges, in this sample, from 0.53% to 9.87%. It stayed below 1% for over a decade (1935–1946) and, at the end of the sample, stayed generally well above 5% for over a decade. In spite of this erratic behavior, the correlation coefficient between p^* computed from (15) and p^* computed from (16) was .996, and $\sigma(p_t^*)$ was 250.5 and 268.0 by (15) and (16), respectively. Thus the linearization (16) can be quite accurate. Note also that while these large movements in $\bar{r}_t$ cause p_t^* to move much more than was observed in figure 5.2, $\sigma(p^*)$ is still less than half of $\sigma(p)$. This suggests that the variability $\bar{r}_t$ that is needed to save the efficient markets model is much larger yet, as we shall see.

To put a formal lower bound on $\sigma(\bar{r})$ given the variability of Δp, note that (16) makes $\hat{p}_t^*$ the present value of z_t, z_{t+1}, ... where $z_t \equiv \hat{d}_t - \hat{r}_t E(d)/E(\bar{r})$. We thus know from (13) that $2E(\bar{r})\text{var}(\Delta p) \leqslant \text{var}(z)$. Moreover, from the definition of z we know that $\text{var}(z) \leqslant \text{var}(d) + 2\sigma(d)\sigma(\bar{r})E(d)/E(\bar{r}) + \text{var}(\bar{r})E(d)^2/E(\bar{r})^2$, where the equality holds if $\hat{d}_t$ and $\bar{r}_t$ are perfectly negatively correlated. Combining these two inequalities and solving for $\sigma(\bar{r})$ one finds

$$\sigma(\bar{r}) \geqslant (\sqrt{2E(\bar{r})}\sigma(\Delta p) - \sigma(d))E(\bar{r})/E(d). \tag{17}$$

This inequality puts a lower bound on $\sigma(\bar{r})$ proportional to the discre-

Table 5.2
Sample statistics for price and dividend series[a]

	Data set 1: Standard and Poor's: 1871–1979	Data set 2: modified Dow industrial: 1928–1979
1. $E(p)$	145.5	982.6
$E(d)$	6.989	44.76
2. $\bar{r}$	.0480	0.456
$\bar{r}_2$	.0984	.0932
3. $b = \ln \lambda$	.0148	.0188
$\hat{\sigma}(b)$	(.0011)	(1.0035)
4. $\mathrm{corr}(p, p^*)$	.3918	.1626
$\sigma(d)$	1.481	9.828
Elements of inequalities:		
inequality (1)		
5. $\sigma(p)$	50.12	355.9
6. $\sigma(p^*)$	8.968	26.80
inequality (11)		
7. $\sigma(\Delta p + d_{-1} - \bar{r}p_{-1})$	25.57	242.1
$\min(\sigma)$	23.01	209.0
8. $\sigma(d)/\sqrt{\bar{r}_2}$	4.721	32.20
inequality (13)		
9. $\sigma(\Delta p)$	25.24	239.5
$\min(\sigma)$	22.71	206.4
10. $\sigma(d)/\sqrt{2\bar{r}}$	4.777	32.56

a. In this table, E denotes sample mean, σ denotes standard deviation and $\hat{\sigma}$ denotes standard error. Min(σ) is the lower bound on σ computed as a one-sided χ^2 95% confidence interval. The symbols p, d, $\bar{r}$, $\bar{r}_2$, b, and p^* are defined in the text. Data sets are described in the appendix. Inequality (1) in the text asserts that the standard deviation in row 5 should be less than or equal to that in row 6, inequality (11) that σ in row 7 should be less than or equal to that in row 8, and inequality (13) that σ in row 9 should be less than that in row 10.

pancy between the left-hand side and right-hand side of the inequality (13).[17] It will be used to examine the data in the next section.

5.5 Empirical Evidence

The elements of the inequalities (1), (11), and (13) are displayed for the two data sets (described in the appendix) in table 5.2. In both data sets, the long-run exponential growth path was estimated by regressing $\ln(P_t)$ on a constant and time. Then λ in (3) was set equal to e^b, where b is the coefficient of time (table 5.2). The discount rate $\bar{r}$ used to compute p^* from (4) is estimated as the average d divided by the average p.[18] The terminal value of p^* is taken as average p.

With data set 1, the nominal price and dividend series are the real Standard and Poor's Composite Stock Price Index and the associated dividend series. The earlier observations for this series are due to Alfred Cowles, who said that the index is "intended to represent, ignoring the elements of brokerage charges and taxes, what would have happened to an investor's funds if he had bought, at the beginning of 1871, all stocks quoted on the New York Stock Exchange, allocating his purchases among the individual stocks in proportion to their total monetary value and each month up to 1937 had by the same criterion redistributed his holdings among all quoted stocks" [1938, p. 2]. Standard and Poor later restricted the sample to 500 stocks, but the series continues to be value weighted. The advantage to this series is its comprehensiveness. The disadvantage is that the dividends accruing to the portfolio at one time may not correspond to the dividends forecasted by holders of the Standard and Poor's portfolio at an earlier time, due to the change in weighting of the stocks. There is no way to correct this disadvantage without losing comprehensiveness. The original portfolio of 1871 is bound to become a relatively smaller and smaller sample of U.S. common stocks as time goes on.

With data set 2, the nominal series are a modified Dow Jones Industrial Average and associated dividend series. With this data set, the advantages and disadvantages of data set 1 are reversed. My modifications in the Dow Jones Industrial Average assure that this series reflects the performance of a single unchanging portfolio. The disadvantage is that the performance of only 30 stocks is recorded.

Table 5.2 reveals that all inequalities are dramatically violated by the sample statistics for both data sets. The left-hand side of the inequality is always at least five times as great as the right-hand side, and as much as thirteen times as great.

The violation of the inequalities implies that "innovations" in price as we measure them can be forecasted. In fact, if we regress $\delta_{t+1}p_{t+1}$ onto (a constant and) p_t, we get significant results: a coefficient of p_t of $-.1521$ ($t = -3.218$, $R^2 = .0890$) for data set 1 and a coefficient of $-.2421$ ($t = -2.631$, $R^2 = .1238$) for data set 2. These results are not due to the representation of the data as a proportion of the long-run growth path. In fact, if the holding period return H_t is regressed on a constant and the dividend-price ratio D_t/P_t, we get results that are only slightly less significant: a coefficient of 3.533 ($t = 2.672$, $R^2 = .0631$) for data set 1 and a coefficient of 4.491 ($t = 1.795$, $R^2 = .0617$) for data set 2.[19]

These regression tests, while technically valid, may not be as generally useful for appraising the validity of the model as are the simple volatility comparisons. First, as noted above, the regression tests are not insensitive to data misalignment. Such low R^2 might be the result of dividend or commodity price index data errors. Second, although the model is rejected in these very long samples, the tests may not be powerful if we confined ourselves to shorter samples, for which the data are more accurate, as do most researchers in finance, while volatility comparisons may be much more revealing. To see this, consider a stylized world in which (for the sake of argument) the dividend series d_t is absolutely constant while the price series behaves as in our data set. Since the actual dividend series is fairly smooth, our stylized world is not too remote from our own. If dividends d_t are absolutely constant, however, it should be obvious to the most casual and unsophisticated observer by volatility arguments like those made here that the efficient markets model must be wrong. Price movements cannot reflect new information about dividends if dividends never change. Yet regressions like those run above will have limited power to reject the model. If the alternative hypothesis is, say, that $\hat{p}_t = \rho\hat{p}_{t-1} + \varepsilon_t$, where ρ is close to but less than one, then the power of the test in short samples will be very low. In this stylized world we are testing for the stationarity of the p_t series, for which, as we know, power is low in short samples.[20] For example, if postwar data from, say, 1950–1965 were chosen (a period often used in recent financial markets studies) when the stock market was drifting up, then clearly the regression tests will not reject. Even in periods showing a reversal of upward drift the rejection may not be significant.

Using inequality (7), we can compute how big the standard deviation of real discount rates would have to be to possibly account for the discrepancy $\sigma(\Delta p) - \sigma(d)/(2\bar{r})^{1/2}$ between table 5.2 results (rows 9 and 10) and the inequality (13). Assuming table 5.2 $\bar{r}$ (row 2) equals $E(\bar{r})$ and that sample variances equal population variances, we find that the standard deviation of $\bar{r}_t$ would have to be at least 4.36 percentage points for data set 1 and 7.36 percentage points for data set 2. These are very large numbers. If we take, as a normal range for $\bar{r}_t$ implied by these figures, a $\pm$ 2 standard deviation range around the real interest rate $\bar{r}$ given in table 5.2, then the real interest rate $\bar{r}_t$ would have to range from -3.91% to 13.52% for data set 1 and -8.16% to 17.27% for data set 2! And these ranges reflect lowest possible standard deviations consistent with the model only if the real rate has the first-order autoregressive structure and perfect negative correlation with dividends!

These estimated standard deviations of ex-ante real interest rates are roughly consistent with the results of the simple regressions noted above. In a regression of H_t on D_t/P_t and a constant, the standard deviation of the fitted value of H_t is 4.42% and 5.71% for data sets 1 and 2, respectively. These large standard deviations are consistent with the low R^2 because the standard deviation of H_t is so much higher (17.60% and 23.00%, respectively). The regressions of $\delta_t p_t$ on p_t suggest higher standard deviations of expected real interest rates. The standard deviation of the fitted value divided by the average detrended price is 5.24% and 8.67% for data sets 1 and 2, respectively.

5.6   Summary and Conclusions

We have seen that measures of stock price volatility over the past century appear to be far too high—five to thirteen times too high—to be attributed to new information about future real dividends if uncertainty about future dividends is measured by the sample standard deviations of real dividends around their long-run exponential growth path. The lower bound of a 95% one-sided χ^2 confidence interval for the standard deviation of annual changes in real stock prices is over five times higher than the upper bound allowed by our measure of the observed variability of real dividends. The failure of the efficient markets model is thus so dramatic that it would seem impossible to attribute the failure to such things as data errors, price index problems, or changes in tax laws.

One way of saving the general notion of efficient markets would be to attribute the movements in stock prices to changes in expected real interest rates. Since expected real interest rates are not directly observed, such a theory can not be evaluated statistically unless some other indicator of real rates is found. I have shown, however, that the movements in expected real interest rates that would justify the variability in stock prices are very large—much larger than the movements in nominal interest rates over the sample period.

Another way of saving the general notion of efficient markets is to say that our measure of the uncertainty regarding future dividends—the sample standard deviation of the movements of real dividends around their long-run exponential growth path—understates the true uncertainty about future dividends. Perhaps the market was rightfully fearful of much larger movements than actually materialized. One is led to doubt this, if after a century of observations nothing happened that could remotely justify the stock price movements. The movements in real dividends the market feared must have been many times larger than those observed in the Great Depression of the 1930s, as was noted above. Since the market did not know in advance with certainty the growth path and distribution of dividends that was ultimately observed, however, one cannot be sure that they were wrong to consider possible major events that did not occur. Such an explanation of the volatility of stock prices, however, is "academic," in that it relies fundamentally on unobservables and cannot be evaluated statistically.

Appendix

A. Data Set 1: Standard and Poor Series

Annual 1871–1979. The price series P_t is Standard and Poor's Monthly Composite Stock Price index for January divided by the Bureau of Labor Statistics wholesale price index (January WPI starting in 1900, annual average WPI before 1900 scaled to 1.00 in the base year 1979). Standard and Poor's Monthly Composite Stock Price index was extended back to 1871 as the Cowles Commission Common Stock index developed by Alfred Cowles and Associates [1938]. The index is currently based on 500 stocks.

The Dividend Series D_t is total dividends for the calendar year accruing to the portfolio represented by the stocks in the index divided by the average wholesale price index for the year (annual average WPI scaled to 1.00 in the base year 1979). Starting in 1926 these total dividends are the series "Dividends per share ... 12 months moving total adjusted to index" from Standard and Poor's statistical service. For 1871 to 1925, total dividends are Cowles series Da-1 multiplied by .1264 to correct for change in base year.

B. Data Set 2: Modified Dow Jones Industrial Average

Annual 1928–1979. Here P_t and D_t refer to real price and dividends of the portfolio of 30 stocks comprising the sample for the Dow Jones Industrial Average when it was created in 1928. Dow Jones averages before 1928 exist, but the 30 industrials series was begun in that year. The published Dow Jones Industrial Average, however, is not ideal in that stocks are dropped and replaced and in that the weighting given an individual stock is affected by splits. Of the original 30 stocks, only 17 were still included in the Dow Jones Industrial Average at the end of our sample. The published Dow Jones Industrial Average is the simple sum of the price per share of the 30 companies divided by a divisor that changes through time. Thus, if a stock splits two for one, then Dow Jones continues to include only one share but changes the divisor to prevent a sudden drop in the Dow Jones average.

To produce the series used in this chapter, the *Capital Changes Reporter* was used to trace changes in the companies from 1928 to 1979. Of the original 30 companies of the Dow Jones Industrial Average, at the end of our sample (1979), 9 had the identical names, 12 had changed only their names, and 9 had been acquired, merged or consolidated. For these latter 9, the price and dividend series are continued as the price and dividend of the shares exchanged by the acquiring corporation. In only one case was a cash payment, along with shares of the acquiring corportion, exchanged for the shares of the acquired corportion. In this case, the price and dividend series were continued as the price and dividend of the shares exchanged by the acquiring corporation. In four cases, preferred shares of the acquiring corporation were among shares exchanged. Common shares of equal value were substituted for these in our series. The number of shares of each firm included in the total is determined by the splits, and effective splits effected by stock dividends and merger. The price series is the value of all these shares on the last trading day of the preceding year, as shown on the Wharton School's Rodney White Center Common Stock tape. The dividend series is the total for the year of dividends and the cash value of other distributions for all these shares. The price and dividend series were deflated using the same wholesale price indexes as in data set 1.

Notes

1. The stock price index may look unfamiliar because it is deflated by a price index, expressed as a proportion of the long-run growth path and only January figures are shown. One might note, for example, that the stock market decline of 1929–1932 looks smaller than the recent decline. In real terms, it was. The January figures also miss both the 1929 peak and 1932 trough.

2. The price and dividend series as a proportion of the long-run growth path are defined below at the beginning of section 5.1. Assumptions about public knowledge or lack of knowledge of the long-run growth path are important, as shall be discussed below. The series p^* is computed subject to an assumption about dividends after 1978. See text and figure 5.3.

3. Some people will object to this derivation of (1) and say that one might as well have said that $E_t(p_t) = p_t^*$, i.e., that forecasts are correct "on average," which would lead to a reversal of the inequality (1). This objection stems, however, from a

misinterpretation of conditional expectations. The subscript t on the expectations operator E means "taking as given (i.e., nonrandom) all variables known at time t." Clearly, p_t is known at time t and p_t^* is not. In practical terms, if a forecaster gives as his forecast anything other than $E_t(p_t^*)$, then his forecast is not optimal in the sense of expected squared forecast error. If he gives a forecast that equals $E_t(p_t^*)$ only on average, then he is adding random noise to the optimal forecast. The amount of noise apparent in figure 5.1 or 5.2 is extraordinary. Imagine what we would think of our local weather forecaster if, say, actual local temperatures followed the dotted line and his forecasts followed the solid line!

4. This analysis was extended to yields on preferred stocks by Christine Amsler [1980].

5. It should not be inferred that the literature on efficient markets uniformly supports the notion of efficiency put forth there, for example, that no assets are dominated or that no trading rule dominates a buy and hold strategy, (for recent papers see S. Basu [1977]; Franco Modigliani and Richard Cohn [1979]; William Brainard, John Shoven and Lawrence Weiss [1980]; and the papers in the symposium on market efficiency edited by Michael Jensen [1978]).

6. No assumptions are introduced in going from (2) to (3), since (3) is just an algebraic transformation of (2). I shall, however, introduce the assumption that d_t is jointly stationary with information, which means that the (unconditional) covariance between d_t and z_{t-k}, where z_t is any information variable (which might be d_t itself or p_t), depends only on k, not t. It follows that we can write expressions like var(p) without a time subscript. In contrast, a realization of the random variable the conditional expectation $E_t(d_{t+k})$ is a function of time since it depends on information at time t. Some stationarity assumption is necessary if we are to proceed with any statistical analysis.

7. Taking unconditional expectations of both sides of (3) we find

$$E(p) = \frac{\overline{\gamma}}{1 - \overline{\gamma}} E(d);$$

using $\overline{\gamma} = 1/1 + \overline{r}$ and solving we find $\overline{r} = E(d)/E(p)$.

8. It follows that var(u) = var(δp)/$(1 - \overline{\gamma}^2)$ as LeRoy and Porter noted. They base their volatility tests on our inequality (1) (which they call theorem 2) and an equality restriction $\sigma^2(p) + \sigma^2(\delta p)/(1 - \overline{\gamma}^2) = \sigma^2(p^*)$ (their theorem 3). They found that, with postwar Standard and Poor earnings data, both relations were violated by sample statistics.

9. Of course, all indeterministic stationary processes can be given linear moving average representations, as Hermann Wold showed. However, it does not follow that the process can be given a moving average representation in terms of its own innovations. The true process may be generated nonlinearly or other information besides its own lagged values may be used in forecasting. These will generally result in a less perfect correlation of the terms in (5).

10. The empirical fact about the unconditional distribution of stock price changes is not that they have infinite variance (which can never be demonstrated with any finite sample), but that they have high kurtosis in the sample.

11. With any stationary process X_t, the existence of a finite var(X_t) implies, by Schwartz's inequality, a finite value of cov(X_t, X_{t+k}) for any k, and hence the entire autocovariance function of X_t, and the spectrum, exists. Moreover, the variance of $E_t(X_t)$ must also be finite, since the variance of X equals the variance of $E_t(X_t)$ plus the variance of the forecast error. While we may regard real dividends as having finite variance, innovations in dividends may show high kurtosis. The residuals in a second-order autoregression for d_t have a studentized range of 6.29 for the Standard and Poor series and 5.37 for the Dow series. According to the David-Hartley-Pearson test, normality can be rejected at the 5% level (but not at the 1% level) with a one-tailed text for both data sets.

12. For simplicity, in this example, the assumption elsewhere in this chapter that d_t is always known at time t has been dropped. It follows that in this example $\delta_t p_t \neq \Delta p_t + d_{t-1} - rp_{t-1}$ but instead $\delta_t p_t = p_t$.

13. For another illustrative example, consider $\hat{d}_t = \bar{\gamma}\hat{d}_{t-1} + \varepsilon_t$ as with the upper bound for the inequality (11) but where the dividends are announced for the next n years every $1/n$ years. Here, even though $\hat{d}_t$ has the autoregressive structure, ε_t is not the innovation in d_t. As n goes to infinity, $\sigma(\delta p)$ approaches zero.

14. LeRoy and Porter [1981] do assume price as present value of earnings but employ a correction to the price and earnings series that is, under additional theoretical assumptions not employed by Miller and Modigliani [1961], a correction for the double counting.

15. To understand this point, it helps to consider a traditional continuous time growth model, so instead of (2) we have $P_0 = \int_0^\infty D_t e^{-rt}\, dt$. In such a model, a firm has a constant earnings steam I. If it pays out all earnings, then $D = I$ and $P_0 = \int_0^\infty I e^{-rt}\, dt = I/r$. If it pays out only s of its earnings, then the firm grows at rate $(1 - s)r$, $D_t = sIe^{(1-s)rt}$, which is less than I at $t = 0$, but higher than I later on. Then $P_0 = \int_0^\infty sIe^{(1-s)rt}e^{-rt}\, dt = \int_0^\infty sIe^{-srt}\, dt = sI/(rs)$. If $s \neq 0$ (so that we are not dividing by zero), $P_0 = I/r$.

16. James Pesando [1979] has discussed the analogous question: how large must the variance in liquidity premiums be in order to justify the volatility of long-term interest rates?

17. In deriving the inequality (13) it was assumed that d_t was known at time t, so by analogy this inequality would be based on the assumption that r_t is known at time t. However, without this assumption the same inequality could be derived anyway. The maximum contribution of $\bar{r}_t$ to variance of Δp occurs when $\bar{r}_t$ is known at time t.

18. This is not equivalent to the average dividend-price ratio, which was slightly higher (.0514 for data set 1, .0484 for data set 2).

19. [Regressions on D_t/P_t are, however not strictly valid as tests of (2) since D_t (total dividends for year t) are not fully known in January when P_t is measured. See instead table 1.2 on page 34.]

20. If dividends are constant (let us say $d_t = 0$), then a test of the model by a regression of $\delta_{t+1}p_{t+1}$ on p_t amounts to a regression of p_{t+1} on p_t with the null hypothesis that the coefficient of p_t is $(1 + \bar{r})$. This appears to be an explosive model for which t-statistics are not valid yet our true model, which in effect assumes $\sigma(d) \neq 0$, is nonexplosive.

References

Amsler, Christine, 1980. "An American Consol: A Reexamination of the Expectations Theory of the Term Structure of Interest Rates," unpublished manuscript, Michigan State Univ.

Basu, S., 1977. "The Investment Performance of Common Stocks in Relation to their Price-Earnings Ratios: A Test of the Efficient Markets Hypothesis," *Journal of Finance* 32:663–682.

Box, G. E. P. and G. M. Jenkins, 1970. *Time Series Analysis for Forecasting and Control*, San Francisco: Holden-Day.

Brainard, William C., John B. Shoven, and Laurence Weiss, 1980. "The Financial Valuation of the Return to Capital," *Brookings Papers* 2:243–502.

Cootner, Paul H., 1964. *The Random Character of Stock Market Prices*, Cambridge: MIT Press.

Cowles, Alfred and Associates, 1938. *Common Stock Indexes, 1871–1937*, Cowles Commission for Research in Economics, Monograph No. 3, Bloomington: Principia Press.

Fama, Eugene F., 1970. "Efficient Capital Markets: A Review of Theory and Empirical Work," *Journal of Finance* 25:383–420.

Fama, Eugene F., 1965. "The Behavior of Stock Market Prices," *Journal of Business, Univ. Chicago* 38:34–105.

Granger, C. W. J., 1975. "Some Consequences of the Valuation Model When Expectations are Taken to be Optimum Forecasts," *Journal of Finance* 30:135–145.

Jensen, M. C. et al., 1978. "Symposium on Some Anomalous Evidence Regarding Market Efficiency," *Journal of Financial Economics* 6:93–330.

LeRoy, Stephen, and Richard Porter, 1981. "The Present Value Relation: Tests Based on Implied Variance Bounds," *Econometrica* 49:555–574.

Miller, Merton H., and Franco Modigliani, 1961. "Dividend Policy, Growth and the Valuation of Shares," *Journal of Business, Univ. Chicago* 34:411–433.

Modigliani, Franco, and Richard Cohn, 1979. "Inflation, Rational Valuation and the Market," *Financial Analysts Journal* 35:24–44.

Pesando, James, 1979. "Time Varying Term Premiums and the Volatility of Long-Term Interest Rates," unpublished paper, Univ. Toronto.

Samuelson, Paul A. 1977. "Proof that Properly Discounted Present Values of Assets Vibrate Randomly," in Hiroaki Nagatani and Kate Crowley, eds., *Collected Scientific Papers of Paul A. Samuelson*, Vol. IV, Cambridge: MIT Press.

Shiller, Robert J. 1979. "The Volatility of Long-Term Interest Rates and Expectations Models of the Term Structure," *Journal of Political Economy* 87:1190–1219.

6

The Use of Volatility
Measures in Assessing
Market Efficiency

6.1 Introduction

Recently a number of studies have used measures of the variance or
"volatility" of speculative asset prices to provide evidence against simple
models of market efficiency. These measures were interpreted as implying
that prices show too much variation to be explained in terms of the random
arrival of new information about the fundamental determinants of price.
The first such use of the volatility measures was made independently by
LeRoy and Porter [1981] in connection with stock price and earnings data,
and myself [1979], in connection with long-term and short-term bond
yields. Subsequently, further use of these measures was made to study
efficient markets models involving stock prices and dividends (Shiller
[1981b]—chapter 5), yields on intermediate and short-term bonds (Shiller
[1981a], Singleton [1980]), preferred stock dividend-price ratios and short-
term interest rates (Amsler [1980]), and foreign exchange rates and money
stock differentials (Huang [1981], Meese and Singleton [1980]). My intent
here is to interpret the use of volatility measures in these papers, to
describe some alternative models that might allow more variation in prices,
and to contrast the volatility tests with more conventional methods of
evaluating market efficiency.

My initial motivation for considering volatility measures in the efficient
markets models was to clarify the basic smoothing properties of the models
to allow an understanding of the assumptions which are implicit in the
notion of market efficiency. The efficient markets models, which are described in section 6.2, relate a price today to the expected present value of
a path of future variables. Since present values are long weighted moving

Reprinted with minor editing from *Journal of Finance* 36 (1981): 291–304; © 1981 the
American Finance Association.

averages, it would seem that price data should be very stable and smooth. These impressions can be formalized in terms of inequalities describing certain variances (section 6.3). The results ought to be of interest whether or not the data satisfy these inequalities, and the procedures ought not to be regarded as just "another test" of market efficiency. Our confidence of our understanding of empirical phenomena is enhanced when we learn how such an obvious property of data as its "smoothness" relates to the model, and to alternative models (section 6.4).

On further examination of the volatility inequalities, it became clear that the inequalities may also suggest formal tests of market efficiency that have distinct advantages over conventional tests. These advantages take the form of greater power in certain circumstances of robustness to data errors such as misalignment and of simplicity and understandability. An interpretation of volatility tests versus regression tests in terms of the likelihood principle is offered in section 6.5.

6.2   The Simple Efficient Markets Hypothesis

The structure common to the various models of market efficiency noted in the introduction can be written

$$p_t = \sum_{k=0}^{\infty} \gamma^{k+1} E_t d_{t+k} = E_t p_t^* \tag{1}$$

where p_t is a price or yield and $p_t^* \equiv \sum_{k=0}^{\infty} \gamma^{k+1} d_{t+k}$ is a perfect foresight or ex-post rational price or yield not known at time t. E_t denotes mathematical expectation conditional on information at time t, and γ is a discount factor $\gamma \equiv 1/(1 + r)$, where r is the (constant) discount rate. Information includes current p_t, d_t, and their lagged values, as well as other variables. In the application of the basic structure (1) that shall be emphasized here (from Shiller [1981b]—chapter 5), p_t for 1871–1979 is the Standard and Poor Composite Stock Price Index for January (deflated by the wholesale price index scaled to base year $T = 1979$) times a scale factor λ^{T-t} (see figure 6.1). The parameter λ equals one plus the long-term growth rate of the real value of the portfolio (1.45% per annum) and the scale factor has the effect of eliminating heteroskedasticity due to the gradually increasing size of the market. The variable d_t for 1871–1978 is the total real dividends paid over the year times λ^{T-t-1} (figure 6.1). The discount rate r was estimated as average d divided by average p, or 4.52% (while the average dividend price ratio was 4.92%). In LeRoy and Porter [1981] the approach is similar except that real earnings rather than real dividends are used. As is well known, one

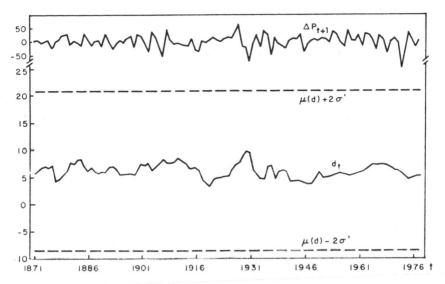

Figure 6.1

(Upper plot) Δp_{t+1} where p_t is the real Standard and Poor Composite Stock Price Index for January scaled (to eliminate heteroskedasticity) by multiplying by $\exp(.0145(1979 - t))$. (Lower plot, d_t) Real dividends for the p_t series times $\exp(.0145(1978 - t))$. Here $\hat{\sigma}(d) = 1.28$. The dividend series here ranges from 3.31 to 9.62, a range of nearly 5 standard deviations. The dashed lines mark off a $+2$ standard deviation range from the mean $\mu(d)$ where the standard deviation is $\sigma' = 7.30$, or the lower bound allowed for $\sigma(d)$ by inequality (I-2), given $\sigma(\Delta p) = 24.3$. In order to justify this magnitude of $\sigma(\Delta p)$, the true $\sigma(d)$ would have to be at least this high according to (I-2).

cannot claim price as the present value of expected earnings without committing a sort of double counting unless earnings are corrected for investment. Usually, such a correction means subtracting retained earnings from earnings, which would convert the earnings series into the dividend series (Miller and Modigliani [1961]). Instead, LeRoy and Porter correct both the price and earnings series by dividing by the capital stock, which is estimated as the accumulated undepreciated real retained earnings. Since the resulting series appear stationary over their shorter (postwar) sample period, they make no further scale correction.

In Shiller [1979] (chapter 15), p_t is the yield to maturity on a long-term bond such as a consol times $\gamma/(1 - \gamma)$, and corrected for a constant liquidity premium, while d_t is the one-period yield. This model is derived as an approximation to a number of different versions of the expectations model of the term structure. In Amsler [1980] the same model is applied using instead of the yield on long-term bonds her dividend price ratio series on high quality preferred stock which she argues is a proxy for a perpetuity yield. In Shiller [1981a] and Singleton [1980] p_t is related to the yield to maturity on intermediate term bonds and the model is modified slightly by truncating the summation in (1) at the maturity date.[1] In Huang [1981] p_t is the spot exchange rate and d_t is the nominal money stock differential adjusted for the real income differential between domestic and foreign countries. His model is implied by the well-known theory of the monetary approach to the balance of payments.

Although the models considered here are so simple they may be considered excessively restrictive, the econometric issues raised here are relevant to the study of alternative hypotheses as well, such as the hypotheses considered in section 6.3.

An implication of the structure (1) is that the innovation in price $\delta_{t+1} p_{t+1}$, which is unforecastable based on information available at time t,[2] equals $\Delta p_{t+1} + d_t - r p_t$ so that

$$E_t(\Delta p_{t+1} + d_t - r p_t) = 0. \tag{2}$$

In the context of the stock price and dividend series application, this innovation is the change in price corrected for price movements in response to short-run dividend variations (e.g., corrected for the predictable ex-dividend day movement in stock prices). That the innovation in stock prices is not very forecastable (i.e., the correlation coefficient between $\delta_{t+1} p_{t+1}$ and information available is small) is certainly well known, as a result of the well-known tests of the random-walk hypothesis. For example, with our data, $\delta_{t+1} p_{t+1}$ is significantly negatively correlated over 1871–1978 with p_t, but the R^2 is only .08.[3] With relatively short time series, the correlation coefficient is not statistically significantly different from zero. To detect a slight correlation statistically, one must use a great deal of data. Such results with the century of data are generally not viewed with much interest, however. It is commonly felt that such small correlations detected in long historical data are of questionable relevance to modern conditions and of minor interest given possible errors in data from remote times in history.

If we could summarize the results of the tests of the random walk hypothesis with recent data by saying that (2) held *exactly*, then, using an additional assumption that prices are not explosive, we could conclude that (1) was proven. Rearranging (2) one gets the first order rational expectations model $p_t = \gamma E_t(p_{t+1} + d_t)$. One can solve this model by recursive substitution. Substituting the same expression led for one period gives us $p_t = \gamma E_t(\gamma E_{t+1}(p_{t+2} + d_{t+1}) + d_t) = \gamma^2 E_t(p_{t+2}) + \gamma^2 E_t d_{t+1} + \gamma d_t$. One may then substitute for p_{t+2} in this expression and so on. The result is expression (1) as long as the additional requirement that $\gamma^k E_t(p_{t+k})$ goes to zero as k goes to infinity is satisfied. That the terminal condition holds in the stock price application seems quite reasonable since the dividend price ratio shows no particular trend, while on an explosive path p and d should diverge.

There is a big difference, however, between the statement that (2) holds approximately and (2) holds exactly. Expression (2) can hold approximately if movements Δp_{t+1} are so large as to swamp movements in $(rp_t - d_t)$, even if the movements in p do not reflect information about future d at all. For example, suppose stock prices are heavily influenced by fads or waves of optimistic or pessimistic "market psychology." Suppose this means that demeaned $p_t = \rho p_{t-1} + \varepsilon_t$, where $0 < \rho < 1$ and ε_t is unforecastable noise and d is constant. If ρ is, say, .95, changes in p will not be highly autocorrelated, and hence $\delta_{t+1} p_{t+1}$ as defined in (2) would not be very correlated with information (the theoretical R^2 of $\delta_{t+1} p_{t+1}$ on p_t and a constant would, for $r = .045$, be .08). The fact that in short samples one would have trouble proving the existence of such correlation is a reflection of the fact that with such an alternative it takes a very long time to take effective advantage of the profit opportunity implied by the fad. It may take, say, 10 or 20 years for the fad to end, and hence one does not have the opportunity to observe this to happen very many times.

Such a fads alternative may be detectable using the volatility tests discussed in the next section. The reasons why such tests may be more powerful than a regression test will be indicated formally in section 6.5. Before turning to these matters, however, it is important to reflect on the importance of the terminal condition discussed above. The terminal condition in (1) is essential to consider if we want to examine the question raised in the introduction to this chapter: are movements in speculative prices too large, or are they justified by subsequent movements in dividends? If p_t were generated by the autoregressive process $p_{t+1} = (1 + r)p_t + d_t + \varepsilon_{t+1}$, where ε_{t+1} is an unforecastable white noise, then (2) would be satisfied regardless of the size of $\sigma(\varepsilon)$. Thus, (2) itself is consistent with any degree of variability of prices. This autoregressive process is, however, necessarily explosive unlesss ε_t represents information about (i.e., is offset by) future d.

If we wish to derive formal tests of the restrictions, then we must represent the model in terms that allow us to derive the likelihood function of our observations and to represent the restrictions on the likelihood function implied by the model. A first step in this direction is to assume that the variables (or some transformations of the variables) are jointly covariance stationary. A random vector x_t is considered covariance stationary if the mean of x_t and the covariance between x_t and x_{t+k} are finite and do not depend on t. Our assumption that $[p_t, d_t]$ is covariance stationary thus rules out an explosive path for p_t, and incorporates the assumption of the terminal condition. The terminal condition could also be imposed by assuming $[\Delta p_t, \Delta d_t]$ is covariance stationary, since on an explosive path Δp would diverge. However, the terminal condition would not be represented by the assumption only that the proportional changes $[\Delta p/p, \Delta d/d]$ are stationary, since these could have constant variances along an explosive path for p. On the other hand, the assumption that $\Delta p/p$, $\Delta d/d$, and p/d are stationary would rule out an explosive solution to (2). Such an assumption may be more attractive than that made here, and may lead to similar results, but is less convenient analytically because it is a nonlinear transformation of data in a linear model and variance inequalities like those derived in the section below would depend on the distribution assumed for the variables.

Stationarity, and hence the terminal condition, is part of the maintained hypothesis and the motivation for the volatility tests is not that these tests will reject when p (or Δp) is explosive in the sample. Quite to the contrary, the stationarity assumption suggests tests which may reject far more decisively than a regression test even when p (or Δp) is not divergent in the sample at all, as will be seen in section 6.5.

6.3   Derivation of Variance Inequalities

Since p^* is a weighted moving average of d, one can use simple principles of spectral analysis to put restrictions on the spectrum of p^*: its spectrum must be relatively much more concentrated in the lower frequencies than the spectrum of d, and must be everywhere below the spectrum of d/r except at the zero frequency. Thus, informally, p^* series ought to be "smoother" than d series. It was shown in Shiller [1979] (chapter 15) that the same formal characterization does not apply to the spectrum of p; yet there is a sense in which p ought to be "smooth." The inequality restrictions on the spectra of p and d implied by the model in fact concern weighted integrals of the spectra, and these inequality restrictions can be stated more simply in terms of variance inequalities.

The variance inequalities implied by the model (1) can be derived from (1) the equality restrictions between variances and covariances imposed by the model, (2) the inequality restrictions regarding variances and covariances implied by positive semidefiniteness of variance matrices, and (3) the stationarity assumption for the random processes. Several simple inequalities will be considered here. The first (used by LeRoy and Porter [1981], and Shiller [1979]—chapter 15, [1981b]—chapter 5, as well as Amsler [1980], Singleton [1980] and Meese and Singleton [1980]) puts a limit on the standard deviation of p in terms of the standard deviation of p^*:

$$\sigma(p) \leqslant \sigma(p^*). \tag{I-1}$$

The second (Shiller [1981b]—chapter 5), which is analogous to inequalities used in Shiller [1979]—chapter 15, Amsler [1980], Shiller [1981a], and Singleton [1980], puts a limit on the standard deviation of Δp in terms of the standard deviation of d:

$$\sigma(\Delta p) \leqslant \sigma(d)/\sqrt{2r}. \tag{I-2}$$

The third, which is analogous to inequalities used in Shiller [1979] (chapter 15) and Huang [1981], puts a limit on the standard deviation of Δp in terms of the standard deviation of Δd:

$$\sigma(\Delta p) \leqslant \sigma(\Delta d)/\sqrt{2r^3/(1 + 2r)}. \tag{I-3}$$

The third inequality has the advantage that it applies even if p and d are integrated processes, i.e. the variance of the levels does not exist. An example of an integrated process is a random walk, though if d_t followed a random walk the model would imply a tighter bound on $\sigma(\Delta p)$.

It is trivial to prove the first inequality. The model implies that $p_t^* - p_t \equiv u_t$ is a forecast error which must be uncorrelated with p_t. Hence, $\mathrm{var}(p_t^*) = \mathrm{var}(p_t) + \mathrm{var}(u_t)$. Since positive semidefiniteness requires $\mathrm{var}(u_t) \geqslant 0$, it follows that $\mathrm{var}(p_t^*) \geqslant \mathrm{var}(p_t)$. The derivation of the other inequalities may proceed in much the same way, though the previous papers used a somewhat different derivation. To prove the second, note that the model implies that the innovation $\Delta p_{t+1} + d_t - r p_t$ is a forecast error that must be uncorrelated with p_t. Hence $\mathrm{cov}(p_{t+1}, p_t) + \mathrm{cov}(d_t, p_t) - (1 + r)\mathrm{var}(p_t) = 0$. Stationarity requires that $\mathrm{var}(p_{t+1}) = \mathrm{var}(p_t)$, and hence $\mathrm{cov}(p_{t+1}, p_t) = \mathrm{var}(p_t) - \frac{1}{2}\mathrm{var}(\Delta p_t)$. If this is substituted into the restriction we get $-r\,\mathrm{var}(p_t) - \frac{1}{2}\mathrm{var}(\Delta p_t) + \mathrm{cov}(d_t, p_t) = 0$, or, in terms of standard deviations and the correlation coefficient ρ between d_t and p_t, $r\sigma(p)^2 - \rho\sigma(d)\sigma(p) + \frac{1}{2}\sigma^2(\Delta p) = 0$. Positive semidefiniteness can be interpreted as requiring all standard deviations to be positive and $|\rho| \leqslant 1$. One easily verifies that if $\sigma(\Delta p)$ exceeds the upper bound of the inequality (I-2) then no values of $\sigma(p)$ or ρ can be consistent with the model restriction and positive semidefiniteness. Solving the quadratic expression for $\sigma(p)$ one finds $\sigma(p) = (\rho\sigma(d) \pm \sqrt{\rho^2\sigma(d)^2 - 2r\sigma(\Delta p)^2})/2r$. If a real value of $\sigma(p)$ is to satisfy the model restriction, then the expression inside the square root operator (discriminant) must be nonnegative, $\rho^2\sigma(d)^2 \geqslant 2r\sigma(\Delta p)^2$, which in turn implies, since $\rho^2 \leqslant 1$, the inequality (I-2). To prove the third inequality, note first that if Δd_t is jointly stationary with information variables, then the model (1) implies that both Δp_t and $rp_t - d_t$ are also jointly stationary. The forecast error $\Delta p_{t+1} - (rp_t - d_t)$ must be uncorrelated with information at time t and hence with $(rp_t - d_t)$, and so the model implies the restriction $\text{cov}(\Delta p_{t+1}, (rp_t - d_t)) - \text{var}(rp_t - d_t) = 0$. Stationarity implies $\text{cov}(\Delta p_{t+1}, (rp_t - d_t)) = \{2\,\text{cov}(\Delta d_t, (rp_t - d_t)) - \text{var}(r\Delta p_t) + \text{var}(\Delta d_t)\}/2r$. One then finds, converting to standard deviations that the model restriction can be written $2r\sigma(rp_t - d_t)^2 - 2\rho\sigma(\Delta d_t)\sigma(rp_t - d_t) + r^2\sigma(\Delta p)^2 - \sigma(\Delta d)^2 = 0$, where ρ is the correlation coefficient between Δd_t and $(rp_t - d_t)$. One can then verify that this restriction cannot be satisfied for $|\rho| < 1$ and positive standard deviations if (I-3) is violated, by solving the quadratic expression in $\sigma(rp_t - d_t)$ as with the proof of (I-2).

Intuitive interpretations of the inequalities are also possible. For the first, we require that at any point of time p_t is an unbiased forecast of p_t^*, which means, roughly speaking, that p_t^* must be equally likely to be above or below p_t. If p_t had a higher variance than p_t^*, then in periods when p_t was especially high (or low) it would tend to lie above (below) p_t^* and hence in these periods would be an upwardly (downwardly) biased forecast of p_t^*. For the second, one must bear in mind that if $\sigma(\Delta p)$ is large, then either $\sigma(p)$ is very large or Δp is highly forecastable. Changes in p which are not highly forecastable would cumulate into big swings in p, while on the other hand, if p were confined to relatively narrow range, then the successive movements in Δp would have to show strong negative correlation and hence be forecastable. Either way, if $\sigma(\Delta p)$ is above the upper bound in (I-2), then the excess returns $\Delta p_{t+1} + d_t - rp_t$ would be forecastable, either because Δp_{t+1} makes large predictable movements relative to dividend and price movements or because rp_t moves a lot relative to d_t and the predictable component of Δp_{t+1}. For the third, note that if $\sigma(\Delta p)$ is very large relative to $\sigma(\Delta d)$, then either $\sigma(rp_t - d_t)$ is very large or Δp_{t+1} is highly forecastable; either way the forecast error $\Delta p_{t+1} - (rp_t - d_t)$ would be forecastable.

The first two of these inequalities were compared with the Standard and Poor data described over the 1871–1979 sample period in my paper on stock prices (Shiller [1981b]—chapter 5). The variable p^* was computed by recursive substitution from a terminal value of p^* equal to the average p over the sample. With these data the estimated standard deviation of p, $\hat{\sigma}(p)$, was 47.2 and $\hat{\sigma}(p^*) = 7.51$ so that (I-1) was dramatically violated by sample statistics. The $\hat{\sigma}(d)$ over the entire sample was 1.28, while $\hat{\sigma}(\Delta p)$

was 24.3. The upper bound on the standard deviation of Δp allowed by the inequality (I-2) was thus (disregarding sampling error in the estimation of standard deviations) 4.26, so that the upper bound was exceeded by almost sixfold. Putting it another way, the standard deviation of d would have to be at least 7.30, which is greater than the sample mean of d, in order to justify $\sigma(\Delta p)$.[4] Figure 6.1 gives an impression as to how dramatically (I-2) is violated.

On the other hand (I-3) (which was not reported in that paper) was not violated by the annual data. Since $\hat{\sigma}(\Delta d)$ was .768 for this data, the upper bound on $\sigma(\Delta p)$ allowed by (I-3) is 59.0, which is greater than the sample $\sigma(\Delta p)$. Of course, we do not expect the data to violate all inequalities even if the model is wrong. Moreover, the choice of annual data was arbitrary, and the inequality is violated when longer differencing intervals are used. The definition of p^* implies $p_t^* = \sum_{k=0}^{\infty} \bar{\gamma}^{k+1} \bar{d}_{t+nk}$, where n is any integer greater than one, $\bar{\gamma} = \gamma^n$ and $\bar{d}_t = d_t(1 + r)^{n-1} + d_{t+1}(1 + r)^{n-2} + \cdots + d_{t+n-1}$, or the accumulated dividends over n periods. Defining the n-period rate $\bar{r}$ implicitly by $\bar{\gamma} = 1/(1 + \bar{r})$, we see that for data sampled at n-period intervals (I-3) becomes[5] $\sigma(p_t - p_{t+n}) \leqslant \sigma(\bar{d}_t - \bar{d}_{t+n})/\sqrt{2\bar{r}^3/(1 + 2\bar{r})}$. Using n of ten years, for example, annual data from 1871 to 1969 produces $\hat{\sigma}(p_t - p_{t+10}) = 69.4$ and $\hat{\sigma}(\bar{d}_t - \bar{d}_{t+10}) = 16.5$ so that the upper bound on $\hat{\sigma}(p_t - p_{t+10})$ is 40.8, which is violated by the data.

A sampling theory for these standard deviation and formal tests of the model can be derived if we further specify the model with distributional assumptions for d_t and p_t. If Δp_t is assumed normal and serially uncorrelated, the lower bound of a χ^2 one-sided confidence interval for $\sigma(\Delta p)$ is 21.9, which is still over 5 times the maximum given by (I-2) using the sample $\sigma(d)$, so that we can safely conclude tht the model requires a much bigger standard deviation for d than was observed in the sample. It is possible, however, that we could adopt distributional assumptions for d_t that would imply that the sample standard deviation of d is not a good measure of the population standard deviation, as will be discussed in the next section. Other distributional assumptions and formal tests were employed by LeRoy and Porter [1981] and Singleton [1980].

6.4   Some Alternative Hypotheses

The only alternative discussed above to the efficient markets model was a "fads" alternative. Such an alternative seems appealing, given the observed tendency of people to follow fads in other aspects of their lives and based on casual observation of the behavior of individual investors. Such fads do not necessarily imply any quick profit opportunity for investors not vulnerable to fads. It is worthwhile exploring, however, alternatives more in accordance with economic theory and with rational optimizing behavior.

Another alternative to the simple efficient markets model is one in which real price is the expected present value of real dividends discounted by a time varying real discount factor $\gamma_t = 1/(1 + r_t)$:

$$p_t = E_t\left(\sum_{k=0}^{\infty} \left(\prod_{j=0}^{k} \gamma_{t+j}\right) d_{t+k}\right). \tag{3}$$

One might study this model by seeking some measure of time varying real interest rates. In one paper (Grossman and Shiller [1981]—chapter 21) consumption data and an assumed utility function were used to provide a measure of the marginal rate of substitution between present and future consumption. A more parsimonious approach is to treat the discount rate as an unobserved variable and ask merely how big its movements will have to be if information about future real rates accounts for the stock price movements not accounted for by dividend movements according to the above analysis. Since with the stock data mentioned above the standard deviation of Δp is 18% of the mean of p, if we are to attribute most of the variance of Δp to changes in one-period real interest rates, movements in r_t must be quite large. Expression (3) effectively contains a moving average that ought to average out the movements in the one-period real interest rate. Based on a linearization that makes p equal to an expected present value of dividends plus a term related to a "present value" of real interest rates, it was concluded in Shiller [1981b] (chapter 5) that the expected one-year real interest r_t in percent would have a standard deviation in excess of 5 percentage points to account for the variance of Δp.[6] This number is substantially in excess of the standard deviation of nominal short-term interest rates over the sample period and in fact implies a $\pm$ two standard deviation range of over 20 percentage points for the expected real interest rate.

Because of the very large movements in real interest rates required to explain the observed variance of Δp by this model, some have reacted by claiming that the historical standard deviations of real dividends around their trend are inherently poor measures of subjective uncertainty about dividends. One can propose alternative models for dividends for which, say, the actual $\sigma(d)$ is infinite, yet of course sample standard deviations will be finite and spurious as a measure of population standard deviations. The most commonly mentioned specific alternative hypothesis is that d_t is an unforecastable random walk with normal increments. We saw in the preceding section that even such a model, where $\sigma(\Delta d)$ is finite, can be subjected to volatility tests. In the particular case of an unforecastable random walk, $p_t = d_t/r$ and $\sigma(\Delta p) = \sigma(\Delta d)/r$. With our data using one year differencing $\hat{\sigma}(\Delta p) = 24.3$ and $\hat{\sigma}(\Delta d)/r = 17.0$ while with ten year differencing (as described above) $\hat{\sigma}(p_t - p_{t+10}) = 69.4$ and $\hat{\sigma}(\bar{d}_t - \bar{d}_{t+10})/\bar{r} = 29.6$. Prices appear to be too volatile for either differencing interval; the dividend ratio is not constant but moves so as to cause p to be relatively more volatile than dividends One should also ask whether such an alternative hypothesis is plausible. Since $\hat{\sigma}(\Delta d)$ is only 8 times the sample mean, this hypothesis would imply that aggregate dividends often stood a substantial chance of hitting zero in a matter of years (and then forecasted dividends would also be zero), and that the apparent resemblance of d_t to an exponential growth path over the century[7] was due to chance rather than the physical process of investment and technical progress. It seems that a more plausible alternative hypothesis should be sought. Other integrated processes (i.e., processes stationary in Δd but not d) do not look promising, given that (I-3) appears violated for long differencing intervals. There are, however, certainly hypothetical forms for the d process that imply that the volatility tests are incorrect; the question is whether such alternatives are plausible.

   In discussions about plausible alternative hypotheses the hypothesis has been repeatedly suggested to me that the market may indeed be legitimately concerned with a major disaster with low probability each period that would, let us say, completely destroy the value of all stock. The fact that such a disaster did not occur in the last century in the United States and that dividends roughly followed a growth path does not prove that disaster was not a distinct possibility. Such disasters might include nationalization, punitive taxation of profits, or conquest by a foreign power. Similar events are not uncommon by world standards, and my selection of the long uninterrupted U.S. stock price series may involve a selection bias. In the context of foreign exchange market efficiency studies, the possibility of such a disaster has been called the "Peso problem," referring to the fluctuation in the peso forward rate in anticipation of a devaluation that did not occur in the sample period (Krasker [1980]).

   To evaluate this possibility, suppose that the probability of a disaster ("nationalization") *during* period t as evaluated at the beginning of period t is given by a stochastic π_t, $0 \leqslant \pi_t \leqslant 1$, and suppose π_t is independent of an underlying dividend process d_t in the absence of disaster. If the disaster occurs, the stock is worthless and d_t will not received. This means that the expected value as of time of the dividend *received* at time $t + k$ is $E_t[(\prod_{j=0}^{k}(1 - \pi_{t+j}))d_{t+k}]$, where $E_t \prod_{j=0}^{k}(1 - \pi_{t+j})$ is the probability that no disaster occurs between time t and $t + k$. Thus, the model (1) should be modified as

$$p_t = E_t \sum_{k=0}^{\infty} \left(\prod_{j=0}^{k} (\gamma(1 - \pi_{t+j})) \right) d_{t+k}. \tag{4}$$

This model is identical to the model (3) if we set $\gamma_{t+j} = \gamma(1 - \pi_{t+j})$, and collapses to our basic model (1) if the probability of disaster is constant, except that our estimated γ ought to be interpreted as the estimate of $\gamma(1 - \pi)$. Clearly, then, the disaster model can explain the volatility of stock prices only if the probability of disaster changes substantially from period to period. Indeed, using the earlier conclusion about real interest rate variation the standard deviation of the probability that disaster will occur *within the current year* must have exceeded .05 if movements in p_t are to be attributed to new information about current and future π. One wonders whether the probability of disaster in a single year could have changed so much. At the very least the theory relies very heavily on the selection bias for its plausibility since such a standard deviation for π_t implies π_t must often be high. If the probability of disaster is, say, .1 each year, then the probability that no disaster occurred over 108 years is roughly one in 100,000.

6.5 Regression Tests of the Model

The most obvious way to test the model (1) as noted above is to run a regression to see whether innovations are forecastable. Such a procedure would be to regress $y_t = (p_{t+1} + d_t)$ on a constant term and independent variables p_t and d_t. The coefficient of p_t is, by our model, $(1 + r)$ (which is greater than one) and the constant term and coefficient of d_t are zero. One could perform an F-test on these coefficient restrictions. Why, one might ask, ought one to examine the volatility measures as a way of evaluating the model?

There are potentially many ways of justifying a test other than a regression test. For example, one may justify it by claiming special interest in an alternative hypothesis (e.g., a "fads" alternative) implying excess volatility, or one may justify it on the basis of robustness or simplicity. Here, however, I will emphasize a sort of data alignment problem for the motivation. Since the distributed lead in (1) is infinitely long, movements in p may be due to information about dividends in the indefinite future. However, we have data about dividends only for the relatively short sample period. The price movements corresponding to information regarding the dividends in the sample period may have occurred before our sample began. The price movements during the sample may reflect information about dividends beyond the sample. Of course, one might doubt that dividends beyond the sample ought to be so important. This, however, is just the point of the volatility tests, a point in effect missed by the regression tests.

For the purpose of motivating the discussion below, consider the simplest example of a rational expectations model in which $x_t = E_t y_t$ and the maintained hypothesis is that $[x_t, y_t]$ is jointly normal with zero mean and successive observations are independent. Suppose the data are *completely* misaligned, and there are T observations on x_t (for 1950–1960, say) and T nonoverlapping observations on y_t (for 1970–1980, say). Clearly, it is not possible to test the model by regressing y_t on x_t. It does not follow that the model cannot be tested. The likelihood function is then

$$l(\sigma_x, \sigma_y | X, Y) = (2\pi\sigma_x\sigma_y)^{-T} \exp\left(-\frac{\sum x^2}{2\sigma_x^2} - \frac{\sum y^2}{2\sigma_y^2}\right).$$

The model imposes only one restriction on this likelihood function, namely that $\sigma_x \leqslant \sigma_y$. The likelihood ratio test statistic is then

$$\lambda = \begin{cases} 1 & \text{if} \quad \hat{\sigma}_x \leqslant \hat{\sigma}_y \\ \left(\dfrac{\sqrt{\hat{\sigma}_x^2 \hat{\sigma}_y^2}}{(\hat{\sigma}_x^2 + \hat{\sigma}_y^2)/2}\right)^T & \text{if} \quad \hat{\sigma}_x > \hat{\sigma}_y, \end{cases}$$

where $\hat{\sigma}$ denotes sample standard deviation about zero. The likelihood ratio test that is the unique uniformly most powerful test with this data thus works out to be a volatility test. Since if $\sigma_x = \sigma_y$, the distribution of $-2 \log \lambda$ is asymptotically a mixture of a χ^2 with one degree of freedom and a spike at the origin, one can easily find an approximate 95% critical value for λ for a given level of significance. The test may enable us to reject the model with confidence. If $\hat{\sigma}_y = 0$ and $\hat{\sigma}_x \neq 0$, $-2 \log \lambda$ is infinite, so that the hypothesis would be rejected at any significance level. The power of the test approaches one as σ_y/σ_x approaches zero.

In contrast, if the data were perfectly aligned, the likelihood ratio test would amount to a t test that the coefficient is 1.00 in a regression of y on x. If the data were only partially aligned, the likelihood function would be the product of a likelihood function of the aligned observations and the likelihood of the unaligned observations. Regression tests with the overlapping observations would be suggested by looking only at the first factor, and volatility tests by looking only at the second, while the true likelihood ratio test would be a hybrid of the two. Reliance on the likelihood of the unaligned observations alone (or, more properly, treating all observations as if unaligned) might be justified if data alignment is considered inaccurate, or if a simple and easily applied test is desired.

The structure (1) is a little different from this simple example since the expectations variable p_t relates to an infinite weighted moving average of the expected variable partly within the sample and partly without, and successive observations are not independent. Since the purpose is exposition here, let us assume that the data consists of T *independent* normal observations of the vector $z_t = [p_{\tau_t+1}, p_{\tau_t}, d_{\tau_t}]$. Imagine that, for some reason, we have observations on this vector so widely spaced in time (e.g., $z_1 = [p_{1801}, p_{1800}, d_{1800}]$. $z_2 = [p_{1901}, p_{1900}, d_{1900}]$, $z_3 = [p_{2001}, p_{2000}, d_{2000}], \ldots$) that we regard separate observations as independent. Our analysis of that data set can be extended routinely to the case where observations are not widely spaced and p_t and d_t are parameterized as autoregressive or moving average processes, but this analysis would be messier and so is omitted here. A discussion of this more general case in the context of the expectations model of the term structure of interest rates is in Shiller [1981a]. In that paper it is shown that the likelihood ratio test employed by Sargent [1979] to test the expectations model of the term structure does not impose the kinds of restrictions implied by the model that are considered here.

The likelihood function for the T observations on the vector z_t can be written in the usual form: $l(\mu, \Omega | z) = (2\pi)^{-3T/2} |\Omega|^{-t/2} \exp(-\frac{1}{2} \sum_{t=1}^{T} (z_t - \mu) \Omega^{-1} (z_t - \mu)')$, where z is the $T \times 3$ matrix of observations, μ is the 1×3 vector of means, and Ω the 3×3 covariance matrix. Since Ω is symmetric, the model has nine parameters: the three means, the three variances, and the three covariances. However, because of the stationarity assumption $E(p_t) = E(p_{t+1})$ and $\text{var}(p_t) = \text{var}(p_{t+1})$ there are only seven independent parameters, a fact we shall consider below.

Given the vector z_t, we can by a linear transformation derive the vector $w_t = [p_{t+1} + d_t, p_t, d_t]$ that has as its first element the dependent variable in the regression described above and the same second and third elments. Since z_t is normally distributed, w_t is also. We can therefore write the likelihood function for w_t by a change of variables from the likelihood function (of z_t). This likelihood function can be written in various ways. For our purposes, it is convenient to write the likelihood function for w in a factored from that makes it easy notationally to consider regression tests of the model. Partitioning w_t into $w_t = [w_{1_t}, w_{2_t}]$ where w_{1_t} is a 1×1 and w_{2_t} is a 1×2, and letting w, w_1 and w_2 denote the matrices of observations of orders $T \times 3$, $T \times 1$ and $T \times 2$, respectively, and defining a T element vector Y, $Y = w_1$ of dependent variables and a $T \times 3$ matrix X, $X = [L\, w_2]$ of independent variables where L is a column vector of 1's, then the likelihood function is

$$l(\sigma^2, \beta, \Phi, \mu | w) = l(\sigma^2, \beta | w_1, w_2) l(\Phi, \mu | w_2)$$

$$= (2\pi\sigma^2)^{-T/2} \exp(-(Y - X\beta)'(Y - X\beta)/2\sigma^2)$$

$$\cdot (2\pi)^{-T} |\Phi|^{-T/2} \exp\left(-\sum_{t=1}^{T} (w_{2_t} - v)\Phi^{-1}(w_{2_t} - v)'/2 \right),$$

$$(5)$$

where σ^2 is the variance of the residual in a theoretical regression of Y on X, β is the 3-element vector of theoretical regression coefficients of Y on X, v is the 2-element vector of means of p and d and Φ the 2×2 variance matrix for the vector w_{2_t}. The nine parameters of the multivariate normal distribution for z_t are here transformed into the 3 elements of β, the 2 elements of μ, the two diagonal and one off-diagonal element of Φ, and σ^2. The first factor in the likelihood function is the usual expression for the likelihood of a regression of Y on X, while the second factor is the usual expression for the likelihood of a bivariate normal vector.

The factorization (5) of the likelihood function then makes it transparent why, if we disregard the requirement that $E(p_t) = E(p_{t+1})$ and $\mathrm{var}(p_t) = \mathrm{var}(p_{t+1})$, it is appropriate to test the model by regressing the variable $(p_{t+1} + d_t)$ on information available at time t, i.e., on the constant, p_t and d_t, and testing the restrictions on the regression coefficient β. The efficient markets model restricts only the first factor of the likelihood function. The likelihood ratio test statistic is the ratio of the maximized unconstrained likelihood to the maximum constrained likelihood. The likelihood is the product of the maxima of the two factors and so the second factor will be the same in both numerator and denominator and hence will cancel out, leaving us with (a transformation of) the ordinary regression test statistic. A Bayesian posterior odds procedure will similarly produce the posterior odds of the simple regression of Y on X so long as there is no prior dependency between the parameters of the two factors.

In fact, however, there is a constraint across the coefficients in the two factors due to the fact that $E(p_t) = E(p_{t+1})$ and $\mathrm{var}(p_t) = \mathrm{var}(p_{t+1})$. It was emphasized above that it is these constraints that represent the requirement that price movements be justified in terms of future dividends. One can rewrite these constraints in terms of the parameters of the likelihood of z_t. The mean restriction becomes $\beta_1 = (1 - \beta_2)\mu_p - \beta_3\mu_d$ and the variance restriction becomes $\sigma^2 = (1 - \beta_2^2)\,\mathrm{var}(p) + 2\beta_2(1 - \beta_3)\,\mathrm{cov}(p, d) - (1 - \beta_3)^2\,\mathrm{var}(d)$. With these restrictions across the two factors of the likelihood function the second factor is no longer irrelevant to the likelihood ratio, and regression tests are no longer approriate. If we make minus two times the log likelihood ratio our test statistic, then the power of the test approaches one as $\sigma(d)$ goes to zero so long as $\sigma(p)$ does not equal zero. If $\sigma(d)$ equals zero, the above variance restriction reduces to $\sigma^2 = (1 - \beta_2^2) \text{var}(p)$. Under the null hypotheses, $\beta_2 = 1 + r > 1$, so this restriction cannot be satisfied unless p does not vary, which is rejected with probability one if $\sigma(p) > 0$. In this case, as in our simple example with non-overlapping observations, the sample will give $-2 \log \lambda = \infty$, while, whether or not p appears explosive in the sample $-2 \log \lambda$ for the regression test will not be infinite. The likelihood ratio test thus has power of one in a region of the parameter space where the regression test does not. In this region, the volatility test, using (I-2) and a test statistic $\hat{\sigma}(\Delta p)/\hat{\sigma}(d)$ also has power equal to one. Thus, if volatility tests reject decisively and regression tests do not, one may infer that in fact the parameters are likely to lie near this region.

6.6   Conclusion and Summary

The various papers discussed here, which attempted to provide evidence against simple efficient markets models by showing that prices are too volatile, share a common econometric motivation. By assuming that both p_t (real stock prices in our main example) and d_t (real dividends), or some transformations of these, are stationary stochastic processes, it is possible to inquire whether the movements in p_t are "too big" to be explained by the model. With these assumptions, the conventional regression tests of the model are no longer suggested by the likelihood ratio principle and volatility tests have distinctly more power in certain regions of the parameter space. In the papers discussed here, the movements in p_t indeed appear to be too big. Figure 6.1 illustrates how dramatically our stock price and dividend data appear to violate one of the inequalities, (I-2). Roughly speaking, if the efficient markets model holds, and if the large movements of Δp are to be justified in terms of information about future d, then the d_t series ought to range over an area equal to the space between the dashed lines, while in fact it appears confined to a fraction of the area. Commonly used hypotheses that have been advanced to reconcile this data with efficient markets—a random walk model for d_t or a disaster theory—do not appear to be promising. Other possibilities are that ex-ante real interest rates show very large movements or, alternatively, that markets are irrational and subject to fads.

Notes

1. The former paper (Shiller [1981a]) did not find any significant evidence of excess volatility with bonds maturing in less than two years.

2. The innovation operator is defined as $\delta_t = E_t - E_{t-1}$, where E_t is the expectation operator at time t.

3. This regression was added in response to John Lintner's comments. The return $(\Delta p_{t+1} + d_t)/p_t$ is significantly positively correlated with d_t/p_t, but the R^2 is only .05.

4. Even though dividends cannot be negative, $\sigma(d)$ could exceed $\mu(d)$ if the distribution of d were sufficiently skewed.

5. It is easily verified that if p_t and d are stationary indeterministic processes this inequality approaches (I-1) as n goes to infinity.

6. An alternative approach to the same issues is used by Pesando [1980].

7. A regression of log (d_t) on a constant, $\log(d_{t-1})$ and time for 1872–1978 gives $\log(d_{t-1})$ a coefficient of .807 with an estimated standard deviation of .058. This regression would always forecast that log d_t should return half way to the trend in three years. According to table 8.5.1 in Fuller [1976], if $\log(d_t)$ were a Gaussian random walk, the probability in a sample of this size of obtaining a smaller coefficient for $\log(d_{t-1})$ is .05.

References

Amsler, Christine. 1980. "The Term-Structure of Interest Rates in an Expanded Market Model," unpublished Ph.D. dissertation, University of Pennsylvania.

Fuller, Wayne A. 1976. *Introduction to Statistical Time Series*, John Wiley & Sons, New York.

Grossman, Sanford, and Robert Shiller. 1981. "The Determinants of the Variability of Stock Prices," *American Economic Review* 71:222–227.

Huang, Roger D. 1981. "The Monetary Approach to the Exchange Rate in an Efficient Foreign Exchange Market: Tests Based on Volatility," *Journal of Finance* 36:31–41.

Krasker, William. 1980. "The Peso Problem in Testing the Efficiency of Forward Markets," *Journal of Monetary Economics* 6:269–276.

LeRoy, Stephen, and Richard Porter. 1981. "The Present Value Relation: Tests Based on Implied Variance Bounds," *Econometrica* 49:555–574.

Meese, Richard A. and Kenneth J. Singleton. 1980. "Rational Expectations, Risk Premia and the Market for Spot and Forward Exchange," mimeographed, Board of Governors of the Federal Reserve System.

Miller, Merton H. and Franco Modigliani. 1961. "Dividend Policy, Growth and the Valuation of Shares," *Journal of Business* 34:411–433.

Pesando, James E. 1980. "On Expectations, Term Premiums and the Volatility of Long-Term Interest Rates," unpublished paper, University of Toronto.

Sargent, Thomas J. 1979. "A Note on the Maximum Likelihood Estimation of the Term Structure," *Journal of Monetary Economics* 5:133–143.

Shiller, Robert J. 1981a. "Alternative Tests of Rational Expectations Models: The Case of the Term Structure," *Journal of Econometrics* 16:17–87.

Shiller, Robert J. 1981b. "Do Stock Prices Move Too Much to be Justified by Subsequent Changes in Dividends?" *American Economic Review* 71:421–436.

Shiller, Robert J. 1979. "The Volatility of Long-Term Interest Rates and Expectations Models of the Term Structure," *Journal of Political Economy* 87:1190–1219.

Singleton, Kenneth. 1980. "Expectations Models of the Term Structure and Implied Variance Bounds," *Journal of Political Economy* 88:1159–1176.

7

The Probability of Gross Violations of a Present Value Variance Inequality

One way of evaluating the simple efficient markets model of stock prices is to compare the volatility of the "perfect-foresight" price per share P_t^* with that of the actual price per share P_t. The perfect-foresight price P_t^* is the present value at time t of actual future dividends D_{t+k}, $k \geqslant 0$, discounted at constant rate r. The simple efficient markets model asserts that $P_t = E_t P_t^*$, which implies (if detrended series p_t and p_t^* are stationary) that $\sigma^2(p^*) \geqslant \sigma^2(p)$. I found [Shiller 1981] (chapter 5) evidence suggesting gross violation of this and other such variance inequalities. With annual U.S. data from 1871–1979, $s(p)/s(p^*) = 5.59$. (Here, σ and s denote population and sample standard deviations, respectively.)

Allan Kleidon [1986] criticizes such methods of evaluating efficiency. By Monte Carlo methods he computes the probability that $s(p)/s(p^*) > 5$ with 100 observations under the simple efficient markets hypothesis and assuming that $\log(D_t) = \mu + \log(D_{t-1}) + \varepsilon_t$, where ε_t is independent normal $N(0, \sigma^2)$ and μ is a constant. He finds that the probability may be substantial, as high as .397.

In each of his 1,000 Monte Carlo iterations, Kleidon first generated 100 observations of a random normal variable with $\mu = .0095$ and $\sigma = .218$. He cumulated and exponentiated these to produce a real dividend series D_t. He produced a price series from the dividend series by multiplying by $(1 + g)/(r - g)$, where r is the discount factor and g is the expected growth of dividends, equal to $\exp[\mu + (\sigma^2/2)]$. Duplicating the procedure in my original paper, he estimated a trend by regressing $\ln(P_t)$ on time t. With the slope coefficient b in this regression, he produced detrended series $d_t = D_t \exp(-bt)$ and $p_t = P_t \exp(-bt)$. He then produced detrended p_t^* recursively with $p_t^* = (p_{t+1}^* + d_{t+1})/(1 + r)$ working backward from $p_T^* = p_T$,

Reprinted with minor editing from *Journal of Political Economy* 96 (1988):1089–1092;

where T is the terminal date. In his table 2 he provides statistics on $s(p)/s(p^*)$ in the 1,000 iterations. I succeeded in replicating his results (table 7.1, case A).

There are two respects in which Kleidon's calculations of this probability are possibly misleading or incorrect. First, he does not adjust his discount factor r for detrending. Second, and more important, he uses assumptions that produce unrealistic dividend-price ratios.

For the first point note that the recursion that I used in my original paper to generate p_t^* was $p_t^* = (p_{t+1}^* + d_{t+1})/[(1 + r)\exp(-b)]$. With my recursion, the model $P_t = E_t P_t^*$ implies $p_t = E_t p_t^*$. With his, it does not. He is in effect using a higher discount rate for p^* than for p, which should have the effect of creating spurious volatility in his simulations for p. Case B of table 7.1 redoes Kleidon's simulations with this change in the recursion. The probability of "gross violations," column 2, is reduced somewhat.

For the second point, note that we can estimate the discount factor r in the model merely by taking the average real return in the market R_t. With the annual U.S. data in my original paper for 1871–1979, the mean of R is 7.848% with a standard error of 1.711%. Kleidon's choices for his tables of $r = 5\%$, 6.5%, and 7.5% are thus a little on the low side but are not unreasonable: none is more than two standard errors below the mean. However, the implied constant dividend-price ratios $(r - g)/(1 + g)$ are often unreasonable: with his estimate of g of 3.382%, these are 1.565%, 3.016%, and 3.983%, respectively. The mean actual dividend-price ratio with this sample is 5.138% with a standard error of 0.389% based on an AR(1) model for the dividend-price ratio. His dividend-price ratios are extreme because as he varies r in his simulations he holds g constant. Yet most of the uncertainty about the population mean of $R_t \equiv (P_{t+1} - P_t)/P_t + (D_t/P_t)$ is due to uncertainty about the growth, the mean of $(P_{t+1} - P_t)/P_t$, rather than to uncertainty about the mean of the dividend-price ratio, D_t/P_t. When he varies r he should vary μ and hence g as well, holding $(r - g)/(1 + g)$ as the average dividend-price ratio.

Assuming too low a dividend-price ratio has the effect in his simulations of overstanding the variability of price, by a factor of over three in the case of $r = 5\%$. The fault in his procedure can be seen by *reductio ad absurdum*: for $r = 3.382\%$ the standard deviation of price would be *infinite*. Of course, in principle price could be much more volatile than dividends if r approaches g and the dividend-price ratio approaches zero, but that is hardly the route toward justifying the actual volatility of prices relative to dividends when the actual dividend-price ratio is around 5%.

Table 7.1
Summary statistics of the distribution of the ratio of sample standard deviation of detrended price p to sample standard deviation of detrended "perfect-foresight" price p^* (1,000 replications)

r	Number of violations		Ratio mean	Ratio standard deviation	Minimum ratio	Maximum ratio	Percentile		
	Ratio >1 (1)	Ratio >5 (2)	(3)	(4)	(5)	(6)	50th (7)	90th (8)	95th (9)
					Case A. Replication of Kleidon's results[a]				
.05	910	370	4.172	2.961	.537	17.431	3.140	8.341	9.431
.065	897	137	3.183	1.734	.560	11.901	3.319	5.354	6.183
.075	908	55	2.872	1.337	.544	9.526	2.914	4.478	5.057
					Case B. Adjusting discount factor for detrending				
.05	867	290	3.754	2.809	.118	13.894	2.816	8.110	9.103
.065	894	109	2.849	1.602	.162	9.041	2.617	5.085	5.674
.075	914	44	2.660	1.265	.123	7.383	2.658	4.287	4.845
					Case C. Adjusting also growth factor g with r				
.05	921	8	2.363	.978	.411	5.988	2.353	3.629	4.076
.065	930	6	2.386	.961	.308	7.219	2.355	3.619	3.917
.075	923	7	2.349	.977	.381	5.852	2.308	3.601	3.984

a. The replications in case A use the same assumptions as in Kleidon [1986], table 2, case ii.

Part C of table 7.1 reports Monte Carlo results that are identical to those in part B except that μ was varied with r so that $(r - g)/(1 + g)$ equals .05138 (the sample average dividend-price ratio for 1871–1978). The results in part C, column 2, show that for any of these discount rates, a gross violation has a probability of less than 1%.

The random walk case for log dividends assumed here is extreme: some other unit root models for dividends give much lower probabilities.

References

Kleidon, Allan W. 1986. "Variance Bounds Tests and Stock Price Valuation Models." *Journal of Political Economy* 94:953–1001.

Shiller, Robert J. 1981. "Do Stock Prices Move Too Much to Be Justified by Subsequent Change in Dividends?" *American Economic Review* 71:421–436.

8

Stock Prices, Earnings,
and Expected Dividends

In this chapter we present estimates indicating that data on accounting earnings, when averaged over many years, help to predict the present value of future dividends. This result holds even when stock prices themselves are taken into account. The data are the real Standard and Poor Composite Index and associated dividend and earnings series 1871–1987. Our estimates indicate to what extent dividend-price ratios and returns on this index behave in accordances with simple present-value models, and allow us to shed new light on earlier claims that stock prices are too volatile to accord with such models (LeRoy and Porter [1981], Shiller [1981 and chapter 5], Mankiw, Romer, and Shapiro [1985], Campbell and Shiller [1987, 1988, and chapter 16] and West [1988]).

It seems appropriate to consider earnings data for forecasting dividends, since earnings are constructed by accountants with the objective of helping people to evaluate the fundamental worth of a company. However, the precise economic meaning of earnings data is not clearly defined; accounting definitions are complicated and change through time in ways that are not readily documented. Because of this, many studies of financial time series have avoided the use of earnings data and have thus omitted relevant information about fundamental value from the analysis.[1]

Our approach is to introduce earnings, measured either annually or as an average over a number of years, as an information variable in a vector-autoregressive (VAR) framework. Any errors in measurement in earnings are accounted for automatically by the estimation procedure, which allows earnings to enter the model only insofar as they are useful in forecasting. The VAR framework, developed originally in Campbell and Shiller [1987, 1988, and chapter 16], enables us to answer two questions. First,

Coauthored with John Y. Campbell. Reprinted with minor editing from *Journal of Finance* 43 (1988):661–676; © 1988 the American Finance Association.

what component of stock returns can be *predicted* given the information used in the VAR system? Second, what component of stock returns can be *accounted for* ex-post by news about future dividends? The existing literature addresses the first question, but the second question is also important for evaluating present-value models. As Shiller [1984] (chapter 1) and Summers [1986] have shown, it is possible to construct a model in which only a small fraction of one-period stock returns is predictable, but in which news about fundamental value accounts for only a small part of the variability of ex-post returns.

Our approach reveals that stock returns and dividend-price ratios are too volatile to be accounted for by news about future dividends. Further, this excess volatility is closely related to the predictability of multiperiod returns. It has recently been shown that stock returns are more highly predictable when they are measured over intervals of several years, rather than over short intervals of a year or less. Fama and French [1987, 1988] have made this point most forcefully, although the result can also be found in Flood, Hodrick, and Kaplan [1986] and Poterba and Summers [1987]. (See also DeBondt and Thaler [1985].) These papers found that 20% or 30% of the variance of four- or five-year stock returns can be explained by variables such as lagged multiyear stock returns or dividend-price ratios. The explained variances are higher when dividend-price ratios are used than when lagged returns are used.

It may be helpful, by way of motivation, to give at the outset a simple story indicating why excess volatility is fundamentally related to this forecastability of multiperiod returns. Let us consider the simplest argument for excess volatility given in the original LeRoy and Porter [1981] and Shiller [1981 and chapter 5] papers. It was argued in those papers that if, as the present-value model asserts, price P_t is the expectation of P_t^*, the present value of actual future dividends, then the data must satisfy the variance inequality $\text{var}(P_t^*) \geq \text{var}(P_t)$. The proof that the model implies this variance inequality was as follows. Since P_t is known at time t, we may write $P_t^* = P_t + u_t$, where u_t is a forecast error. A forecast error must be uncorrelated with the corresponding forecast, so u_t must be uncorrelated with P_t. Therefore $\text{var}(P_t^*) = \text{var}(P_t) + \text{var}(u_t)$. Since variances cannot be negative, the variance inequality follows. This argument can be reversed to show that if the variance inequality is violated in U.S. data, then it must be that $P_t^* - P_t$ is forecastable. We will show below that $P_t^* - P_t$ may itself be considered a sort of infinite-period return. Hence, excess volatility directly implies forecastability of infinite-period returns.

While the above simple story is illustrative of the nature of our argument, we will restate it below in terms of dividend-price ratios to allow for nonstationary dividends and prices, we will avoid any comparisons of P_t and P_t^* estimated with a terminal condition, we will take account of earning data, and we will allow for a simple form of time variation in the real discount rate on stock. These advances are made possible by our use of the VAR framework discussed above. In our earlier work using this framework (Campbell and Shiller [1988]), we found that our rejection of the hypothesis that one-period returns are unforecastable was much less strong than our rejection of the hypothesis that the dividend-price ratio equals the theoretical dividend-price ratio given the present-value model. We will see that this is essentially the same result as noted by Fama and French and others that the one-period return is much less forecastable than the multiperiod return. The limit of their excess-return regression, where returns are computed over an infinite period of time, is essentially our test the stock price equals the expected present value of future dividends. Thus we argue that excess volatility and predictability of multiperiod returns are not two phenomena, but one.

The organization of the chapter is as follows. In section 8.1 we discuss our data and show that dividend-price and earnings-price ratios predict stock returns measured over several years. We also present an approximation to the continuously compounded stock return, which we need to use in our VAR analysis. We show that predictability of approximate returns is close to that of exact returns. In section 8.2 we explain our VAR methodology and relate it to research on multiperiod returns. In section 8.3 we present basic VAR results, and in Section 8.4 we use them to compare the historical behavior of stock prices and returns with the behavior implied by the present-value model. Section 8.5 checks the robustness of our results to changes in specification. Section 8.6 concludes.

8.1   Predicting Stock Returns Using Prices, Dividends, and Earnings

The data set used in this chapter consists of annual observations on prices, dividends and earnings for the Standard and Poor Composite Stock Price Index, extended back to 1871 by using the data in Cowles [1939]. The series on prices and dividends are also used in Campbell and Shiller [1987] (chapter 6), and in much of the literature on volatility tests. Campbell and Shiller [1988] show that the properties of the post-1926 data are very similar to those of the CRSP series on the value-weighted New York Stock

Exchange Index, while Wilson and Jones [1987] have carefully analyzed the pre-1926 data. The nominal earnings series for 1926 to 1986 is the Standard and Poor earnings per share adjusted to index, total for the year. For earlier years, our nominal earnings series is earnings-price ratio series R-1 (Cowles [1939], pp. 404–405) times the annual average Standard and Poor Composite Index for the year. We deflate nominal series using a January Producer Price Index (annual average before 1900), 1967 = 100.

We write the real price of the stock index, measured in January of year t, as P_t. The real dividend paid on the index during period t is written D_t. The realized log gross return on the portfolio, held from the beginning of year t to the beginning of year $t + 1$, is $h_{1t} \equiv \log((P_{t+1} + D_t)/P_t) = \log(P_{t+1} + D_t) - \log(P_t)$. The realized log gross return over i years, from the beginning of year t to the beginning of year $t + i$, is

$$h_{it} \equiv \sum_{j=0}^{i-1} h_{1,t+j}. \tag{1}$$

We also wish to study excess returns on common stock over short debt. The short-term interest rate we use is the annual return on 4–6 month prime commercial paper, rolled over in January and July. If we write the realized log real return on commercial paper in year t as r_t, and aggregate to a multiperiod return r_{it} in the manner of equation (1), then the excess return on stock over i periods is $h_{it} - r_{it}$. Working with excess returns has the advantage that price deflators cancel so that results are not contaminated by measurement error in the deflators.

We begin our empirical work by regressing real and excess stock returns on some explanatory variables that are known in advance (at the start of year t). For real returns, we consider the following variables:[2] the log dividend-price ratio, $\delta_t \equiv d_{t-1} - p_t$ (the dividend is lagged one year to ensure that it is known at the start of year t); the lagged dividend-growth rate, Δd_{t-1}; log earnings-price ratio $\varepsilon_t \equiv e_{t-1} - p_t$; and two log earnings-price ratios based on moving averages of earnings. The latter two are a ten-year moving average of log real earnings minus current log real price, $\varepsilon_t^{10} \equiv (e_{t-1} + \cdots + e_{t-10})/10 - p_t$, and a thirty-year moving average of log real earnings minus current log real price, $\varepsilon_t^{30} \equiv (e_{t-1} + \cdots + e_{t-30})/30 - p_t$.

The ratio variables are used here with the same motivation that we see in the financial press, as indicators of fundamental value relative to price. The notion is that if stocks are underpriced relative to fundamental value, returns tend to be high subsequently, the converse holds if stocks are overpriced. A moving average of earnings is used because yearly earnings are quite noisy as measures of fundamental value; they could even be negative while fundamental value cannot be negative. The use of an average of earnings in computing the earnings-price ratio has a long history. Graham and Dodd [1934] recommended an approach that "shifts the original point of departure, or basis of computation, from the current earnings to the average earnings, which should cover a period of not less than five years, and preferably seven to ten years" (*Security Analysis*, p. 452). We push their averaging scheme even further, to thirty years, in recognition of the substantial decadal variability of earnings, under the supposition that fundamental value may be less variable than this decadal variability.

We regress real stock returns on each of these variables individually, and also on the combination $(\delta_t, \Delta d_{t-1}, \varepsilon_t^{30})$. For excess stock returns, the procedure is similar except that we use the excess of dividend growth over the commercial-paper rate, $\Delta d_{t-1} - r_{t-1}$, in place of the real dividend-growth rate.

Table 8.1 presents regression results for the period 1871–1987 (truncated where necessary at the end of the sample to allow computation of multiperiod returns, and at the beginning of the sample to allow computation of ε_t^{10} and ε_t^{30}). Returns are measured over one, three, and ten years. The left side of panel A gives results for real returns, and the left side of panel B gives results for excess returns. For each regression the table reports the R^2 statistic, and in parentheses the significance level for a Wald test of the hypothesis that all coefficients (other than a constant) are zero. The Wald test corrects for the moving-average structure of the equation errors when the dependent variable is a multiperiod return, but it does not correct for heteroscedasticity.[3]

The table shows that several of the variables in our list have a striking ability to predict returns on the Standard and Poor Index. This is true whether returns are measured in real terms or as an excess over commercial-paper rates. The variables with predictive power are those that include the stock price itself: the log dividend-price ratio δ_t, and the three earnings-price ratios ε_t, ε_t^{10}, and ε_t^{30}. The forecasting power of these variables is statistically significant at conventional levels for one-period returns, but the fraction of variance explained is modest at this horizon: 3.9% of the variance of one-year real returns is explained by the log dividend-price ratio, for example. As the number of years used to compute the return increases, however, the fraction of variance explained also increases, and the constant-expected-return model is rejected more strongly. The log dividend-price ratio explains 26.6% of the variance of ten-year real returns, for example, and the thiry-year moving-average earnings-price ratio explains 56.6% of this variance. These results confirm and extend the findings

Table 8.1
Predicting stock returns, 1871–1987[a]

Explanatory variable	Exact returns [expression (1), text]			Discounted returns [expression (4), text]		
	1-year	3-year	10-year	1-year	3-year	10-year
A. Real returns						
δ_t	0.039	0.110	0.266	0.048	0.135	0.327
	(0.033)	(0.015)	(0.001)	(0.017)	(0.006)	(0.000)
Δd_{t-1}	0.000	0.004	0.003	0.000	0.004	0.003
	(0.964)	(0.522)	(0.485)	(0.977)	(0.568)	(0.537)
ε_t	0.019	0.090	0.296	0.023	0.104	0.303
	(0.143)	(0.027)	(0.000)	(0.100)	(0.017)	(0.000)
ε_t^{10}	0.040	0.111	0.401	0.047	0.130	0.423
	(0.036)	(0.031)	(0.000)	(0.022)	(0.019)	(0.000)
ε_t^{30}	0.067	0.195	0.566	0.079	0.225	0.615
	(0.013)	(0.008)	(0.000)	(0.007)	(0.004)	(0.000)
$\delta_t, \Delta d_{t-1}, \varepsilon_t^{30}$	0.076	0.204	0.637	0.088	0.235	0.667
	(0.073)	(0.046)	(0.000)	(0.041)	(0.022)	(0.000)
B. Excess returns						
δ_t	0.016	0.080	0.184	0.022	0.101	0.246
	(0.180)	(0.037)	(0.033)	(0.114)	(0.019)	(0.010)
$\Delta d_{t-1} - r_{t-1}$	0.026	0.027	0.000	0.026	0.026	0.001
	(0.082)	(0.127)	(0.811)	(0.082)	(0.134)	(0.758)
ε_t	0.011	0.054	0.195	0.015	0.066	0.206
	(0.261)	(0.083)	(0.009)	(0.194)	(0.053)	(0.005)
ε_t^{10}	0.052	0.145	0.341	0.060	0.168	0.399
	(0.017)	(0.010)	(0.003)	(0.010)	(0.005)	(0.001)
ε_t^{30}	0.051	0.187	0.480	0.074	0.218	0.548
	(0.017)	(0.007)	(0.002)	(0.009)	(0.003)	(0.000)
$\delta_t, \Delta d_{t-1} - r_{t-1}, \varepsilon_t^{30}$	0.086	0.195	0.493	0.096	0.229	0.553
	(0.046)	(0.045)	(0.011)	(0.028)	(0.022)	(0.004)

a. The numbers reported are the R^2 in the regression of return on the explanatory variables, and in parentheses the significance level of a Wald test of the hypothesis that all coefficients in the regression are zero. The Wald test adjusts for overlapping data in regressions with multiperiod returns, but does not adjust for heteroskedasticity. The sample period is 1871–1987, truncated at the end where necessary to compute multiperiod returns.

of Fama and French [1988] for a longer data set, and establish that a very high proportion of multiperiod returns is forecastable using a long moving average of earnings.[4]

The lagged rate of dividend growth, by contrast, does not predict stock returns at any horizon. This is true whether we deflate it with a price index or use the commercial-paper rate. Also the system of three variables does not achieve an R^2 statistic that is much greater than that for ε_t^{30} alone.

In what follows, we will be concerned with the relationship between the realized log one-period return h_{1t}, the dividend-growth rate Δd_t, and the log dividend-price ratio δ_t. The exact relationship between these variables is nonlinear. It takes the form

$$h_{1t} = \log(\exp(\delta_t - \delta_{t+1}) + \exp(\delta_t)) + \Delta d_t. \tag{2}$$

However, this equation can be linearized by a first-order Taylor expansion around the point $\delta_t = \delta_{t+1} = \delta$. We argued in Campbell and Shiller [1988] that the log dividend-price ratio follows a stationary stochastic process, so that it has a fixed mean that can be used as the expansion point δ. We will also define the interest rate implicit in the chosen δ as $r = g + \ln(1 + \exp(\delta))$, where g is the mean Δd. We obtain

$$h_{1t} \approx \xi_{1t},$$
$$\xi_{1t} \equiv \delta_t - \rho\delta_{t+1} + \Delta d_t + k = (1 - \rho)d_t + \rho p_{t+1} - p_t + k, \tag{3}$$

where $\rho = 1/(1 + \exp(\delta)) = \exp(-(r - g))$, and $k = \log(1 + \exp(\delta)) - \delta\exp(\delta)/(1 + \exp(\delta))$.

Equation (3) says that the log one-period return on the stock portfolio, h_{1t}, can be approximated by a variable ξ_{1t} that is linear in the log dividend-price ratios δ_t and δ_{t+1} and the dividend-growth rate Δd_t. The approximation in (3) replaces $\log(P_{t+1} + D_t)$ with $\rho\log(P_{t+1}) + (1 - \rho)\log(D_t)$, where ρ is a parameter related to the mean ratio of prices to dividends.

We now define a multiperiod extension of (3). For the purpose of showing the relation between the excess-volatility literature and the multiperiod-return forecasting literature, it is helpful to define this slightly differently than would be natural given (1). We define the discounted i-period return ξ_{it} as

$$\xi_{it} \equiv \sum_{j=0}^{i-1} \rho^j \xi_{1,t+j}. \tag{4}$$

The variable ξ_{it} is the *discounted* sum of approximate returns from t to $t + i - 1$. It has the convenient property that it depends only on δ_t, δ_{t+i}, and dividend-growth rates from t to $t + i$; log dividend-price ratios for times between t and $t + i$ do not appear. While the summation in (1) approaches infinity as i increases, the summation in (4) instead approaches under the assumption that δ_t and Δd_{t-1} and jointly stationary) a well-defined limit, a stationary stochastic process. We can thus speak of an infinite-period log return, which we will see below is related to the log dividend-price ratio; this is why use of the definition (4) ties the multiperiod-return literature to our own earlier study of the behavior of the dividend-price ratio.

One interpretation of the discounted i-period return ξ_{it} is that it is (up to a constant term that depends on i) a linearization of an exact i-period log return H_{it}, where dividends paid are reinvested not in the stock itself but in an instrument than pays a fixed real return.[5] H_{it} can be written in terms of the log dividend-price ratio and log dividend-growth rates:

$$H_{it} = \ln \left\{ \exp \left(\delta_t - \delta_{t+1} + \sum_{j=0}^{i-1} \Delta d_{t+j} \right) \right.$$

$$\left. + \sum_{j=0}^{i-1} \exp \left(\delta_t + \sum_{k=0}^{j} \Delta d_{t+k} \, r(i - j - 1) \right) \right\}.$$

The first term inside the curly brackets is the price relative P_{t+i}/P_t. The subsequent terms give the terminal value of total dividends received between t and $t + i - 1$ divided by P_t. Note that since reinvestments are not made in the stock, dividend-price ratios between t and $t + i$ do not enter the expression, as also with (4). Let us linearize the above expression around $\delta_t = \delta$ and $\Delta d_{t+j} = g$, for all j. This gives us the discounted i-period return ξ_{it} defined in equation (4), plus a constant that increases with i.

Naturally equations (3) and (4) do not give actual log returns exactly; since they were derived from a linearization, there is some approximation error. In Campbell and Shiller [1988], we presented considerable evidence that in practice the error is quite small for one-period returns. Here we supplement that analysis by repeating the regressions discussed above using discounted multiperiod returns ξ_{it} rather than exact returns h_{it}. We treat the parameter ρ as fixed, and set it equal to 0.936 following Campbell and Shiller [1988].[6]

The results are given in the right side of table 8.1. They are generally similar to those discussed before; while there is a slightly greater tendency to reject the constant-expected-return model with discounted returns (indicating that the approximation error is correlated with the explanatory variables), the difference is relatively minor. This confirms that we can

speak of our definition of multiperiod returns (4) as roughly interchange-
able, for present purposes, with the definition (1) used by Fama and French
[1987, 1988] and others.

8.2   A Vector-Autoregressive Approach

In the previous section we derived an approximation to the log return on
stock that is linear in log dividend-price ratios and dividend-growth rates.
We now exploit this linearity in analyzing stock price movements.

First, we write the discounted i-period log return as an explicit linear
function of δ_t, δ_{t+i} and Δd_{t+j}, $j = 0, \ldots, i-1$. From equations (3) and (4)
we have

$$\xi_{it} = \delta_t - \rho^i \delta_{t+i} + \sum_{j=0}^{i-1} \rho^j \Delta d_{t+j} + k(1 - \rho^i)/(1 - \rho). \tag{5}$$

Equation (5) shows that the discounted i-period return is higher, the higher
the dividend-price ratio is when the investment is initiated, the lower the
dividend price ratio is when the investment is terminated, and the higher
dividend growth is between those two dates.[7]

We can also use this equation to see the relationship between multiperiod returns and the literature on price volatility. If we take the limit of
(5) as i increases, assuming that $\lim_{i \to \infty} \rho^i E_t \delta_{t+i} = 0$ (which follows from
the stationarity of δ_t), we find that we have

$$\lim_{i \to \infty} \xi_{it} = (1 - \rho) \sum_{j=0}^{\infty} \rho^j d_{t+j} - p_t + k/(1 - \rho).$$

The first term on the right-hand side of this expression is the present
discounted value of log dividends, which is a log-linearization of P_t^*, while
the second term is the log of P_t. Thus, as noted in the introduction, the
infinite-period discounted log return is a log-linearization of the variable
$P_t^* - P_t$, which is the subject of the volatility literature. Moreover, for finite
i, ξ_{it} is a log-linear representation of $P_t^* - P_t$ where P_t^* is computed under
the assumption that the present value in period $t + i$ of dividends from
$t + i$ onward equals P_{t+i}. This assumption was used in the volatility literature to obtain an estimate of P_t^* with a finite record of dividends.

Equation (5) makes it easy to compute the implication of a returns model
for the dividend-price ratio. For example, suppose our model is that expected real one-period stock returns are constant: $E_t \xi_{1t} = r$. Then $E_t \xi_{it} =$
$r(1 - \rho^i)/(1 - \rho)$. Taking conditional expectations of the left- and right-
hand sides of (5) and rearranging, we have

$$\delta_t = -\sum_{j=0}^{i-1} \rho^j E_t \Delta d_{t+j} + \rho^i E_t \delta_{t+i} + (r - k)(1 - \rho^i)/(1 - \rho). \tag{6}$$

This equation says that the log dividend-price ratio at time t is determined by expectations of future real dividend growth over i periods, by the i-period-ahead expected dividend-price ratio, and by the constant required return on stock. If we take the limit as i increases, assuming as before that $\lim_{i \to \infty} \rho^i E_t \delta_{t+i} = 0$, we obtain

$$\delta_t = -\sum_{j=0}^{\infty} \rho^j E_t \Delta d_{t+j} + (r - k)/(1 - \rho). \tag{7}$$

Equation (7) expresses the log dividend-price ratio as a linear function of expected real dividend growth into the infinite future.

A similar approach can be used when our returns model is that expected *excess* returns on stock, over some alternative asset with return r_t, are constant: $E_t \xi_{1t} = E_t r_t + c$. In our empirical work, we take r_t to be the real return on commercial paper. For this model we have

$$\delta_t = \sum_{j=0}^{i-1} \rho^j E_t [r_{t+j} - \Delta d_{t+j}] + \rho^i E_t \delta_{t+i} + (c - k)(1 - \rho^i)/(1 - \rho), \tag{6'}$$

and taking the limit as i increases,

$$\delta_t = \sum_{j=0}^{\infty} \rho^j E_t [r_{t+j} - \Delta d_{t+j}] + (c - k)/(1 - \rho). \tag{7'}$$

This relation is what Campbell and Shiller [1988] call the "dividend-ratio model." It may also be described as a dynamic Gordon model, after the simple growth model proposed by Myron Gordon [1962], which makes the dividend-price ratio equal the interest rate minus the growth rate of dividends. The original Gordon model did not specify how the dividend-price ratio should change through time if interest rates or growth rates change through time: equation (7') says that the dividend-price ratio is related to a present value of expected one-period interest rates and dividend-growth rates.

The linearity of these relationships makes it possible to test them as restrictions on a vector autoregression. This procedure has several advantages over the straightforward multiperiod-regression approach discussed in the previous section. First, one need only estimate the VAR once: then one can conduct Wald tests of (6) or (6') for any i, without reestimating the system. Second, as i increases, the regression approach forces one to shorten the sample period. This becomes quite serious when returns are calculated over five to ten years. The VAR, by contrast, can be estimated over the whole sample. Third, the VAR can be used to test the restrictions of (7) or (7′), which are the limits of (6) and (6′) as i increases. This is important because (7) and (7′) directly state the implications of the returns model for the dividend-price ratio. Finally, the VAR approach enables us to characterize the historical behavior of the dividend-price ratio in relation to an unrestricted econometric forecast of future dividends and discount rates. It is important to note that if the present-value model is correct, then this theoretical value, which we call δ'_t, should equal the log dividend-price ratio δ_t no matter how much information market participants have. The reason for this is that δ_t, which is included in the VAR system, is a sufficient statistic for market participants' information about the present value of future dividends.

A detailed account of the VAR framework is given in Campbell and Shiller [1987] (chapter 16), [1988]. Here we briefly summarize it for the constant-expected-returns case. Consider estimating a VAR for the variables δ_{t+1}, Δd_t and ε^{30}_{t+1}. The last variable, a moving-average earnings-price ratio, is included only as a potential predictor of stock returns. If the VAR has only one lag, then the system estimated is

$$
\begin{bmatrix} \delta_{t+1} \\ \Delta d_t \\ \varepsilon^{30}_{t+1} \end{bmatrix} = \begin{bmatrix} a_{11} & a_{12} & a_{13} \\ a_{21} & a_{22} & a_{23} \\ a_{31} & a_{32} & a_{33} \end{bmatrix} \begin{bmatrix} \delta_t \\ \Delta d_{t-1} \\ \varepsilon^{30}_t \end{bmatrix} + \begin{bmatrix} u_{1t+1} \\ u_{2t+1} \\ u_{3t+1} \end{bmatrix} \tag{8}
$$

where the variables in the vector are demeaned. This can be written more compactly, in matrix form, as $z_{t+1} = Az_t + v_{t+1}$.

Now a first-order vector autoregression has the desirable property that to forecast the variables ahead k periods, given the history $H_t = \{z_t, z_{t-1}, \ldots\}$, one just multiplies z_t by the kth power of the matrix A:

$$
E[z_{t+k}|H_t] = A^k z_t. \tag{9}
$$

This makes it easy to translate equations (6) and (7) into restrictions on the VAR. First, define vectors $e1 = [1\ 0\ 0]'$, so that $e1'z_t = \delta_t$, and $e2 = [0\ 1\ 0]'$, so that $e2'z_t = \Delta d_{t-1}$. Next, take the expectation of equation (6), conditional on H_t:

$$
\delta_t = -\sum_{j=0}^{i-1} \rho^j E[\Delta d_{t+j}|H_t] + \rho^i E[\delta_{t+i}|H_t] + (r-k)(1-\rho^i)/(1-\rho). \tag{6″}
$$

The left-hand side is unaffected, because δ_t is in the information set H_t, and the right-hand side becomes an expectation conditional on H_t.

Finally, apply the multiperiod forecasting formula (9):

$$e1'z_t = -\sum_{j=0}^{i-1} \rho^j e2' A^{j+1} z_t + \rho^i e1' A^i z_t + (r-k)(1-\rho^i)/(1-\rho). \tag{10}$$

If (10) is to hold for arbitrary z_t, we must have

$$e1'(I - \rho^i A^i) = -e2'A(I - \rho A)^{-1}(I - \rho^i A^i). \tag{11}$$

These are complicated restrictions on the coefficient-matrix A, but they do simplify in two special cases, which are emphasized in Campbell and Shiller [1988]. First, if $i = 1$ then we have a set of *linear* restrictions that one-period returns are unpredictable: $e1'(I - \rho A) = -e2'A$. In terms of the individual coefficients, the restrictions are $a_{21} = \rho a_{11} - 1$, $a_{22} = \rho a_{12}$ and $a_{23} = \rho a_{13}$. The coefficients in the equation for the earnings-price ratio, a_{31}, a_{32}, and a_{33}, are unrestricted. Second, if $i = \infty$, then we have a set of non-linear but simple restrictions that the log dividend-price ratio δ_t equals the unrestricted VAR forecast of real dividend growth into the infinite future, which we will call δ_t'. The restrictions are $\delta_t \equiv e1'z_t = -e2'A(I - \rho A)^{-1} z_t \equiv \delta_t'$, which requires that $e1' = -e2'A(I - \rho A)^{-1}$. We will compare the historical behavior of δ_t', the VAR forecast of future real dividend growth, with that of the log dividend-price ratio δ_t.

Of course, the restrictions for all i are algebraically equivalent. If $e1'(I - \rho A) = -e2'A$, then one can postmultiply by $(I - \rho^i A^i)$ for any i to get the i-period restriction. The reverse is also possible since stationarity of the VAR guarantees nonsingularity of $(I - \rho^i A^i)$. This algebraic equivalence reflects the fact that if one-period returns are unpredictable, then i-period returns must also be, and vice versa. Nevertheless, Wald tests on the VAR may yield different results depending on which value of i is chosen, just as regression tests did in table 8.1.

The VAR approach can easily be modified to handle different specifications. To test the model in which expected excess returns are constant, one simply replaces Δd_t with $\Delta d_t - r_t$ and proceeds as before. To handle higher order VAR behavior, one estimates the higher order system and then stacks it into first-order "companion" form as discussed by Sargent [1979] and Campbell and Shiller [1987 (chapter 16), 1988]. When z_t, A, $e1$ and $e2$ are suitably redefined, the restriction (11) remains correct.

8.3   Results of the VAR Procedure

In table 8.2 we apply the VAR method to our data on stock prices, dividends and earnings over the period 1871–1987. The sample period is truncated at the beginning to allow for construction of a thirty-year moving average of earnings, but it need not be truncated at the end even though we will test for unpredictability of multiperiod returns. We estimate first-order VARs, using real dividend growth in panel A (to test the constant-expected-*real*-return model), and the excess of dividend growth over the commercial-paper rate in panel B (to test the constant-expected-*excess*-return model). We devote most of our attention to the results in panel A, discussing the panel B results briefly in section 8.5.

The VAR coefficients, a_{ij} for $i, j = 1, 2, 3$ are reported at the top of the table. Below each coefficient is an asymptotic standard error in parentheses. The coefficients in the second row (the dividend-growth equation) are perhaps of special interest; they show that the dividend-price ratio has strong forecasting power for dividend growth, and the earnings-price ratio ε_t^{30} is also highly significant. These results suggest that some improvement is possible in the dividend-growth equation proposed by Marsh and Merton [1986, 1987], which does not use the long average of earnings variable.

The hypothesis that expected real returns on stock are constant restricts the coefficients in the first two rows, the equations for the dividend-price ratio and real dividend growth respectively. We should have $a_{21} = \rho a_{11} - 1$, $a_{22} - \rho a_{12}$ and $a_{23} = \rho a_{13}$. As before, we fix the parameter ρ at 0.936.

These restrictions do not hold exactly, and the differences $a_{21} - \rho a_{11} + 1$, $a_{22} - \rho a_{12}$ and $a_{23} - \rho a_{13}$ are the coefficients obtained in a regression of ξ_{1t} on the VAR explanatory variables. Coefficients from such a regression are reported in table 8.2 below the VAR results. (This regression was also used in table 8.1, panel A.)

Wald tests of the model restriction (11), for $i = 1, 2, 3, 5, 7, 10$, and ∞, are reported next in table 8.2. The test statistic for $i = 1$ is numerically identical to the statistic obtained from the regression of ξ_{1t} on the VAR explanatory variables; its significance level of 0.041 is therefore identical to the one reported in table 8.1, panel A. When $i > 1$, the exact equivalence of the regression test and the VAR is broken, but the general nature of the results is the same. The VAR tests, like the multiperiod regression tests, reject more and more strongly as the return horizon increases. In the limit, at $i = \infty$, the null hypothesis is that the log dividend-price ratio δ_t equals the unrestricted VAR forecast of the present value of future real dividend growth δ_t'. This hypothesis can be rejected at better than the 0.1% level.

Table 8.2
One-lag VAR results, 1871–1987[a]

A. Real returns			

Dependent variable	Explanatory variable			
	δ_t	Δd_{t-1}	ε_t^{30}	R^2
δ_{t+1}	0.610	0.210	0.086	0.503
	(0.134)	(0.175)	(0.093)	
Δd_t	−0.418	0.332	0.209	0.361
	(0.067)	(0.087)	(0.046)	
ε_{t+1}^{30}	0.008	−0.104	0.874	0.791
	(0.125)	(0.163)	(0.087)	
ξ_{1t}	0.011	0.135	0.129	0.088
	(0.118)	(0.154)	(0.082)	

Significance levels for VAR tests of unpredictability of returns: number of years over which returns are computed

1	2	3	5	7	10	∞
0.041	0.023	0.012	0.002	0.000	0.000	0.000

Some implications of the VAR estimates:

$$\delta_t' = 1.032\delta_t - 0.078\Delta d_{t-1} - 0.776\varepsilon_t^{30}$$

$\qquad$ (0.076) $\qquad$ (0.046) $\qquad$ (0.101)

$\sigma(\delta_t')/\sigma(\delta_t) = 0.672,$ $\qquad$ corr$(\delta_t', \delta_t) = 0.175$

$\qquad$ (0.074) $\qquad\qquad\qquad$ (0.146)

$\sigma(\xi_{1t}')/\sigma(\xi_{1t}) = 0.269,$ $\qquad$ corr$(\xi_{1t}', \xi_{1t}) = 0.915$

$\qquad$ (0.067) $\qquad\qquad\qquad$ (0.064)

B. Excess returns			

Dependent variable	Explanatory variable			
	δ_t	$\Delta d_{t-1} - r_{t-1}$	ε_t^{30}	R^2
δ_{t+1}	0.619	0.482	0.087	0.541
	(0.126)	(0.164)	(0.087)	
$\Delta d_t - r_t$	−0.393	0.235	0.179	0.339
	(0.066)	(0.086)	(0.045)	
ε_{t+1}^{30}	−0.024	0.256	0.908	0.796
	(0.121)	(0.158)	(0.083)	
$\xi_{1t} - r_t$	0.028	−0.216	0.097	0.096
	(0.114)	(0.149)	(0.078)	

Significance levels for VAR tests of unpredictability of returns: number of years over which returns are computed

1	2	3	5	7	10	∞
0.028	0.013	0.005	0.000	0.000	0.000	0.000

Table 8.2 (continued)

B. Excess returns (cont.)

Some implications of the VAR estimates:

$\delta_t' = 0.927\delta_t + 0.046(\Delta d_{t-1} - r_{t-1}) - 0.634\varepsilon_t^{30}$
  (0.144)   (0.086)   (0.217)

$\sigma(\delta_t')/\sigma(\delta_t) = 0.580,$ $\qquad\qquad$ corr$(\delta_t', \delta_t) = 0.309$

$\qquad\qquad$ (0.136) $\qquad\qquad\qquad\qquad\qquad$ (0.341)

$\sigma(\xi_{1t}' - r_t)/\sigma(\xi_{1t} - r_t) = 0.485,$ $\qquad$ corr$(\xi_{1t}' - r_t, \xi_{1t} - r_t) = 0.733$

$\qquad\qquad$ (0.044) $\qquad\qquad\qquad\qquad\qquad\qquad$ (0.188)

a. Results are for vector autoregressions with three-element vector including ε_t^{30}. The first group of numbers reported are regression coefficients, with standard errors in parentheses. (In the δ_t' column the numbers are implied coefficients from the VAR, with asymptotic standard errors calculated numerically.) Also reported are R^2 statistics from the regressions. Below this are significance levels for Wald tests of restrictions (11), with $i = 1, 2, 3, 5, 7,$ 10, and ∞. The Wald test at $i = \infty$ is a test of the hypothesis that $\delta_t = \delta_t'$. Below this are some implied statistics computed from the VAR, with asymptotic standard errors calculated numerically in parentheses.

8.4 Comparison of Historical and Theoretical Stock Prices and Returns

In this section we use the VAR estimates in table 8.2 to compare actual stock prices and returns with their theoretical counterparts. We find that with the constant-expected-real-return model, the log dividend-price ratio δ_t has only a weak relation to its theoretical counterpart δ_t', a result that strongly contradicts the model. The variables δ_t' and δ_t have a correlation of only 0.175 (this estimate has a standard error of 0.146), and δ_t' is less variable than δ_t (see the bottom of table 8.2, panel A). Its standard deviation is 0.672 times that of δ_t, with a small standard error of 0.074. This would suggest that the dividend-price ratio is unrelated to the theoretical value implied by the constant-expected-real-return model. However, a plot of δ_t and δ_t' (figure 8.1) shows a suggestion of *short-run* coherence, even though the overall correlation between the two is virtually zero. Our VAR results also indicate that the dividend-price ratio helps to forecast *short-run* dividend changes.

One-period returns ξ_{1t} are about four times as variable as they should be given the model. To see this, we computed a variable $\xi_{1t}' \equiv \delta_t' - \rho\delta_{t+1}' + \Delta d_t$. This is our estimate of what the one-year return on stock *would* be, if the constant-expected-real-return model held so that δ_t equaled δ_t'. Note that ξ_{1t} should equal ξ_{1t}' even if the market has superior information not available to econometricians. We find that ξ_{1t}' has a standard deviation only

0.269 as large as that of ξ_{1t}. This appears to be a strong result, as the standard error on this ratio of standard deviations is only 0.067. This result is good evidence that returns on stocks are far too volatile to accord with the constant-expected-real-return present-value model, confirming the earlier claims of the volatility literature.

Although returns seem to be too volatile, we do estimate a remarkably high correlation coefficient between actual returns ξ_{1t} and their theoretical counterparts ξ'_{1t}, equal to 0.915. Returns may be too volatile, but they appear to be on track in the sense that they correlate very well with their theoretical values.

This result is due to the same feature of the data that gives the short-run coherence between δ_t and δ'_t observed in figure 8.1. It is easy to see where the result comes from if we use the derived equation defining δ'_t, as shown in table 8.2, panel A. This equation defines δ'_t as $\delta'_t = 1.032\delta_t - 0.078\Delta d_{t-1} - 0.776\varepsilon_t^{30}$. Let us define p'_t as the theoretical log real price implied by the model, $p'_t = d_{t-1} - \delta'_t$. The present-value model implies that p'_t should equal p_t, even if economic agents have superior information not observed by econometricians. By contrast, our estimates imply that $p'_t = 0.776e_t^{30} + 0.256p_t + 0.046d_{t-1} - 0.078d_{t-2}$, where e_t^{30} is the thiry-year moving average of log real earnings. This shows that p'_t is essentially three

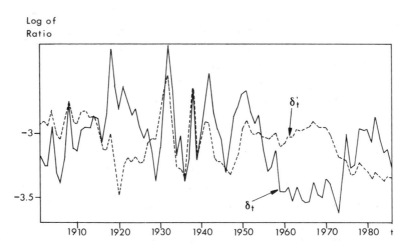

Figure 8.1
Log dividend-price ratio δ_t (solid line), and theoretical counterpart δ'_t (dashed line), 1901–1986. The variable δ'_t is the optimal forecast of the present value of future real dividend-growth rates (constant discount rate), based on the vector-autoregressive model as given in table 8.2, panel A. That is, $\delta'_t = -e2'A(I - \rho A)^{-1}z_t = 1.032\delta_t - 0.078\Delta d_{t-1} - 0.776\varepsilon_t^{30}$.

fourths of the long moving average of real log earnings plus one fourth of the current price. It is a weighted average of the moving average of log real earnings and of log real price with most of the weight on the moving average.

A plot of p_t and p_t' over the period 1901–1986 is shown in figure 8.2. The variable p_t' is strikingly smoother than p_t and at the same time shows short-run movements that are highly correlated with it. This is as we would expect: the long moving average of real earnings is very smooth, since long moving averages smooth out the series averaged. Hence, most of the short-run fluctuations in p_t are seen, in an attenuated form, in p_t'. Since returns ξ_{1t} and ξ_{1t}' are essentially changes in p_t, their behavior is dominated by the short-run movements in the series so that they are highly correlated with each other. Dividend-price ratios δ_t and δ_t', on the other hand, are determined by the levels of p_t and p_t' and are not very correlated.

8.5   How Robust Are the Results to Changes in Specification?

In panel B of table 8.2, we repeat all these exercises using dividend growth deflated by the commercial-paper rate rather than the inflation rate of the producer price index. The null hypothesis here is that expected excess

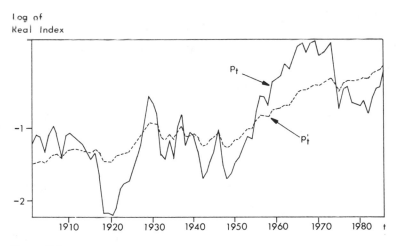

Figure 8.2
Log real stock price index p_t (solid line) and theoretical log real price index p_t' (dashed line), 1901–1986. The theoretical log real price index p_t' is the optimal forecast of the log-linearized present value (constant rate of discount) of real dividends based on the vector-autoregressive forecasting model presented in table 8.2, panel A. The variable p_t' is computed as $d_{t-1} - \delta_t'$, where δ_t' is the series plotted in figure 8.1.

returns on stock over commercial paper are constant. We obtain results that are similar to, though for the most part somewhat less dramatic than, those in panel A. The correlation between δ_t and δ'_t is small, at 0.309. The standard deviation of ξ'_{1t} is just under half that of ξ_{1t}, and the two have a substantial correlation, of 0.733. The implied variable p'_t now places a weight of 0.634 on e_t^{30} and 0.293 on p_t. Again, the long moving average of earnings dominates the stock price in forecasting dividend growth adjusted for commercial-paper rates.

We also checked to see whether our VAR results are robust to increases in the lag length of the VAR. We estimated VARs of order 1–5. Except for the fact that the significance levels in the one-period-return regression decline with lag length, the conclusions for the most part do not seem to be very sensitive to the order of the estimated VAR. We also checked to see whether a shorter ten-year moving average of earnings gives similar results to those reported in table 8.2. We estimated that $p'_t = 0.423e_t^{10} + 0.455p_t + 0.246d_{t-1} - 0.114d_{t-2}$. The correlation between δ'_t and δ_t is higher than in table 8.2, but the correlation drops dramatically as lag length is increased towards 5. Finally, we estimated the VAR system in table 8.2 for the shorter sample 1927–1986. We obtained results that were very similar to those for the full sample period.

8.6   Conclusion

Our results indicate that a long moving average of real earnings helps to forecast future real dividends. The ratio of this earnings variable to the current stock price is a powerful predictor of the return on stock, particularly when the return is measured over several years. We have shown that these facts make stock prices and returns much too volatile to accord with a simple present-value model. Yet annual returns do seem to carry some information and are correlated with what they should be given the model.

Whenever a new variable is introduced into an analysis, in this case the long moving average of earnings, and the new variable plays an important role in the results, it is natural for critics to wonder if the new variable really belongs in the analysis. There is always the possibility that many different variables were attempted, until the results changed, and only the one that changed the results was reported. However, we think that it can be argued that a long moving average of earnings is a very natural variable to use to represent fundamental value, and that there are not many competitors for this role. We note also that we found evidence of excess volatility in earlier research (Campbell and Shiller [1988]) that did not use the information in earnings.

In evaluating our results, it should also be borne in mind that (disregarding small-sample considerations) if we find one variable that destroys the model, then introducing new variables can never save the model. Since the log dividend-price ratio δ_t is in the information set assumed, it should get a unit coefficient and all other variables should get zero coefficients in the equation for the theoretical log dividend-price ratio δ_t'. Adding more variables can never bring us back to this situation, so long as the earnings variable is included. Another way to put this, recalling our argument that excess volatility is the same as forecastability of multiperiod returns, is that once a forecasting variable is found that predicts multiperiod returns, adding new forecasting variables can never make them unforecastable.

Notes

1. There is a large accounting literature on the response of securities prices to earnings announcements; see Kormendi and Lipe [1987] for a list of references. However, with a few exceptions, notably Kormendi and Lipe, this literature does not ask whether the response is consistent with a particular fundamental valuation model for the security price.

2. In this chapter lowercase letters indicate natural logs of the corresponding uppercase letters.

3. As in our previous paper (Campbell and Shiller [1988]), the results are hardly changed by using White's [1984] heteroskedasticity correction for standard errors.

4. When we use the Fama-French sample periods, 1927–1986, we find that the dividend-price ratio explains 21.9% of the variance of exact four-year real returns. (Four years was the longest horizon they reported.) This roughly confirms their estimated R^2 of 29%. The 30-year average of earnings does only slightly better than the dividend-price ratio over this sample period and return horizon, explaining 22.6% of the variance of returns. When we extend the horizon to ten years, however, the 30-year earnings average explains 47.5% and the dividend-price ratio only 24.8% of the variance of returns.

5. We assume this reinvestment rate of return is equal to the rate of return r implicit in the ρ used in the linearization, that is, $r = g - \ln(\rho)$.

6. In that paper we showed that varying ρ in a plausible range did not greatly affect our conclusions. Here, too, when we set $\rho = 1$ in equation (4) [but retain $\rho = 0.936$ in equation (3)], so that ξ_{it} becomes the simple sum which approximates h_{it}, we obtain very similar results to those reported.

7. Note that as i grows larger, less weight is given in (5) to the terminal dividend-price ratio δ_{t+i}, and hence to the terminal price. One might wonder why the

terminal price is downweighted in an approximate expression for log total return over $t + i$. The reason is that as i is increased, the component of total return due to reinvestment of intervening dividends at the fixed rate grows larger, causing the slope of the log function at the point of linearization to approach zero as i is increased.

References

Campbell, John Y. and Robert J. Shiller. 1987. "Cointegration and Tests of Present Value Models," *Journal of Political Economy* 95:1062–1088.

Campbell, John Y. and Robert J. Shiller. 1988. "The Dividend-Price Ratio and Expectations of Future Dividends and Discount Factors," *Review of Financial Studies* 1:195–228.

Cowles, Alfred and Associates. 1939. *Common-Stock Indexes*, 2nd ed. Bloomington, Indiana: Principia Press.

DeBondt, Werner and Richard Thaler. 1985. "Does the Stock Market Overreact?" *Journal of Finance* 60:793–805.

Fama, Eugene F. and Kenneth R. French. 1988. "Permanent and Temporary Components of Stock Prices," *Journal of Political Economy* 96:246–273.

Fama, Eugene F. and Kenneth R. French. 1987. "Dividend Yields and Expected Stock Returns." *Journal of Financial Economics* 22:3–25.

Flood, Robert P., Robert J. Hodrick, and Paul Kaplan. 1986. "An Evaluation of Recent Evidence on Stock Market Bubbles." NBER Working Paper No. 1971.

Gilles, Christian and Stephen F. LeRoy. 1987. "The Variance-Bounds Tests: A Critical Survey." Unpublished paper, University of California Santa Barbara.

Gordon, Myron J. 1962. *The Investment, Financing and Valuation of the Corporation.* Homewood, Illinois: Irwin.

Graham, Benjamin and David L. Dodd. 1934. *Security Analysis*, 1st ed. New York: McGraw-Hill.

Gregory, Allan W. and Michael R. Veall. 1985. "Formulating Wald Tests of Nonlinear Restrictions," *Econometrica* 53:1465–1468.

Kleidon, Allan W. 1986. "Variance Bounds Tests and Stock Price Valuation Models," *Journal of Political Economy* 94:953–1001.

Kormendi, Roger C. and Robert Lipe. 1987. "Earnings Innovations, Earnings Persistence and Stock Returns," *Journal of Business* 60:323–345.

LeRoy, Stephen F. and Richard D. Porter. 1981. "Stock Price Volatility: Tests Based on Implied Variance Bounds," *Econometrica* 49:97–113.

Mankiw, N. Gregory, David Romer, and Matthew D. Shapiro. 1985. "An Unbiased Reexamination of Stock Market Volatility," *Journal of Finance* 40:677–687.

Marsh, Terry A. and Robert C. Merton. 1986. "Dividend Variability and Variance Bounds Tests for the Rationality of Stock Market Prices," *American Economic Review* 76:483–498.

Marsh, Terry A. and Robert C. Merton. 1987. "Dividend Behavior for the Aggregate Stock Market," *Journal of Business* 60:1–40.

Poterba, James M. and Lawrence H. Summers. 1987. "Mean Reversion in Stock Prices· Evidence and Implications." Unpublished paper, Harvard University.

Sargent, Thomas J. 1979. "A Note on the Estimation of the Rational Expectations Model of the Term Structure," *Journal of Monetary Economics* 5:133–43.

Shiller, Robert J. 1981. "Do Stock Prices Move Too Much to be Justified by Subsequent Changes in Dividends?" *American Economic Review* 71:421–436.

Shiller, Robert J. 1984. "Stock Prices and Social Dynamics," *Brookings Papers on Economic Activity* 2:457–498.

Summers, Lawrence H. 1986. "Does the Stock Market Rationally Reflect Fundamental Values?" *Journal of Finance* 41:591–601.

West, Kenneth D. 1988. "Dividend Innovations and Stock Price Volatility," *Econometrica* 56:37–61.

White, Halbert. 1984. *Asymptotic Theory for Econometricians*. Orlando, Florida: Academic Press.

Wilson, Jack W. and Charles P. Jones. 1987. "A Comparison of Annual Common Stock Returns: 1871–1925 with 1926–85," *Journal of Business* 60:239–258.

9

The Dividend Ratio Model and Small Sample Bias: A Monte Carlo Study

In this chapter, we evaluate the estimates and tests of the present value model in the log linear vector autoregressive dividend ratio model formulation of Campbell and Shiller [1988a,b] (chapter 8). The data generating processes for the simulations are cointegrated vector autoregressive processes that are consistent with the efficient markets model. An estimated vector autoregressive model and an alternative model with an imposed unit eigenvalue are both used.

9.1 The Dividend Ratio Model

The dividend ratio model (Campbell and Shiller [1988a, 1988b, and chapter 8]) states that the log dividend-price ratio δ_t (equal to $d_{t-1} - p_t$, where d_{t-1} is the log dividends per share paid the period before time t and p_t is the log price per share at the beginning of time t) is given by

$$\delta_t = E_t \delta_t^*, \tag{1}$$

$$\delta_t^* = \sum_{j=0}^{\infty} \rho^j [r_{t+j} - \Delta d_{t+j}] - k/(1 - \rho), \tag{2}$$

where r_t is the one-period discount rate at time t. The model was derived by linearizing the exact expression for δ_t, and the constant k equals $\ln(1 + \exp(\delta)) - \delta \exp(\delta)/(1 + \exp(\delta))$, where δ is the point of linearization.

9.2 The Data Generating Processes

Two data generating processes were estimated. The first was estimated subject to the constraint that the present value model holds with a constant

Coauthored with John Y. Campbell. Reprinted with minor editing from *Economics Letters* 29 (1989):325–331; © 1989 Elsevier Science Publications.

discount rate. The second was estimated subject to the constraint that the present value model holds with discount rate varying through time with the commercial paper rate.

Let us consider the first data generating process. The vector for the vector autoregression was $z_t = [\delta_{t+1}, \Delta d_t, \varepsilon_{t+1}^{30}]'$ where ε_t^{30} is a log earnings price ratio based on a thirty year moving average of earnings, as in campbell and Shiller [1988b (chapter 8)]. Let us suppose that z_t is a Gaussian vector first-order auto-regressive (AR1) process:

$$z_t = A z_{t-1} + v_t. \tag{3}$$

As was shown in Campbell and Shiller [1988b] (chapter 8), the efficient markets model (1) requires that

$$e1'(I - \rho A) = -e2'A, \tag{4}$$

where $e1' = [1, 0, 0]$ and $e2' = [0, 1, 0]$. Equation (4) may be interpreted as requiring that the linearized one-period return $\xi_t = \delta_t - \rho\delta_{t+1} + \Delta d_t$ be unforecastable. The restriction (4) can be written in another way:

$$e1' = -e2'A(I - \rho A)^{-1}. \tag{4'}$$

It is a feature of the Wald test that the test statistic depends on the way the restrictions are written. In our previous paper we referred to a Wald test of the restriction (4') as a test that $\delta_t = \delta_t'$, where $\delta_t' = -e2'A(I - \rho A)^{-1}z_t$ or as a test that infinite-period returns are unforecastable. Here, we refer to a Wald test using (4) as the linear Wald test of the model, since (4) is linear in the parameter matrix A, and to a Wald test using (4') as a nonlinear Wald test of the model.

An estimate of the vector autoregression parameters was derived by ordinary least squares subject to the restriction (4).[1] The estimated A and Σ using the full data set in Campbell and Shiller [1988b (chapter 8)] (regressions containing 86 observations, with ξ_t from 1901 to 1986) were

$$A = \begin{bmatrix} 0.6101 & -0.2103 & 0.0862 \\ -0.4289 & -0.1969 & 0.0806 \\ 0.0079 & 0.1041 & 0.8741 \end{bmatrix}$$

$$\Sigma = \begin{bmatrix} 0.0415 & 0.0076 & 0.0338 \\ 0.0076 & 0.0134 & -0.0025 \\ 0.0338 & -0.0025 & 0.0362 \end{bmatrix}$$

The (real) eigenvalues of A are 0.8681, 0.7254, and -0.3062. The largest is fairly close to one, so that its half life is five years. Such eigenvalues are to be expected, as the variables δ_t and ε_t^{30} show some persistence through time.[2]

The matrix Σ is not terribly ill-conditioned, its condition number (the ratio of largest to smallest eigenvalue) is 76.09. Thus, we are not in a situation in which there is a linear dependence among the rows of z_t, as would happen in the case of "no superior information." The no superior information case occurs when the log real price carries only information that is in the other variables in the regression. In that case the only information relevant to forecasting the future comes from dividend changes (Δd_{t-1}), the spread between the current log real dividend and the 30-year moving average of log real earnings ($\delta_t - \varepsilon_t^{30}$), and their lagged values, so that log real price is linear in these and its innovations therefore linear in their innovations. The "no-superior information" case has figured prominently in Monte Carlo evaluations of volatility tests (see, for example, Kleidon [1986], Mattey and Meese [1986], and Fama and French [1988]). In the present case, a component of innovations in δ_t uncorrelated with the other innovations feeds into future movements in dividends. (The moving average representation of the system would give weight to this component in the determination of future dividend changes). The example here can therefore be interpreted as one in which economic agents have some information relevant to predicting future dividends beyond dividends and earnings.

The second data generating process, which assumes that the present value model (1) holds where discount rates move through time with the commercial paper rate, was estimated in the same way, except that the vector $z_t = [\delta_{t+1}, \Delta d_t - r_t, \varepsilon_{t+1}^{30}]$ (all variables demeaned), where r_t is the prime commercial paper rate. In this vector, Δd_t is measured in nominal terms; in effect the interest rate is used to deflate the change in dividends. With this change in data, the same constraint (4) or (4') applies here. The least squares estimates of A and Σ were

$$A = \begin{bmatrix} 0.5840 & -0.2735 & 0.1068 \\ -0.4539 & -0.2560 & 0.1000 \\ 0.0087 & 0.0824 & 0.8743 \end{bmatrix},$$

$$\Sigma = \begin{bmatrix} 0.0410 & 0.0072 & 0.0338 \\ 0.0072 & 0.0129 & -0.0025 \\ 0.0338 & -0.0025 & 0.0363 \end{bmatrix},$$

which are fairly similar to those of the constant discount rate case.

9.3   The Present Value Model Tests

The methods used in Campbell and Shiller [1988a, 1988b, and chapter 8] are to estimate the vector autoregression for z_t and to test restriction (4) or (4') by an ordinary Wald test. The theoretical log ratio $\delta'_t = -e2'A(I - \rho A)^{-1}z_t$ is computed and compared with the actual dividend-price log ratio δ_t. Finally, the theoretical linearized return $\xi'_t = \rho\delta'_{t+1} + \Delta d_t - \delta'_t$ is computed and compared with the actual linearized return ξ_t.

The Campbell-Shiller results [1988b] (chapter 8) for the constant discount rate case are reproduced in table 9.1, panel A. The linear Wald test rejects the restrictions (4) at the 4.1% level; the nonlinear Wald test rejects at a much higher significance level (with a Wald statistic of 104.424 and three degrees of freedom, the computed significance level is 1.545×10^{-9}). The equation determining δ'_t in terms of the vector z_t does not put a coefficient of 1.000 on δ_t and zero on the other two variables, as the efficient markets model requires. The equation determining δ'_t may be interpreted as an equation determining p'_t (equal to $d_{t-1} - \delta'_t$): $p'_t = .776e_t^{30} + 0.256p_t + 0.046d_{t-1} - 0.078d_{t-2}$, where e_t^{30} is a thirty-year moving average of real earnings. This equation does not put all the weight in determining p'_t on p_t as efficient markets would require; rather it puts roughly three-quarters of the weight on e_t^{30} and only one-quarter of the weight on the price p_t. We see that δ'_t is somewhat less variable than δ_t and has little correlation with it. The variable ξ'_t is much less variable than ξ_t but is highly correlated with it. These results were interpreted as indicating a substantial failure of the efficient markets model (1), in the direction of excess volatility for stock returns.

The stochastic simulation results (table 9.1, panel B) are generally supportive of this interpretation of the results. While the size of the 5% linear Wald test is really 8.6%, the rejection of the hypothesis with the actual data occurred at a significance level of 4.1%, and such a rejection occurred in 7.2% of the iterations. Thus, we can say in light of the stochastic simulations that the linear Wald test with our data rejects at roughly the 7% level. The size of the nonlinear Wald test is more problematic: the 5% nonlinear Wald test rejected 23.4% of the time. But the rejection of the nonlinear Wald test with the actual data was so dramatic that in none of the 1,000 iterations was the significance level of the Panel A results achieved. While there is a bias that puts some weight on the extraneous variable e_t^{30} in determining p'_t, the average weight put on e_t^{30} in the stochastic simulations is only 0.215, not, as in the estimated equation, 0.776. There is also a downward bias in the standard deviation of ξ'_t: the

Table 9.1
Vector autoregression results—constant discount rate (real returns)

A. Actual results (from table 8.2, panel A)

Linear Wald test (test of unpredictability of 1-period returns):
significance level = 0.041

Nonlinear Wald test (test that $\delta_t = \delta_t'$):
significance level = 0.000

$\delta_t' = 1.032\delta_t - 0.078\Delta d_{t-1} - 0.776\varepsilon_t^{30}$

$\quad(0.076)\quad\quad(0.046)\quad\quad\quad(0.101)$

$\sigma(\delta_t')/\sigma(\delta_t) = 0.672,\quad\quad \text{corr}(\delta_t', \delta_t) = 0.175$

$\quad\quad(0.074)\quad\quad\quad\quad\quad\quad\quad(0.146)$

$\sigma(\xi_t')/\sigma(\xi_t) = 0.269,\quad\quad \text{corr}(\xi_t', \xi_t) = 0.915$

$\quad\quad(0.067)\quad\quad\quad\quad\quad\quad\quad(0.064)$

Note: Figures in parentheses are standard errors.

B. Simulated results where efficient markets model is true using estimated constrained
VAR model: 1,000 iterations

Linear Wald test: rejection at

5% level: 0.086,　　1% level: 0.021,　　Significance level obtained panel A: 0.072

Nonlinear Wald test: rejections at

5% level: 0.234,　　1% level: 0.147,　　Significance level obtained in panel A: 0.000

$\delta_t' = 1.066\delta_t - 0.034\Delta d_{t-1} - 0.215\varepsilon_t^{30}$

$\quad(0.564)\quad\quad(0.250)\quad\quad\quad(0.634)$

$\sigma(\delta_t')/\sigma(\delta_t) = 0.926,\quad\quad \text{corr}(\delta_t', \delta_t) = 0.946$

$\quad\quad(0.251)\quad\quad\quad\quad\quad\quad\quad(0.063)$

$\sigma(\xi_t')/\sigma(\xi_t) = 0.878,\quad\quad \text{corr}(\xi_t', \xi_t) = 0.950$

$\quad\quad(0.211)\quad\quad\quad\quad\quad\quad\quad(0.049)$

Note: Ratios and coefficients are means across iterations; figures in parentheses are standard
deviations across iterations.

Table 9.2
Vector autoregression results—time-varying discount rate (excess returns)

A. Actual results (from table 8.2, panel B)

Linear Wald test (test of unpredictability of 1-period returns):
significance level = 0.028

Nonlinear Wald test (test that $\delta_t = \delta_t'$):
significance level = 0.000

$$\delta_t' = 0.927\delta_t + 0.046(\Delta d_{t-1} - r_{t-1}) - 0.634\varepsilon_t^{30}$$

$\quad$ (0.144) $\quad$ (0.086) $\qquad\qquad$ (0.217)

$\quad\sigma(\delta_t')/\sigma(\delta_t) = 0.580,$ $\qquad\qquad$ corr$(\delta_t', \delta_t) = 0.309$

$\qquad\qquad$ (0.136) $\qquad\qquad\qquad\qquad$ (0.341)

$\sigma(\xi_t' - r_t)/\sigma(\xi_t - r_t) = 0.485,$ $\qquad$ corr$(\xi_t' - r_t, \xi_t - r_t) = 0.733$

$\qquad\qquad$ (0.044) $\qquad\qquad\qquad\qquad$ (0.188)

Note: Figures in parentheses are standard errors.

B. Simulated results where efficient markets model is true using estimated constrained
VAR model: 1,000 iterations

Linear Wald test: rejections at

5% level: 0.079, $\quad$ 1% level: 0.019, $\quad$ Significance level obtained panel A: 0.046

Nonlinear Wald test: rejections at

5% level: 0.214, $\quad$ 1% level: 0.133, $\quad$ Significance level obtained in panel A: 0.009

$$\delta_t' = 1.045\delta_t - 0.026(\Delta d_{t-1} - r_{t-1}) - 0.187\varepsilon_t^{30}$$

$\quad$ (0.571) $\quad$ (0.254) $\qquad\qquad$ (0.641)

$\quad\sigma(\delta_t')/\sigma(\delta_t) = 0.922,$ $\qquad\qquad$ corr$(\delta_t', \delta_t) = 0.948$

$\qquad\qquad$ (0.262) $\qquad\qquad\qquad\qquad$ (0.065)

$\sigma(\xi_t' - r_t)/\sigma(\xi_t - r_t) = 0.882,$ $\qquad$ corr$(\xi_t' - r_t, \xi_t - r_t) = 0.952$

$\qquad\qquad$ (0.216) $\qquad\qquad\qquad\qquad$ (0.046)

Note: Ratios and coefficients are means across iterations; figures in parentheses are standard
deviations across iterations.

procedure tends to conclude that returns ought to be less variable than they are even when the model is correct. Both of these biases might be interpreted as manifestations of the same general phenomenon reported by Flavin [1983], Kleidon [1986], Marsh and Merton [1986], and others. However, the extent of the bias is not enough to give a likely reconciliation between the model and the estimated regression. Not once in the 1,000 iterations was an estimated standard deviation of ξ_t' less than 0.3 times the standard deviation of actual ξ_t.

Another aspect of table 9.1 is well worth nothing. The stochastic simulations uniformly put a high correlation between δ_t and δ_t': the average correlation was 0.946 with a standard deviation of only 0.063. The actual correlation, at 0.175, was dramatically below this.

Table 9.2 shows the same results for the time-varying discount rate case. The results are very similar to those shown in table 9.1. The rejection of the efficient markets model with the actual data was somewhat less dramatic than in the constant discount rate case: with the actual data the standard deviation of $\xi_t' - r_t$ was almost half that of $\xi_t - r_t$. In only 1.7% of the simulation iterations was the standard deviation of ξ_t' less than half that of ξ_t.

While these results are quite favorable to the interpretation of results in Campbell and Shiller [1988b (chapter 8)], it should be noted that alternative data generating processes are available that give substantially worse small sample performance to the estimators and tests. To show this, we altered the A matrix so that the largest eigenvalue equaled 1.000. This was done by increasing the single element $A(3, 3)$, a parameter that is not involved in the restrictions (4). To achieve a unit eigenvalue, the parameter $A(3, 3)$ had to be increased by 1.413 standard errors in the constant discount rate case, not an implausible amount. Note that the small sample properties of the tests diverge even more from those suggested by our asymptotic distribution theory that assumed stationarity for z_t. Most strikingly, the nonlinear Wald test rejects more than half the time at the 5% level. Still, rejections of the efficient markets model in the constant discount rate case at the significance level found in the actual data occurred less than 1% of the time. In none of the 1,000 iterations was the the estimated standard deviation of ξ_t' less than .3 times the actual standard deviation, as observed with the actual data in table 9.1, panel A.

With the time-varying discount rate case (table 9.4), the unit eigenvalue process small sample properties show about as much discrepancy from the asymptotic properties as we saw in table 9.3. In some respects, the situation looks somewhat worse: 13.4% of the time the nonlinear Wald test rejects at the significance level we observed with the actual data, and 23.8% of the

Table 9.3
Stochastic simulation—unit eigenvalue imposed, constant discount rate (real returns):
1,000 iterations

	Linear Wald test: rejections at	
5% level: 0.210,	1% level: 0.071,	Significance level of table 9.1, panel A: 0.189
	Nonlinear Wald test: rejections at	
5% level: 0.603,	1% level: 0.493,	Significance level of table 9.1, panel A: 0.009

$\delta_t' = 1.060\delta_t - 0.049(\Delta d_{t-1} - r_{t-1}) - 0.459\varepsilon_t^{30}$

$\quad(0.256)\qquad(0.141)\qquad\qquad\qquad(0.378)$

$\sigma(\delta_t')/\sigma(\delta_t) = 0.886,\qquad \mathrm{corr}(\delta_t', \delta_t) = 0.533$

$\qquad\quad(0.361)\qquad\qquad\qquad(0.297)$

$\sigma(\xi_t')/\sigma(\xi_t) = 0.658,\qquad \mathrm{corr}(\xi_t', \xi_t) = 0.914$

$\qquad\quad(0.212)\qquad\qquad\qquad(0.088)$

Note: Ratios and coefficients are means across iterations; figures in parentheses are standard deviations across iterations.

Table 9.4
Stochastic simulation—unit eigenvalue imposed, time varying discount rate (excess returns): 1,000 iterations

	Linear Wald test: rejections at	
5% level: 0.195,	1% level: 0.071,	Significance level of table 9.2, panel A: 0.136
	Nonlinear Wald test: rejections at	
5% level: 0.589,	1% level: 0.484,	Significance level of table 9.2, panel A: 0.134

$\delta_t' = 1.043\delta_t - 0.036(\Delta d_{t-1} - r_{t-1}) - 0.437\varepsilon_t^{30}$

$\quad(0.246)\qquad(0.122)\qquad\qquad\quad(0.345)$

$\qquad\sigma(\delta_t')/\sigma(\delta_t) = 0.828,\qquad\qquad \mathrm{corr}(\delta_t', \delta_t) = 0.533$

$\qquad\qquad\qquad(0.272)\qquad\qquad\qquad\qquad(0.318)$

$\sigma(\xi_t' - r_t)/\sigma(\xi_t - r_t) = 0.660,\qquad \mathrm{corr}(\xi_t' - r_t, \xi_t - r_t) = 0.919$

$\qquad\qquad(0.206)\qquad\qquad\qquad\qquad\quad(0.081)$

Note: Ratios and coefficients are means across iterations; figures in parentheses are standard deviations across iterations.

time the estimated standard deviation of $\xi_t' - r_t$ is less than half that of $\xi_t - r_t$. Here, we do not have a very significant rejection of the efficient markets model.

The unit eigenvalue case that was the basis of tables 9.3 and 9.4 is an extreme one. It implies that dividend-price ratios, earnings-price ratios, and dividend growth rates are all nonstationary stochastic processes. It has not been suggested in the literature that these are nonstationary. We believe that the encouraging results in tables 9.1 and 9.2 are more likely to be relevant to the actual data, which appear to be stationary.

Notes

1. By a change of variables, we define $\tilde{z}_t = Sz_t$, where S is the matrix

$$S = \begin{bmatrix} 1 & 0 & 0 \\ \rho & -1 & 0 \\ 0 & -0 & 1 \end{bmatrix}.$$

Now, $\tilde{z}_t = \tilde{A}\tilde{z}_t + \tilde{v}_t$, where $\tilde{A} = SAS^{-1}$. One imposes the restriction that ξ_t is unforecastable on the coefficients of the second equation, estimates $\tilde{A}$ and $\tilde{\Sigma}$ and then recovers A and Σ.

2. If we were using similar methods to evaluate a VAR-p model with p greater than 1, using the first order autoregressive companion from $z_t = Az_{t-1} + v_t$, then the restrictions (2) would imply that there is a zero eigenvalue for A. This is because one of the rows of A would be $e1'$. However, in the first order case the martix A need not be singular.

References

Campbell, John Y., and Robert J. Shiller. 1988a. "The Dividend-Price Ratio and Expectations of Future Dividends and Discount Factors," *Review of Financial Studies* 1:197–228.

Campbell, John Y., and Robert J. Shiller. 1988b. "Stock Prices, Earnings and Expected Dividends," *Journal of Finance* 43:661–676.

Fama, Eugene F., and Kenneth R. French. 1988. "Permanent and Temporary Components of Stock Prices," *Journal of Political Economy* 96:256–273.

Flavin, Marjorie. 1983, "Excess Volatility in the Financial Markets: A Reassessment of the Empirical Evidence," *Journal of Political Economy*, 91:929–956.

Kleidon, Allan W. 1986, "Variance Bounds Tests and Stock Price Valuation Models, *Journal of Political Economy* 94:953–1001.

Marsh, Terry A., and Robert C. Merton. 1986, "Dividend Variability and Variance Bounds Tests for the Rationality of Stock Market Prices," *American Economic Review* 76:483–498.

Mattey, Joe, and Richard Meese. 1986, "Empirical Assessment of Present Value Relations," *Econometric Reviews* 5(2):171–234, 1986.

10

Comovements in Stock
Prices and Comovements
in Dividends

On October 19–20, 1987, the level of stock prices in all the major stock markets of the world made similar spectacular drops. Some observers have stated that it seems unlikely that negative information about fundamentals appeared in all these diverse economies during the crash. The crash is, however, only one episode. Can stock price comovements overall be justified by comovements in dividends and real interest rates?[1]

Figure 10.1, upper panel shows real dividend indexes for the United Kingdom and the United States for years 1919–1987. Figure 10.1, lower panel, shows the corresponding real price indexes for the United Kingdom and the United States for the end of each year. (These data, which are the basis for the empirical work here, are defined below.) There is some apparent resemblance between the dividend series as well as between the price series. But simple comparisons of such plots do not enable us to ask whether prices covary more than would be implied by efficient markets models. More theoretical apparatus is needed.

10.1 Comovements in The Efficient Markets Model

The efficient markets model is

$$\tilde{P}_{it} = E_t \tilde{P}_{it}^*. \tag{1}$$

Here $\tilde{P}_{it}$ is the price (or transformed price) of a unit of asset i (which may be portfolio i or of index i) and $\tilde{P}_{it}^*$ is the ex-post value corresponding to this asset. E_t denotes mathematical expectation conditional on all publicly available information at time t. In the application below, $\tilde{P}_{it}$ is the detrended real stock price index i and $\tilde{P}_{it}^*$ is the detrended present value at time t of

Reprinted with minor editing from *Journal of Finance* 44 (1989):719–729; © 1989 the American Finance Association.

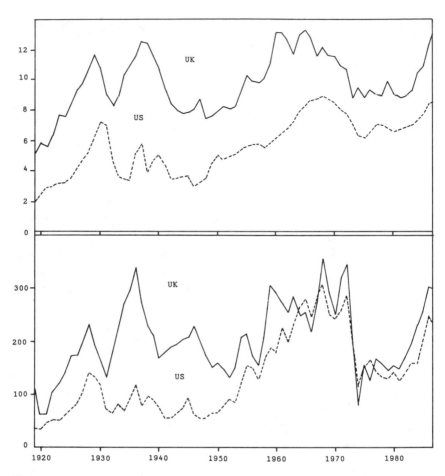

Figure 10.1
Comparisons of annual real dividends and real prices in the United Kingdom and the
United States. (Upper panel) Real Dividend Indexes per share, 1919–1987. (Lower panel)
Real Price Indexes, year end, 1919–1987. See text for source of data.

dividends represented by the stock price index i starting with time t and into the future.[2]

Now, it should first be recognized that, under this model, for two assets i and j, $\text{cov}(\tilde{P}_{it}, \tilde{P}_{jt})$ can exceed $\text{cov}(\tilde{P}_{it}^*, \tilde{P}_{jt}^*)$.

It is in fact possible under the efficient markets model (1) that $\tilde{P}_{it}$ and $\tilde{P}_{jt}$ can be perfectly correlated with each other even if $\tilde{P}_{it}^*$ and $\tilde{P}_{jt}^*$ are perfectly uncorrelated with each other. Suppose that $\tilde{P}_{it}^*$ and $\tilde{P}_{jt}^*$ are independent of each other, and have the same unconditional mean and unconditional variance, and that some information variable I_t is available that reveals the sum: $I_t = P_{it}^* + \tilde{P}_{jt}^*$. The breakdown of the sum into the components is not available; i.e., the information about the two present values is pooled. By the usual errors-in-variables formula (and assuming we have subtracted means from all variables), both $\tilde{P}_{it}$ and $\tilde{P}_{jt}$ will equal $.5I_t$, and hence the two are perfectly correlated. Since the information pooling is positive, the correlation is positive. We can just as well construct an example where the two are perfectly *negatively* correlated with each other. To do that, we would need only to suppose that I_t equals $\tilde{P}_{it}^* - \tilde{P}_{jt}^*$, a case of negative information pooling.

Let us arrange the asset prices $\tilde{P}_{it}$, $i = 1, \ldots, k$, into a k-element vector $\tilde{\mathbf{P}}_t$, and the ex-post values $\tilde{P}_{it}^*$, $i = 1, \ldots, k$, into another k-element vector $\tilde{\mathbf{P}}_t^*$. Then, in vector form, the efficient markets model is

$$\tilde{\mathbf{P}}_t = E_t \mathbf{P}_t^*. \tag{2}$$

Writing $\tilde{\mathbf{P}}_t^* = \tilde{\mathbf{P}}_t + \tilde{\mathbf{U}}_t$, where $\tilde{\mathbf{U}}_t$ is a $k \times 1$ vector of forecast errors, and using the fact that prices at time t are in the information set at time t, we know that the vectors $\tilde{\mathbf{P}}_t$ and $\tilde{\mathbf{U}}_t$ are uncorrelated. Therefore

$$\text{var}(\tilde{\mathbf{P}}_t^*) = \text{var}(\tilde{\mathbf{P}}_t) + \text{var}(\tilde{\mathbf{U}}_t), \tag{3}$$

where $\text{var}(\ )$ denotes a $k \times k$ variance matrix. The ith diagonal element of the above expression is

$$\text{var}(\tilde{P}_{it}^*) = \text{var}(\tilde{P}_{it}) + \text{var}(\tilde{U}_{it}). \tag{4}$$

Diagonal elements of $\text{var}(\tilde{U}_t)$ must be nonnegative because of the positive semidefinite requirement for variance matrices. Therefore

$$\text{var}(\tilde{P}_{it}^*) \geqslant \text{var}(\tilde{P}_{it}). \tag{5}$$

This variance inequality was used by LeRoy and Porter [1981] and Shiller [1981] (chapter 5) to claim that aggregate stock price indexes appear to be too volatile to accord with the present value models. Essentially, stock price indexes $\tilde{P}_{it}$ appear to be more volatile than the ex-post values $\tilde{P}_{it}^*$.

The econometric work in these papers was criticized by Flavin [1983], Kleidon [1986], Marsh and Merton [1986], and others for the stationarity assumptions or small sample properties of estimators. There is some validity to their criticisms, yet the basic conclusion of excess volatility appears to survive them; see below. No one has questioned that (5) is an implication of present value models if the variances shown exist, so we may proceed for the moment under this assumption.

The ijth (off-diagonal) element of (3) is

$$\text{cov}(\tilde{P}_{it}^*, \tilde{P}_{jt}^*) = \text{cov}(\tilde{P}_{it}, \tilde{P}_{jt}) + \text{cov}(\tilde{U}_{it}, \tilde{U}_{jt}). \tag{6}$$

This model does not imply that $\text{cov}(\tilde{P}_{it}^*, \tilde{P}_{jt}^*) \geqslant \text{cov}(\tilde{P}_{it}, \tilde{P}_{jt})$ because positive semidefiniteness does not require that the *off* diagonal elements of $\text{var}(\tilde{U}_t)$ be nonnegative. $\text{Cov}(\tilde{P}_{it}, \tilde{P}_{jt})$ can exceed $\text{cov}(\tilde{P}_{it}^*, \tilde{P}_{jt}^*)$ and be consistent with the model (1) if and only if $\text{cov}(\tilde{U}_{it}, \tilde{U}_{jt}) < 0$, a case that may be referred to as the positive information pooling case.

A negative correlation between $\tilde{U}_{it}$ and $\tilde{U}_{jt}$ may be referred to as a case of positive information pooling because the negative correlation between the error terms implies that there is an advantage in predicting the sum $\tilde{P}_{it}^* + \tilde{P}_{jt}^*$ over the separate components $\tilde{P}_{it}^*$ and $\tilde{P}_{jt}^*$. The prediction $\tilde{P}_{it} + \tilde{P}_{jt}$ of $\tilde{P}_{it}^* + \tilde{P}_{jt}^*$ has an error whose variance is less than the sum of the variances of $\tilde{U}_{it}$ and of $\tilde{U}_{jt}$. In this case the information in $\tilde{P}_{it}$ and $\tilde{P}_{jt}$ may be described as more about a broader aggregate than about either $\tilde{P}_{it}^*$ or $\tilde{P}_{jt}^*$. Of course, if the efficient markets model is wrong, a negative correlation between $\tilde{U}_{it}$ and $\tilde{U}_{jt}$ need not have any interpretation in terms of pooling of information.

If $\text{cov}(\tilde{P}_{it}^*, \tilde{P}_{jt}^*) < \text{cov}(\tilde{P}_{it}, \tilde{P}_{jt}) + \text{cov}(\tilde{U}_{it}, \tilde{U}_{jt})$, then $\text{cov}(\tilde{U}_{it}, \tilde{P}_{jt}) + \text{cov}(\tilde{U}_{jt}, \tilde{P}_{it}) < 0$. This inequality means that the forecast error in the price of one asset tends to be negatively related to the price of the other asset. When one asset has a high price, the other asset tends to be overpriced relative to ex-post value. This implication of the efficient markets model will be tested in table 10.2.

A.   Portfolios of Stocks

Another way of generalizing the original variance inequality (5) to include covariance is to check the condition implied by (1) that

$$\text{var}(\tilde{\mathbf{P}}_t^*) - \text{var}(\tilde{\mathbf{P}}_t) \text{ is positive semidefinite.} \tag{5'}$$

This condition says that for any portfolio of assets (whose prices are elements of $\tilde{\mathbf{P}}_t$) with portfolio price $\tilde{P}_{pt}$ and portfolio ex-post value $\tilde{P}_{pt}^*$,

$\text{var}(\tilde{P}_{pt}^*) \geqslant \text{var}(\tilde{P}_{pt})$; i.e., it is impossible to construct a portfolio with excess volatility. Now, violation of this condition could happen if $\text{var}(\tilde{P}_t^*) - \text{var}(\tilde{P}_t)$ is neither positive semidefinite nor negative semidefinite, which would mean that some portfolios show excess volatility, $\text{var}(\tilde{P}_{pt}^*) < \text{var}(\tilde{P}_{pt})$, but some portfolios do not. For example, it could be that components of the vector $\tilde{P}_t$ show excess volatility but that some portfolios diversify away this excess volatility. Or, it could be that no components of $\tilde{P}_t$ show excess volatility, but because covariances between prices $\tilde{P}_{it}$ and P_{jt} are large relative to covariances between ex-post values $\tilde{P}_{it}^*$ and $\tilde{P}_{jt}^*$, portfolios can be constructed that show excess volatility. This would be a case where blame for failure of the present value model could be placed squarely on the excess covariances rather than excess variances. Violation of the condition (5′) could also happen if $\text{var}(\tilde{P}_t^*) - \text{var}(\tilde{P}_t)$ were negative semidefinite. This would mean that all conceivable portfolios show excess volatility.

We can compute the portfolio weights that minimize excess volatility, i.e., the vector $\mathbf{x}$ that maximizes $\mathbf{x}'(\text{var}(\tilde{P}_t^*) - \text{var}(\tilde{P}_t))\mathbf{x}$ subject to the restriction that $\mathbf{wx} = 1$ where $\mathbf{w}$ is the $1 \times k$ vector whose elements are all one. If a maximum exists, $\mathbf{x}^*$ indicates the importance of excess comovements relative to excess volatility of individual assets.

B.   Individual Stocks

Suppose we made the vector $\tilde{\mathbf{P}}_t$ the vector of prices of all stocks, so that $\tilde{\mathbf{P}}_t$ has thousands of elements, and form the corresponding vectors $\tilde{\mathbf{P}}_t^*$ and $\tilde{\mathbf{U}}_t$. Then an equally weighted market index $\tilde{P}_{\text{indext}}$ is $\mathbf{w}\tilde{\mathbf{P}}_t/k$. The variance of the market index is then $1/k$ times the average variance $\text{var}(\tilde{P}_{it})$ plus $(k - 1)/k$ times the average covariance, $\text{cov}(\tilde{P}_{it}, \tilde{P}_{jt})$. Since k is very large and since covariances are not negligible relative to variances (the market component is a substantial component of individual stock price variance), the variance of the market index $\tilde{P}_{\text{indext}}$ is approximately equal to the average covariance of individual stocks. Similarly, the variance of the market index fundamental $\tilde{P}_{\text{indext}}^*$ is approximately equal to the average covariance between ex-post values $\text{cov}(\tilde{P}_{it}^*, \tilde{P}_{jt}^*)$. Thus, an observation that indexes are excessively volatile is itself an observation that individual stocks covary too much on average to accord with the efficient markets model. Earlier articles (LeRoy and Porter [1981], Shiller [1981]—chapter 5) that claimed to find excess volatility of stock market indexes have shown (if they are right) evidence of excess covariance among individual stocks. But these studies did not provide evidence whether there was excess covariance between U.K. and U.S. stock prices, or between major subindexes.

10.2 Data Analysis

The prices used for the econometric work were detrended by dividing by a long moving average of lagged dividends. This kind of detrending was discussed in Campbell and Shiller [1988b (chapter 8)], where a long moving average of earnings, rather than of dividends, was used to detrend. Our results were similar if dividends or prices were used in place of earnings in the moving average. Since these long moving averages are fairly smooth and trendlike, dividing price by such a moving average is essentially a method of detrending or of removing low-frequency components. Since only lagged (before time t) dividends are used, no future information is used to detrend the price per share at time t. Thus, certain criticisms made in the literature on the use of variance inequalities in econometric work are obviated. Under various nonstationary models for price and dividend discussed in the literature, the detrended price and detrended $\tilde{P}_{it}^*$ will be stationary stochastic processes. There are of course still potential small sample problems in the use of these inequalities to test the model; these will be addressed below.

Two versions of the present value model are considered here. In version I, the discount rate is a constant, equal to the average of the log of one plus the real return on an investment in the portfolio represented by the index. In version II, the discount rate is a short-term interest rate plus a constant term so that the average discount rate is the same as in version 1.

The detrended ex-post value $\tilde{P}_{it}^*$ was computed according to

$$\tilde{P}_{it}^* = \left[\sum_{k=0}^{T-t-1} D_{it+k+1} \prod_{j=0}^{k} \frac{1}{1 + r_{t+j}} + P_{iT} \prod_{j=0}^{T-t-1} \frac{1}{1 + r_{t+j}} \right] \Big/ \bar{D}_{it}, \qquad T \geqslant t. \tag{7}$$

In this formula, the present value of dividends starting with the end of the sample, $t = T$, is proxied by the terminal real price P_T. The moving average of real dividends $\bar{D}_t$ that was used to detrend was an exponentially weighted distributed lag on past real dividends, $\bar{D}_{it} = (1 - \rho) \sum_{k=0}^{\infty} \rho^k D_{it-k}$. The parameter ρ is taken as $\exp(-R)$, where R is the average of the log of one plus the real return on an investment in the portfolio represented by the index, and ρ is the same as the discount factor in version I of the model. For the United Kingdom, the estimated ρ was 0.935, for the United States it was 0.936. The "trend" is just the present value formula worked backward in time rather than forward, and the trend as a forecast of the present value of future dividends is just a forecast that the future will be like the past. The trend was computed recursively from an initial condition by $\bar{D}_{it} = \rho\bar{D}_{it-1} + (1 - \rho)D_{it}$. The detrended price $\tilde{P}_{it}$ is defined as $P_{it}/\bar{D}_{it}$.

This method of detrending, essentially initiated in Campbell and Shiller [1988b] (chapter 8), represents a substantial improvement over previous discussions of the alleged excess volatility of stock prices. If we are to consider whether stock prices move too much or comove too much, we are in effect claiming that stocks should be priced differently. It is important to have in mind some simple different pricing rule that shows less movement or less comovement. In my original paper [1981] (chapter 5) the alternative was a linear trend line for price. In Mankiw, Romer, and Shapiro, [1985] it was a proportional-to-dividend rule for price. These alternatives are less attractive: no one would seriously consider a linear trend or a constant as a forecast for ex-post value, and real dividend series are not at all smooth.

As an alternative to using an arbitrary detrending rule, one may compute an optimal forecasting rule for future dividends derived from a cointegrated time series model. This was done in Campbell and Shiller [1987, (chapter 16)] using a low-order vector autoregressive model. However, by construction, such a model is incapable of forecasting that the present value of future dividends will depend on a long average of past dividends, since lags are limited by the length of the autoregression. When an ARIMA(1, 1, 1) model for aggregate U.S. real dividends was estimated (Shiller [1984])—chapter 1—it was found that the optimal forecast of the present value of future dividends did depend on a log exponentially weighted distributed lag on past dividends, like the one used here to detrend.

The present chapter aims to make a point in the simplest way possible, without reference to complicated time series models and the linearizations needed to make these serve our purposes when there are time-varying interest rates. The simple detrending rule should be interpreted in this light.

A.   The Data

It was felt that a very long span of data was needed to examine the propositions considered here, data covering many decades. Obtaining many observations by sampling frequently will not give us enough data for our purposes. There is a growing recognition of the need for a long time span in financial data—see, for example, Fama and French [1986].

Finding stock price data with very long time spans is difficult. Most individual stocks do not continue for very long in unchanged form. Fama and French examined "survivor" companies that had stayed in business since 1926, but these companies may be different from others. To obtain really long time series of representative stocks we are forced to deal with portfolios of stocks rather than individual stocks, and these can be represented by stock price indexes. Time series index data for prices and dividends in the United States are available back to 1871. Among major countries, only for the United Kingdom was it possible to find a clean, uninterrupted dividend and price series that was nearly as long. Long time series on prices and dividends in Japan are available, but there is a break at World War II, after which major holders of stocks, the Zaibatsu, saw much of their holdings frozen and then sold by the Supreme Command of the Allies in the Pacific. They were given in exchange nontransferable fixed-yen long-term government bonds, which were then effectively expropriated by the postwar inflation. The effect on their net worth is hard to measure. Long time series data on stocks in Germany are also available, but again there is a break at World War II. It is a difficult matter to describe what happened to investments over this break, as treatment of property in the aftermath of the war differed across the four zones. (In the Soviet zone the treatment was disastrous.) It was decided therefore not to use these countries in this study. Of course, omitting them does not necessarily solve the problem: U.K. and U.S. investors must have been aware of the possibility of confiscation of their holdings should the war have ended differently. There is no statistical method to consider infrequent big events that did not occur in the sample.

The U.K. real stock price index P_{UKt} 1919–1987 is the BZW Equity Index (produced by Barclay's de Zoete Wedd) for the end of the year divided by the price deflator (1929 = 1.00) for the year from Friedman and Schwartz [1982], table 4.9, column 4, pp. 132–134 and updated.[3] The BZW Equity Index is an arithmetic market-capitalization-weighted index. The index was created retrospectively for earlier years. Beginning with 1918, the index was constructed from end-of-year share prices of thirty of the largest publicly quoted British industrial and retail companies, excluding financial, mining, and oil companies and companies whose activities were primarily overseas. For years after 1918, changes in the 30 companies were made, in order to make the index as representative as possible of British industry, but in 1962 the index still included 24 of the original 30 companies. Starting with 1963, the index becomes the same as the FT Actuaries All Share Index for December. For version II of the model, the

U.K. nominal short-term interest rate is the three-month treasury bill rate, for the end of the year.

For the United States, the annual real stock price index P_{USt} 1871–1987 is the December Standard and Poor Composite Stock Price Index divided by the December producer price index, and the real dividend series D_{USt} is the corresponding dividends (total for year) divided by the producer price index. The Standard and Poor Composite Stock Price Index and corresponding dividends per share adjusted to index, starting 1926, are from Standard and Poor Statistical Service. Before 1926, the dividends per share are from Cowles [1939]. The producer price index starting in 1913 is the December all commodities producer price index from the U.S. Bureau of Labor Statistics. For years before 1913, it is linked to the December index of all commodities prices from Warren and Pearson [1935] pp. 13–14. For version II of the model, the short rate is the annual return on 4–6-month prime commercial paper, computed from January and July figures under the assumption of a 6-month maturity. These data are from the same sources as in Campbell and Shiller [1988a, 1988b, and chapter 8], and differ from the data used in those papers in that December, rather than January, stock prices and producer price indexes were used. December was chosen to correspond to the specification of the available U.K. stock price and dividend series.

For the United Kingdom a shorter dividend history is available than for the United States. Therefore, different methods were used for the two countries for choosing the initial value for $\bar{D}_{it0}$, where $t0$ is the beginning of the sample used to compute variance matrices. In the United States, dividend series are available for years back to 1871. $\bar{D}_{it0}$ was therefore taken as $(1 - \rho)\sum_{j=1}^{\infty} \rho^{j-1} D_{t0-j}$, where D_{1871} was used to proxy for real dividends before 1871. In the United Kingdom, the real dividend series begins in 1918; however, real price series are available much earlier.[4] Under the assumption that the average dividend-price ratio was the same before 1918, $\bar{D}_{UKt0}$ was taken as $(1 - \rho)\delta\sum_{j=1}^{\infty} \rho^{j-1} P_{UKt0-j}$, where δ is the average prices before 1871. Since a long average smooths over short-term fluctuations, this value for $\bar{D}_{UKt0}$ is likely to be a good proxy for the true value if there is no long term trend in the dividend price ratio, even though δP_{UKt} would be a poor proxy for the dividend in a given year.

B.   Results

Table 10.1 shows variance matrices for the United Kingdom and United States in expression (3). Standard errors, shown in parentheses, are based

Table 10.1
Variance matrices[a]

A. Version I: constant discount rate case					
$\mathrm{var}(\tilde{P}^*_{\mathrm{UK}t}, \tilde{P}^*_{\mathrm{US}t})$		$\mathrm{var}(\tilde{P}_{\mathrm{UK}t}, \tilde{P}_{\mathrm{US}t})$		$\mathrm{var}(\tilde{U}_{\mathrm{UK}t}, \tilde{U}_{\mathrm{US}t})$	
10.63	6.42	46.05	39.73	63.53	53.27
(7.68)	(7.27)	(11.82)	(15.43)	(18.52)	(21.57)
6.42	12.40	39.73	126.59	53.27	116.56
(7.27)	(10.67)	(15.43)	(38.30)	(21.57)	(36.81)

$A = \mathrm{var}(\tilde{P}^*_{\mathrm{UK}t}, \tilde{P}^*_{\mathrm{US}t}) - \mathrm{var}(\tilde{P}_{\mathrm{UK}t}, \tilde{P}_{\mathrm{US}t})$ is negative definite.

x^* (which maximizes $x'Ax$ subject to $wx = 1$): $[0.975, 0.025]'$.

B. Version II: time varying discount rate case					
$\mathrm{var}(\tilde{P}^*_{\mathrm{UK}t}, \tilde{P}^*_{\mathrm{US}t})$		$\mathrm{var}(\tilde{P}_{\mathrm{UK}t}, \tilde{P}_{\mathrm{US}t})$		$\mathrm{var}(\tilde{U}_{\mathrm{UK}t}, \tilde{U}_{\mathrm{US}t})$	
18.64	41.75	46.05	39.73	33.38	60.97
(13.41)	(29.67)	(11.82)	(15.43)	(7.56)	(20.88)
41.75	126.84	39.73	126.59	60.97	307.41
(29.67)	(79.66)	(15.43)	(38.30)	(20.88)	(114.49)

$A = \mathrm{var}(\tilde{P}^*_{\mathrm{UK}t}, \tilde{P}^*_{\mathrm{US}t}) - \mathrm{var}(\tilde{P}_{\mathrm{UK}t}, \tilde{P}_{\mathrm{US}t})$ is neither positive definite nor negative definite.

x^* (which maximizes $x'Ax$ subject to $wx = 1$): $[0.057, 0.943]'$.

a. Annual data 1918–1987, 70 observations. Figures in parentheses are standard errors estimated by bootstrap Monte Carlo simulation, based on an estimated VAR(2) model for the 2-element vector whose variance matrix is estimated, and 1,000 replications.

on stochastic simulations using an estimated model, which is a second-order autoregressive model for each pair of variables whose variance matrix is estimated.[5] The error terms in the simulations were constructed with a bootstrap method, so that normality was not assumed. Panel A shows the constant real discount rate case, version I. Panel B shows the time-varying discount rate case, version II.

In version I, we see from the variance matrices shown that there appears to be not only excess volatility in the individual countries' stock markets [$\mathrm{var}(\tilde{P}_{it}) > \mathrm{var}(\tilde{P}^*_{it})$] but also that the stock price variables move together a lot more than do the ex-post values [$\mathrm{cov}(\tilde{P}_{it}, \tilde{P}_{jt}) > \mathrm{cov}(\tilde{P}^*_{it}, \tilde{P}^*_{jt})$]. There is no evidence of the positive information pooling that might justify the covariance of prices exceeding that of fundamental, that is, $\mathrm{cov}(\tilde{U}_{it}, \tilde{U}_{jt}) > 0$. It was noted above, by viewing figure 10.1, that there is a broad similarity in appearance between the U.K. and U.S. real price series and between the U.K. and U.S. real dividend series. The excess comovement might be described as just the same excess volatility in two closely related countries. The U.S. market shows rather more excess volatility than does the U.K. market, and the portfolio that minimizes excess volatility puts almost all the weight on the U.K. market.

In version II, where time varying interest rates are taken into account, there is weaker evidence that $\text{var}(\tilde{P}_{it}) > \text{var}(\tilde{P}_{it}^*)$ in the United Kingdom and no evidence for this in the United States. The reason is that real interest rates have been quite variable and positively autocorrelated in both countries. A protracted period of predominantly low or predominantly high real interest rates has, by expression (7), a substantial cumulated effect on $\tilde{P}_{it}^*$. In version II we also no longer find evidence that $\text{cov}(\tilde{P}_{it}, \tilde{P}_{jt}) > \text{cov}(\tilde{P}_{it}^*, \tilde{P}_{jt}^*)$ between the two countries. The ex-post values move together more than do the price variables. Real interest rates behaved broadly similarly in the two countries. In both countries, real rates were high in the 1920s, generally negative or negligibly positive in the late 1930s and 1940s, positive in the late 1950s and early 1960s, negative in the 1970s, and high in the 1980s.

Table 10.2 shows regressions of the forecast error $\tilde{P}_{it}^* - \tilde{P}_{it}$ onto the price variable $\tilde{P}_{jt}$. In panel A, where version I of the model is tested, the coefficient of the price variable is always negative, indicating both excess volatility and excess comovement between the United Kingdom and the United States. The coefficient is usually near -1.00. In the own-country regressions such a value for the coefficient indicates that any movements in the price variable are totally due to forecast error. The coefficient is significant at the 5% level in both United Kingdom and United States when forecast errors in one country are regressed on the price variable in the same country ($i = j$). It is also significant at the 5% level when U.S. forecast errors are regressed on the U.K. price variable, but it is not significant when the U.K. forecast errors are regressed on the U.S. price variable. In panel B, we see that when forecast errors in one country are regressed on the price variable in that country the coefficient is substantially negative and significant in both countries. This means that while real interest rate movements are big enough possibly to account for the movements in the stock price variable $\tilde{P}_{it}$, the real interest rate movements in fact do not account for the actual movements. Simply put, it means that when prices are high, they tend also to be high relative to ex-post value. When forecast errors in one country are regressed on the price variable in the other country in panel B, the coefficient is also negative but smaller and statistically insignificant. There is thus a suggestion of excess comovement in the time-varying interest rate case, but there are not enough data to be able to establish this with any authority.

Table 10.2
Regression of forecast error on price variable: $\tilde{P}_{it}^* - \tilde{P}_{it} = a + b\tilde{P}_{jt} + \varepsilon_t$ [a]

		A. Version I: constant discount rate case			
i	j	a	b	R^2	σ_ε
U.K.	U.K.	23.195	−1.074	0.837	3.245
		(2.632)	(−3.504)		
U.K.	U.S.	7.710	−0.348	0.241	6.995
		(0.692)	(−1.063)		
U.S.	U.K.	20.285	−0.924	0.337	8.854
		(2.008)	(−2.638)		
U.S.	U.S.	23.411	−0.911	0.902	3.402
		(1.827)	(−2.431)		
		B. Version II: time varying discount rate case			
i	j	a	b	R^2	σ_ε
U.K.	U.K.	15.903	−0.660	0.595	3.676
		(1.900)	(−2.267)		
U.K.	U.S.	11.309	−0.396	0.597	3.693
		(1.069)	(−1.277)		
U.S.	U.K.	14.759	−0.189	0.005	17.614
		(1.390)	(−0.513)		
U.S.	U.S.	42.96	−1.211	0.606	11.085
		(3.189)	(−3.077)		

a. Annual data 1918–1987, 70 observations. Estimation method is ordinary least squares. Figures in parentheses are t-statistics, corrected for overlapping observations as described in Shiller [1988].

Notes

1. Pindyck and Rotemberg [1988] have analyzed whether there is excess comovement of commodity prices relative to comovements in fundamentals. Their analysis is rather different, in that they did not directly measure the fundamentals.

2. Detrending here is different from that in earlier papers that were criticized for possible spurious trend estimation.

3. The BZW Index was also used by Bulkley and Tonks [1987] in their study of the efficiency of the U.K. stock market.

4. To obtain a price index before 1918, the London and Cambridge Economic Service Index of Industrials (K. C. Smith and G. F. Horne [1934]) was spliced to the de Zoete and Wedd Index by multiplying it by the ratio of the indexes in 1918.

5. With other assumed stochastic processes, of course, the uncertainty about these variance matrices may be even higher. For reasons stressed by Kleidon [10] and others, there may be a bias toward finding excess volatility in small samples. With the log-normal random walk assumption for dividends that Kleidon stressed, there is a tendency for the variance of P_{it} to be greater than that of P_{it}^*, but not so much greater than is actually observed in the United States. See Shiller [1988a] and Campbell and Shiller [1989].

References

Bulkley, George and Ian Tonks. 1987. "Are UK Stock Prices Excessively Volatile?" London School of Economics, Financial Markets Group.

Campbell, John Y. and Robert J. Shiller. 1987. "Cointegration and Tests of Present Value Models," *Journal of Political Economy* 95 : 1062–1088.

Campbell, John Y. and Robert J. Shiller. 1988a. "The Dividend-Price Ratio and Expectations of Future Dividends and Discount Factors," *Review of Financial Studies* 1 : 195–228.

Campbell, John Y. and Robert J. Shiller. 1989. "The Dividend-Ratio Model and Small Sample Bias," *Economics Letters* (forthcoming).

Campbell, John Y. and Robert J. Shiller. 1988b. "Stock Prices, Earnings, and Expected Dividends," *Journal of Finance* 43 : 661–676.

Cowles, Alfred, and Associates. 1939. *Common Stock Indexes*, 2nd ed., Principia Press, Bloomington.

Fama, Eugene F. and Kenneth R. French. 1986. "Permanent and Temporary Components of Stock Prices." *Journal of Political Economy* 96 : 256–273.

Flavin, Marjorie A. 1983. "Excess Volatility in the Financial Markets: A Reassessment of the Empirical Evidence." *Journal of Political Economy*, 91, 929–956.

Friedman, Milton and Anna J. Schwartz. 1982. *Monetary Trends in the United States and the United Kingdom*. Chicago: The University of Chicago Press.

Kleidon, Allan W. 1986. "Variance Bounds Tests and Stock Price Valuation Models," *Journal of Political Economy* 94 : 953–1001.

LeRoy, Stephen F. and Richard D. Porter. 1981. "The Present-Value Relation: Tests Based on Implied Variance Bounds," *Econometrica* 49 : 555–574.

Mankiw, N. Gregory, David Romer, and Matthew D. Shapiro. 1985. "An Unbiassed Reexamination of Stock Market Volatility," *Journal of Finance* 40 : 677–687.

Marsh, Terry A. and Robert C. Merton. 1986. "Dividend Variability and Variance Bounds Tests for the Rationality of Stock Market Prices," *American Economic Review* 76 : 483–498.

Pindyck, Robert S. and Julio J. Rotemberg. 1988. "The Excess Co-Movement of Commodity Prices." National Bureau of Economic Research Working Paper No. 2671.

Shiller, Robert J. 1981. "Do Stock Prices Move Too Much to Be Justified by Subsequent Changes in Dividends?" *American Economic Review* 71:421–436.

Shiller, Robert J. 1988a. "The Probability of Gross Violations of a Present Value Variance Inequality," *Journal of Political Economy* 96:1089–1092.

Shiller, Robert J. 1988b. "A Scott Type Regression Test of the Dividend Ratio Model," *Review of Economics and Statistics* (forthcoming).

Shiller, Robert J. 1984. "Stock Prices and Social Dynamics." *Brookings Papers on Economic Activity* (2):457–498.

Smith, K. C. and G. F. Horne. 1934. "An Index Number of Securities 1867–1914." London and Cambridge Economic Service, Special Memorandom No. 37.

Warren, George F. and Frank A. Pearson. 1935. *Gold and Prices*, New York: John Wiley and Sons.

11   Factors and Fundamentals[1]

Individual stock returns show certain tendencies to move together in tandem. Most important, there is a tendency for *all* stocks' returns to rise and fall together. That is, there is a strong market factor in stock returns.[2] This fact, and the observation that different stocks load somewhat differently onto the market factor, i.e., have somewhat different though generally positive betas, has provided the motivation for the capital asset pricing model (CAPM) in finance. Individual stock returns also tend to move together in groups, apart from the market factor. When one railroad stock price falls relative to the market, other railroad stock prices tend to do so also. That is, there are other factors, besides the market factor, in stock returns. This fact, and the observation that a small number of factors dominate, has provided motivation for the arbitrage pricing theory (APT) in finance.

The presumption in much of the CAPM and APT literature seems to be that these comovements in returns or prices are justified in terms of simple efficient markets models. It is presumed that optimal use of information about future dividends or discount factors would imply this pattern of comovements. For the *market* factor or first principal component this assumption has been drawn into question with empirical work, as we saw in previous chapters. This means that there appears to be too much overall or market comovements in stock returns.

This chapter will repeat such comparisons using other principal components of returns beside the market factor, to see whether comovements of stocks within groups can be justified in terms of comovements in their respective present values. Such comparisons have apparently not been made before. Indeed, data sets used by those who did factor analysis of stock returns (Roll and Ross [1980], Chen [1983], and Chen, Roll, and Ross [1986]) did not span enough time to allow study of the relatively low-frequency movements through time in prices, dividends, and discount factors. If we want to learn whether the various "bull markets" that lasted for many years were justified, we need to have observed many of these bull markets. It is not enough to get many observations by sampling frequently from a short time span (see Shiller and Perron [1985] and Summers [1986]). Roll and Ross [1980] used only 10 years' data, Chen [1983] used only 16 years of data, and Chen, Roll, and Ross [1983] used only 25 years' data. There is good reason why these studies used a short span of data. Individual stocks often do not last very long as separate entities doing a certain kind of business. They may be acquired by other companies, or acquire other companies in different lines of business. Even when there are no mergers or acquisitions, the nature of the business a particular company does may change through time. Thus, we may not expect to see a stable factor structure over long periods of time for individual companies.

There is perhaps a better chance of finding long time series with a stable factor structure when looking at indexes of stocks, rather than at individual stocks. The three component indexes of the composite index maintained by Standard and Poor's back to 1871 are industrials, railroads, and utilities. Of these three, railroads represents a well-defined line of business, essentially unchanged over the whole sample period. (Unfortunately, the Standard and Poor's railroads index was discontinued after 1981, which requires terminating all three data sets in 1981 for this chapter.[3]) The nature of business conducted by the industrials may be considered to have changed substantially since 1871, but broadly to comprise the "smokestack industries," foods, and retailing for much of the period. In the 1870s the Standard and Poor industrials index was comprised primarily of coal, mining, smelting, railway equipment, shipping, and shipbuilding companies. By the turn of the century the industrials index had broadened to include a much richer variety of industries, including foods, retailing, and household products. The utilities indexes also comprise a fairly consistent line of business throughout the century-long sample. Utilities today are electric and gas, gas transmission, telephone, and water companies. Very roughly, they are energy and communications companies. For the early 1870s the Standard and Poor utilities index was composed of water, gas, telegraph, canal, and mail steamship companies. Telegraph companies were offering essentially the same service as do telephone companies today. Canal and mail steamship companies would not be classified as utilities today, but they are in the Standard and Poors Utilities index only until the turn of the century, when they are replaced by electric power companies. Street and elevated railway companies were also in the Standard and Poor's Utilities index for years after the 1890s; these companies were also producers of electric power.

Fama and French [1988] have looked at individual stocks and portfolios of stocks for evidence, in effect, of excess volatility. They too perceived the problem of finding long time series of individual stocks; they described their sample of individual firms as a sample of survivors. Their sample was 60 years long, about a half as long as the 110-year sample used here. However, if we were to do the analysis here on a 60-year sample, then, after allowing for a 30-year moving average of earnings to be described below, we would be left with only 30 years data for testing the model, as opposed to the 80 years here.

In section 11.1, the data will be analyzed as were the U.K. and U.S. stock market data in chapter 10. In section 11.2, principal components of the variance matrix of the component returns will be extracted and the corresponding portfolios of stocks will be examined for excess volatility, i.e., for evidence that the comovements represented by factors other than the first are excessive relative to fundamentals. In section 11.3, a modified version of a regression test used by Scott [1985] is used to do formal significance tests of the efficient markets model using the principal components. In section 11.4, the cointegrated vector-autoregressive methodology described in my work with John Campbell (chapter 8) is used with the principal components to further give indication of the extent of excess covariance in stock prices.

11.1   Covariances in the Simple Efficient Markets Model

This chapter will use the linearized version of the expected present value model that John Campbell and I studied, as described in chapters 4 and 8. The detrended log price $\bar{p}_t$ is defined for each index as $p_t - e_t^{30}$, where e_t^{30} is the thirty-year moving average of lagged log real earnings for that index (as in chapter 8).[4] Table 11.1, panel A, shows covariance matrices in expression (3) of chapter 10 for the three components of the Standard and Poor stock price indexes—industrials, railroads, and utilities—where the discount rates r_t are constant through time and equal to the average return for the component. Data sources are described in the appendix to this chapter. The parameter ρ was taken as 0.949, the log of which is the mean change in real log dividends minus the mean real log return for the Standard and Poor Composite Index 1871–1987.[5] To produce an estimate of the ex-post value $\bar{p}_t^* \equiv p_t^* - e_t^{30}$, $\bar{p}_{1981}^*$ was used in place of the present value of dividends starting in 1981. Table 11.1, panel B, shows the same

Table 11.1[a]

Variance matrices—constant real rates case

A. Discount rate r_t constant and equal to average real return over sample

var(p_t^*)			var($\bar{p}_t$)			var(u_t)			var(ζ_t)		
.027	−.024	.013	.194	.024	.174	.158	.076	.152	.043	.038	.033
−.024	.070	.004	.024	.291	.157	.076	.163	.115	.038	.052	.035
.013	.004	.032	.174	.157	.262	.152	.115	.200	.033	.035	.049

Eigenvalues:

var(p_t^*)			var($\bar{p}_t$)			var(u_t)			var(ζ_t)		
.081	.040	.009	.501	.226	.021	.409	.091	.022	.118	.016	.009

Matrix whose columns are eigenvectors of var(u_t):

.413	.444	−.795	.438	.629	−.642	.556	.491	−.670	.554	−.193	.810
−.910	.236	−.341	.570	−.747	−.342	.487	−.846	−.215	.609	−.569	−.552
.036	.864	.501	.695	.216	.686	.673	.206	.710	.568	.799	−.198

B. Discount rate r_t varying and equal to prime commercial paper rate plus a constant so that mean (r_t) = mean nominal return over sample

var(p_t^*)			var($\bar{p}_t$)			var(u_t)			var(ζ_t)		
.132	.022	.092	.194	.024	.174	.183	.123	.171	.047	.040	.030
.022	.057	.024	.024	.291	.157	.123	.231	.155	.040	.052	.029
.092	.024	.086	.174	.157	.262	.171	.155	.213	.030	.029	.038

Eigenvalues:

var(p_t^*)			var($\bar{p}_t$)			var(u_t)			var(ζ_t)		
.210	.051	.013	.501	.226	.021	.510	.093	.024	.113	.015	.009

Matrix whose columns are eigenvectors of var(u_t):

.768	−.250	.590	.438	.629	−.642	.538	.515	−.667	.607	−.115	.787
.206	.968	.143	.570	−.747	−.342	.579	−.801	−.151	.626	−.540	−.562
.607	−.011	−.795	.695	.216	.686	.612	.305	.730	.489	.834	−.256

a. $\tilde{p}_t$, $t = 1902\text{--}1981$, is a three-element vector whose first element corresponds to industrials, second to railroads, and third to utilities, all Standard and Poor's indexes. Each element is log real price minus the thirty-year average of lagged log real earnings. $\tilde{p}_t^*$ is the three-element vector whose elements are the corresponding log real ex-post value p_t^* minus the thirty-year average of log real earnings. The ex-post value p_t^* is defined as in chapter 4, equation 2′ on p. 93, and the assumption that ex-post value in 1981 equals the 1981 price. For panel A, real dividends are discounted by a constant real rate; for panel B, nominal dividends are discounted by a nominal interest rate and p_t^* then deflated. The vector u_t equals $\tilde{p}_t^* - \tilde{p}_t$.

results where the discount rate is not constant, but equals the prime commercial paper rate plus a constant risk premium, set so that the average discount rate equals the average return on the component. The analysis of the variance matrices in chapter 9 carries over without modification here.

In both panels A and B of table 11.1 the diagonal elements of $\text{var}(\tilde{p}_t)$ are always greater than the diagonal elements of $\text{var}(\tilde{p}_t^*)$. Thus, within each of the three component indexes there appears to be excess volatility, or, equivalently, excess comovement of stock prices within each component index. This confirms for the component indexes earlier results with market indexes. In both panels A and B of table 11.1 the covariances between the price earnings ratios $\tilde{p}_{it}$ and $\tilde{p}_{jt}$ are always greater than the covariances of the ex-post values $\tilde{p}_{it}^*$ and $\tilde{p}_{jt}^*$, and there is never evidence of the positive information pooling (defined in chapter 10) that might justify the discrepancy.

Since $\text{cov}(u_{it}, u_{jt})$ is always positive, it follows that $\text{cov}(P_{it}, u_{jt}) + \text{cov}(P_{jt}, u_{it}) < 0$ for all $i \neq j$. This means that the price of any one component tends to be negatively correlated with forecast errors of another component. This is evidence of excess comovement, relative to the simple efficient markets model. When a price of one component is high, other components tend to be too high, tending to produce negative forecast errors.

The table 11.1 results do not look much different if a thirty-year average of real prices or a thirty-year average of real dividends is used to detrend. Nor do the results depend critically on the length of the moving average, so long as it is a long moving average.

11.2   Factor Portfolios

The three component indexes are highly correlated with each other; to focus attention on the discrepancies between the three indexes it is helpful to look at principal components of the indexes, which are mutually orthogonal.

Expression (3) in chapter 10 contains three variance matrices, with three different sets of eigenvectors. There is yet a fourth variance matrix, that of the excess one-year returns $\zeta_t = \xi_t - r_t$,[6] which may have yet another set of eigenvectors. To accord with past usage in the literature, we shall look at eigenvectors of the variance matrix of excess returns ζ_t, a variance matrix that under the efficient markets model is proportional to the variance matrix of u_t. The proportionality follows from the efficient markets model since the estimated $u_t = \sum_{j=0}^{T-t-1} \rho^j \zeta_{t+j}$ $t < T$, where T is the terminal date equal to 1981 and since the model requires that ζ_t be serially uncorrelated. In practice, of course, the estimated matrices will not have exactly the same eigenvectors.

Eigenvectors and eigenvalues of all four matrices are shown in the bottom half of panels A and B of table 11.1. Note that for all matrices except the variance matrix of $\tilde{p}_t$ the highest eigenvalue corresponds to an eigenvector with approximately equal weight to all three component indexes. This confirms that the market index dominates in prices, though not so strongly in ex-post values. The other eigenvalues are substantially smaller than the first, indicating that the other components of returns have much smaller amplitude than does the first. Very roughly speaking, the second principal component based on eigenvectors of $\text{var}(\zeta_t)$ is utilities minus rails. Also, very roughly, the third principal component based on eigenvectors of $\text{var}(\zeta_t)$ is industrials minus rails.

Letting γ_k denote the kth eigenvector of $\text{var}(\zeta_t)$, let us form the three principal component portfolio log price-earnings ratios $\tilde{p}_{kt} = \tilde{p}_t'\gamma_k$, $k = 1, 2, 3$, and their corresponding ex-post values $\tilde{p}_{kt}^* = \tilde{p}_t^{*'}\gamma_k$, $k = 1, 2, 3$, from data described in the preceding section. The returns on these three principal component "portfolios" will be mutually uncorrelated under the efficient markets model.[7]

Plots of $\tilde{p}_{kt}^*$ and $\tilde{p}_{kt}$ through time for $k = 1, 2, 3$ are shown in figure 11.1 for the constant discount rate case and in figure 11.2 for the time-varying discount rate case.[8] There is strong suggestion of excess volatility only for the case of the first principal component. The excess volatility appears less pronounced in the time-varying interest rate case largely because of the sharp comovement in both plotted series after World War I and into the early 1920s. This comovement is entirely due to the sharp movements in the producer price index over this period, when nominal interest rates did not reflect the producer price index movements.

The second principal component also seems to show some excess volatility, especially if allowance is made for the fact that much of the variance of $\tilde{p}_{2t}^* - e_{2t}^{30}$ in the sample is due to the terminal condition used to compute $\tilde{p}_{2t}^*$.

11.3 Scott-Type Regression Tests

One way of testing for the significance of the apparent excess volatility revealed in figures 11.1 and 11.2 is to regress $\tilde{p}_{kt}^*$ onto $\tilde{p}_{kt}$ and a constant term, $k = 1, 2, 3$. The coefficient of $\tilde{p}_{kt}$ should, under efficient markets,

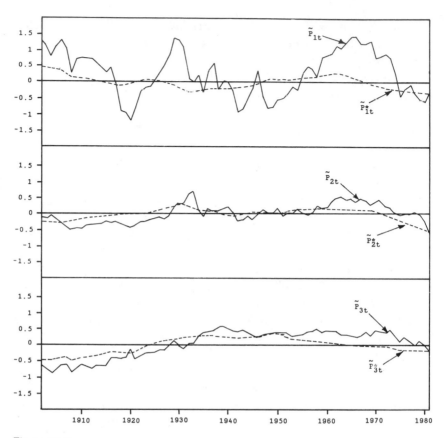

Figure 11.1
Principal components $\tilde{p}_{kt}^*$ and $\tilde{p}_{kt}$—Constant discount rate case, 1902–1981. The first principal component is on top, the second is in the middle, and the third is on bottom. Each series is plotted as a deviation from the mean of the corresponding $\tilde{p}_{kt}^*$.

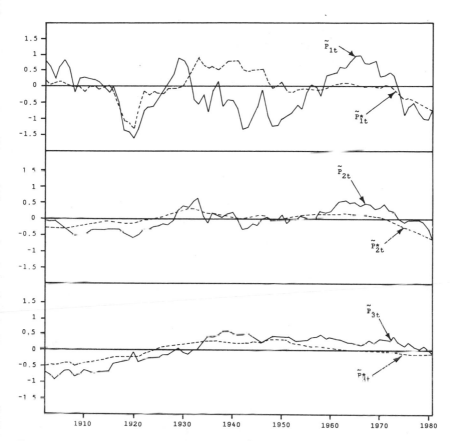

Figure 11.2
Principal components $\tilde{p}_{kt}^*$ and $\tilde{p}_{kt}$—time-varying discount rate case, 1902–1981. The first principal component is on top , the second is in the middle, and the third is on bottom. Each series is plotted as a deviation from the mean of the corresponding $\tilde{p}_{kt}^*$.

be 1.00. Ordinary t-tests for the significance of a departure from 1.00 are not, however, valid, because of serial correlation in residuals. Scott [1985] showed how one can compute asymptotic standard errors for the coefficient of $\tilde{p}_{kt}$ in such regressions. A modification (Shiller [1988]) of Scott's approach will be adopted here.

We know from the model the serial correlation properties of the error term u_t. Now, $u_t = \sum_{j=0}^{T-t-1} \rho^j \zeta_{t+j}$, $t < T$, where ζ_t is the linearized excess return equal to $\xi_t - r_t$, or, from chapter 4, equation (9), $\rho(p_{t+1} - p_t) + (1-\rho)(d_t - p_t) - r_t$ plus a constant and T is the terminal date, here 1981.[9] Since the efficient markets model requires that ζ_t be serially uncorrelated, the serial correlation structure of u_t can be calculated, which may then be used to correct the standard errors of the coefficient estimates. We have

$$\text{cov}(u_i, u_j) = \frac{\sigma^2(1 - \rho^{2(T-\max(i,j))})\rho^{|i-j|}}{1 - \rho^2}, \tag{1}$$

where σ^2 is the variance of ζ_t. Under the efficient markets (null) hypothesis, a regression coefficient $\beta = (X'X)^{-1}X'Y$, where Y is a vector whose ith element is $\tilde{p}_{kt}^*$ and X is a matrix whose ith row is the vector $[1, \tilde{p}_{kt}]$ has a standard error variance matrix given by $(X'X)^{-1}X'\Omega X(X'X)^{-1}$, where Ω is the variance matrix of u composed from (1). For the kth regression in table 11.2, σ^2 was taken as the squared sample standard deviation of ζ_{kt} for the kth principal component.

Table 11.2 shows that for the first principal component, the coefficient of $\tilde{p}_{kt}$ is much less than one, and very significantly so. For the constant r case, this coefficient is 0.130; for the time-varying r case it is 0.155. This is just another manifestation of the excess volatility described in earlier chapters for market indexes. For principal components 2 and 3, the estimated coefficients are also less than one—always less than a half. However, the regression coefficients are not significantly less than one at the conventional 5% level.

The regressions shown in table 11.2 are equivalent to regressions for the kth principal component of the ex-post value p_{kt}^* onto a constant and actual log real price p_{kt} and the 30-year moving average of log real dividends, e_{kt}^{30}, where the coefficients of p_{kt} and e_{kt}^{30} are constrained to sum to one. The coefficient of p_{kt} is then the same as the coefficient of $p_{kt} - e_{kt}^{30}$ shown in table 11.2, and the coefficient of e_{kt}^{30} is equal to one minus the coefficient of $\tilde{p}_{kt}$. Thus, we see that for the first principal component almost all of the weight is put on e_{kt}^{30}; its estimated coefficient is between 0.8 and 0.9 in both the constant and time-varying discount rate cases. For the second and third

Table 11.2
Regressing kth principal component $\tilde{p}_{kt}^{*}$ onto a constant and $\tilde{p}_{kt}$, annual data, 1902–1981[a]

A. Constant real rate used to compute $\tilde{p}_{kt}^{*}$			
	Constant	$\tilde{p}_{kt}$	R^2
First principal component	3.569 (1.537)	0.130 (0.304)	0.205
Second principal component	0.070 (0.232)	0.369 (0.444)	0.334
Third principal component	0.228 (0.216)	0.471 (0.276)	0.693
B. Time-varying discount rate used to compute $\tilde{p}_{kt}^{*}$			
	Constant	$\tilde{p}_{kt}$	R^2
First principal component	3.918 (1.522)	0.155 (0.303)	0.063
Second principal component	0.316 (0.306)	0.403 (0.388)	0.383
Third principal component	0.111 (0.177)	0.468 (0.270)	0.719

a. Modified Scott-type standard errors, as described in text, are in parentheses.

principal components, roughly equal weight is put onto $\tilde{p}_{kt}$ as on $e_{kt}^{*\text{''}}$ in explaining $\tilde{p}_{kt}^{*}$.

Some caution should be maintained in interpreting the test results, as the small sample properties of the tests may be unreliable. Sampling properties of the modified Scott regression test were evaluated by stochastic simulation for century-long sample sizes (Shiller [1988]). In the case where annual real log dividends are a first-order autoregressive process with autoregressive coefficient equal to 0.9, the standard errors given using the above analysis are very close to actual standard errors, and there is little bias in the estimated coefficient. In the log random walk case for real dividends, a case singled out by Kleidon [1986] as particularly bad for the volatility tests, the test rejected too often. However, the estimated coefficient of $\tilde{p}_{kt}$ was less than 0.15 in only 1.4% of the trials, so that we can say that even in this random walk case we can safely reject the efficient markets model for the first principal component. In the random walk case, t-statistics for the hypothesis that the coefficient of $\tilde{p}_{kt}$ equals 1.000 that were over 2.5 in absolute value occurred in 5.7% of the iterations, so that 2.5 is roughly the critical value for tests at the 5% level. The t-statistic for the first principal component was 2.86, so that rejection is clearly valid at the 5% level even in the random walk case. Clearly, in the Kleidon case the coefficients of $\tilde{p}_{kt}$ are not significantly different from one for the other two principal components.

A Linearized Vector-Autoregressive Formulation

A more general vector autoregressive framework, like the one John Campbell and I developed in chapter 8, will make it possible to take into account a large measure of the stochastic properties of prices, dividends, and discount factors to evaluate whether the covariance of stock prices or returns is justified in terms of the efficient markets model. The vector-autoregressive framework takes account in a different way of the fact that ex-post values (p_t^* above) are not observed because dividends beyond the end of the sample are not known. Rather than using the terminal price to proxy for the present value of these dividends, the vector-autoregressive model will be in effect used to provide a forecast of these dividends.

In chapter 8 Campbell and I used a cointegrated vector-autoregressive formulation, where the vector z_t contained the three elements δ_t ($= d_{t-1} - p_t$), $r_{t-1} - \Delta d_{t-1}$, and $\tilde{p}_t$, all demeaned. Using that vector-autoregressive framework, we were able to compute the optimal forecast δ_t' of the δ_t^* in the efficient markets model based on the information set represented in the vector autoregression. If z_t follows a first-order vector autoregression, $z_t = Az_{t-1} + \varepsilon_t$ [essentially as in chapter 8, equation (8)], then the model implies that $\delta_t' = -e2'A(I - \rho A)^{-1}z_t$. Since the actual dividend-price ratio δ_t is an element of the vector z_t, and thus in the information set, it should equal δ_t'. Moreover, the log real price p_t should equal p_t' defined as $d_{t-1} - \delta_t'$ and the excess return ζ_t should equal ζ_t' given by $\zeta_t' = \rho(p_{t+1}' - p_t') + (1 - \rho)(d_t - p_t') - r_t$.

Table 11.3 shows the results for the constant discount rate case. For the first principal component we see that the model shows striking evidence of excess volatility. The equation defining δ_t' puts a weight of 0.802 onto $\tilde{p}_t$; in terms of p_t' this equation implies that $p_t' = .802e_t^{30} + .215p_t + .034d_{t-1} - 0.51d_{t-2}$. Theoretical price is about 80% determined by the long moving average of earnings, and only 20% by actual price. Since the thirty-year average is a very smooth series through time, this means that the theoretical price is much more smooth and trendlike than is the actual price, but that short-run wiggles in p_t' and p_t are highly correlated. The standard deviation of the theoretical excess return ζ_t' is only a quarter that of the actual excess return ζ_t. The theoretical log dividend-price ratio δ_t', has a correlation with it of only 0.202. These are essentially the same results that

Table 11.3
Vector autoregression results—constant discount rate[a]

A. First principal component

VAR test of unpredictability of returns:
significance level $= 0.009$

$\delta_t' = 1.017\delta_t - 0.051\Delta d_{t-1} + 0.802\tilde{p}_t$
$\quad\;\;(0.058)\quad\;\;(0.030)\quad\quad\;\;(0.084)$

$\sigma(\delta_t')/\sigma(\delta_t) = 0.889,\qquad \mathrm{corr}(\delta_t', \delta_t) = 0.202$
$\quad\quad\quad(0.000)\qquad\qquad\qquad\quad(0.092)$

$\sigma(\zeta_t')/\sigma(\zeta_t) = 0.237,\qquad \mathrm{corr}(\zeta_t', \zeta_t) = 0.871$
$\quad\quad\quad(0.063)\qquad\qquad\qquad\quad(0.082)$

B. Second principal component

VAR test of unpredictability of returns:
significance level $= .100$

$\delta_t' = 1.014\delta_t + 0.074\Delta d_{t-1} + 0.511\tilde{p}_t$
$\quad\;\;(0.114)\quad\;\;(0.090)\quad\quad\;\;(0.188)$

$\sigma(\delta_t')/\sigma(\delta_t) = 1.050,\qquad \mathrm{corr}(\delta_t', \delta_t) = 0.783$
$\quad\quad\quad(0.133)\qquad\qquad\qquad\quad(0.125)$

$\sigma(\zeta_t')/\sigma(\zeta_t) = 0.482,\qquad \mathrm{corr}(\zeta_t', \zeta_t) = 0.955$
$\quad\quad\quad(0.156)\qquad\qquad\qquad\quad(0.038)$

C. Third principal component

VAR test of unpredictability of returns:
significance level $= .022$

$\delta_t' = 0.727\delta_t - 0.008\Delta d_{t-1} + 0.182\tilde{p}_t$
$\quad\;\;(0.127)\quad\;\;(0.058)\quad\quad\;\;(0.222)$

$\sigma(\delta_t')/\sigma(\delta_t) = 0.532,\qquad \mathrm{corr}(\delta_t', \delta_t) = 0.881$
$\quad\quad\quad(0.083)\qquad\qquad\qquad\quad(0.333)$

$\sigma(\zeta_t')/\sigma(\zeta_t) = 0.605,\qquad \mathrm{corr}(\zeta_t', \zeta_t) = 0.790$
$\quad\quad\quad(0.142)\qquad\qquad\qquad\quad(0.128)$

a. Standard errors are in parentheses.

with it of only 0.202. These are essentially the same results that Campbell and I found in chapter 8 for the Standard and Poor Composite Index.

For the second principal component, the results also suggest excess volatility, but less dramatically. The implied equation for p'_t puts about equal weight on p_t and e_t^{30}. The theoretical excess return ζ'_t is about half as variable as the actual excess return. For the third principal component, the evidence for excess volatility is even weaker still.

Table 11.4 reports results for the time-varying discount rate case. For the first principal component there is again substantial evidence of excess volatility. Almost all of the weight in determining p'_t is given to e_t^{30}, and little to actual price. Theoretical excess returns ζ'_t are less than half as variable as actual excess returns; the evidence for excess volatility is less dramatic than in the case of the constant discount rate. The results for the second and third principal components are similar to those in the constant discount rate case; the sum of the elements in the eigenvectors used to form the principal components are approximately zero, so the variable r_t representing time variation of the discount rate nearly drops out of the second and third principal components.

John Campbell and I did Monte Carlo evaluation of the small sample properties of the statistics reported in table 11.3 and 11.4; these are reported in chapter 9. Under the assumptions of the simulation, the small sample properties are not unreliable, and so we can take the estimated ratios in tables 11.3 and 11.4 of $\sigma(\zeta'_t)/\sigma(\zeta_t)$ as evidence for excess volatility in the second and third principal components. However, as the Monte Carlo experiments are not conclusive evidence as to the small sample properties of the estimators, some caution sould be taken before asserting that there is evidence of excess volatility in principal components other than the first.

11.4   Conclusion

The evidence for excess volatility for principal component portfolios other than the first was substantially weaker than for the first principal component portfolio, or market portfolio.

We should not, however, overgeneralize from this result to assume that there is not substantial excess volatility for groupings of stocks other than the principal components portfolios studied here. The construction of the principal components portfolios here relied on the aggregation of stocks by index number producers into the broad categories industrials, rails, and utilities. There may not have been any excess volatility in the differences in prices between these groupings, if investor attitudes did not single out

Table 11.4
Vector autoregression results—varying discount rate[a]

A. First principal component

VAR test of unpredictability of excess returns:
significance level = 0.010

$$\delta'_t = 0.991\delta_t - 0.149(\Delta d_{t-1} - r_{t-1}) + 0.872\bar{p}_t$$
$$\quad\;\; (0.095) \quad\;\; (0.056) \qquad\qquad (0.163)$$

$\sigma(\delta'_t)/\sigma(\delta_t) = 0.976,\qquad \text{corr}(\delta'_t, \delta_t) = 0.102$
$\qquad\quad (0.168) \qquad\qquad\qquad (0.147)$

$\sigma(\zeta'_t)/\sigma(\zeta_t) = 0.447,\qquad \text{corr}(\zeta'_t, \zeta_t) = 0.339$
$\qquad\quad (0.070) \qquad\qquad\qquad (0.285)$

B. Second principal component

VAR test of unpredictability of excess returns:
significance level = .114

$$\delta'_t = 1.088\delta_t + 0.094(\Delta d_{t-1} - r_{t-1}) + 0.470\bar{p}_t$$
$$\quad\;\; (0.141) \quad\;\; (0.106) \qquad\qquad (0.225)$$

$\sigma(\delta'_t)/\sigma(\delta_t) = 1.094,\qquad \text{corr}(\delta'_t, \delta_t) = 0.832$
$\qquad\quad (0.157) \qquad\qquad\qquad (0.127)$

$\sigma(\zeta'_t)/\sigma(\zeta_t) = 0.585,\qquad \text{corr}(\zeta'_t, \zeta_t) = 0.924$
$\qquad\quad (0.193) \qquad\qquad\qquad (0.069)$

C. Third principal component

VAR test of unpredictability of excess returns:
significance level = .009

$$\delta'_t = 0.584\delta_t - 0.051(\Delta d_{t-1} - r_{t-1}) + 0.129\bar{p}_t$$
$$\quad\;\; (0.185) \quad\;\; (0.091) \qquad\qquad (0.338)$$

$\sigma(\delta'_t)/\sigma(\delta_t) = 0.784,\qquad \text{corr}(\delta'_t, \delta_t) = 0.970$
$\qquad\quad (0.461) \qquad\qquad\qquad (0.113)$

$\sigma(\zeta'_t)/\sigma(\zeta_t) = 0.865,\qquad \text{corr}(\zeta'_t, \zeta_t) = 0.771$
$\qquad\quad (0.208) \qquad\qquad\qquad (0.134)$

a. Standard errors are in parentheses.

these groupings for attention. In short, there may have been speculative excesses and collapses for various categories of stocks as well as the market index, without there being such for railroad stocks and utilities stocks as groups apart from the market index. Alternatively, one might say that the results are consistent with the notion that much of the volatility of stock prices is due to changes through time in a market-wide rate of discount r_t, which, subject to the log-linear approximation, does not impinge on log relative prices.

The evidence for excess volatility is weaker for other principal components. The point estimates do, however, indicate that for portfolios other than the first the optimal forecast of the present value of future log real dividends estimated here puts no more than half of the weight on current log real price, and at least half on the crude moving average of lagged log real earnings.

Appendix: Sources of Data

The industrial, railroad, and utilities price indexes starting 1871 as well as the dividend and earnings series starting 1926 are from Standard and Poor's Statistical Service, Security Price Index Record. Prices are averages for January, dividends and earnings are four quarter totals. For years before 1926 the dividend and earning series are derived from Alfred Cowles [1939]. The Cowles price series are identical to the Standard and Poor's series before 1926, except for a rescaling due to change in base year. The interest rate is from chapter 26, table 26.1, series 4. The price deflator is the from chapter 26, table 26.2, series 5.

Notes

1. This chapter draws heavily on previous joint work with John Campbell, who also made helpful suggestions.

2. In this chapter, the term "factor" is used loosely; the empirical work here uses principal components analysis rather than factor analysis per se.

3. The postwar period has seen increasing concentration and government involvement in the railroad industry. While the railroad index shows the lowest growth of the three indexes in the postwar period, it has not shown a sharp drop in real value.

4. Since earnings are available starting in 1872 for all three indexes, the first year for which a moving average of 30 years of lagged earnings is available is 1902.

5. The choice of the parameter ρ is not terribly critical for the log linear model used here, see Campbell and Shiller [1988a]. Since growth-adjusted interest rates cannot

be forecasted well into the distant future, the weighting given the distant future does not affect regressions of $\tilde{p}_t^*$ onto $\tilde{p}_t$ very much. Thus, the same value of ρ is used for all three component indexes.

6. Here, ξ_t is an approximation to $\ln((P_{t+1} + D_t)/P_t)$, as defined in chapter 8.

7. These are not true portfolio prices since combinations of logs rather than levels are taken.

8. Note that $\tilde{p}_{kT} = \tilde{p}_{kT}^*$, $k = 1, 2, 3$, where $T = 1981$. This is so by construction, since the terminal $\tilde{p}_{kT}$ was used to proxy for the present value in 1981 of dividends starting in 1981.

9. This relation is the log linear model analog of equation (7) of chapter 4, since ζ_t is proportional to the innovation in log price at time $t + 1$.

References

Campbell, John Y., and Robert J. Shiller. 1987. "Cointegration and Tests of Present Value Models," *Journal of Political Economy* 95 : 1062–1088.

Campbell, John Y., and Robert J. Shiller. 1988a. "The Dividend-Price Ratio and Expectations of Future Dividends and Discount Factors," *Review of Financial Studies* 1 : 195–228.

Campbell, John Y., and Robert J. Shiller. 1988b. "Stock Prices, Earnings, and Ex pected Dividends," *Journal of Finance* 43 : 661–676.

Chen, Nai-Fu. 1983. "Some Empirical Tests of the Theory of Arbitrage Pricing," *Journal of Finance* 38 : 1393–1414.

Chen, Nai-Fu, Richard Roll, and Stephen A. Ross. 1986. "Economic Forces and the Stock Market," *Journal of Business* 59 : 383–403.

Cowles, Alfred, III, and Associates. 1939. *Common-Stock Indexes*, Second Edition, Bloomington Indiana: Principal Press.

Fama, Eugene F., and Kenneth R. French. 1988a. "Dividend Yields and Expected Stock Returns," *Journal of Financial Economics* 22 : 3–25.

Fama, Eugene F., and Kenneth R. French. 1988b. "Permanent and Temporary Components of Stock Prices," *Journal of Political Economy* 96 : 246–273.

Flood, Robert P., Robert J. Hodrick, and Paul Kaplan. 1986. "An Evaluation of Recent Evidence on Stock Market Bubbles," NBER Working Paper No. 1971.

Gilles, Christian, and Stephen F. LeRoy. 1987. "The Variance-Bounds Tests: A Critical Survey," unpublished paper, University of California Santa Barbara.

Gordon, Myron J. 1962. *The Investment, Financing and Valuation of the Corporation*, Homewood, Illinois: Irwin.

Hansen, Lars Peter, and Robert J. Hodrick. 1980. " Forward Exchange Rates as Optimal Predictors of Future Spot Rates: An Econometric Analysis," *Journal of Political Economy* 88:829—853.

Kleidon, Allan W. 1986. "Variance Bounds Tests and Stock Price Valuation Models," *Journal of Political Economy* 94:953—1001.

LeRoy, Stephen F., and Richard D. Porter. 1981. "Stock Price Volatility: Tests Based on Implied Variance Bounds," *Econometrica* 49:97—113.

Mankiw, N. Gregory, David Romer, and Matthew D. Shapiro. 1985. "An Unbiased Reexamination of Stock Market Volatility," *Journal of Finance* 40:677—687.

Marsh, Terry A., and Robert C. Merton. 1986. "Dividend Variability and Variance Bounds Tests for the Rationality of Stock Market Prices," *American Economic Review* 76:483—498.

Marsh, Terry A., and Robert C. Merton. 1987. "Dividend Behavior for the Aggregate Stock Market," *Journal of Business* 60:1—40.

Poterba, James M., and Lawrence H. Summers. 1988. "Mean Reversion in Stock Prices: Evidence and Implications," *Journal of Financial Economics* 22:26—59.

Pindyck, Robert S., and Julio J. Rotemberg. 1987. "The Excess Co-Movement of Commodity Prices," reproduced, Massachusetts Institute of Technology.

Roll, Richard, and Stephen A. Ross. 1980. "An Empirical Investigation of the Arbitrage Pricing Theory," *Journal of Finance* 35:1073—1103.

Sargent, Thomas J. 1979. "A Note on the Estimation of the Rational Expectations Model of the Term Structure," *Journal of Monetary Economics* 5:133—143.

Scott, Louis O. 1985. "The Present Value Model of Stock Prices: Regression Tests and Monte Carlo Results," *Review of Economics and Statistics* 67:599—605.

Shea, Gary. 1988. "Ex-Post Rational Price Approximations and the Empirical Reliability of the Present Value Relation," presented at the NATO Advanced Research Workshop, A Reappraisal of the Efficiency of Financial Markets, Sesimbra, Portugal.

Shiller, Robert J. 1988. "A Scott-Type Regression Test of the Dividend-Ratio Model," Review of Economics and Statistics (forthcoming).

Shiller, Robert J., and Pierre Perron. 1985. "Testing the Random Walk Hypothesis: Power versus Frequency of Observation," *Economics Letters* 18:381—386.

Summers, Lawrence H. 1986. "Does the Stock Market Rationally Reflect Fundamental Values?" *Journal of Finance* 41:591—601.

West, Kenneth D. 1988. "Dividend Innovations and Stock Price Volatility," *Econometrica* 56:37—61.

III

The Bond Market

12　　　　Overview

Long-term bonds are assets whose prices show the same sort of mysterious volatility that we see in the stock market. While short-term debt is very safe if there is little default risk, long-term bonds tend to fluctuate greatly in value from day to day, since the price at which one can sell the bond tomorrow to another investor is not well tied down by the maturity value many years hence. Analysts have the same difficulty explaining long-term bond price movements, even after the fact, that they have for stock price movements. It is natural to suspect that popular models may induce the same sort of excess volatility in the bond market as they appear to do in the stock market.

Simple efficient markets theories claim that the fluctuations in the bond market are explainable with theoretical models that resemble those applied in the stock market. Here, it is more convenient to talk in terms of the long-term interest rate, the yield to maturity that is computed from the price of the long-term bond, rather than of price itself. The efficient markets theories can be described as asserting that the long-term interest rate R_t is the optimal forecast of its perfect foresight value or ex-post value R_t^*. The latter depends on economic variables between time t and the maturity date. In this part of the book, two efficient markets theories are considered: the simple expectations theory of the term structure of interest rates, and the Fisher theory of inflationary expectations. The two theories differ in their specification of R_t^*.

By the simple expectations theory of the term structure, R_t^* is a sort of average of short-term interest rates from time t until the maturity of the bond (plus a constant risk premium). The reason for considering such an R_t^* is simple. If short-term interest rates were expected to be a lot lower than the long rate on average over this period, then borrowers would have an incentive not to borrow long (i.e., not to issue long term bonds) and instead to borrow at a short rate, refinancing repeatedly until the maturity date. If short-term interest rates were expected to be a lot higher than the long rate on average over this period, then lenders would have an incentive not to lend long (i.e., not to buy long term bonds) and instead to invest in a series of short bonds. These tendencies will tend to enforce a relationship between long and short rates that can be described by saying that R_t optimally forecasts R_t^*: $R_t = E_t R_t^*$. Those mysterious movements in long-term interest rates are, by this theory, just due to new information about the average of future short rates. R_t and R_t^* by the expectations theory are plotted together here in the next chapter (figure 13.3) and in chapter 15 (figure 15.3).

By the other efficient markets theory, the Fisher theory, R_t^* is a sort of average of *inflation* rates (rates of change in the price of a market basket of goods), rather than short-term interest rates, from time t until maturity (plus a constant). The reason to expect R_t to equal $E_t R_t^*$ is the same as with the simple expectations theory of the term structure, except that the alternative to investing at the long rate would be investing in the market basket of goods or a proxy for that. R_t and R_t^* by the Fisher theory are plotted together in chapter 14 (figure 14.4).

The chapters in this part of the book consider the evidence on the efficient markets theories that are revealed by these data, concluding that the evidence is rather mixed, supporting the simple expectations theory of the term structure incompletely but more strongly denying the Fisher theory. The next chapter (chapter 13) is a survey chapter, which is relatively nontechnical and graphical in its approach, and which introduces the succeeding chapters. Chapter 14, written with Jeremy Siegel in 1977, is a study of the Fisher theory and the associated phenomenon, the positive correlation between long rates and prices associated with the term "Gibson Paradox." Chapter 15, which I wrote in 1979, is a study of the simple expectations theory of the term structure, and is the first paper to set forth the basic variance bounds tests. Chapter 16, written with John Campbell in 1987, uses a cointegrated vector-autoregressive methodology to study the expectations theory. (This chapter also includes a discussion of the stock market.) Note that some of the rather negative conclusions on the expectations theory stated in chapter 15 are modified in chapters 13 and 16, written subsequently.

Bonds differ from common stocks in that the "dividends" (here called coupons and principal) are prespecified in nominal terms. Thus, time variation in real dividends can be ascribed solely (disregarding the possibility of default or call) to changes in the price level measure used to convert nominal dividends into real dividends. This means that the real dividend series in the bond market looks a lot different from that in the stock market. Studying the bond market may give us some largely independent evidence about market volatility.

Another important difference between the stock markets and the bond markets is the alternative to the efficient markets hypothesis that we will want to consider. The investing public puts bonds in a very different mental category from stocks, and has a different set of popular models to understand the bond market. Thus, we might expect that the results of tests of market efficiency may be very different in the bond market.

Of course, yet another difference between bonds and stocks is that most bonds are not perpetuities and have a maturity date. For long-term bonds the maturity date is so far removed (typically 25 or more years) that this difference may not be important. The chapters in this book on the bond market emphasize such long-term bonds and perpetuities (British consols). Most of the empirical literature on the term structure of interest rates (which I have surveyed elsewhere—Shiller [1989]) has emphasized much shorter bonds, notes, or bills. The longer instruments perhaps more closely resemble common stocks in that their value is not tied down in the near future by the principal at maturity.

Since bonds are basically like stocks as claims on a long well-measured sequence of dividends, an analysis of bond market volatility can proceed in much the same terms as stock market volatility. The theoretical literature generally applies the same kinds of models to both. However, studies of the bond market are typically conducted in rather different terms, in terms of yield to maturity rather than price. Yield to maturity is of course a nonlinear transformation of price, given coupon and maturity. The common time series data on finite maturity bonds do not follow individual bonds (whose time to maturity would decline as time proceeds) but show yields on bonds of fixed maturity.

The chapters on the bond market in this book primarily consider two theories of the bond market: a linearized rational expectations theory of the term structure and a linearized rational Fisher model (after Irving Fisher [1930]). Both of these theories are analogues of models for the stock market considered in the overview chapter on the stock market (chapter 3). The linearized rational expectations model of the term structure [chapter 15, equation (1)] relates long rates to a long weighted average of expected future short rates, with weights that decline into the future. This is essentially the bond market application of the version of the model in chapter 4 that related price to the rationally expected present value of nominal dividends discounted by nominal short interest rates (and represented for the stock market in figures 4.2 and 4.4). Obviously, since nominal dividends are constant the model is a relation among interest rates of different maturities only. The linearized rational expectations Fisher model [derived by Jeremy Siegel and myself in chapter 14, equation (1)] relates long rates to a weighted average of expected future inflation rates with weights that decline into the future. It is essentially the bond market application of the model developed in chapter 4 in which price is related to the present value of real dividends discounted by constant discount rates (and represented for the stock market in figures 4.1 and 4.3). Obviously, since real dividends in the bond market change through time only due to inflation, this is a theory about the relation of long-term interest rates to expected future inflation rates.

This chapter will describe the research on the volatility of the bond market, both my own research and the relevant literature, in an intuitive rather than technical manner. Simple plots will be used here to make points when possible.

13.1 The Expectations Theory of the Term Structure

While the expectations theory of the term structure is analogous to an efficient markets theory applied to the stock market, when one looks at the data, there is a striking contrast. There are senses in which the long-term interest rate appears to be largely justified in terms of expectations of future short-term interest rates. It was found in Shiller [1972] and Modigliani

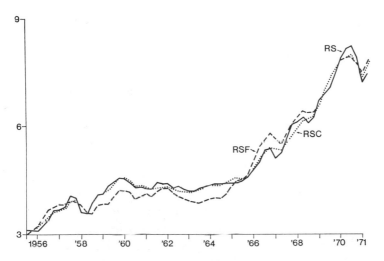

Figure 13.1
Plot of Moody Aaa Corporate Bond Yield Average (RS) with the estimated forecast (RSF) of the weighted average of future short rates based on current and lagged short rates and inflation rates, and with fitted values (RSC) in a distributed lag regression on inflation and short-term interest rates. Source: Modigliani and Shiller [1973].

and Shiller [1973] that for 1956 to 1971 the long-term interest rates behave similarly through time to the optimal forecast of the present value of one-period interest rates based on a simple vector-autoregressive forecasting mechanism. This can be seen clearly in a plot in Modigliani and Shiller [1973], reproduced in this chapter as figure 13.1. In this figure, the optimal forecast of the present value of future short-term interest rates RSF is plotted with the actual long-term interest rate RS and the fitted values RSC in a regression of RS on the information set used in the forecast RSF. The similarity between the long rate RS and the optimal forecast RSF suggests some element of truth to the rational expectations model. RS and RSF are much more similar in appearance than are the long rate and the short rate, even though RSF is itself largely determined by current and past short rates. The similarity of RS and RSC suggests that movements in long rates are actually a response to this information set. Long-term interest rates are fairly well described as a long weighted average (or distributed lag) on short rates and inflation rates, and this weighted average is approximately optimal in the context of the rational expectations model.[1]

The original idea for this rational expectations model came from Richard Sutch, who had written a Ph.D. dissertation under Modigliani a few years earlier [1967], and made the basic point that the long rate looks something like an optimal forecast of an average of future short rates based on a univariate autoregressive forecasting model.

Sutch did not promote his results. He did not dwell long on it in his dissertation and did not publish the results. He wrote several papers with Franco Modigliani on the term structure of interest rates, and none mentioned his rational expectations model of the term structure.

Although I published the results with Modigliani, I really was not a strong promoter of these results either, and later tried to knock them down. I think perhaps that the biggest reason why I did not fully believe the results is extrapolation from evidence about the stock market and other speculative markets, where rational expectations models really did not seem to be performing well. It did not seem at all likely that the long-term interest rate would really be set using fully optimal forecasts of future short-term interest rates. Another reason I felt this was that when I tried the procedure with a short pre–World War II sample period, the results were not at all encouraging.[2] It was not until much later that I tried the methods on long sample periods with a variety of data sets [1987] and found less reason to be discouraged.

Another issue that caused me to doubt that the results were genuine had to do with a unit roots problem. In order for the procedure to produce reliably good results, I had to impose a unit root on the autoregressive equation for the short rate—imposing that the sum of coefficients in the regression of short rates on their lagged values would sum to one. When this was not imposed, sometimes the results were apparently far less encouraging for the rational expectations model. I knew that the sum of the coefficients was not well enough measured to allow good estimation of the distributed lag that the long rate *should* have on the short rate.

These results led me to try another tack and try to find evidence *against* the expectations model.

13.2   Variance Bounds Tests of the Expectations Hypothesis

My 1979 article (chapter 15) asserted that the variance of the short rate must be higher than the sample variance if the kind of volatility of long-term interest rates we observe is to be explained in terms of the expectations model of the term structure. This point sounds analogous to the claim for excess volatility I made for the stock market, and one might be inclined to interpret the evidence as suggesting "fashions and fads" in financial markets. However, in my paper it was reported that the variance inequalities are all only on the borderline of being violated for the sample periods other than short sample periods in the interval between 1956 and 1977. Thus, the paper did not find strong evidence of such excess volatility.

The inequality (I-1) [which is analogous to inequality (5) or (6) in chapter 4] in chapter 15 was strongly violated for the 1966–1977 period in the United States or the 1956–1977 period in the United Kingdom: the standard deviation of holding period yields was about twice the upper limit given by the inequality.[3] But short-term interest rates rose much further than ever before in history after 1977. Shortly after I finished this paper, the Federal Reserve announced its "new operating procedures," which made short-term interest rates much more volatile; short rates also soared to new record levels in the United Kingdom around the same time. Moreover, both U.S. and U.K. short-term interest rates were extremely low in the years of the '30s and '40s. Extending the sample back to 1935 and up to the present substantially increases the sample standard deviation of the short rate, but has much less effect on the standard deviation of the holding period yield, both for the United States and the United Kingdom, tending sharply to reduce the extent of violation of the inequality (I-1).

Interest rate data are of course available going back very far in time. Long historical series on long rates R_t and short rates r_t are plotted in figure 13.2 for the United States (top) and for the United Kingdom (bottom). For the United States the series are biannual from 1857-1 to 1988-1; for the United Kingdom the series are annual 1824–1987. With these data, the inequality (I-1) is only mildly violated for either the United States or the United Kingdom here with the full sample and the sample mean long rate as the point of linearization.[4] For U.S. data 1857–1987 the sample standard deviation of holding period yields $\sigma(H)$ is 1.14 times the upper bound given by (I-1).[5] This violation is too narrow to be accorded much significance. For U.K. data, over the years 1824–1986 the sample standard deviation of holding period yields $\sigma(H)$ is 1.57 times the upper bound given by (I-1). But of course, judging from the plot, the sharp upturn in interest rates in the postwar period suggests nonstationarity, so that perhaps we can not measure the variances that enter the inequalities well. There is a long period of time in which U.K. short rates look much more stationary—say, 1824–1930. In this period with the U.K. data there is a slight violation of the inequality (I-1): the left-hand side of the inequality is about 1.13 times the right-hand side. But one might counter that the movements in the long rates in this period might not be excessive if people thought then that the short rates might at any time break into something like their post-1930 behavior.

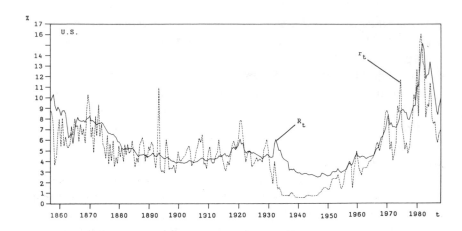

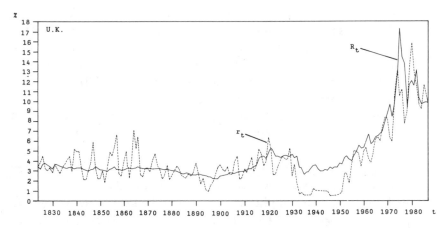

Figure 13.2
Interest rates: Long term (R_t) and short term (r_t). (Top) U.S. long-term corporate bond
yields R_t (solid line) and U.S. 4–6-month commercial paper rate r_t (dashed line), biannual
data 1857-1 to 1988-1. (Bottom) U.K. consol yield R_t (solid line) and U.K. 3-month bank
bill rate r_t (dashed line), annual data 1824–1987. See appendix for sources of data.

In my 1979 paper (chapter 15), I presented a plot (figure 15.3) of the "perfect foresight" long-term interest rate R_t^* and the actual long-term interest rate R_t. R_t^* looked much less variable than the actual long rate R_t, contrary to the theory that R_t is the conditional expectation of R_t^*. Unfortunately, the plot was presented only for a very short sample period, that of the first quarter of 1966 to the second quarter of 1977. Here, I repeat this plot using the much longer time series for the United States and the United Kingdom. Figure 13.3 shows the corresponding ex-post values R_t^* as well as R_t. For the United States (top), R_t^* is the yield to maturity at time t on a 25-year current coupon bond whose price is the present value of future coupons and principal discounted by the short rate r_{t+k}, $k = 0, \ldots, 49$, plus a constant risk premium equal to the mean of R over the sample minus the mean of r over the sample. For the United Kingdom (bottom), R_t^* is the yield to maturity on a perpetuity whose price is the present value of coupons discounted by the actual future short rates r_{t+k}, $k = 0, \ldots, \infty$, plus the constant risk premium. In both cases, short rates after the end of the sample are assumed equal to the long rates at the end of the sample, so that R_t and R_t^* converge there by construction.[6] With these long time series, the volatility of R_t is roughly on par with that of R_t^*. There is no substantial evidence that R_t is more variable than R_t^* from these plots.

Using these data, it is instructive to regress $R_t^* - R_{t-1}$ on $R_t - R_{t-1}$ and a constant term. With the full sample for the United States, the estimated slope coefficient is 1.156 (with a standard error of 0.253)—remarkably close to the theoretical value, under the efficient markets model, of 1.000. This is essentially a confirmation of the basic truth revealed for a shorter sample in figure 13.1. However, for the United Kingdom the results are much worse—the estimated slope coefficient is 0.347, which, with a standard error of 0.178, is significantly below 1.000.[7]

Marjorie Flavin [1983] did some calculations of small sample properties of the variance bounds tests used in my 1979 paper (chapter 15) under the assumption that the short-term interest rate is a first-order autoregressive stochastic process with autoregressive coefficient equal to 0.95 when data are sampled annually. With such a stochastic process there is substantial positive serial correlation in the short rate series, and hence the sample standard deviation is a downward biased measure of the true (population) standard derivation that enters the inequalities. She found that the evidence for excess volatility of long-term interest rates that I produced was substantially less dramatic than was suggested by the point estimates alone. From her results, we should not be surprised that the variance bounds are in fact less strongly violated with a bigger sample.[8]

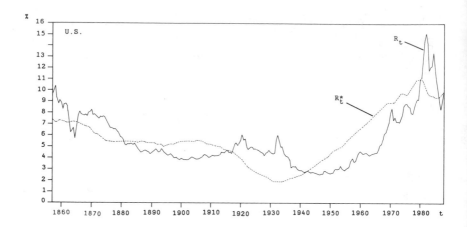

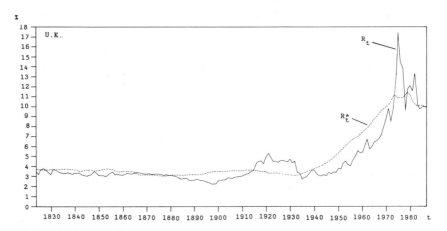

Figure 13.3

Long rates R_t and ex-post values R_t^*: (top) U.S. data; (bottom) U.K. data. Series are based on data shown in figure 13.2. R_t^*, the perfect-foresight yield, is the yield to maturity on a 25-year current coupon bond whose price is the present value of coupons and principal. Discount rates are the actual future short rates augmented by a constant risk premium that brings the mean discount rate equal to the sample mean long rate.

Flavin presented her results as if they were disputing mine, but actually she and I described the results in rather similar terms from the outset. My 1979 article (chapter 15) states in its conclusion that there is reason to doubt that the variance of the short rate can be reliably measured in short samples. There may be unobserved variance of interest rates. The violation of the variance inequalities was construed only as saying that we *must* rely on unobserved variance if we are to accept the expectations models.

Given this, why did I think that the violation of the variance inequalities was interesting for the short sample that I used? First, the high interest rates that succeeded 1976 were as yet in the future. Second, the short-term interest rates of the late '30s and early '40s seemed largely to be perceived as an anomaly—something to do with the depression that would not be repeated. It seemed interesting to note that volatility of long-term interest rates like that actually observed would in effect *require*, given the efficient markets model, that information be accruing about such "anomalous" behavior of interest rates. There is a tendency for people to think that data remote in time are irrelevant, as if they come from a different regime; if we accept this then, the volatility of long rates can only be explained in terms of information about possible regime changes. And of course, since there is reason to think that the actual volatility of long-term interest rates is affected somewhat by the opinion change that characterizes stock prices, it is worth noting that the variance bounds are not violated more dramatically.

13.3   The Slope of the Term Structure Gives Wrong Signals

Another observation made in my 1979 paper (chapter 15)—and later confirmed in Shiller, Campbell, and Schoenholtz [1983] and Mankiw [1986]—was that the spread between the long rate and a short rate, i.e., the slope of the term structure, gives the wrong prediction as to the short-run change in long-term interest rates. For example, when the spread between the long-term interest rate and the three-month rate is unusually high, the long rate tends to fall over the next three months, rather than rise as predicted by the expectations theory. This observation provides a sense in which the rational expectations theory of the term structure of interest rates is fundamentally wrong. It means that three-month holding returns on long bonds indeed tend to be high when long rates are above the three-month rates, as a naive theory, but not the sophisticated expectations theory, would predict.

Such a result could be due to extraneous fashions and fads in the market for long-term bonds, causing an independent short-run noise component in long-term interest rates. If long rates are subjected to random noise that is mean reverting, then when long rates are disturbed upward by such noise they tend to be high relative to short rates and also tend to fall subsequently. The result therefore sounds like it might be evidence for extraneous excess volatility of long-term interest rates. This interpretation should, however, be qualified. Subsequent work (Shiller [1988]) showed that while the problem may indeed be described in terms of mean-reverting short-run noise in the long rate relative to the optimal forecast of future short rates, a substantial part of this short-run noise is actually largely described by a function of current and lagged interest rates. It was found in that paper that the distributed lag regression of the long rate on current and lagged short rates appears to be actually too smooth, not choppy enough, to accord with the expectations model, and that this smooth distributed lag seems to be the source of the "wrong signals" given by the short-term interest rate. This might be due to a tendency of investors to price bonds using their memories, and to blur the past history of short-term interest rates. This departure from market efficiency may then be due to a popular model of the time series properties of interest rates that oversimplifies the forecasting rule. The departures of this popular model from a rational expectations model are rather different from the "fashions and fads" noise story that seemed to be suggested by the analysis of the aggregate stock market.[9]

Interpreting a distributed lag regression of long rates on short rates partly in terms of sluggishness of investors' reaction is of course making a guess as to the causes of a correlation. The distributed lag relation observed could be affected at least in part by something else, e.g., the policy rule that the Federal Reserve uses. Still, the investor reaction story has some appeal. That investors are to a substantial extent just forming averages of lagged short rates as a guide to pricing long-term bonds is somewhat appealing from casual observations of the popular models that investors seem to be using. This story of sluggish investor behavior has in its favor at least that it accords with the way investors often seem to talk. Whether such sluggish behavior of the long rate represents underreaction or overreaction depends on the stochastic properties of short rates, which may change through time as will be discussed below.

13.4   The Slope of the Term Structure Gives the Right Signals

While the departure from market efficiency is certainly important, in other dimensions the efficient markets theory works well. While the "noise" in the long rate described above may be significant enough to cause the slope of the term structure to give wrong signals as to the course of long-term interest rates over the next three months, the slope may yet give correct signals as to the course of short-term interest rates over the life of the long-bond. John Campbell and I found (chapter 16) that the long-short spread behaves quite similarly to the optimal forecast of the present value of future short rates.[10] The estimation method was based on a vector-autoregressive model of interest rates, as pioneered by Sargent [1979].

The basic truth revealed by my work with Campbell (chapter 16) can be represented by merely plotting $R_t - r_t$ and $R_t^* - r_t$ (see figure 13.4).[11]

The former should be a forecast of (and hence less variable than) the latter. What we see is a substantial correlation between the two series, and $R_t^* - r_t$ is indeed more volatile than $R_t - r_t$. One might call this a striking confirmation of some basic truth of the efficient markets model or expectations model of the term structure. When $R_t^* - r_t$ is regressed on $R_t - r_t$ and a constant term with the full data sets shown in figure 13.4, the coefficient of $R_t - r_t$ is significantly greater than zero. With the U.S. data, the coefficient is 0.690 with a standard error of 0.188; with the U.K. data, the coefficient is 0.622 with a standard error of 0.379.[12]

Of course, the theory says that the coefficient *should* be 1.000, and these coefficient estimates are far enough below 1.000 to suggest some substantial departures from the efficient markets model. When one also takes account of possible downward bias in the estimated coefficient,[13] we must conclude that there is not substantial evidence here against the expectations theory of the term structure.

13.5   Evidence of Excess Volatility of Long Rates before 1930

On the other hand, one might say that much of what figure 13.4 reveals is that the long rate moves more sluggishly than the short rate, as it should indeed by the expectations theory, but perhaps there is nothing to be amazed about here. For the United Kingdom, the correlation between $R_t - r_t$ and $R_t^* - r_t$ is especially striking for the first half of the sample. Note that in this part of the sample neither R_t nor R_t^* does much of anything, when compared with the noisy ups and downs of the short rate. Even if the long rate were much more variable than it should be, the short rate in that period is obviously so much more variable that there would still be a substantial correspondence between $R_t - r_t$ and $R_t^* - r_t$.

We can see that this is indeed the case if we regress R_t^* directly onto R_t for the first part of the sample; the slope coefficient should be 1.000 by the

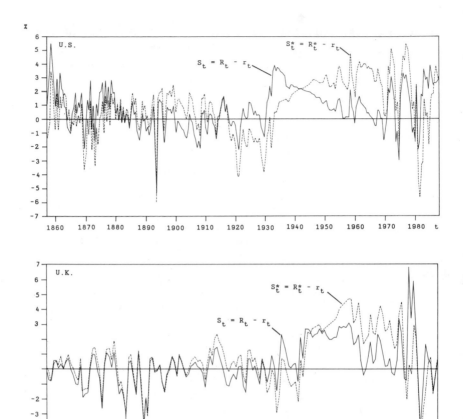

Figure 13.4
Spread $R_t - r_t$ and ex-post value spread $R_t^* - r_t$: (top) U.S. data; (bottom) U.K. data. Data
are spreads between the R_t or R_t^* shown in figure 13.3 and the short rate r_t shown in figure
13.2.

rational expectations model. If we take the period from the beginning of the sample through 1930, interest rates in the United States and the United Kingdom do not look nonstationary, and with the gold standard in force through much of this period, perhaps there is reason to expect stationary nominal interest rates. In this period, the coefficient of R_t is significantly below 1.000 for both the United States and the United Kingdom (0.480 with standard error 0.266 for the United States, 0.000 with a standard error of 0.276 for the United Kingdom). It appears then that in the period of apparently stationary interest rates the long rate, while substantially less variable than the short rate so that the spread comparisons in figure 13.4 look encouraging, still showed too much variability relative to its ability to forecast the short rate.[14]

John Campbell and I [1984] concluded, with post–World War II data, that long rates tended to underreact in a sense to short rates. Using the same method, I found that long rates overreacted to short rates before World War II [1987].

13.6   The Rational Expectations Fisher Model

An alternative way to compute ex-post value R_t^* is to use the inflation rate, based on a wholesale price index, in place of the short term interest rate. The theory that R_t is the expectation at time t of R_t^* may be called a rational expectations Fisher model, after Irving Fisher [1930]. A plot of R_t^* so computed along with the actual rate R_t appears in the 1977 paper that Jeremy Siegel and I wrote (chapter 14, figure 14.4).[15] Since available data on inflation rates extend further back in time than do available data on short-term interest rates, this diagram extends all the way back to 1729. There is really no substantial suggestion of violation of simple variance inequalities here either; the striking fact is that R_t and R_t^* are negatively correlated with each other. The long rate is excessively volatile in the sense that if it were totally scaled down—that is, replaced with a constant—it would do a better job of forecasting R_t^*.

The reader may be puzzled to note that chapter 14 concludes that the rational expectations Fisher model [equation (1) in that chapter with an expectations operator E_t before the summation on the right-hand side] implies there cannot be a positive correlation between R_t and p_t (where p_t is the price index used to convert nominal quantities into real quantities) regardless of the stochastic properties of p_t. The Gibson Paradox, it will be recalled, is an observed positive association between R_t and p_t. From the consideration of the restrictions imposed by rational expectations, one would think that one needs to know the stochastic properties of p_t before discussing the relation of R_t and p_t implied by the theory. In fact (and this is not explained well in that chapter) the nonpositive correlation follows from positive semidefiniteness inequalities. Note that from equation (1) of chapter 14, R_t can be written as $R_t = \bar{\rho} + (1 - \exp(-\bar{\rho}))^2 E_t \sum_{k=0}^{\infty} \exp(-k\bar{\rho})(p_{t+k} - p_t)$. Positive semidefiniteness of the autocovariance function for p_t requires $\text{cov}(p_t, p_{t+k} - p_t) \leq 0$ for all k, from which (using the fact that the correlation between R_t and p_t must be the same as the correlation between ex-post value R_t^* and p_t) the result follows.

13.7 Conclusion

There is a distinct sense in which the rational expectations theory of the term structure has an element of truth to it, as suggested in the simple plots in figure 13.4. Since this figure is analogous to figure 4.3 for the stock market, by comparison one can see that the bond market shows more signs that the efficient markets theory holds than does the stock market.

This positive evidence does not extend to the rational expectations Fisher model, for which the corresponding plot that Siegel and I made (figure 14.4) shows the theory running strongly contrary to the data.

Note that the evidence for the rational expectations theory in figure 13.4, while suggesting that there is some truth to the model, is still consistent with the notion that there is substantial noise in the long-short spread, relative to the rational expectations term structure model. The estimated regression slope coefficient when $R_t^* - r_t$ is regressed on $R_t - r_t$ is poorly measured, and has a substantial standard error that leaves open the possibility that the coefficient could be even less than one-half. We just do not have enough evidence in the available data to get a good fix on this coefficient, even though the data span well over a century. There is some transient noise in long rates, which is part of the reason that the slope of the term structure gives wrong signals as to short-run changes in long rates and contributes to the rather narrow violation of the variance bounds inequality (I-1) of chapter 15.

There is strong evidence, in the regressions of the ex-post value R_t^* onto the long rate R_t, of excess volatility of long rates in the period before 1930. This was a period of relatively quickly mean-reverting short-term interest rates, and while long rates were less volatile then, they still showed too much response to current short rates. The same kind of evidence does not work against the rational expectations model of the term structure in the post-1930 period; it is harder to make the case that short rates are mean reverting, and it is correspondingly harder to make a case that long rates show excess volatility.

Appendix: Data Sources

The U.S. interest rate series are biannual, for January and July of each year. The short rate 1857–1936 is the commercial paper rate in New York City from Macaulay [1938], table 10, column 3, pages A141–A161. For January 1857–July 1923 these are choice 60–90-day two–name paper; for January 1924–July 1936, 4–6-month prime-double and single-name paper. After 1936 the short rate is the prime commercial paper rate from the Board of Governors of the Federal Reserve System, 4–6-month through 1979, 6-month starting 1980. The U.S. long rate 1857–1936 is the unadjusted railroad bond yield from Macaulay, table 10, column 4, pages A141–A161. Thereafter, the long rate is Moody's AAA seasoned corporate bond yield average.

The U.K. interest rates are annual, 1824–1987. The long rate is a consol yield at the beginning of the year spliced together from several sources. For 1824–1896 the long rate is the early-January British consol yield from Peter Garber [1986], table 2, page 1019, the column labeled "yield-gold." His table contains minor errors for the years 1883–1896; I used corrected data that he gave me. For the years 1897–1944 I used early January yields on the consols, issued 1888, that promised 2.75% until 1903, and thereafter 2.5%. I derived these yields to maturity from prices reported in January issues of *The Economist*. For the years 1945–1987 I used flat yields for the last working day of the preceding year on the War Loan perpetual $3\frac{1}{2}$s issued in 1932, as reported in the *Bank of England Statistical Abstract*, table 30, pages 174–178, and the *Bank of England Quarterly Bulletin*. The U.K. short rate 1824–1987 is the annual average 3-month prime bank bill rate described in chapter 14.

Notes

1. Phillips and Pippenger [1976] argued that the significance of regressions Modigliani and I ran of long rates on current and lagged short rates may be spurious due to a serially correlated error term. However, the Phillips and Pippenger solution to estimating the projection of long rates onto a distributed lag of short rates—first differencing interest rates and rerunning the regression—will not produce consistent estimates of the projection of the long rates on information.

2. The bad performance of the expectations model in the United States in the 1930s and 1940s is readily apparent in the top part of figure 13.4, to be discussed below.

3. Chapter 15, table 1, page 270.

4. Singleton [1980] asserted that the violations in the 1959–1971 period were statistically significant; however, his asymptotic distribution theory assumed that processes were stationary around the estimated trends. Also for the short sample,

Amsler [1984] rejected time-varying risk premiums (in terms of a model of risk premiums based on the capital asset pricing model) as a possible source of the variance bounds violation.

5. The violations of (I-1) with actual holding period yield data on current coupon bonds (such as I used for the shorter postwar sample periods in chapter 15), rather than holding period yields inferred from bond yield averages, are likely to be somewhat stronger. Evidence from the postwar period shows that the U.S. bond yield averages are somewhat artificially smoothed due to nontrading, and the yields are less volatile than current coupon yields due to tax effects (see Shiller and Modigliani [1973]).

6. The terminal value assumption differs from that used in figure 15.3. Moreover, figure 15.3 differed in that it was based on the linearization (1) rather than the exact present value of coupons.

7. The standard error takes account of serial correlation of the error term, as in Shiller [1988] drawing on Scott [1985], as discussed in chapter 11.

8. Shea [1988] simulated a nonstationary model of coupon-bearing interest rates that is consistent with Cox, Ingersoll, and Ross's [1981] local expectations hypothesis and concluded that the volatility test using I-3 of my 1979 paper (chapter 15) rejects often. However, his result does not affect the conclusions of that paper; the inequality (I-3) was *not* one that was violated in the results of that chapter.

9. Stock prices are less well explained as a distributed lag on earnings (chapter 1) than are long rates explained as a distributed lag on short rates (Modigliani and Shiller [1973]).

10. See also Fama and Bliss [1987] and Froot [1987].

11. Figure 16.1 suggests an even more dramatic success for the expectations model of the term structure. In that plot, the long-short spread $R_t - r_t$, there called S_t, is plotted with the theoretical spread S_t', the latter defined as the optimal forecast, according to our vector-autoregressive forecasting model, of $R_t^* - r_t$. The information set used in the model to forecast $R_t^* - r_t$ included $R_t - r_t$ and its lagged values and some other noisy variables; since $R_t^* - r_t$ is a smooth series, it is hard to judge how surprised one should be that the fitted value resembles the smooth independent variable $R_t - r_t$.

12. Standard errors take account of the serial correlation of residuals; they are computed by a method (Shiller [1988]) that is a modification of a method of Scott [1985].

13. A downward bias in the analogous coefficient for stocks data was documented using an estimated vector-autoregressive model to generate data in Shiller [1988].

14. In Shiller [1988] the less volatile behavior of the long rate in the earlier part of the sample when compared with the later part of the sample was taken as encouraging evidence for the rational expectations model of the term structure, given the changed stochastic structure of the short rate between the two periods.

However, that paper found (with a method different from that used here) evidence of excess responsiveness of long rates to short rates in that period. Mankiw, Miron, and Weil [1987] also found that the distributed lag regression of U.S. long rates on short rates showed appropriately smaller coefficients in the years before the founding of the Federal Reserve.

15. The idea of plotting an ex-post rational long-term interest rate and comparing this with the actual long-term interest rate was due originally to Jeremy Siegel, in an unpublished manuscript [1969].

References

Amsler, Christine. 1984. "Term Structure Variance Bounds and Time Varying Liquidity Premia," *Economics Letters* 16:137–144.

Campbell, John Y., and Robert J. Shiller. 1984. "A Simple Account of the Behavior of Long-Term Interest Rates," *American Economic Review* 74:44–48.

Cox, John C., Jonathan E. Ingersoll, and Stephen A. Ross. 1981. "A Reexamination of Traditional Hypotheses about the Term Structure of Interest Rates," *Journal of Finance* 36:769–799.

Fama, Eugene F., and Robert R. Bliss. 1987. "The Information in Long-Maturity Forward Rates," *American Economic Review* 77:680–692.

Fisher, Irving. 1930. *The Theory of Interest*, New York: Macmillan.

Flavin, Marjorie. 1983. "Excess Volatility in the Financial Markets: A Reassessment of the Empirical Evidence," *Journal of Political Economy* 91:929–956.

Flavin, Marjorie. 1984. "Time Series Evidence on the Expectations Hypothesis of the Term Structure," *Carnegie-Rochester Conference Series on Public Policy* 20:211–238.

Froot, Kenneth A. 1987. "New Hope for the Expectations Hypothesis of the Term Structure of Interest Rates," reproduced, Sloan School of Management, M.I.T.

Garber, Peter M. 1986. "Nominal Contracts in a Bimetallic Standard," *American Economic Review* 76:1012–1030.

Macaulay, Frederick R. 1938. *Some Theoretical Problems Suggested by the Movements of Interest Rates, Bond Yields, and Stock Prices in the United States since 1856*, New York: National Bureau of Economic Research.

Mankiw, N. Gregory. 1986. "The Term Structure of Interest Rates Revisited," *Brookings Papers on Economic Activity* 1:61–96.

Mankiw, N. Gregory, Jeffrey A. Miron, and David N. Weil. 1987. "The Adjustment of Expectations to a Change in Regime: A Study of the Founding of the Federal Reserve," *American Economic Review* 77:358–374.

Modigliani, Franco, and Robert J. Shiller. 1973. "Inflation, Rational Expectations, and the Term Structure of Interest Rates," *Economica* 40:12–43.

Modigliani, Franco, and Richard Sutch. 1966. "Innovations in Interest Rate Policy," *American Economic Review* 56:178–197.

Modigliani, Franco, and Richard Sutch. 1967. "Debt Management and the Term Structure of Interest Rates," *Journal of Political Economy* 75:569–589.

Phillips, Llad, and John Pippenger. 1976. "Preferred Habitat vs. Efficient Market: A Test of Alternative Hypotheses," *Federal Reserve Bank of St. Louis Review* 58:11–19.

Sargent, Thomas J. 1979. "A Note of the Estimation of the Rational Expectations Model of the Term Structure," *Journal of Monetary Economics* 5:133–143.

Scott, Louis O. 1985. "The Present Value Model of Stock Prices: Regression Tests and Monte Carlo Results," *Review of Economics and Statistics* 67:599–605.

Shea, Gary S. 1988. "Qualms about the Linearized Expectations Hypothesis and Variance Bounds Studies of the Interest Rate Term Structure," reproduced, Pennsylvania State University.

Shiller, Robert J. 1981. "Alternative Tests of Rational Expectations Models: The Case of the Term Structure," *Journal of Econometrics* 16:17–87.

Shiller, Robert J. 1987. "Conventional Valuation and the Term Structure of Interest Rates," in Rudiger Dornbusch, Stanley Fischer and John Bossons, editors, *Macroeconomics and Finance: Essays in Honor of Franco Modigliani*, Cambridge, MA: MIT Press.

Shiller, Robert J. 1988. "A Scott-Type Regression Test of the Dividend Ratio Model," reproduced, Yale University.

Shiller, Robert J. 1989. "The Term Structure of Interest Rates," in Frank Hahn and Benjamin Friedman, editors, *Handbook of Monetary Economics*.

Shiller, Robert J., John Y. Campbell, and Kermit L. Schoenholtz. 1983. "Forward Rates and Future Policy: Interpreting the Term Structure of Interest Rates," *Brookings Papers on Economic Activity* I:173–217.

Shiller, Robert J., and Franco Modigliani. 1979. "Coupon and Tax Effects on New and Seasoned Bond Yields and the Measurement of the Cost of Debt Capital," *Journal of Financial Economics* 7:297–318.

Siegel, Jeremy J. 1969. "Inflation, Interest Rates, and British Consol Yields," reproduced, Massachusetts Institute of Technology.

Singleton, Kenneth J. 1980. "Expectations Models of the Term Structure and Implied Variance Bounds," *Journal of Political Economy* 88:1159–1176.

Sutch, Richard. 1967. *Expectations, Risk and the Term Structure of Interest Rates*, unpublished Ph.D. Dissertation, Massachusetts Institute of Technology.

14   The Gibson Paradox and Historical Movements in Real Interest Rates

For the past quarter of a millennium for which British data are available, there is a strong positive correlation between the price level, as measured by a (log) price index, and the long-term interest rate, as measured by the yield to maturity of long-term bonds. This phenomenon is named by Keynes [1930] the "Gibson Paradox," after A. H. Gibson [1923], the man Keynes thought had discovered the relationship. The long-term interest rate R and the log of the price level P as we measure them are plotted together for comparison in figure 14.1 (see appendix for source of data). The similarity of the two series is most impressive, especially when one considers the major changes in social, political, and economic structure that took place over this period.[1] Keynes called this correlation "one of the most completely established empirical facts in the whole field of quantitative economics" [1930, 2: 198].

Over the shorter time period for which good British data on short-term interest rates are available, there is also a substantial but less pronounced positive correlation between short-term interest rates and prices. The short-term interest rate I is plotted in figure 14.2, with the same price series P. The correlation is not only less pronounced than that in figure 14.1;[2] it also takes a different form. The relation between I and P is much stronger over the short term than that between R and P. We will refer to this short-term correlation with the short rate of interest as the Kitchin Phenomenon, after Joseph Kitchin, who noted it in 1923.

A correlation between interest rates and prices of this significance must certainly have been noted many times in the past, and indeed it has been an empirical regularity that has been of great importance in the development of monetary theory. The correlation was apparently first described

Coauthored with Jeremy J. Siegel. Reprinted with minor editing from *Journal of Political Economy* 85 (1977):891–907; © 1977 The University of Chicago.

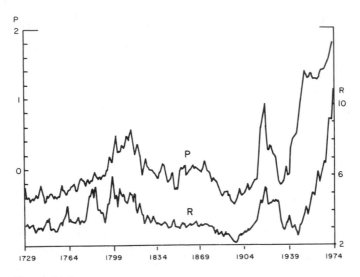

Figure 14.1
The log of the price index (*P*) and the long-term interest rate (*R*), British data. See the appendix for the source of data.

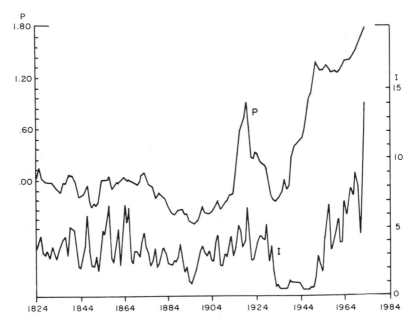

Figure 14.2
The log of the price level (*P*) and the short (3-month) interest rate (*I*), British data. See the appendix for the source of data.

by Tooke [1844]. He used it to criticize the Thornton-Ricardo view that an increase in the money supply is transmitted to an increase in prices by a decline in the interest rate and to defend the real bills doctrine. Alternative views of the phenomenon were developed by Wicksell [1898, 1962] and by Hawtrey [1913]. Renewed interest in the phenomenon was then prompted by the "discovery" of the relation of long rates to prices by Gibson [1923], and of the relation of short rates to prices by Kitchin [1923] and Peake [1928]. Kitchin compared the peaks and troughs of I and P and noted that the turning points that occur together occur about 40 months apart, a phenomenon that has come to be known as the "Kitchin Cycle." Unfortunately, what is best known today is Kitchin's conclusion that a 40-month cycle is discernible from the I or P series individually.

A number of theories have been proposed to explain the positive correlation between interest rates and prices, notably by Fisher [1930], Keynes [1930], MacCaulay [1938], and Sargent [1973]. In this chapter we analyze these theories and propose alternative explanations of the Gibson Paradox and Kitchin Phenomenon.

14.1   Analysis of the British Data

Spectral analysis of the time series appearing in figures 14.1 and 14.2 gives us a more precise description of the pheomena described above:[3]

1. The squared coherence (which is essentially a squared correlation coefficient at each frequency) between R and P, as shown in the top of figure 14.3, is stronger at the lower frequencies, where it is significant at the 5% level. The squared coherence between I and P shown in the bottom of figure 14.3 is concentrated, in contrast, more in the higher frequencies and peaks very near the Kitchin frequency of .300 (40 months), where it is also significant at the 5% level. In both cases the phase angle is nearly zero wherever coherence is strong (i.e., the relations are essentially unlagged).

2. Considered individually, none of the series shows a spectrum that is very concentrated at any particular (nonzero) frequency; that is, there is little evidence of predominant business cycle for prices and interest rates. The spectra of both R and P are typical of the kind of spectra that, as elaborated by Granger [1966], are commonly found among economic time series, in that their most striking feature is the considerable power at the lower frequencies. Box-Jenkins analysis suggests that both series might be represented as integrated processes. Since Klein [1975] found major changes in the behavior of prices after the end of the gold standard, we

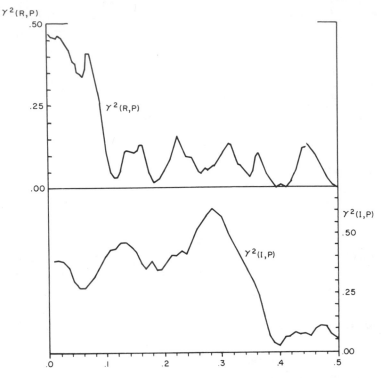

Figure 14.3
Plot of squared coherence (vertical axis) against frequency in cycles per year (horizontal axis). (Top) Squared coherence between R and P; critical coherence squared at 5% level is .350. (Bottom) Squared coherence between I and P; critical coherence squared is .472. See note 3 for details of estimation.

tried dividing the sample period rather arbitrarily at 1913. As a first approximation, it is useful to regard both of these series as random walks for the period up through 1913, and as positively serially correlated IMA(1, 1) (integrated moving average processes) for 1914–1974. Thus, as Klein emphasized, our impression that inflation is forecastable is valid for the present time, but not for most of the period covered by our data. The appearance to the eye of "trends" in figure 14.1 before 1914 is the usual illusion given by random walks. These Box-Jenkins representations, however, do not perfectly correspond to the observed spectra. The long rate spectrum also shows small humps in the middle frequencies, peaking at frequencies .23 and .32. The short rate series I, in contrast to the above, has a spectrum much less concentrated in the low frequencies, as evidenced by the relatively choppy appearance of the series in figure 14.2. Again, there are no important humps in the spectrum. There is a small hump in the Kitchin frequency of .30, but other humps that are just as large occur at lower frequencies.

14.2   Theories Based on a Response in Interest Rates to Inflationary Expectations

Irving Fisher in his classic *The Theory of Interest* (published in 1930) has given the most popular explanation of the Gibson Paradox. Fisher stated that the market rate of interest at time t, R_t, on long-term bonds is the sum of a more or less constant real rate of interest $\bar{\rho}$ plus an expected "long run" rate of inflation at time t, π_t, so that $R_t = \bar{\rho} + \pi_t$. He asserted that the Gibson phenomenon arises because π_t is positively correlated with the price level, and he attempted to provide a plausible theory of expectations that would give this result.[4]

According to this theory, if we assume knowledge of future prices the price V_t of a consol paying coupons of C dollars each time period is the present value of its real coupons (in time t prices) discounted by a constant real rate $\bar{\rho}$. The yield $R_t = \log(1 + C/V_t)$ of the consol can be approximated by linearizing around $\Delta P(t + n) = 0$, $n = 1, 2, \ldots$ see Shiller [1972] to obtain

$$R_t = \bar{\rho} + [1 - \exp(-\bar{\rho})] \sum_{k=1}^{\infty} \exp(-k\bar{\rho}) \Delta P_{t+k}. \tag{1}$$

Thus, consol yields are given approximately as $\bar{\rho}$ plus a weighted average of future rates of inflation, the weights declining geometrically with time. This weighted average we refer to as an "expected long-run rate of inflation." In effect, the long-run rate of inflation is related to the "present value" of future one-period rates of inflation discounted by the real rate of interest.

Fisher claimed that expected long-run inflation rates π_t could be represented as a distributed lag on past actual inflation rates. If the distributed lag is exponential, this gives.

$$R_t = \bar{\rho} + b \sum_{k=1}^{\infty} \exp(-ak) \Delta P_{t-k}, \tag{2}$$

a model that resembles (1) except that the weighted average includes lagged ΔP rather than led ΔP. As an expectations mechanism, it sounds superficially plausible that individuals should form expectations as a weighted average of lagged inflation rates. Moreover, if a is very small we can be sure that the model will fit the data very well since

$$\sum_{k=1}^{\infty} \exp(-ak)\Delta P_{t-k}$$

is essentially the price level itself, thus such a "model" becomes a simple restatement of the Paradox.[5] We know that R will fit π so defined very well.[6]

Although the model fits well, however, it is not a plausible one from the standpoint of investor rationality. To see this, we look at expression (1). Since R here is a linear function of P_t, P_{t+1}, ..., we can derive the cross-spectrum between R and P.[7] It turns out that the phase angle from P to R is for high frequencies (short cycles) near 180°, implying that high-frequency components of P are matched by high-frequency changes in R in the opposite direction. The intuitive explanation is simple: in the short-run the price of the bond must move with the price level for real returns to be kept constant for short holding periods. In short periods of time the coupon payments are negligible and can be disregarded. Keynes suggested this point in his *Treatise on Money*. For long cycles, on the other hand, the phase angle approaches 90°. At these frequencies yield becomes uncorrelated with the price level. Hence, there is thus nothing to suggest a phenomenon like the Gibson Paradox.

A more graphic way to see the "paradox" involved here is to compute what interest rates would have been had investors known with certainty what future prices actually transpired. We will define an "ex-post rational yield" as the yield on a bond whose price is the present value of its real coupons discounted by $\bar{\rho}$. If R^* is the yield on such a consol, then we have from the definition of yield the recursive relation

$$R_t^* = \log\{1 + \exp(\bar{\rho} + \Delta P_{t+1}) \cdot [1 - \exp(-R_{t+1}^*)]\}. \tag{3}$$

Given a value for $\bar{\rho}$ and a terminal value for R^*, which we took to be 3% and the actual yield for 1973, respectively, we can compute an ex-post rational yield for all earlier dates for which we have price data. This is plotted at the top of figure 14.4. This ex-post rational yield guarantees that holding period real returns for *all* period be 3%. Clearly the ex-post rational yield moves *opposite* actual yields, which appear in the middle of figure 14.4. The correlation between ex-post rational yields and actual yields from 1729 to 1950 (a period chosen to exclude the most recent values of our ex-post rational yield that are heavily influenced by the arbitrary terminal value chosen) was −.30.

Figure 14.4
Ex-post rational yields, R_t^*, actual yields R_t, and ex-post real long-term rates of interest ρ, British data.

The ex-post long-term rate ρ_t is that rate of interest that discounts the real coupons to the *actual* real value of the bond. In the case of a consol whose price is V_t and that carries coupon C per time period, the ex-post real long-term rate ρ_t at time t is defined implicitly by

$$V_t = C \sum_{n=1}^{\infty} \exp(-\rho_t n - \sum_{m=1}^{n} \Delta P_{t+m}). \qquad (4)$$

This implicit function for ρ_t in terms of C, V_t, and future ΔP cannot in general be solved for ρ_t. However, if inflation rates are not large, then, based on a linearization around $\bar{\rho}$, we derive the approximation

$$\rho_t = R_t - (R_t^* - \bar{\rho}), \qquad (5)$$

where $\bar{\rho}$ is the real rate used in the computation of R^*, the ex-post rational yield. The ex-post real long rate is here essentially the nominal rate minus the ex-post long-run rate of inflation that is implicit in R^*. The values of ρ_t computed from the R^* at the top of figure 14.4 are plotted at the bottom of figure 14.4. By construction, the rate ρ_t approaches $\bar{\rho}$ (3%) at the final date. The standard deviation from 1729 to 1950 of ρ_t is 217 basis points. If R_t had been constant over this period, then using R^* and (5) we compute that the standard deviation of ρ_t over this period would have been 182 basis points; that is, as we have noted, the movements in R aggravated, rather than mitigated, the effect of changes in P on real yields.

The ex-post real long rate of interest is strongly negative in the depression of the 1930s, which means that the real value of the bond then was greater than the simple sum of its real coupon payments up to 1973 plus its real value in 1973. Real rates of interest hit zero during the depression of the 1890s, and were relatively low during the last part of the nineteenth century. The secular deflation then was not severe enough to offset the low nominal yields.

Of course, individuals do not possess perfect foresight. Based on the stochastic properties of the price level alone, before 1914 investors should have projected a near zero rate of inflation consistently, since the price level displayed little upon which to project future rates of inflation. When there were external circumstances that should have given rise to nonzero projections, as during the war years 1810–1815, the Napoleonic Wars, and especially the 1920 World War I peak, it would appear that investors consistently forecast prices in the wrong direction. The same could be said for the depression period of the 1930s and the governmental suppression of inflation during World War II.

In conclusion, the Fisherian hypothesis that price expectations account for the Gibson Paradox and the real rate is constant cannot be maintained on the basis of a rational expectation mechanism for generating inflationary expectations. If the price level follows a random walk and expectations of future inflation are based only on past inflation, then the interest rate series we see is in fact the real rate of interest.

14.3   Theories That Rely on Interest Sensitive Demand or Supply of Money

A completely different approach to the explanation of the Gibson Paradox was taken by several other authors, who combined a characterization of an interest-sensitive demand for or supply of money with a characterization of the time path of exogenous variables. Keynes [1930] and Wicksell [1962] proposed explanations that, while differing in details, both relied on an interest-sensitive money supply. Sargent [1973] proposed a model of the Gibson Paradox that relied instead on an interest-elastic *demand* for money.

We may summarize both types of explanation in terms of the two-equation model

$$\log(M) = \log[\mu(r)] + \log(H), \qquad \text{money supply,} \qquad (6)$$

$$\log(M) + \log[V(r)] = P + \log(y), \qquad \text{money demand,} \qquad (7)$$

where M is the money supply, $\mu(r)$ is the interest-sensitive money multiplier, $\mu'(r) > 0$, H is the supply of high-powered money, $V(r)$ is the interest-sensitive velocity of money, $V'(r) > 0$, and y is real national product. The interest rate r could be either the short-term interest rate I or the long-term interest rate R. Let us for the moment assume it is R. If we assume demand equals supply we may derive from (6) and (7) the reduced form for P:

$$P = \log[V(r)] + \log[\mu(r)] + \log(H/y)$$

or   (8)

$$P = \log V_H(r) + \log(H/y),$$

where $\log V_H(r) = \log[V(r)] + \log[\mu(r)]$ is the velocity of high powered money. This result divides the log of the price level into two or three components; all components are directly observable; $V(r) = Y/M$, where Y is money income, and $[\mu(r)]$ is M/H. Sargent's model asserts that $\log[\mu(r)]$ and $\log(H/y)$ are relatively constant, and the Gibson Paradox arises because $V(r)$ moves with R. Wicksell's and Keynes's models assert that $\log V(r)$ and $\log(H/y)$ are relatively constant, and the Gibson Paradox arises because $[\mu(r)]$ moves with R. All of these theories assert that the variation in P must be due primarily to variations in the velocity of high-powered money $V_H(r)$. One way of evaluating these theories is thus to check which of the components of P in (8) account for movements in P.

Before we do this, we must decide on the definition of high-powered money H. If we take the conventional definition, which includes Bank of England notes as well as gold, then it is neither $V(r)$ nor $\mu(r)$ that does most to explain P; it is instead the third component, $\log(H/y)$, as can be seen from figure 14.5. The correlation between P and $\log(H/y)$ is an extraordinary .972. The log of the velocity of high-powered money $\log(Y/H)$ plotted at the bottom of figure 14.5 accounts for only a small part of the variation in P. This is not to say that the velocity of high-powered money is not sensitive to the interest rate, since the correlation coefficient between the consol yield series and the log of Y/H is .348, but the changes in this velocity are not very important in explaining price movements compared

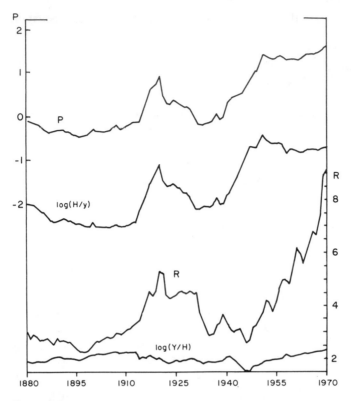

Figure 14.5
(Upper plots) The log price level P and the log of the ratio of high-powered money to real GDP, $\log(H/y)$; scale for these plots is at left. (Lower plots) The long-term interest rate R and the log of the velocity of high-powered money, $\log(Y/H)$; scale for these plots is at the right.

to changes in the money stock. In particular, one notes that the high prices and interest rates during World War I cannot be associated with an increase in the velocity of high-powered money.[8]

The data thus indicate that neither Sargent's theory nor Wicksell's theory can be the principal explanation of the Gibson phenomenon. On the other hand, if we define high-powered money to be reserves of the Bank of England, as Keynes at least clearly intended in this context, then these data are entirely consistent with Keynes's explanation. The possibility that Keynes suggested is that governments or central banks will respond to increases in interest rates by increasing the money supply.[9] If the central bank seeks, with less than complete success, to stabilize the long-term interest rate with its handling of the money supply, then the Gibson phenomenon might emerge. Keynes [1930] argued, as an element of his explanation of the Gibson Paradox, that central banks have long behaved in this manner.

The clearest case for such behavior occurs during wartime. Debt-financed war expenditures are an attempt to shift part of the burden of the war to the future. To the extent that individuals do not discount all future tax liabilities arising from the issuance of debt, current government borrowing will not be met by an equivalent increase in saving unless the real rate rises to equilibrate the financial market. The central bank may succumb to the political pressure of keeping the interest rate from rising by increasing high-powered money and hence causing inflation. Thus, during wartime the correlation between interest and prices arises because each, in turn, is causally linked to two other variables that are correlated: government interest-bearing debt and high-powered money.[10]

This explanation is capable of explaining the Kitchin Phenomenon as well as the Gibson Paradox. Since the coherence between P and the log of H/y is high for all frequencies, both the low-frequency coherence between P and R and the high-frequency coherence between P and I could be explained with an appropriate model linking H/y to both I and R. If we suppose that the monetary authority attempts to stabilize short-term cycles in the short rate of interest and long-term cycles in the long rate of interest, then both the Gibson and Kitchin phenomena would emerge. This type of policy might arise if the central bank responds only to large movements in either series, since our spectral analysis demonstrates that large movements in R are associated with long cycles and large movements in I with short cycles.

14.4   Theories that Depend on Effects of Unanticipated Price Changes on Contracts Made in Nominal Terms

Changes in the price level that do not affect relative prices should have no real effects and should hence not affect the real interest rate if no intertemporal contracts are made in nominal terms. Traditionally, a very large variety of contracts are made specifying payments to be made at different times that are denominated in money terms. When such contracts are made, unanticipated price changes have the effect of redistributing income across individuals and possibly inducing real effects.

We now develop a model in which these price-induced wealth redistributions can give rise to the Gibson Paradox or Kitchin Phenomenon.[11] In this model, we assume that the economy is initially in stochasic equilibrium. Individuals will be divided into two groups. One group (demanders) wishes to hold net long positions in nominally denominated assets such as consols. For simplicity we shall assume that the net supply of these assets is zero, so a second group (suppliers) must necessarily be short in these assets. For instance, a firm whose real captial stock is partially financed by bonds has the property that equity holders are net short in those bonds. Assume that the interest rate on bonds equilibrates the demand and supply.

When the price level has risen unexpectedly, the wealth position of those long in bonds will have decreased, and the wealth position of those short will have increased by the the same amount. Assume that each group wishes to maintain a certain fraction of its total wealth in long or short positions in bonds. An unexpected price rise will reduce the real supply of nominal debt in existence, but the demanders of nominal debt will seek to increase their bond positions by only a fraction of this change in supply once their wealth has decreased. The net suppliers of debt will wish to increase the supply by more than the drop in the value of the bonds since their wealth position has been enhanced. Hence, at the initial equilibrium interest rate there will be an excess supply of bonds, and the interest rate will have to rise to equilibrate the market.

We may, although it is not necessary, associate those who demand bonds as relatively "risk averse" and those who supply bonds (lever their investments) as relatively "risk taking." If this is the case, then unexpected changes in the price level change the relative wealth positions of the relative risk averse and relative risk takers in the economy. An unexpected upward movement in prices would tend to change the risk characteristics in the economy toward the preferences of the risk takers and conversely in the case of unexpected price declines.

A change in the rate of interest on bonds hence may not be associated with any real change in the productive technique or quantity of capital in the economy,[12] but only reflect changes in the income distribution the economy caused by unanticipated price movements. An increase in, say, risk aversion resulting from an unanticipated price fall will cause "sure" claims to trade at a higher price (and lower rate) than risky capital. This last point is particularly important since, if we interpret the market rate of interest as the real rate of interest (as the data up to World War I suggest), then a deterministic model will suggest results that may not exist in a stochastic world. A deterministic model would predict that the capital-output ratio in the economy would move inversely to the real rate of interest, and hence we would expect that the capital-output ratio would conform inversely to the historical interest rate pattern. Available evidence does not suggest any such countercyclical movements of capital intensity—no deepening during the latter half of the nineteenth century or "thinning" thereafter. Certainly during the depression of the 1930s the capital stock did not rise. As mentioned above, changes in aggregate distribution of income (and possibly risk preferences) can bring about such changes without any concomitant changes in the capital stock.

A result of this theory is that the rate of return on real, unlevered equity need not follow the pattern of the long-term nominal bond rate even if this rate corresponds to the real rate of interest. Interestingly, evidence that supports constant unlevered returns also supports one of Fisher's assumptions: that expected real rates were constant. We are also suggesting in this analysis that there may be a constant expected real asset return, but differ from Fisher in that we suppose that the expected real risk-free rate is one that will fluctuate with the (unanticipated) movements of the price level due to distribution effects and not inflationary anticipations.

Our distribution-effects explanation is consistent with the coherence pattern that characterizes the Kitchin Phenomenon, if we add the assumption that there is some, say, white noise affecting supply and demand for credit and hence I, the short-term interest rate. The distributional effects of unanticipated price changes are likely to be temporary, if for no more reason than that generations are finite lived. The high power of P at the lowest frequencies is thus not transmitted to I, and so because of the other noise in I at those frequencies coherence is low there. Moreover, since the power of P is low at the highest frequencies, it is also probable that the hypothesized noise in I might swamp out the influence of P on I at these frequencies, again producing low coherence. Thus, the inverted U-shaped coherence pattern at the bottom of figure 14.3, which is high only at the middle frequencies, might well emerge.

We might also assume some noise component in the supply and demand for long-term bonds to explain why coherence is low for the higher frequencies between R, the long-term bond rate, and P. It is more difficult, however, to make a case for the concentration in the extreme low frequencies of the coherence between R and P. To explain this, we would have to assume that the effect of movements in P on the distribution of wealth is attenuated very slowly.

14.5   Conclusion

Our analysis confirms a long-cycle correlation between *long-term* interest rates and prices, popularly termed the Gibson Paradox, and a short-cycle correlation between *short-term* interest rates and prices that we term the Kitchin Phenomenon. Long-term interest rates and prices display no significant short-cycle correlation; hence any "business-cycle" explanations of the Gibson Paradox are invalid.

Our results suggest that it is proabably unreasonable to suppose, as many have, that historical changes in long-term interest rates can be attributed largely to changes in inflationary expectations. Thus, historical movements in nominal yields are probably a reflection of movements in the expected real long-term rate of interest. Second, it is also unreasonable to attribute historical movements in the price level to changes in the velocity of money. Long-run movements in the price level arise instead primarily from changes in the supply of high-power money, so an explanation of the Gibson Paradox that relies on interest rate induced shifts in velocity or the money multiplier cannot be maintained. However, it is possible that central bank behavior, in attempting to attenuate interest rate changes, will result in a correlation between high-powered money and interest rates and hence give rise to the Gibson Paradox.

Another possible explanation involves changes in interest rates that arise due to the effects of unanticipated changes in the price level on contracts made in money terms. A price rise distributes wealth from creditors to debtors, which changes the interest rate that equilibrates demand and supply for nominally denominated assets. The extent to which this explanation explains the Gibson Paradox as well as the Kitchin Phenomenon depends on how quickly economic agents readjust altered wealth positions.

Appendix: Sources of Data

Price data come primarily from Mitchell and Deane [1962] and Mitchell and Jones [1971]. The Wholesale Price Index (whose log is P) for 1846–1966 is the Sauerbeck-Statist Overall Price Index, which is the index used by Keynes in his discussion of the Gibson Paradox. The series was extended by linking to it other series, multiplied by the ratio of the two series for one overlapping year. In this manner, the Gayer Rostow and Schwartz Monthly Index of British Commodity Prices was linked to it for the years 1790–1846. To this in turn was linked Elizabeth Schumpeter's Consumer Goods Price Index for the period 1727–1790. Since the Statist series was discontinued in 1966, the wholesale price index number of output of manufactured products, total sales from the Central Statistical Office, was linked to the Statist Index for the period 1967–1973.

The yield series R is basically that on British Perpetual Annuities from 1727 to 1973, compiled by Homer [1963, tables 13, 19, and 57]. Beginning with 1753, there are yields of 3% consols, redeemable at the option of the government. In the 1880s yields fell below 3%, so that the yields were prevented from falling much further by the possibility of redemption. After the refunding of 1888, the 3% consols were replaced with new consols yielding $2\frac{3}{4}$% until 1903, and thereafter $2\frac{1}{2}$%. Since the yields on consols were thus abnormally high in the 1880s, we here follow Homer's suggestion and use yields on $2\frac{1}{2}$% government annuities for the years 1881–1888, consol yields thereafter.

Bill rates I are taken primarily from Mitchell and Deane [1962, p. 460]. From 1824 to 1844 we use Overend and Gurney's rates from Mitchell and Deane [1962] for first-class 3-month bills. From 1845 to 1938 we use the average of the annual means of the monthly means of the highest and lowest rates of each day on 3-month bank bills [Mitchell and Deane 1962, p. 460, part B]. From 1939 to 1965 we use the annual mean of the market buying rate on working days of 3-month bank bills quoted in Mitchell and Jones [1971, p. 182]. The most recent data were the 3-month prime bank bill rate averaged over the year, from the Central Statistical Office Abstract of Financial Statistics.

Gross Domestic Product (Y) for the United Kindgom for the years 1870–1965 are those given in Feinstein [1972, table 3, col. 9, pp. T10–T11]. Real Gross Domestic Product (y) was formed from Y by dividing Y by our price index P.

The high-powered money supply series H and the money supply series M are basically those given in Sheppard [1971]. The actual data we used, however, were supplied to us by Anna J. Schwartz. Her series involves some minor judgmental changes and updates Sheppard's series based in part on recent data supplied her by Sheppard.

Notes

1. The Gibson Paradox appears in data from other countries as well. Fase [1971] concluded that the paradox holds in the Dutch economy. The paradox also appears over the shorter time period for which data are available in the United States and Canada. For the U.S. data, the relation between a long-term bond yield series and

prices is again a long-term one, and shorter-run movements in the series show little relationship. One may not, of course, regard the experience of these other countries as independent observations, since their interest rates and prices are related through financial markets. There is, however, substantial variation between U.S. and British price series and U.S. and British bond yield time series. The data show that U.S. federal government bond yields were dramatically above the British consol yields during the War of 1812 and the Civil War, and these periods corresponded to periods of very high prices in the United States relative to Britain. Experiences of some other countries, however, may be construed as disconfirming the Gibson Paradox. For instance, the price level in France rose during World War II to a plateau that was, in the 1950s, 2,500% higher than in 1937. Interest rates did not rise to a new higher plateau. We could find similar counterexamples in the experience of certain Latin American countries with dramatically unstable price levels.

2. The correlation between the R and P data in figure 14.1 is .743, while that between R and ΔP (the rate of inflation) is .045. The correlation between I and P in figure 14.2 is .421, between I and ΔP is $-.01$.

3. The sample period is 1730–1973 in all estimates except those involving I, for which a sample period of 1826–1937 was used. The shorter sample period was necessitated by lack of good data before 1820 and by the unusual controls on short rates around World War II, whose effect in drastically lowering short rates can be readily seen in figure 14.2. In computing the cross-spectra, the data were quasi first-differenced (with filter $[1 - .8L]$), and then Fourier transformed (without prior padding with zeroes). The cross-periodogram was smoothed with a wrap triangular filter. In computing the cross-spectra between R and P the data were initially detrended, but this was unnecessary for I and P. The range of the filter for R and P was 18, and the band width was .065. The range of the filter for I and P was 12, and the band width was .102. Since Box-Jenkins analysis suggested that R and P may be represented as random walks for the greater part of the sample period, the series may not be stationary, so that their spectra would not be defined. Even if this is so, the spectra remain useful characterization of the data. Using the filter $(1 - .8L)$ on all the data produced spectra of R and P that were whitened considerably (and a spectrum of I with much reduced lower frequencies), so that the coherence pattern of the first differenced series would not be substantially different.

4. The Fisher theory has spawned an enormous literature [see, for example, Roll, 1972; Modigliani and Shiller, 1973; Sargent, 1973; Fama, 1975].

5. For small a the theoretical gain from P to R according to (2) is essentially flat and the phase angle zero for all but the lowest frequencies.

6. There is an extensive literature on the estimation of the parameters of (2), although the relation is often modified by making $\bar{\rho}$ a function of other variables [see Roll, 1972]. Some authors have not found the distributed lag significant for certain subperiods and estimation procedures [see Cargill and Meyer, 1974].

7. The phase angle is given by

$$\phi(w) = \arctan\left\{\frac{(1 - e^{-\bar{p}})}{(1 + e^{-\bar{p}})} \cdot \frac{\sin(2\pi w)}{[\cos(2\pi w) - 1]}\right\},$$

and the gain is given by

$$g(w) = (1 - e^{-\bar{p}})\{[2 - 2\cos(2\pi w)]/[1 - 2e^{-\bar{p}}\cos(2\pi w) + e^{-2\bar{p}}]\}^{.5}.$$

8. Cagan [1965] has also emphasized the importance of H/y in determining P based on U.S. data.

9. In the United States also, even before the Federal Reserve System, the government has had influence over high-powered money. In the Civil War, the U.S. printed "greenbacks" not immediately redeemable in gold. Moreover, during the War of 1812 (even though there was no central bank, the charter of the Bank of the United States having expired in 1811) banks in the middle states had suspended specie payments and the federal government was able to obtain loans of their unredeemable paper notes from them, thus effectively increasing the money supply.

10. Hawtrey [1932] observed this tendency clearly: "Governments do not want to borrow from their central banks (apart from quite legitimate overdrafts for a few days) except at a time of overwhelming financial strain, and at such a time the central banks *never* resist their demands. . . . In face of the exigencies of war, no reliance can be placed on an independent central bank to resist demands from the government. At such a time the government is accepted by public opinion as the sole authoritative exponent of the national needs. If the directors of the central bank raise objections to the government's financial measures, they will be overborne."

11. Much of this explanation is drawn from Siegel [1975]. Other price-induced distributional explanations have relied on the existence of fixed nominal wages. Hawtrey [1913] theorized that unanticipated price changes result in shifts of wealth between workers and entrepreneurs because of sticky money wages in such a way as to cause corresponding shifts in capital productivity and the return on capital, but his theory appears poorly developed. MacCaulay [1938], who resolutely rejected Irving Fisher's explanation, felt that distribution effects, through their influence on levered firms' profitability, were responsible for the Gibson Paradox. It should be noted, as Keynes [1930] so aptly states, that any short-run or business cycle explanation of the Gibson Paradox is insufficient due to its long-run nature.

12. For a more detailed discussion of this, see Siegel and Warner [1977].

References

Cagan, Phillip. 1965. *Determinants and Effects of Changes in the Stock of Money 1875–1960*. New York: Columbia Univ. Press (for Nat. Bur. Econ. Res.).

Cargill, Thomas F., and Meyer, Robert A. 1974. "Interest Rates and Prices since 1950." *International Economic Review* 15:458–471.

Fama, Eugene F. 1975. "Short Term Interest Rates as Predictors of Inflation." *American Economic Review* 65:269–282.

Fase, M. M. G. 1972. "Bond Yields and Expected Inflation." *Econ. Quarterly Review* 30:5–10.

Feinstein, C. H. 1972. *National Income Expenditure and Output of the United Kingdom.* Cambridge: Cambridge Univ. Press.

Fisher, Irving. 1930. *The Theory of Interest.* New York: Macmillan.

Gibson, A. H., 1923. "The Future Course of High Class Investment Values." *Banker's Magazine* (London) 115:15–34.

Granger, C. W. J. 1966. "The Typical Spectral Shape of an Economic Variable," *Econometrica* 34:150–161.

Hawtrey, R. G. 1913. *Good and Bad Trade.* London: Constable.

Hawtrey, R. G. 1932. *The Art of Central Banking.* London: Longmans, Green.

Homer, Sidney. 1963. *A History of Interest Rates.* New Brunswick, N.J.: Rutgers Univ. Press.

Keynes, J. M. 1930. *A Treatise on Money.* New York: Macmillan.

Kitchin, Joseph. 1923. "Cycles and Trends in Economic Factors." *Review of Economics and Statistics* 5:10–16.

Klein, Benjamin. 1975. "Our New Monetary Standard: The Measurement and Effects of Price Uncertainty, 1880–1973," *Economic Inquiry* 13:461–483.

MacCaulay, Frederick. 1938. *Some Theoretical Problems Suggested by the Movements of Interest Rates, Bond Yields, and Stock Prices in the United States since 1856.* New York: Nat. Bur. Econ. Res.

Mitchell, B. R., and P. Deane. 1962. *Abstract of British Historical Statistics.* Cambridge: Cambridge Univ. Press.

Mitchell, B. R., and Jones, H. 1971. *Second Abstract of British Historical Statistics.* Cambridge: Cambridge Univ. Press.

Modigliani, Franco, and Robert Shiller. 1973. "Inflation, Rational Expectations, and the Term Structure of Interest Rates," *Economica* 40:12–43.

Peake, E. G. 1928. *Bankers Magazine* (London) 125:720.

Roll, Richard. 1972. "Interest Rates on Monetary Assets and Commodity Price Index Changes," *Journal of Finance* 27:251–277.

Sargent, Thomas J. 1973. "Interest Rates and Prices in the Long Run: A Study of the Gibson Paradox," *Journal of Money, Credit and Banking* 4:385–449.

Sheppard, David K. 1971. *The Growth and Role of UK Financial Institutions*. London: Methuen.

Shiller, Robert J. 1972. "Rational Expectations and the Structure of Interest Rates." Ph.D. dissertation, Massachusetts Inst. Tech.

Siegel, Jeremy J. 1975. "The Correlation between Interest and Prices: Explanations of the Gibson Paradox." Unpublished manuscript, Univ. Pennsylvania.

Siegel, Jeremy J., and Jerold Warner. 1977. "Indexation, the Risk-Free Asset, and Capital Market Equilibrium," *Journal of Finance*.

Tooke, Thomas. 1844. *An Inquiry into the Currency Question*. London: Longman.

Wicksell, Knut. 1898. *Geldzins und Guterpreise [Interest rates and prices]*. Jena: Fischer.

Wicksell, Knut. 1962. *Lectures on Political Economy*. London: Routledge & Kegan Paul. (Lectures given in 1911.)

15

The Volatility of Long-
Term Interest Rates and
Expectations Models of
the Term Structure

15.1 Introduction

An argument that often seems to be implicit in popular criticisms of
rational expectations models of the term structure of interest rates is that
long-term interest rates are too "volatile" to accord with the averaging
inherent in the models. With these expectations models, the long-term
interest rate can be approximately represented as a long average of rationally expected future short-term rates plus a liquidity premium term.
Long linear moving averages tend to smooth out the series averaged,
and this tendency would seem to extend to nonlinear averaging schemes
inherent in alternative versions of the model. In addition, if rational expectations represent a conditional mean or "conditional average," they should
tend to change dramatically only when important new information arrives,
which could not be too often. This tendency would seem to extend to
alternative measures of conditional central tendency that might be used to
represent public expectations. It would thus seem that observed volatility
of interest rates would have to be ascribed to factors not usually represented in these models. The liquidity premium is usually described as
reflecting public attitudes toward and perceptions of risk and is usually
assumed constant or modeled as slow moving.

Observed long-term interest rates series are not much smoother than
short-rate series, as can be seen, for example, in figure 15.1, which displays
a long-rate series for high-grade bonds with over 20 years to maturity
(solid line) and a 4–6 month short-rate series (dotted line).[1] As a result of
the choppy behavior of long-term interest rates, the short-term holding
yield on long-term bonds, which is related to the percentage change in the

Reprinted with minor editing from *Journal of Political Economy* 87 (1979):1190–1219;
©1979 The University of Chicago.

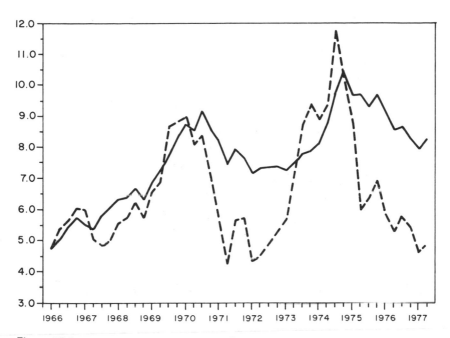

Figure 15.1
U.S. long-term interest (R) (solid line) and short-term interest rate (r) (dotted line)
quarterly, 1966:1–1977:II. See appendix B, data set 1.

long-term interest rate, has a very high variance. Figure 15.2 shows the approximate annualized one-quarter holding yield on long-term bonds, as computed from the long-term interest rate series from figure 15.1 (solid line),[2] and the same short-term interest rate (dotted line). Note that the vertical axis in figure 15.2 has smaller units than that of figure 15.1, because the one-period holding yield is so volatile. The standard deviation of the holding yield is in fact 18.6 percentage points, and the holding yield ranges in this sample from −29% to +42%. Recent U.K. data also show great short-term holding-yield volatility. For British consols, for which the time to maturity is infinite, the standard deviation of the annualized quarterly holding yield from 1956:II to 1977:II is 25.8 percentage points, and the holding yield ranges from −53% to +108%.[3] Culbertson [1957], in his well-known critique of expectations models of the term structure, remarked in connection with a graph of holding yields like our figure 15.2, "what sort of expectations, one might ask, could possibly have produced this result?"[4]

My purpose here is to develop the robust properties of a broad class of expectations models for the random behavior of long-term interest rates,

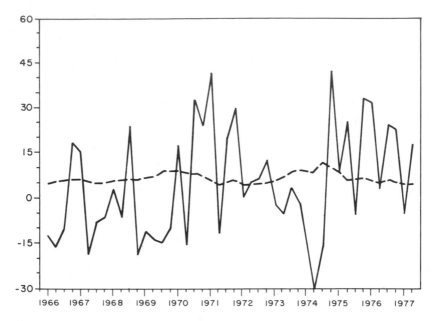

Figure 15.2
Approximate one-quarter holding yield (*H*) on the long-term bonds from figure 15.1 (solid line) and the short-term interest rate (*r*) (dotted line) quarterly, 1966:I–1977:II. See appendix B, data set 1, and note 2.

and to examine whether observed rates are too volatile to accord with these models. LeRoy and Porter [1979] have independently shown ways of evaluating such a model in the context of their analogous claim that stock prices are too volatile to accord with a model that makes stock prices equal the present discounted value of expected earnings. I have also found support [Shiller, 1979] (chapter 5) for a similar claim regarding common stock price volatility using methodology that draws on this paper. The volatility of bond prices is in a sense more basic an issue than that of stock prices, since (high-quality) bond-price movements depend only on variations in the rate of discount, whereas stock prices can change due either to a change in the rate of discount or to a change in expected earnings.

Any claim that long-term interest rates (or, in the case of the other papers, stock prices) are too volatile contradicts a large literature confirming "market efficiency" or "random-walk" behavior of certain sequences. The claim that bond markets are efficient or that long-term interest rates are approximately random walk was made, for example, by Granger and Rees [1968], Bierwag and Grove [1971], Laffer and Zecher [1975], Phillips and Pippenger [1976], Sargent [1976, 1979], Mishkin [1978], and Pesando [1978]. However, we shall see that even if long-term interest rates are much too volatile, conventional tests of "market efficiency" may be weak. Other studies have, in any event, provided evidence contrary to some forms of simple models of bond-market efficiency [Roll, 1970; Sargent, 1972; Cargill, 1975; and Fama, 1976], so the claim that market efficiency fails due to excess volatility should not be regarded as highly improbable based on past literature.

In section 15.2 I will discuss the basic linearized model and show how it can be derived as an approximation from a number of different versions of the expectations model. In section 15.3 I will derive some inequality restrictions that show in what sense the expectations model implies long-term interest rate series must be stable and smooth, and I will contrast this with observed behavior of long rates.

In section 15.4 I test some market-efficiency restrictions by running simple regressions. If long rates are too volatile to accord with the theory, then they must also be forecastable in a way inconsistent with the theory, and this is tested here. Implications of the model for the spectral density of interest rates are derived in appendix A.

15.2   A Linearized Expectations Model

The linearized model we shall study relates the n-period interest rate (yield to maturity on n-period bonds) $R_t^{(n)}$ to a weighted average of expected future one-period (short-term) interest rates $r_t, r_{t+1}, \ldots$:

$$R_t^{(n)} = \frac{1 - \gamma}{1 - \gamma^n} \sum_{K=0}^{n-1} \gamma^K E_t(r_{t+k}) + \Phi_n, \tag{1}$$

where γ is a constant $0 < \gamma < 1$ and Φ_n is a constant "liquidity premium."[5] Here, E_t is the expectations operator conditional on information available at time t, which includes all current and lagged interest rates. Linear models relating long rates to expected future short rates should be familiar to most readers; however, the precise form I have chosen here requires some explanation, since the form is important for the analysis that follows. Most simple linear term structure models relate long-term interest rates to an unweighted simple average of expected short rates. Those models are indeed appropriate for pure (no coupon) discount bonds. In contrast, this equation involves weights that describe a truncated exponential (or "Koyck") distribution scaled so that the sum of the coefficients is one. Expected short-term interest rates in the near future carry more weight in determining the long yield than do expected short-term interest rates in the more distant future. We will set $\gamma = 1/(1 + \bar{R})$, and then (1) relates $R_t^{(n)}$ to the "present value" of future short-term interest rates discounted by $\bar{R}$. This model is intended for coupon-carrying bonds that are selling par, or for consols with $n = \infty$. Since longer-term bonds that are available do carry coupons, and since yield series for bonds selling near par or for consols are available, this expression suits our purposes.

Note that our model is not specific to a particular time interval chosen, for example, whether quarterly or annual. If the model holds for a given time interval, then it holds for a higher time interval as well. By regrouping terms in (1) where m is replaced by mn and then using (1) again where n is replaced by m, it is easily verified that

$$R_t^{(mn)} = \frac{1 - \hat{\gamma}}{1 - \hat{\gamma}^n} \sum_{K=0}^{n-1} \hat{\gamma}^K E_t[R_{t+Km}^{(m)}] + \hat{\Phi}_n,$$

where $\hat{\gamma} = \gamma^m$ and $\hat{\Phi}_n = \Phi_{mn} - \Phi_m$. Hence, mn-period rates are related to a truncated Koyck average of expected m-period rates over the next n time intervals, where time intervals are m periods long.

Expression (1) is a linearization of any of a number of versions of the rational expectations model as applied to bonds that carry coupons and mature in n periods. To see this, we begin with a few definitions. For coupon-carrying bonds, for which we normalize the principal at maturity at 1.00, and for which coupon rate per period is denoted by C, the present value $V_t^{(n)}$ of future coupons and principal is defined by

$$V_t^{(n)} \equiv C \sum_{K=0}^{n-1} \prod_{j=0}^{K} (1 + r_{t+j})^{-1} + \prod_{j=0}^{n-1} (1 + r_{t+j})^{-1} \equiv V^{(n)}(\mathbf{r}_t), \tag{2}$$

where $\mathbf{r}_t$ is defined as the vector $(r_t, r_{t+1}, \ldots, r_{t+n-1})$, and $V^{(n)}(\cdot)$ will refer to the present value function here defined. I have assumed here that coupons are paid once per period starting after one period. The first term in the expression is the present value of the stream of coupon payments; the second term is the present value of the payment of principal ($\$1.00$) at maturity.

The yield to maturity or long-term interest rate $R_t^{(n)}$ on an n-period bond is determined by the requirement that the price $P_t^{(n)}$ of the bond is the present value of coupons and principal discounted by $R_t^{(n)}$; that is,[6]

$$P_t^{(n)} = V^{(n)}[R_t^{(n)}] = \frac{C}{R_t^{(n)}} + \frac{R_t^{(n)} - C}{R_t^{(n)}[1 + R_t^{(n)}]^n}. \tag{3}$$

If $R_t^{(n)} = C$, $P_t^{(n)} = 1$, and conversely. Such bonds, whose price today equals the principal paid at maturity, are selling "at par." Since new bonds are issued at par, our newly issued and recently offered bond yield averages refer to such bonds.

The one-period holding yield $H_t^{(n)}$ is equal to the capital gain $P_{t+1}^{(n-1)} - P_t^{(n)}$ (note than an n-period bond at time t becomes an $[n - 1]$-period bond at time $t + 1$) plus the coupon payment C at the end of the period divided by the price $P_t^{(n)}$ at time t (to convert to a rate of return):[7]

$$H_t^{(n)} = \frac{P_{t+1}^{(n-1)} - P_t^{(n)} + C}{P_t^{(n)}}. \tag{4}$$

This may be rewritten, using (3), in terms of the yields to maturity $R_t^{(n)}$ and $R_{t+1}^{(n-1)}$:[8]

$$H_t^{(n)} = \left\{ C + \frac{C}{R_{t+1}^{(n-1)}} + \frac{R_{t+1}^{(n-1)} - C}{R_{t+1}^{(n-1)}[1 + R_{t+1}^{(n-1)}]^{n-1}} \right\}$$

$$\Big/ \left\{ \frac{C}{R_t^{(n)}} + \frac{R_t^{(n)} - C}{R_t^{(n)}[1 + R_t^{(n)}]^n} \right\} - 1. \tag{5}$$

The simplest way to motivate expression (1) is to consider a model that relates the expected one-period holding yield to the short-term interest rate:

$$F_t[H_t^{(n)}] = r_t + \phi^{(n)}, \tag{6}$$

where $\phi^{(n)}$ is a constant. In the one-period Sharpe-Lintner mean-variance capital asset pricing model, as applied to the bond market by Roll [1971], McCallum [1975], and Friend, Westerfield, and Granito [1978], $\phi^{(n)}$ will equal $\beta^{(n)}[E(R_m) - r]$, where R_m is the return on the market portfolio and $\beta^{(n)}$ is equal to the covariance between $H_t^{(n)}$ and the return on the market portfolio divided by the variance of the return on the market portfolio. The capital asset pricing model itself does not necessarily imply that $\phi^{(n)}$ is constant, although the usual tests of the capital asset pricing model as in Friend and Blume [1970] or Black, Jensen, and Scholes [1972], as well as the above cited applications to the bond market, assume this is true, at least over certain time intervals. If we make this assumption, then substituting (5) into (6) gives us a first-order nonlinear rational expectations model relating $R^{(n)}$ and r. The nonlinearities, however, create fundamental problems. Our approach will be to linearize expression (5) around $R_t^{(n)} = R_{t+1}^{(n-1)} = \bar{R} = C$ (i.e., take a Taylor expansion truncated after the linear term) to give us a linearized holding yield $\tilde{H}_t^{(n)}$ that will approximate $H_t^{(n)}$. This procedure gives us[9]

$$\tilde{H}_t^{(n)} = \frac{R_t^{(n)} - \gamma_n R_{t+1}^{(n-1)}}{1 - \gamma_n}, \tag{7}$$

where $\gamma_n = \{1 + \bar{R}[1 - 1/(1+\bar{R})^{n-1}]^{-1}\}^{-1} = \gamma(1-\gamma^{n-1})/(1-\gamma^n)$. Substituting this expression for $\tilde{H}_t^{(n)}$ in place of $H_t^{(n)}$ in (6) and rearranging gives

$$R_t^{(n)} = \gamma_n E_t[R_{t+1}^{(n-1)}] + (1 - \gamma_n)[r_t + \phi^{(n)}],$$

which is a first-order linear rational expectations difference equation in $R_t^{(n)}$ with variable coefficients. Such a model may be solved using familiar methods in the rational expectations literature—as surveyed, for example, in Shiller [1978]—by a method of recursive substitution and with a terminal value condition for the maturity date. To do this, one merely substitutes in place of $E_t R_{t+1}^{(n-1)}$ in the above expression the expected value of the expression obtained by replacing t by $t+1$ and n by $n-1$. After doing this, one then replaces $E_t[R_{t+2}^{(n-2)}]$ in the resulting expression, and so on. The resulting solution (involving a terminal value condition that $R_{t+n-1}^{(1)} = r_{t+n-1}$, or that, in effect, the price of the bond is 1.00 at $t+n$) is expression (1) with

$$\Phi_n = \frac{1-\gamma}{1-\gamma^n} \sum_{K=0}^{n-1} \gamma^K \phi^{(n-K)}. \tag{8}$$

The model (1) is thus a consequence of the capital asset pricing model under our linearization assumption coupled with the additional assumption introduced by the terminal condition. The capital asset pricing model itself is not (in contrast to model [1]) invariant to changes in the time interval chosen, that is, to the investment horizon of the representative investor. Roll [1971], in his capital asset pricing model of the bond market, tried to find from the data what is the "representative" investment horizon of investors. My linearization sidesteps this problem.

The linear expression (1) may also serve as an approximation to a number of other versions of the expectations model of the term structure, so long as interest rates do not vary too much. The model discussed above, in which expected one-period holding yields $H_t^{(n)}$ equal the short rate plus a constant, may be written as $P_t^{(n)} = E_t V^{(n)}(r_t + \phi)$, where $\phi = [\phi^{(n)}, \phi^{(n-1)}, \ldots, \phi^{(1)}]$. An alternative model is one in which forward rates equal expected future spot rates plus a liquidity premium, which can be written as $P_t^{(n)} = V^{(n)}(E_t r_t + \phi)$. Other models include a model in which the expected total return from holding a bond n periods (reinvesting coupons at the short rate) equals the expected total return from investing in a sequence of shorts for n periods,

$$P_t^{(n)} = E_t \left[V^{(n)}(\mathbf{r}_t) \prod_{i=0}^{n-1} (1 + r_{t+i}) \right] \Big/ E_t \left[\prod_{i=0}^{n-1} (1 + r_{t+i}) \right],$$

or a model in which the yield $R_t^{(n)}$ equals the expected yield from holding a sequence of shorts that are liquidated in a manner that matches the coupon principal payout structure of par long-term bonds, $P_t^{(n)} = V^{(n)}[R_t^{(n)}]$, where

$$R_t^{(n)} = E_t \left\{ \left[1 - \prod_{i=0}^{n-1} (1 + r_{t+i})^{-1} \right] \Big/ \sum_{K=0}^{n-1} \prod_{j=0}^{K} (1 + r_{t+j})^{-1} \right\}. \text{[10]}$$

All of these models have the common property that if the expectations operator is replaced by the number 1, the models reduce to $P_t^{(n)} = V^{(n)}(\mathbf{r}_t + \boldsymbol{\phi})$ for some vector $\boldsymbol{\phi}$; that is, under perfect certainty they reduce (except for the liquidity premium) to the present-value formula itself. One can readily verify that if the present-value expression (2) is linearized around $\mathbf{r}_t = \bar{R} = C$, we get

$$V_t^{(n)} \cong 1 - \sum_{K=0}^{n-1} \left(\frac{1}{1 + \bar{R}} \right)^{K+1} (r_{t+K} - \bar{R}).$$

If the variation in interest rates is not too large, all of the above models can thus be written as[11]

$$P_t^{(n)} \cong 1 - \sum_{K=0}^{n-1} \left(\frac{1}{1 + \bar{R}} \right)^{K+1} [E_t r_{t+K} + \phi^{(n-K)} - \bar{R}].$$

Similarly, the expression (3) for yield can be linearized around $R_t^{(n)} = \bar{R} = C$ as

$$P_t^{(n)} \cong 1 - \frac{1}{\bar{R}} \left[1 - \frac{1}{(1 + \bar{R})^n} \right] [R_t^{(n)} - \bar{R}].$$

Equating the above two expressions and solving for $R_t^{(n)}$ yields expression (1) with $\gamma = 1/(1 + \bar{R})$ and Φ as given by expression (8). Expression (1) is thus an accurate characterization of all these rational expectations models of the term structure whenever the variation in short-term interest rates is not too large. Our results below concerning the relative volatility of long rates when compared to that of short rates will be robust characterizations of all these models whenever the level of interest rate volatility is not too high.

15.3 The Volatility of Interest Rates in the Linearized Expectations Model

We will assume now for ease of exposition that the long-term bond under consideration is a perpetuity, that is, $n = \infty$, so that $\gamma_n = \gamma$, and we will drop superscripts for R and H. Results here can be routinely extended to the case of finite maturity bonds.

The simplest (albeit unrealistic) assumption one can make regarding the formation of expectations is that there is perfect knowledge of future one-period rates of interest and hence perfect knowledge of future long-term rates as well. Then, $R_t = R_t^*$, where R_t^* is an "ex-post rational rate" analogous to that defined in Shiller and Siegel [1977] (chapter 14) given by

$$R_t^* = (1 - \gamma) \sum_{K=0}^{\infty} \gamma^K r_{t+K}, \qquad (9)$$

which is just expression (1) for $n = \infty$ and $\Phi = 0$ where the expectations operator has been dropped. Here R_t^* is a weighted moving average of r_t.

In figure 15.3 I have plotted the ex-post rational rate R^* based on the short-rate series shown in figure 15.1 and the assumption that $\gamma = .98$ and R^* at the end of the sample equals the average short rate over this sample. That is, I used $R_t^* = \gamma R_{t+1}^* + (1 - \gamma)r_t$, working backward from the terminal value of R^*. One notes the dramatically reduced amplitude for this long-rate series R^* compared with that actually observed for the long-rate series R, and that the short-run movements in the long rate R that we observed in figure 15.1 seem totally absent from R^*. This is entirely as we would expect, since we know (see appendix A) that the moving average in (9) reduces cycles of wavelength 5–6 years by a factor of about .08 and of very short wavelengths by a factor of about .01.[12]

One might also note a curious aspect of the behavior of the long-term interest rate in figure 15.3. Whenever the long rate is above the short rate it is rising, and whenever it is below it, it is falling. The greater the spread between the long rate and the short rate, the greater the rate of increase of the long rate. The reason for this behavior is not hard to find. Whenever the long rate is above the short rate, the long bond has a higher current yield (coupon divided by price), which must be offset by an expected capital loss if expected holding-period returns are to be equalized. A capital loss of course requires an increase in long rates. Conversely, when long rates are low relative to short rates, there must be an expected capital gain, that is, a decline in long rates. If one compares this behavior in figure 15.3

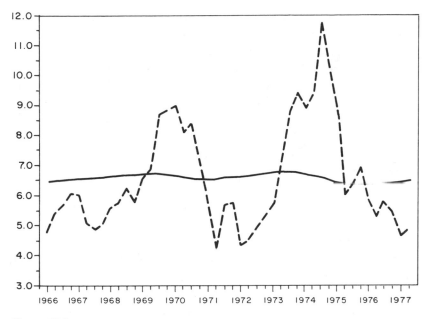

Figure 15.3
Ex post rational long term interest rate (R^*) (solid line), or what long rates would have been if bonds were priced at present value with actual subsequent short rates (r) (dotted line). See expression (9) and short rate from figure 15.1.

with the actual behavior of the long rate in figure 15.1, one again sees a striking difference.

These striking differences between the behavior of the long rate implied by (9) and that actually observed suggest that the model (1) is incorrect too. However, we shall see that the inclusion of the expectations operator in the model (1) causes nontrivial complications, and when these are taken into account the case for excess volatility is not as simple to prove as one might have expected.

The model (1) makes $R_t = E_t R_t^* + \Phi$. This means the forecast error $R_t^* + \Phi - R_t$ must be uncorrelated with information known at time t, which includes all current and lagged interest rates:

$$E[(R_t^* + \Phi - R_t) \cdot R_{t-\tau}] = 0, \qquad \tau \geq 0;$$
$$E[(R_t^* + \Phi - R_t) \cdot r_{t-\tau}] = 0, \qquad \tau \geq 0. \qquad (10)$$

Here, the t subscript on the expectations operator has been dropped since these are unconditional expectations. Implications of these restrictions for the spectrum of the bivariate process (R_t, r_t) are discussed in appendix A. One might think of testing these restrictions by regressing $R_t^* - R_t$ onto a constant and R_t, R_{t-1}, R_{t-2}, and r_t, r_{t-1}, r_{t-2}, ... (or any subset of these). The theoretical regression coefficients (except for the intercept) must be zero. It should be obvious that, with the data plotted in the figures, not all coefficients would be zero. Since R_t^* is very stable, and R_t very volatile, movements in $R_t^* - R_t$ correspond closely to movements in R_t, and hence $R_t^* - R_t$ and R_t would show correlation approaching -1. The residuals in such regressions are, however, serially correlated so ordinary significance tests are not valid. Along lines suggested by generalized least squares, the data may be transformed to eliminate the serial correlation by subtracting γ times the led value from the current value of all variables. Such a "generalized least-squares" regression would then amount to regressing $\tilde{H}_t - r_t$ onto transformed right-hand variables.[13] Except for a constant due to Φ, $\tilde{H}_t - r_t$ is, like $R_t^* - R_t$, a forecast error that should be uncorrelated with all information at time t but that, unlike $R_t^* - R_t$, is serially uncorrelated since its lagged value is known at time t. There is, however, still one important difference between this model and the usual generalized least-squares model, namely, the residual $\tilde{H}_t - r_t$ is uncorrelated with all current and past, but not future, interest rates, and hence the variables $R_t - \gamma R_{t+1}$ and $r_t - \gamma r_{t+1}$ cannot be included in the regression. The correct procedure to test the model is then to regress $\tilde{H}_t - r_t$ onto a constant and $R_{t-1} - \gamma R_t$, $R_{t-2} - \gamma R_{t-1}, \ldots$, and $r_{t-1} - \gamma r_t$, $r_{t-2} - \gamma r_{t-1}, \ldots$, or, just onto a constant and R_t, $R_{t-1}, \ldots, r_t, r_{t-1}, \ldots$, and do a significance test such as a conventional F-test on the coefficients. I will perform tests along these lines in section 15.4. For the remainder of this section, we will concern ourselves instead with the implications of (10) for the volatility of interest rates.

The first implication of (10) for interest rate volatility has already been suggested. If a regression of $R_t^* - R_t$ onto a constant and R_t is to yield a zero coefficient for R_t, then var(R) must be less than var(R^*), as Shiller [1972] and LeRoy and Porter [1979] noted. Since $(R_t^* - R_t)$ must be uncorrelated with R_t, var$(R_t^*) = $ var$(R_t) + $ var$(R_t^* - R_t)$. Moreover, since R_t^* is a moving average of r_t, it must have a smaller variance than r_t, and hence var$(R_t) \leqslant$ var$(R_t^*) \leqslant$ var(r).

This means that the model (1) must imply an even smaller amplitude for the long-term interest rate than that predicted by equation (9). It seems clear, then, that the large amplitude of movements of the long rate as observed in figure 15.1 could not be reconciled with the behavior of short rates if short rates are expected to swing up and down in the future with repeated episodes roughly like those observed in cycles from 1967 to 1971 and 1972 to 1976. We cannot rule out, however, that other behavior of the short rate is expected, unless we model the stochastic behavior of the short rate. If r is expected to have some very slow (long-cycle) movements in the future, then these movements will not be effectively reduced by the moving average (9), so R^* and R may yet have a fairly high variance.

The inequality $\text{var}(R) < \text{var}(R^*)$ puts limits on the total amplitude of the long-rate series. It does not tell us whether the long-rate series need be a "smooth" series. Intuition would suggest that the smoothness observed in figure 15.3 should extend, at least in some sense, to the model (1). We can show that this is the case by finding an upper bound to the variance of the linearized holding-period yield $\tilde{H}$ or $\tilde{H} - r$. In doing this, we make no assumptions, it should be emphasized, about the nature of the random processes or the information used in forecasting, such as the bivariate ARIMA forecasts assumed by LeRoy and Porter [1979]. We assume only (10) and that processes are stationary.

From (10) and our discussion above, we know that $\text{cov}(\tilde{H}_t - r_t, R_t) = 0$. Using the definition (7) of $\tilde{H}_t$ for $n = \infty$ (so that $\gamma_n = \gamma$), we then see that

$$\text{cov}(R_{t+1}, R_t) = \frac{1}{\gamma} \text{var}(R_t) - \frac{(1-\gamma)}{\gamma} \rho_{rR} \sqrt{\text{var}(R_t)} \sqrt{\text{var}(r_t)}, \tag{11}$$

where ρ_{rR} is the correlation coefficient between r_t and R_t. We then take the expression for the variance of the holding yield $\tilde{H}_t$:[14] $\text{var}(\tilde{H}_t) = \text{var}[(R_t - \gamma R_{t+1})/(1 - \gamma)] = [(1 + \gamma^2) \text{var}(R_t) - 2\gamma \text{cov}(R_t, R_{t+1})]/(1 - \gamma)^2$ and substitute into this expression the expression (11) for $\text{cov}(R_t, R_{t+1})$ and maximize (by differentiating and setting to zero) the resulting expression with respect to $\text{var}(R_t)$. The second derivative must be negative, since our model implies $\rho_{rR} > 0$. We find that the maximum is $V_{\tilde{H}} = \text{var}(r) \rho_{rR}^2/(1 - \gamma^2)$. Since positive semidefiniteness requires that $\rho_{rR}^2 \leqslant 1$, our model then implies that

$$\sigma(\tilde{H}_t) \leqslant a\sigma(r_t), \tag{I-1}$$

where $a = (1 - \gamma^2)^{-1/2}$ and σ denotes standard deviation. Since $\rho_{rR}^2 \text{var}(r) = \text{var}(\hat{r})$, where $\hat{r}$ is the fitted value of a regression of r_t on R_t, we also have the stronger inequality

$$\sigma(\tilde{H}_t) \leqslant a\sigma(\hat{r}_t). \tag{I-1'}$$

The coefficient a may be rather larger than the one expected (for $\gamma = .98$ with quarterly data, $a \cong 5$), so fairly high holding-yield volatility is consistent with the model. Still a is finite and (I-1) and (I-1') can be tested. The coefficient a depends on our choice of $\gamma = 1/(1 + \bar{R})$ and depends ultimately on the interest rate $\bar{R}$ we linearize around. However, for small $\bar{R}$, $a \cong 1/\sqrt{2\bar{R}}$, so that a is not highly sensitive to the choice of $\bar{R}$. If we varied the log of $\bar{R}$ by as much as $\pm.30$, the log of a would vary only by about $\pm.15$. This will generally not affect our results.

These inequalities quantify the smoothing behavior of the model, since $\sigma(\tilde{H}_t)$ is high when R is a choppy unsmooth series. Clearly, the permissible standard deviation of $\tilde{H}$ increases with the standard deviation of r, and only that component of the variance of r, namely, the variance of $\hat{r}$, that correlates with R is relevant. The correlation coefficient ρ_{rR} measures how much information about future r is implicit in current r_t. If ρ_{rR} is one, then the r process is first-order autoregressive $\tilde{r}_t = \lambda \tilde{r}_{t-1} + \varepsilon_t$ and $E_t(\tilde{r}_{t+j}) = \lambda^j \tilde{r}_t$, $j \geqslant 0$, and $\tilde{R}_t = \tilde{r}_t (1 - \gamma)/(1 - \gamma\lambda)$, where the tilde denotes demeaned series. The maximum possible $\sigma(\tilde{H})$ for given $\sigma(r)$ then occurs with $\lambda = \gamma$, and here $\sigma(R) = \sigma(r)/(1 + \gamma) \cong \frac{1}{2}\sigma(r)$.[15]

By the same sort of reasoning, we can also show that restrictions on the smoothness of the long-rate series can be found that do not require knowledge of $\mathrm{var}(r_t)$ and would hold, technically, even if $\mathrm{var}(r_t)$ were infinite (r_t is unstationary) so long as $\mathrm{var}(\Delta r_t)$ is known and finite.[16] As long as Δr_t is stationary, $\tilde{H}_t - r_t$ and $R_t - r_t$ will also be stationary, and we can put limits on $\mathrm{var}(\tilde{H}_t - r_t)$ given $\mathrm{var}(\Delta r_t)$.

To show this, we use the restriction $\mathrm{cov}(\tilde{H}_t - r_t, R_t - r_t) = 0$, which follows, as before, from (10). This restriction implies, instead of (11), that

$$\mathrm{cov}(R_t - r_t, R_{t+1} - r_{t+1}) = \frac{1}{\gamma}\mathrm{var}(R_t - r_t) - \mathrm{cov}(R_t - r_t, \Delta r_{t+1}). \tag{11'}$$

One may then substitute (11') into $\mathrm{var}(\tilde{H}_t - r_t) = (1 - \gamma)^{-2}\mathrm{var}[(R_t - r_t) - \gamma(R_{t+1} - r_{t+1}) - \gamma\Delta r_{t+1}]$, which yields

$$\mathrm{var}(\tilde{H}_t - r_t) = (1 - \gamma)^{-2}[(\gamma^2 - 1)\mathrm{var}(R_t - r_t) + \gamma^2\mathrm{var}(\Delta r_t)$$

$$+ 2\gamma^2\rho_{R_t - r_t, \Delta r_t}\sqrt{\mathrm{var}(R_t - r_t)}\sqrt{\mathrm{var}(\Delta r_t)}].$$

If we maximize this expression with respect to both $\mathrm{var}(R_t - r_t)$ and $\rho_{R_t - r_t, \Delta r_t}$, we get an upper bound to $\mathrm{var}(\tilde{H}_t - r_t)$. Our model then implies that

$$\sigma(\tilde{H}_t - r_t) \leqslant b\sigma(\Delta r_t),$$

$$b = \gamma(1 - \gamma^2)^{-1/2}/(1 - \gamma) = a\gamma/(1 - \gamma) = a/\bar{R}. \tag{I-2}$$

The upper bound is obtained if $\rho_{R_t - r_t, \Delta r_t} = 1$ and, in a case analogous to that which gave rise to the upper bound in (I.1), Δr_t is first-order autoregressive, $\Delta r_t = \gamma \Delta r_{t-1} + \varepsilon_t$, and $E_t(\Delta r_{t+j}) = \gamma^j \Delta r_t$, $j \geqslant 0$. This upper bound, which is quite high, is obtained only when r_t is very strongly unstationary. In fact, for all of our data sets Δr_t is negatively correlated with $R_t - r_t$. If we require that $\rho_{R_t-r_t,\Delta r_t}$ be less than or equal to zero, the maximum $\mathrm{var}(\tilde{H}_t - r_t)$ comes when $\mathrm{var}(R_t - r_t) = 0$, and so our model implies:

$$\sigma(\tilde{H}_t - r_t) \leqslant c\sigma(\Delta r_t),$$

$$c = \gamma/(1 - \gamma) = 1/\bar{R}.$$

(I-3)

The upper bond occurs when Δr_t is white noise, r_t is a random walk, and $R_t = r_t + \Phi$.

The elements in the inequalities (I-1), (I-1′), (I-2), and (I-3) are examined for six data sets in table 15.1. All of the six data sets involve bonds that have a sufficiently large time to maturity that they may be approximated for our purposes as consols, and $\gamma_n \cong \gamma$.[17] However, γ_n (using for n the maturity of a representative bound in the sample and for $\bar{R}$ the average value of R over the sample) was substituted for γ in the above formulas so as not to overstate the holding-yield variance.[18]

We see from the sample standard deviations that for five of the six data sets $\sigma(\tilde{H}) > a\sigma(r)$, violating the inequality (I-1), and for all six data sets $\sigma(\tilde{H}) > a\sigma(\hat{r})$, violating the inequality (I-1′).[19] One also notes that for two data sets $\sigma(R) > \sigma(r)$. The inequalities (I-2) and (I-3) are, however, satisfied by the data.

That the inequalities (I-1) and (I-1′) are violated by the data constitutes some evidence against the model (1). That (I-2) and (I-3) are satisfied means that one cannot find evidence contrary to the model based only on the knowledge of $\sigma(\Delta r)$ and the simple arguments alluded to before about the smoothing imposed by the averaging in (1). In simple terms, it is conceivable that even if $\sigma(\Delta r)$ is very small, $\sigma(r)$ may be large, if r is expected to drift far above its historical range in the future (and Φ is sufficiently negative that R is not large). The short-run movements in R might reflect genuine new information about the large values of r that will come in the future.

Since $\tilde{H}_t - r_t$ and $\tilde{H}_t$ are approximately serially uncorrelated, we can put a lower bound on $\sigma(\tilde{H} - r)$ and $\sigma(\tilde{H})$ by computing a one-sided 95% confidence interval for them based on the χ^2 sampling distribution.[20] The lower bounds in table 15.1 are denoted $\sigma_m(\tilde{H} - r)$ and $\sigma_m(\tilde{H})$. Then if we accept that the true standard deviations lie above these values, $\sigma_m(\tilde{H})/a$ is the lowest possible value for $\sigma(r)$ and $\sigma(\hat{r})$ if the model (1) is to hold. For

Table 15.1
Standard deviations of interest rates and holding-period returns[a]

Data set, country, and period	γ_n / n	$\sigma(R)$ / $\sigma(\Delta R)$	$\sigma(r)$ / $\sigma(\Delta r)$	$\sigma(H)$ / $\sigma_m(H)$	$\sigma(\hat{H})$ / $\sigma_m(\hat{H})$	$a\sigma(\hat{r})$ / $a\sigma(r)$	$\sigma(\hat{H} - r)$ / $\sigma_m(\hat{H} - r)$	$b\sigma(\Delta r)$ / $c\sigma(\Delta r)$
1. U.S., beginning of quarter, 1966:I–1977:II	.978 / 100	1.39 / .429	1.78 / .999	18.6 / 15.8	19.5 / 16.5	4.75 / 8.55	19.7 / 16.8	213 / 44.4
2. U.S., beginning of month, 1969:I–1974:I	.992 / 288	.433 / .206	1.77 / .512	27.7 / 24.0	27.4 / 23.6	6.25 / 14.03	27.5 / 23.8	503 / 63.5
3. U.S., beginning of year, 1960–1976	.925 / 25	1.85 / .760	1.39 / 1.29	9.09 / 7.09	9.82 / 7.65	2.93 / 3.66	9.69 / 7.55	41.9 / 15.9
4. U.S., beginning of year, 1919–1958	.940 / 25	1.04 / .327	1.86 / .950	5.21 / 4.36	5.48 / 4.58	4.73 / 5.44	5.31 / 4.44	43.5 / 14.8
5. U.K., end of quarter, 1956:I–1977:II	.980 / ∞	3.31 / .689	2.84 / 1.36	25.8 / 22.9	34.4 / 30.4	12.3 / 14.3	34.3 / 30.4	335 / 66.7
6. U.K., annual average, 1824–1929	.968 / ∞	.596 / .159	1.17 / 1.20	4.27 / 3.82	4.95 / 4.43	2.28 / 4.66	4.97 / 4.44	144 / 36.2

a. The top row of terms in the column heads refers to the top line of each data set. The second row of terms refers to the second line of each data set. See appendix B for description of data sets 1–6. The σ denotes sample standard deviation: σ_m denotes the lower bounds of a one-sided 95% confidence interval for the standard deviation, assuming observations are normal and uncorrelated. Except for data set 2 (for which see appendix B), H is computed from expression (5) using n indicated and $C = R_t$. For all data sets, $\hat{H}$ is computed from expression (7) using γ_n indicated; γ_n is computed as in (7) with n indicated using for R the mean of R over the sample period. All rates are expressed in percent per annum in this and subsequent tables and must be converted to rate per period to accord with notation in the text. The parameter a is defined as in inequality (I-1), b in (I-2) and c in (I-3), with γ as given in the first column.

data sets 1, 2, 3, and 5 the standard deviation of the short rate would have to be roughly twice its historically observed value in order to justify this standard deviation of $\tilde{H}$, given the inequality (I-1).

15.4   Testing Equality Restrictions on the Cross-Covariance Function

We have seen that in all data sets the sample standard deviations of $\tilde{H}_t$ and r_t do not satisfy the inequality (I-1'). This implies that the sample covariances do not satisfy the equality restriction $\text{cov}(\tilde{H}_t - r_t, R_t) = 0$, which was used to prove (I-1') (at least as long as the sample variance of R_t approximately equals the sample variance of R_{t+1}). Yet we have noted that many authors have studied some of the covariance restrictions implied by the model (by running appropriate regressions) for various samples and concluded in favor of the rational expectations model. Why then was it not discovered by these authors that this covariance restriction was violated in the sample? I will offer two explanations. First (and foremost), even if the holding-period yield variance is much too high, the R^2 in the regressions that would reveal this may be very low. Second, many authors have not run the right regressions, that is, they tested some restrictions that are not relevant to the holding-yield variance inequalities.

To see the first point, consider, for example, the monthly data for which the point is most dramatic. With monthly data, the parameter γ_n will be very nearly one. In data set 2, it is .992. The maximum standard deviation of the one-period holding yield consistent with the rational expectations model occurs when R_t is given by the simple autoregression $R_t = \gamma_n R_{t-1} + \varepsilon_t$, and then the standard deviation of $\tilde{H}_t$ is about 12 times the standard deviation of R_t. If, on the other hand, the correlation of R_t with its own lagged value is only slightly smaller, then the standard deviation of the one-period holding yield may be much higher. For example, if the correlation of R_t with R_{t+1} is .96, then the standard deviation of $\tilde{H}$ is about 35 times that of R_t. In this situation, if ΔR_{t+1} is regressed on R_t, the R^2 (i.e., the proportion of the variance of ΔR_{t+1} explained by R_t) is only .02. This R^2 turns out to be very small (and may remain small if other independent variables are added), so that it is unlikely to be significant in small samples. Hence many would be led to conclude that R_t is approximately a random walk.

The second point is that many of the most elaborate studies of the covariance restrictions implied by the model, such as those by Sutch [1968], Shiller [1972], and Modigliani and Shiller [1973], simply did not test these particular restrictions. These studies tested, in essence, whether a regression of R onto current and lagged r and current and lagged inflation rates produces an equation (the "term-structure equation") that is the same as an optimal forecasting equation for R^* based on the same variables. Neither R nor $R - r$ appeared on the right-hand side of the equations. In fact, the serially uncorrelated residual in the term-structure equation (which was ascribed in part to exogenous shocks to supply and demand in various "habitats") meant that high R or high $R - r$ would indeed imply high $\tilde{H} - r$.

Sargent [1979], on the other hand, did test (in essence) these restrictions, along with others implied by the model, using a likelihood ratio test. His tests did not reject the hypothesis that all restrictions hold, perhaps due to low power of this test for the particular restrictions that we are concerned with here and perhaps to his use of a relatively short-term (5-year) bond to represent a long bond.

We now proceed to test restrictions in (10) by running regressions as described above. When one contemplates running such regressions, one must confront the fact that there are potentially an infinite number of coefficients in the model, yet only a finite amount of data. One must eliminate variables before running a regression. Since all coefficients are zero, it does not matter from the standpoint of the model which variables are eliminated. My approach was to eliminate all but R_t (table 15.2) or $(R_t - r_t)$ (table 15.3). It is good statistical methodology to concentrate the power of one's test onto an interesting alternative hypothesis. I have attempted to do this in consideration of the volatility arguments noted above (these restrictions produced the inequalities) and the understandability and simplicity of the alternative hypothesis. Sargent's [1979] regressions included, in effect, eight right-hand-side variables: the current and three lagged values of both R and r.[21]

The regressions were run for each of the data sets using both $\tilde{H}_t$ and H_t. Results were very similar with the two different measures of one-period holding yields, and I chose to present in table 15.2 those using $H_t - r_t$ and R_t and in table 15.3 those using $\tilde{H}_t - r_t$ and $R_t - r_t$. In table 15.3, the results are reported as a regression of $R_{t+1} - R_t$ on $R_t - r_t$, and since $R_{t+1} - R_t$ is a linear combination of $\tilde{H}_t - r_t$ and the independent variable, it amounts to the same regression. The coefficient of $R_t - r_t$ should then equal $(1 - \gamma_n)/\gamma_n$, which is greater than zero.

One notes, since R_t enters positively into the determination of H_t and $\tilde{H}_t$, that R_t in effect appears on both sides of all of these equations. This might seem to suggest an upward "bias" for the slope coefficient in the

Table 15.2
Regression of spread between short-term holding yield of long-term bonds and short rate on the long rate $(H_{1t} - r_t = A + B \cdot R_t + e_t)^a$

Data set, country, and period	A (t_A)	B (t_B)	R^2	SE	D-W
1. U.S., beginning of quarter, 1966:I–1977:II	−40.2 (−2.72)*	4.97 (2.62)*	.155	17.7	1.63
2. U.S., beginning of month, 1969:I–1974:I	−139 (−2.28)*	18.2 (2.27)*	.080	26.9	2.01
3. U.S., beginning of year, 1960–1976	−8.81 (−1.14)	1.32 (1.11)	.076	8.81	1.48
4. U.S., beginning of year, 1919–1958	−1.14 (−.373)	.748 (.954)	.023	5.08	1.59
5. U.K., end of quarter, 1956:I–1977:II	−14.7 (−2.03)*	1.54 (1.86)*	.040	25.2	1.88
6. U.K., annual average, 1824–1929	−2.50 (−1.51)	.646 (.913)	.008	4.32	1.25

* Significant at the 5% level with a one-sided test. See appendix B for source of data.
a. Numbers in parentheses are t-statistics.

Table 15.3
Regression of change in long rate on long rate–short rate spread $(R_{t+1} - R_t = A + B \cdot [R_t - r_t] + e_t)$

Data set, country, period, and dates	A (t_A)	B (t_B) $[t'_B]$	R^2	SE	D-W
1. U.S., beginning of quarter, 1966:I–1977:II	.211 (2.97)*	−.125 (−3.33)* [−3.93]*	.201	.388	2.21
2. U.S., beginning of month, 1969:I–1974:I	.039 (1.27)	−.020 (−1.22) [−1.68]*	.024	.206	2.17
3. U.S., beginning of year, 1960–1976	.451 (1.49)	−.187 (−1.10) [−1.58]	.075	.755	1.88
4. U.S., beginning of year, 1919–1958	.005 (.068)	−.028 (−.582) [−1.90]*	.009	.323	2.12
5. U.K., end of quarter, 1956:I–1977:II	.164 (2.06)*	−.120 (−2.81)* [−3.29]*	.086	.662	2.27
6. U.K., annual average, 1824–1929	.011 (.715)	.002 (.183) [−2.32]*	.0003	.162	1.46

* Significant at the 5% level with a one-sided test.
a. Numbers in parentheses are t-statistics; $[t'_B]$ is the t-statistic for the hypothesis $B = (1 - \gamma_n)/\gamma_n$, where γ_n is as given in table 15.1.

regressions. In fact, however, under the rational expectations hypothesis the error term in the regressions is uncorrelated with the independent variable, and so under this hypothesis there is no bias. If, on the other hand, the rational expectations hypothesis is only partly true and R_t is influenced by other factors not in the rational expectations model, then we should not be surprised if such a "bias" emerges and the slope coefficient turns out to be significant.

Unfortunately, an upward bias in the coefficient of R_t or $(R_t - r_t)$ might also emerge in some of the data sets even if the rational expectations model is true. It is possible that measurement error in the R_t series could induce an upward bias in the coefficient of R_t or $(R_t - r_t)$. However, there should be little measurement error in these series. It is true, of course, that not all bonds of the same maturity and coupon sell for exactly the same price, so that different bond yield series may differ slightly, but this is not so much measurement error as a reflection of the very deviation from the rational expectations model that we are interested in describing.[22]

In table 15.2 we observe a significant positive coefficient (based on a one-tailed test at the 5% level) for R_t in data sets 1, 2, and 5.[23] Although other data sets were not significant at the 5% level, the pattern appears to be the same for all six data sets: a negative intercept and a positive slope coefficient.[24]

The R^2 is small in all of the table 15.2 regressions, as we would expect. The coefficients, however, are not small. For example, with data set 1 the coefficient of 4.97 means that if R_t rises by 1 percentage point, then the expected annualized one-quarter holding yield on long bonds relative to short returns rises by 4.97 percentage points. The R^2 is still small since there is so much unpredictable variation in the short-term holding yield.

In table 15.3, the coefficients of $R_t - r_t$ have a negative sign (contrary to the implication of the model [1]) in data sets 1–5 and are significantly below the theoretical value of $(1 - \gamma_n)/\gamma_n$ at the 5% level based on a one-tailed test for all data sets except data set 3.

The results in table 15.3 contradict what may be thought of as the essential characteristic of rational expectations models: that long-term interest rates tend on average to move in such a way as to equalize short-term holding yields. This characteristic, which we noted in connection with the perfect-certainty model illustrated in figure 15.3, carries over to our model (1) in the sense that long rates should rise on average when long rates are high relative to short rates and decline on average when long rates are low relative to short rates. Instead, long rates if anything move in the opposite direction, which means that when long rates are high relative to short rates they tend to move down in the subsequent period. The capital gain thus produced augments (rather than offsets) the advantage to holding long-term bonds when these bonds have higher current yield. This behavior is not consistent with our rational expectations models but is instead what we would expect to find if long rates are influenced by noise that causes long rates temporarily to rise relative to short rates and then fall to a more "normal" level.[25]

15.5 Summary and Conclusions

The goal that was set for this chapter was in some ways ambitious. I sought to find simple ways of understanding whether the data are well described by any of a number of expectations models of the term structure. I was guided, however, by a plain fact that seemed to stand in glaring contradiction to these models: the fact that actual long-rate series (as illustrated in figure 15.1) look completely different from ex-post rational long-rate series (as illustrated in figure 15.3).

Since the ex-post rational long-rate series was very smooth, it seemed likely that a robust implication of the expectations models of the term structure would be that actual long-rate series should be similarly smooth. It is not easy, however, to give formal content to this implication for all of these models. The linearization that produced expression (1) enabled me to derive some inequalities that do this, subject, however, to the approximation error in the linearization. The upper bounds on the volatility of the long-rate series that these inequalities impose occur only in worst possible cases where the short rate has a specific autocovariance function. In using these inequalities to examine the model, we passed up the possibility of using the actual autocovariance function in conjunction with the expectations model to put a tighter limit on the volatility of the long-rate series.

Based on sample standard deviations (table 15.1), the inequalities (I-1) and (I-1') implied by the linearized expectations model appear violated by the data. If we wish to test whether the population standard deviations violate the inequalities, then we must inquire whether the terms in the inequalities can be reliably measured under general assumptions in small samples. It was felt that it is reasonable to suppose that we can put a lower bound on the left side of the inequalities by a usual χ^2 one-sided confidence interval, since the variable whose standard deviation is measured is approximately serially uncorrelated. It is another matter to put an upper bound on the right-hand side of the inequalities, since we have no real information in small samples about possible trends or long cycles in interest rates.

Indeed, some would claim that short-term interest rates may be unstationary and hence have infinite variance. The fact that the lower bound on the left-hand side exceeds the sample value of the right-hand side may be interpreted as safely telling us, then, that we must rely on such unobserved variance or expected explosive behavior of short rates if we wish to retain expectations models. This conclusion appears to hold for earlier time periods as well as the more recent.

The inequalities that characterize the smoothing behavior are not the only avenues for constructing tests of the model that are powerful against an alternative hypothesis that long rates are too volatile, and in fact small sample tests are available. Such regression tests (tables 15.2 and 15.3) do generally reject the expectations model in favor of an alternative hypothesis that long rates are disturbed by transient effects unrelated to expectations. The regression results might still be construed as offering some support for the expectations models in the sense that the R^2 are small. However, based on the results reported here, there is nothing more to be said for the expectations model. My table 15.3 regressions show that movements in long rates tend to be in a direction opposite to that predicted by the expectations models.

These negative results on the expectations model may be contrasted with earlier positive results by Sutch [1968], Shiller [1972], Modigliani and Shiller [1973], and Sargent [1979]. Some interpretation of the contrast, in terms of the residual of the term-structure equation, was offered above. An attempt at further reconciliation of these apparently conflicting results will be the subject of another paper.

Appendix A: Model Restrictions on the Spectral Densities of Interest Rates

The ex-post rational long rate R_t^* is defined in expression (9) as a moving average of r_t. The squared gain of this moving average, or "linear filter," is $g^2(\omega) = (1 - \gamma)^2/[1 - 2\gamma \cos(\omega) + \gamma^2]$, where ω is frequency $-\pi \leqslant \omega \leqslant \pi$. The squared gain is 1.00 at $\omega = 0$, declines monotonically as frequency increases, and reaches $[(1 - \gamma)/(1 + \gamma)]^2$ at $\omega = \pi$.[26] If γ is close to 1.00, the decline will be very dramatic, as my example illustrated. The spectrum of R^* thus lies below the spectrum of r everywhere except at $\omega = 0$, and is relatively much more concentrated in the lower frequencies. Spectral analysis of actual interest rate time series, however [e.g., Granger and Rees, 1968], does not reveal any such attenuation of the high-frequency components in long-rate series.

One might have thought that our results with the perfect-certainty model (9)—that the spectrum of R^* must be more concentrated in the lower frequencies and must lie everywhere below the spectrum of r—should also carry over to the

R in the general model (1). However, this is not the case, as a simple example will illustrate. Suppose r_t is a first-order moving average of a white-noise process ε_t: $\tilde{r}_t = \varepsilon_t + \theta \varepsilon_{t-1}$, $0 < \theta < 1$, and suppose the ε_t is also serially independent and no other information is available for forecasting, so that the optimal forecast is linear in current and lagged r. Then, in this special case, $E_t(\tilde{r}_{t+1}) = \theta \varepsilon_t$ and $E_t(\tilde{r}_{t+K}) = 0$, $K > 1$, so that $\tilde{R}_t = (1 - \gamma)[(1 + \gamma\theta)\varepsilon_t + \theta\varepsilon_{t-1}]$ will appear less smooth than r_t since the moving average weights for R_t are relatively more concentrated on ε_t. More precisely, the squared gain from r to R (which is also the ratio of their spectra) is $g^2(\omega) = (1 - \gamma)^2[(1 + \gamma\theta)^2 + \theta^2 + 2\theta(1 + \gamma\theta)\cos(\omega)]/[1 + \theta^2 + 2\theta\cos(\omega)]$, which is a function that increases monotonically with ω for $0 \leqslant \omega \leqslant \pi$. One might also note that as θ approaches one, $g^2(\omega)$ approaches infinity at $\omega = \pi$. This illustrates that there is no limit to the ratio of the spectra at a particular frequency, and that the spectrum of R need not lie everywhere below the spectrum of r as does the spectrum of R^*.

In spite of this counterexample, it remains true that R_t cannot have too much power at the high frequencies. In the above example, the variance of R_t is very small, so that even though the spectrum of R is relatively more concentrated in the higher frequencies and may have absolutely more power at the highest frequencies, the total power in the spectrum of R at the higher frequencies is still small. Inequality restrictions on the total power at the high frequencies for R_t can be derived from the restrictions that the model (1) places on the autocovariance function of the bivariate process (r_t, R_t).

The covariance restrictions (10) can be rewritten in terms of the cross-covariance functions:

$$C_{RR}(\tau) = (1 - \gamma) \sum_{K=0}^{\infty} \gamma^K C_{rR}(K + \tau), \qquad \tau \geqslant 0, \tag{A1}$$

$$C_{rR}(-\tau) = (1 - \gamma) \sum_{K=0}^{\infty} \gamma^K C_{rr}(K + \tau), \qquad \tau \geqslant 0, \tag{A2}$$

where for any pair of variables x and y, $C_{xy}(\tau)$ will refer to $E[x_t - E(x)] \cdot [y_{t-\tau} - E(y)]$. These expressions give all restrictions imposed by our model on the autocovariance function of the bivariate process (r_t, R_t). Since $C_{rR}(\tau)$ is not generally an even function of τ (as $C_{RR}[\tau]$ and $C_{rr}[\tau]$ are), these expressions do not suffice to define $C_{RR}(\tau)$ given $C_{rr}(\tau)$, and hence the spectrum of R_t is not determined by the spectrum of r_t as it was in the perfect-certainty case or first-order moving-average case discussed above. This is as we would expect, since we have not specified all of the information used in forecasting. Both of the special cases considered above are in fact consistent with the above equalities, though in each case additional restrictions are also involved. When future short-term interest rates are known with certainty, the relations (A1) and (A2) hold for all τ. When the expected future short rates are optimal linear forecasts based on current and lagged short rates only (as in the moving-average case considered above), then other restrictions can be shown to characterize the cross-covariance function; that is, R does not cause r in the Granger [1969] or Sims [1972] sense. Neither of these restrictions is assured in the general case, however, and I do not assume them here.

We can now see in what sense the restrictions (A1) and (A2) may be described as putting a limit on the high-frequency variance of R_t. Since the holding-period yield $\tilde{H}_t$ is derived by passing R_t through the linear filter $(1 - \gamma F)/(1 - \gamma)$, then the spectrum of $\tilde{H}_t$, $S_{\tilde{H}}(\omega)$, equals the spectrum of R_t, $S_R(\omega)$, times the squared gain of this filter which is $g^2(\omega) = [1 + \gamma^2 - 2\gamma \cos(\omega)]/(1 - \gamma)^2$. This gain function rises monotonically with the absolute value of frequency. Squared gain is 1.0 at $\omega = 0$ and rises, for $\gamma = .98$ (corresponding to $\bar{R} = 8\%$ per annum with quarterly data), to about 10,000. The variance of $\tilde{H}_t$ is the integral from $-\pi$ to π of its spectrum, which is then the integral from $-\pi$ to π of $g^2(\omega)$ times the spectrum of R, so that, by (I-1)

$$\int_{-\pi}^{\pi} \frac{1 + \gamma^2 - 2\gamma \cos(\omega)}{(1 - \gamma)^2} S_R(\omega)\,d\omega \leqslant \frac{\operatorname{var}(r_t)}{1 - \gamma^2}.$$

The left hand side of this expression is a weighted integral of the spectrum of R_t with very high weights for high frequencies. Thus, an observation that the holding-period yield variance does not satisfy the inequality may generally be described as an observation that the high-frequency components of R_t are too strong to be consistent with the model (1).

Restrictions (I-2) and (I-3) may similarly be interpreted as inequality restrictions on a weighted integral of the spectrum of the bivariate process $(\Delta r_t, R_t - r_t)$. Our observation that the variance of R must be less than the variance of R^* is also of this form. Other (presumably less easily interpreted) inequality restrictions of this form can also be derived from (A.1) and (A.2).

Appendix B: Sources of Data

Data are from the macro data library of the Federal Reserve System or the Federal Reserve *Bulletin* unless otherwise noted.

Data set 1 (quarterly, 1966:1–1977:III): The long-term interest rate R is the Federal Reserve recently offered AAA utility bond yield series (constructed by Kichline, Laub, and Stevens [1973]), and the short-term interest rate r is the 4–6-month prime commercial paper rate. Both series are for the first week of the quarter.

Data set 2 (monthly, 1969:1–1974:II): The long-term interest rate R is a series produced by Salomon Brothers for yields on the first of the month of a composite portfolio of Aa utilities and industrials (Leibowitz and Johannesen 1975, table XII). The annualized 1-month holding yield H (Leibowitz and Johannesen 1975, table XV) is not computed from the R series but from an average price series for the bonds using the actual average coupon and average maturity. The short-term interest rate r is the 90–119 day prime commercial paper rate starting in June 1972, and the 4–6-month prime commercial paper rate before that date, both for the first week of the month.

Data set 3 (annual, 1960–77): The long-term interest rate R is the Federal Reserve new issue Aaa utility yield series for the first month of the year, and the short-term interest rate r is the 12-month U.S. Treasury bill rate averaged over the first month of the year.

Data set 4 (annual, 1919–1959): The long-term interest rate R is the Moody Aaa corporate bond yield average, and the short-term interest rate r is the 4–6 month prime commercial paper rate, both for the first month of the year. The sample was ended in 1959 to provide estimates over a sample period which does not overlap with those of data sets 1−3.

Data set 5 (quarterly, 1956:1−1977:III): The long-term interest rate R is the flat yield on $2\frac{1}{2}\%$ British Consols as reported in *Financial Statistics* from the Central Statistical Office starting in 1962 and in the *London Times* for the earlier years. Observations are taken at the last Friday of the quarter. The coupon is paid on the fifth day of the following quarter. The short-term interest rate series r is the 3-month local authorities temporary loan rate for the last Friday of the quarter starting 1960:III and for the last Saturday before that as reported in the *Bank of England Statistical Abstract, Number I* [1970], table 29, and subsequent issues of the *Bank of England Quarterly Bulletin*.

Data set 6 (annual 1824−1930): The long-term interest rate R is the annual average rate of 3% British Consols through 1888 and on $2\frac{1}{2}\%$ government annuities starting in 1889 (Homer 1963, table 19, col. 2, and table 57, col. 2). The short-rate r is, for 1824−1844, Overend and Gurney's annual average first-class 3-month bill rates and, after 1844, the annual average rates (averaging maximum and minimum) for 3-month bank bills, both from Mitchell and Deane [1962, p. 460]. The data series were terminated here in 1930 to provide an estimate for the period before the great depression.

Notes

1. This is a plot of data set 1, described in appendix B.

2. Computed using expression (5), below where $R_t^{(n)}$ is the long-term interest rate in figure 15.1 (divided by 400) and $R_{t+1}^{(n-1)}$ is the long-term interest rate for the following quarter (divided by 400), and C is taken as $R_t^{(n)}$. After computation, the holding yield is remultiplied by 400 to convert to annual percent. See note 9 concerning approximation error in this measure of holding yield.

3. Computed from the expression in note 7 without the approximation error referred to in note 2, using data set 5 described in appendix B. The range divided by standard deviation is high, indicating heteroscedasticity as discussed below.

4. See Culbertson [1957, p. 508]. Culbertson, however, did not clearly state the argument we make here.

5. Throughout this chapter, superscripts are distinguished from exponents by superfluous parentheses. Here $r_t = R_t^{(1)}$. I use lowercase r_t to denote the one-period rate, for notational convenience. Later, I shall use unsuperscripted uppercase R to denote the perpetuity rate, i.e., $R_t = R_t^{(\infty)}$.

6. The $V^{(n)}[R_t^{(n)}]$ refers to the function $V^{(n)}$ in which $R_t^{(n)}$ is substituted for each of $r_t, r_{t+1}, \ldots, r_{t+n-1}$; $R_t^{(n)}$ is the single real positive root to equation (3).

7. It has been pointed out that if numerator and denominator in the ratio (4) are jointly normally distributed, the ratio will not have a finite variance. One should not be misled by this fact. If the mean of the denominator is large relative to its

standard deviation, the distribution function of the ratio approximates the normal. Anyway, the denominator cannot be normally distributed since price cannot be negative.

8. If the bond is a perpetuity, $n = \infty$ and expression (5) reduces to $H_t = R_t - \Delta R_{t+1}/R_{t+1}$.

9. The approximation error introduced by the linearization (7) is not large. The correlation coefficients between H and $\tilde{H}$ for data sets 1–6 as computed in table 15.1 are .993, .994, .990, .997, .947, and .978, respectively. Models which describe pure discount bonds and which equalize expected log holding yields seem to avoid the necessity for such approximation. That apparent advantage is illusory, however, for if these models are to be similarly robust to variations in assumptions, as discussed below, the same sort of linearization arguments must be made. Another approximation error, which affects our estimated holding-period yields based on newly issued or recently offered yield series, even without the linearization, is introduced by my practice of substituting the yield average at time t for $R_t^{(n)}$ and the yield average at time $t + 1$ for $R_{t+1}^{(n-1)}$ in expression (5) or (7). The problem with this practice is that the maturity date and coupon are not kept constant from period to period in the yield averages, and, in fact, coupons roughly equal current yields. The error introduced by failing to keep the maturity date constant is certainly negligible. There is no measurable difference in yield between, e.g., 25-year bonds and $25\frac{1}{4}$-year bonds. A bigger error is introduced by the fact that the coupon rate is not kept constant between t and $t + 1$ in the yield averages. There is a relationship between coupon and yield for individual bonds, as a study by Shiller and Modigliani (1979) concluded. The relationship, which appears to be due to the differential taxation of capital gains versus income, works in the direction of causing our measures H and $\tilde{H}$ to slightly overstate actual holding yields by, in effect, purifying our series from tax effects.

10. The four special cases considered here are the four versions of the rational expectations model of the term structure suggested by Cox, Ingersoll, and Ross [1977], although their analysis considered only pure discount bonds. With coupon bonds, the last model mentioned is a little more difficult to understand, since one cannot ex ante plan such a sequence of shorts. Ex post, one can see how one could have invested \$1.00 at time t in shorts, withdrawn C dollars at each subsequent period, and be left with \$1.00 at maturity. This model sets $R_t^{(n)}$ to the ex ante expectation of the C which will achieve this.

11. All of these models can be written in the form $P_t^{(n)} = g^{(n)}(E_t, \mathbf{r}_t)$ such that $g^{(n)}(1, \mathbf{r}_t) = V^{(n)}(\mathbf{r}_t + \boldsymbol{\phi})$. They can then be linearized using a two-step procedure. First, one linearizes all subexpressions in $g^{(n)}(E_t, \mathbf{r}_t)$ that do not contain (but are premultiplied by) E_t around $r_t + \phi^{(n)} = r_{t+1} + \phi^{(n-1)} = \cdots = r_{t+n-1} + \phi^{(1)} = \bar{R} = C$. The expectations operator that premultiplies the expressions can then be brought inside (using the distributive law), yielding an approximate expression for P_t^n in $E_t[r_t + \phi^{(n)}]$, $E_t[r_{t+1} + \phi^{(n-1)}] \cdots E_t[r_{t+n-1} + \phi^{(1)}]$. The second step is to linearize this approximate expression for $P_t^{(n)}$ around $E_t[r_t + \phi^{(n)}] = E_t[r_{t+1} + \phi^{(n-1)}] = \cdots = E_t[r_{t+n-1} + \phi^{(1)}] = \bar{R} = C$. This yields an expression which is linear in $E_t(\mathbf{r}_t + \boldsymbol{\phi})$. Since we know that $g^{(n)}(1, \mathbf{r}_t) = V^{(n)}(\mathbf{r}_t + \phi)$, we know that this

linearization evaluated at $E_t = 1$ is just the linearization of $V^{(n)}(r_t + \phi)$ around $r_t + \phi^{(n)} = r_{t+1} + \phi^{(n-1)} = \cdots = r_{t+n-1} + \phi^{(1)} = \bar{R} = C$. Hence, our linearized $g^{(n)}(E_t, r_t)$ must be E_t times the linearized $V^{(n)}(r_t + \phi)$.

12. Figure 15.3 is based on a perpetuity assumption, but the basic result on the smoothing of long cycles carries over to finite maturity bonds. Based on the gain of the filter in expression (1) for $n = 100$ quarters and $\gamma = .98$ (appropriate for this data set), we find that for frequencies in the vicinity of 5 years amplitude is reduced by a factor of $.065-.085$, roughly as illustrated in figure 15.3. The reason for the similarity is clear: 100 quarters is close enough to infinity ($.98^{100} = .13$) that the bond is approximately a consol. Since R_t^* varies little, the linearization (7) that underlies (9) is quite accurate. The exact yield of a consol whose price is given by the present value formula $V(r + \phi)$ (rather than our linearized approximation) under the perfect-certainty assumption and an assumption about Φ consistent with the $\bar{R}$ chosen in figure 15.3 looks virtually indistinguishable, differing (except for Φ) by no more than one basis point throughout from the series plotted here. If the linearization (7) is not accurate enough over the range that actual R varies, then that fact itself is a disconfirmation of the model, not of our use of the linearization in describing the model. If we had chosen a higher terminal value for R^*, then we would in effect add an exponential trend to the R^* plotted in figure 15.3, and figure 15.3 would then represent deviations from the trend. Thus, R^* is smooth regardless of our assumptions about interest rates beyond the sample.

13. We can write $R_t^* = G(F)r_t$, where F is the forward operator defined by $F^K r_t = r_{t+K}$, and $G(F)$ is a polynomial in the forward operator. Then, $G(F) = (1 - \gamma)/(1 - \gamma F)$. One can invert the polynomial and one finds $r_t = G(F)^{-1}R_t^* = [(1 - \gamma F)/(1 - \gamma)]R_t^*$. The linearized holding-period yield $\tilde{H}_t$ can be written $\tilde{H}_t = [(1 - \gamma F)/(1 - \gamma)]R_t$, and hence $R_t = [(1 - \gamma)/(1 - \gamma F)]\tilde{H}_t$. Therefore, $(R_t - R_t^*) = [(1 - \gamma)/(1 - \gamma F)](\tilde{H}_t - r_t)$. Since by our model $(\tilde{H}_t - r_t)$ is a forecast error whose lagged values are known at time t, $\tilde{H}_t - r_t$ is serially uncorrelated, and hence the generalized least-squares transformation yields serially uncorrelated residuals. This also implies that $\text{var}(R_t - R_t^*) = [(1 - \gamma)^2/(1 - \gamma^2)] \cdot \text{var}(\tilde{H}_t - r_t)$, as was noted by LeRoy and Porter [1979] and formed the basis of the test by which they rejected their model of stock prices.

14. Stationarity requires $\text{var}(R_t) = \text{var}(R_{t+1})$. Stationarity means, in the theory of stochastic processes, that the unconditional distribution of R_t does not change, and hence that R does not explode. The conditional variance $E_t(R_t - \bar{R})^2$ may yet change.

15. If r_t is regressed on a constant and r_{t-1}, the coefficient of r_{t-1} is .843, .966, .588, .845, .885, and .502 for data sets 1–6, respectively, always substantially below the corresponding γ_n in table 15.1.

16. If r is expected to drift too far over the relevant horizon, our linearization argument for (1) may break down. This appears not to be a problem in our samples, since the value of R_t remained fairly near $\bar{R}$.

17. A couple of other features of the data deserve mention. The bonds are callable, though for the Federal Reserve Series there is 5-year call protection, and for

consols in data set 5 the call price is prohibitively high. Consideration of call provisions only strengthens our case. Call provisions ought to reduce the volatility of bond prices by shortening the effective maturity or putting an upper barrier on price. Differential taxation of interest and capital gains might, if our time period is long enough so that capital gains rates apply, suggest that $P_{t+1}^{(n-1)} - P_t^{(n)}$ in expression (4) be multiplied by $(1 - g)/(1 - i)$, where g is the effective rate of taxation on capital gains and i is the income tax rate of the "representative" bond investor (see Shiller and Modigliani, 1979). This consideration again strengthens our case. Offering a tax advantage for capital gains means bond prices do not have to move as much to achieve equalization of (after-tax) returns.

18. The approximation error in our use of finite maturity bonds then comes only in our use of $R_{t+1}^{(n)}$ rather than $R_{t+1}^{(n-1)}$ in computing $\tilde{H}_t^{(n)}$. This error should be negligible for long-term bonds. The inequalities where γ_n is substituted for γ can be derived in the same way for finite maturity bonds after n is substituted for $n - 1$ in the expression for $\tilde{H}_t^{(n)}$.

19. The sample period for which the results are weakest is that from 1919 to 1959 in the United States, data set 4, apparently largely because of the period of the depression and World War II, when short rates were low and then officially pegged near zero, but long rates failed to fall so far. In this abnormal situation the market apparently correctly anticipated that the peg would end, and so here the expectations theory does the best. If the years of low short rates 1933–1951 are omitted from the sample, $a\sigma(\tilde{r})$ falls to 3.82, $a\sigma(r)$ to 4.32, and $\sigma(\tilde{H})$ rises to 6.81. That the inequality (I-1) is violated by this shorter sample is not due to the 1920–1921 episode. Although short-term holding yields made large movements then, the short rate also moved dramatically. If the years 1920–1921 are also omitted (as well as the years 1933–1951) from data set 4, $\sigma(\tilde{H})$ falls from 6.81 to 6.09, but $a\sigma(r)$ falls even further, from 4.32 to 3.33, causing (I-1) to be violated even more strongly.

20. The χ^2 confidence interval depends on the normality assumption, which is open to question. Normality appears satisfied for most data sets (see note 23).

21. This interpretation does not appear in Sargent's paper, which emphasizes that his model tests some complicated nonlinear restrictions on the coefficients of an autoregression for (r_t, R_t). The nonlinearity of the restrictions is introduced by his use of the assumption that the R_t series refers to finite maturity pure discount bonds. Since time to maturity is constant, $H_t^{(n)}$ cannot be expressed as a linear function of his $R_t^{(n)}$ series. We have eliminated the nonlinearity by discussing consols or long-term coupon-carrying bonds which may be approximated as consols. Our model then places simple linear restrictions on the autoregressive coefficients for (r_t, R_t), which are in effect summarized in (10).

22. Suppose the true unobserved long rate (which we shall denote by $\tilde{R}_t$) behaves in accordance with the expectations theory, and that (for table 15.3) $\tilde{R}_{t+1} - \tilde{R}_t = a + b(\tilde{R}_t - r_t) + U_t$, where $b = (1 - \gamma_n)/\gamma_n$. If the error in measurement $e_t = R_t - \tilde{R}_t$ is uncorrelated with all other variables (including its own lagged values), and if U_t is uncorrelated with $R_t - r_t$, then the coefficients whose esti-

mates appear in table 15.3 will be $\hat{b} = [b \operatorname{var}(\bar{R} - r) - \operatorname{var}(e)]/[\operatorname{var}(\bar{R} - r) +$ $\operatorname{var}(e)]$. Using $\operatorname{var}(R - r) = \operatorname{var}(\bar{R} - r) + \operatorname{var}(e)$ and solving for $\operatorname{var}(e)$ we find $\operatorname{var}(e) = [(b - \hat{b}) \operatorname{var}(R - r)]/(1 + b)$. We can, using this expression, deduce how big the measurement error would have to be if it were to account for our results in table 15.3. Setting $b = (1 - \gamma_n)/\gamma_n$ from table 15.1, we then find that for data sets 1–6 the standard deviation of the measurement error would have to be 58, 27, 55, 32, 62, and 17 basis points, respectively. It is inconceivable that true measurement error could be this high. A 4 standard deviation range would be over 2 percentage points for several series. Discrepancies between different bond-yield averages purporting to measure roughly the same thing are nowhere near this high, and, as noted above, even these discrepancies are not due primarily to measurement error but instead to variations in actual price among similar high-quality bonds.

23. Another potential problem in the evaluation of the t-statistics here is that the error term may be nonnormal. The studentized range test recommended by Fama and Roll [1971] as a test of normality gives statistics for $H_t - r_t$, for data sets 1–6, of 3.97, 4.61, 3.18, 4.40, 6.81, and 6.94, respectively. The ratio shows no evidence for nonnormality for data sets 1–4, but is significant at the 0.5% level for data sets 5 and 6. Examining the data suggests that for data set 5 the problem is one of increasing variance through time, rather than leptokurtosis. The equations for data set 5 were thus reestimated by generalized least squares by scaling the observations by $e^{-0.1t}$, $t = 1, \ldots, 86$. The t-statistic in the regression then drops to 1.33 in table 15.2, which is no longer significant at the 5% level, but t_b and t'_b in table 15.3 remain significant ($t_b = -1.88$ and $t'_b = -2.40$).

24. Basu [1977] found an analogous result that price-earnings ratios are negatively correlated with corporate stock returns.

25. This observation (which was first pointed out to me by Franco Modigliani) is analogous to one reported early by Shiller and Siegel [1977] (chapter 14) that long-term bond yields move on average in a direction that exacerbates rather than mitigates the effect of inflation on real returns. Mishkin [1978] has further confirmed table 15.2 (as well as table 15.3) with high-quality U.S. short-term holding-yield data on intermediate term bonds, and with a heteroskedasticity correction, although his table 3 results are somewhat less significant than those reported here for roughly the same sample.

26. If the interest rates r_{t+K} do not have finite second moments (as claimed, e.g., by Roll [1970] for forward rates), then we cannot use this analysis. It remains true if, as these authors estimated, the characteristic exponent is greater than one, that the dispersion of the rates will be reduced by averaging. Clark [1973], in any event, showed that a finite variance model explains speculative price data well.

References

Basu, Sanjoy. 1977. "The Investment Performance of Common Stocks in Relation to Their Price-Earnings Ratios: A Test of the Efficient Markets Hypothesis," *Journal of Finance* 32:663–682.

Bierwag, G. O., and Grove, M. A. 1971. "A Model of the Structure of Prices of Marketable U.S. Treasury Securities," *Journal of Money, Credit and Banking* 3 : 605—629.

Black, Fischer; Jensen, Michael; and Scholes, Myron. 1972. "The Capital Asset Pricing Model: Some Empirical Tests." In *Studies in the Theory of Capital Markets*, edited by Michael Jensen. New York: Praeger.

Cargill, Thomas. 1975. "The Term Structure of Interest Rates: A Test of the Expectations Hypothesis," *Journal of Finance* 30 : 761—771.

Clark, Peter K. 1973. "A Subordinated Stochastic Process Model with Finite Variance for Speculative Prices," *Econometrica* 41 : 135—155.

Cox, John C.; Ingersoll, Jonathan E., Jr.; and Ross, Stephen A. 1977. "A Theory of the Term Structure of Interest Rates and the Valuation of Interest-Dependent Claims." Mimeographed. Stanford Univ.

Culbertson, John M. 1957. "The Term Structure of Interest Rates," *Quarterly Journal of Economics* 71 : 485—517.

Fama, Eugene F. 1976. "Foreward Rates as Predictors of Future Spot Rates," *Journal of Financial Economics* 3 : 361—377.

Fama, Eugene F., and Roll, Richard. 1971. "Parameter Estimates for Symmetric Stable Distributions," *J. American Statis. Assoc.* 66 : 331—338.

Friend, Irwin, and Blume, Marshall E. 1970. "Measurement of Portfolio Performance under Uncertainty," *American Economic Review* 60 : 561—575.

Friend, Irwin; Westerfield, Randolf; and Granito, Michael. 1978. "New Evidence on the Capital Asset Pricing Model," *Journal of Finance* 33 : 903—917.

Granger, C. W. J. 1969. "Investigating Causal Relations by Econometric Models and Cross-spectral Methods," *Econometrica* 37, no. 3 : 424—438.

Granger, C. W. J., and Rees, H. J. B. 1968. "Spectral Analysis of the Term Structure of Interest Rates," *Review of Economic Studies* 35 : 67—76.

Homer, Sidney. 1963. *A History of Interest Rates.* New Brunswick, N.J.: Rutgers Univ. Press.

Kichline, James L.; Laub, P. Michael; and Stevens, Guy V. G. 1973. "Obtaining the Yield on a Standard Bond from a Sample of Bonds with Heterogeneous Characteristics." Staff Econ. Study no. 77, Board Governors Federal Reserve System.

Laffer, Arthur B., and Zecher, Richard. 1975. "Some Evidence on the Formation, Efficiency and Accuracy of Anticipations of Nominal Yields," *Journal of Monetary Economics* 1 : 327—342.

Leibowitz, Martin L., and Johannesen, Richard I., Jr. 1975. "Introducing the Salomon Brothers Total Performance Index for the High Grade Long-Term Corporate Bond Market." Mimeographed. New York: Salomon Brothers.

LeRoy, Stephen, and Porter, Richard. 1979. "The Present Value Relation: Tests Based on Implied Variance Bounds." Mimeographed. Board Governors Federal Reserve System.

McCallum, John S. 1975. "The Expected Holding Period Return, Uncertainty and the Term Structure of Interest Rates," *Journal of Finance* 30:307–323.

Mishkin, Frederic S. 1978. "Efficient Markets Theory: Its Implications for Monetary Policy," *Brookings Papers on Economic Activity* 3:707–752.

Mitchell, Brian R., and Deane, Phyllis. 1962. *Abstract of British Historical Statistics.* Cambridge: Cambridge Univ. Press.

Modigliani, Franco, and Shiller, Robert. 1973. "Inflation, Rational Expectations, and the Term Structure of Interest Rates," *Economica* 40:12–43.

Pesando, James E. 1978. "On the Efficiency of the Bond Market: Some Canadian Evidence," *Journal of Political Economy* 86:1957–1076.

Phillips, Llad, and Pippenger, John. 1976. "Preferred Habitat vs. Efficient Market: A Test of Alternative Hypotheses," *Federal Reserve Bank St. Louis Review* 58:11–19.

Roll, Richard. 1970. *The Behavior of Interest Rates: An Application of the Efficient Market Model to U.S. Treasury Bills.* New York: Basic.

Roll, Richard. 1971. "Investment Diversification and Bond Maturity," *Journal of Finance* 26:51–66.

Sargent, Thomas J. 1972. "Rational Expectations and the Term Structure of Interest Rates," *Journal of Money, Credit and Banking* 4:74–97.

Sargent, Thomas J. 1976. "A Classical Macroeconometric Model for the United States," *Journal of Political Economy* 84:207–237.

Sargent, Thomas J. 1979. "A Note on Maximum Likelihood Estimation of the Rational Expectations Model of the Term Structure," *Journal of Monetary Economics* 5:133–143.

Shiller, Robert J. 1972. "Rational Expectations and the Term Structure of Interest Rates." Ph.D. dissertation, MIT.

Shiller, Robert J. 1978. "Rational Expectations and the Dynamic Structure of Macroeconomic Models," *Journal of Monetary Economics* 4:1–44.

Shiller, Robert J. 1979. "Do Stock Prices Move Too Much to Be Justified by Subsequent Changes in Dividends?" Mimeographed. Univ. Pennsylvania.

Shiller, Robert J., and Modigliani, Franco. 1979. "Coupon and Tax Effects on New and Seasoned Bond Yields and the Measurement of the Cost of Debt Capital," *Journal of Financial Economics* 7, no. 3.

Shiller, Robert J., and Siegel, Jeremy J. 1977. "The Gibson Paradox and Historical Movements in Real Interest Rates," *Journal of Political Economy* 85:891–908.

Sims, Christopher A. 1972. "Money, Income and Causality," *American Economic Review* 62:540–552.

Sutch, Richard C. 1968. "Expectations, Risk and the Term Structure of Interest Rates." Ph.D. dissertation, MIT.

16

Cointegration and Tests
of Present Value Models

Present value models are among the simplest dynamic stochastic models of economics. A present value model for two variables, y_t and Y_t, states that Y_t is a linear function of the present discounted value of expected future y_t:

$$Y_t = \theta(1 - \delta) \sum_{i=0}^{\infty} \delta^i E_t y_{t+i} + c, \tag{1}$$

where c, the constant, θ, the coefficient of proportionality, and δ, the discount factor, are parameters that may be known a priori or may need to be estimated. Here and in what follows, E_t denotes mathematical expectation, conditional on the full public information set $\mathbf{I}_t$, which includes y_t and Y_t themselves and in general exceeds the information set $\mathbf{H}_t$ available to the econometrician. Models of this form include the expectations theory for interest rates (Y_t is the long-term yield and y_t the one-period rate), the present value model of stock prices (Y_t is the stock price and y_t the dividend), and, with some modification, the permanent income theory of consumption.[1]

Despite the simplicity of their structure, there is a surprising degree of controversy about the validity of present value models for bonds, stocks, and other economic variables.[2] The controversy seems to be stimulated by three problems that arise in testing equation (1). First, there are several test procedures in the literature: these include single-equation regression tests, tests of cross-equation restrictions on a vector autoregression (VAR), and variance bounds tests. It is not clear how these alternative approaches are related on one another.

Second, a statistical rejection of the model (1) may not have much economic significance. It is entirely possible that the model explains most of the variation in Y_t even if it is rejected at the 5% level. Most work on

Coauthored with John Y. Campbell. Reprinted with minor editing from *Journal of Political Economy* 95(1987):1062–1088. © 1987 The University of Chicago.

present value models concentrates on statistical testing rather than informal evaluation of the "fit" of the models.

Finally, the variables y_t and Y_t usually require some transformation before the theory of stationary stochastic processes can be applied. One approach is to remove a deterministic linear trend, but this can bias test procedures against the model (1) if in fact y_t and Y_t are nonstationary in levels.[3]

In this chapter we develop a test of the present value relation that is valid when the variables are stationary in first differences.[4] Hansen and Sargent [1981a], Mankiw et al. [1985], and West [1986, 1987] have also studied this case. We follow Hansen and Sargent and differ from Mankiw et al. and West by using a relatively large information set H_t. We include in H_t current and lagged values not just of y_t but also of Y_t.

Our choice of information set has several advantages. By including Y_t in the vector stochastic process for analysis, we in effect include *all* relevant information of market participants, even if we econometricians do not observe all their information variables. We can test *all* the implications of the model for the bivariate (y_t, Y_t) process, giving a natural extension of Fama's [1970] notion of a "weak-form" test. We can exploit the recently developed theory of cointegrated processes [Phillips and Durlauf, 1986; Phillips and Ouliaris, 1986; Engle and Granger, 1987; Stock, 1987]. Our test procedure can be interpreted as a single-equation regression or as a test of restrictions on a VAR. We propose a way to assess the economic significance of deviations from (1), comparing the forecast of the present value of future y_t embodied in Y_t with an unrestricted VAR forecast. Because the information set H_t includes Y_t, the two forecasts should be equal if the model is true.

We examine the present value models for bonds and stocks, while a companion piece by one of us [Campbell, 1987] studies the permanent income theory of consumption. The chapter is organized as follows. Section 16.1 discusses alternative tests of the present value relation when y_t and Y_t are stationary in first differences rather than levels. Section 16.2 is an introduction to the literature on cointegration, summarizing the results we use in testing the present value model. Section 16.3 applies the method to data on bonds and stocks. Section 16.4 presents conclusions.

16.1   Alternative Tests of the Present Value Relation

One straightforward way to test the model (1) is to use it to restrict the behavior of the variable $\xi_t \equiv Y_t - (1/\delta)[Y_{t-1} - \theta(1 - \delta)y_{t-1}]$. Substitution from (1) shows that

$$\xi_t = Y_t - E_{t-1} Y_t + c\left(1 - \frac{1}{\delta}\right). \tag{2}$$

Apart from a constant, ξ_t is the true innovation at time t in Y_t (i.e., the innovation with respect to the full market information set I_t). The model has the striking implication that this innovation is observable when only Y_t, Y_{t-1}, y_{t-1}, and the parameters c, θ, and δ are known.[5] In the applications of this paper, ξ_t, has the economic interpretation of an asset return. In the term structure it is the excess return on long bonds over short bills, while in the stock market it is the excess return on stocks over a constant mean, multiplied by the stock price.

Since the right-hand side of (2), adjusted for a constant, is orthogonal to all elements of the information set I_{t-1}, one can test the present value relation by regressing ξ_t on variables in this set and testing that the coefficients are jointly zero. This approach is standard in the literature and seems attractively simple. However, there are some econometric pitfalls and issues of interpretation that need careful handling.

First, the regressors used to predict ξ_t must be stationary if conventional asymptotic distribution theory is to apply. Of course, there are many stationary elements of I_{t-1}, but one may want to choose variables that summarize the joint history of y_t and Y_t. It is not clear how the stationarity requirement can be reconciled with this objective if y_t and Y_t are themselves nonstationary.

Second, while (1) implies (2), the reverse is not true. Equation (2) is consistent with a more general form of (1) that includes a "rational bubble," a random variable b_t satisfying $b_t = \delta E_t b_{t+1}$. Recently there has been considerable interest in testing (1) against the alternative that Y_t is influenced by a rational bubble [Blanchard and Watson, 1982; Hamilton and Whiteman, 1985; Quah, 1986; West, 1987].

Third, it is not clear what are the implications for Y_t of nonzero coefficients in a regression of ξ_t on information. Predictability of returns has consequences for asset price behavior, and one may want to calculate these explicitly.

Further insight into these issues can be gained by defining a new variable $S_t \equiv Y_t - \theta y_t$. We will refer to S_t as the "spread." In the case of the term structure, it is just the spread between long- and short-term interest rates; for stocks, it is the difference between the stock price and a multiple of dividends. The spread can also be written as a linear combination of the variables ΔY_t, Δy_t, and ξ_t: $S_t = [1/(1 - \delta)]\Delta Y_t - \theta\Delta y_t - [\delta/(1 - \delta)]\xi_t$.

The present value model (1) implies two alternative interpretations of the spread. Subtracting θy_t from both sides of equation (1) and rearranging, one obtains

$$S_t = E_t S_t^* + c, \tag{3}$$

where

$$S_t^* = \theta \sum_{i=1}^{\infty} \delta^i \Delta y_{t+i},$$

and

$$S_t = \left(\frac{\delta}{1-\delta}\right) E_t \Delta Y_{t+1} + c. \tag{4}$$

Equation (3) says that the spread is a constant plus the optimal forecast of S_t^*, a weighted average of future changes in y; equation (4) says that the spread is linear in the optimal forecast of the change in Y.

Equation (4) can be used in an alternative test of the present value model, in which one regresses ΔY_t on a constant, S_{t-1}, and other variables. The coefficient on S_{t-1} should be $(1 - \delta)/\delta$, and the coefficients on the other variables should be zero. This regression is just a linear transformation of the regression that has ξ_t as the dependent variable, and it yields the same test statistic.

Equations (3) and (4) help to resolve the issues raised above. If Δy_t is stationary, it follows from (3) that S_t stationary; (4) then implies that ΔY_t is stationary. Thus one can use S_t and Δy_t, or S_t and ΔY_t, as stationary variables that summarize the bivariate history of y_t and Y_t in a regression test of the model. (The pair Δy_t and ΔY_t is also stationary, but by using these one would lose information on the relative levels of y_t and Y_t.) Our strategy is to work with S_t and Δy_t.

The effect of a "rational bubble" alternative is easily seen using (3) and (4). If a term b_t is added to the right-hand side of equation (1), satisfying $b_t = \delta E_t b_{t+1}$, it appears on the right-hand side of (3) but does not affect equations (2) and (4). The term b_t is explosive by construction, as it causes explosive behavior of S_t by (3), and this is passed through to ΔY_t by (4).[6]

One way to test for the importance of rational bubbles is therefore to test the stationarity of S_t and ΔY_t. This approach has been proposed by Diba and Grossman [1984], among others. As we noted above, S_t can be written as a linear combination of ΔY_t, Δy_t, and ξ_t. Therefore, independent of any model, if three of the variables S_t, ΔY_t, Δy_t, and ξ_t are stationary, the fourth must be also. This linear dependence needs to be taken into account in testing for stationarity.

Finally, (3) and (4) suggest a way to compute the implications for Y_t of predictable ξ_t. Consider estimating a VAR representation for Δy_t and S_t (with their means removed):

$$
\begin{bmatrix} \Delta y_t \\ S_t \end{bmatrix} = \begin{bmatrix} a(L) & b(L) \\ c(L) & d(L) \end{bmatrix} \begin{bmatrix} \Delta y_{t-1} \\ S_{t-1} \end{bmatrix} + \begin{bmatrix} u_{1t} \\ u_{2t} \end{bmatrix}, \tag{5}
$$

where the polynomials in the lag operator $a(L)$, $b(L)$, $c(L)$, and $d(L)$ are all of order p. This VAR can be used for multiperiod forecasting of Δy_t, and it includes the variable S_t, which, according to (3), is the optimal forecast of the present value of future Δy_t.

To simplify notation, (5) can be stacked into a first-order system

$$
\begin{bmatrix} \Delta y_t \\ \cdot \\ \cdot \\ \Delta y_{t-p+1} \\ S_t \\ \cdot \\ \cdot \\ S_{t-p+1} \end{bmatrix} = \begin{bmatrix} a_1 \ldots a_p & b_1 \ldots b_p \\ 1 & \\ & \cdot \\ & 1 \\ c_1 \ldots c_p & d_1 \ldots d_p \\ & 1 \\ & \cdot \\ & 1 \end{bmatrix} \begin{bmatrix} \Delta y_{t-1} \\ \cdot \\ \Delta y_{t-p} \\ S_{t-1} \\ \cdot \\ S_{t-p} \end{bmatrix} + \begin{bmatrix} u_{1t} \\ 0 \\ \cdot \\ 0 \\ u_{2t} \\ 0 \\ \cdot \\ 0 \end{bmatrix} \tag{6}
$$

where blank elements are zero. This can be written more succinctly as $z_t = A z_{t-1} + v_t$. The matrix A is called the companion matrix of the VAR. For all i, $E(z_{t+i}|H_t) = A^i z_t$, where H_t is the limited information set containing current and lagged values of y_t and Y_t or, equivalently, of z_t. As elsewhere in the chapter, we are taking conditional expectations to be linear projections on information.

We can now discuss the implications of the present value relation for the VAR system. A rather weak implication is that S_t must linearly Granger-cause Δy_t unless S_t is itself an exact linear function of current and lagged Δy_t (which is a stochastic singularity we do not observe in the data; it would require, e.g., that the variance-covariance matrix of u_{1t} and u_{2t}, Ω, be singular).

The intuitive explanation for this result is that S_t is an optimal forecast of a weighted sum of future values of Δy_t, conditional on agents' full information set. Therefore, S_t will have incremental explanatory power for future Δy_t if agents have information useful for forecasting Δy_t beyond the history of that variable. If agents do not have such information, they form S_t as an exact linear function of current and lagged Δy_t.[7]

The full set of restrictions of the present value model is more demanding. We obtain these restrictions by projecting equation (3) onto the information set H_t, noting that the left-hand side is unchanged because S_t is in H_t and rewriting as

$$g'z_t = \theta \sum_{i=1}^{\infty} \delta^i h' A^i z_t,$$

where g' and h' are row vectors with $2p$ elements, all of which are zero except for the $p + 1$st element of g' and the first element of h', which are unity. If this expression is to hold for general z_t (i.e., for nonsingular Ω), it must be the case that

$$g' = \theta \sum_{i=1}^{\infty} \delta^i h' A^i = \theta h' \delta A (I - \delta A)^{-1}. \tag{7}$$

Here the second equality follows by evaluating the infinite sum, noting that it must converge because the variables Δy_t and S_t are stationary under the null.[8]

The restrictions of equation (7) appear to be highly nonlinear cross-equation restrictions of the type described by Hansen and Sargent (1981b) as the "hallmark" of rational expectations models. However, it turns out that (7) can be simplified so that (taking θ and δ as given) its restrictions are linear and easily interpreted. Postmultiplying both sides of (7) by $(I - \delta A)$, one obtains

$$g'(I - \delta A) = \theta h' \delta A. \tag{8}$$

From the structure of the matrix A, the constraints imposed by (8) on individual coefficients are $c_i = -\theta a_i$, $i = 1, \ldots, p$; $d_1 = (1/\delta) - \theta b_1$; and $d_i = -\theta b_i$, $i = 2, \ldots, p$. By adding $\theta \Delta y_t$ to S_t, one can interpret these restrictions. They state that $\xi_t = S_t - (1/\delta)S_{t-1} + \theta \Delta y_t$ is unpredictable given lagged Δy_t and S_t, which is what equation (2) implies for the information set H_t. In our empirical application, we obtain a Wald test statistic for equation (8) that is numerically identical to the Wald test statistic for a regression of ξ_t on lagged Δy_t and $S_.$.[9]

The major advantage of the VAR framework is that it can be used to generate alternative measures of the economic importance, not merely the statistical significance, of deviations from the present value relation. To see this more clearly, suppose that the present value model is false so that $E_t \xi_{t+i} \neq 0$ for $i \geq 1$. Then equations (3) and (4) no longer hold. We define the "theoretical spread," S'_t, as the optimal forecast, given the information set H_t, of the present value of all future changes in y:

$$S'_t \equiv E(S^*_t | H_t) = \theta h' \delta A (I - \delta A)^{-1} z_t. \tag{9}$$

We then have, ignoring constant terms,

$$S_t - S_t' = \sum_{i=1}^{\infty} \delta^i E(\xi_{t+i}|\mathbf{H}_t) \tag{10}$$

and

$$S_t - \left(\frac{\delta}{1-\delta}\right) E(\Delta Y_{t+1}|\mathbf{H}_t) = \left(\frac{1}{1-\delta}\right) E(\xi_{t+1}|\mathbf{H}_t). \tag{11}$$

Equations (10) and (11) measure deviations from the model in two different ways. The metric of equation (11) is the difference between S_t and the optimal forecast, given the information set $\mathbf{H}_t$, of the one-period change in Y. Equation (11) shows that this difference is large if excess returns are predictable one period in advance.

The metric of equation (10) is the difference between S_t and the theoretical spread, which is large if the present value of all future excess returns is predictable. By this measure, a large deviation from the model requires not only that movements in ξ be predictable one period in advance but that they be predictable many periods in advance. Loosely speaking, predictable excess returns must be persistent as well as variable.[10]

We use the VAR framework not only to conduct statistical tests of the present value relation but also to evaluate its failures using the metric of equation (10). We display time-series plots of the spread S_t and the theoretical spread S_t', the unrestricted VAR forecast of the present value of future changes in y. If the present value model is true, these variables should differ only because of sampling error. Large observed differences in the time-series movements of the two variables imply (subject to sampling error) economically important deviations from the model.

The VAR framework can also be used to test the present value model against more specific alternatives. Volatility tests, for example, are designed to test against the alternative that Y_t or some transformation of it "moves too much."

We present two different volatility tests. The first is just a test that the ratio $\text{var}(S_t)/\text{var}(S_t')$ is unity. This ratio, together with its standard error, can be computed from the VAR system. Under the present value model, the ratio should be one but would be larger than one if the spread is too volatile relative to information about future y. A statistic that complements this is the correlation between S_t and S_t' since if the variance ratio and correlation both equal one, then S_t must equal S_t' and the model is satisfied.[11]

We obtain a second volatility test, following West [1987], as follows. Let us define ξ_t' as θ times the innovation from $t-1$ to t in the expected present value of Δy, conditional on the VAR information set:

$$\xi'_t \equiv \theta \sum_{i=0}^{\infty} \delta^i [E(\Delta y_{t+i} | \mathbf{H}_t) - E(\Delta y_{t+i} | \mathbf{H}_{t-1})]$$

$$= S'_t - \left(\frac{1}{\delta}\right) S'_{t-1} + \theta \Delta y_t. \tag{12}$$

Under the present value model, $\xi'_t = \xi_t$ since $S'_t = S_t$. We construct the ratio $\text{var}(\xi_t)/\text{var}(\xi'_t)$, again with standard error.[12] The model implies that this ratio should be one, while the notion that stock prices are too volatile suggests that it will be greater than one. We call the first of our variance ratios the "levels variance ratio" and the second the "innovations variance ratio."

The fact that a linear combination S_t of y_t and Y_t is stationary in its level, even though y_t and Y_t are individually stationary only in first differences, turns out to be important for understanding present value models. In the language of time-series analysis, the vector $\mathbf{x}_t = (y_t Y_t)'$ is cointegrated. Cointegrated vectors have a number of important properties, which we now discuss.

16.2 Properties of Cointegrated Vectors

In this section we summarize the theory of cointegrated processes and show how it applies to present value models.

DEFINITION [Engle and Granger 1987] A vector $\mathbf{x}_t$ is said to be cointegrated of order (d, b), denoted $\mathbf{x}_t$ $\text{CI}(d, b)$, if (i) all components of $\mathbf{x}_t$ are integrated of order d (stationary in dth differences) and (ii) there exists at least one vector $\alpha(\neq 0)$ such that $\alpha' \mathbf{x}_t$ is integrated of order $d - b$, $b > 0$.

When y_t is stationary in first differences, the vector $\mathbf{x}_t = (y_t Y_t)'$ is $\text{CI}(1, 1)$ if the present value model holds. The $\text{CI}(1, 1)$ case is the one that has been studied almost exclusively in the theoretical literature, and the results that follow apply to it.

Cointegrated systems of order $(1, 1)$ have two unusual properties. These concern the existence of well-behaved vector time-series representations for the cointegrated variables and the estimation of unknown elements of the vector α. Both properties turn out to be relevant for testing present value models.

The first important property of a cointegrated vector is that the vector moving average (VMA) representation of the first difference $\Delta \mathbf{x}_t$ is non-invertible. Equivalently, the spectral density matrix of $\Delta \mathbf{x}_t$ is singular at zero frequency. This singularity is what "holds together" the elements of $\mathbf{x}_t$ so that a linear combination is stationary.

More formally, write $\Delta \mathbf{x}_t = \mathbf{K}(L)\varepsilon_t = \mathbf{I}\varepsilon_t + \mathbf{K}_1 \varepsilon_{t-1} + \cdots$. The matrix $\mathbf{M} = \mathbf{K}(1)\mathbf{K}(1)'$, where $\mathbf{K}(1) = \mathbf{I} + \mathbf{K}_1 + \mathbf{K}_2 + \cdots$, is the spectral density matrix of $\Delta \mathbf{x}_t$ at zero frequency. Now if the variance of $\boldsymbol{\alpha}' \mathbf{x}_t$ exists, it will be given by

$$\text{var}(\boldsymbol{\alpha}' \mathbf{x}_t) = \sum_{i=0}^{\infty} \boldsymbol{\alpha}' \mathbf{C}_i \mathbf{V} \mathbf{C}_i' \boldsymbol{\alpha},$$

where $\mathbf{V}$ is the variance-covariance matrix of ε_t and $\mathbf{C}_i = \mathbf{I} + \mathbf{K}_1 + \cdots + \mathbf{K}_i$. Ignoring the degenerate case in which $\mathbf{V}$ is singular, the summation above converges only if $\boldsymbol{\alpha}' \mathbf{C}_i$ converges to zero. But the limit of $\mathbf{C}_i$ as $i \to \infty$ is $\mathbf{K}(1)$, so for convergence we must have $\boldsymbol{\alpha}' \mathbf{K}(1) = 0$, which requires $\mathbf{K}(1)$, and hence $\mathbf{M}$, to be singular.

It follows from this that if an economic theory imposes cointegration on a set of nonstationary variables, simple first differencing of all the variables can lead to econometric problems. Noninvertibility of the VMA destroys the usual argument for using a finite VAR representation, that a finite VAR can approximate the true VMA arbitrarily well. Intuitively, the problem arises because a cointegrated system has fewer unit roots than variables, so first differencing all the variables amounts to overdifferencing the system.[13]

Fortunately, there is a simple solution to the difficulty, which is to include $\boldsymbol{\alpha}' \mathbf{x}_t$ in a VAR along with a subset of the elements of $\Delta \mathbf{x}_t$. An equation that relates the change in an elements of $\mathbf{x}_t$ to its own lags and lags of $\boldsymbol{\alpha}' \mathbf{x}_t$ is called an error-correction model for that element of $\mathbf{x}_t$. The VAR proposed in the previous section to test present value models is an error-correction model for y_t, along with an equation describing the evolution of $\boldsymbol{\alpha}' \mathbf{x}_t$.

The second major result from the theory of cointegration concerns the "cointegrating vector" $\boldsymbol{\alpha}$. In a present value model, $\boldsymbol{\alpha}$ is unique up to a scalar normalization and is proportional to $(-\theta \quad 1)'$. Stock [1987] and Phillips and Ouliaris [1986] prove that a variety of methods provide estimates that converge to the true parameter at a rate proportional to the sample size T (rather than $\sqrt{T}$ as in ordinary cases). The reason for this is that, asymptotically, all linear combinations of the elements of $\mathbf{x}_t$ other than $\boldsymbol{\alpha}' \mathbf{x}_t$ have infinite variance.

The practical implication is that an unknown element of $\boldsymbol{\alpha}$ may be estimated in a first-stage regression and then treated as known in second-stage procedures, whose asymptotic standard errors will still be correct. This is extremely useful in carrying out the VAR tests of the previous section. In the case of stock prices, for example, the present value model constrains $\theta = \delta/(1 - \delta)$, so one can estimate the discount factor from a preliminary regression and then treat it as known in testing the model.

Two types of preliminary regression have been proposed for estimating the unknown parameter θ. The first, called the cointegrating regression by Engle and Granger [1987], is just a regression of Y_t on y_t. The second is an "error-correction" regression of Δy_t or ΔY_t on lagged changes in and levels of y_t and Y_t. In the first case, one estimates θ as the coefficient on y_t, while in the second case one takes the ratio of the coefficient on lagged y_t to that on lagged Y_t.

One might argue that use of the error-correction regression is preferable because it accounts more fully for the short-run dynamics of Y_t and y_t. However, it has an important disadvantage. For any cointegrated vector with two elements, there are two possible error-correction regressions, one for Δy_t and one for ΔY_t. Cointegration alone does not rule out that, in one of these regressions, lagged Y_t and y_t have zero coefficients in the population, so that the coefficient ratio fails to identify the desired parameter.[14] Of course, under the present value model the error-correction equation for Δy_t has nonzero coefficients (because $\alpha' x_t$ Granger-causes Δy_t), but this is not implied by all plausible alternatives. Accordingly, we rely primarily on the cointegrating regression to identify θ.

One may want to conduct a formal statistical test of the null hypothesis that x_t is not cointegrated. This turns out to pose some difficult statistical problems. If a candidate for the cointegrating vector α is available, the null hypothesis is that $\alpha' x_t$ is nonstationary, and one can use a modified Dickey-Fuller [1981] test, regressing the change in $\alpha' x_t$ on a constant and a single lagged level. The t-statistics and F-statistic are corrected for serial correlation in the equation residual as proposed by Phillips and Perron [1986] and Phillips [1987] and then compared with significance levels computed numerically by Dickey and Fuller. If the statistics are sufficiently high, the null hypothesis is rejected.

If the cointegrating vector is not known but must be estimated from a cointegrating regression, the Dickey-Fuller significance levels are no longer appropriate. Engle and Granger [1987] analyze a variety of tests that use the residual from the cointegrating regression, an estimate of $\alpha' x_t$. We report two of their test statistics, one based on the Dickey-Fuller regression and one that augments that regression with four lagged dependent variables. Engle and Granger provide significance levels for these tests, based on a Monte Carlo study.[15]

Phillips and Ouliaris [1986] propose an alternative test procedure for the null hypothesis of no cointegration. Their method involves computing the matrix M, the spectral density matrix at zero frequency, nonparametrically. As discussed above, this matrix will be nonsingular under the null and singular under the alternative of cointegration. Unlike the Engle-Granger procedures, their test statistics have a distribution that is asymptotically free of nuisance parameters. They applied their methods to our data, and we note their results below.

16.3 Testing the Model in Bond and Stock Markets

In this section we apply the methods developed above to test present value models for bonds and stocks. The model for bonds, usually referred to as the "expectations theory of the term structure," is a special case of equation (1) in which the parameters θ and δ are known a prior (θ equals one, and δ is a parameter of linearization), while the constant c is a liquidity premium unrestricted by the model.[16]

We test the present value model for bonds on a monthly U.S. Treasury 20-year yield series, available from 1959 to 1983 from Salomon Brothers' *Analytical Record of Yields and Yield Spreads*. The short rate used is a 1-month Treasury bill rate, obtained from the *Treasury Bulletin* for dates prior to 1982 and from the *Wall Street Journal* thereafter.[17] These data were previously studied in Campbell and Shiller [1984]; Shiller et al. [1983] worked with very similar data. We present empirical results both for the full sample 1959:1–1983:10 and for a short sample ending in 1978:8, which is more likely to correspond to a single interest rate regime.[18]

The present value model for stocks is a special case of equation (1) in which θ is known to equal $\delta/(1 - \delta)$. The model restricts the constant c to be zero. The discount factor δ is not known a priori but can be inferred by estimating the cointegrating vector for stock prices and dividends; a consistent estimate is also provided by the sample mean return on stocks.[19]

One difficulty with this formulation for stocks is that Y_t and y_t are not measured contemporaneously. The term Y_t is a beginning-of-period stock price, and y_t is paid sometime within period t. Literal application of the methods outlined in section 16.1 would require us to assume that y_t is known to the market at the start of period t; but, as pointed out by West [1987] and others, this might lead us to a spurious rejection of the model if in fact y_t is known only at the start of period $t + 1$. Intuitively, it is not hard to "predict" excess returns using ex-post information. In order to avoid this problem, we modify the procedures of section 16.1 by constructing a variable $SL_t \equiv Y_t - \theta y_{t-1}$. We use this variable in our tests and alter the cross-equation restrictions appropriately. The dependent variables in the VAR are now SL_t and Δy_{t-1}, both of which are in the information set at the start of time t but not at the start of time $t - 1$ under our conservative assumption about the market's information.[20] Since $SL_t = S_t + \theta \Delta y_t$, it is of course stationary if S_t and Δy_t are.

We tested the model for stocks using time-series data for real annual prices and dividends on a broad stock index from 1871 to 1986. The term Y_t is the Standard and Poor's composite stock price index for January, divided by the January producer price index scaled so that the 1967 producer price index equals 100. (Before 1900 an annual average producer price index was used.) The nominal dividend series is, starting in 1926, dividends per share adjusted to index, four-quarter total, for the Standard and Poor's composite index. The nominal dividend before 1926 was taken from Cowles [1939], who extended the Standard and Poor's series back in time.[21] Finally, y_t is the nominal dividend series, divided by the annual average producer price index scaled so that the 1967 producer price index equals 100.

As shown in table 16.1 parts A and B, we ran unit root tests on our raw data and the various linear combinations discussed in section 16.1. This is an important preliminary because our approach is appropriate only if y_t is integrated of order one. We present test statistics that are based on the t-statistic on the lagged level in a Dickey-Fuller regression, corrected for fourth-order serial correlation as proposed by Phillips and Perron [1986] and Phillips [1987].[22] We ran the Dickey-Fuller regression with and without a time trend; the former is appropriate when the alternative hypothesis is that the series is stationary around a trend, the latter when the alternative is that the series is stationary around a fixed mean.

The results in part A of table 16.1 are generally supportive of the view that short- and long-term interest rates are cointegrated, with the cointegrating vector equal to $[-1 \quad 1]$ as implied by the expectations theory. Over the short sample 1959–1978, one cannot reject the hypothesis that short and long rates have a unit root at even the 10% level; however, there is strong evidence that *changes* in interest rates are stationary. The hypothesis that the long-short spread has a unit root is rejected at the 10% level when a trend is estimated and at the 5% level when the trend is excluded from the regression. Finally, the excess return ξ_t also appears stationary; this, together with the results for Δy_t and ΔY_t,

Table 16.1
Unit root tests (test statistic $zt\alpha$)[a]

Variable	With trend	Without trend
A. In the term structure		
Sample 1959–1978		
y_t	−2.78	−1.72
Y_t	−2.76	−.46
Δy_t	−17.40 (1%)	−17.44 (1%)
ΔY_t	−15.30 (1%)	−15.32 (1%)
S_t	−3.15 (10%)	−3.08 (5%)
ξ_t	−15.22 (1%)	−15.25 (1%)
Sample 1959–1983		
y_t	−3.83 (2.5%)	−2.32
Y_t	−2.51	−.50
Δy_t	−17.05 (1%)	−17.08 (1%)
ΔY_t	−15.27 (1%)	−15.29 (1%)
S_t	−4.77 (1%)	−4.67 (1%)
ξ_t	−15.18 (1%)	−15.19 (1%)
B. In the stock market		
y_t	−2.88	−1.28
Y_t	−2.19	−1.53
Δy_t	−8.40 (1%)	−8.44 (1%)
ΔY_t	−9.91 (1%)	−9.96 (1%)
$\theta = 31.092$		
SL_t	−4.35 (1%)	−4.31 (1%)
ξ_t	−9.93 (1%)	−9.99 (1%)
$\theta = 12.195$		
SL_t	−2.68	−2.15
ξ_t	−9.76 (1%)	−9.69 (1%)

a. Test statistics for a variable X_t are based on the t-statistics on α in the regression $\Delta X_t = \mu + \beta t + \alpha X_{t-1}$ with (trend) or the regression $\Delta X_t = \mu + \alpha X_{t-1}$ (without trend). The t-statistic is corrected for serial correlation in the equation residual in the manner proposed by Phillips and Perron [1986] and Phillips [1987]. Significance levels are: with trend: 10%, −3.12; 5%, −3.41; 2.5%, −3.66; 1%, −3.96; without trend: 10%, −2.57; 5%, −2.86; 2.5%, −3.12; 1%, −3.43.

Table 16.2
Estimation of the cointegrating vector and test for cointegration in the stock market[a]

	R^2	Estimate of θ	Implied discount rate (%)
1. $Y_t = -12.979 + 31.092y_t$	.842	31.092	3.2
2. $\Delta y_t = .101 + .165\Delta y_{t-1} + .010\Delta Y_t$			
$\quad -.157y_{t-1} + .004Y_t$	.373	37.021	2.7
3. Sample mean return = 8.2%	—	12.195	8.2

a. Tests of no cointegration: Engle and Granger [1987] ξ_2 statistic for equation (1) residual, 3.58; significance levels: 10%, 3.03; 5%, 3.37; 1%, 1.07. Engle and Granger [1987] ξ_3 statistic for equation (1) residual, 2.64.; significance levels: 10%, 2.84; 5%, 3.17; 1%, 3.77.

is indirect evidence for stationarity of the spread because of the linear dependence discussed in section 16.1

Results are fairly similar over the full sample 1959–1983. There is even stronger evidence that the spread is stationary, and the unit root hypothesis for short rates can be rejected unless a trend in interest rates is ruled out on a priori grounds.[23]

In part B of the table, we repeated these tests for the stock market data. Once again y_t and Y_t appear to be integrated of order one. In the stock market, the parameter θ is not determined by the present value model as it is in the term structure. Therefore, we must compute SL_t and ξ_t using estimates of θ obtained from the data. Strictly speaking, this invalidates the Phillips-Perron tests for SL_t and ξ_t, but we report the statistics as data description.

Table 16.2 gives details of alternative estimation procedures for θ. The cointegrating regression estimates θ at 31.092; the corresponding real discount rate (the reciprocal of θ) is 3.2%, which is lower than the average dividend-price ratio and considerably lower than the sample mean return of 8.2%.[24] The error-correction regression delivers a fairly similar estimate of θ, 37.021 with an implied real discount rate of 2.7%. We proceed to construct SL_t using discount rates of 8.2% and 3.2% as a check on the robustness of our methods.

Engle and Granger's tests for no cointegration, based on the residual from the cointegrating regression, give mixed results: the ξ_2 statistic rejects at the 5% level, while the ξ_3 statistic narrowly fails to reject at the 10% level. The Phillips-Perron tests in part B of table 16.1 are also mixed. Both SL_t and ξ_t appear to be stationary when the 3.2% discount rate is used, but at an 8.2% discount rate the tests fail to reject the unit root null for SL_t even

Table 16.3
Tests of present value model

A. In the term structure

Sample 1959–1978

  Akaike criterion selects 11-lag VAR

  Δy equation $R^2 = .216$; S Granger-causes Δy at 0.01% level

  S equation $R^2 = .877$; Δy Granger-causes S at 0.3% level

  Test of present value model: $\chi^2(22) = 83.02$; P-value $< 0.005\%$

  Summary statistics

$E(\Delta y) = .016$	$\sigma(S) = 1.060$
$E(S) = 1.144$	$\text{var}(S)/\text{var}(S') = .987(.360)$
$E(S') = .016$	$\text{corr}(S, S') = .978(.011)$
$\sigma(\Delta y) = .442$	$\text{var}(\xi)/\text{var}(\xi') = 1.160(1.146)$

Sample 1959–1983

  Akaike criterion selects six-lag VAR

  Δy equation $R^2 = .171$; S Granger-causes Δy at 0.3% level

  S equation $R^2 = .772$; Δy Granger-causes S at 1.3% level

  Test of present value model: $\chi^2(12) = 35.63$; P-value $= 0.03\%$

  Summary statistics

$E(\Delta y) = .021$	$\sigma(S) = 1.320$
$E(S) = 1.138$	$\text{var}(S)/\text{var}(S') = 3.394(3.948)$
$E(S') = .021$	$\text{corr}(S, S') = .956(.098)$
$\sigma(\Delta y) = .793$	$\text{var}(\xi)/\text{var}(\xi') = .502(.506)$

though they reject for Δy_t, ΔY_t, and ξ_t. There seems to be some evidence for cointegration between stock prices and dividends, but it is weaker than the evidence for cointegration in the term structure.[25]

The results in table 16.1 do not suggest that a "rational bubble" is present in the term structure or the stock market since a bubble would cause both ΔY_t and S_t to be nonstationary. Accordingly, we interpret the test statistics below in terms of predictable excess returns.

In table 16.3, part A, we report summary statistics for a VAR test of the expectations theory of the term structure. The VAR includes Δy_t and S_t as variables, and the number of lags is chosen by the Akaike information criterion (AIC).[26] White's [1984] heteroskedasticity-consistent covariance matrix estimator is used in constructing standard errors and test statistics. The VARs are estimated for the short sample 1959–1978 and the full sample 1959–1983; they have 11 and 6 lags, respectively.

Table 16.3 (continued)

B. In the stock market

Sample 1871–1986
$\theta = 12.195$ (8.2% discount rate): Akaike criterion selects four-lag VAR

Δy equation $R^2 = .400$; SL Granger-causes Δy at $<0.001\%$ level

SL equation $R^2 = .837$; Δy Granger-causes SL at 63.3% level

Test of present value model with mean restriction: $\chi^2(9) = 15.74$; P-value = 7.2%

Test of present value model without mean restriction: $\chi^2(8) = 15.72$; P-value = 4.7%

Summary statistics

$E(\Delta y) = .017$	$\sigma(SL) = 15.51$
$E(SL) = 16.07$	var(SL)/var(SL') = 67.22(86.04)
$E(SL') = 2.563$	corr(SL, SL') = $-.459(.801)$
$\sigma(\Delta y) = .168$	var(ξ)/var(ξ') = 11.27(4.49)

$\theta = 31.092$ (3.2% discount rate): Akaike criterion selects two-lag VAR

Δy equation $R^2 = .378$; SL Granger-causes Δy at $<0.001\%$ level

SL equation $R^2 = .516$; Δy Granger-causes SL at 1.8% level

Test of present value model with mean restriction: $\chi^2(5) = 14.90$; P-value = 1.1%

Test of present value model without mean restriction: $\chi^2(4) = 5.75$; P-value = 21.8%

Summary statistics

$E(\Delta y) = .017$	$\sigma(SL) = 9.937$
$E(SL) = -12.52$	var(SL)/var(SL') = 4.786(5.380)
$E(SL') = 16.66$	corr(SL, SL') = $.911(.207)$
$\sigma(\Delta y) = .167$	var(ξ)/var(ξ') = 1.414(.441)

In both sample periods the lagged variables have a fair degree of explanatory power for the change in short rates. The R^2 for the Δy_t equation is 21.6% in the short sample and 17.1% in the full sample. This argues against the view of Mankiw and Miron (1986) that short-rate changes are essentially unpredictable in the postwar period in the United States. Furthermore, there is strong evidence that spreads Granger-cause short-rate changes, as they should do if the expectations theory is true. The hypothesis of no Granger causality can be rejected at the 0.01% level for the short sample and the 0.3% level for the full sample.

A formal test of the expectations theory restrictions in equation (8) rejects very strongly. The null that excess returns on long bonds are unpredictable can be rejected at less than the 0.005% level in the short sample and at the 0.03% level in the full sample. The R^2 values for excess returns are 26.3% and 16.7% respectively.[27] In the corresponding regression (4), which has the change in the long rate as its dependent variable, the coefficient on the spread has the wrong sign (-0.020 in the short sample and -0.039 in the full sample).[28]

Despite these negative results, the summary statistics in table 16.3, part A, suggest that there is an important element of truth to the expectations theory of the term structure. The spread does seem to move very closely with the theoretical spread, the unrestricted forecast of the present value of future short-rate changes. In both sample periods the variance of the spread is insignificantly different from the variance of the theoretical spread (i.e., our "levels variance ratio" does not reject), and the two variables have similar innovation variances and an extremely high correlation. In the 1959–1978 period the correlation between the actual and theoretical spreads is 0.978 with a standard error of 0.011, while in the 1959–1983 period it is 0.956 with a standard error of 0.098. Figure 16.1 illustrates the comovement of S_t and S_t' in the short sample.[29]

What this suggests is that tests of predictability of returns are highly sensitive to deviations from the expectations theory—so sensitive, in fact, that they may obscure some of the merits of the theory. An example illustrates the point. Suppose long and short rates differ from the expectations theory in the following manner: $S_t = S_t' + w_t$, where w_t is serially uncorrelated noise. As Campbell and Shiller [1984] point out, excess bond returns will be predicted by S_t, and a regression of ΔY_{t+1} on S_t may find that the coefficient has the opposite sign from that predicted by (4), even if the variance of w_t is quite small. However, a regression of S_t^* on S_t will find that the coefficient has the same sign as predicted by (3), and downward bias caused by w_t will be small if the variance of w_t is small. Moreover, the variance ratios $\mathrm{var}(S_t)/\mathrm{var}(S_t')$ and $\mathrm{var}(\xi_t)/\mathrm{var}(\xi_t')$ may not be much greater than one. In this example the spread predicts short-rate movements almost correctly, even though it badly misforecasts long-rate movements. Deviations from the present value model are transitory rather than persistent, so the metric of equation (10) reveals the strengths of the expectations theory that are obscured by the metric of equation (11).[30]

In part B of table 16.3, we repeated the exercises above for stock prices and dividends. We worked with one sample period but two discount rates. The Akaike criterion selected a four-lag representation for the data when the sample mean discount rate 8.2% was used and a two-lag representation when the cointegrating regression discount rate 3.2% was used.

The VAR estimates suggest that dividend changes are rather highly predictable; the R^2 values for the equations that explain them are around 40%. There is very strong evidence that price-dividend spreads Granger-

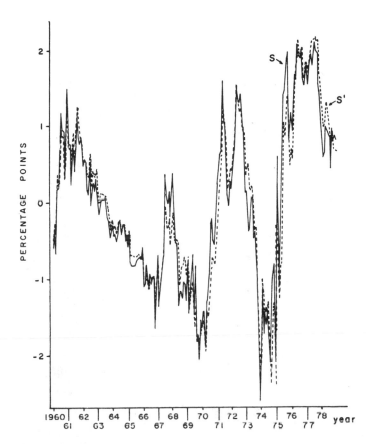

Figure 16.1
Term structure: deviations from means of long-short spread S_t and theoretical spread S_t'.

cause dividend changes, which is what one would expect if there is any truth to the present value model for stock prices.

We conducted two formal tests of the model. The first restricted the mean of the price-dividend difference, while the second left the mean unconstrained and restricted only the dynamics of the variable. (In the case of the term structure, the mean spread is always unconstrained because we allowed a constant risk premium.)

The results of these tests include some statistical rejections at conventional significance levels, but they are not nearly as strong as the rejections in the term structure. The pattern of results is sensitive to the choice of discount rate. When the sample mean return is used, the mean restriction on SL_t is satisfied almost exactly. Therefore, the test of only the dynamic restrictions in equation (8) rejects more strongly, at the 4.7% level as compared with the 7.2% level for the full set of restrictions. When the discount rate from the cointegrating regression is used, the complete set of restrictions is rejected at the 1.1% level while the significance level for the dynamic restrictions is only 21.8%.[31] For both discount rates, a regression of ΔY_{t+1} on SL_t gives a coefficient estimate with a negative sign rather than the positive sign implied by the present value model.[32]

These tests are "portmanteau" tests of the present value model against an unspecified alternative. We also present variance ratios in order to test against the specific alternative that stock prices "move too much" in levels or innovations. The point estimate of the levels variance ratio $\text{var}(SL_t)/\text{var}(SL_t')$ is dramatically different from unity, at 67.22, when the sample mean discount rate is used. Not surprisingly, the variance ratio is smaller when future dividend changes are discounted at the lower rate estimated by the cointegrating regression, but it is still considerable at 4.79. However, the asymptotic standard errors on these ratios are huge, and one cannot reject the hypothesis that both of them equal unity.

The innovations variance ratios $\text{var}(\xi_t)/\text{var}(\xi_t')$ are also estimated larger than unity, and here the standard errors are less extreme. In the sample mean discount rate case, one can reject at the 5% level the hypothesis that the innovation variance ratio is unity; it is estimated to be 11.27, with a standard error of 4.49. With the lower discount rate, the ratio is estimated at 1.41, with a standard error of 0.44.

Plots of the price-dividend difference and the unrestricted VAR forecast of dividend changes give a visual image of these variance results. At an 8.2% discount rate (figure 16.2), SL_t and SL_t' are negatively correlated (but there is a very large standard error on the correlation) and the excess volatility of the spread is very dramatic. At a 3.2% discount rate (figure 16.3), SL_t and SL_t' have a correlation of 0.911 (with standard error 0.207) and the excess volatility is much less dramatic.[33]

To compare our results on volatility with results using earlier methods, we also computed sample values of S_t^* using the terminal condition $S_T^* = S_T$, where T is the last observation in our sample. We computed SL_t^* analogously. Equation (3) implies $\sigma(S_t^*) > \sigma(S_t)$ and $\sigma(SL_t^*) > \sigma(SL_t)$. For the bond data in the period 1959–1978, $\sigma(S_t^*) = 1.217$, while $\sigma(S_t) = 1.060$, so the inequality is satisfied. For the stock data at an 8.2% discount rate, $\sigma(SL_t^*) = 7.928$, while $\sigma(SL_t) = 15.506$, so the inequality is sharply violated. The inequality is again satisfied by the stock data at a 3.2% discount rate, where $\sigma(SL_t^*) = 12.888$ and $\sigma(SL_t) = 9.937$.

Following Scott [1985], we also regressed S_t^* on S_t and a constant. If the present value model is true, the coefficient on S_t should be one. The same

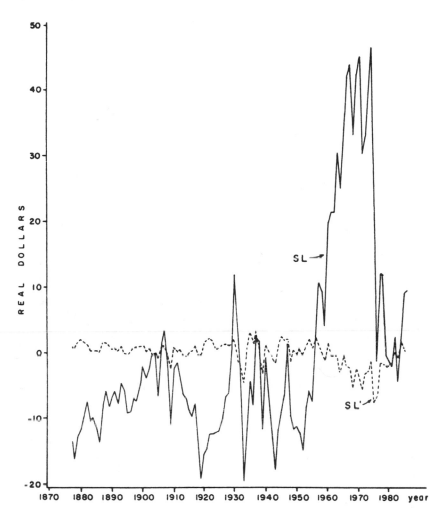

Figure 16.2
Stock market: deviations from means of actual spread ($SL_t = \text{Price}_t - \theta \cdot \text{Dividend}_{t-1}$) and theoretical spread SL'_t, $\theta = 12.195$.

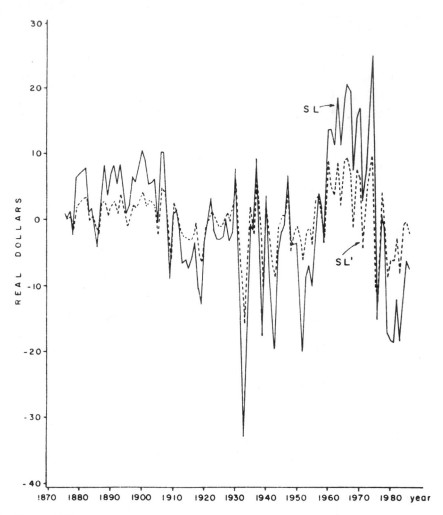

Figure 16.3
Stock market: deviations from means of actual spread ($SL_t = \text{Price} - \theta \cdot \text{Dividend}_{t-1}$)
and theoretical spread SL_t', $\theta = 31.092$.

holds for the corresponding regression with SL_t^* and SL_t. For bonds in 1959–1978, we estimated the coefficient at 0.81; for stocks at an 8.2% discount rate we estimated it at 0.16, while for stocks at a 3.2% discount rate we estimated it at 0.02. Thus the results using S_t^* and SL_t^* generally support the conclusion that the present value model for bonds fits the data comparatively well, whereas the model for stocks has a poor fit even though it cannot be rejected statistically at high levels of confidence.

We close with a caveat about the plots and summary statistics generated by the VAR system. The VAR simulation method may be misleading if the wrong value of θ is chosen so that the spread variable is nonstationary. For example, if θ is chosen too large, the movements of S_t are dominated by the movements of $-\theta y_t$. The VAR results are then approximately those one would get if one regressed Δy_t and $-\theta y_t$ on lagged values of these variables. It is well known that in finite samples estimates of autoregressive parameters for nonstationary variables are biased downward, and this problem will afflict the VAR if θ is too large.

In a simple case in which y_t follows an AR(1) process with a unit root and the VAR includes one lag only, one can show that the estimated VAR companion matrix will have first column zero and second column $((1 - \rho)/\theta, \rho)'$, where ρ is a downward-biased estimate of the unit root. This companion matrix satisfies the restrictions of equation (9) almost exactly, whatever the behavior of the variable Y_t. A symptom of this misspecification would be that mean returns would not obey the model, even though the dynamics of returns would appear to satisfy the restrictions.

It is possible that a problem of this sort affects our results for the stock market when we use a low 3.2% discount rate corresponding to a high θ of 31.092. The cointegrating regression that generates this θ estimate—a regression of the level of Y on the level of y—is dominated by the enormous postwar hump in stock prices. Since this hump coincided with a much milder hump in real dividends, the regression estimates a coefficient for y that is much larger than the historical average price-dividend ratio. The negative intercept prevents the fitted value from overpredicting Y over the sample period as a whole. As a result, over the bulk of the sample period, the spread SL_t is distinctly negatively correlated with the lagged dividend.[34] The VAR estimates place considerable weight on this earlier part of the sample period because the dividend equation is specified in terms of dividend changes that are more variable before 1946. Thus the high correlation of SL_t and SL_t' may be to some extent spurious.

This view is supported by the results from regressing SL_t^* on SL_t. This is a levels regression that is dominated by the postwar hump in stock prices, and here we find the coefficient to be essentially zero rather than one as required by the model. Further support comes from the fact that we strongly reject the implications of the model for the mean of the data when we impose a 3.2% discount rate.

16.4   Conclusion

In this chapter we have shown how a present value model may be tested when the variables of the model, y_t and Y_t, follow linear stochastic processes that are stationary in first differences rather than in levels. If the present value model is true, a linear combination of the variables—which we call the spread—is stationary. Thus y_t and Y_t are cointegrated. The model implies that the spread is linear in the optimal forecast of the one-period change in Y_t and also in the optimal forecast of the present value of all future changes in y_t. We have shown how to conduct formal Wald tests of these implications.

We have also proposed an informal method for evaluating the "fit" of a present value model. A VAR is used to construct an optimal unrestricted forecast of the present value of future y_t changes, and this is compared with the spread. If the model is true, the unrestricted forecast or "theoretical spread" should equal the actual spread. We computed the variances and correlation of the two variables and plotted their historical movements.

We applied our methods to the controversial present value models for stocks and bonds. We found that both models can be rejected statistically at conventional significance levels, with much stronger evidence for bonds. However, in our data set, the spread between long- and short-term interest rates seems to move quite closely with the unrestricted forecast of the present value of future short-rate changes. This can be interpreted as evidence that deviations from the present value model for bonds are transitory. In contrast, our evaluation of the present value model for stocks indicates that the spread between stock prices and dividends moves too much and that deviations from the present value model are quite persistent, although the strength of the evidence for this depends sensitively on the discount rate assumed in the test.

Notes

1. The discounted sum in equation (1) extends to an infinite horizon. Most of the methods in this chapter can be applied to the finite horizon case, at the cost of some additional complexity. Throughout this chapter we will treat conditional expectations as equivalent to linear projections on information.

2. For bonds, see Sargent [1979]. Shiller [1979 (chapter 15), 1981a, 1987]. Hansen and Sargent (1981a), Shiller, Campbell, and Schoenholtz [1983], and Campbell and Shiller [1984]. For stocks, see LeRoy and Porter [1981], Shiller [1981b (chapter 5), 1984], Mankiw, Romer, and Shapiro [1985], Scott [1985], Marsh and Merton [1986], and West [1986, 1987].

3. This point is made for stocks by Kleidon [1986] and Marsh and Merton [1986], Mankiw and Shapiro [1985] present a similar argument for the permanent income theory of consumption.

4. It might be attractive to model the variables y and Y as stationary in log first differences. However, since the model (1) is linear in levels, a log specification is intractable unless one is willing to focus on a special case [Kleidon 1986] or to approximate the model [Campbell and Shiller, 1986]. Also see chapter 4, pp. 92–94.

5. The variable ξ_t can also be written as a constant plus the true innovation in the expected present value of all future y_t. We note, however, that in general the model does *not* identify the true innovation in y_t itself.

6. Quah [1986] gives an example in which b_t satisfies $b_t = \delta E_t b_{t+1}$ but is stationary. However, this example violates the equivalence of conditional expectations and linear projections, which we assume here.

7. A formal proof is as follows. Suppose that S_t does not Granger-cause Δy_t. Then $E(\Delta y_{t+i}|\mathbf{H}_t) = E(\Delta y_{t+i}|\Delta y_t, \Delta y_{t-1}, \ldots)$ for all i, and from (3), $E(S_t|\mathbf{H}_t) = E(S_t|\Delta y_t, \Delta y_{t-1}, \ldots)$, an exact linear function of current and lagged Δy_t. But because S_t is itself in the information set $\mathbf{H}_t$, $S_t = E(S_t|\mathbf{H}_t)$.

8. Under an explosive bubble alternative this infinite sum will not converge, and the matrix $(\mathbf{I} - \delta\mathbf{A})$ will be singular.

9. However, this statistic is not numerically identical to the Wald statistic for a test of equation (7), even though (7) and (8) are algebraically equivalent restrictions. Nonlinear transformations of restrictions can change the numerical values of Wald statistics and, as Gregory and Veall [1985] point out, can dramatically alter their power. We report Wald statistics for (8) in the tables that summarize our empirical results and Wald statistics for (7) in notes.

10. The terminology of our earlier paper [Campbell and Shiller, 1984] may be helpful in understanding (10) and (11). The right-hand side of (11) is proportional to what we called the one-period "holding premium," and the right-hand side of (10) is what we called the "rolling premium."

11. We compute the levels variance ratio and correlation from the sample moments of S_t and S_t'. We report numerical standard errors that are conditional on the sample moments of z_t and take account of sampling error only in the coefficients of the estimated VAR.

12. We use the estimated variance-covariance matrix of the VAR to compute the innovations variance ratio. The standard error takes account of sampling error in this matrix as well as in the VAR coefficients.

13. Shiller (1981a) and Melino [1983] criticized Sargent [1979] on this ground (and on the ground that he failed to test implications of the model for the relative levels of y_t and Y_t). Baillie, Lippens, and McMahon [1983] also overdifferenced their system. Hansen and Sargent [1981a] corrected the problems with Sargent's procedure.

14. Cointegration does rule out that the coefficients are zero in both error-correction regressions.

15. The Monte Carlo results are based on 10,000 replications of 100 observations of independent random walks, with four lagged residual changes included in the test.

16. The linearization required to write the expectations theory in this form is explained in Shiller [1979 (chapter 15)] and Shiller et al. [1983].

17. The *Treasury Bulletin* and *Wall Street Journal* data are consistent with one another at dates when they are both available.

18. For both samples, the parameter of linearization δ is set equal to $1/(1 + R)$, with R at 0.0587/12 (the mean 20-year bond rate in the short sample, expressed at a monthly rate). Our subsequent empirical results are conditional on a fixed value of δ.

19. The sample mean return converges to the population mean only at rate $\sqrt{T}$ and therefore should not strictly be taken as known in second-stage procedures. However, we ignore this problem in our empirical work.

20. Engle and Watson (1987) did some regressions similar to ours, using a similar data set on stock prices and dividends. They used the variable S_t rather than SL_t. Their results differ from ours in that they found no evidence of Granger causality from S_t to Δy_t, but they did not reject the present value model more strongly than we do.

21. The dividend data differ slightly from those used in Shiller [1981b (chapter 5)], Mankiw et al. [1985], West [1987], and others. It has recently come to our attention that the second [1939] edition of Cowles's book contains some corrections to the dividend series presented in the original 1938 edition, and these corrections have been incorporated here.

22. The results are qualitatively unchanged by looking at other statistics from the Dickey-Fuller regression or by varying the order of the serial correlation correction between 1 and 10.

23. The results in table 16.1, part A, are more favorable to the hypothesis of cointegration between long and short rates than are the results reported by Phillips and Ouliaris [1986]. They reject the null hypothesis of no cointegration at only the 15% level (their table 6). However, their procedure does not impose the cointegrating vector a priori, and this may involve a loss of power.

24. The estimate of θ that corresponds to the sample mean return is 12.195. The higher estimate in the cointegrating regression is associated with a negative

constant term; under the present value model, the constant should be proportional to the unconditional mean change in dividends, so it should be positive rather than negative. An estimated discount rate lower than the mean dividend-price ratio is consistent with the model only if dividends are expected to decline through time, the historical rise being due to sampling error.

25. Phillips and Ouliaris [1986] did not reject the null hypothesis of no cointegration between stock prices and dividends at even the 25% level (their table 6). Campbell and Shiller [1986] report unit root tests for log dividends, log prices, and the log dividend-price ratio. There is some evidence for trend stationarity of log dividends, no evidence against the unit root null for log prices, and strong evidence for stationarity of the dividend-price ratio.

26. That is, we pick the number of lags to minimize ($-\ln$ likelihood + number of parameters) in the VAR. Sawa [1978] has argued that the AIC tends to choose models of higher order than the true model but states that the bias is negligible when $p < T/10$, as it is here. The test statistics in table 16.3 are not highly sensitive to small changes in the lag length of the VAR system.

27. Nonlinear Wald tests of equation (7) reject at significance levels of less than 0.005% in the short sample and 8.4% in the full sample.

28. This is consistent with the results of Shiller et al. [1983].

29. The high correlation of these variables in postwar U.S. data might also have been inferred from results in Modigliani and Shiller [1973] (figure 13.1 on p. 221, from that article). Despite the evidence reported in Modigliani and Shiller and in the present chapter, one of us [Shiller, 1979] (chapter 15) presented evidence suggesting that long-term interest rates are too volatile to accord with the expectations theory. By contrast with Modigliani and Shiller and this chapter, Shiller [1979] (chapter 15) assumed that *levels* of short rates are stationary, an assumption more clearly appropriate for prewar data sets.

30. We do not claim that this example is literally correct for our data. The model $S = S' + w$ can be tested, for any MA(q) process for w, by regressing ξ on information known $q + 2$ periods earlier. We found that this test rejected the model for q up to 8 using the bond data for 1959–1978.

31. Nonlinear Wald tests of the dynamic restrictions in the form (7), rather than (8), reject at less than the 0.005% level for the 8.2% discount rate and at the 7.3% level for the 3.2% discount rate.

32. The coefficient is -0.064 for the 8.2% discount rate and -0.079 for the 3.2% discount rate.

33. It should be emphasized that excess volatility of the spread SL_t is not quite the same as the excess volatility discussed in Shiller [1981b] (chapter 5). That analysis suggested that stock prices should very nearly follow a trend. If that were in fact what was observed, the spread SL_t would be quite volatile because of dividend movements.

34. Over the period 1871–1946, the spread has a correlation of −0.7 with the lagged dividend when θ is set equal to 31.092.

References

Baillie, Richard T.; Lippens, Robert E.; and McMahon, Patrick C. 1983. "Testing Rational Expectations and Efficiency in the Foreign Exchange Market," *Econometrica* 51:553–563.

Blanchard, Olivier J., and Watson, Mark W. 1982. "Bubbles, Rational Expectations and Financial Markets." In *Crises in the Economic and Financial Structure: Bubbles, Bursts and Shocks*, edited by Paul Wachtel. Lexington, Mass.: Lexington.

Campbell, John Y. 1987. "Does Saving Anticipate Declining Labor Income? An Alternative Test of the Permanent Income Hypothesis," *Econometrica* 55:1249–1273.

Campbell, John Y., and Shiller, Robert J. 1984. "A Simple Account of the Behavior of Long-Term Interest Rates," *American Economic Review* 74:44–48.

Campbell, John Y., and Shiller, Robert J. 1986. "The Dividend-Price Ratio and Expectations of Future Dividends and Discount Factors," Working Paper no. 2100. Cambridge, Mass.: NBER.

Cowles, Alfred. 1939. *Common-Stock Indexes*. 2d ed. Bloomington, Ind.: Principia.

Diba, Behzad T., and Grossman, Herschel I. 1984. "Rational Bubbles in the Price of Gold," Working Paper no. 1300. Cambridge, Mass.: NBER.

Dickey, David A., and Fuller, Wayne A. 1981. "Likelihood Ratio Statistics for Autoregressive Time Series with a Unit Root," *Econometrica* 49:1057–1072.

Engle, Robert F., and Granger, Clive W. J. 1987. "Cointegration and Error-Correction: Representation, Estimation and Testing," *Econometrica* 55:251–276.

Engle, Robert F., and Watson, Mark W. 1987. "The Kalman Filter: Applications to Forecasting and Rational Expectations Models," in Truman Bewley, ed., *Advances in Econometrics*, Fifth World Congress, Vol. 1. Cambridge, England: Cambridge University Press.

Fama, Eugene F. 1970. "Efficient Capital Markets: A Review of Theory and Empirical Work," *Journal of Finance* 25:383–417.

Gregory, Allan W., and Veall, Michael R. 1985. "Formulating Wald Tests of Nonlinear Restrictions," *Econometrica* 53:1465–1468.

Hamilton, James D., and Whiteman, Charles H. 1985. "The Observable Implications of Self-fulfilling Expectations," *Journal of Monetary Economics* 16:353–373.

Hansen, Lars Peter, and Sargent, Thomas J. 1981a. "Exact Linear Rational Expectations Models: Specification and Estimation," Staff Report no. 71. Minneapolis: Fed Reserve Bank, November.

Hansen, Lars Peter, and Sargent, Thomas J. 1981b. "Linear Rational Expectations Models for Dynamically Interrelated Variables." In *Rational Expectations and Econometric Practice*, edited by Robert E. Lucas, Jr., and Thomas J. Sargent. Minneapolis: Univ. Minnesota Press.

Kleidon, Allan W. 1986. "Variance Bounds Tests and Stock Price Valuation Models," *Journal of Political Economy* 94:953–1001.

LeRoy, Stephen F., and Porter, Richard D. 1981. "The Present-Value Relation: Tests Based on Implied Variance Bounds," *Econometrica* 49:555–574.

Mankiw, N. Gregory, and Miron, Jeffrey A. 1986. "The Changing Behavior of the Term Structure of Interest Rates," *Quarterly Journal of Economics* 101:211–228.

Mankiw, N. Gregory; Romer, David; and Shapiro, Matthew D. 1985. "An Unbiased Reexamination of Stock Market Volatility," *Journal of Finance* 40:677–687.

Mankiw, N. Gregory, and Shapiro, Matthew D. 1985. "Trends, Random Walks, and Tests of the Permanent Income Hypothesis," *Journal of Monetary Economics* 16:165–174.

Marsh, Terry A., and Merton, Robert C. 1986. "Dividend Variability and Variance Bounds Tests for the Rationality of Stock Market Prices," *American Economic Review* 76:483–498.

Melino, Angelo. 1983. "Essays on Estimation and Inference in Linear Rational Expectations Models." Ph.D. dissertation, Harvard Univ.

Modigliani, Franco, and Shiller, Robert J. 1973. "Inflation, Rational Expectations and the Term Structure of Interest Rates," *Economica* 40:12–43.

Phillips, P. C. B. 1987. "Time Series Regression with Unit Roots," *Econometrica* 55:277–302.

Phillips, P. C. B., and Durlauf, Stephen N. 1986. "Multiple Time Series Regression with Integrated Processes," *Review of Economic Studies* 53:473–495.

Phillips, P. C. B., and Ouliaris, Sam 1986. "Testing for Cointegration." Discussion Paper no. 809. New Haven, Conn.: Yale Univ., Cowles Foundation.

Phillips, P. C. B., and Perron, Pierce 1986. "Testing for Unit Roots in Time Series Regression." Discussion Paper. New Haven, Conn.: Yale Univ., Cowles Foundation.

Quah, Danny. 1986. "Stationary Rational Bubbles in Asset Prices." Manuscript. Cambridge: MIT.

Sargent, Thomas J. 1979. "A Note on Maximum Likelihood Estimation of the Rational Expectations Model of the Term Structure," *Journal of Monetary Economics* 5:133–143.

Sawa, Takamitsu. 1978. "Information Criteria for Discriminating among Alternative Regression Models," *Econometrica* 46:1273–1291.

Scott, Louis O. 1985. "The Present Value Model of Stock Prices: Regression Tests and Monte Carlo Results," *Review of Economics and Statistics* 67:599–605.

Shiller, Robert J. 1979. "The Volatility of Long-Term Interest Rates and Expectations Models of the Term Structure," *Journal of Political Economy* 87:1190–1219.

Shiller, Robert J. 1981a. "Alternative Tests of Rational Expectations Models: The Case of the Term Structure," *Journal of Econometrics* 16:71–87.

Shiller, Robert J. 1981b. "Do Stock Prices Move Too Much to Be Justified by Subsequent Changes in Dividends?" *American Economic Review* 71:421–436.

Shiller, Robert J. 1984. "Stock Prices and Social Dynamics," *Brookings Papers on Economic Activity*, no. 2, pp. 457–498.

Shiller, Robert J. 1987. "Conventional Valuation and the Term Structure of Interest Rates." In *Macroecomonics and Finance: Essays in Honor of Franco Modigliani*, edited by Rudiger Dornbusch, Stanley Fischer, and John Bossons. Cambridge, Mass.: MIT Press 63–68.

Shiller, Robert J.; Campbell, John Y.; and Schoenholtz, Kermit L. 1983. "Forward Rates and Future Policy: Interpreting the Term Structure of Interest Rates," *Brookings Papers on Economic Activity*, no. 1, pp. 173–217.

Stock, James H. 1987. "Asymptotic Properties of Least Squares Estimates of Cointegrating Vectors," *Econometrica* 56:1035–1036.

West, Kenneth D. 1986. "A Specification Test for Speculative Bubbles," *Quarterly Journal of Economics* 102:553–580.

West, Kenneth D. 1987. "Dividend Innovations and Stock Price Volatility," *Econometrica* 56:37–61.

White, Halbert. 1984. *Asymptotic Theory for Econometricians*. Orlando, Fla.: Academic Press.

IV

The Real Estate Market

17   Overview

Markets for real estate are subject to dramatic price fluctuations that are often as hard to explain as are price movements in the stock and bond markets. But we face a problem in studying the volatility in these markets along the same lines as in the stock and bond markets: there are not such long and high quality time series on prices and on the rents that correspond to the dividends for real estate. It was argued in chapter 4 that we need price and dividend series that span many decades to do the kind of analysis of volatility that was feasible for the stock market.

Price series in real estate are hard to construct, because most real estate is not a standard commodity. The nature or quality of real estate on the market at any one time may be different from that of real estate on the market at another time. For example, sales of larger homes may tend to come in phase with the school year, when families with children are more likely to move. The quality of real estate tends to change through time as the results of, for example, depreciation or (unmeasured) funds spent on improvements.

Not trusting in existing housing price series, Karl Case and I went back to data on repeat sales of individual houses for which we had information on the kind and quality of house. With this information, we were able to throw out of our sample any houses that showed substantial change in characteristics. But we were unable to find such data in a machine-readable form before 1970.

The actual rent earned by most houses is not actually observed, since most houses are used by the owner and do not pass through rental markets. The owner-occupant of a home earns instead an implicit rent in the form of housing services, on which there is no market valuation. The best proxy for such implicit rents that we appear to have here are rental indexes (computed from data on rental properties) published by the U.S. Bureau of Labor Statistics.

While the volatility tests used for the stock and bond markets are not feasible for the housing market, it may yet be possible to find substantial evidence of inefficiency in these markets even with these short data series. The markets may show striking inefficiency, in the form of serial correlation of price changes. There are smaller opportunities for "smart money" to operate in these markets so as to make the markets more efficient. The results in the next chapter do find some evidence of such inefficiency.

Agricultural land data are available for substantial periods, and some authors have sought to apply simple volatility tests to these markets. Colling and Irwin [1988] used real U.S. aggregate farm asset values and income from assets for the period 1910–1986 from the *Agricultural Finance Databook* published by the Board of Governors of the Federal Reserve System. Farm assets consist primarily of land, but include structures and equipment as well. They used methods apparently identical to those I used in chapter 5 to analyze these data, and found that the standard deviation of detrended price P_t was 2.39 times that of detrended ex-post value P_t^*, that is, inequality (1) of chapter 5 was substantially violated. A plot of their data reveals that most of the variability of P_t^* comes from the first decade of their sample, when both P_t^* and P_t were falling sharply. A depression of land values occurred in the 1930s and early 1940s, unmatched by any decline in P_t^*. The 1970s saw a dramatic runup of asset values, and the 1980s a rapid decline, while P_t^* remained fairly steady.[1] However, the violation is less striking than for the stock market example, and since their sample is somewhat shorter, the evidence for excess volatility must be considered weak.

Falk [1988] exploited different data sources to obtain Iowa farmland values, 1921–1986. He spliced together two Iowa farm price series, from the U.S. Department of Agriculture Economic Research Service 1921–1941 and from the Iowa State University Extension Service *Iowa Land Value Survey* 1942–1986. Cash rent on whole farms in Iowa were provided by the USDA Economic Research Service based on data from the Iowa Crop and Livestock Reporting Service.

His data look broadly similar to those of Colling and Irwin, showing the same real price runup in the 1970s and collapse in the 1980s, the same lack of action in P_t^*. He strongly rejects the present value model, using methods like those Campbell and I used (chapter 16). It is interesting to note that he found a negative correlation between the spread S_t and the theoretical spread S_t', just as we did with the stock market when the discount rate had a reasonable value (table 16.3, panel B, $\theta = 12.195$). The reason that this happens appears to be the tendency of price to overreact to dividends, as noted in chapter 1. Consider a post-World War II period, where the pattern is striking. Falk's data show that both price and rents had a fairly similar hump-shaped pattern through time in the 1970s through 1986, but the hump was much bigger and more pronounced in price than it was in rents. The upside of the hump in price came after that of rents, and when it did come it was much bigger and sharper. When real rents started falling (the downside of the hump), real prices fell much more sharply. The postwar performance of stock prices in the United States can also be described, though less accurately, in the same terms. The hump in aggregate real stock prices in the United States, rising from 1950 to 1973 and falling sharply into 1975, was bigger and sharper than the hump in real dividends, rising gently from 1950 to the late 1960s, then falling gently (see figure 10.1).

Note

1. The plot of real land values in figure 19.1, page 347, stops just short of the sharp drop of land values in the 1980s.

References

Colling, Phil L., and Scott H. Irwin, 1988. "Has the Farm Asset Market Been Too Volatile?" Economic and Sociology Occassional Paper #1350, Department of Agricultural Economics and Rural Sociology, Ohio State University.

Falk, Barry. 1988. "The Search for Speculative Bubbles in Farmland Prices," reproduced, Department of Economics, Iowa State University.

The Efficiency of the Market for Single Family Homes

There is good reason to think that the market for single family homes ought to be less efficient than are financial markets. The market is dominated by individuals trading in the homes they live in. Because of transactions costs, carrying costs, and tax considerations, professionals find it relatively difficult to take advantage of profit opportunities in this market. For these reasons, it is commonly casually asserted that the market for single family homes is inefficient, and "bull markets" in housing (i.e., temporary upwards inertia in housing prices) are frequently alleged. But it is hard to find scholarly work confirming whether this is so.

We have found surprisingly little in the literature on the testing of the efficiency of real estate markets. A computer search turned up only three recent papers, by George Gau and Peter Linneman. Gau describes his two papers [1984, 1985] as the "first rigorous testing" of real estate market efficiency.[1] His data, however, were confined to commercial real estate and to the Vancouver area for the years 1971–1980. He concluded that prices in the Vancouver market were well described as a random walk. Linneman [1984], who asserts that "there are no empirical studies of the efficiency of the housing market,"[2] did a study using observations on individual owners' assessments of house value (rather than actual sales prices) in Philadelphia for two times: 1975 and 1978. He found that houses that were undervalued relative to a 1975 hedonic regression (i.e., that had negative residuals in a regression of price on housing characteristics) tended to increase in value subsequently, but that because of transactions costs only an insignificant number of units appear to present profitable arbitrage candidates. Robert Engle, David Lilien, and Mark Waston [1985] estimated a model of the resale housing market using data on retail house sales in San

Coauthored with Karl E. Case. Reprinted with minor editing from *American Economic Review* 79 (1989): 125–137. © 1989 the American Economics Association.

Diego for 1973–1980. They concluded that much of the overall movement in housing prices in this period could be explained in terms of such factors as demographically driven changes in the cost of housing services, Proposition 13, and the inflation-driven change in marginal tax rates. But they did not investigate directly whether the market was efficient.

This chapters performs test of the efficiency of this market using data from the Society of Real Estate Appraisers tapes for the years 1970–1986 for Atlanta, Chicago, Dallas, and San Francisco/Oakland (see appendix). The tapes contain actual sale prices and other information about the homes. We extracted from the tapes for each city a file of data on houses sold twice for which there was no apparent quality change and for which conventional mortgages applied. For each house the data we used consisted of the two sales prices and the two dates (quarters) in which the sales occurred. The total number of observations on such double sales of relatively unchanged homes was 39,210 (8,945 for Atlanta, 15,530 for Chicago, 6,669 for Dallas, and 8,066 for San Franciso). None of the other studies had actual repeat sales price data on individual homes at all, let alone such a large number, and none of the studies spanned the time interval and geographical area of our study. Moreover, the present study presents some statistical-methodological improvements over the Gau studies in its effort to test the random walk theory for housing prices.

18.1   The WRS Index

In a companion paper [1987] we discuss our method of price index construction, which we call the Weighted Repeat Sales (WRS) method. The method is a modification of the regression method proposed by Martin J. Bailey, Richard Muth, and Hugh Nourse (hereafter, BMN). The BMN method produces estimates and standard errors for an index of housing prices by regressing, using ordinary least squares, the change in log price of each house on a set of dummy variables, one dummy for each time period in the sample except for the first. Each value of the log price index BMN (t) is represented by a regression coefficient, except for the first value of the log price index, which is set to zero as a normalization. The dummy variables are zero except when the dummy is $+1$, corresponding to the second time period when the house was sold, and when the dummy is -1, corresponding to the first time period when the house was sold (unless this is the first time period). Bailey, Muth, and Nourse argued that if the log price changes of individual houses differ from the citywide log price change by an independent, identically distributed noise term, then by the Gauss-

Markov theorem their estimated index is the best linear unbiased estimate of the citywide log price.

Our procedure differs from the BMN procedure because we feel that the house-specific component of the change in log price is probably not homoskedastic but that the variance of this noise increases with the interval between sales. The motivation for our WRS method was the assumption that the log price P_{it} of the ith house at time t is given by

$$P_{it} = C_t + H_{it} + N_{it}, \tag{1}$$

where C_t is the log of the citywide level of housing prices at time t, H_{it} is a Gaussian random walk (where ΔH_{it} has zero mean and variance σ_h^2) that is uncorrelated with C_T and H_{jT}, $i \neq j$ for all T, and N_{it} is an identically distributed normal noise term (which has zero mean and variance σ_N^2) and is uncorrelated with C_T and H_{jT} for all j and T and with N_{jT} unless $i = j$ and $t = T$. Here, H_{it} represents the drift in individual housing value through time, and N_{it} represents the noise in price due to imperfections in market for housing.[3] Presumably, the value that a house brings when it is sold depends on such things as the random arrival of interested purchasers, the behavior of the real estate agent, and other random factors, so that the sale price is not identical to true value. Moreover, there may be some change in true value that may be bunched at the purchase date.

A three-step weighted (generalized) least squares procedure was undertaken. In the first step, the BMN procedure was followed exactly, and a vector of regression residuals was calculated. In the second step, the squared residuals in the first step regression were regressed on a constant and the time interval between sales.[4] The constant term was the estimate of σ_N^2, and the slope term was the estimate of σ_H^2. In the third step, a generalized least squares regression (a weighted regression) was run by first dividing each observation in the step-one regression by the square root of the fitted value in the second stage regression and running the regression again.

The estimated WRS index WRS(t) and its accuracy are discussed in our companion paper. The level of the index is quite well measured, the quarterly first difference of the index is not well measured, and the annual difference of the index is fairly well measured. One way of describing how well these variables are measured is to compute the ratio of the standard deviation of a variable to the average standard error for the variable. For the log index in levels, this ratio is 13.87 for Atlanta, 24.52 for Chicago, 9.94 for Dallas, and 28.03 for San Francisco/Oakland. Thus, we can make very accurate statements about the level of house prices in the cities. For the quarterly difference of the log indexes, the ratios are 1.64, 1.61, 1.35, and 1.54, respectively. We thus cannot accurately describe the quarterly changes in the log prices, though the index will give a rough indication. For the annual difference of the log index, the ratios are 2.73, 3.99, 2.90, and 3.62 respectively; we can make fairly accurate statements about the annual change in log housing prices.

Other existing housing price indexes are widely interpreted as showing even monthly changes in housing prices. We argue in our companion paper that these indexes (for which no standard errors are provided) are likely to be less accurate than ours.

18.2   Seasonality, City Influence, and Beta

Table 18.1A gives sample statistics for $W(t) = \text{WRS}(t) - \ln(\text{CPI}_t)$. $W(t)$ is the real WRS index in each city, deflated by the city-specific consumer price index. The growth in real price was less than 1% per quarter for all cities, even San Francisco, where a real estate "boom" took place. The standard deviation in quarterly real price changes is less than 3% per quarter, or on the order of a third of the standard deviation of quarterly changes in comprehensive real stock price indexes.

Individual housing prices are like many individual corporate stock prices in the large standard deviation of annual percentage change, close to 15% a year for individual housing prices. But housing prices in our sample differ from stock prices in that the individual prices are not so heavily influenced by the aggregate market price. When one-year changes in real individual house prices are regressed on contemporaneous one-year changes in the real WRS index, R^2 is only .066 for Atlanta, 0.158 for Chicago, 0.121 for Dallas, and 0.270 for San Francisco.

While second-quarter price changes tend to be high and third-quarter changes low, the difference is small and only in Chicago is seasonality statistically significant at the 5% level. The National Association of Realtors series on the median price of existing single family homes appears to show more pronounced seasonality; we argued elsewhere that much of this may be due to seasonality in the composition of houses sold over the year (see our companion paper). Still, the NAR and WAR indexes do agree that prices are highest at midyear (the NAR index tends to peak in July).

The beta (estimated for each of the cities by regressing the quarterly change in the log nominal WRS index on the corresponding change in the log Standard and Poor Composite Index) is always virtually zero (table 18.1B). This confirms the results of Gau.

Table 18.1
Summary statistics[a]

A. Quarterly changes in real WRS log price index: $z = W(t) - W(t-1)$

City	All quarters: mean z, std. z[b]	Mean z for quarter t				H_0: all quarters, same mean, F probability
		$t = 1$ (t-statistic)	$t = 2$ (t-statistic)	$t = 3$ (t-statistic)	$t = 4$ (t-statistic)	
Atlanta	0.0001	−0.0013	0.0050	−0.0043	0.0006	0.33
	0.0270	(−0.2040)	(0.7694)	(−0.6461)	(0.0888)	0.85
Chicago	0.0007	0.0088	0.0071	−0.0019	−0.0115	3.32
	0.0218	(1.6456)	(1.3682)	(−0.3571)	(−2.1970)	0.02
Dallas	0.0050	0.0031	0.0114	0.0024	0.0028	0.43
	0.0265	(0.4612)	(1.7788)	(0.3586)	(0.4172)	0.79
San Francisco	0.0092	0.0100	0.0161	0.0024	0.0082	0.84
	0.0254	(1.5040)	(2.5822)	(0.3621)	(1.2317)	0.51

B. Regression of nominal WRS index changes on changes in log Standard and Poor Composite Index: $WRS(t) - WRS(t-1) = \alpha + \beta(LSP(t) - LSP(t-1)) + u(t)$

City	Number of observations, S.E.E.	α (t)	β (t)	R^2, $\bar{R}^2$
Atlanta	65	0.017	−0.022	0.003
	0.025	(5.264)	(−0.454)	−0.013
Chicago	65	0.017	−0.014	0.002
	0.018	(7.418)	(−0.393)	−0.013
Dallas	65	0.023	−0.066	0.026
	0.027	(6.698)	(−1.289)	0.010
San Francisco	66	0.025	0.035	0.006
	0.028	(7.259)	(0.643)	−0.009

a. WRS(t) is the quarterly WRS index (in logs) described in the text. W(t) is WRS(t) deflated by the city-specific consumer price index averaged over the quarter. LSP(t) is the log of the Standard and Poor Composite Index, quarterly average of daily prices. Sample is 1970-second quarter to 1986-second quarter (65 observations), except for San Francisco, where the data are 1970-second quarter to 1986-third quarter (66 observations).
b. std. means standard deviation.

18.3   Testing for Market Efficiency

One might think that we could test the random walk property of prices by regressing the change in the index on lagged changes in the index. But there is a problem, the noise in the estimated index. To see this point, consider the very simple case where we have two observations only on log housing prices. House A was sold in period 0 and period 1, while house B was sold in period 0 and period 2. The estimated changes in the log price index (using either the original BMN or WRS procedure, since in this example the number of observations equals the number of coefficients) are, for period 1,

$$P_{A1} - P_{A0} = C_1 - C_0 + H_{A1} - H_{A0} + N_{A1} - N_{A0},$$

and for period 2

$$(P_{B2} - P_{B0}) - (P_{A1} - P_{A0}) = C_2 - C_1 - (H_{A1} - H_{A0} + N_{A1} - N_{A0})$$
$$+ H_{B2} - H_{B0} + N_{B2} - N_{B0}.$$

The index change between 0 and 1 is negatively correlated with the change between 1 and 2 because of common terms appearing with opposite signs.

There may also be positive serial correlation of estimated changes in the log price index. Suppose we have three houses in our sample: house A was sold in periods 1 and 3, house B was sold in periods 0 and 2, and house C was sold in periods 0 and 3. The estimated changes in the log price index (again, using either the original BMN procedure or the WRS procedure with the full sample) are, for period 1, $(P_{C3} - P_{C0}) - (P_{A3} - P_{A1})$, and for period 3, $(P_{C3} - P_{C0}) - (P_{B2} - P_{B0})$. These two estimated changes will be positively correlated in our model because house C appears with the same sign in both expressions, while the specific shocks to the other two houses are independent. The three-house example also makes clear that there may be serial correlation between noncontiguous price changes.

Gau's procedure for testing the efficiency of the Vancouver commercial real estate market involved building three price indexes (not repeat-sales indexes): sales price divided by square footage, sales price divided by gross income, and sales price divided by number of suites. For each month he chose a single transaction for his index. His method of construction of a price series is likely to induce the same spurious serial correlation in price changes. His conclusion that his price index was approximately a random walk might be spurious.[5]

18.4   A Simple Expedient for Dealing with Estimation Error

We have seen that we cannot test efficiency of the housing market by regressing real changes in the WRS index onto lagged changes, and testing for significance of the coefficients, because the same noise in individual house sales contaminates both dependent and independent variables. A simple expedient for dealing with this problem is to split the sample of individual house sales data and estimate two WRS indexes. For each city, houses were randomly allocated between samples A and B, and log price indexes WRS_A and WRS_B were estimated using the respective samples. Then efficiency is tested by regressing changes in the real log index $W_A(t) = WRS_A(t) - \ln(CPI(t))$ on lagged changes in the real index $W_B(t) = WRS_B(t) - \ln(CPI(t))$, where $CPI(t)$ is the consumer price index for the city for quarter t (quarterly average).[6] Both sides of the equation are contaminated by noise, but since the same houses do not enter into the indexes on the two sides of the equation, these noise terms will not be correlated. If the slope coefficients are statistically significant, we can reject weak form efficiency.

Table 18.2 presents such regressions. For each city, we report first the regression of annual change with real log index A on the contemporaneous annual change in real log index B, as a diagnostic on our methods. The coefficient should be 1.00 if the indexes were measured perfectly, but should tend to be less than one for estimated indexes, due to the errors in variables problem. Fortunately, the estimated coefficients are never too far below 1.00. For each city, we then report the regression of the real annual change in the real index for sample A on the one-year-lagged real annual change in the real index for sample B, and then the same regression with samples A and B reversed. These coefficients are always positive and substantial, and statistically significant at the 5% level for Chicago and San Francisco. The greater significance in Chicago may be due to the greater number of observations on individual houses for that city, so that the measurement error problem is less severe.

We interpret these results as substantial evidence that there is inertia in housing prices, increases in prices over any year tending to be followed by increases in the subsequent year.

The table 18.2 regressions show that real price changes are forecastable, but do not show that there are any predictable excess returns to be had in investing in real estate. It is in principle possible that the forecastability of price changes is due to nothing more than the forecastability of real interest rates or of the dividend on housing. Table 18.3 reports analogous

Table 18.2
Regression of changes in real log index estimated with one half of sample on changes in real log index estimated with other half of sample: $W_j(t) - W_j(t-4) = \beta_0 + \beta_1(W_k(t-L) - W_k(t-4-L)) + u(t)$, $t = 1972:I–1986:II$ (1986:III San Francisco)[a]

City parameters	Number of observations, S.E.E.	β_0 (t)	β_1 (t)	R^2, $\bar{R}^2$
Atlanta				
$j = A, k = B, L = 0$	58	0.001	0.857	0.629
	0.028	(0.074)	(5.981)	0.622
$j = A, k = B, L = 4$	58	−0.003	0.215	0.045
	0.045	(−0.279)	(0.991)	0.028
$j = B, k = A, L = 4$	58	−0.004	0.191	0.046
	0.041	(−0.408)	(1.051)	0.029
Chicago				
$j = A, k = B, L = 0$	58	−0.001	0.871	0.836
	0.024	(−0.208)	(9.337)	0.833
$j = A, k = B, L = 4$	58	−0.001	0.412	0.183
	0.053	(−0.076)	(1.953)	0.169
$j = B, k = A, L = 4$	58	−0.000	0.502	0.234
	0.054	(−0.011)	(2.226)	0.220
Dallas				
$j = A, k = B, L = 0$	58	0.002	0.730	0.658
	0.029	(0.317)	(6.264)	0.652
$j = A, k = B, L = 4$	58	0.011	0.254	0.090
	0.047	(0.857)	(1.474)	0.074
$j = B, k = A, L = 4$	58	0.012	0.312	0.046
	0.052	(0.874)	(1.460)	0.029
San Francisco				
$j = A, k = B, L = 0$	59	0.017	0.608	0.313
	0.063	(0.947)	(3.061)	0.301
$j = A, k = B, L = 4$	59	0.030	0.255	0.055
	0.074	(1.435)	(1.093)	0.038
$j = B, k = A, L = 4$	59	0.021	0.430	0.220
	0.062	(1.206)	(2.462)	0.206

a. Houses were randomly allocated into two separate samples of half original size, samples A and B. $W_A(t)$ is the real WRS index estimated using sample A only. $W_B(t)$ is the real WRS index estimated using sample B only. Both series are deflated using the real city-specific consumer price index.

Table 18.3
Regression of after-tax excess returns estimated with one half of sample on after-tax excess returns estimated with other half of sample: $\text{Excess}_j(t) = \beta_0 + \beta_1 \text{Excess}_k(t - L) + u(t + 4)$[a]

City parameters	Number of observations, S.E.E.	β_0 (t)	β_1 (t)	R^2, $\bar{R}^2$	Trading profits
Atlanta					
$j = A, k = B, L = 0$	58	0.012	0.831	0.673	
	0.030	(1.036)	(6.171)	0.667	
$j = A, k = B, L = 4$	58	0.041	0.327	0.113	0.009
	0.049	(2.159)	(1.556)	0.097	
$j = B, k = A, L = 4$	58	0.038	0.348	0.135	0.010
	0.041	(2.141)	(1.782)	0.120	
Chicago					
$j = A, k = B, L = 0$	58	0.004	0.915	0.862	
	0.026	(0.452)	(9.848)	0.859	
$j = A, k = B, L = 4$	58	0.020	0.661	0.449	0.021
	0.052	(1.086)	(3.577)	0.439	
$j = B, k = A, L = 4$	58	0.017	0.706	0.479	0.024
	0.051	(0.959)	(3.774)	0.470	
Dallas					
$j = A, k = B, L = 0$	58	0.010	0.856	0.762	
	0.036	(0.735)	(7.555)	0.757	
$j = A, k = B, L = 4$	58	0.037	0.526	0.286	0.014
	0.061	(1.570)	(2.778)	0.273	
$j = B, k = A, L = 4$	58	0.038	0.549	0.286	0.017
	0.063	(1.550)	(2.737)	0.273	
San Francisco					
$j = A, k = B, L = 0$	59	0.029	0.759	0.461	
	0.082	(0.991)	(3.881)	0.451	
$j = A, k = B, L = 4$	59	0.055	0.507	0.203	0.024
	0.100	(1.502)	(2.130)	0.189	
$j = B, k = A, L = 4$	59	0.046	0.550	0.379	0.029
	0.079	(1.708)	(3.474)	0.368	

a. Houses were randomly allocated into samples A and B. $\text{Excess}_A(t)$ is the city excess return estimated using sample A only. $\text{Excess}_B(t)$ is the city excess return estimated using sample B only. Rental index (used to compute returns) was scaled so that average dividend-price ratio was .05. Assumed income tax rate was 0.30. $T = 1971:I-1985:II$ (1985:III for San Francisco). Trading profits are average extra return for the sample (A or B) as a proportion of the value of the house for the trading rule in the text.

regressions, where the dependent variable is the after-tax excess nominal return on housing over the one-year Treasury bill rate, using one index, and the independent variable is the after-tax excess nominal return using the other index. The after-tax excess return for sample A or B was defined by

$\text{Excess}_j(t)$

$$= \frac{\exp(\text{WRS}_j(t+4)) + C_j\{R(t) + R(t+1) + R(t+2) + R(t+3)\}}{\exp(\text{WRS}_j(t))}$$

$$-1 - (1-\tau)r(t)/100, \qquad j = A, B,$$

where $\text{WRS}_j(t)$ is the nominal (uncorrected for inflation) WRS index (in logs) estimated using sample j, $R(t)$ is the city-specific index, residential rent, from the U.S. Bureau of Labor Statistics, τ is the marginal personal income tax rate (assumed to be 0.30), and $r(t)$ is the one-year Treasury bill rate, secondary market.[7] The constant C_j was chosen to make the average "dividend-price ratio" $C_j\{R(t) + R(t+1) + R(t+2) + R(t+3)\}/$ $\exp(\text{WRS}_j(r))$ equal to .05. We are using the residential rent index to indicate the implicit "dividend" (in the form of housing services) on houses, and must guess at the factor of proportionality between the index and the actual dividend. The assumptions about taxes are that neither the capital gain nor the implicit rent are subject to income taxes, but that interest is deducted from taxable income.[8]

As seen in table 18.3, excess returns are even more forecastable than real price changes. The greater forecastability holds up even when we adjust the constant C_j to make the average dividend-price ratio either 0.0 or 0.1, adjust the tax rate τ up to 0.50, and whether we substitute the residential mortgage rate for the interest rate $r(t)$. Apparently, the greater forecastability of excess returns comes about largely because of the forecastability of real interest rates over this period, and because housing prices do not take account of information about predicted real interest rates. That real interest rates are quite forecastable may surprise some readers, who remember Eugene Fama's assertion that real interest rates are almost unforecastable. Fama's sample period in that paper was 1953–1971, which hardly overlaps with our sample period. Since 1971 real interest rates have shown major persistent movements and have been much more forecastable. Real interest rates shifted from positive to negative in the early 1970s, and sharply shifted up to large positive values following the October 1979 change in the operating procedures of the Federal Reserve System [see John Huizinga and Frederic Mishkin, 1986]. The forecastability of real interest rates is likely to have more impact on the forecastability of excess returns in citywide housing returns over the risk free rate than on the excess returns between corporate stock indexes over the risk free rate, just because the variability of corporate stock price indexes is so much higher than the variability of citywide housing price indexes.

18.5   Exploiting Serial Dependence in the Housing Market

Observed serial dependence, of course, does not by itself imply that a market is inefficient in the full sense of the term. There must be some way of exploiting that dependence. The institutional structure of the housing market makes it appear at first glance that exploitation would be difficult. First, there is no market for future contracts and there are no short sales, so that there are no profit opportunities to exploit if the market is expected to decline. Second, transactions costs are high. Selling real estate traditionally involves a brokerage commission, typically 6%, which covers sellers' search costs. Since the product is heterogeneous, buyers incur high search costs. For a portfolio investor to realize gains from appreciation, a capital gains tax must be paid. For those buying a property to live in, there are moving costs.

The absence of a futures market or short sales means only that forecast decreases in home prices cannot be exploited. If excess returns are expected to be positive because of appreciation, there is nothing to preclude a buy-and-hold strategy.

Those interested in exploiting potential positive excess returns fall into three categories: (1) first time home buyers who intend to live in the unit; (2) homeowners who live in their units who desire to trade up, or increase the size of their holding; and (3) those who buy and sell properties in which they do not intend to live, as portfolio investments. The institutional impediments to exploiting accurately forecast excess returns in case 3 differ from those in cases 1 and 2.

Buyers in case 1 pay no brokerage fees, since these are borne by sellers, and no capital gains tax as long as they remain homeowners. A buyer who wants to execute a purchase can also do so very quickly. Purchase and sale agreements can be negotiated in a matter of minutes if buyer and seller agree on price. There is, of course, a lag between purchase and sale and closing, but since price is fixed at time of purchase and sale, appreciation during the closing period accrues to the buyer. In case 2, the buyer is also a seller and must pay a brokerage fee on the sale of an earlier residence. Again, however, no capital gains tax liability is normally incurred.

Transactions costs for the portfolio investor or the speculator are higher since costs are incurred at the time of purchase and at the time of sale. At point of sale, the portfolio investor must pay a capital gains tax—during the period of this study, the maximum effective tax rate on capital gains was 20%.

To explore the potential for actually exploiting profit opportunities revealed by the forecasting regression in table 18.3, we simulate a simple trading rule. Consider a first time home buyer (case 1) or a homeowner who wants to trade up (case 2), and suppose that this buyer is indifferent, given personal and financial considerations other than forecastable variations in excess returns, between buying now or waiting another year. We establish the following trading rule: buy now if the excess return predicted by the regression in table 18.3 is greater than the mean excess return; otherwise delay purchase for one year. Implementing this rule does not require estimates of the parameters in table 18.3 beyond the sign of the slope coefficient, of course—only the mean of the independent variable, the excess return. In this case we can disregard transactions costs since the purchase will be made anyway. We can also disregard capital gains taxes since we are assuming the gains are on a principal residence and they will be continuously rolled over. The rightmost column of table 18.3 gives the average trading profits (as a proportion of the value of the house) individuals would have earned had they followed this trading rule over the sample period. The average trading profit is the proportion of quarters in the sample that are early buys given the trading rule times the difference between the mean excess return in those periods where an early buy is signaled by the regression and the mean excess return for the entire sample. The average trading profit can also be viewed as approximately equal to one-half times the mean of the "rectified" excess return. For a given quarter, rectified excess return is equal to the actual excess return if the trading rule gave a buy-early signal: otherwise it is equal to minus excess return.

The average trading profits are between 2.4% and 2.9% for San Francisco, which suggests that it would have been worthwhile for some potential purchasers to attend to the trading rule. This is the average over all quarters, and of course for roughly half the quarters, when an early buy was indicated, the average excess profits were twice as high. (Sometimes the predicted excess return differed from the mean excess return by over 10 percentage points.) For Chicago and Dallas, the average trading profits fell in the 1.4–2.4% range. For Atlanta, the city with the least volatile prices, the average trading profits were only around 1%. But even here, there were quarters where the forecasting regression would predict much higher excess profits. (Sometimes the predicted excess return deviated from the mean excess return by over four percentage points.)

18.6   Forecasting Individual House Sales Data

A second procedure for testing the efficiency of the market for single family homes is to regress changes in *individual* housing prices between time t and a subsequent period on information available at time $t - 1$. The log price index we construct appears only as an explanatory variable in these regressions, and so any spurious serial correlation in it will have no effect on our results. Under the efficient markets hypothesis, anything in the information set at time t should have no explanatory power for individual house price changes subsequent to that date. It is natural to set up the testing of the efficient markets hypothesis in this way: we are concerned with forecasting individual housing prices, and if people were to use past price data to forecast these prices, the forecasting variable would be an index like ours.

To assure that the individual price changes are predicted only using lagged information, we reestimated the WRS index anew for each quarter, using only data available up to that quarter. That is, we reestimated the entire WRS index for all N quarters in each sample, thus providing N different estimated price indexes, with from 1 to N time periods. In our forecasting regressions where past price indexes were used as explanatory variables, only those past values in the price index were used that were estimated using data up to and including the quarter before the quarter of the first sale of the house.[9]

Doing regression tests of the efficient markets hypothesis by regressing individual house log price changes does pose a potential problem in that many of the observations of price changes are for time intervals that overlap with each other. Thus, we cannot assume that residuals are uncorrelated with each other, even if they are uncorrelated with the independent variables.

To deal with this overlap problem, we use the model (1) again where the null hypothesis of market efficiency is taken to be that C_t is a random walk that is independent of anything in the information set at time $t - 1$. Consider two different houses in a city, house A sold at time t and t' and house B sold at time T and T'. The variance of the residual in the regression of the log real price change on lagged information (under the null hypothesis of market efficiency this residual is just the change in price) for house A is $(\sigma_C^2 + \sigma_h^2)(t' - t) + 2\sigma_N^2$, and the covariance between the residual for house

A and for house B is $n\sigma_C^2$, where n is the length of overlap of the two time intervals. The testing procedure was as follows. A preliminary ordinary least squares regression (where $t' - t$ was fixed at a constant for all observations in the regression) was performed to get a vector of estimated residuals. The parameter $(\sigma_C^2 + \sigma_h^2)(t' - t) + 2\sigma_N^2$ was estimated as the average square value of the residuals. The parameter σ_C^2 was estimated by forming all possible products of residuals for different houses where the time intervals overlap, dividing each by the length of the overlap, and forming the average of these. The variance matrix Ω was constructed using these estimates, and the variance matrix of the ordinary least squares estimates was taken as $(X'X)^{-1}X'\Omega X(X'X)^{-1}$. This variance matrix was used to construct t tests and X^2 tests of market efficiency.

18.7 Results with Individual House Data

The regression results generally do not find statistical significance (tables 18.4 and 18.5). The magnitudes of coefficients estimated in table 18.4 are, however, roughly consistent with those found in table 18.2 and the distributed lag pattern in table 18.5 shows a crude indication of an expo-

Table 18.4
Individual house log price changes on lagged real index change: $P(i, t_i + 4) - P(i, t_i) = \beta_0 + \beta_1(W(t_i - 1, t_i - 1) - W(t_i - 1, t_i - 5)) + u(t + 4)^a$

City	Number of observations, S.E.E.	β_0 (t-statistic)	β_1 (t-statistic)	R^2
Atlanta	246	0.0380	0.2392	0.002
	0.141	(2.6875)	(0.6155)	
Chicago	596	0.0416	0.3437	0.012
	0.137	(2.261)	(1.0588)	
Dallas	202	0.0874	0.0763	0.001
	0.146	(3.7157)	(0.2268)	
San Francisco	332	0.1000	0.3337	0.028
	0.125	(3.183)	(1.0108)	

a. In the regressions, each observation i corresponds to a house that was sold twice 4 quarters apart, and t_i denotes the quarter of the first sale for house i. Prices are in real terms: $P(i, t)$ is the natural log price of the ith home at time t minus the natural log of the city consumer price index for time t. $W(t, t')t' < t$, is the WRS log price index for time t' estimated with data up to time t and minus the natural log of the city consumer price index for time t'. Figures in parentheses are t-statistics computed taking into account the serial correlation of error terms induced by overlapping intervals between sales.

Table 18.5

Regressions of real log price change on lagged index changes: $P(i, t_i + 4) - P(i, t_i) = \beta_0 + \Sigma(j = 1,\ldots,4)\beta_j(W(t_i - 1, t_i - j) - W(t_i - 1, t_i - j - 1)) + u(i, t + 4)$[a]

City	N	β_0	β_1	β_2	β_3	β_4	S.E.E.	R^2	χ^2
Atlanta	246	0.037	0.432	0.283	-0.009	-0.029	0.142	0.006	1.154
		(2.919)	(1.033)	(0.602)	(-0.019)	(-0.075)			
Chicago	596	0.044	1.055	0.663	-0.253	-0.149	0.136	0.032	7.692
		(2.494)	(2.254)	(1.309)	(-0.565)	(-0.296)			
Dallas	202	0.089	0.430	0.220	0.094	-0.483	0.145	0.019	3.259
		(4.841)	(0.992)	(0.487)	(0.213)	(-1.172)			
San Francisco/Oakland	332	0.099	0.652	0.511	0.118	-0.106	0.125	0.036	2.822
		(3.325)	(1.465)	(1.173)	(0.222)	(-0.214)			

a. χ^2 is chi-squared statistic (4 degrees of freedom) for null hypothesis that all slope coefficients are zero. The χ^2 tests are computed taking into account the serial correlation of error terms induced by overlapping intervals between sales. See also notes to table 18.4.

nential decay pattern that gives most weight to the most recent quarterly index change. There appears to be a substantial response in individual house prices to lagged index changes, but there is so much noise in individual houses (the standard deviation of annual price changes is comparable to that on the aggregate stock market) that we do not generally find statistical significance.

One reason that the regressions did not disclose stronger or more consistent evidence of inertia in housing prices is inadequate data. While we had hundreds of observations of individual house sales for each forecast horizon, we have only 16 years of data. The serial correlation correction in effect does not assume a great number of "degrees of freedom" despite the large number of observations.

Errors in the WRS index as a measure of citywide prices are a problem tending to bias our coefficients, probably toward zero. The index is reestimated anew every quarter, and there is always substantial measurement error in the most recent observations of the index.[10]

To attempt to deal with this problem, a model with time-varying errors in the variables was estimated. It is well known in the errors-in-variables literature that if there is an independent measurement error in a single independent variable, the estimated coefficient tends to be biased toward zero by a factor of proportionality called the reliability ratio [see, for example, Fuller, 1987]. The reliability ratio is the ratio of the variance of the correctly measured independent variable to the sum of the variance of the correctly measured independent variable and the variance of the measurement error. We have information (in the form of estimated standard errors) on the size of the measurement error; this size varies through time, and we can assess movements in the reliability ratio through time. Reestimating table 18.4 where the independent variable was a time-varying estimated reliability ratio (thereby downweighting inaccurately measured observations) did not substantially improve the significance of the results.

18.8   Conclusion

There is substantial persistence through time in rates of change in indexes of real housing prices in the cities. A change in real citywide housing prices in a given year tends to predict a change in the same direction, and one-quarter to one-half as large in magnitude, the following year. Predictable movements in real interest rates do not appear to be incorporated in prices. Our experiments with a variety of assumptions about rental rates and taxes indicate that citywide after-tax excess returns are forecastable.

While we have suggested a trading rule for individual homeowners that appears to be profitable, there are still some doubts about the results. We cannot measure the dividend on housing accurately. Our measure of the dividend on housing, the BLS residential rent index, is estimated from data on rental properties that may differ in quality from owner-occupied housing, and we do not know the constant of proportionality for the index. We have given only rudimentary attention to the effects of tax laws.

There is little hope of proving definitively whether the housing market is not efficient. We see no way of obtaining an accurate historical time series on implicit rents of owner-occupied houses. Available property tax series appear to have major deficiencies. There is not just a single income tax bracket, so any effort to model tax effects runs into definitional problems.

From the standpoint of forecasting excess returns of individual houses, such factors may be of only secondary importance anyway. The noise in individual housing prices is so great relative to the standard deviation of changes in citywide indexes that any forecastability of individual housing prices due to forecastability of citywide indexes will tend to be swamped by the noise. Of course, this conclusion may not apply to periods of extraordinary price movements, such as have been observed over the last few years in the northeast United States and in California.

Appendix: Constructing the Multiple Sales Files

The multiple sales files were constructed from several basic data sets containing large amounts of information on recorded sales of just under a million individual housing units between 1970 and 1986 (221,876 for Atlanta, 397,183 for Chicago, 211,638 for Dallas, and 121,909 for San Francisco). The San Francisco data were actually drawn from the eastern part of the metropolitan area including Oakland, Berkeley, Piedmont, Hayward, and the rest of Alameda County. The data from the other three cities were drawn from the entire metropolitan areas.

The data from Atlanta, Chicago, and Dallas, as well as the data from before 1979 from San Francisco, were obtained from the Society of Real Estate Appraisers' Market Data Center in Atlanta. The data from San Francisco between 1979 and 1986 were obtained from the California Market Data Cooperative in Glendale, California, a licensee of the Society.

The data in the basic data sets were collected by members of the Society, who include many real estate agents, bank officials, and appraisers. When a transaction occurs (at the closing), members fill out a long data sheet and submit it to the Society. We have no information about how representative the membership is. We do know that the data seem to be uniformly distributed across each areas and that they contain a large number of both high-priced and low-priced properties.

Information coded for each observation includes the exact street address, the sales price, the closing date, and the type of financing, as well as between 25 and 40 characteristics of the property depending on the city and the time period. Characteristics include numerous structural and parcel descriptors such as number of rooms, condition, and lot size. To complete our raw data set 16 separately coded files were merged.

The process of identifying repeat sales involved several steps. First, an exact match was done on the address fields. Next, properties identified as anything other than a single family home, such as a condominium or a cooperative unit, were dropped. Third, pairs were excluded if there was evidence that the structure had been physically altered. This was done by checking the total number of rooms, the number of bedrooms, the indicated condition, and whether any rooms had been modernized.

The condition and modernization variables were recorded differently in the various data sets that had to be merged. For condition, most used ratings of excellent, good, average, fair, and poor. Because the ratings were subjective and given by different people, often many years apart, we decided to ignore small changes. Thus, a property that went from good to average was retained. Any unit that indicated a jump of two categories between sales, such as a drop from good to fair, was excluded. All properties listed in poor condition in either period were excluded on the grounds that the rate of physical deterioration was likely to be high, and that there could well be unobservable problems reflected in price.

Whether the kitchen or a bathroom had been "modernized" was also recorded on the forms in a variety of ways. Records that indicated a modernized room were flagged, and if a flag appeared at the time of the second sale but not at the time of the first sale, the record was dropped. Of the total of 39,267 clean pairs, 57 observations appeared to be data entry errors; the two sales prices differed by a factor close to 10.

Notes

1. George Gau [1984] p. 301

2. Peter Linneman [1986], p. 140.

3. Cary Webb [1988] has a similar model, except that $\sigma_N = 0$.

4. Because the errors in this regression are likely to be larger for houses for which the time interval between sales is larger, a weighted regression was used, downweighting the observations corresponding to large time intervals.

5. It should be noted that a strength of Gau's [1984] approach relative to ours is that he could research the properties more thoroughly. He used detailed descriptions of debt liens from provincial land title records to adjust for financing with below-market interest rates. We did not have such information on the SREA tapes. He also controlled for other quality differences by his choice of properties to include.

6. Since quarterly data were used and price index changes were measured over four

quarters, error terms in the regression are not independent under the random walk assumption, but follow an MA-3 process. A method of Lars Hansen and Robert Hodrick was used to correct the standard errors of the ordinary least squares estimates.

7. The residential rent index is computed by the U.S. Bureau of Labor Statistics every other month only. For quarters where two months are available, $R(t)$ is the average of the two figures. When only one month is available, $R(t)$ is the figure for the middle month. The interest rate $r(t)$ is the quarterly average of the monthly series Treasury bills, secondary market, one-year, from the Board of Governors of the Federal Reserve System.

8. We should properly also account for changes through time in the property tax rate. However, existing data series do not appear to allow us to measure well changes in this rate for the cities and sample period studied.

9. Note that all three steps of the WRS estimation procedure were run separately for each quarter, using only data available in that quarter, so that no future information would creep into the constructed price index. In some instances (especially for the earlier quarters, that is, using small amounts of data) the step 2 estimated coefficient of the interval between sales had the wrong sign. When this happened, it was set to zero, so that the procedure then reduces to ordinary least squares in step 3.

10. For example, with the San Francisco/Oakland data, there is, when the index is estimated with data through 1980-II, an estimated decline in real housing prices of 6.20% between 1980-I and 1980-II (the actual decline, not an annualized rate). When data through 1986-III are used to estimate, the index between those two quarters is estimated to increase 2.53%.

References

Bailey, Martin J., Richard F. Muth, and Hugh O. Nourse. 1963. "A Regression Method for Real Estate Price Index Construction," *Journal of the American Statistical Association* 58:933—942.

Case, Karl E., and Robert J. Shiller. 1987. "Prices of Single Family Homes since 1970: New Indexes for Four Cities," *New England Economic Review*, 45—56.

Engle, Robert F., David M. Lilien, and Mark Watson. 1985. "A DYMIMIC Model of Housing Price Determination," *Journal of Econometrics* 28:307—326.

Fama, Eugene F. 1975. "Short-Term Interest Rates as Predictors of Inflation," *American Economic Review* 65:269—282.

Fuller, Wayne A. 1987. *Measurement Error Models*, Wiley, New York.

Gau, George W. 1984. "Weak Form Tests of the Efficiency of Real Estate Investment Markets," *The Financial Review* 19:301—320.

Gau, George W. 1985. "Public Information and Abnormal Returns in Real Estate Investment," *AREUEA Journal* 13 : 15–31.

Hansen, Lars Peter, and Robert J. Hodrick. 1980. "Forward Exchange Rates as Optimal Predictors of Future Spot Rates: An Econometric Analysis," *Journal of Political Economy* 88 : 829–853.

Huizinga, John, and Frederic S. Mishkin. 1986. "Monetary Policy Regime Shifts and the Unusual Behavior of Real Interest Rates," *Carnegie Rochester Conference Series on Public Policy* 24 : 231–274.

Linneman, Peter. 1986. "An Empirical Test of the Efficiency of the Housing Market," *Journal of Urban Economics* 20 : 140–154.

U.S. Department of Labor, Bureau of Labor Statistics, *CPI Detailed Report*, Washington: U.S. Government Printing Office.

Webb, Cary. 1988. "A Probabilistic Model for Price Levels in Discontinuous Markets," in W. Eichhorn, ed., *Measurement in Economics*, Physica-Verlag, Heidelberg.

V   The Aggregate Economy

19   Overview

The same questions as to the sources of fluctuations in speculative prices may be posed for macroeconomic variables other than speculative prices. What, ultimately, is behind the movements we observe in gross national product? In the unemployment rate? In the inflation rate? There seems to be little more agreement on these questions than on the questions of the ultimate sources of speculative price variability. A broad view of these questions is given in chapter 20. The conclusion is that many qualitatively different factors are likely to be behind movements in these macroeconomic variables. Among these are some of the same opinion or psychological forces, the same changing popular models, that drive speculative markets.[1]

The aggregate stock market has long been reputed to move with the business cycle. To the extent that this is so, macroeconomic and stock fluctuations would appear to have the same source. It was argued in chapters 5, 6, and 8 that the movements in the present value of dividends are not big enough to account for the movements in stock prices, and the conclusion was that the business cycle is unlikely to have its effect on stock prices through this. So what might account for the common movements?

It could be that the business cycle affects the demand for stocks dramatically, so that, since the supply of stocks is relatively fixed, the price of stocks must adjust, even if the outlook for future dividends does not change appreciably over the business cycle. In times of recession, it could be that the demand for stock at its old price would be relatively low. In temporary recessions people have an incentive to sell stocks to help tide them over in their personal expenditures. Thus, price should tend to be low in recessions, and the rate at which future dividends are discounted high. In boom times, people should have a relatively great incentive to save, and

Portions of this chapter © 1989 Elsevier Science Publications.

part of this demand might be directed to stocks, causing their price to be relatively high and the rate of discount low.

Sanford Grossman and I (chapter 21), drawing on earlier theoretical work of Lucas and Breeden, examined an empirical model of the above business cycle effects, and found that there was somewhat more promise to this model of stock prices than the simple model that makes price the present value of future dividends discounted by a constant discount rate. If a parameter called the coefficient of relative risk aversion were high enough, the data on the variability of consumption suggest that volatility of the price of stocks might be explained.[2] Hansen and Singleton [1983] later used a similar analysis, which presented much smaller estimates of the coefficient of relative risk aversion, but they rejected the model for other reasons.[3]

One problem with the analysis of consumption and aggregate fluctuations is that consumption is not measured at a specific time, as is the consumption in the abstract theoretical model. Most researchers have disregarded this discrepancy, but it may lead to some biased estimates. Grossman, Melino, and Shiller [1987] attacked this problem by estimating a continuous-time model from unit-averaged data.[4] However, that model did not perform well with the data.

There is a fundamental problem with the model that makes stock prices move substantially with the business cycle because of discount rate changes due to demand fluctuations. Real interest rates do not appear to behave properly in connection with these models. Prices of other speculative assets, such as bonds, land, or housing, do not show movements that correspond very much at all to movements in stock prices, as is seen in figure 19.1. We would expect the price for these assets to move with the stock market if the price of stocks was driven heavily by business-cycle-related changes in the rate of discount. While the dividend series are all different for these other assets, and are not even well observed for the real estate series, so long as the present value of future dividends is fairly smooth we would expect to see similar behavior in these different prices at least at times of sudden sharp price movements. For example, if the stock market decline of 1929–1932 was due to a sudden increase in the rate of discount, we would expect to see that markets for other speculative assets crashed too at that time. If the stock market crashed in 1929 because people would want to sell stocks (if price did not fall) to consume the proceeds, then the same would plausibly happen in other speculative markets. A look at figure 19.1 reveals that the stock market crash is not reflected

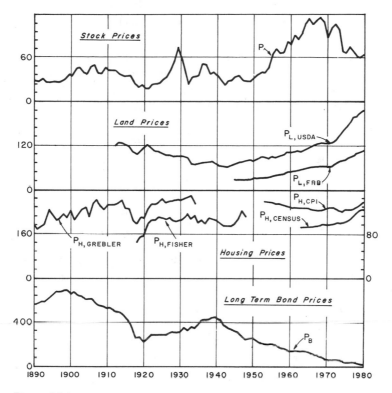

Figure 19.1
Real prices of corporate stock, land, housing, and long term bonds. All series are divided by the consumption deflator for nondurables and services (1972 = 1.0). (Upper panel) P, Standard and Poor's Composite Stock Price Index. (Second panel) $P_{L,FRB}$, Federal Reserve Board land value series from the balance sheets for the U.S. economy, year and outstandings, national net worth, in ten billions of dollars; $P_{L,USDA}$, the USDA index number of average value of farm real estate per acre, 1967 = 100. (Third panel) $P_{H,Grebler}$, Grebler-Blank-Winnick price index for one-family owner occupied houses, 1929 = 100; $P_{H,Fisher}$, Fisher's median asking price for existing one-family houses, Washington, D.C., in hundreds of dollars; $P_{H,CPI}$, home purchase component of Consumer Price Index for all urban consumers, 1967 = 100; $P_{H,Census}$, Census Bureau price index of new one-family houses sold, 1972 = 100 (the scale for $P_{H,CPI}$ and $P_{H,Census}$ is at right). (Bottom panel) P_B, price of a 5% 25-year bond whose yield is the Macaulay Railroad Bond Yield Arithmetic index (1890–1935) and Moody Aaa Corporate Bond Yield Average (1936–1980). Source: Robert J. Shiller, "Consumption, Asset Markets, and Macroeconomic Fluctuations," *Carnegie Rochester Conference Series on Public Policy*, 17 (1982), p. 224.

in real prices of land, housing, or bonds, nor are other major stock price movements.

One attempt to explain the poor performance of the consumption based asset pricing model is to assume that consumption yields utility for more than one period, so that, in effect, consumption is a durable good (Eichenbaum, Hansen, and Singleton [1988]), or that there is habit formation in consumption (Ferson and Constantinides [1988]). But these alternatives would appear to be incapable of explaining both the high variability of stock prices and the relative independence of stock prices from prices of other assets.

It is likely that these analyses of asset prices and consumption have an element of truth in them, but they put too much reliance on the expected utility maximization paradigm. What we know about popular models in consumption does not suggest that consumption is chosen very well at all so as to optimize lifetime utility as hypothesized by these models. Some synthesis of these models with behavioral alternatives would likely be productive.

Notes

1. Hall [1988] uses methodology analogous to that used to assess excess volatility in financial markets to develop estimates, in the context of a model of output and investment, of the noise component of GNP.

2. However, we found, using Euler equation methods [1980], that the coefficient of relative risk aversion had implausibly large values. LeRoy and LaCivita [1981] independently argued that the volatility of stock prices might be explained in terms of risk aversion in a model like the one decribed here. See also Michener [1982].

3. Cechetti, Lam, and Mark [1988] studied the implications of such models for measures of mean reversion and forecastability of long-horizon returns.

4. Since the Grossman-Melino-Shiller paper was published, an error was discovered in data sets 1 and 2, the annual data set with the long sample period 1980–1981. In place of the log of real consumption, we mistakenly substituted the level of real consumption. This error did not affect data sets 3–6, the quarterly data sets in the postwar period. The basic conclusion for data sets 1 and 2 that a high value of the coefficient of relative risk aversion was required is still true, given the results in Grossman and Shiller [1980], table 1.

References

Cechetti, Stephen G., Pok-Sang Lam, and Nelson C. Mark. 1988. "Mean Reversion in Equilibrium Asset Prices," reproduced, Columbus, OH: Ohio State University.

Eichenbaum, Martin S., Lars Peter Hansen, and Kenneth J. Singleton. 1988. "A Time Series Analysis of Representative Agent Models of Consumption and Leisure Choice under Uncertainty," *Quarterly Journal of Economics* 103:51–78.

Ferson, Wayne E., and George M. Constantinides. 1988. "Habit Formation and Durability in Aggregate Consumption: Empirical Tests," reproduced, University of Chicago.

Grossman, Sanford J., and Robert J. Shiller. June 1980. "Preliminary Results on the Determinants of the Variability of Stock Market Prices," reproduced, University of Pennsylvania.

Grossman, Sanford J., Angelo Melino, and Robert J. Shiller. July 1987. "Estimating the Continuous-Time Consumption-Based Asset Pricing Model," *Journal of Business and Economic Statistics* 53:315–327.

Hall, Robert E. 1988. "Spontaneous Volatility of Output in the Business Sector," Lecture 2 of the Okun Memorial Lectures presented at Yale University.

Hansen, Lars Peter, and Kenneth J. Singleton. 1983. "Stochastic Consumption, Risk Aversion, and the Temporal Behavior of Asset Returns," *Journal of Political Economy* 91:249–265.

LeRoy, Stephen and C. J. LaCivita. 1981. "Risk Aversion and the Dispersion of Asset Prices," *Journal of Business* 54:535–547.

Michener, Ronald W. 1982. "Variance Bounds in a Simple Model of Asset Prices," *Journal of Politicial Economy* 90:166–175.

Shiller, Robert J. 1982. "Consumption, Asset Markets, and Macroeconomic Fluctuations," *Carnegie-Rochester Conference Series on Public Policy* 17:203–238.

20   Ultimate Sources of Aggregate Variability

Any empirical model of the macroeconomy tells a story about the exogenous shocks that are ultimately responsible for changes from year to year in macroeconomic variables. The characterization of these sources of aggregate variability is of fundamental importance. Economic theory cannot be applied to data unless we know which economic relations are *not* themselves shocked, or at least unless we know something about the shocks.[1]

Recent models have differed widely in their characterizations of these ultimate sources of aggregate variability. Finn Kydland and Edward Prescott [1982] and others proposed models of the business cycle in which the *only* shocks to the macroeconomy are certain kinds of shocks to technology. Robert Barro [1977] proposed a model in which 78% of the variance of a (transformed) U.S. unemployment rate 1946–1973 is due to unexpected changes in the money stock, and military employment and minimum wage variables. David Lilien [1982] argued that most of the unemployment fluctuations in the United States in the 1970s were due to "unusual structural shifts," such as changes in the demand for produced goods relative to services. James Hamilton [1983] argued that dramatic oil price shocks preceded all but one of the recessions in United States since World War II, and that these oil price shocks were in turn caused by events such as the nationalization of Iranian assets, the Suez crisis, and strikes by oil and coal workers.

Other have offered analyses that, while not necessarily claiming to isolate the major source of aggregate fluctuations, do suggest that qualitatively very different exogenous shocks may be quite important: changes in desired consumption [Robert Hall, 1986], breakdowns in the process of

Reprinted with minor editing from *American Economic Review* 77(1987):87–92. © 1987 the American Economics Association.

borrowing and lending [Ben Bernanke, 1981], breakdowns or establishments of cartels [Julio Rotemberg and Garth Saloner, 1986], or variations in attitudes toward union membership [Olivier Blanchard and Lawrence Summers, 1986]. Moreover, any of these shocks might occur in a foreign country, and be transmitted by trade relations to the domestic economy. Some analyses have even emphasized that something that ought to be, by any fundamental logic, truly irrelevant to the macroeconomy, may well importantly influence it if people think it does [for example, Michael Woodford, 1987]. The potential importance of such variables may be even more important than suggested in some papers in the theory literature if we allow for "near-rational expectations" as well as the strictly rational expectations.

Recent evidence [John Campbell and N. Gregory Mankiw, 1987] suggests that innovations in real gross national product (GNP) show little tendency to be reversed subsequently, and that the apparent tendency of GNP to be trend-reverting may be due to spurious trend estimation. To the extent that this is right, then variations in the same sources that explain long-run growth (and explain why the United States is wealthier than India or China) would also play a role in explaining short-run movements. If cultural or institutional factors influencing the dissemination and application of learning are the reason, then changes in these factors may play a role. If economies of scale are a factor determining intercountry differences, then the discovery of new industries or regions of production functions where such economies obtain might also play a role. Other possible factors are changes in government expenditure on "infrastructure" formation, government policies and other factors encouraging or discouraging initiative, or just population growth and natural resource discoveries and depletion.

There seem to be a bewildering array of possibilities for ultimate sources. It is important to understand that it is in principle possible that they might all contribute substantially. It is technically possible that 10 different independent shocks each might make a contribution whose standard deviation is 32% ($= \sqrt{0.1}$) of the standard deviation of the aggregate. Thus, for each of the 10 factors there may be evidence that it is often very important and occasionally dominates aggregate fluctuations. Or, it is possible that 100 independent factors each may make a contribution whose standard deviation is 10% of the aggregate standard deviation.

One is naturally led to wonder if there is not any systematic way to determine what is the relative importance of different sources of macroeconomic variability.

20.1   Pigou's Analysis of Ultimate Sources

A. C. Pigou's remarkable book *Industrial Fluctuations* [1929] appears to be the most recent effort until now to provide such a systematic breakdown of sources. He grouped these sources into three broad categories. "Real causes" are "changes that have occurred, or are about to occur, in actual industrial conditions and expectations based on these are true or valid expectations." The principal real causes he cites are (1) harvest variations, (2) inventions, (3) industrial disputes, (4) changes in fashion, (5) wars, and (6) foreign demand and foreign openings for investment. "Psychological causes" are "changes that occur in men's attitude of mind, so that, on a constant basis of fact, they do not form a constant judgment." "Autonomous monetary causes" are events affecting money, such as gold discoveries, or changes in monetary or banking policies (p. 35). He thought that removal of either the autonomous monetary or the psychological causes might reduce the amplitude of industrial fluctuations by about a half. Removal of harvest variations might reduce amplitude by about a quarter. He thought that other real causes, such as inventions or work stoppages, had much less effect.[2]

Of the above sources, only one, the psychological, appears largely absent from contemporary macroeconomics, though it might be interpreted as present in some macroeconometric models in the form of error terms. Pigou here describes swings in optimism or pessimism affecting investment that arise "spontaneously," though perhaps ultimately as a "psychological reflex" from some of the same factors that he calls "real" causes (p. 73). He emphasized that the swings occur simultaneously over a large number of people, because of "psychological interdependence," "sympathetic or epidemic excitement," or "mutual suggestion" (p. 86).[3] He denied what we now call "rational expectations" because there is "instability in the facts being assumed," though he admitted that "if everything were absolutely stable, recurring every year with exact similarity or in a perfectly regular progression, people could not fail to be aware of the relevent facts and to form correct judgments" (p. 74).

What sort of evidence might Pigou have that his list comprises the important sources? Although he made some use of statistics, his method involves judgment that appears to be based on anecdotal and narrative historical evidence. Such a method may in fact be of some use for this purpose. A rough sense of proportion about some economic mechanisms may suggest that if certain factors would change exogenously, there would be important macroeconomic consequences. If these factors did indeed change historically, then the only question that remains is whether such a change could be purely endogenous, that is, caused ultimately by other economic variables. We may then have some idea whether these factors are likely to be determined reliably by such other economic variables.

Consider, for example, the case of the autonomous monetary causes. In the contemporary context, we know that the Federal Reserve (the Fed) can and does move interest rates, which have a major impact on the economy. Of course, the announced goal of the Fed currently is to stabilize the economy, and their efforts may ideed attenuate the effects of other shocks. But since their methods are judgmental and imprecise, it is to be expected that they must also serve to *add* shocks themselves. By analogy, if we analyzed the movements of an airplane in rough weather, we would expect to find that a component of the airplane's movements is ultimately due to the pilot.

Methods like Pigou's are suggestive, but one might hope for something more objective and quantitative.

20.2   Evidence from Large-Scale Macroeconometric Models

The large-scale macroeconometric models in the Keynesian tradition appear to be the only models detailed enough to allow a decomposition of output variability into a variety of constituent shocks as broad as that proposed by Pigou. In these models, all macroeconomic fluctuations can be traced ultimately to equation residuals or exogenous variables.

Ray Fair [1986] has undertaken stochastic simulations of Fair model of the U.S. economy to show what are the important shocks to the model. The Fair model is similar to most large-scale macroeconometric models in that it includes consumption and investment functions, and a national income identity to yield an IS curve, and demand for money equations that gives rise to an LM curve. Monetary policy is modeled by a Fed reaction function, but fiscal policy is taken to be exogenous.

To take account of shocks to exogenous variables, he added simple autoregressive forecasting equations for 23 exogenous variables to the 30 structural equations in his model, producing a 53-equation model with basically no exogenous variables. Taking as given data through 1981:II, a stochastic simulation, the base simulation, was run using a 53 × 53 (block diagonal, with a 30 × 30 and 23 × 23 block) variance covariance matrix residuals, and the variance of actual real GNP for one to eight quarters ahead (i.e., 1981:III through 1983:II). He then set residuals for the eight quarters to zero in each of the 53 equations, one at time and then in groups, and ran new stochastic simulations. The variance in real GNP in any one of these simulations as a percent of the variance in the base simulation is a measure of the importance of the residual that is analogous to the square of the relative amplitudes described by Pigou.

What is striking about the results is that the conclusions differ substantially between one-quarter-ahead simulations and eight-quarter-ahead simulations. For example, if we drop the error term to the inventory investment equation, real GNP variance falls by 29% relative to the base simulation in the one-quarter-ahead simulations, but by only 4% in the eight-quarter-ahead simulations. If we drop the error term in all investment equations (consumer durables, housing, inventories, and business fixed investment) the corresponding figures are 50.6% and 13.4%. Thus, failure to predict investment accounts for most of the model's difficulty in forecasting one quarter ahead, but relatively little of the difficulty in making longer-run forecasts. Other sources of variability grow faster with time horizon, so that uncertainty about investment is swamped out.

The story told by the Fair model is a complicated one, with no single source of variability dominating. Consider the percentage variance declines in the eight-quarter-ahead simulations for real GNP. Dropping all exogenous variables' shocks reduced variance by 44%, the remainder being accounted for by equation residuals. The principal grouping of exogenous variables was government expenditure and transfers (federal, state, and local), for 21% and after that, exports, for 19%. Among endogenous variables, dropping residuals on consumption on services and nondurables reduced variance by 10%, on the wage and price sector by 11%, and on import demand by 7%. Dropping Federal Reserve policy shocks reduced variance by only 3%.

What sort of evidence is behind the Fair model that gave rise to these variance decompositions? The modeling effort relied on the assumption that a large list of variables is exogenous. Many of these are not plainly exogenous to the model, though one might suppose that their relation to economic activity is in some cases tenuous, complicated, and involving long lags. The modeling effort also relied on a set of restrictions on coefficients that vastly overidentified the model. Because of these overidentifying restrictions, the estimate of the reduced form was not at all the same as if it had been estimated by merely regressing endogenous variables on exogenous and predetermined variables. The restrictions sometimes have the effect, for example, of inferring an effect of an exogenous variable on GNP from an observed effect on a component of GNP.

These overidentifying restrictions were usually not explicitly discussed in the description of the model. Their specification appears to have largely intuitive origins, just as was the case with the theory of Pigou. One would wish that there were a method that was more capable of producing a consensus in the profession as to ultimate sources.

20.3   Partial Specifications of Exogenous Sources

Many doubt the assumptions of the large-scale macroeconometric models. But, certainly *some* of their assumptions must be uncontroversial. Certainly *some* variables (for example, the weather) would be judged genuinely exogenous by just about everyone. It would be progress if we could all agree that such a variable explains x percent of macroeconomic variability, even if x is very small. Might not a Granger or Sims causality test for causality from such a variable to real GNP produce such an agreement?

But it is hard to think of any single measurable clearly exogenous variable that seems likely to have much impact on the aggregate economy. We have a wealth of data at a finely disaggregated level, for example, information on individual patents each of which represents a component of technological progress. But how to aggregate this information into a data series that might be found to cause GNP? We cannot regress GNP on hundreds of exogenous variables each of which explains a component of it, since we would have more independent variables than available observations.

Weather variables are probably the most obvious candidates for a truly exogenous variable that might really cause macroeconomic aggregates. Regression models explaining individual crop yields [for example, Wolfgang Baier, 1977] show that weather variables explain a substantial portion of year-to-year crop variability. Often the R^2 is over 0.5. But to achieve such R^2 for individual crops the researcher uses finely focused weather variables that differ across crops, such variables as "estimated June potential evapotranspiration," or "mean soil moisture reserves (mm) at heading stage in 0–100 cm. depth of soil." To explain aggregates well, these weather variables should be measured at all the appropriate times and sites for the specific crops to which they pertain. To explain weather effects on nonagricultural productive activities would require yet very different weather variables. To explain housing starts, we may use number of days in the year where temperature is below freezing, to explain restaurant meals the number of evenings of inclement weather and highway conditions in urban areas, to explain electricity demand an average of a nonlinear function of summer temperatures above 75°, to explain heating fuel demand an average of a nonlinear function of winter temperatures below 60°.[4] It is not easy to find a good aggregator of these shocks other than GNP (or its analogues) itself.

20.4 . Models as Aggregators

Finding an aggregator of very many exogenous shocks means building a highly disaggregated model that explains many components of GNP and shows how they interact to produce the total. If models are to be judged as aggregators, then models may be deemed successful even if they have known structural defects that would cause them to be rejected by conventional criteria. An aggregator model might be only a naive or crude model. For example, we might build a large Leontief input-output model. Data on the implementation of technological innovations, on weather or on other known exogenous shocks could be used to adjust the elements of the input-output matrix and the matrix of factor-input requirements. We might find that an index of structural change in the model aggregates successfully (for example, Granger-causes GNP) even though we know that the assumption of fixed proportions is highly restrictive.

Large macroeconometric model projects that deal laboriously with details may thus yield insight into sources of variability. Existing large-scale macroeconometric models may be viewed, even by those who accept some of the well-known criticism of their theory, as having shown some such success already (see Fair and Shiller, 1987). It is natural to expect that further progress can be made along these lines, taking account of developments in economic theory and data, if people are willing to do more work at a detailed level, and for many different countries.

20.5   Interpretation

There is as yet no consensus in the profession as to the quantitative importance of *any* of the various ultimate sources. In my judgment, however, the existing literature does suggest that a great multiplicity of sources is at work: shocks to tastes as well as technology, shocks in government policy, demographic shocks, shocks to organizations in labor or industry, and "psychological" shocks of the kind described by Pigou and others.

Currently popular methodology results in models that attempt to make do with very few shocks. These models are valuable as special cases but should be interpreted as exploratory exercises. We should not consider it an objective of research to simplify or reduce the array of exogenous shocks. Simplicity is of course a virtue, but simple models cannot be construed as an objective if the world is not simple.

Notes

1. Peter Garber and Robert King [1983] pointed out that contemporary Euler equation estimation methods always assume that the shocks come in somewhere else in the model, but that this assumption will not do for every equation in the model.

2. See pp. 219–225. Note that Pigou's breakdown denies independence of factors: he thought eliminating one may reduce the impact of another.

3. On this point, compare Woodford [1987].

4. Donald Deere and Jeffrey Miron [1986] regressed U.S. layoff rates by state and industry on state-specific (but not finely focused) weather variables and other variables. The weather variables were significant at the 90% level in about 25% of the regressions, and were very significant overall.

References

Baier, Wolfgang, 1977. "Crop-Weather Models and their Use in Yield Assessments," Technical Note No. 151, World Meteorological Organization.

Barro, Robert J., 1977. "Unanticipated Money Growth and Unemployment in the United States," *American Economic Review* 67: 101–115.

Bernanke, Ben S., 1981. "Bankruptcy, Liquidity, and Recession," *American Economic Review Proceedings*, 71, 155–159.

Blanchard, Olivier and Summers, Lawrence, 1986. "Hysteresis and the European Unemployment Problem," reproduced, MIT.

Campbell, John Y. and Mankiw, N. Gregory, 1987. "Permanent and Transitory Components in Macroeconomic Fluctuations," *American Economic Review Proceedings* 77: 111–117.

Deere, Donald R. and Miron, Jeffrey A., 1986. "The Cross Sectional Impact of Unemployment Insurance on Layoff, Employment and Wages," reproduced, Texas A&M University.

Fair, Ray C., 1986. "Sources of Output and Price Variability in a Macroeconometric Model," reproduced, Yale University.

Fair, Ray C., and Shiller, Robert J., 1987, "Econometric Modelling as Information Aggregation," reproduced, Yale University.

Garber, Peter M. and King, Robert G., 1983. "Deep Structural Excavation? A Critique of Euler Equation Methods," NBER Technical Working Paper No. 31.

Hall, Robert E. 1986. The Role of Consumption in Economic Fluctuations," in Robert J. Gordon, ed., *The American Business Cycle: Continuity and Change*, NBER, Chicago: University of Chicago Press.

Hamilton, James D., 1983. "Oil and the Macroeconomy since World War II," *Journal of Political Economy* 91:228–248.

Kydland, Finn E. and Prescott, Edward C. 1982. "Time to Build and Aggregate Fluctuations," *Econometrica* 50:1345–1370.

Lilien, David M. 1982. "Sectoral Shifts and Cyclical Unemployment," *Journal of Political Economy* 90:777–793.

Pigou, Arthur C. 1929. *Industrial Fluctuations*, 2nd. ed., London: Macmillan.

Rotemberg, Julio J. and Saloner, Garth. 1986. "A Supergame-Theoretic Model of Price Wars during Booms," *American Economic Review* 76:390–407.

Woodford, Michael, 1987. "Self-Fulfiling Expectations and Business Cycles," *American Economic Review Proceedings* 77:93–98.

21

The Determinants of the Variability of Stock Market Prices

The most familiar interpretation for the large and unpredictable swings that characterize common stock price indices is that price changes represent the efficient discounting of "new information." It is remarkable given the popularity of this interpretation that it has never been established what this information is about. Recent work by Shiller [1981] (chapter 5), and Stephen LeRoy and Richard Porter [1981], has shown evidence that the variability of stock price indices cannot be accounted for by information regarding future dividends since dividends just do not seem to vary enough to justify the price movement. These studies assume a constant discount factor. In this chapter, we consider whether the variability of stock prices can be attributed to information regarding discount factors (i.e., real interest rates), which are in turn related to current and future levels of economic activity.

The appropriate discount factor to be applied to dividends that are received k years from today is the marginal rate of substitution between consumption today and consumption k periods from today. We use historical data on per capita consumption from 1890 to 1979 to estimate the realized value of these marginal rates of substitution Theoretically, as LeRoy and C. J. La Civita [1981] have also noted independently of us, consumption variability may induce stock price variability whose magnitude depends on the degree of risk aversion.

Robert Hall [1978] also studied these marginal rates of substitution and concluded that consumption is a random walk. We show that if current consumption and dividends are the best predictors of future consumption and dividends in Hall's sense, then the discount factor applied to stock prices would not vary. The variability of stock prices implies they do vary, so we conclude that consumers must have a better method for forecasting

Coauthored with Sanford J. Grossman. Reprinted with minor editing from *American Economic Review* 71 (1981):222–227. © 1981 the American Economics Association.

future consumption than using only current consumption (for example, consumers may know when the economy is in a recession).

21.1   Stock Returns and the Marginal Rate of Substitution

Consider a consumer who can freely buy or sell asset i and whose utility can be written as the present discounted value of utilities of consumption in future years, $U_t = \sum_{k=0}^{\infty} \beta^k u(C_{t+k})$, where $\beta = 1/(1 + r)$ and r is the subjective rate of time preference. A necessary condition for his holdings of the asset at t to be optimal, given that the consumer maximizes the expectation at time t, of this utility function is

$$u'(C_t)P_{it} = \beta E[u'(C_{t+1})(P_{it+1} + D_{it+1})|I_t], \tag{1}$$

where P_{it} is the real price (in terms of the single consumption good or "market basket" C_t) of asset i and D_{it+1} is the real dividend paid at $t + 1$ to holders of record at t. The term E denotes mathematical expectation, conditional here on I_t, which is all the information about the future that the agent possesses at time t. The left-hand side of (1) is the cost in terms of forgone current consumption of buying a unit of the asset, while the right-hand side gives the expected future consumption benefit derived from the dividend and capital value of the asset. This relation plays a central role in modern theoretical models of optimal dynamic consumption and portfolio decisions, such as those of Robert Lucas [1978].

Since $u'(C_t)$ and P_{it} are known at time t (in contrast to P_{it+1}, D_{it+1}, and C_{t+1}, which are not), we can rewrite (1) as

$$1 = E(R_{it}S_t|I_t), \tag{2}$$

where $S_t = \beta u'(C_{t+1})/u'(C_t)$ is the marginal rate of substitution between present and future consumption (the reciprocal of the usual measure), and $R_{it} = (P_{it+1} + D_{it+1})/P_{it}$ is the return (or rather one plus the rate of return as it is usually calculated). Note that the expectation in (2) conditional on information I_t is always 1. Hence it does not depend on I_t. Therefore, it equals the unconditional or simple expectation

$$1 = E(R_{it}S_t). \tag{3}$$

Thus, the proper stochastic interpretation of the familiar two-period diagram is that the expected product of the uncertain return and the uncertain marginal rate of substitution is one. This means that $E(R_{it})$ need not equal the subjective rate of time preference, nor need it be the same for all assets ("expected profit opportunities" may exist). Instead, (3) says that a *weighted* expectation of returns, with weights corresponding to marginal rates of substitution, is the same for all assets. Returns that come in periods of low marginal utility of consumption (i.e., when consumption is high) are given little weight, because they do little good in terms of utility. Returns that come in periods of high marginal utility are given a lot of weight. The same expression can also be written another way, using the fact that the expected product of two variables is the product of their means plus their covariance:

$$E(R_{it}) = E(S_t)^{-1} \cdot (1 - \text{cov}(R_{it}, S_t)) \tag{4}$$

Equation (4) states that the expected return of an asset depends on the covariance of the asset's return with the marginal rate of substitution. An asset is very "risky" if its payoff has a high negative covariance with S. (Douglas Breeden [1979] has recently persuasively argued for the use of consumption correlatedness as the appropriate measure of risk.)

The theory of asset returns embodied in each of expressions (1)–(4) is very powerful because it can be applied so generally. It holds for *any* asset, or portfolio of assets. It holds for *any* individual consumer who has the option of investing in stocks (even if he chooses not to hold stocks), and thus it must hold for aggregate consumption as long as some peoples' consumption is well represented by the aggregate consumption. It holds even if the individual's choices regarding other assets are constrained (for example, the individual cannot trade in his "human capital," is constrained by institutional factors in housing investment, or is unable to borrow money) so long as such constraints do not affect his ability to change his saving rate through stock purchases or sales. It incorporates all sorts of uncertainty that people consider in making investment decisions, since these factors are reflected in consumption. The model holds for any time interval, whether a month, a year, or a decade.

21.2 Perfect Foresight Stock Prices

By iterating (1), we find that price P_{it} at time $t < n$ is the expected present value of dividends and a terminal price P_{in} discounted by the marginal rates of substitution:

$$P_{it} = E\left[\sum_{j=1}^{n-t} \beta^j \frac{u'(C_{t+j})}{u'(C_t)} D_{it+j} + \beta^{n-t} \frac{u'(C_n)}{u'(C_t)} P_{in} \Big| I_t \right]. \tag{5}$$

It is useful to define the perfect foresight stock price P_{it}^*, which is the price at t given that the consumer knows the whole future time path of consumption, dividends, and the terminal price P_{in}:

$$P_{it}^* = \sum_{j=1}^{n-t} \beta^j \frac{u'(C_{t+j})}{u'(C_t)} D_{it+j} + \beta^{n-t} \frac{u'(C_n)}{u'(C_t)} P_{in}. \tag{6}$$

Clearly (5) states that $P_{it} = E[P_{it}^*|I_t]$. Further, we assume that $u(C)$ is of the constant relative risk aversion form

$$u(C) = \frac{1}{1-A} C^{1-A}, \qquad 0 < A < \infty, \tag{7}$$

where A is the "coefficient of relative risk aversion," which is a measure of the concavity of the utility function or the disutility of consumption fluctuations.

Figure 21.1 shows a plot of P_t from 1889 to 1979, where P_t is the annual average Standard and Poor's Composite Stock Price Index divided by the consumption deflator. On the same figure, we plot the perfect foresight real price P_t^* for $A = 0$ and $A = 4$ using (6) and (7), where we use actual realized real annual dividends for the Standard and Poor series, the Kuznets-Kendrick-U.S. NIA per capita real consumption on nondurables and services and the terminal data $n = 1979$. For each A, we generate a value of β so that (3) holds, as estimated by the sample mean. The case $A = 0$ is revealing; this is the case of risk neutrality, and of a constant discount factor. Notice that with a constant discount factor, P_t^* just grows with the trend in dividends; it shows virtually none of the short-term variation of actual stock prices. The larger A is, the bigger the variations of P_t^* and $A = 4$ was shown here because for this A, P, and P^* have movement of very similar magnitude. Irwin Friend and Marshall Blume [1975] estimated A to be about 2 under the assumption that the only stochastic component of wealth is stock returns. Irwin Friend and Joel Hasbrouck estimated A to be about 6 when stock returns and human capital are the stochastic components of wealth. We also computed a P^* series using after-tax returns. It did not look much different from the P^* shown here in the first half of the sample when income taxes were generally unimportant, and did not seem to fit P any better in the second half.

The rough correspondence between P^* and P (except for the recent data) shows that if we accept a coefficient of relative risk aversion of 4, we can to some extent reconcile the behavior of P with economic theory even under the assumption that future price movements are known with certainty. In a world of certainty, the marginal rate of substitution S_t would equal the inverse of one plus the real interest rate, ρ_t. Hence our equilibrium condition becomes $(P_{t+1} + D_{t+1}) + P_t = 1 + \rho_t$. Thus it can be shown that real stock prices as well as real prices of other assets whose dividend is stable

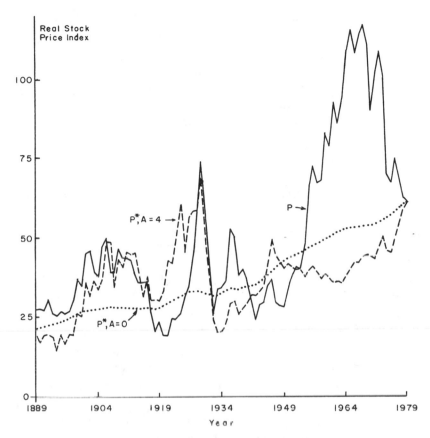

Figure 21.1
Actual and perfect foresight stock prices, 1889–1979. The solid line P_t is the real Standard
and Poor Composite Stock Price Average. The other lines are: P_t^* [as defined by
expression (6) and (7)], the present value of actual subsequent real dividends using the
actual stock price in 1979 as a terminal value. With $A = 0$ (dotted line) the discount rates
are constant, while with $A = 4$ (dashed line) they vary with consumption.

in real terms will rise dramatically over periods when real interest rates are very high. Real interest rates will be high when C_{t+1} is high relative to C_t, for example, in periods of depression when C_t is abnormally low. Hence it is an equilibrium for P_t to be low (relative to P_{t+1}) because otherwise people will desire to dissave (for example, by selling stock at t) in order to maintain their consumption level. Movements in real interest rates that are necessary to equilibrate desired savings to actual savings will lead to changes in stock prices even if dividends are unchanged. It is these movements that are brought out in the figure when P^* with $A = 4$ is compared with P^* with $A = 0$.

The correlation between P^* and P is perhaps not altogether surprising, given the correlation between the stock market and aggregate economic activity over the business cycle noted long ago by many people (see, for example, Arthur Burns and Wesley Mitchell). However, P_t^* is not merely a proxy for aggregate economic activity or consumption at time t. If we assume, as an approximation, that dividends follow a growth path $D_t = D_0 \delta^t$ and if we set $n = \infty$ in (6) to ignore the terminal price, then P_t^* is given by $P_t^* = D_0 \delta^t [C_t^A \sum_{k=0}^{\infty} (\beta \delta)^k C_{t+k}^{-A}]$. This says that P_t^* follows a growth path times the *ratio* of C_t^A to a weighted harmonic average of future C^A. The weights decline exponentially into the future. Thus, for example, P^* declines gradually between 1907 and 1919 not because consumption declined, since real per capita consumption remained more or less level over this period, but because the gap between current consumption and the longer-run outlook widened. In other words, P^* fell at this time because the perfect-foresight individual, knowing his economic fortune would eventually improve following the war period, wished to try to smooth his consumption over this period. This kind of relationship between P and C would not have been visible by looking at raw stock price and economic activity index series alone, as the earlier scholars did. On the other hand, the short-run correspondence between P and P^* around such episodes as the panics of 1893 or 1907 was in effect noted by these authors.

Our construction implies that P^* (as well as P) is a leading indicator of future levels of economic activity, but it does not suggest the conventional notion of a fixed lead of a few months to a year between P and aggregate economic activity. However, such a fixed lead has never been quantitatively established (see C. W. J. Granger and M. Hatanaka, [1964]).

Once we drop the assumption of perfect foresight, there need not be a close relationship between P_t and P_t^*. If consumers have no information about P_t^*, then P_t will be a constant and P_t^* will vary. We can write $P_t^* = P_t + U_t$ where $U_t = P_t^* - E[P_t^*|I_t]$ is a forecast error. Since P_t is in the information set I_t, U_t must be uncorrelated with P_t, so that the variability of the stochastic process $\{P_t^*\}$ will be *larger* than that of the stochastic process $\{P_t\}$. Further, if we consider any subset of the information set at t, say I_t^s, then $\text{var}(P_t^*|I_t^s) \geqslant \text{var}(P_t|I_t^s)$. If we make the assumption that the variability of the stochastic processes $\{P_t\}$ and $\{P_t^*\}$ can be estimated from the sample variability of observed P_t and P_t^*, then the figure can give some evidence in favor of the hypothesis that A is at least 4. From the figure, it is clear that with $A = 0$ the variance inequality is reversed: P_t^* varies *less* than P_t. This is evidence against the hypothesis that the discount factor does not vary. Once we raise A to, say, $A = 4$, then the variability of the discount factor forces P_t^* to vary a lot. The larger A is, the larger is the variability induced in P_t^* by changes in consumption path. Another way that the reader can see that discount factor variability is important is to apply the above variance inequality with $I_t^s = D_t$, yielding $\text{var}(P_t^*|D_t) \geqslant \text{var}(P_t|D_t)$. If the discount factor was constant, then this states that current dividends should be a better predictor of the current stock price than current dividends can predict weighted future dividends. Casual observation suggests this is false. Current dividends are a very good forecaster of future dividends, and a terrible forecaster of the current stock price. Once we permit the discount factor to vary, the inequality has a much greater chance of being true, since the current dividend is a poor forecaster of future discount factors.

If it is accepted that the variability of the discount factor is important, then we can use this to provide evidence against Hall's assertion that short-term movements in consumption are not forecastable by consumers. To see this, write the jth term in the summation in (5) as $E(\beta^j u'(C_{t+j})/u'(C_t)|I_t) E(D_{t+j}|I_t) + \text{cov}(\beta^j u'(C_{t+j})/u'(C_t),D_{t+j}|I_t)$. If neither the expectation of $\beta^j u'(C_{t+j})/u'(C_t)$ nor its covariance with dividends is forecastable (depends on I_t) then this term varies only due to changes in the expectation of D_{t+j}, i.e., due to information about dividends. If, moreover, $E(\beta^j u'(C_{t+j})/u'(C_t)|I_t) = \gamma^j$ (as might be suggested by Hall's random walk hypothesis), then P_t equals $E(\hat{P}_t^*|I_t)$ where $\hat{P}_t^* = \sum \gamma^j D_{t+j}$ (plus a deterministic term due to the covariance). $\hat{P}_t^*$ has a *constant* discount factor and is proportional to P^* in figure 21.1 with $A = 0$. Because P_t^* with $A = 0$ fails the variance test as mentioned previously, we tend to reject models with constant discount factors. Hence we conclude that consumption changes are forecastable. This implies that expected real interest rates vary (contrary to the claims of Eugene Fama [1975] and others).

This conclusion does not contradict Robert Hall's [1978] assertions (i) that to an *econometrician* who does not know as much as consumers, the marginal utility of consumption is a random walk, and (ii) that income may be a proxy for lagged consumption in econometric models that have shown that consumption is very sensitive to income. The fact that stock prices vary so much with consumption suggests that consumers have more information about consumption than is contained in current consumption, and this leads expected real interest rates to vary with information.

21.3   Further Research

We have some preliminary results on the estimation of A and β. Estimates of both parameters can be derived using expression (3) for two different assets, which we took as stocks and short-term bonds. Unfortunately, the estimates of A for the more recent subperiods seem implausibly high. This breakdown of the model mirrors the divergence between P^* and P since the early 1950s, as well as the extremely low real return on short-term bond rates in this period. There was an enormous rise in stock prices in that period that cannot be explained by changes in realized dividends or in marginal rates of substitution. Preliminary results show that it cannot be explained by taxes. Friend and Blume noticed an extremely high excess return of stocks over bonds in this period relative to all other subperiods from 1890 to date. Their estimated market price of risk was twice as high in the decade 1952–1961 as the highest of any other decade. While the divergence between P_t and P_t^* might be considered an enormous forecast error, we do not have any idea as to why $E(P_t^*|I_t)$ should have changed so much.

References

D. Breeden. 1979. "An Intertemporal Asset Pricing Model With Stochastic Consumption and Investment Opportunities," *Journal of Financial Economics* 7: 265–296.

Arthur F. Burns and Wesley C. Mitchell. 1956. *Measuring Business Cycles*, New York.

E. Fama. 1975. "Short-Term Interest Rates as Predictors of Inflation," *American Economic Review* 65:296–282.

I. Friend and M. Blume. 1975. "The Demand for Risky Assets," *American Economic Review* 65:900–923.

I. Friend and J. Hasbrouck. 1980. "Effect of Inflation on the Profitability and Valuation of U.S. Corporations," Univ. Pennsylvania.

C. W. J. Granger and M. Hatanaka. 1964. *Spectral Analysis of Economic Time Series*, Princeton.

R. Hall. 1978. "Stochastic Implications of the Life Cycle-Permanent Income Hypothesis," *Journal of Political Economy* 6:971–988.

S. LeRoy and R. Porter. 1981. "The Present Value Relation: Tests Based on Implied Variance Bounds," *Econometrica*, forthcoming.

S. LeRoy and C. J. La Civita. 1981. "Risk Aversion and the Dispersion of Asset Prices," *Journal of Business*, forthcoming.

R. E. Lucas. 1978. "Asset Prices in an Exchange Economy," *Econometrica* 46: 1429–1445.

R. Shiller. 1981. "Do Stock Prices Move Too Much to be Justified by Subsequent Changes in Dividends?," *American Economic Review*, forthcoming.

VI Popular Models and Investor Behavior

22   Overview

Let us now return to a theme described in the introduction: the systematic collecting of information about popular models of speculative markets, the models or theories of the markets that the general public has. There is, of course, not just one popular model but a pool of such models, and the frequency of any given model in that pool changes through time. Snapshots of the pool of popular models at certain times can be obtained through questionnaire surveys of the general investing public. Such questionnaire surveys can also give information about parameters of investor behavior, such as reaction times, communications patterns, and information sources, that help us to interpret the effects of popular models on economic variables. Having obtained some such information, it is possible to proceed tentatively to some models of the dynamics of speculative markets, even to feedback models of speculative bubbles.

22.1   Surveys of Market Partipants

The two chapters in this part use survey methods to look at unusual situations in which the social psychology of markets may be especially important. The first, chapter 23, which I wrote in November 1987, concerns the stock market crash of October 19, 1987; the second, chapter 24, written jointly with Karl E. Case, concerns local booms in real estate in the 1980s.

The stock market crash was a national event that riveted popular attention. It followed a boom period in which stock prices, by some accounts, reached unusual heights. The study in chapter 23 finds that the initial price drops themselves were the most important news event that triggered the crash; the timing of the crash is not explained as the reaction to any particular news break at that time. Certain themes were shown to be on the minds of a broad spectrum of investors, the most notable being a theme that stocks were overpriced, another being that program trading had made markets fundamentally different, a third being that there was too much indebtedness in the aggregate economy. The popular models of the crash tended to emphasize investor psychology. From this evidence, the timing of the crash appears related to themes that had created a popular model in the minds of investors that made them unusually reactive to price movements. A survey of Japanese institutional investors (Shiller, Konya, and Tsutsui [1988]) shows that they were similar in many dimensions to U.S. investors at the time of the crash; they were reacting largely to price movements as well, and most respondents interpreted events in terms of investor psychology.

One criticism of these surveys is that the market move may have been caused by a relatively small number of very large investors who would probably be missed in such a survey. The President's Task Force on Market Mechanisms (Brady Commission) [1988] concluded that the top 15 sellers in the stock market accounted for "about 20 precent of total sales" October 19; the top 10 sellers in the futures market accounted for "roughly 50 percent of non-market maker total volume," on that date.[1] This does not necessarily mean, however, that such investors, who accounted for a minority of trading volume, were in any sense a *cause* of the crash, nor does it mean that their behavior was fundamentally different from the behavior of the broader cross section of investors. The *Wall Street Journal* reported that one such large actor was Fidelity Investments which sold "nearly one billion in equities" on October 19. These sales came because "Investors had peppered Fidelity over the weekend to cash in some fund shares."[2]

The various studies (Brady Commission [1988], Chicago Mercantile Exchange, Miller, Hawke, Malkiel, and Scholes, [1988], Commodity Futures Trading Commission [1988], Securities and Exchange Commission [1988]) have concluded that the automated selling, due to portfolio insurance, was an important factor in the crash. According to the Brady Commission [1988], "Out of total NYSE sales [October 19] of just under $21 billion, sell programs by three portfolio insurers made up just under $2 billion ... In the futures market, portfolio insurer sales amounted to the equivalent of $4 billion of stocks, or 34,500 contracts, equal to over 40% of futures volume, exclusive of locals' transactions."[3] However, the portfolio insurance selling, which also accounted for a minority of volume of trade, is done only in reaction to price declines, and does not initiate a crash by itself. Moreover, in searching for the ultimate causes of the crash, we should not regard portfolio insurance as an exogenous event, like those thrust upon society at times by technological innovations. Rather, portfolio insurance should itself be regarded as a consequence of the growth of certain popular models in the public. I have argued this elsewhere [1988].

Certainly, the behavior of the broad mass of investors, individual and institutional, is a factor that ought to be considered in seeking the origins of the crash. The major studies (with the exception of the Brady Commission report) generally admit that they have not tried as I did to learn about this behavior.

Another, more focused, criticism of my paper was that the conclusion that most investors thought the market overpriced *before* the crash was reached by polling them *after* the crash. Although the question asked was very explicit in asking for the opinion before the crash, it is clearly plausible that their memories are influenced by the crash. Polls had been taken before the crash that shed some light on investors ideas then, although I have not found that the very same question was asked.

Richard B. Hoey and his colleagues at Drexel, Burnham Lambert have been conducting regular monthly polls of institutional investment managers. They asked whether they thought that "three months from today, market will be in bull market," "neutral phase," or "bear market." Respondents were strongly bullish in September 1987, just before the crash: 47.9 percent chose "bull," and 24.5 percent chose "bear." They had been similarly bullish throughout most of the four year prior to the 1987 crash. But the proportion who were bullish dropped sharply in their first survey after the crash: in November 1987 only 19.9 percent chose "bull," 42.4 percent chose "bear."[4]

Is a bullish attitude consistent with the impression reported in my surveys that the market was overpriced? I think that it may be. William Feltus of Market Consensus Surveys. Inc., and I conducted telephone surveys of investment professionals on the week before the unusually large increase in the stock market on the Tuesday after Memorial Day, May 31, 1988 (when the Dow Jones Industrial Average increased 74.68 points or 3.82% in a day). We asked respondents to forecast the Dow one month hence. The average expectation was that there would be virtually no change. Yet respondents did tend to feel that the market was oversold: 54% thought it was oversold; 24% thought it was overbought; the remainder did not know. Why did they not expect the market to go up in a month if they thought it was oversold? Apparently investors were alert for an increase, but there was apparently no news event to trigger buying, until the beginnings of the stock market price increase on May 31. (No other notable news event appears to have reported in the media that day.)

There is another, much earlier, study that concludes that investor reaction to price changes plays a major role in a crash. The Securities and Exchange Commission [1947] interviewed persons who traded large amounts of common stock following the sharp stock market decline of September 3, 1946, when stock prices fell 6.1% in one day. They coded the major reason for selling into 17 categories. The category coded most often, at 43% of sellers, was "declining prices on September 3." No other category was coded nearly as often. The category coded second most often, "Dow Theory," another popular model, was coded for only 13 percent of sellers.

The second chapter in this part (in joint work with Karl E. Case) is on the real estate boom in California in the late 1980s and in the northeastern United States in the mid-1980s. The local nature of these booms is an advantage from the standpoint of basic research; because the booms are geographically concentrated, we can make comparisons by sending out questionnaires to other cities: identical questionnaires at the identical point in history to boom cities, a postboom city, and a control city experiencing little price volatility. Thus, the research in this chapter has an advantage over the research concerning the stock market crash, where there was no comparison with a precrash state. This study found no more evidence of an exogenous "trigger" to the housing price boom than did the study of the stock market crash (the ultimate source of the sudden price moves remaining unexplained). It did find evidence of strong investment motivation and of higher price expectations in the boom cities than in the control city, expectations that respondents did not show any ability to justify in their answers to open-ended questions. An important difference between the popular models uncovered with respect to the stock market crash and with respect to the California real estate boom is that only in the former did popular models represent the price changes as primarily due to investor psychology.

Both of these survey studies, the stock market crash study and the real estate boom study, concluded that feedback of price changes to subsequent price changes were likely to be important factors in price dynamics. In the case of the stock market crash, the feedback occurred very rapidly, as downward price movements attracted attention and produced further selling pressure within a day or less. In the case of the real estate boom, upward price movements attracted attention, and contributed an ambience of gradually increasing prices over a period of a year or more.

22.2   Dynamic Feedback Models

The evidence on these two episodes suggests that simple feedback models, in which price depends on lagged price changes, amplifying price changes in a vicious circle, play a role in price dynamics. The evidence suggests that price is determined in part from its own lagged values, increases in price tending at times to foster further increases. Formally, this vicious circle can be described as a difference equation. But it is not a difference equation with parameters that are constant through time. The parameters of the difference equations depend on circumstances and may change from time to time or place to place, depending on popular models of the time.

Despite the likely complexity of actual feedback mechanisms, it is instructive to look at some special cases that at least awaken us to possibilities. For example, see De Long et al. [1989].

One important fact to bear in mind is that feedback models do not necessarily imply positive serial correlation of price changes. There are examples in which feedback from past price changes to present price greatly increases the variance of price, but in which there is little, even a negative, serial correlation of price changes. The appendix at the end of this chapter gives one such example.

Feedback does not necessarily take the form of reaction to price. There can also be a feedback loop in which demand for stocks creates more demand through direct interpersonal communications. John Pound and I [1989] considered contagion models, like the classic general epidemic model of Kermack and McKendrick [1927] used to represent the spread of contagious diseases, which has also been employed to model the time pattern of rumors, attitudes, or fads (Bartholomew [1982]). Contagion models are attractive because research in social psychology has shown that direct interpersonal communications among peers is of great importance in promoting attitude change (see McGuire [1969] or Adler and Adler [1984]).

The contagion model in its simplest form asserts that the number I_t of infectives is increased by an amount per unit of time equal to an infection rate b_t times the number of infectives, while b_t is itself proportional to the number S_t of susceptibles. Infectives lose their ability to carry the disease at a rate equal to a constant removal rate g times the number of infectives. If an equilibrium is hit by a shock at a single time, I_t can show a hump shaped pattern through time, rising at first and then falling, or a decaying form in which the number of infectives declines steadily. But the positive serial correlation of price changes suggested by this single-shock story is no more a necessary part of these models than it is of the price feedback models. If the source of the epidemic is a series of serially uncorrelated shocks, the outcome, in terms of the number of infectives, may in some cases resemble a random walk.

John Pound and I obtained a rough idea of the infection rates and removal rates directly from survey data. But perhaps the most important conclusion of our survey results was just some evidence on the extent of contagion. Respondents, both individual investors and investment professionals, report that their interpersonal communications influenced them and appeared to influence others. They tend to buy investments that their friends are making. For most individual investors and most institutional investors in stocks undergoing rapid price increase, initial attention to particular investments is not the outcome of a systematic search, but the result of prompting by others.

All of this emphasis on feedback loops should not obscure the fact that a substantial component of prices in speculative markets is driven by fundamentals, whether appropriately or not. It was noted in chapter 1 that stock prices correlate with earnings substantially. Mankiw and Weil [1988] have shown evidence that demographics have an impact on housing prices, although this evidence suggested that markets are not efficient because they do not anticipate the predictable changes in national demographics due to aging population. Moreover, speculative prices do sometimes show a tendency to anticipate future developments in earnings, as efficient markets theories assert. In practice, all these stories—feedback loop stories, direct response to economic variables, and anticipatory response to information—are likely to be operative simultaneously.

Appendix

It was asserted above that feedback of price change to subsequent price change may increase volatility without inducing much serial correlation of price changes.

Suppose demand for shares by investors is given by $D_t = a - bP_t + c\sum_{k=0}^{\infty} \rho^k \Delta P_{t-k} + V_t$, where $0 < \rho < 1.00$ and V_t is an exogenous shock to demand. Let us also suppose that the shock to the system V_t is a first-order autoregressive process, $V_t = \rho V_{t-1} + u_t$ where u_t is serially uncorrelated. Supposing that the supply of shares is fixed ($S_t = 1$), and solving, we find that this model is consistent with price following a first-order autoregressive process, with autoregressive coefficient equal to $\lambda = (b\rho - c)/(b - c)$, and with error term $u_t/(b - c)$. Increasing the feedback coefficient c has the effect of lowering the autoregressive coefficient and raising the variance of the error term. The variance of price is given by $\text{var}(P) = \text{var}(u)/((b - c)^2 - (b\rho - c)^2)$ and the correlation of ΔP_t with ΔP_{t-1} is $-(1 - \lambda)^2/(2 - 2\lambda)$. If $\rho = 0.98$, $b = 0.5$, and $c = 0$ (no feedback), then $\lambda = 0.98$, the variance of price is 101.0, and the correlation of ΔP_t with ΔP_{t-1} is -0.010. If c is changed to 0.2, so that there is positive feedback, then λ drops to 0.966, the variance of P increases to 169.5, and the correlation of ΔP_t with ΔP_{t-1} is -0.017. We see that feedback substantially increases the variance of price without inducing very much autocorrelation. The correlation coefficient is in fact negative (and is negative if data is sampled at any other time interval for the purpose of computing autocorrelation).

In this example, the dynamics of the bubble are determined by the lag of demand on past price changes. This form of the distributed lag, which decays gradually as the lag is increased, is taken to reflect the decay of memory of investors, or the tendency of fewer investors to focus on the longer differencing intervals.

Notes

1. Brady Commission [1988], p. 36.

2. *Wall Street Journal,* "Black Monday: What Really Ignited the Market's Collapse after Its Long Climb," p 1, col 6, December 16, 1987

3. Brady Commission [1988], p. 36.

4. Richard B. Hoey et al. [1988], p. 8.

5. I am indebted to Merton Miller for pointing out to me this study.

References

Adler, Patricia A., and Peter Adler. 1984. *The Social Dynamics of Financial Markets.* Greenwich, CT: JAI Press.

Bailey, Norman T. J. 1975. *The Mathematical Theory of Infectious Diseases.* London: Griffin.

Bartholomew, D. J. 1982. *Stochastic Models for Social Processes,* 3rd edition. Chichester: John Wiley & Sons.

Commodity Futures Trading Commission, Division of Economic Analysis.1987. *A Review of Stock Index Futures Trading on January 23, 1987.* Washington: Commodity Futures Trading Commission.

Commodity Futures Trading Commission, Division of Economic Analysis, Division of Trading and Markets. 1987. *Interim Report on Stock Index Futures and Cash Market Activity During October, 1987.* Washington: Commodity Futures Trading Commission.

Daley, D. J., and D. G. Kendall. 1965. "Stochastic Rumors," *Journal of the Institute of Math. Appl.,* 1:42–55.

DeBondt, W. F. M. and R. Thaler. 1985. "Does the Stock Market Overreact?" *Journal of Finance* 40:793–805.

De Long, J. Bradford, Andrei Schleifer, Lawrence H. Summers, and Robert J. Waldman. 1989. "Positive Feedback Investment Strategies and Destabilizing Speculation," reproduced, Harvard University.

Hoey, Richard B., David Rolley, and Helen Hotchkiss, August 30, 1988. *Decision Makers Poll.* New York: Drexel, Burnham Lambert.

Kermack, W. O., and A. G. McKendrick. 1927. "Contributions to the Mathematical Theory of Epidemics," *Proceedings of the Royal Society*, A115, 700–721.

Mankiw, N. Gregory, and David N. Weil. 1988. "The Baby Boom, the Baby Bust, and the Housing Market," Cambridge, MA: National Bureau of Economic Research, Working Paper No. 2794.

McGuire, William J. 1969. "The Nature of Attitudes and Attitude Change," in Gardner Linzey and Elliot Aronson, eds., *The Handbook of Social Psychology*, 2nd edition, vol. III, Reading, MA: Addison Wesley.

Miller, Merton H., John D. Hawke Jr., Burton Malkiel, and Myron Sholes. 1987. "Preliminary Report of the Committee of Inquiry Appointed by the Chicago Mercantile Exchange to Examine the Events Surrounding October 19, 1987," Chicago: Chicago Mercantile Exchange.

Presidential Task Force on Market Mechanisms (Brady Commission). January 1988. *Report*, Washington: U.S. Government Printing Office.

Shiller, Robert J. 1984. "Stock Prices and Social Dynamics," *Brookings Papers on Economic Activity* II : 457–497.

Shiller, Robert J. 1988. "Portfolio Insurance and Other Investor Fashions as Factors in the 1987 Stock Market Crash," in Stanley Fischer, ed., *NBER Macroeconomics Annual 1988*, Cambridge MA: National Bureau of Economic Research.

Shiller, Robert J., and John Pound. 1989. "Survey Evidence on Diffusion of Interest and Information among Investors," forthcoming, *Journal of Economic Behavior and Organization*.

Shiller, Robert J., Fumiko Konya, and Yoshiro Tsutsui. 1987. "Investor Behavior in the October 1987 Stock Market Crash: The Case of Japan," Cambridge MA: National Bureau of Economic Research.

U.S. Securities and Exchange Commission. 1987. "The Role of Index-Related Trading in the Market Decline of September 11 and 12, 1986," Washington.

U.S. Securities and Exchange Commission, Trading and Exchange Division. 1947. *A Report on Stock Trading on the New York Stock Exchange On September 3, 1946*. Washington: Securities and Exchange Commission.

23　Investor Behavior in the October 1987 Stock Market Crash: Survey Evidence

On Monday, October 19, 1987, the Dow Jones Industrial Average fell 508 points, a drop of 22.6% in one day. This crash was unprecedented in stock market history. The next biggest one day drop in the Dow Jones Industrial Average, on Monday, October 28, 1929, was only 12.8%.[1] The October 19, 1987, stock market crash was preceded by three drops in the Dow Jones Industrial Average, on Wednesday, October 14, Thursday, October 15, and Friday, October 16, of 95, 58, and 108 points respectively.

I have for some time been using questionnaire survey methods to learn about investor behavior. As part of the Investor Behavior Project at Yale University, John Pound and I have done several surveys of investors to learn general patterns of behavior (Pound and Shiller [1986]; Shiller and Pound [1987]). I have undertaken pilot questionnaire surveys immediately after a couple of major stock market drops (Shiller [1987]) to see what can be learned about these drops. We have found that questionnaire surveys aimed at collecting specific facts about individual behavior are useful research methods. We learned among other things that well-posed open-ended questions (where the respondents are asked to write their own replies) do help us to learn things not obtainable from traditional questionnaires. The questionnaire format seems often to provoke thoughtful responses, as the frequent and sometimes extensive answers indicate.

To try to understand what happened on October 19, 1987, and surrounding dates, I undertook four different mail questionnaire surveys: two small pilot surveys (PILOT1 and PILOT2) both mailed out before 5:00 P.M,. October 19, and then a major survey of individual investors (INDIV) (mostly sent out by 5:00 P.M., October 21) and a major survey of institutional investors (INSTI). All questionnaires were mailed before 5:00 P.M., October 23, 1987, so that investors would receive them while their memories were

---

This chapter was circulated in November 1987 as NBER working paper No. 2446.

fresh. In total, there were 3,250 questionnaires sent out and 991 completed questionnaires received, for an overall response rate (adjusting for 227 addressee unknown or deceased returns) of 32.8%.

In this chapter, I report on general survey results, and then provide interpretations and conjectures for what happened on October 19, 1987.[2]

23.1   Prior Pilot Surveys

The structure of the questionnaires sent out in the week of October 19 was informed by the results of previous questionnaire surveys following market drops. It is useful, then, to indicate briefly what was learned from these.

September 11-12, 1986

On September 11 and 12, 1986, the Dow Jones Industrial Average dropped a total of 120.78 points, or 6.43%. The September 11 drop of 86.61 points in the Dow was the steepest one-day drop in percentage terms since May 28, 1962. Desiring to see if anything could be learned about the events on those days, I sent out immediately after the drop in the market a short pilot questionnaire to 175 institutional investors and 125 individual investors (the latter, from a list of those from a random sample of high-income Americans, provided by Survey Sampling, Inc., who indicated in response to a previous questionnaire that they held common stocks). The questionnaire asked among other things, "Can you remember any reason to buy or sell that you thought about *on those days* [September 11–12]? (Please try hard to remember. Don't give something you thought or talked about later)." Of those who responded (38% of those polled) there was near-total absence in the answers of any "story" about the market decline, that is, any repeated reference to a concrete news break or rumor on those days, except for the decline in the market itself. No more than three respondents seemed to refer to any one other economic theory or fact on those days (see Shiller [1986]).

January 23, 1987

Between 1:30 and 3:00 P.M., January 23, 1987, the Dow Jones Industrial Average dropped 115 points and then rose 60 points. I wanted to see if survey methods could shed light on what went on in that $1\frac{1}{2}$-hour period. Thinking that stockbrokers may have a good feel for investor concerns, I tried this time a pilot survey of 1,000 stockbrokers selected at random from throughout the United States. The idea this time was to tabulate "key words" that were used at various times of the day. I asked respondent to tabulate "rumors, stories, theories, names, words, facts, or expressions, that people used in conversations at various times of that day." The response rate for the survey was only 8.2%, perhaps in part because the survey was difficult or unappealing to respondents and because the survey was mailed out rather late after the market drop, so that they could not remember. For what it is worth, however, the only key words found in the 1:30–3:00 period were "program trading," "profit taking," "madness," and "buying panic," and the only other repeated theme of conversations was estimates of how many years ago this last happened.

These pilot surveys suggested that there is no concrete story for big market drops. The answers to open-ended questions suggested people were reacting to price changes themselves, so that the price drop fed on itself in a vicious circle. I spent some time thinking about and soliciting opinions on how to write a questionnaire that would provide information about the importance and nature of this and related phenomena. Thus, I was prepared with a different questionnaire formulation for the market drop surrounding October 19, 1987.

23.2   The Four Surveys of the October, 1987, Crash

The four surveys were

1. PILOT1: Pilot study regarding October 14–16. After the precipitous downturn in the stock market October 14–16, a pilot questionnaire was sent out, this time to the same 125 individual investors who were used in the September 11–12, 1986, pilot survey. These were mailed out early on the morning of October 19, 1987. Of those sent out, 51 completed questionnaires were received.

2. PILOT2: Pilot study regarding October 19. After the 200 point drop in the Dow Jones Industrial Average on the morning of October 19, 1987, it was apparent that the pilot survey mailed out that morning had missed a much bigger stock market drop, although the full magnitude of the October 19 drop was still not known. It was a simple matter to repeat the mailing of that morning, with the primary change that the questionnaire pertained to October 19 rather than October 14–16. These were mailed at about the time that the markets closed on October 19. There were 51 completed questionnaires.

3. INDIV: Full study of individual investors. After the closing of the market October 19, 1987, when the magnitude of the crash was known, it

was decided to go ahead with a major survey. The questionnaire was revised to take account of the news of that day and suggestions of several colleagues. The questionnaire was mailed out to 2,000 individuals on October 20–22. The list of names was from W. S. Ponton, and entitled "High-Grade Multi-Investors" with a random selection from the entire United States. There were 605 completed responses.

4. *INSTI*: Full study of institutional investors. A questionnaire nearly the same as that of the October 19 survey of individuals was prepared and mailed to 1,000 investment managers sampled at random from the section "Investment Managers, Alphabetical Index" from the *Money Market Directory of Pension Funds and Their Investment Managers 1987*. There were 284 completed responses.

The PILOT1 and PILOT2 sample is more likely than are the others to be representative of all high-income persons who hold stocks, and since the surveys were sent out very early, the results rely on fresher memories. However, the sample size is small. The INDIV sample should be representative of *active* wealthy individual investors, and has the largest sample size. The INSTI sample should be representative of officers of all ranks in investment management groups, and is not aimed particularly at the managers of large portfolios.

23.3   Results

Breakdown into Buyers and Sellers

Respondents for the INDIV and INSTI questionnaires were asked whether they were net purchasers or sellers on various dates (see table 23.1).[3] Of course, institutional investors trade much more frequently than do individual investors. On October 19, the number of net buyers approximately equaled the number of net sellers both for institutional and individual investors. For the month before the crash, September 12–October 12, institutional investors who changed their holdings generally reported decreasing their holdings, individual investors increasing their holdings. Between October 19 and October 20 this was reversed, institutional investors buying and individual investors selling. For other time periods, both institutional investors and individual investors report moving the same way; this can happen of course with numbers of buyers and sellers even though the value of the amount bought by all buyers must equal the value of the amount sold by all sellers. The survey also missed certain

Table 23.1
Buyers versus sellers[a]

A. Did you buy or sell either individual corporate stocks, index futures or stock options on that October 19, 1987?

	I bought (mostly)	I sold (mostly)	I did not buy or sell
INDIV ($n = 549$)	2.9	2.3	94.8
	(0.7)	(0.6)	(0.9)
INSTI ($n = 277$)	17.7	13.4	69.0
	(2.3)	(2.0)	(2.8)

B. What was the change in your holdings in 1987 of stocks (in terms of number of shares or contracts, not value) between each of the following dates (at close of market):

	Holdings increased	No change	Holdings decreased
a. Between September 12 and October 12			
INDIV ($n = 383$)	18.0	72.3	9.7
	(2.0)	(2.3)	(1.5)
INSTI ($n = 262$)	11.1	44.3	44.7
	(1.9)	(3.1)	(3.1)
b. Between October 12 and October 19			
INDIV ($n = 383$)	4.4	85.6	9.9
	(1.0)	(2.2)	(1.5)
INSTI ($n = 262$)	7.6	64.9	27.5
	(1.6)	(2.9)	(2.8)
c. Between October 19 and October 20			
INDIV ($n = 383$)	4.7	85.9	9.4
	(1.1)	(1.8)	(1.5)
INSTI ($n = 262$)	20.6	66.7	12.6
	(2.5)	(2.9)	(2.1)
d. Between October 20 and later in week			
INDIV ($n = 383$)	15.4	76.7	7.8
	(1.8)	(2.2)	(1.4)
INSTI ($n = 262$)	33.6	50.0	16.4
	(2.9)	(3.1)	(2.3)

a. Figures are in percent. Standard errors are shown in parentheses.

Table 23.2
Importance of new items[a]

	Individual (INDIV)					Institutional (INSTI)				
	All	Buyers		Sellers		All	Buyers		Sellers	
		October					October			
	12–19	12–19	19	12–19	19	12–19	12–19	19	12–19	19

A. Please tell us how important each of the following news items was to you personally on October 19, 1987, in your evaluation of stock market prospects. Please rate them on a one-to-seven scale, 1 indicating that the item was completely unimportant, 4 indicating that it was of moderate importance, 7 indicating that it was very important. Please tell how important *you* then felt these were, and not how others thought about them.

a. Drop in U.S. stock prices October 14–16, 1987

4.54	5.29	5.12	5.13	5.38	5.23	4.85	5.18	5.77	5.83
(0.07)	(0.35)	(0.41)	(0.29)	(0.46)	(0.09)	(0.45)	(0.22)	(0.15)	(0.21)

b. Drop in Japanese or London stock prices that preceded October 19, 1987

3.74	4.19	4.53	4.55	5.00	4.78	4.90	4.83	5.11	5.14
(0.08)	(0.47)	(0.45)	(0.32)	(0.47)	(0.09)	(0.33)	(0.25)	(0.18)	(0.25)

c. The 200 point drop in the Dow the morning of Monday, October 19

5.14	5.69	5.76	5.32	6.54	5.93	6.05	5.86	6.24	6.08
(0.08)	(0.36)	(0.39)	(0.30)	(0.26)	(0.08)	(0.23)	(0.19)	(0.13)	(0.21)

d. Trade deficit figures announced Wednesday October 14, 1987

4.21	3.94	4.24	4.50	4.62	4.21	4.40	4.14	4.75	4.39
(0.08)	(0.43)	(0.33)	(0.30)	(0.46)	(0.09)	(0.33)	(0.24)	(0.19)	(0.28)

e. Producer price index figures announced Friday, October 16, 1987

3.26	3.13	3.47	3.13	3.23	3.17	3.00	3.22	3.38	3.03
(0.07)	(0.32)	(0.43)	(0.28)	(0.45)	(0.08)	(0.32)	(0.21)	(0.18)	(0.24)

f. Prechter's short-run sell signal the morning of Wednesday, October 14

2.17	2.07	3.00	2.49	2.45	2.59	2.80	2.37	3.10	2.94
(0.07)	(0.34)	(0.43)	(0.29)	(0.53)	(0.10)	(0.35)	(0.22)	(0.18)	(0.21)

g. Chemical Bank raising prime rate Thursday, October 15

4.14	4.18	4.00	4.58	4.77	3.95	4.25	3.82	4.51	4.28
(0.08)	(0.48)	(0.41)	(0.28)	(0.44)	(0.10)	(0.36)	(0.22)	(0.18)	(0.25)

h. Treasury bond yields hit 10.5%

4.27	4.56	4.41	4.46	4.46	5.57	5.85	5.84	6.01	5.64
(0.08)	(0.49)	(0.42)	(0.34)	(0.47)	(0.08)	(0.22)	(0.16)	(0.15)	(0.25)

i. Baker suggested that the dollar should slip further

4.04	4.50	4.05	4.11	5.31	4.84	4.45	4.67	5.41	5.39
(0.08)	(0.49)	(0.46)	(0.32)	(0.51)	(0.10)	(0.33)	(0.25)	(0.20)	(0.25)

Table 23.2 (continued)

	Individual (INDIV)				Institutional (INSTI)			
All	Buyers		Sellers		All	Buyers		Sellers	
	October					October			
	12–19	19	12–19	19		12–19	19	12–19	19
j. U.S. attack on Iranian oil station Monday, October 19, 1987									
3.73	3.13	3.53	3.70	3.46	3.32	3.30	2.96	3.61	3.28
(0.08)	(0.49)	(0.39)	(0.31)	(0.39)	(0.10)	(0.33)	(0.25)	(0.20)	(0.25)
k. Other (fill in)									

B. Suppose that as of October 19, 1987, the same news had occurred except for the news of price drops. Would your evaluation of the market or decisions to buy or sell on October 19 have been substantially different?

18.3	12.5	37.5	29.7	53.9	34.0	40.0	48.0	39.1	40.0
(1.6)	(8.3)	(12.1)	(7.5)	(13.8)	(2.9)	(10.9)	(7.2)	(5.9)	(8.2)

a. Standard errors are in parentheses. For question B, figures, percent, give yes answers relative to those answering question.

categories of buyers or sellers (e.g., foreign investors and New York Exchange specialists).

All results in the remaining tables are broken down between buyers and sellers as described in this section.

No Clear-Cut Reaction to News

In an effort to assess directly what it was that people were reacting to, I included in this survey a list of news stories that were claimed in the media as possible determinants of the stock market declines October 14–19, 1987, and asked respondents to rate their importance. They were asked to rate on a 1–7 scale (one completely unimportant, seven very important) "how important each of the following news items was to you personally on October 19, 1987.... Please tell how important *you* then felt these were, and not how others thought about them." The question here departs from the format in my earlier questionnaires, in that this time I suggested the news stories, and used an open-ended question format only for the last category, "other."

The news items are shown in table 23.2, question A; investors seem to think that just about everything is at least somewhat relevant. There is a broad similarity in results between individual (INDIV) and institutional (INSTI) investors. The 200-point drop in the Dow on the morning of October 19 is the most important for both groups, and the price drops of the preceding week are second or third for both. Treasury bond yields hitting 10.5% are second or third for both groups. For both groups Prechter's sell signal is given lowest importance, the producer price index figures the second lowest, and the U.S. attack on the Iranian oil station the third lowest. The low importance given to the producer price index announcement confirms that there is some accuracy to the answers: the announcement was not out of the ordinary at all and not substantive news; people knew that. The low importance given to the attack on the Iranian oil station is significant: it seems to be the best candidate for an important news event that become public knowledge right on October 19 or over the weekend.[4]

Not many in either group wrote in an answer under "other." When they did, the items entered were highly varied. They rarely mentioned current news stories. A "too much indebtedness" theme seemed to be most common: they referred to such things as the federal deficit, national debt, budget deficit, or taxes. Of the 90 individual investors who wrote in an answer, 33.3% mentioned such a theme; of the 55 institutional investors, 20.0% mentioned this theme.

The *Barron's* survey (Palmer [1987]) included a question that was somewhat similar. Respondents were read a list of "things that have been mentioned as possible causes of the recent fluctuations in the stock market— particularly the 508 point drop on October 19," and were asked to rate the importance of each of them. One important distinction between their question and mine is that they are asking for opinions held *after* the crash, and not asking them to recall what they were reacting to then. Their question also did not emphasize that what was wanted was a personal opinion, and not just a distillation from the postcrash media accounts. According to their survey, the most important items were the budget deficit and program trading, and everyone getting nervous at the same time about the way the economy is going, followed by the trade deficit and investor speculation, and everyone getting nervous at the same time about the high stock market and government economic policies. Their respondents did not think that banks announcing an increase in interest rates was important at all, whereas in the results I report in table 23.2, this had moderate importance. *Barron's* also found that the decline in the dollar and the recent merger and takeover activities were unimportant.

In the results reported here in table 23.2, there was little difference between buyers' and sellers' ratings of the news events, with minor exceptions: sellers October 19 were somewhat more impressed than others with Treasury Secretary Baker's statement that the dollar should slip further, and slightly more impressed with the rise of the prime rate.

That nothing stood out in the table 23.2 results beyond the price declines may be thought of as perhaps consistent with the general conclusion I was inclined to from previous surveys: that investors may be reacting to price movements themselves on days of big market drops, and not to any specific news stories. However, some of the nonprice news stories were rated as almost as important as the news of the price drop itself. Moreover, one question that I wrote with the expectation that it might confirm that people reacted to price movements did not go as I expected. I asked, "Suppose that as of October 19, 1987, the same news had occurred except for the news of price drops. Would your evaluation of the market or decisions to buy or sell on October 19 have been substantially different?" Only 18.3% of the individual investors and 34.0% of the institutional investors agreed with this statement (table 23.2, question B.). Perhaps the question was too subtle, and open to alternative interpretations.

Other evidence also suggests that people were not reacting to concrete news stories. In the PILOT2 survey, respondents were asked, "Was any news story that you read in the paper then, heard from an advisory service, etc., or from anyone else, or any rumor on your mind over the weekend or on that day as a reason to buy or sell that day?" Of the 48 respondents who answered, 9, or 19.7%, said yes, the remainder, no. These were then asked, "If yes, can you describe the story or rumor? (Be sure you're describing something you heard on that day. Please try hard to put *something* down, but don't put something down that really wasn't on your mind then.)" Only 3 put down a genuine news story. Among the others one wrote, "A friend who is a securities analyst had informed me two weeks earlier he had pulled all of his clients out of the market." Another wrote, "News media stories about 'panic'/'free fall,' 1929 etc.," another that "I discussed with my broker on 10/15 and decided to stay calm," and another that "news commentators looked grim—like trying hard not to panic people." In PILOT1, respondents were asked the same question regarding the days October 14–16. Of these, 21.6% said yes, but few of these entered any news story, and nothing consistent emerged. Almost all of the responses reported not news stories but advice of brokers and friends, or predictions others made about the future course of the market.

Much Talk, Much Anxiety, Little Action

The survey revealed a remarkable amount of concern and involvement in the stock market among individual and institutional investors, while very few individual investors and only a moderate number of institutional investors actually changed their holdings on October 19.

Almost everyone (96.7%) in the random sample INDIV of individual investors who responded said they had heard of the market crash on the day of the crash. Of these, the average time when the investor became aware of "above average stock market drops" was 1:56 P.M. Eastern Daylight Time, remarkably early for individuals in the nation as a whole when one considers that this is only 10:56 A.M. Pacific Daylight Time. Only 18.4% of the individual investors in INDIV did not hear of the drop until after 5:00 P.M. local time (as would be the case if they learned of it on the evening news). For institutional investors (INDIV) the average time when they became aware was 10:32 A.M. Eastern Daylight Time. Roughly speaking, they were almost all aware as the event unfolded.

The average individual investor in INDIV reported talking to 7.4 other people on the day of the crash, the average institutional investor 19.7 other people. The average individual investor (INDIV) checked the price of stocks 3.2 times on that day. The average institutional investor (INSTI) checked the price of stocks 35.0 times that day.[5]

Many of these people were emotionally involved in the market. The questionnaire asked about actual *symptoms* of anxiety experienced by respondents (see table 23.3, question A): difficulty concentrating, sweaty palms, tightness in chest, irritability, or rapid pulse. Fully 20.3% of the individual investors in INDIV and 43.1% of the institutional investors answered yes for the date Monday, October 19; substantial percentages answered yes for adjacent days. It is remarkable that such a proportion of the general population reported such specific symptoms of real anxiety at one time.

Moreover, 23.0% of the individual investors and 40.2% of the institutional investors reported experiencing a contagion of fear from other investors. Among individual investors who sold on October 19, 53.9% reported experiencing contagion of fear. Moreover, 35.0% of the individual investors and 53.2% of the institutional investors report talking of events of 1929 on the few days before October 19. The percents who spoke of 1929 were even higher for those who sold on October 19 (see table 23.3, questions B and C).

Table 23.3
Investor anxieties[a]

	Individual (INDIV)				Institutional (INSTI)			
All	Buyers		Sellers		All	Buyers		Sellers	
	October					October			
	12–19	19	12–19	19		12–19	19	12–19	19

A. On which of the following dates did you experience any unusual symptoms of anxiety (difficulty concentrating, sweaty palms, tightness in chest, irritability, or rapid pulse.) regarding the stock market?

Wednesday–Friday October 14–16, 1987

3.7	5.9	12.5	13.0	7.7	13.1	5.0	12.5	23.6	22.2
(0.8)	(5.7)	(8.3)	(7.4)	(7.4)	(2.0)	(4.8)	(4.8)	(5.0)	(6.9)

The weekend October 17–18

3.3	5.9	12.5	0	23.2	15.0	5.0	14.6	31.9	30.6
(0.7)	(5.7)	(8.3)	—	(11.7)	(2.2)	(4.8)	(5.1)	(5.5)	(7.7)

Monday, October 19, 1987

20.3	17.6	18.8	31.6	30.8	43.1	30.0	45.8	51.4	44.4
(1.7)	(9.2)	(9.8)	(7.5)	(12.8)	(3.0)	(10.2)	(7.2)	(5.9)	(8.3)

Tuesday, October 20, 1987

12.3	5.9	18.8	23.7	30.8	30.3	25.0	37.5	37.5	27.8
(1.4)	(5.7)	(9.8)	(6.9)	(12.8)	(2.8)	(9.7)	(7.0)	(5.7)	(7.5)

Wednesday–Friday October 21–23

7.0	5.9	12.5	13.2	7.7	29.2	25.0	39.5	34.7	30.6
(1.1)	(5.7)	(9.8)	(5.5)	(7.4)	(2.8)	(9.7)	(7.1)	(5.6)	(7.7)

B. Do you think you may have personally experienced contagion of fear from other people on October 14–19?

23.0	31.3	35.2	31.6	53.9	40.2	42.1	44.9	47.1	45.7
(7.7)	(11.6)	(11.9)	(7.5)	(13.8)	(3.0)	(11.3)	(7.1)	(6.1)	(8.4)

C. Do you remember thinking or talking about events of 1929 on the few days *before* October 19, 1987?

35.0	17.6	31.3	42.1	46.2	53.2	55.0	61.2	54.0	63.9
(2.0)	(9.2)	(11.6)	(8.0)	(13.8)	(3.0)	(11.1)	(7.1)	(5.9)	(8.0)

a. Figures are percent of respondents selecting the item or answering yes from the respondents who answered the question. Standard errors are in parentheses.

Despite all this anxiety, most people did not change their holdings of stocks. As we saw from table 23.1, only 5.2% of the individual investors surveyed reported actually being net buyers or sellers of either individual corporate stocks, index futures, or stock options on October 19. (A higher proportion reported having changed their holdings between October 12 and 19.) There were almost four times as many who experienced the symptoms of anxiety. With institutional investors, 31.1% changed their holdings on October 19; slightly less than the percentage reporting experiencing symptoms of anxiety. Thus, there was a lot of talk and anxiety, little action.[6]

Many Investors Thought They Knew What the Market Would Do

I asked a question aimed at discovering whether investors thought on October 19 that they knew when a rebound was to occur (table 23.4, question A). The point of this question was to learn the motivation of buyers that day. Among individual investors fully 29.2% (or ten times the number of people who actually bought that day) reported yes. Among institutional investors, 28.0% reported yes, well over the percent who bought that day. Respondents were then asked, "If yes, what made you think you knew when a rebound would occur?" Many individual investors said "intuition" or "gut feeling" or just "knew there would be a rebound." Often individual investors mentioned theories of what the "big" investors were doing. There was often a suggestion that the market tends to rebound when certain conditions were met, but only infrequent references to technical analysis. Institutional investors usually did not explain why they expected a rebound. When they did, the answers were usually similar to those of individual investors, simple intuitive statements: "gut feel," "historical evidence and common sense," "market psychology."

A common theme in answers to this question among institutional investors was that the magnitude of the decline was prima facie evidence of a rebound: "too far too fast for it not to rebound," "logic (wishful thinking perhaps) that such a decline has *never* occurred without a corresponding up reaction." Of the 73 institutional investors who explained why they expected a rebound, 37.0% volunteered such an argument. The theme was the magnitude of the decline, not the bargains that were created by the decline. Among institutional investors who answered, only 13.7% cited the low prices themselves as reason to expect a rebound. Individual investors were less likely to mention either theme as reason to expect a rebound: 13.6% of the 154 individual investors who explained

Table 23.4
Investor outlook[a]

	Individual (INDIV)				Institutional (INSTI)			
All	Buyers		Sellers		All	Buyers		Sellers	
	October					October			
	12–19	19	12–19	19		12–19	19	12–19	19

A. Did you think at any point on October 19, 1987 that you had a pretty good idea when a rebound was to occur?

All	Buyers		Sellers		All	Buyers		Sellers	
29.2	23.5	47.1	31.6	46.1	28.0	25.0	47.9	28.2	16.7
(1.9)	(10.3)	(12.1)	(7.5)	(13.8)	(2.7)	(9.7)	(7.2)	(5.3)	(6.2)

B. Did you have a sense just before the crash (around October 12, 1987) that the market was overpriced relative to fundamental value? (Try hard to remember what you thought *then*.)

All	Buyers		Sellers		All	Buyers		Sellers	
71.7	76.5	88.9	62.2	91.0	84.3	89.5	87.0	85.7	88.5
(2.2)	(10.2)	(10.5)	(8.0)	(8.7)	(2.2)	(7.0)	(5.0)	(4.8)	(5.4)

C. Do you think you were bullish and optimistic, relative to other investors, on October 12 (before the beginning of the crash)?

All	Buyers		Sellers		All	Buyers		Sellers	
36.1	23.5	55.6	54.0	60.0	22.2	25.0	22.2	20.3	20.0
(2.4)	(10.3)	(16.5)	(8.2)	(15.4)	(2.6)	(9.7)	(6.9)	(4.8)	(6.8)

D. Was your thinking on October 19 influenced by the stock market dropping through a 200-day moving average or similar long-term trend line?

All	Buyers		Sellers		All	Buyers		Sellers	
37.3	43.8	43.8	52.8	58.3	33.2	30.0	34.7	49.3	37.1
(2.0)	(12.4)	(12.4)	(8.3)	(14.2)	(2.8)	(10.2)	(6.7)	(6.0)	(8.2)

a. Figures are percent of respondents answering yes from the respondents who answered the question. Standard errors are in parentheses.

why they expected a rebound volunteered that the magnitude of the drop itself was a reason to expect a rebound, and 8.4% cited the low prices.

Only one institutional respondent and only one individual respondent mentioned portfolio insurance and only one institutional respondent mentioned index arbitrage in answer to this question. The absence of mention of these is surprising; one might expect such program trading to be part of a theory of rebounds since program trading was widely held to be the reason for the stock market drops. A few institutional investors mentioned that the stock market decline included many quality equities, allegedly a sign of a rebound. A few institutional and individual investors mentioned a psychological theory that the close of the market would exhaust the panic.

The pilot questionnaire also had a related question. In answer to the question "Did you at any point feel that prices had fallen too far, and that bargains had been created?" yes answers were given by 48% of the PILOT1 respondents and 74% of the PILOT2 respondents, the latter a far higher percent than thought they had a pretty good idea when a rebound would occur among INDIV investors. Perhaps the difference in answers has to do with the absence of the words "pretty good idea" in the INDIV question. Moreover, a "bargain" does not imply a "rebound," and as we shall see next, opinion of over- or undervaluation do not seem to be the basis for most trade.

The Average Investor Thought the Market Was Overvalued before the Crash

Fully 71.7% of the INDIV investors and 84.3% of the INSTI investors reported that they thought around October 12, just before the crash, that the market was overpriced relative to fundamental value (table 23.4, question B). The question said, "Try hard to remember what you thought *then*" [October 12]. Of course it is quite possible that their reporting of their own past thoughts was colored by the events that followed October 12.

Consistent with their report that they thought the market was overpriced, only 36.1% of the INDIV investors and 22.2% of the INSTI investors described themselves as bullish and optimistic relative to other investors on this date (table 23.4, question C).

Thus, few people in the INDIV and INSTI thought they were more optimistic about the stock market than average. It was as if people did not realize how many others shared the view that the market was overpriced. Apparently the view did not dissuade many people from buying stocks nonetheless.

What is particularly interesting about their answers is that those people who reported net buying between September 12 and October 12 were just as likely to think that the market was overpriced on October 12: 68.1% of the individual investors in INDIV who were buying then and 93.1% of the institutional investors in INSTI buying then. There are various reasons why some investors might buy when they think the market is overpriced. For example, many investors apparently think that they can time the market, and buy while it is still going up. One institutional investor who had been increasing holdings between September 12 and October 12 agreed that the market had been overpriced but volunteered, "Although we thought this to be true, we followed the 'trend is your friend' philosophy. " Another who had not changed holdings over the interval wrote, "Not expecting such a dramatic decline—expecting lower price to develop over the next 3–6 months." Some follow a policy of reinvesting dividends. Others may follow the popular "dollar-cost averaging" plan of buying equal amounts of money at regular intervals, which is often described as a sober and responsible plan that will cause the investor to acquire fewer shares when stocks are overpriced.

Weekend Effect

Both the October 19, 1987, and October 28, 1929, crashes occurred on a Monday after a preceding week of great market turmoil. It is plausible that the magnitude of the drops had something to do with the fact that a weekend gave people the time to reach decisions to act on Monday. We have seen above that actual symptoms of anxiety extended into the weekend for many investors; in our samples of both individual and institutional investors the number of people who reported such symptoms over the weekend was roughly comparable to the number who sold on Monday. The percent showing anxiety over the weekend was even higher for those who sold on October 19: 23.2% of these individual investors and 30.6% of these institutional investors. And the symptoms of anxiety reported are rather pronounced; there are likely to have been many more people who thought quite seriously about the market without such symptoms.

In the PILOT2 questionnaire it was asked, "Did you at any point over the weekend or on October 19 feel that prices were likely to fall dramatically soon?" Of those who answered, 39% said yes. Some of the respondents' comments are suggestive of such a weekend effect. One respondent who answered yes wrote, "Saturday was a day of soul searching to resist the absolute fear that Monday could have dealt. Do we sell out Monday or ride it out?" Of those who answered no, there was often as much anxiety over the weekend; they merely had a difference of opinion as to the likely direction of the market. One who answered no wrote, "I thought the market would *rebound* on Monday!"

Investors Thought Investor Psychology Moved the Markets

Investors were asked, "Can you remember any specific theory you had about the causes for the price declines October 14–19, 1987?" The most common theme overall in the theories written in response to this question was the overpricing of the market before the crash. Among individual investors, 33.9% of the 342 who wrote theories mentioned this theme;

among institutional investors, 32.6% of the 184 who wrote theories mentioned this theme. Another important theme was an institutional stop-loss theme (identified by key words institutional selling, program trading, stop-loss, or computer trading): 22.8% individual, 33.1% institutional.[7] Also present was an investor irrationality theme (that investors were crazy or that the fall was due to investor panic or capricious change in opinion): 25.4% individual, 24.4% institutional.

The next question on the questionnaire was, "Which of the following better describes your theory about the declines: a theory about investor psychology, [or] a theory about fundamentals such as profits or interest rates?" Here, 67.5% ($n = 530$) of the INDIV sample of individual investors and 64.0% ($n = 267$) of the institutional investors said the theory was about investor psychology. This is in contrast to results obtained earlier (Pound and Shiller [1987]) with a random sample of institutional investors, where a very similar question referred not to the stock market on a day of a crash but to an individual stock the respondent held on a normal day. There, 79% of the random sample of institutional investors said that the theory that led them to hold the stock was a theory about fundamentals.

Unfortunately, the interpretation of the question is somewhat ambiguous, as respondents' written theories show. Many who said that the market was very much overpriced before the crash, and needed to come more in line with fundamentals, classified this as a theory about fundamentals. It is hard to think, however, that someone who thought that the market crash was due to bad news about the fundamental economic data would classify the theory as one about investor psychology. The bias would seem to be against investor psychology as an answer.

That so many investors think that market psychology is the reason for market movements is consistent with their holding stocks when they also thought they were overpriced.

Technical Analysis Played a Role

Investors were asked whether they were influenced by price dropping through a 200-day moving average or other long-term trend line. This trend line is an example of a technical indicator. About a third in both the individual INDIV and institutional INSTI samples answered yes (table 23.4, question D).

In the PILOT2 questionnaire, respondents were asked, "Was any technical factor on your mind in this connection on that day (channel, oscillator, support level, etc)?" Of the 47 who answered, 17.0% said yes.

Since important news about fundamentals does not seem to appear on a daily basis, any day-to-day formal analysis of price movements is likely to focus on technical analysis, which uses price data as information. That is probably why daily reports in places like the "Heard on the Street" column of the *Wall Street Journal* report so many references to technical indicators, and why we can be confident technical analysis plays a role itself in market movements.

Portfolio Insurance Is but the Tip of the Iceberg

Only 5.5% of those institutional investors who answered the questionnaire answered yes to the question, "Do you follow an explicit portfolio insurance scheme?" A portfolio insurance scheme is a predetermined rule that investors may use to limit losses. The rule specifies trade in index futures that causes index futures contracts to be sold continually as stock prices go down, thereby hedging the portfolio against further losses. The rule follows a mathematical formula that has certain optimality properties.

Although the proportion who use explicit portfolio insurance is small, the proportion of institutional and individual investors who have a policy of limiting losses is around 10%, and among those who sold on October 19, close to 40% individual, close to 20% institutional (see table 23.5, question A). One can limit losses without an explicit portfolio insurance scheme by adopting buy or sell points, i.e., deciding in advance when to sell on either the cash or futures markets, by stop-loss orders or puts.

One common misconception about portfolio insurance is that, since it typically involves computers, it is importantly faster than other means of limiting losses. However, people can respond quite fast themselves relative to a day of market drops, without any computers (assuming that they can get in touch with their brokers and have their orders executed). Moreover, we have seen above that on October 19, they did indeed find out about record market movements in time to be a factor in these movements.

Studies of the September 11–12, 1986, drop (SEC [1987]) and of the January 23, 1987, drop (CFTC [1987]), as well as preliminary newspaper accounts (Cox [1987]) of a CFTC study of the October 19 drop, all conclude that portfolio insurance was not big enough in impact to account for much of the drop on those days. CFTC Commissioner Robert Davis was quoted as saying that "the activity was not exceptional, and didn't have much impact on the overall stock market" (Cox [1987]).

Since the behavior rule implicit in portfolio insurance is so well-defined as to be executable by a computer, it is readily analyzable by economists.

Table 23.5
Investor policies[a]

	Individual (INDIV)					Institutional (INSTI)			
All	Buyers		Sellers		All	Buyers		Sellers	
	October					October			
	12–19	19	12–19	19		12–19	19	12–19	19
A. Did you have, as of October 19, 1987, a policy of holding losses to a certain amount (by deciding in advance to sell at a certain point, by stop-loss orders, buying puts, or other forms of portfolio insurance)?									
10.1	6.3	17.7	31.6	38.5	10.2	5.3	16.3	18.3	18.9
(1.3)	(6.1)	(9.2)	(7.5)	(13.4)	(1.8)	(5.1)	(5.3)	(4.6)	(6.4)
B. If yes, had you adopted this policy shortly before or on October 19?									
44.4	—	—	69.2	50.0	28.0	0	10.0	40.9	50.0
(6.3)	—	—	(12.7)	(20.4)-	(6.3)	—	(9.4)	(10.5)	(13.3)
C. Did you abandon a policy of investing for the long term (value investing, contrarian investing or the like) shortly before or on October 19?									
13.2	12.5	24.6	27.0	38.5	6.6	0	4.3	19.4	27.8
(1.5)	(8.2)	(10.3)	(7.3)	(13.5)	(1.6)	—	(2.9)	(4.7)	(7.4)
D. Try to imagine that you heard exactly the same news about price declines that you heard October 19, without the other news, on a Monday six months ago. Would your reaction have been less intense?									
19.9	11.8	12.5	26.3	23.1	22.2	20.0	22.5	23.1	29.4
(1.6)	(7.8)	(8.3)	(7.5)	(11.6)	(2.5)	(8.9)	(7.2)	(5.1)	(7.6)

a. Figures are percent of respondents answering yes from the respondents who answered the question. Standard errors are in parentheses.

We should avoid the temptation, however, to overemphasize the importance of behaviors that we know well relative to behaviors that are not precisely defined.

Changes in Investment Strategy

If the stock market crash was due to investors reacting to price drops themselves, then one might expect that they were more reactive at the time of the crash than at other times. That would then explain why the crash was so big on that day. I sought evidence whether this was so. I asked whether they had adopted their policy of holding losses to a certain amount shortly before the crash. Of those who had such a policy, 44.4% of the individual investors and 28.0% of the institutional investors said yes (table 23.5, question B). Those who said yes were asked when they adopted this policy: some put down years, but 46.4% of these individual investors and 50% of the institutional investors adopted the policy within a month of the crash.[8]

Respondents were also asked whether they had abandoned a policy of investing for the long term just before the crash: 13.2% of the individual investors and 6.6% of the institutional investors said yes (table 23.5, question C). Among those who sold October 19, the percentages were 38.5% individual and 27.8% institutional. One institutional respondent who said yes and who abandoned the policy on October 16 wrote, "The 95 point drop is a sure indicator of much higher risk on the downside. As things turned out, it was a precursor to the GREAT QUAKE on Monday. "Another institutional investor who claimed the policy was abandoned October 19 wrote, "The market was in a free fall and therefore unable to make proper investment decisions."

Respondents were also asked whether their response to the price declines would have been less intense if the declines had occurred six months ago (table 23.5, question D). I thought perhaps many would answer yes, indicating a heightened responsiveness of investors to market prices now, but most did not. Perhaps more would have answered yes if the question had not specified the "same news about price declines" but instead "a 30-point drop in the Dow." Perhaps the 508 point drop is so large that respondents feel they would react intensely to it at any time.

23.4   Interpretation and Conjectures

Something must have been different on October 19, 1987, that caused the behavior of the market to be very different from other days. What *was* different on that day? To answer that question, one must look for something that happened on exactly that day, not general considerations that characterize many days. Thus, for example, it is not enough to say that "portfolio insurance did it," since portfolio insurance has been around for years.

Sometimes big market movements are related to specific identifiable newsbreaks. However, the survey did not turn up anything really important to investors that became public on October 19 or over the weekend, other than the price decline itself and the behavior of investors reacting to it and previous declines. There is of course the possibility that a group of investors —missed or underweighted in the survey—was responsible for the stock market drop, and that these were responding to some important news event that the broader group of investors surveyed did not appreciate. The questionnaire was not directed to foreign investors, or to specialists, nor did the survey weight results by size of investor.

While no important news story appears to have broken right at the time of the stock market drop, we can identify news stories that preceded the drop by a number of days, and that were on investors' minds. Institutional investors were most concerned about the recent rise in interest rates and about Treasury Secretary James A. Baker's October 15 threat to push the dollar lower in response to increases in German interest rates. Both individual and institutional investors were confident that the market was overpriced, worried about program trading, and were concerned about the national debt and taxes. These concerns and worries certainly affected individual behavior on October 19, but do not explain the events of that day.

In interpreting the lack of an identifiable proximate cause for the drop, it should be borne in mind that there is a growing literature that calls into question the "efficient markets" theory that all price movements must be interpretable by information about economic fundamentals: (e.g., Shiller [1984 and chapter 1]; Campbell and Shiller [1987, and chapter 16]; DeBondt and Thaler [1985]; Fama and French [1986]; Mankiw, Romer, and Shapiro [1986]; Poterba and Summers [1987]; West [1986]). Increasingly, there is statistical evidence that suggests the stock market may have a life of its own to some extent, unrelated to economic fundamentals.[9]

Since no news story or any other recognizable event outside the market appears to be immediately responsible for the market crash, we will thus turn to consideration of a theory of the crash as being determined endogenously by investors: that the timing of the crash was related to some internal dynamics of investor thinking, investor reactions to price and to each other. The survey results give us some information about investors that help us to think about these investor dynamics.

There were two channels by which price declines could feed back into further price declines: first, a price-to-price channel—investors on October 19 were reacting to price changes; second, a social-psychological channel—investors were directly reacting to each other.[10] From the information collected on the frequency with which investors checked prices and talked with each other on October 19, both feedback channels were operating fast enough among the broad masses of investors to play an important role in the hour-to-hour movements of the market: the communications proceeded rapidly, and prices were checked with great frequency. This was especially so among those investors who were net buyers or sellers on October 19.

The extent of communications as well as the amount of anxiety reported suggests that this event was not unlike other alarming national events that seize the public attention, and push aside much everyday activity for attention. As such, the significance of the event should not be interpreted solely in terms of the quantitative measure of the amount of wealth lost in the market drop. The changes in individual perceptions are more fundamental and are likely to be lasting, even if the decline in wealth is reversed.

Investors had expectations before the 1987 crash that something like a 1929 crash was a possibility, and comparisons with 1929 were an integral part of the phenomenon. It would be wrong to think that the crash could be understood without reference to the expectations engendered by this historical comparison. In a sense many people were playing out an event again that they knew well.

Many investors thought that they could time the market. Technical analysis played an important role in their predictions, and thus in the decline in demand October 19. On the other hand, few investors, institutional or individual, *volunteered* any references to technical analysis in their answers to open-ended questions. They often wrote "gut feeling" as their forecasting method, and often seemed to say that they were guessing about the psychology of other investors. Investors appear to believe they have some internal sense of magnitude or direction for the market, and investors are highly divided on this sense of direction. Many investors thought that the sheer magnitude of the price drops on October 14–16 made it common sense that a rebound should come on Monday. At the same time, many other investors thought that the tremendous drops that came on those days raised issues that the market may be headed for a 1929-style crash. Most of those who held to either belief did nothing about it. Of the small number who did, the "crash" theory holders happened to outnumber the "rebound" theory holders.

The actual decision to buy or sell on October 19 seems to be only weakly related to interpretations of recent news events that investors rated as important: there was little difference between buyers and sellers on the importance rating that was given to news events. Respondents apparently did not have a clear theory how these past news events translated into predictions of market price movements on October 19, yet very many respondents still had predictions. It would thus be wrong to say, as many have done, that the market drop on October 19, 1987, ought to be interpreted as a statement of public opinion about some fundamental economic factor, e.g., that there is lack of confidence in the White House or

Congress. At best, any such opinions probably played a role in the crash mainly as they affected the vague intuitive assessments people under great stress made about the tendency of prices to continue or reverse, or about how other investors will react to the current situation.

Appendix: Sources of Mailing Lists

PILOT1, PILOT2 (High Income Individuals, n = 125 Each)
Survey Sampling, Inc., random sample of high income investors in the continental United States whose income predicted by a regression was $70,000 a year or more. This is a list of high income individuals, not investors. In a previous survey (Shiller and Pound [1986]) using this list we achieved (by repeated followup mailings urging prompt response) a response rate of 59%. Of those who responded, we asked, "Have you, or someone in your household, ever bought shares of common stock (not preferred stock) in a corporation?" Of those who answered, 55% answered yes. The PILOT1 and PILOT2 lists were drawn from those respondents who answered yes to this question.

INDIV (Individual Investors, n = 2,000)
W. S. Ponton, (5149 Butler Street, The Ponton Building, Pittsburgh, PA 15201): "High-Grade Multi-Investors" with a random selection from the entire United States. This list is described in the Ponton *Investor List Catalog* Vol. VIII by "names on three (3) or more lists—net worth of generally over $250,000.00," (p. 4). Harvey A. Rabinowitz (president of W. S. Ponton) explained to me that they maintain many mailing list of investors. The high grade multi-investor list consists of people who are on three or more of their lists that are suggestive of high income, active investors. Most lists described in their catalog are used. Sources of lists include "clippings from almost every daily, weekly and religious newspaper in the United States, legal journals, business directories & magazines, public court house records, replies to space ads in all types of business & investment publications, investment seminar attendees, trade-offs with stock brokerage firms & business/financial & investment publications, a few corporate stockholder lists, purchase of lists from some investment firms that are no longer in business, & many private & personal sources (*Investor List Catalog*, p. 23). However, Rabinowitz said there was no use made of some of their more unusual lists (their lists of gamblers, cattle or new movie investors). Rabinowitz thought that the high grade multi-investor list should resemble a random sample of all high income active investors. The average income of respondents was $136,700.

INSTI (Institutional Investors, n = 1,000)
"Investment Managers, Alphabetical Index," from the *Money Market Directory of Pension Funds and Their Investment Managers 1987*, T. H. Fitzgerald, Ed., Mcgraw-Hill. Categories are Investment Counsel Firms, U.S. Bank and Trust Companies, U.S. Insurance Companies, and Independent Real Estate Advisors. Names were selected randomly from this, without regard to kind of firm or position within the firm.

Notes

1. The combined drop October 28–29, 1929, was 23.1%.

2. *Barron's* magazine also did a poll of investors in the closing days of October (Palmer [1987]). Their poll did not include institutional investors.

3. Of PILOT respondents, 3.9% bought and 5.9% sold October 14–16; 9.0% bought and 5.9% sold on October 19. These percentages are slightly higher than among the INDIV investors, though not statistically significantly higher. The difference may be due to the wording of the question. Some of the INDIV or INSTI respondents who both bought and sold in the interval may put down "No Change" in the questionnaire, even though they traded.

4. The attack occurred at about 7:00 A.M. Eastern Daylight Time.

5. The figure is the number who provided an answer to the question; many did not answer but wrote in the margin "very many times" or "continuously."

6. A *Wall Street Journal*/NBC News poll November 17–18, 1986, queried 271 adults who said they have an account with a stockbroker. Of these, 67% said they traded financial securities three times a year or less, 16% four to ten times a year, and 10% more than ten times a year; 7% were unsure (*Wall Street Journal*, Nov. 5, 1987, p. 2).

7. The *Barron's* survey asked individual investors who they thought triggered the stock market crash. The results were institutional investors 56%, foreign investors 26%, and individual investors, 9% (Palmer [1987]). The dominance of institutional investors in the answers here does not seem to square with answers to open-ended questions I read, which often seemed to refer to other individual investors. Perhaps individual investors will say that institutional investors are extremely important when explicitly asked about institutional investors, but at other times imagine that others like themselves are important.

8. As a percent of total respondents, these are only 2.1% and 2.1%, respectively—not a large percent.

9. There are of course critics of this view as well. See, for example, Terry Marsh and Robert Merton [1987].

10. The fields of sociology and social psychology offer many insights into the latter of these two channels—see, for example, Adler and Adler [1984], Katona [1975], and McGuire [1969].

References

Adler, Patricia A., and Peter Adler, eds., 1984. *The Social Dynamics of Financial Markets*, Greenwich, Connecticut: JAI Press.

Campbell, John Y., and Robert J. Shiller. 1987. "Cointegration and Tests of Present Value Models," *Journal of Political Economy* 95 : 1062–1088.

Commodity Futures Trading Commission (CFTC), Division of Economic Analysis, "A Review of Stock Index Futures Trading on January 23, 1987," reproduced.

Cox, Paul. 1987. "CFTC Believes Futures-Related Strategies Had Limited Part in Stock Market Plunge," *Investors Daily*, p. 35.

DeBondt, Werner F. M., and Richard Thaler. 1985. "Does the Stock Market Overreact?" *Journal of Finance* 40:793—805.

Fama, Eugene F., and Kenneth R. French. 1986. "Permanent and Transitory Components of Stock Prices," Center for Research in Securities Prices, Working Paper No. 178, University of Chicago.

Katona, George. 1975. *Psychological Economics*, Elsevier.

LeRoy, Stephen, and Richard D. Porter. 1981. "The Present Value Relation: Tests Based on Implied Variance Bounds," *Econometrica* 49:555—574.

Mankiw, N. Gregory, David Romer, and Matthew Shapiro. 1985. "An Unbiassed Reexamination of Stock Price Volatility," *Journal of Finance* 40:677—687.

McGuire, William J. 1969. "The Nature of Attitudes and Attitude Change," in Gardner Lindzey and Elliot Aronson, Eds., *Handbook of Social Psychology*, Addison Wesley.

Palmer, Jay. 1987. "What Do You Think? A Nationwide Poll of Reaction to the Crash," *Barrons*, Nov. 9, 16ff.

Pound, John, and Robert J. Shiller. 1987. "Are Institutional Investors Speculators?" *Journal of Portfolio Management*, Spring, 46—52.

Shiller, Robert J. 1984. "Stock Prices and Social Dynamics," *Brookings Papers on Economic Activity* II: 457—498.

Shiller, Robert J. 1986. "Survey Evidence Regarding the September 11—12 Stock Market Drop," reproduced, Yale University.

Shiller, Robert J. and John Pound. 1987. "Survey Evidence on the Diffusion of Interest and Information Among Investors," reproduced.

U.S. Securities and Exchange Commission (SEC), Division of Market Regulation, 1987, "The Role of Index-Related Trading in the Market Decline of September 11 and 12, 1986," reproduced.

West, Kenneth D. 1987. "Dividend Innovations and Stock Price Volatility," *Econometrica* 56:37—61.

The Behavior of Home Buyers in Boom and Post-Boom Markets

A recent development in the U.S. market for single-family homes has provided an ideal laboratory in which to study the sources of volatility in home prices: prices have been moving in dramatically different ways at the same time in different parts of the country. A boom in housing prices has appeared in California, with price increases from late 1987 to mid-1988 exceeding 20% in many cities. At the very same time, a post-boom market exists in the Northeast. A remarkable boom occurred between 1983 and mid-1987 in many places from New York to Boston, where housing prices more than doubled in those three and one-half years. That boom appears to be over, with prices actually falling in late 1987. At the same time, it is possible to observe a housing market in the Midwest that has had no sign of a boom for the past five years.

We exploited this opportunity by collecting data about the behavior of home buyers in these different markets using questionnaire survey methods. Identical questionnaires were sent to those who bought homes in May of 1988 in each of four markets: Anaheim (Orange County) and San Francisco, California (two "boom" markets); Boston, Massachusetts (a "post-boom" market); and Milwaukee, Wisconsin (a "control" sample, representing more normal housing market conditions). Since the questionnaires were identical and were sent out at the same time, differences in answers across cities can be attributed only to differences in the local market for housing and not to differences in the wording or order of questions or to national economic conditions.

We sought information that would help answer some nagging questions about the nature and causes of booms in housing markets. Most fundamentally, what causes sudden and often dramatic and sustained price

Coauthored with Karl E. Case. Reprinted with minor editing from *New England Economic Review* (1988): 29–46. © 1988 the Federal Reserve Bank of Boston.

movements? Although questionnaire survey methods can never provide a definitive answer to such a question, they can provide information that helps us begin to understand the process: What are home buyers thinking about, and what sources of information are used to decide how much to pay for a house? How motivated are they by investment considerations, and how do they assess investment potential? Is destabilizing speculation affecting housing prices?

Second, why does a state of excess demand tend to occur in boom markets, where some people reportedly stand in line to make offers on the day that a house is listed for sale, often making bids that are above the asking price? Why is it that sellers do not just increase their asking prices until the excess demand disappears?

Third, why does a state of excess supply seem to occur in post-boom markets, where people reportedly take substantial periods of time to sell their homes? Why is it that people do not just cut their asking prices to eliminate the excess supply?

Housing price booms have raised a number of concerns. A boom in housing prices represents a major redistribution of wealth. Those who own see their equity increase while those who do not face higher rents and reduced probability of owning. This redistribution seems capricious and unfair to many. Some have also expressed concern that high housing prices have made it more difficult for firms to attact labor to the boom regions. A special report in the *Harvard Business Review* spoke of a "convulsion in U.S. housing" that has begun to affect American business.[1] The report cites examples of firms in Boston and New York that have experienced severe problems recruiting. Many have chosen to relocate outside the region as a result.

Others are concerned that if speculators are pushing housing prices up temporarily, then housing prices may fall rapidly, creating turmoil among homeowners and homebuilders and in the banking system. On August 22, 1988, the front page of *Barron's* contained a full-page sketch of a home falling off a cliff with the headline "The Coming Collapse of Home Prices." A few cities in recent years have in fact witnessed falling home prices. The best known example is Houston, where the median price of existing single-family homes dropped 24% in two years, contributing to the insolvency of large savings and loan institutions and multi-billion-dollar payouts by the Federal Savings and Loan Insurance Corporation.

Given the seriousness of the problems associated with rising and falling housing prices, surprisingly little research has been done on the questions we pose here. Most models of housing price movements have focused on macroeconomic variables such as interest rates, income, and national demographic trends. But the simple fact that the most dramatic examples of price booms have taken place in well-defined geographic areas while prices were not rising in most of the country suggests that macro variables offer only a partial explanation.

The causes of these booms are still not understood. A study by one of us suggests that housing booms cannot be attributed to rational fundamental factors. In a 1986 article on this subject, Case [1986] sought to explain the Boston experience using data on economic fundamentals. His model included such demand-side and supply-side variables as population growth, employment growth, interest rates (short-term and long-term), construction costs, income growth, tax rates, and the like. Estimated with data from 10 cities over a 10-year period, that model failed to explain more than a fraction of the observed increase in Boston housing prices. Case then put forward a conjecture that the boom was essentially driven by expectations.

Section 24.1 of this chapter describes the behavior of prices in the four metropolitan areas surveyed. Section 24.2 describes the survey, including samples and response rates for each city, section 24.3 presents some interpretations and conjectures.

24.1 Housing Prices in Four Metropolitan Areas

The survey (described in section 24.2) was sent to people who bought homes or condominiums during the month of May 1988. By selecting buyers from a narrow time window, we sought to control for national macroeconomic factors such as interest rates and national income growth. Four metropolitan areas were targeted for the survey. The four were chosen because of what we perceived to be dramatic differences in recent price behavior.

Table 24.1 presents National Association of Realtors data on the median price of existing single-family homes in each metropolitan area quarterly since 1983 and table 24.2 shows annual price increases. Figure 24.1 plots indexes derived from table 24.1 for the same time period. Although we have shown in earlier work (Case and Shiller, 1987) that these are less than perfect measures of appreciation, they are the only source consistent enough to allow such a cross-city comparison.

Orange County and San Francisco

The experience of these two very different California metropolitan areas has been similar. Both experienced a period of rapid increases in home

Table 24.1
Median price of existing single-family homes, 1983–1988 ($)[a]

Year	Orange County	San Francisco	Boston	Milwaukee
1983	134,900	129,500	82,600	68,000
1984:1	133,500	126,600	89,400	69,800
2	135,100	130,500	95,600	68,100
3	134,900	132,600	102,000	69,600
4	130,600	130,400	104,800	64,100
1985:1	132,100	134,500	108,600	66,600
2	135,400	141,100	131,000	66,700
3	137,800	143,800	138,800	66,700
4	139,600	n.a.	144,800	68,100
1986:1	138,000	n.a.	145,600	67,600
2	149,400	n.a.	156,200	71,000
3	149,600	164,900	163,000	70,800
4	152,400	164,800	167,800	69,200
1987:1	156,100	161,300	170,000	67,800
2	167,300	169,900	176,200	71,700
3	167,700	175,900	182,200	70,900
4	174,500	176,000	177,500	70,800
1988:1	183,800	178,800	176,900	72,600
2	204,000	196,300	182,900	71,500

Source: National Association of Realtors. *Home Sales*, monthly.
a. n.a. = not available.

prices during the late 1970s. That came to an end in 1981. Beginning in late 1984, prices began rising again in San Francisco; Orange County picked up in late 1986. While prices in Boston were cooling in 1987 and 1988, San Francisco and Orange County began booming. Table 24.3 and figure 24.2 show the pattern in Orange County and table 24.3 gives annual figures for several other areas in California as well.

The height of the boom seems to have come in May 1988. Between May and June, a single month, the California Association of Realtors reported a 10.2% increase in the median price of single-family homes in San Francisco and a 4.1% increase in Orange County. Such rates of increase drew national attention. On June 1, 1988, the *Wall Street Journal* carried a headline on the front page reading "Buyers' Panic Sweeps California's Big Market in One-Family Homes." The *Journal* article speaks of "a buying frenzy that extends to every segment of the market" and

Table 24.2
Annual increases in median prices of single-family homes, 1983−1988 (%)

Metropolitan area	1983−1984[a]	1984−1985	1985−1986	1986−1987	1987−1988
Orange County	.1	.2	10.3	12.0	21.9
San Francisco	.8	8.1	8.5[b]	11.0[b]	15.5
Boston	15.7	37.0	19.2	12.8	3.8
Milwaukee	0	−2.2	6.6	1.0	−.3

Source: National Association of Realtors data shown in table 24.1.
a. All changes are from second quarter to second quarter except the change for 1983−1984, which is the change from the 1983 annual figure to the 1984 second quarter figure.
b. Data for San Francisco were not available for the second quarter of 1986; the changes presented are estimates.

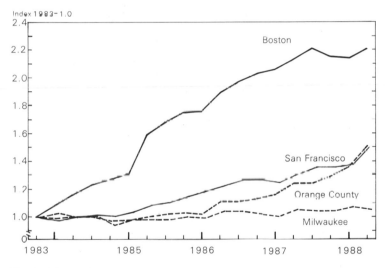

Figure 24.1
Median price of existing single-family homes, 1983−1988. Source: National Association of Realtors, *Home Sales*, monthly.

Table 24.3
Home prices, sales activity in California

	Median sales price			June sales activity	
Region	June 1988 ($)	June 1987 ($)	Percent increase	Percent change from May	Percent change from year ago
Orange County	211,038	170,163	24.0	+25.2	+18.6
Los Angeles	182,364	148,670	22.7	+6.4	+5.8
San Francisco	209,687	173,098	21.1	+9.4	−2.6
San Diego	147,605	125,488	17.6	+14.3	+15.1
Sacramento	92,708	87,276	9.7	+15.7	−8.5
Riverside/ San Bernardino	108,567	96,922	12.0	+7.3	+15.8
Ventura	195,209	160,303	21.8	+2.6	−13.3
California	167,428	140,620	19.1	−7.8	+4.8

Source: California Association of Realtors as presented in the *Los Angeles Times*, July 26, 1988.

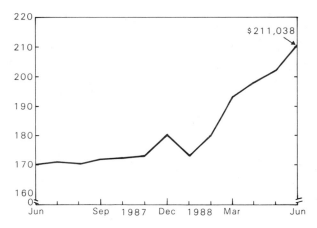

Figure 24.2
Medium resale price of homes in Orange County California, 1987–1988. Source: California Association of Realtors, as published in *Los Angeles Times*, July 26, 1988.

describes lines of 150 cars waiting to buy houses. Articles on the real estate market appeared in the *Los Angles Times* and the *San Francisco Chronicle* an average of more than four times per week during the summer of 1988, carrying such leads as "The real estate market is getting so frenzied, prospective home owners are offering more than asking price" (*Chronicle*, 7/6/88). The president of the Alameda County Board of Realtors is quoted in the same article: "The market is hotter than a pistol....I went to a presentation last night in Fremont for a $400,000 home that had been on the market for five days. There were five offers, and the winning bid was more than the asking price."

Boston

The Boston housing price boom began in 1983. The most rapid growth occurred between 1984 and 1985 when growth rates neared 40% per year. Multiple sales data presented in Case (1986) confirmed rapid acceleration of prices beginning in the first quarter of 1984, peaking in the third quarter of 1985, and slowing steadily through 1986 and 1987. Housing prices doubled between the beginning of 1984 and mid-1987.

Median price fell in Boston in both the fourth quarter of 1987 and the first quarter of 1988. The *Boston Globe* reported the dip with great fanfare. On February 17, 1988, the business page carried the full-page headline "Boston-Area Houses Register a $3,000 Price Drop." It was also reported in that article that the inventory of single-family homes offered for sale through [the Greater Boston Real Estate Board's] multiple listing service has increased from 2,512 to 4,814. The average stay on the market has increased from 58 to 80 days....Long gone are the days when asking prices were extremely exuberant but home buyers met them anyway."[2]

Milwaukee

Milwaukee was chosen for its remarkable record of price stability. The median home price series for Boston presented in table 24.1 has a standard deviation of $34,743. The same statistic for the Milwaukee series is $2,210. Since 1983 median price has risen an average of less than 1% per year, from $68,000 to $71,500.

24.2   The Survey

The universe, the samples, and the response rates on the survey are described in table 24.4. A mailing list of 3,871 persons who bought homes

Table 24.4
Survey universe, samples, and response rates

City/metropolitan area (3-digit ZIP)	Universe	Sample	Bad address	Returned unusable[a]	Net sample	Returns tabulated	Response rate (%)
Anaheim (928)	576	500	21	12	467	241	51.6
San Francisco (941)	1,297	530	18	6	506	199	39.3
Boston (021)	1,383	500	67	12	421	200	47.5
Milwaukee (532)	615	500	36	7	457	246	53.8
	3,871	2,030	142	37	1,851	886	47.9

a. Returned unusable included numerous notes that the property had only been refinanced; several cases where properties were out of state, but the owner resided in state; three land deals; and several replies that claimed never to have bought a home.

in May 1988 was purchased from Dataman, Inc., a research and marketing firm in Atlanta. Dataman collects names, addresses, and selling prices from public records of closings. The data are made available by 3-digit zip code. The lists for Boston and Milwaukee contained addresses drawn from the entire metropolitan areas. The California zip codes were for the cities of San Francisco and Anaheim in Orange County.

From the universe, samples of 500 were drawn at random for Boston, Anaheim, and Milwaukee; 530 were drawn for San Francisco. The survey followed methods described by Dillman (1978). Each household in the sample was sent a 10-page questionnaire with a personalized cover letter hand-signed by both authors. The original mailing was sent on July 17 and 18. This was followed up with a postcard reminder mailed to the entire sample on July 26. A third mailing to those who did not respond was sent on August 16 and 17. The third mailing contained a duplicate questionnaire (for those who had misplaced the first) and a new personalized cover letter. As an incentive to participate, we offered to send survey results to those who requested them.

A total of 142 surveys (7%) were returned "delivery attempted—not known" by the Post Office. Another 37 were returned by recipients but were inappropriate for use in the survey. Among these were replies from several who had only refinanced their homes, some who has bought land only, others who had actually bought property out of state, and a few who claimed not to have been involved in a sale at all. With these excluded, the net sample size was 1,851.

In total, 886 responses were coded and tabulated. Response rates were above 50% in Milwaukee and Anaheim, close to 50% in Boston, and 39% in San Francisco. Such response rates are about what we would expect given the extensive follow-up and personalized format. The questionnaire was long and fairly detailed, taking close to half an hour to complete, but the subject of the questionnaire was likely to be of interest to recent home buyers.

The Questionnaire

We did some pretest interviews of a small number of home buyers in the cities in our sample. We used some of their responses as the base for adding questions to the survey.

The questions are worded in everyday language. In some cases questions may seem, to an economist, to be ill-defined or to suggest fallacious concepts. We included such questions purposely, as a way of documenting

Table 24.5
General description of survey respondents' home purchases (percent of responses)

Description	Anaheim	San Francisco	Boston	Milwaukee
Single-family home	70.0	55.9	39.7	71.1
Condo or coop	22.1	20.5	43.7	11.4
First-time purchase	35.8	36.2	51.5	56.9
Bought to live in as a primary residence	88.4	72.7	92.0	88.2
Bought to rent to others	3.7	12.1	3.0	4.1

how people express themselves. We will discuss the results of the survey in several parts. First, we will explore what the responses suggest about the spread of high expectations for investment potential during booms. Second, we will describe how people seem to interpret the booms. Third, we discuss the question of upward rigidity and excess demand. Finally, we turn to the issue of excess supply and downward price stickiness, focusing on seller behavior.

Table 24.5 presents a brief description of the respondents' purchases. In two of the cities, Milwaukee and Anaheim, about 70% of the properties were single-family homes. Boston had the lowest percentage at 39.7, while San Francisco stood at 55.9. Boston had the largest proportion of condomimiums and cooperatives. What was not a single-famly home, a cooperative or a condo was either a duplex or "other." The properties listed as "other" included triple deckers, three- and four-family homes, apartments, and town houses. In all cities except San Francisco, nearly 90% of the properties were bought as primary residences. A significant number in San Francisco were purchased to rent to others.

Expectations and Investment in the Housing Market
Without question, home buyers in all four cities looked at their decision to buy as an investment decision. Table 24.6 presents tabulations of three questions that shed some light on the extent to which home buyers were motivated by investment considerations.

In both California cities, over 95% said that they thought of their purchase as an investment at least in part. In Boston, the figure was 93.0%, and in Milwaukee, 89.7%. A surprisingly large number in San Francisco, 37.2%, said that they bought the property "strictly" for investment purposes.

Clearly, one's willingness to pay for an asset depends in part on the perceived degree of risk associated with it. Very few home buyers in any

Table 24.6
Housing as an investment (percent of responses in each category)

Question	Boom markets		Post-boom	Control
	Anaheim	San Francisco	Boston	Milwaukee
"In deciding to buy your property, did you think of the purchase as an investment?"	(N = 238)	(N = 199)	(N = 200)	(N = 243)
"It was a major consideration"	56.3	63.8	48.0	44.0
"In part"	40.3	31.7	45.0	45.7
"Not at all"	4.2	4.5	7.0	10.3
"Why did you buy the home that you did?"	(N = 238)	(N = 199)	(N = 199)	(N = 246)
"Strictly for investment purposes"	19.8	37.2	15.6	18.7
"Buying a home in _____ today involves:"	(N = 237)	(N = 192)	(N = 197)	(N = 237)
"A great deal of risk"	3.4	4.2	5.1	5.9
"Some risk"	33.3	40.1	57.9	64.6
"Little or no risk"	63.3	55.7	37.1	29.5

of the four cities thought that the housing market involved a great deal of risk. Even in Boston, where newspapers have been openly speculating about the possibility of a crash, 37.1% said that buying a home involves little or no risk. The degree of risk perceived is clearly lowest in the boom markets. Rising prices seem to dampen fears, and that may well fuel the boom. In Anaheim a full 63.3% said that their purchase was essentially risk-free.

It is important to keep in mind from the outset that the sample is a sample of actual *home buyers*. That is, the people who were surveyed were the ones who went out and bought homes in May. It can be assumed that they would have significantly higher expectations than the general population of *potential* home buyers. In addition, they are likely to have a lower perception of risk than the general population of potential buyers. We did not sample, and indeed could not have sampled, those who decided not to buy because they were worried about future losses and risks.

Table 24.7 presents responses to a number of questions designed to probe the actual price expectations of buyers. First, virtually every buyer in our California cities and the vast majority of buyers in Boston and Milwaukee believe that prices will rise. As you would expect, those in the

Table 24.7
Current price expectations (% of responses—except as indicated)

Question	Boom markets		Post-boom	Control
	Anaheim	San Francisco	Boston	Milwaukee
"Do you think that housing prices in the _____ area will increase or decrease over the next several years?"	(N = 240)	(N = 199)	(N = 194)	(N = 233)
"Increase"	98.3	99.0	90.2	87.1
"Decrease"	1.7	1.0	9.8	12.9
"How much of a change do you expect there to be in the value of your home over the next 12 months?"	(N = 217)	(N = 185)	(N = 176)	(N = 217)
Mean %	15.3	13.5	7.4	6.1
(Standard error)	(.8)	(.6)	(.6)	(.5)
"*On average* over the next 10 years, how much do you expect the value of your property to change each year?"	(N = 208)	(N = 181)	(N = 177)	(N = 211)
Mean %	14.3	14.8	8.7	7.3
(Standard error)	(1.2)	(1.4)	(.6)	(.5)
"Which of the following best describes the trend in home prices in the _____ area since January 1988?"	(N = 239)	(N = 196)	(N = 198)	(N = 230)
"Rising rapidly"	90.8	83.7	3.0	8.7
"Rising slowly"	8.8	12.8	34.3	53.0
"Not changing"	.4	3.1	37.4	23.9
"Falling slowly"	0	.5	22.2	11.7
"Falling rapidly"	0	0	3.0	2.6
"It's a good time to buy because housing prices are likely to rise in the future"	(N = 206)	(N = 180)	(N = 171)	(N = 210)
"Agree"	93.2	95.0	77.8	84.8
"Disagree"	6.8	5.0	22.2	15.2
"Housing prices are booming Unless I buy now, I won't be able to afford a home later."	(N = 200)	(N = 167)	(N = 169)	(N = 194)
"Agree"	79.5	68.9	40.8	27.8
"Disagree"	20.5	31.1	59.2	72.2

Table 24.7 (continued)

| Question | Boom markets | | Post-boom | Control |
	Anaheim	San Francisco	Boston	Milwaukee
"There has been a good deal of excitement surrounding recent housing price changes. I sometimes think that I may have been influenced by it."	($N = 230$)	($N = 191$)	($N = 181$)	($N = 233$)
"Yes"	54.3	56.5	45.3	21.5
"No"	45.7	43.5	54.7	78.5
"In conversations with friends and associates over the last few months, conditions in the housing market were discussed."	($N = 238$)	($N = 195$)	($N = 198$)	($N = 235$)
"Frequently"	52.9	49.7	30.3	20.0
"Sometimes"	38.2	39.0	55.1	50.2
"Seldom"	8.0	9.7	12.1	25.1
"Never"	.8	1.5	2.5	4.7

boom cities are more optimistic than those in Boston and Milwaukee. Of 440 respondents from California, only two said prices were falling and five thought prices were not changing.

When asked how much they thought that their property would appreciate over the next 12 months and over the next 10 years, the respondents' answers were enormously varied. There were significant modes at 5, 10, and 15% in all four cities for both questions. In California, there were significant modes at 10, 15, and 20%. The average expected annual increase for buyers in California was in the 15% range, while for Milwaukee and Boston, the figures were roughly half as high.

Three questions probed whether expected price increases actually influenced the decisions to buy. The answer seems to be an overwhelming yes. Even in Boston, 77.8% reported that it was a good time to buy because prices were likely to rise in the future. For Milwaukee the figure was 84.8%, while it was well over 90% in both California cities. At least one-quarter of the buyers in all markets and at least two-thirds of California buyers expressed a fear of being unable to afford to buy a home in the future. Over half of the buyers in the boom cities worried that they might have been influenced by the excitement surrounding recent housing price movements.

Table 24.8
Popular themes mentioned in interpreting recent price changes (% of all tabulated questionnaires, by city)

| Question[a] | Boom markets | | Post-boom | Control |
	Anaheim	San Francisco	Boston	Milwaukee

"What do you think explains recent changes in home prices in _____? What ultimately is behind what's going on?"

"Was there any event (or events) in the last two years that you think changed the trend in home prices?"

References to fundamentals

National

	Anaheim	San Francisco	Boston	Milwaukee
Interest rate changes	31.7	39.5	24.5	27.0
Stock market crash	1.7	2.1	25.0	2.0
Demographics—baby boom	1.3	5.1	4.0	1.2
Tax law changes	1.3	4.1	3.0	2.0
Other national economic changes	1.7	5.1	8.5	2.9

Regional

	Anaheim	San Francisco	Boston	Milwaukee
Region is a good place to live	16.7	17.9	6.0	2.4
Immigration or population change	20.4	8.2	11.0	2.4
Asian investors	2.9	27.2	0	0
Asian immigrants	2.1	13.8	.5	0
Income growth	2.5	1.5	2.0	1.2
Anti-growth legislation	10.8	3.1	0	0
Not enough land	7.5	18.5	2.0	.4
Local taxes	2.9	0	4.0	9.8
Increasing black population	.4	0	0	6.6
Rental rates and vacancies	.8	2.6	6.5	2.0
Traffic congestion	3.8	7.2	0	0
Local economy—general	25.4	4.6	29.5	18.4

	Anaheim	San Francisco	Boston	Milwaukee
Psychology of the housing markets[b]	5.4	7.1	18.0	.8
Quantitative evidence[c]	0	0	0	0
No answer	15.8	17.9	20.0	18.4

Table 24.8 (continued)

a. To tabulate these two open-ended questions, 60 questionnaires from each of two cities, Anaheim and San Francisco, were independently coded by two coders. In addition, 60 questionnaires from the Boston sample were coded by three coders. Intercoder reliability was tested by calculating the simple correlation coefficient between the raw number of responses in each category across coders. The correlation for Anaheim was .986 and for San Francisco .969. For Boston, three coefficients could be calculated: .953, .976, and .985. For cities used in the reliability test, the final score in each category is the simple average across coders. The remaining questionnaires were coded by just one coder.

b. Any references to panic, frenzy, greed, apathy, foolishness, excessive optimism, excessive pessimism, or other such factors were coded in this category.

c. Coders were asked to look for any reference at all to any numbers relevant to future supply or demand for housing or to any professional forecast of supply or demand. The numbers need not have been presented, so long as the respondent seemed to be referring to such numbers.

Finally, the enthusiasm expressed in the boom cities seems to have a social basis. There is significantly more discussion among friends and associates in the California markets surveyed.

Interpretations of Booms

A number of specific questions were designed to probe people's interpretations of price movements and possible triggers that changed their opinions. It is critical to distinguish between mob psychology, excessive optimism, and a situation in which a solid reason to expect price increases exists. Since most people expressed a strong investment motive, one would assume significant knowledge of underlying market fundamentals. The efficient markets hypothesis assumes that asset buyers make rational decisions based on all available information and based on a consistent model of underlying market forces.

The survey reveals little real knowledge of or agreement about the underlying causes of price movements. Rather than citing any concrete evidence, people retreat into clichés and images. Table 24.8 presents a tabulation of two important open-ended questions. Respondents were asked to explain recent price changes and also to report on any specific events that changed the trend in prices. Nearly all respondents read these questions to be asking for the same information, so we tabulated them together.

In all four cities, interest rate changes are cited as a major factor. First of all, interest rates are virtually identical everywhere, and housing prices have been relatively stable in the regions between the coasts. Second, while there has been some recent movement upwards in interest rates, forecasters are hardly unanimous in their predictions about future movements. Finally, housing price movements in Boston and Milwaukee have been dramatically different from price movements in California. It is hard to understand how price changes in all four cities can be driven by interest rates.

Second in overall frequency were general comments about the local economy, such as "strong local economy" or "growing regional economy." None of these references cited any specific evidence of such strength or any detail about its character. It may be that further probing was needed to expose more specifics, but since there was plenty of space to write on the questionnaire we must take the responses at face value.

The responses to questions in this section leave the strong impression that people look to observed price movements to form their expectations and then look around for a logic to explain and reinforce their beliefs: "It's a nice place to live"; "Asians are buying up our land"; "The economy is strong." Irrelevant stories that make a vivid impression tend to be cited: "There is just too much traffic around here."

Among the most popular clichés were "The region is a good place to live" and "There is not enough land." Neither of these is news and neither could explain a sudden boom. We also asked *explicitly* whether the boom was due to the area's being a desirable place to live, and whether the real problem was that there was not enough land available (table 24.9). (We asked these questions because we had observed in pretesting telephone interviews that people in boom cities tended to say this.) Respondents in boom cities very largely answered yes to these questions. We were careful to ask the open-ended questions at the beginning of the questionnaire and the explicit ones at the end to ensure that we did not suggest answers. It should be noted, moreover, that it is one of the strengths of our method that the same questionnaire was distributed in the different cities. Very few people mentioned these clichés in Milwaukee.

Most participants in housing markets do not attribute market events to the psychology of other investors. We see from table 24.8 that "psychology of the market" was mentioned by housing market participants in fewer than 10% of the responses, except for Boston, where the figure was 18%. We also asked explicitly whether respondents preferred to describe their own theory about recent trends as one about psychology or one about economic fundamentals (table 24.9). In all four cities fewer than a quarter picked psychology. This is also consistent with evidence in Pound and Shiller [1987] about institutional investors in corporate stocks, most of whom thought that prices were driven by fundamentals, even in a stock whose price had boomed and had high price-earnings ratios. However, a similar question was put to investors right after the stock market crash of October 1987, and the answers were quite different. About two-thirds of both

Table 24.9
Buyers' Interpretations of recent events (% of responses)

| Question | Boom markets | | Post-boom | Control |
	Anaheim	San Francisco	Boston	Milwaukee
"Housing prices have boomed in _____ because lots of people want to live here."	(N = 210)	(N = 178)	(N = 181)	(N = 193)
"Agree"	98.6	93.3	69.6	16.1
"Disagree"	1.4	6.7	30.4	83.9
"The real problem in _____ is that there is just not enough land available."	(N = 197)	(N = 174)	(N = 168)	(N = 192)
"Agree"	52.8	83.9	54.2	17.2
"Disagree"	47.2	16.1	45.8	82.8
"When there is simply not enough housing available, price becomes unimportant."	(N = 197)	(N = 165)	(N = 171)	(N = 193)
"Agree"	34.0	46.0	26.9	20.7
"Disagree"	66.0	59.4	73.1	79.3
"Which of the following better describes your theory about recent trends in home prices in _____?"	(N = 226)	(N = 180)	(N = 188)	(N = 215)
"It is a theory about the psychology of home buyers and sellers."	11.9	16.7	21.3	10.7
"It is a theory about economic or demographic conditions, such as population changes, changes in interest rates or employment."	88.1	83.3	78.7	89.3
"In a hot real estate market, sellers often get more than one offer on the day they list their property. Some are even over the asking price. There are also stories about people waiting in line to make offers. Which is the best explanation?"	(N = 210)	(N = 177)	(N = 176)	(N = 211)
"There is panic buying, and price becomes irrelevant."	73.3	71.2	61.4	34.6
"Asking prices have adjusted slowly or sluggishly to increasing demand."	26.7	28.8	38.6	65.4

individual and institutional investors in the United States thought the crash was due to market psychology [Shiller, 1987, and chapter 23], while three-quarters of Japanese institutional investors thought the crash was due to market psychology [Shiller, Konya, and Tsutsui, 1988]. Perhaps popular boom theories emphasize fundamentals as causes of upward price movements (despite the fact that irrational behvior is thought to be present), while sudden crashes are thought to be due to panic.

An especially striking feature of the coded answers in table 24.8 is that not a single respondent referred to explicit quantitative evidence relevant to future supply of or demand for housing. We did not ask explicitly for such evidence, but among 886 responses one would expect some to volunteer such evidence if it figured prominently in their views.

Excess Demand and Upward Rigidity in Asking Prices

In boom cities, newspaper accounts feature stories of homes that sold well above the asking price, interpreting this phenomenon as evidence of investor frenzy or panic. Recall the examples of such newspaper accounts from our discussion of the current boom in California. The view that excess demand is evidence of investor panic is also very popular among market participants in the boom cities, as the last question in table 24.9 indicates. It is likely that the local media had some success in spreading the notion that prices above asking prices are evidence of panic, since this view was much more common in the boom cities than in the control city.

The news media seem to exaggerate the importance of such sales above asking price. In fact, houses selling above the asking price were reported in all our cities (table 24.1), so the fact that a newspaper reporter can find examples is not much evidence of a boom market. The incidence of such sales was higher in the boom cities than in our control city, but was still only about 6–10%. The prevalence of such examples is better at discriminating between boom and post-boom cities; fewer than 1% of houses in our sample sold above the asking price in Boston.

We also sought evidence why some sellers did not raise their asking price more (table 24.10). Those who thought they might have asked more often agreed that notions of intrinsic worth or fairness played a role in their decision.

Real estate agents in the boom cities told us that, because of the excess demand situation, they found it profitable to spend more time soliciting listings, rather than showing houses to potential buyers. The responses to the last question in table 24.10 largely confirm that real estate agents were behaving as this would suggest.

Table 24.10
Upward rigidity in asking prices (% of responses—except as indicated)

Question	Boom markets		Post-boom	Control
	Anaheim	San Francisco	Boston	Milwaukee
"Did you finally settle on a price that was:"	(N = 237)	(N = 194)	(N = 200)	(N = 242)
"Above the asking price"	6.3	9.8	.5	3.3
"Equal to the asking price"	38.0	26.8	23.5	22.7
"Below the asking price"	55.7	63.4	76.0	74.0
"If you had asked 5 to 10 percent more for your property, what would the likely outcome have been?"	(N = 89)	(N = 64)	(N = 61)	(N = 43)
"It wouldn't have sold."	21.3	23.4	31.1	32.5
"It would have sold, but it would have taken much more time."	44.9	46.9	54.1	37.2
"If buyers had to pay that much, they might not be able to obtain financing (a buyer cannot obtain financing unless an appraiser confirms the worth of the property)."	7.9	9.4	0	9.3
"It probably would have sold almost as quickly	24.7	17.2	11.5	16.3
"Other"	1.1	3.1	3.3	4.7
"If you answered that it would have sold almost as quickly, which of the following (you can check more than one) explains why you didn't set the price higher?"[a]	(N = 37)	(N = 22)	(N = 26)	(N = 16)
"The property simply wasn't worth that much."	32.4	27.3	38.5	25.0
"It wouldn't have been fair to set it that high; given what I paid for it. I was already getting enough for it."	16.2	22.7	15.4	31.3
"I simply made a mistake or got bad advice: I should have asked more."	21.6	18.2	19.2	25.0
"Other"	29.7	31.8	26.9	18.8

Table 24.10 (continued)

Question	Boom markets		Post-boom	Control
	Anaheim	San Francisco	Boston	Milwaukee
"In the six months prior to the time you first listed the property, did you receive any unsolicited calls from a real estate agent or any one else about the possibility of selling your house?"	(N = 89)	(N = 61)	(N = 62)	(N = 48)
"Yes"	71.9	59.0	38.7	52.1
"No"	28.1	41.0	61.3	47.9
Approximate number of calls				
Mean	8.7	5.0	3.9	2.7
(Standard error)	(1.2)	(.3)	(.4)	(.2)

a. Some respondents answered this question even though they had not replied "It probably would have sold almost as quickly" to the previous question. All the responses to this question have been included in the tabulation.

Excess Supply and Downward Rigidity in Asking Prices

A third important aspect of behavior in housing markets is seller behavior in post-boom markets or generally soft markets. There is a good deal of worry that these booms will end, as most stock market booms end, in collapse. If, indeed, what we are observing in Orange County and San Francisco can appropriately be called "bubbles," will they not inevitably burst?

One theory holds that housing prices are downwardly rigid, and that this rigidity is likely to prevent major real estate collapses in the absence of a general economic collapse. Significant reasons exist to predict such rigidity. First, the housing market is very different from the stock market. In the stock market, people can exit their equity positions quickly and almost without cost. The analog of a Treasury Bill in the housing market is moving to a rental unit. For those with considerable equity this would mean paying large capital gains taxes and a 6% brokerage fee as well as putting up with the aggravation of a move. Thus, the transactions costs are very large.

Second, investors have an alleged psychological disposition to sell their winning investments (to have the satisfaction of getting their money), and to hold on to losing investments (to avoid the pain of regret; see Shefrin and Statman, 1985). Ferris, Haugen, and Makhija (1988) have found evidence for this "disposition effect" by documentation that the volume of trade in stock whose value has declined is lower than in stocks that have increased in value.

In addition, the popular impression is that past experience has shown that waiting may pay off, perhaps the best example being California in 1981. After four years of boom, housing prices stopped rising. While it is clear that some people lost money in the real estate market, many simply decided to wait it out; the number of transactions dropped to very low levels, and median price never fell in nominal terms. Since 1983, prices have again been on the rise.

Table 24.11 presents evidence on seller behavior in markets with excess supply. All respondents were asked to react to the first statement on table 24.11. Nearly 70% of respondents in California agreed with the statement that the best strategy in a slow market is to hold on until you get what you want. In Boston and Milwaukee more than half agree.

The remaining questions were asked of those who had sold or tried to sell a property immediately prior to buying the one that they bought. This relatively small sample is likely to be a biased sample of all sellers. Recall that these sellers are the ones who actually bought new homes. If a seller was unable to sell her house, did not lower her price, and ultimately decided not to buy a new house, she is not in our sample. Thus, those who were at least somewhat flexible are likely to be over-represented.

Buyers who had sold or tried to sell a home prior to buying their present unit were 39.6% of the total respondents in Anaheim, 32.6% in San Francisco, 32.8% in Boston, and 21.3% in Milwaukee. Since the vast majority of this group (over 90% in all cities except Milwaukee, where the figure was 84.3%) had actually sold their properties, the only way to probe the issue was with a hypothetical question. We asked, "If you had not been able to sell your property for the price that you received, what would you have done?" Only a very small fraction said that they would lower their price until they found a buyer—the market-clearing solution.

A significant percentage (between 20 and 40%) in each city said that they would lower the price step by step, looking for a buyer. However, when probed further, more than three-quarters in all cities reported that there was a limit to how far they would drop the price: surprisingly the figures were highest in Boston and Milwaukee, 93.1% and 87.5%, respectively. Most of them seemed to have some knowledge of what comparable homes had sold for, and they did not want to sell for less.

The "other" category in the second question reported in table 24.1 reveals two additional sources of downward rigidity. Several respondents mentioned that their employer had a buy-out program for employees who

Table 24.11
Excess supply and downward rigidity in asking prices (% of responses)

Question[a]	Boom markets		Post-boom	Control
	Anaheim	San Francisco	Boston	Milwaukee
"Since housing prices are unlikely to drop very much, the best strategy in a slow market is to hold on until you get what you want for a property."	(N = 174)	(N = 148)	(N = 160)	(N = 180)
"Agree"	69.0	69.6	57.5	50.6
"Disagree"	31.0	30.4	42.5	49.4
"If you had not been able to sell your property for the price that you received, what would you have done?"	(N = 88)	(N = 62)	(N = 61)	(N = 43)
"Left the price the same and waited for a buyer, knowing full well that it might take a long time"	42.0	38.7	32.8	32.6
"Lowered the price step by step hoping to find a buyer"	20.5	38.7	42.6	20.9
"Lowered the price till I found a buyer"	4.5	3.2	4.9	7.0
"Taken the house off the market"	18.2	17.7	11.5	27.9
"Other"[a]	14.8	1.6	8.2	11.6
"If you responded that you *would have* lowered your price, is there a limit to how far you would have gone if the property still hadn't sold?"[b]	(N = 33)	(N = 38)	(N = 29)	(N = 16)
"Yes"	81.8	78.9	93.1	87.5
"If you answered yes to the above question, can you say how you arrived at that limit?" (Open-ended)	(N = 24)	(N = 28)	(N = 21)	(N = 10)
"Based on what I paid"	29.2	21.4	19.0	30.0
"Based on price of another home that I want to buy"	33.3	35.7	38.1	20.0
"Based on what other similar homes have sold for"	37.5	42.9	42.9	50.0

Table 24.11 (continued)

Question[a]	Boom markets		Post-boom	Control
	Anaheim	San Francisco	Boston	Milwaukee
"If your property did not sell presumably it would have if you had lowered your asking price more. If you considered doing so but decided not to, can you say why?	(N = 19)	(N = 18)	(N = 13)	(N = 13)
"My house is worth more than people seem to be willing to pay right now"	15.8	11.1	7.7	38.5
"I can't afford to sell at a lower price"	26.3	33.3	23.1	15.4
"By holding out, I will be able to get more later"	31.6	44.4	15.4	7.6
"Other"[c]	26.3	11.1	53.9	38.5

a. The most frequently mentioned "other" categories were company buy-out provisions and that sellers would rent the property out.
b. Includes responses by those who did not answer the previous question by saying they would have lowered the price.
c. Many of the "other" responses made reference to time, as in "I was in no hurry," "I was not anxious about selling," or "I had no need to sell."

could not sell. What they really meant was a buy-out plan for employees who could not sell at the price that they wanted to get. A number of others reported simply renting out their first property.

Finally, the small group of sellers who had not sold their properties were asked why they did not simply drop their price. Some of the same notions of fairness or intrinsic worth that played a role in the upward rigidity studies above appear to play a role here. Others said they could not afford to sell, and still others expressed optimism that they could sell at a higher price eventually.

24.3 Interpretations and Conjectures

What have we learned about sources of the booms that from time to time appear in local housing markets? Evidence in this chapter supports the view that the suddenness of booms has to be understood in terms of investor reactions to one another, to past price increases, or to other evidence of boom markets, rather than to economic fundamentals. Of course, we did not look at data on fundamentals in this chapter, and the paper that one of us did on the impact of fundamentals on city housing prices [Case, 1986] is certainly not the last word on the subject. But we have in this chapter provided some evidence that investors in housing markets do not know fundamentals. They tend to interpret events in terms of hearsay, clichés, and casual observations. Moreover, we have seen that investment motivations are high on their list of incentives, and that home buyers in booms expect still more appreciation of housing prices and are worried about being priced out of the housing market in the future. It is certainly plausible that expectations heavily influence the prices people are willing to pay in these markets. Because these expectations do not appear to make much sense except as extrapolations of past price changes, we cannot expect price to be rationally determined.

But what *starts* a housing boom; why does it occur in one year and not another? We asked home buyers what they thought was going on, and whether they could name an event that they thought changed the behavior of housing prices. The most popular answer in all cities was a change in interest rates, but interest rates do not *differ* much across cities and so cannot be the explanation of the differing price behavior. Moreover, interest rates were cited as the cause of the boom in California and as the cause of stagnation in Boston. For the most part, respondents did not produce another event. The most plausible-sounding event in Anaheim (proposed antigrowth legislation) was quite different from the most plausible-sounding event in San Francisco (the entrance of Asian investors into the market), and yet the pattern of price changes was similar in the two cities. The events may instead be after-the-fact-rationalizations of the price movements, just as the October 1987 stock market crash was brought up mainly in Boston, where an explanation of a slump was needed.

The trigger is apparently an event or sequence of events not observed by most home buyers. Since the ultimate trigger is not the factor in the minds of investors, it could even be something that was not observed by *any* investors, except through price. For example, demographic change or income growth could cause an intial price increase, to which home buyers reacted. Perhaps home buyers in California in 1987 and 1988 were also more primed to react to a price increase, having heard stories of the boom in the Northeast.

Another puzzle concerns the slowness of the booms: why do booms extend over years, and not accelerate and terminate very quickly? Our survey results offer only marginal help in conjectures regarding this question. The notion expressed by some investors that they were motivated by a sense of intrinsic worth and comparisons with past prices may suggest that there is a psychological resistance to very rapid price increases. It is of course true that there are barriers to professional speculators entering and closing off profit opportunities in the market for single-family homes; that is why we were not surprised to find persistence in price changes in our earlier study of the efficiency of housing prices (Case and Shiller, 1989, and chapter 18). Ordinary individuals, who are not investment professionals, should be expected to take more time before investing. Such action may involve a change in living arrangements, and may well take months or years.

Respondents were somewhat inconsistent in their reporting of their impression that psychological factors were responsible for the booms. We saw that about half of respondents in boom cities thought they themselves were influenced by the excitement, and that most interpreted houses selling above asking prices as evidence of panic. Yet other evidence in tables 24.8 and 24.9 indicates that most investors do not think that market psychology is the best explanation for booms, citing fundamentals instead. Perhaps we should conclude that social psychology is an important factor in transmission of booms, but that individuals' perceptions of the psychology of others are less so.

Some houses sell above asking price in all cities. Apparently newspapers feature such stories in boom cities because they are perceived as relevant to the big story of area-wide price increases. In a city not experiencing such price increases, such occurrences are more likely to be interpreted as evidence of simple errors in setting the asking price, and are not thought to be particularly newsworthy.

If such occurrences reflect mistakes by a small minority of sellers in setting the asking price, then it is to be expected that such errors will occur more frequently in cities that are currently experiencing increases if some sellers are slow to adjust their price. Perhaps occurrences of sales price above asking price ought to be interpreted as noting more than that. On the other hand, some of the answers reported in table 24.10 suggest that notions of a fair price or of intrinsic worth may also play a role in the sluggishness of price changes. Kahneman, Knetsch, and Thaler [1986] have documented the importance of notions of fairness in many economic decisions. The same notions of fairness arise also in answers to questions as to why those who had trouble selling houses did not cut their prices more.

Evidence of price rigidity appeared to be more significant in falling markets than in rising markets. Only about 5% of the respondents in the post-boom city Boston who had not sold their former property said they would continue to lower the price until a buyer was found. One possible explanation of the downward rigidity in housing prices comes from the prospect theory of Kahneman and Tversky [1979]. In their theory, losses and gains are viewed very differently, and the point from which individuals measure whether they have made a gain or loss may be determined by the frame of reference that attracts their attention.[3]

The regret theories of Bell [1982] and Loomis and Sugden [1982] have similar implications. However, as we saw above, other interpretations of the rigidity are possible. Popular impressions as to the likely course of future prices are also at work here. The fact that a high a proportion of home buyers in all cities thought there was little risk in the housing market reflects a popular view that one cannot lose in this market; houses are always a safe investment, so long as one holds out long enough.

Another reason chosen by those who could not sell was that "I can't afford to sell at a lower price." Since all of the respondent sellers had subsequently bought another house, it is likely that an important factor in this judgment was the price of the other house they bought. If all real estate prices are too high, one may find it difficult to cut the asking price on one's own house, since one cannot coordinate this price cut with the seller of the house one wishes to purchase. Part of the problem in downward rigidity of housing prices may then be a coordination problem of the kind that economic theorists have stressed in other contexts.[4] If we could all agree at once to cut the prices of our houses, we might all be happy, but I can't be the first one to cut.

All these reasons for downward rigidity in prices may be interrelated. If the coordination problem prevents prices from falling, this creates an impression that they should not fall and therefore an impression that it pays us to hold out; this impression heightens the regret experienced if one cuts price.

Conclusions

All of this suggests a market for residential real estate that is very different from the one traditionally discussed and modeled in the literature. In a fully rational market, prices would be driven by fundamentals such as income, demographic changes, and national economic conditions. Investors in such a market would use all available information on potential changes in fundamentals to forecast future price movements, making prolonged price swings impossible and profit opportunities rare. Resources including access to popular regions would be efficiently allocated.

The survey results presented here and actual price behavior together sketch a very different picture. While the evidence is circumstantial, and we can only offer conjectures, we see a market driven largely by expectations. People seem to form their expectations on the basis of past price movements rather than any knowledge of fundamentals. This increases the likelihood that price booms will persist as home buyers in essence become destabilizing speculators.

We also found significant evidence that in the absence of a severe economic decline, housing prices are inflexible downward. Combined with upward volatility, this inflexibility has produced a ratcheting effect in some boom cities with complicated distributional consequences, as owners gain at the expense of nonowners at all levels of income.

At this point we are not prepared to offer or even speculate about possible policy conclusions. We only hope that further research will help shed more light on this still puzzling market.

Notes

1. See Dreier, Schwartz, and Greiner [1988]

2. The Boston *Globe*, February 17, 1988, p. B1

3. Kahneman and Tversky write that "this analysis suggests that a person who has not made peace with his losses is likely to accept gambles that would be unacceptable to him otherwise" [1979, p. 287]

4. For example, Keynes's theory of the downward rigidity in wages in a depression was that "since there is, as a rule, no means of securing a simultaneous and equal reduction of money-wages in all industries, it is in the interest of all workers to resist a reduction in their own particular case" [1936, p. 264]

References

Bell, David E. 1982. "Regret in Decision Making Under Uncertainty," *Operations Research* 9: 961–981.

Case, Karl E. 1986. "The Market for Single-Family Homes in Boston," *New England Economic Review* 79: 125–137.

Case, Karl E., and Robert J. Shiller. 1987. "Prices of Single-Family Homes Since 1970: New Indexes for Four Cities, *"New England Economic Review*, September, 46–56.

Case, Karl E., and Robert J. Shiller. 1989. "The Efficiency of the Market for Single-Family Homes," *The American Economic Review*, forthcoming.

Dillman, Don A. 1978. *Mail and Telephone Surveys: The Total Design Method*. John Wiley and Sons.

Dreier, Peter, David C. Schwartz, and Ann Greiner. 1988. "What Every Business Can Do About Housing," *Harvard Business Review*, 52–61.

Ferris, Stephen P., Robert A. Haugen, and Anil K. Makhija. 1988. "Predicting Contemporary Volume with Historic Volume at Differential Price Levels—Evidence Supporting the Disposition Effect," *The Journal of Finance*, 677–679.

Kahneman, Daniel, Jack L. Knetsch, and Richard Thaler. 1986. "Fairness as a Constraint on Profit Seeking: Entitlements in the Market," *The American Economic Review* 76:728–741.

Kahneman, Daniel, and Amos Tversky. 1979. "Prospect Theory: An Analysis of Decision Under Risk," *Econometrica* 47:236–291.

Keynes, John Maynard. 1936. *The General Theory of Employment, Interest and Money*. New York: Harbinger, 1964 edition.

Loomis, Graham, and Robert Sugden. 1982. "Regret Theory: An Alternative Theory of Rational Choice Under Uncertainty," *The Economic Journal* 92:824.

Pound, John, and Robert J. Shiller. 1987. "Are Institutional investors Speculators?" *Journal of Portfolio Management*, Spring, 46–52.

Shefrin, Hersh, and Meir Statman. 1985. "The Disposition to Sell Winners Too Early and Ride Losers Too Long: Theory and Evidence," *The Journal of Finance* 40:777–790.

Shiller, Robert J. 1987. "Investor Behavior in the October 1987 Stock Market Crash: Survey Evidence." National Bureau of Economic Research Working Paper No. 2446.

Shiller, Robert J., Fumiko Konya, and Yoshiro Tsutsui. 1988. "Investor Behavior in the October 1987 Stock Market Crash: The Case of Japan." National Bureau of Economic Research Working Paper no. 2684.

25   Concluding Notes

The mob is easily led and may be moved by the smallest force, so that its agitations have a wonderful resemblance to those of the sea.
Publius Cornelius Scipio[1]

Speculative prices tend to be mixtures of popular opinion and of fact about fundamental value. Price movements can be reflective of opinion changes that are generated when a popular model causes people to overreact to some economic indicator. We saw evidence of this in large movements in stock prices in connection with swings in dividends or earnings. Or price movements can come from opinion changes that are generated among investors themselves, through their communications or through their interaction via price. We saw evidence of this in the stock market crash of 1987 and the housing booms of the 1980s that were studied above. Yet again, price movements can come about because of genuine information about future dividends or earnings. We saw evidence of this in the study of the bond market above. Moreover, if stock prices were set in accordance with efficient markets models they would be fairly volatile, but not as volatile as we actually observe.[2]

25.1   Opinion Change and Market Inefficiency

Scipio's analogy to the sea seems apt in describing the opinion changes in speculative markets. The stock market crash and the real estate booms that were studied above appear to have no more a sensible, discernible trigger than do the storms at sea that surprised ancient sailors. People interact with each other, and winds interact with each other, creating complicated dynamics. What happens today depends on what happened yesterday, which in turn depends on what happened the day before, and so on. What we see today is the accumulation, through these dynamics, of past shocks, any one of which may appear inconsequential. The lesson may be that we can learn more constructively about the dynamics of speculative markets than we can about the ultimate causes.

But it cannot be easy for everyone to make speculative profits by trading against these dynamics; not everyone can be rich. By implication, then, when there are predictable forces tending to move prices, the information about these must be already incorporated in the price. There is no denying that this simple logic has substantial merit, and ought to be something drilled into beginning students of finance as lesson number one.

The great risk has always been overinterpreting the existing evidence of market efficiency. The efficient markets theory is an extreme view that pops up naturally again and again to people looking for simple explanations of speculative markets. It is not, as some finance textbooks imply, basically a sophisticated theory that came from the University of Chicago in the 1960s. It is actually a very old theory.[3]

The efficient markets model may have exaggerated importance in many people's minds just because no concrete alternative, no other well-defined story, is in mind. I have tried here to offer some such concrete alternatives. In chapter 1 I showed a simple model [expressed formally by equation (3)] representing price movements as due to information about both future dividends as well as due to information about future demands by "ordinary investors." The model illustrated that even though changing behaviors of these ordinary investors, as their popular models dictate, are part of speculative price movements, prices do incorporate information about future dividends. The presence of some smart money serves not to eliminate the effect of fashion or opinion change on price, but to reduce the forecastability of price changes and to make price tend to anticipate opinion changes as well as changes in cash flows.

Other formal models were discussed in chapter 22: a simple feedback model, in which price changes respond to past price changes, and a contagion model, in which people interact directly with each other. These models, too, are consistent with the approximate random walk behavior of speculative prices.

These simple models are broadly illustrative of the kind of findings that were reported for the speculative markets studied. In none of the three markets studied—the stock market, bond market, and housing market—was there evidence that short-run price changes were very forecastable. The "random walk" model had an element of truth for all three. And yet the price movements did not generally link up well with any information about fundamentals. The survey evidence of investors during the 1987 stock market crash and of home buyers during recent real estate booms shows a broad tendency to take action in investing based on loosely intuitive popular models and as a reaction to events caused by other investors' actions.

25.2 The Importance of Popular Models

Popular accounts of the importance of market psychology frequently use words like "euphoric" of "panicky" to describe investors.

But the broadly based failures in thinking are not wholly attributable to such spontaneous capriciousness of investors. They instead reflect lack of systematic attention and automatic reliance on popular or intuitive models of the economy.

The surveys in chapters 23 and 24 of the stock market crash and real estate booms found that people willingly admitted to anxieties as well as to influence by the excitement of others. But that does not mean that their judgment was particularly bad at that time; it may mean the opposite— that they were unusually attentive and careful. The views that most people express at any one time, even at the time of a financial "panic," are usually not palpably unreasonable. More likely, the criticism one would make is that they are vague, impressionistic, and cliché ridden.

The periods just before the crashes of 1929 and 1987 are often described, after the fact, as periods of excessive investor optimism or euphoria. But it would not have been at all easy to make an airtight case in either 1929 or 1987 that the market was overpriced. Indeed, Irving Fisher's book [1930] (which must to a large extent have been thought out before the crash, since it went to press only two months later) makes a very sophisticated and cogent argument that the market was not overpriced. Fisher had one of the highest academic reputations at the time; no one could be faulted for valuing his interpretations. But the ultimate evaluation of his arguments relies on some intuitive judgment. There is no objective way to evaluate Fisher's claims that the merger movement of the 1920s would yield future economies of scale, or that new scientific management methods would spur substantial earnings growth in the 1930s. The fault among investors appears to be inconstancy, to be believing him in 1929 and believing the doom-sayers shortly thereafter. Despite great interest in financial and real estate pages in the newspaper, people do not seem to come away with any knowledge of fact that would be the basis for constant judgment about basic issues of market trend. The fault among many investors is being too willing to change beliefs between one expert and another. Such inconstancy of judgment among large numbers of people has been studied by scholars in the field of the sociology of knowledge, such as Karl Mannheim, Emile Durkheim, Maurice Halbwachs, and Pitirim Sorokin.

This kind of inconstancy may result in the kind of excess volatility that appeared so striking for the aggregate stock market in part II above. But, since the inconstancy is due to the popular models and a failure to focus attention, it may not play any role where popular attention has not been attracted. Thus, for example, it was found that principal components other than the first do not appear to be as excessively volatile: people were not so sharply changing their opinions about the spread between the industrials index and the utilities index as they were about the level of either. The media do show less attention to this spread relative to the levels.

Excess volatility is more likely to be generated by a relatively small number of noise factors affecting large groupings of stocks than by a large number of independent shocks striking each individual stock differently. If the latter were the case, a portfolio with a large number of temporarily underpriced stocks would tend consistently to outperform the market, violating the Ross [1976] arbitrage pricing theory. The composition of the large groupings of stocks affected by the respective noise factors is determined by popular models.

Popular models are unobserved by researchers who look only at data on prices and other objective factors. The importance of these models may even be missed by the very people who are carriers of the models, who may feel that they are only responding objectively to the factual situation. The risk social scientists incur in ignoring these models is of interpreting observed behavior as reflecting generalizable patterns of basic human behavior. A very old example will serve to illustrate. In the early days of research on hypnotism, starting with the work of the Marquis de Puysegur in the late eighteenth century, experimental evidence was produced again and again that hypnotism has something to do with magnetism. It was only later discovered, with the work of James Braid in the mid-nineteenth century, that subjects were responding to magnets because they had a popular model, obtained either from the broad public perceptions of hypnotism or from suggestions of the experimenter according to which they should do so.

25.3 Theoretical Models of Speculative Markets

All this suggests that perhaps theoretical models in finance should routinely represent both ordinary investors (or noise traders) and smart money. I think there is a resistance among theorists to such models, perhaps from a feeling that the division of investors into two distinct categories is not a solid construct on which to base theorizing. The "rational" and "irrational" forces are not likely to be cleanly divided between separate groups of investors. Casual evidence suggests that, if anything, all investors have some aspects of "smart money" and of "noise" in their behavior. But how to model such half rational behavior? That is why I think that we must base further modeling efforts on observations of human behavior and on the popular models that inform their behavior. More solid constructs for modeling may come from such research. We cannot anticipate the form such constructs may take.

Still, the simple division of investors into two groups is continuing to yield some important insights. Recent work by De Long, Shleifer, Summers, and Waldman [1987] has made some useful points. They made use of the fact that the wealthiest segment of society may *not* be the smart money; there is instead some tendency for the wealthiest segment of society to be the survivors among those who took foolish risks. Their equilibrium model makes a number of useful points about the origin of the risk premium in returns, the allocation of capital, and regulatory policy. Campbell and Kyle [1988] have shown how we can sensibly get estimates of the importance of noise trading in financial markets.

25.4 Basic Principles for Future Research

The juxtaposition in this book of the study of both rational expectations models and popular models is an effort to deal creatively with a tension in the social sciences over fundamentally different methods of approach. One approach may be called the quantitative or empiricist approach (characteristic of the study of rational expectations models in this book) and the other an interpretive or hermeneutic approach (characteristic of the study of popular models in this book). The former approach, modeled after the physical sciences, looks for patterns in raw, objectively measured data; in the social sciences these data are measures of the acts of people, not the interpretations they place on these acts. The latter approach instead seeks data on the web of social consciousness and meaning. Rabinow and Sullivan [1979] have argued that the former approach has been given too much emphasis in many social sciences—anthropology, political science, psychology, and sociology—and there has been a movement afoot in those disciplines, under the banner of "interpretive social science," to redress the imbalance. The same argument for economics has been advanced forcefully by Berger [1988].

Ideally, survey research would play an important role in understanding much of human history. If we want to know why people do certain things, it is important to *ask* them why they do them, and careful surveys with substantial sample sizes are the only way to accomplish this carefully. Unfortunately, for most of past history this opportunity has been lost, as there are either no surveys, or surveys that ask the wrong questions.

I like to call this the "hat problem" in research. Why did almost all men wear hats 50 to 100 years ago, even in mild weather, while few men do so today? We know that almost all men used to wear hats, as old photographs of random crowds document. If hats were purely fashion accessories, one would think that a substantial proportion of men would forget to bring their hats along. It is natural to speculate that the demand for hats had to do with health issues, i.e., preventing illness. One might call this a popular model of the origins of illness. But while we can document that some popular hygiene books recommended hats for this reason, the opportunity is lost today to find out for sure the real reason men wore hats. Those alive today from that period could not be trusted to remember accurately. A reason that was probably plain and obvious to just about everyone cannot be observed with any assurance today. We will never know for sure why all those people wore hats, just as we will never know for sure what caused the stock market crash of the 1929.

It is important to collect information directly on the popular models that people have with regard to speculative markets, and on the associated investor behavior. If we wish to understand market psychology, it is not enough just to learn about general principles of social psychology, or about common judgmental errors. Direct evidence on investor behavior can be collected either by using experimental methods or by observing investors in the actual investing environment. Both methods have their advantages and disadvantages.

Experimental methods can create a special situation that is designed by us so that we may learn about some specific behavioral parameters. For example, Vernon Smith, Gerry Suchanek, and Arlington Williams [1988] conducted asset market experiments in which subjects were told the true objective probability distribution of dividends on the assets. Because they knew this, there is no possibility that price movements are due to information about some potential but unobserved windfall or disaster, as was discussed in the context of the U.S. stock market in chapter 4, 5, and 6. Even so, when the subjects began trading with each other, "price bubbles" occurred often. Thus, the experimental design allowed them to show that such price bubbles can arise even when investors know that no potential windfall or disaster is possible.[4]

The disadvantage of experimental methods in economics is that they may not duplicate the actual environment in financial markets well enough to produce the kind of economic behavior that occurs there. Subjects in an experiment may be inclined to set aside their popular models, since they may feel that they are in an unusual situation. This problem can be remedied somewhat by making an experiment that resembles the real world. For example, Andreassen [1987] did experiments in which subjects were asked to respond to actual financial data with associated "news stories." Subjects were allowed to keep the money they earned trading. Still, subjects may not resemble those people who have prepared themselves to act in financial markets. They do not have the personal ego involvement in the investing activity as do those who chose the activity themselves. More important, they may not have familiarity with the popular models that inform the judgment of those in the social nexus of investors in the asset under study.

Observing actual investors in actual investing environments may enable us to learn more about their behavior and about these models. If we question investors about their experiences, we of course encounter the well-known limitations of such methods: Answers may not be accurate and truthful, and in the absence of any controlled experiment we may not be able to judge causality. To exploit the advantages of both experimental and survey methods, both methods should be used.

The prevailing opinion among academic researchers in finance has been that work with either experimental or survey methods cannot be productive. Some research discussed in this book may stand as evidence to the contrary. There would appear to be much work to be done on such data collection, as well as on the development of formal models of the impact of popular models on the economy. If we develop a significant body of knowledge on these matters, we may gain a greater depth of understanding of the historical movements in speculative prices, and the result of such an understanding may even be to help rationalize these prices in the future.

Notes

1. In a speech during the war against Hannibal, Scipio asserted that he could find no sensible reason for the insurrection of some of his own soldiers (quoted in Polybius, *Histories*, XI.29.8).

2. John Campbell and I concluded (see table 8.2) that the standard deviation of stock returns should be between a quarter and a half of what it is—much smaller but still substantial.

3. For example, George Gibson wrote 100 years ago that when "shares become publicly known in an open market, the value which they acquire there may be regarded as the judgment of the best intelligence concerning them," (Gibson [1889], 11).

4. Camerer and Weigelt [1986] also produced bubbles in rather different experiments.

References

Andreassen, Paul B. 1987. "On the Social Psychology of the Stock Market: Aggregate Attributional Effects and the Regressiveness of Prediction," *Journal of Personality and Social Psychology*, 53.

Berger, Lawrence A. 1988. "Interpreting the Crash," reproduced, Department of Finance, University of Iowa.

Camerer, Colin F., and Keith Weigelt. 1986. "Tests for Rational Bubbles in Experimental Markets for Infinitely-Lived Assets," University of Pennsylvania Department of Decision Sciences Working Paper.

Campbell, John Y., and Albert S. Kyle. 1988. "Smart Money, Noise Trading, and Stock Price Behavior," Technical Working Paper No. 71, Cambridge National Bureau of Economic Research.

De Long, J. Bradford, Andrei Shleifer, Lawrence Summers, and Robert J. Waldman. 1987. "The Economic Consequences of Noise Traders," Harvard Institute of Economic Research, Discussion Paper No. 1348.

Fisher, Irving. 1930. *The Stock Market Crash—and After*.

Gibson, George R. 1889. *The Stock Exchanges of London, Paris, and New York*, New York: G. P. Putnam's Sons.

Rabinow, Paul, and William M. Sullivan. 1979. *Interpretive Social Science: A Reader*, Berkeley: University of California Press.

Ross, Stephen A. 1976. "The Arbitrage Theory of Capital Asset Pricing," *Journal of Economic Theory* 13:341–360.

Smith, Vernon L., Gerry L. Suchanek, and Arlington W. Williams. 1988. "Bubbles, Crashes and Endogenous Expectations in Experimental Spot Asset Markets," *Econometrica* 56:1119–1151.

An annual series of January values of the Standard and Poor Composite Stock Price Index starting in 1871 was used as the basis of empirical work in chapters 1, 3, 5, 6, 8, 16, and 21. This series (table 26.1, series 1) was taken from Standard and Poor's Statistical Service *Security Price Index Record*, various issues, from tables entitled "Monthly Stock Price Indexes—Long Term."

The dividend and earnings series that correspond to this stock price series are spliced together from two sources. Starting in 1926, the nominal dividend series are dividends per share, 12 months moving total adjusted to index for the last quarter of the year. Starting in 1926, the nominal earnings series are earnings per share, adjusted to index, 4 quarter total, fourth quarter. These are from a table, entitled "Earnings, Dividends and Price-Earnings Ratios—Quarterly," of Standard and Poor's Statistical Service *Security Price Index Record.*

Standard and Poor's does not publish dividend or earnings series before 1926: however, their source for the Standard and Poor Index before 1926, a volume by Cowles [1939], gives a dividend series corresponding to the index, series $D_a - 1$, pp. 388–389, which I multiplied by the ratio of the series in 1926 to adjust for change in base year.[2]

A problem Cowles faced was absence of earnings data for many of the stocks in the Standard and Poor Composite Index. He thus presented series $P_{EA} - 1$—"prices of stocks for which earnings data are available, all stocks," a series of earnings $E - 1$ on these stocks, and the ratio $R - 1$ of these series, the "earnings-price ratio." The Standard and Poor Composite Earnings series were computed here for years before 1926 as series $R - 1$ (Cowles [1939] pp. 404–405) times the annual average Standard and Poor Composite Index for the year. The spliced dividend and earnings series appear in table 26.1 as series 2 and 3.

The absence of earnings data for some stocks is of some importance for the accuracy of the earnings series. One indication of the potential

Table 26.1
Basic data

Year	Series 1: stock prices, January[a]	Series 2: dividends[b]	Series 3: earnings[b]	Series 4: interest (%)
1871	4.44	0.26	0.40	6.35
1872	4.86	0.30	0.43	7.81
1873	5.11	0.33	0.46	8.35
1874	4.66	0.33	0.46	6.86
1875	4.54	0.30	0.36	4.96
1876	4.46	0.30	0.28	5.33
1877	3.55	0.19	0.30	5.03
1878	3.25	0.18	0.31	4.90
1879	3.58	0.20	0.38	4.25
1880	5.11	0.26	0.49	5.10
1881	6.19	0.32	0.44	4.79
1882	5.92	0.32	0.43	5.26
1883	5.81	0.33	0.40	5.35
1884	5.18	0.31	0.31	5.65
1885	4.24	0.24	0.27	4.22
1886	5.20	0.22	0.33	4.26
1887	5.58	0.25	0.36	6.11
1888	5.31	0.23	0.26	5.02
1889	5.24	0.22	0.30	4.68
1890	5.38	0.22	0.29	5.41
1891	4.84	0.22	0.34	5.97
1892	5.51	0.24	0.37	3.93
1893	5.61	0.25	0.26	8.52
1894	4.32	0.21	0.16	3.32
1895	4.25	0.19	0.25	3.09
1896	4.27	0.18	0.21	5.76
1897	4.22	0.18	0.31	3.44
1898	4.88	0.20	0.35	3.55
1899	6.08	0.21	0.48	3.36
1900	6.10	0.30	0.48	4.64
1901	7.07	0.32	0.50	4.30
1902	8.12	0.33	0.63	4.72
1903	8.46	0.35	0.53	5.50
1904	6.68	0.31	0.49	4.34
1905	8.43	0.33	0.67	4.17
1906	9.87	0.40	0.76	5.47
1907	9.56	0.44	0.66	6.23
1908	6.85	0.40	0.58	5.32
1909	9.06	0.44	0.76	3.65
1910	10.08	0.47	0.73	5.26
1911	9.27	0.47	0.59	4.00
1912	9.12	0.48	0.70	4.35
1913	9.30	0.48	0.63	5.65
1914	8.37	0.42	0.52	4.64
1915	7.48	0.43	0.88	3.65
1916	9.33	0.56	1.53	3.64
1917	9.57	0.69	1.28	4.25
1918	7.21	0.57	0.99	5.98
1919	7.85	0.53	0.93	5.56
1920	8.83	0.51	0.80	7.30
1921	7.11	0.46	0.29	7.44
1922	7.30	0.51	0.69	4.58
1923	8.90	0.53	0.98	4.96
1924	8.83	0.55	0.93	4.34
1925	10.58	0.60	1.25	3.87
1926	12.65	0.69	1.24	4.28
1927	13.40	0.77	1.11	4.26
1928	17.53	0.85	1.38	4.64
1929	24.86	0.97	1.61	6.01

Table 26.1 (continued)

Year	Series 1: stock prices, January[a]	Series 2: dividends[b]	Series 3: earnings[b]	Series 4: interest (%)
1930	21.71	0.98	0.97	4.15
1931	15.98	0.82	0.61	2.43
1932	8.30	0.50	0.41	3.36
1933	7.09	0.44	0.44	1.46
1934	10.54	0.45	0.49	1.01
1935	9.26	0.47	0.76	0.75
1936	13.76	0.72	1.02	0.75
1937	17.59	0.80	1.13	0.88
1938	11.31	0.51	0.64	0.88
1939	12.50	0.62	0.90	0.56
1940	12.30	0.67	1.05	0.56
1941	10.55	0.71	1.16	0.53
1942	8.93	0.59	1.03	0.63
1943	10.09	0.61	0.94	0.69
1944	11.85	0.64	0.93	0.72
1945	13.49	0.66	0.96	0.75
1946	18.02	0.71	1.06	0.76
1947	15.21	0.84	1.61	1.01
1948	14.83	0.93	2.29	1.35
1949	15.36	1.14	2.32	1.58
1950	16.88	1.47	2.84	1.32
1951	21.21	1.41	2.44	2.12
1952	24.19	1.41	2.40	2.39
1953	26.18	1.45	2.51	2.58
1954	25.46	1.54	2.77	1.80
1955	35.60	1.64	3.62	1.81
1956	44.15	1.74	3.41	3.21
1957	45.43	1.79	3.37	3.86
1958	41.12	1.75	2.89	2.54
1959	55.62	1.83	3.39	3.74
1960	58.03	1.95	3.27	4.28
1961	59.72	2.02	3.19	2.91
1962	69.07	2.13	3.67	3.39
1963	65.06	2.28	4.02	3.50
1964	76.45	2.50	4.55	4.09
1965	86.12	2.72	5.19	4.46
1966	93.32	2.87	5.55	5.44
1967	84.45	2.92	5.33	5.55
1968	95.04	3.07	5.76	6.17
1969	102.04	3.16	5.78	8.05
1970	90.31	3.14	5.13	9.11
1971	93.49	3.07	5.70	5.66
1972	103.30	3.15	6.42	4.62
1973	118.42	3.38	8.16	7.93
1974	96.11	3.60	8.89	11.03
1975	72.56	3.68	7.96	7.24
1976	96.86	4.05	9.91	5.70
1977	103.81	4.67	10.89	5.28
1978	90.25	5.07	12.33	7.78
1979	99.71	5.65	14.86	10.88
1980	110.87	6.16	14.82	11.37
1981	132.97	6.63	15.36	17.63
1982	117.28	6.87	12.64	14.60
1983	144.27	7.09	14.03	9.37
1984	166.39	7.53	16.64	11.11
1985	171.61	7.90	14.61	8.35
1986	208.19	8.28	14.48	7.31
1987	264.51	8.81	17.50	6.55
1988	250.48			

a. Values 1871–1988 printed with permission of Standard and Poor's Statistical Service.
b. Values 1926–1987 printed with permission of Standard and Poor's Statistical Service.

Table 26.2
Basic data, continued

Year	Series 5: PPI, 1982 = 100, January	Series 6: PPI, 1967 = 100	Series 7: PPI, 1967 = 100, annual Average	Series 8: consumption deflator	Series 9: real consumption
1871	15.39	44.10	44.10		
1872	15.62	45.70	45.70		
1873	15.98	45.40	45.40		
1874	15.27	43.40	43.40		
1875	14.21	40.60	40.60		
1876	13.39	37.60	37.60		
1877	13.51	36.70	36.70		
1878	11.40	33.20	33.20		
1879	10.22	31.80	31.80		
1880	12.33	35.50	35.50		
1881	11.63	34.40	34.40		
1882	12.57	35.00	35.00		
1883	12.33	33.10	33.10		
1884	11.40	30.10	30.10		
1885	10.22	27.80	27.80		
1886	9.87	27.30	27.30		
1887	9.87	27.50	27.50		
1888	10.34	28.30	28.30		
1889	9.87	27.30	27.30	19.30	0.73
1890	9.40	26.70	26.70	19.03	0.71
1891	9.63	26.30	26.30	18.48	0.74
1892	9.05	24.70	24.70	18.11	0.76
1893	9.75	25.30	25.30	18.24	0.76
1894	8.46	22.70	22.70	17.20	0.73
1895	8.11	23.00	23.00	16.89	0.80
1896	8.22	22.00	22.00	16.20	0.78
1897	7.99	22.00	22.00	16.48	0.82
1898	8.22	23.00	23.00	16.68	0.83
1899	8.34	24.70	24.70	17.01	0.90
1900	9.75	26.80	26.70	17.83	0.90
1901	9.52	26.00	26.00	17.55	1.00
1902	9.75	26.50	27.60	18.40	0.98
1903	10.69	27.90	28.30	18.32	1.03
1904	10.22	27.20	29.00	18.78	1.02
1905	10.46	27.40	28.30	19.07	1.05
1906	10.46	29.00	29.30	19.23	1.14
1907	10.93	30.70	30.90	20.13	1.15
1908	10.69	30.20	29.60	20.08	1.07
1909	11.04	29.80	31.90	20.92	1.15
1910	12.22	31.90	33.20	21.51	1.15
1911	11.40	31.00	30.60	21.20	1.19
1912	11.28	31.40	32.60	22.19	1.20
1913	12.10	33.90	32.90	22.07	1.22
1914	11.80	33.20	32.30	22.44	1.18
1915	11.80	33.20	33.30	23.21	1.14
1916	13.30	38.30	41.80	26.08	1.21
1917	17.60	51.90	58.30	32.59	1.16
1918	21.60	62.40	63.90	37.24	1.19
1919	23.20	67.50	67.80	37.17	1.20
1920	27.20	79.00	74.40	41.47	1.24
1921	19.60	57.70	48.40	35.82	1.33
1922	15.70	46.80	49.10	34.30	1.33
1923	17.60	52.90	50.70	35.15	1.40
1924	17.20	51.60	49.40	34.83	1.48
1925	17.70	53.50	52.20	35.71	1.39
1926	17.80	53.60	50.40	36.17	1.48
1927	16.40	50.00	48.10	35.03	1.50
1928	16.60	49.70	48.70	35.36	1.52

Table 26.2 (continued)

Year	Series 5: PPI, 1982 = 100, January	Series 6: PPI, 1967 = 100	Series 7: PPI, 1967 = 100, annual Average	Series 8: consumption deflator	Series 9: real consumption
1929	16.50	50.20	48.00	35.09	1.59
1930	15.90	48.10	43.50	34.26	1.49
1931	13.50	39.80	36.80	30.99	1.43
1932	11.60	34.80	32.70	27.61	1.30
1933	10.50	31.60	33.20	26.47	1.27
1934	12.40	37.40	37.80	28.58	1.30
1935	13.60	40.80	40.30	29.36	1.36
1936	13.90	41.70	40.70	29.67	1.46
1937	14.80	44.40	43.50	30.74	1.51
1938	14.00	41.90	39.60	30.71	1.48
1939	13.30	39.80	38.90	29.97	1.54
1940	13.70	41.10	39.60	30.30	1.58
1941	13.90	41.80	44.00	32.41	1.64
1942	16.50	49.70	49.80	36.25	1.67
1943	17.50	52.70	52.00	39.67	1.71
1944	17.80	53.40	52.40	41.91	1.75
1945	18.10	54.30	53.30	43.45	1.83
1946	18.40	55.40	61.00	46.44	1.95
1947	24.50	73.20	76.50	51.32	1.91
1948	27.70	82.90	82.80	54.37	1.91
1949	27.30	81.60	78.70	54.00	1.90
1950	25.90	77.60	81.80	54.76	1.94
1951	30.50	91.20	91.10	59.93	1.95
1952	30.00	89.70	88.60	60.84	1.98
1953	29.10	87.20	87.40	62.24	2.01
1954	29.40	88.00	87.60	63.41	2.01
1955	29.20	87.40	87.80	63.85	2.07
1956	29.70	88.80	90.70	65.18	2.11
1957	31.00	92.70	93.30	67.27	2.12
1958	31.50	94.30	94.60	69.08	2.13
1959	31.70	94.80	94.80	70.16	2.19
1960	31.80	94.70	94.90	71.69	2.22
1961	31.80	95.20	94.50	72.61	2.24
1962	31.70	95.00	94.80	73.69	2.29
1963	31.60	94.70	94.50	74.85	2.33
1964	31.80	95.20	94.70	76.11	2.41
1965	31.80	95.20	96.60	77.80	2.50
1966	32.90	98.60	99.80	80.57	2.58
1967	33.40	100.10	100.00	82.74	2.63
1968	33.80	101.10	102.50	86.34	2.72
1969	34.80	104.30	106.50	90.39	2.79
1970	36.50	109.30	110.40	95.08	2.84
1971	37.30	111.80	113.90	99.23	2.88
1972	38.80	116.30	119.10	103.26	2.98
1973	41.60	124.50	134.70	110.20	3.05
1974	49.00	146.60	160.10	121.88	3.04
1975	57.40	171.80	174.90	131.60	3.09
1976	59.90	179.40	183.00	138.95	3.20
1977	62.80	188.10	194.20	147.68	3.30
1978	66.80	200.10	209.30	158.38	3.40
1979	73.80	220.80	235.60	172.72	3.47
1980	85.20	254.90	268.80	190.51	3.49
1981	95.20	284.80	293.40	206.93	3.52
1982	99.70	298.30	299.30	218.52	3.54
1983	100.20	299.90	303.10	227.74	3.63
1984	102.90	308.00	310.30	236.55	3.73
1985	103.40	309.50	308.70	250.42	3.71
1986	103.20	308.90	299.80		
1987	100.50	300.90	307.70		
1988	104.50				

importance of their omission can be found by comparing the series $P - 1$ (the Cowles index for all stocks) and the series $P_{EA} - 1$ (the Cowles series prices of stocks for which earnings data are available). The ratio of $P - 1$ to $P_{EA} - 1$, 1871–1925, ranged from 0.98 to 1.27, the biggest discrepancies occurring in the earliest years of the sample. Another suggestion of the importance of the omissions is in Cowles list ([1939], appendix II, pp. 456– 475) of the companies in the index and the years for which the companies' earnings are available. Typically, lack of data on earnings comes for isolated years (as if earnings reported were occasionally missing) or for single years near the begin or end of the inclusion of the company in the index.

Wilson and Jones [1987] have recently examined the Cowles data for accuracy. They found some apparent errors in Cowles' monthly series of cumulated returns (Cowles data implied negative dividends for some months) and produced an alternative monthly return series that attempted to correct these errors. They concluded that "the overall impact of these revisions as compared to the original Cowles Commission data is minimal."[3] The Cowles monthly data that they criticize is not used here; returns are computed on a January-to-January basis assuming dividends are not reinvested during the year.

The nominal interest rate series (table 26.1, series 4) is the total return to investing for six months in January at the January 4–6 month prime commercial paper rate (six months starting January 1980) and for another six months at the July 4–6 month prime commercial paper rate (six months starting July 1980). It is computed as $100[((1 - R_{jan}/200)(1 - R_{jul}/200))^{-1} - 1]$. Data starting 1938 are from the *Federal Reserve Bulletin*. Data before 1938 are from Macaulay [1938], table 10, pp. A142–A160.

The U.S. Bureau of Labor Statistics (BLS) has been emphasizing the Finished Goods Price Index, rather than the All Commodities Product Price Index, ever since the Producer Price Index replaced the Wholesale Price Index in 1978 (see Early [1978]). The Finished Goods Producer Price Index is supposed to be superior since it is not affected by the double counting of intermediate and final goods that infects the All Commodities Producer Price Index. Unfortunately, the Finished Goods Producer Price Index is available only back to 1947. Any earlier series that might be spliced to it would be comparable to the All Commodities Producers Price Index. It was decided, therefore, to continue to use the All Commodities Index shown here, which the BLS makes available on a monthly basis back to 1913.

Starting with January, 1988 the BLS changed the reference base year for the producer price index from 1967 = 100 to 1982 = 100 (see "Producer Price Index—January 1988," *News*, Bureau of Labor Statistics, Feburary 12,

1988.) Table 26.2, series 5, is the January Producer Price Index—All Commodities, with the 1982 bases year starting with 1913. Data from before 1913 are from the January figures from the Warren and Pearson Index [1935], chapter 1, table 1, pp. 11–14, divided by the ratio of the series in 1913.[4]

Previously published papers in this volume use earlier producer price index series with 1967 = 100 (table 26.2, series 6 and 7). These series are built up of component series, by multiplying the earlier series by the ratio of the indexes at the date of the first observation of the succeeding series.

Series 6 is the Producer Price Index for January. For 1947 to the end of the sample the series is the January Producer Price Index, all commodities, 1967 = 100, from the *Survey of Current Business*. For 1924 to 1946 the series used is January Wholesale Price Index (WPI), all commodities, 1926 = 100, from the *Federal Reserve Bulletin*, divided by 1.933. For 1914 to 1923 the series used is January WPI, all commodities, 1913 = 100, from the *Federal Reserve Bulletin*, divided by 2.949. For 1900 to 1913 the series used is January WPI, all commodities, 1890–1899 = 100, from *Wholesale Prices*, BLS Bulletin #149, Government Printing Office, Washington, 1914, divided by 4.1613. For 1871 to 1899 the series is the same as series 7.

The annual average producer price index, series 7, is, for 1947 to the end of the sample, the annual average Producer Price Index, all commodities, 1967 = 100, from the *Survey of Current Business*. For 1924 to 1946 the series used is annual average WPI, all commodities, 1926 = 100, from the *Federal Reserve Bulletin*, divided by 1.9843. For 1914 to 1923 the series used is annual average WPI, all commodities, 1913 = 100, from the *Federal Reserve Bulletin*, divided by 3.038. For 1891 to 1913 the series used is annual average WPI, all commodities, 1913 = 100, from *Wholesale Prices*, BLS Bulletin #320, Government Printing Office, Washington, divided by 3.0395. For 1871 to 1890 the series used is annual average WPI, 1890–1899 = 100, from appendix I of BLS Bulletin #114, divided by 4.1613.

The consumption deflator, 1972 = 100, (table 26.2, series 8) and real per capita consumption (table 26.2, series 9), both for nondurables and services, were used in chapters 16 and 21, as well as Shiller [1982] and Campbell and Shiller [1988]. The data sources are given in Shiller [1982].

Notes

1. Since the chapters in this volume were written at different times over an interval of a dozen years, the basic data series are not always exactly the same from one chapter to the next. Data revisions or rebasing inevitably cause some changes. However, many of the series were essentially unchanged over this time interval.

2. The S&P Composite Index for 1871–1925 is the same as Cowles' "common stock index" series $P - 1$, for all stocks (Cowles [1939], pp. 66–67) times a constant. An earlier edition of the same book (Cowles [1938]) gave a slightly different dividend series, which I used in papers written prior to chapter 7.

3. Wilson and Jones [1987], p. 244.

4. Mankiw, Romer, and Shapiro used for 1890–1912 a monthly series *Index Number of Wholesale Prices on Pre-War Base, 1890–1927* (Washington, GPO, 1928).

References

Campbell, John Y., and Robert J. Shiller. 1988. "The Dividend-Price Ratio and Expectations of Future Dividends and Discount Factors," *Review of Financial Studies* 1:196–228.

Cowles Alfred, III, and Associates. 1939. *Common Stock Indexes*, 2nd Edition, Bloomington, In: Principia Press.

Early, John F. 1978. "Improving the Measurement of Producer Price Change," *Monthly Labor Review* 101:7–15.

Macaulay, Frederic. 1938. *Some Theoretical Problems Suggested by the Movements of Interest Rates, Bond Yields and Stock Prices in the United States Since 1856*, New York: National Bureau of Economic Research.

Shiller, Robert J. 1982. "Consumption, Asset Markets, and Macroeconomic Fluctuations," *Carnegie-Rochester Series on Public Policy* 17:203–238.

Warren, George F., and Frank A. Pearson. 1935. *Gold and Prices*, New York: John Wiley and Sons.

Wilson, J. W. and C. P. Jones. 1987. "A Comparison of Annual Common Stock Returns 1871–1925 with 1926–1985," *Journal of Business* 60:235–258.

Author Index

Subject Index

Abnormal profit opportunity, 52–53
Abnormal returns
  defining of, 52
  and earnings-price ratio, 54
Accounting practices for earnings, 28, 153
Aggregator models, 356
Agricultural land date, 320–321
Akaike information criterion (AIC),
  302, 304, 313n.26
Alignment of data, 109, 123, 143–144
All Commodities Producer Price Index, 442
All Commodities Product Price Index, 442
Alternatives to efficient-market model, 3,
  23–26, 41–42, 139–142. See also
  Bubbles; Fashions or fads; Investor
  psychology
  and "anomalies," 53, 54, 63
  for bonds vs. stocks, 219
  and literature, 8
  and regression tests, 22, 38
Anaheim (Orange County), California
  housing boom in, 403, 405–409, 420,
  423, 426
  housing survey in, 411–425
Analysts (investment), 54–55
Anomalies (efficient markets model), 53, 54,
  63
Anxiety. See Investor anxiety
Approximation error, 93, 281n.9, 283n.18
Arbitrage pricing theory (APT), 197, 434
ARIMA (autoregressive integrated moving
  averages) models, 30–35, 114, 115, 267.
  See also VAR approach
Asset returns, theory of, 361
Atlanta, Georgia, housing market in, 323–
  340
Attitudes, group polarization of, 61–62, 63
Autokinetic effect, 13–14

Automated selling, 372
Autonomous monetary causes, 352, 353
Autoregressive analysis of volatility rela-
  tions, 92–95
Availability heuristic, 61

Baker, James A., 387, 398
Bank of England, 245, 247
Barron's survey after stock market crash,
  386, 401nn.2,7
Betas
  and capital asset pricing model, 197
  consumption, 22
  for housing, 325
Bias in estimation. See Small sample
  properties
Birth rate changes, 20. See also
  Demographics
BMN method, 323–324
Bonds, 219
  and expectations theory of term structure,
  220–231, 232
  present-value models tested for, 298–299,
  309
Bonds, long-term, 217, 219
  and Gibson Paradox, 237–250
  market rate of interest on (Fisher), 241
Booms in housing market. See under
  Housing market
Boston, Massachusetts
  housing boom in, 403, 406, 409, 420
  housing survey in, 411–425
  post-boom market in, 403
Brady Commission, 372, 373
Braid, James, 434
British consols, 219, 257
Brokers' advisory service recommendations,
  55